BOWLING ANALYSIS Second INNINGS of ___

BOWLERS' NAMES	WIDES	NO BALLS	NUMBER OF OVERS AND RUNS MADE FROM EACH BOWLER	OVERS	MAIDENS	RUNS	WIDES	NO BALLS	WICKETS
Cotter				17	1	59			1
				14	2	64			1
w-Laver				20	5	57			0
				8	1	46			0
J-Macleod	1			20	8	38	1		0
-Armstrong				20	8	35			0
S-Noble				20	12	22			1
S-Noble				7	1	31			0
S-Duff				15	2	43			2
rmstrong (Cont)				12	4	10			0

BOWLING ANALYSIS Second INNINGS of Australia

BOWLERS' NAMES	WIDES	NO BALLS	NUMBER OF OVERS AND RUNS MADE FROM EACH BOWLER	OVERS	MAIDENS	RUNS	WIDES	NO BALLS	WICKETS
Arnold				4	2	7			0
				10	1	26			1
Rhodes				20	7	32			0
				12.4	1	39			3
Bosanquet II				20	1	68			5
-Jessop				1	0	1			0
Jackson				5	3	6			0

England won by 213 Runs

Umpires: J. Phillips & J. Carlin

PUBLISHED BY JOHN WISDEN & Co CRICKETING OUTFITTERS. 21. CRANBOURN St. LEICESTER SQUARE, LONDON. W.C.   Entered Stationers Hall

The Illustrated History of the
TEST MATCH

The Illustrated History of the
TEST MATCH

Peter Arnold & Peter Wynne-Thomas

Foreword by
Richie Benaud

First published in Great Britain in 1988
by Sidgwick & Jackson Limited
1 Tavistock Chambers, Bloomsbury Way
London WC1A 2SG

Conceived and produced by
Brian Trodd Publishing House Limited
27 Swinton Street London WC1X 9NW

ISBN 0 283 99618 8

Phototypeset by The Word Factory,
Rawtenstall, Lancashire

Printed in Italy

Contents

FOREWORD

By Richie Benaud

Test cricket is alive and well despite often expressed fears to the contrary, though I do add the qualification that the quality of the game needs to remain high.

Some espouse an argument these days that too much Test cricket is played, but I tend to think this belief merely underlines the fact that the players and cricket followers remain keen and anticipative about the five-day game.

I began my Test career way back in 1952 with what is laughingly known as marginal impact. Running out Frank Worrell was the most startling contribution I made unless, in a moment of massive euphoria, you count that doyen of the number eleven spot, Alfred Valentine, as a scalp to treasure. That match against the West Indies at the SCG produced only 784 runs but it provided a priceless lesson. The giant leap required to move from Sheffield Shield cricket to playing for Australia was something I never forgot as my career unfolded.

I thoroughly enjoy limited-overs cricket and wish I had been lucky enough to play it in addition to Test cricket. There is room for both styles of game but, thankfully, we will always have Sheffield Shield, the County Championship and the nursery competitions of other countries as a lead-up to Test cricket.

There is much at which one can marvel in the life of the modern-day Test player and they probably wonder how we managed travelling by train and ship rather than by sponsored luxury car and jumbo jet, the latter now cutting a tour of England from seven and a half to four months.

The thing I have always loved most about Test cricket though is the tactical battle. The captain who works two overs ahead of the play, the loser who always seems to be putting a man where the ball has just been struck. The batsman who decides to tear apart an attack, or even belt a bowler right out of the game; the bowler who takes a gamble which comes off and makes him a hero.

On every page of any history of Test cricket there is a story. It might be one of triumph or pathos, the start of one career, the sad end of another. There are not many sports about which that can fairly be said!

The Pre-Test Era

The original plans for a cricket team to travel abroad were made as early as 1789, when the great patron of Kent cricket, the Duke of Dorset, arranged for a side under the captaincy of the Surrey wicket-keeper, William Yalden, to go to France. The team arrived in Dover only to meet the Duke fleeing from the French Revolution. The proposed tour was immediately abandoned!

Instead of 'England v France' being the first cricket international, pride of place must go to another title, which to many readers appears almost as strange, 'United States v Canada', played in New York in September 1844.

The match was played almost yearly in the 1840s and 1850s and in 1859, the tenth in the series was regarded as a 'test' for players who would be opposing the England team which was touring the United States and Canada the following month.

This all-professional England side, under the leadership of the Notts captain, George Parr, was the first side from the British Isles to go overseas. Five matches were played,

plus three exhibition games. The five proper matches were all Eleven v Twenty-Two, but despite these odds, the Englishmen were victorious in all.

Two years later, the catering firm of Spiers and Pond tried to persuade George Parr to take an English team to Australia. He and his Notts colleagues all refused the terms offered, but the promoters pressed on with their plans and the Surrey cricketer, H.H. Stephenson, led this first team to the Antipodes. The side won six and lost two of their matches, but financially were most successful and when in 1863 a second opportunity arose for an Australian tour, George Parr quickly accepted the offer. His side returned home undefeated. All matches on these tours were against odds.

The next international exchange occurred in 1868 when a team of Australian aborigines, under the leadership of Charles Lawrence – who had gone to Australia with Stephenson's side and remained out there as coach – toured England. The side was not capable of playing English first-class counties, but opposed strong club sides and in addition to cricket gave exhibitions of boomerang throwing and other similar

attractions. In the same year, Edgar Willsher took a second England side to America and again returned undefeated.

Four years later, the MCC sent an amateur side to America. All matches were against Twenty-Twos and seven of the eight were won, the other being drawn. The famous W.G.Grace captained the third English Team to Australia in 1873/74. The standard of cricket 'Down Under' was now beginning to improve and for two matches the odds were reduced to Eleven v Fifteen, whilst Eighteen of New South Wales actually beat the English Eleven by eight wickets, as did a similar number from Victoria.

American cricket was not making the same progress and, in 1874, the Americans took the courageous step of sending a Baseball Team to tour England – the Baseballers playing cricket matches against fairly good club teams, as well as giving exhibitions of baseball. The visit was not very successful.

James Lillywhite organized and captained the fourth English side to Australia in the autumn of 1876. The team were beaten by Fifteen of New South Wales in their second match and then by Fifteen of Victoria. This was followed by a crushing defeat in the return v Fifteen of New South Wales, who immediately challenged the tourists to an eleven-a-side game. The match was drawn, much in favour of Lillywhite's men, but it set the stage for the first proper eleven-a-side match between 'England' and Australia, which was played when the tourists returned from a visit, in mid-tour, to New Zealand. The match is regarded as the 'First Test'.

The exchange of teams between Australia and New Zealand commenced the following season, when Canterbury toured Victoria and Tasmania and regular exchanges between these two countries continued through the years, though not until 1945–46 did Australia meet New Zealand in a Test.

Canada toured England in 1880 and the United States, under the title of 'Gentlemen of Philadelphia', in 1884. The United States went on to make several 'first-class' visits to England prior to the First World War, but never graduated to Test match status, whilst Canada's only 'first-class' visit to England occurred in much more recent years : 1954.

The first English side went to South Africa in 1888–89 and played an eleven-a-side game against a representative South African side. This is regarded as the first 'England v South Africa' Test, but England was represented by a very weak team, hardly worthy of 'first-class' status. The following year saw the first England tour to India, though in this case Test match status did not come until 1932. India's elevation was therefore preceded by both West Indies (1928) and New Zealand (1929–30).

After the creation of Pakistan, England toured there in 1951–52, but the matches were regarded as 'Unofficial Tests' and Pakistan were not granted Test match status until the following season, when they met India.

The youngest Test playing country is Sri Lanka. They had toured India regularly from the 1880s, but did not rate as 'first-class' until the 1920s and became a Test country only in 1981–82.

England v Australia

1876–77: Australia sets the ball rolling

The first Test match was played on 15, 16, 17 and 19 March 1877. For the first time England toured Australia on their own initiative, i.e. the tour was based on a speculative venture by the British rather than on an invitation from Australian organizers.

James Lillywhite, the Sussex cricketer, arranged the tour, and naturally managed and captained the touring party of twelve players. He was also the selector, and the players were not necessarily England's best – in fact W.G. Grace did not go. The batting would be considered weak by the standards of the best in the country, because the Nottinghamshire players Richard Daft and Arthur Shrewsbury did not tour. The bowling was, however, representative, including the leading bowlers in the country in Alfred Shaw, Allen Hill, Tom Emmett and James Southerton.

The party also included the best wicket-keeper available in Ted Pooley of Surrey, but was to be deprived of his services for the first of all Test matches after he had been arrested in New Zealand. The New Zealand leg of the tour occurred after nine matches in Australia, during which the tourists had played odds matches and had actually been beaten by XV of Victoria and XV of New South Wales, in the latter instance by the convincing margin of 13 wickets. The tourists then had much the better of a draw with XI of New South Wales, who might well have been beaten by an innings had the match continued, before sailing from Sydney for New Zealand where they were to play eight more odds matches.

The New Zealand trip was full of adventure, at one time the cricketers being stuck in their horse-drawn coach in the middle of a swollen river and having not only to swim for it but to rescue the horses.

Pooley's personal misfortune was the result of his being much wiser in the ways of betting on cricket than the locals. All the matches were the subject of constant gambling, and on one of them Pooley bet a spectator that he could forecast the scores of all 22 batsmen on the opposing side. The poor man gave Pooley odds of £1 to 1s (20–1) and Pooley wrote down a duck for each player. It was a ploy well known to practised gamblers, as there was always a reasonable number of ducks, particularly in this kind of odds match. In this case there were 11, so Pooley required of his victim £11 minus 11s, or £10. 9s. The man refused to pay, there was a fight and some damage to property, and this is why England's leading wicket-keeper was awaiting trial in New Zealand when his team-mates played in the first-ever Test in Australia.

As a postscript to this story, Pooley never did rejoin the touring party or play in a Test, and sadly spent many of his last years in the workhouse, but he did not feel too badly about New Zealand as the sporting public there, thinking he had been badly treated, raised a subscription for him which reached about £50.

On returning to Australia the party's 18th match of the tour was at Sydney against a Combined Australian XI, or in effect a combined Melbourne and Sydney XI, these being the rival centres of cricket in Australia at the time. This was the first meeting between England and Australia on level terms, and has been regarded since as the 'first Test match'. There was no such designation at the time. The term 'test match' had been used in cricket earlier than this, but it was not until subsequent years, when cricket's army of statisticians regularized records, that this match came to be the first 'official' Test.

The England team was in bad condition. Everybody was exhausted by the trials and tribulations of New Zealand – the journey from one match to another, in which the players had been forced to swim, also encountered a landslide, and had taken nearly four days. The deputy wicket-keeper, Henry Jupp, was suffering from inflammation of the eyes and a bout of insanity, and was not trusted behind the stumps, although he had to play, there now being only 11 players. Surprisingly he was England's top scorer with 63 after opening the batting. The man who kept wicket for England was the Notts batsman John Selby.

The Australian team, although not in the unfortunate state of the English, was also not quite representative of the best that could be fielded, lacking three of the best bowlers of the day in F.R. Spofforth, Francis Allan and Edwin Evans.

The match followed the day of the tourists' return, when many were still suffering from sea-sickness and not best pleased at having to field.

The first ball in Test cricket was bowled at 1.05 pm on 15 March 1877 by the Notts professional round-arm bowler Alfred Shaw, and Charles Bannerman of New South Wales faced it. The first run was scored by Bannerman off the second ball of

The Australian Test team in 1878-79

Blackham, John McCarthy
Blackham was born on 11 May 1854 at North Fitzroy, Victoria, and having played for Victoria from 1874–75 made his Test debut in the first Test match of all in 1876–77. He was called the 'Prince of Wicket-keepers'. He developed the modern style of keeping, standing over the stumps and taking the ball and whipping off the bails in a single movement. He was on Australia's first eight tours to England, and was captain of the 1893 tourists. In 35 Tests he took 36 catches and made 24 stumpings. He also scored 800 runs, average 15.68. He died on 28 December 1932 in Melbourne.

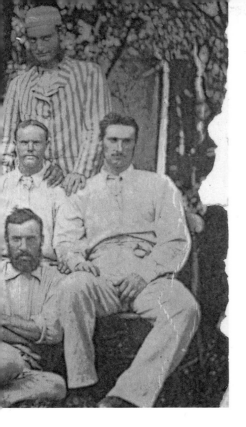

played his last Test in 1930), but having been born on 16 November 1827 Southerton is the 'first-born' of all Test players.

After the tourists had played three up-country matches against sides of 22 players, a return match was played at Melbourne – the second Test. Australia were strengthened by the inclusion of Spofforth, Tom Kelly (another Irishman) and W.L. Murdoch, who was Australian, but like Midwinter later played for England, although in his case it was just one match at the end of his career, against South Africa.

The match was for the benefit of the English touring professionals, and drew about 15,000 spectators, a large number at the time, leading to those gamblers who had lost on betting on England in the first match claiming that it had been 'fixed' to attract a large crowd to the second, claims which were intensified when England duly beat the home side by four wickets.

The England batting in this match was dominated by players from Yorkshire, who scored 329 of England's 383 runs (27 from Surrey, Sussex and Notts and 27 from extras). This percentage of 85.9, although helped by the fact that five of the original 12

tourists were from Yorkshire, is a record for a match in which so many wickets fell.

The tour was a financial success, and helped to establish what was still not yet regarded as 'Test cricket'.

1876–77 1st Series Aus 1, Eng 1
1 MELBOURNE Australia won by 45 runs
Australia 245 (C Bannerman 165) and 104 (A Shaw 5–38, G Ulyett 4–39)
England 196 (H Jupp 63, W E Midwinter 5–78) and 108 (T Kendall 7–55)
2 MELBOURNE England won by 4 wkts
Australia 122 (A Hill 4–27) and 259 (J Southerton 4–46, J Lillywhite 4–70)
England 261 (G Ulyett 52, T Kendall 4–82) and 122–6 (G Ulyett 63)

1878–79: Umpiring controversy, crowd invasion, captain assaulted

The Melbourne Cricket club invited a Middlesex amateur, I.D. Walker, to bring an amateur team to Australia in 1878–79. In order to improve the strength of the side, two professionals, George Ulyett and Tom Emmett were asked to join the tourists. In

---

the first over, overs at that time being of four balls each. Bannerman went on to score the first century in Test cricket, the only first-class century of his career. He was lucky to achieve this corner of fame in cricket's panorama. The England bowling and fielding was appalling and Bannerman was dropped by Tom Armitage, a simple catch being allowed to hit the fielder in what was probably already an upset stomach.

Apart from Bannerman, the Australian batting was not impressive, and when Bannerman was forced to retire hurt when a ball from George Ulyett split his finger, his 165 had come from a total of only 240 for seven. Australia totalled 245, and then dismissed England for 196, William Midwinter taking 5–78.

England bowled better second time round, dismissing Australia for 104, but by scoring only 108 in the last innings themselves, were beaten by 45 runs.

It is interesting to note that Australia's highest scorers in each innings, Bannerman and Tom Horan, were born in Woolwich, England, and Middleton, Eire, respectively, while the leading wicket-takers, Midwinter and Tom Kendall, were born in Gloucestershire and Bedford, England. Midwinter later played Test cricket for England, one of a handful of players who have represented two countries. Nat Thompson was another Australian born in England. Of the rest Bransby Cooper was born in India, while the remaining five were born and bred in Australia.

Bannerman's innings is remarkable in that he scored 67.3 per cent of his side's first-innings total, and that in over 100 years and 1,000 Test matches since, that percentage has not been beaten.

James Southerton, from Petworth in Sussex, was 49 years old when he appeared in this match. He is not the oldest Test cricketer (Wilfred Rhodes was 52 when he

AUSTRALIA V ENGLAND 1877–78
1st Test, Melbourne: Australia won by 45 runs

AUSTRALIA

C. Bannerman	retired hurt	165	b Ulyett		4
N. Thompson	b Hill	1	c Emmett b Shaw		7
T.P. Horan	c Hill b Shaw	12	c Selby b Hill		20
D.W. Gregory*	run out	1	(9) b Shaw		3
B.B. Cooper	b Southerton	15	b Shaw		3
W.E. Midwinter	c Ulyett b Southerton	5	c Southerton b Ulyett		17
E.J. Gregory	c Greenwood b Lillywhite	0	c Emmett b Ulyett		11
J.M. Blackham†	b Southerton	17	lbw b Shaw		6
T.W. Garrett	not out	18	(4) c Emmett b Shaw		0
T. Kendall	c Southerton b Shaw	3	not out		17
J.H. Hodges	b Shaw	0	b Lillywhite		8
Extras	(B 4, LB 2, W 2)	8	(B 5, LB 3)		8
Total		**245**			**104**

ENGLAND

H. Jupp	lbw b Garrett	63	(3) lbw b Midwinter		4
J. Selby†	c Cooper b Hodges	7	(5) c Horan b Hodges		38
H.R.J. Charlwood	c Blackham b Midwinter	36	(4) b Kendall		13
G. Ulyett	lbw b Thompson	10	(6) b Kendall		24
A. Greenwood	c E.J. Gregory b Midwinter	1	(2) c Midwinter b Kendall		5
T. Armitage	c Blackham b Midwinter	9	(8) c Blackham b Kendall		3
A. Shaw	b Midwinter	10	st Blackham b Kendall		2
T. Emmett	b Midwinter	8	(9) b Kendall		9
A. Hill	not out	35	(1) c Thompson b Kendall		0
James Lillywhite*	c and b Kendall	10	b Hodges		4
J. Southerton	c Cooper b Garrett	6	not out		1
Extras	(LB 1)	1	(B 4, LB 1)		5
Total		**196**			**108**

ENGLAND	O	M	R	W	O	M	R	W
Shaw	55.3	34	51	3	34	16	38	5
Hill	23	10	42	1	14	6	18	1
Ulyett	25	12	36	0	19	7	39	3
Southerton	37	17	61	3				
Armitage	3	0	15	0				
Lillywhite	14	5	19	1	1	0	1	1
Emmett	12	7	13	0				
AUSTRALIA								
Hodges	9	0	27	1	7	5	7	2
Garrett	18.1	10	22	2	2	0	9	0
Kendall	38	16	54	1	33.1	12	55	7
Midwinter	54	23	78	5	19	7	23	1
Thompson	17	10	14	1				
D.W. Gregory					5	1	9	0

FALL OF WICKETS

	A	E	A	E
Wkt	1st	1st	2nd	2nd
1st	2	23	7	0
2nd	40	79	27	7
3rd	41	98	31	20
4th	118	109	31	22
5th	142	121	35	62
6th	143	135	58	68
7th	197	145	71	92
8th	243	145	75	93
9th	245	168	75	100
10th	–	196	104	108

the event Walker was unable to go, and Lord Harris captained the party of 13 players.

The tour took in Australia, New Zealand and the USA, and consisted of 15 matches, the third of which, at East Melbourne, was labelled 'Gentlemen of England (with Ulyett and Emmett) v The Australian XI'. This rather strange collection has become accepted as the third Test match. While Australia fielded a stronger side than appeared two years earlier, the England side was not at all representative, including Leland Hone, an Irishman who never played county cricket and was taken to keep wicket, although he was not even a wicket-keeper. For six of the team, including F.A. MacKinnon, more splendidly titled The MacKinnon of MacKinnon, this would be the only Test they played, and it is perhaps unfortunate that this match, featuring a side which never claimed to be anything like 'England', should now be considered a Test match.

England batted first and were soon 26 for 7, with Spofforth taking the first Test hat-trick: Royle, MacKinnon and Emmett. There was a recovery, led by Harris (33) and Absolom (52) to 113, but Australia made 256, and after England's 160 needed only 18 to win, and scored them without loss. Spofforth took 13 wickets in the match.

The tourists also played New South Wales and Victoria twice each on level terms, losing one and winning one with each state. It was in the second New South Wales match at Sydney that the crowd disapproved of a run-out decision against W.L. Murdoch and invaded the pitch. Lord Harris was struck with a whip or stick and had to be rescued by Hornby, a man known for his prowess with his fists. It was suggested that the umpire had bet heavily on a victory for the tourists. There was no further play that day, but eventually the tourists won by an innings.

1878–79 2nd Series Aust 1, Eng 0
1 MELBOURNE Australia won by 10 wkts
England 113 (C A Absolom 52, F R Spofforth 6–48) and 160 (F R Spofforth 7–62)
Australia 256 (A C Bannerman 73, T Emmett 7–68) and 19–0

W.L. Murdoch who led the Australian tourists to England in 1880 for the first Test in England.

Spofforth, Frederick Robert

Born on 9 September 1853 at Balmain, NSW, Spofforth first appeared for his state in 1874–75. Later he also played for Victoria. He played in the second of all Test matches. On his third tour of England he played in the first Test in that country and demolished England in the match that led to the 'Ashes' obituary notice. Spofforth was a right-arm fast bowler, who later became fast-medium, relying on his height of 6ft 2in and his guile rather than speed to bring wickets. His mastery over the best English batsmen was such that he became known as the 'Demon Bowler'. In 18 Tests he took 94 wickets, average 18.41. He died on 4 June 1926 at Long Ditton, Surrey.

1880: The first Test match in England a Graceful affair

An Australian party captained by W.L. Murdoch toured England in 1880. No matches were arranged against an England XI, the English still being unconvinced about the Aussies' ability at cricket, but C.W. Alcock, who was secretary of Surrey CCC, saw the possibilities of a game. Alcock had been instrumental in setting up the Football Association, of which he became secretary, and in organizing the first international soccer match between England and Scotland. Now he arranged for England to play Australia at the Oval on 6, 7 and 8 September 1880, days which had originally been reserved for a match with Sussex. This match has taken its place in history as the first Test in England.

The tourists were without their main bowler, Spofforth, who had damaged a

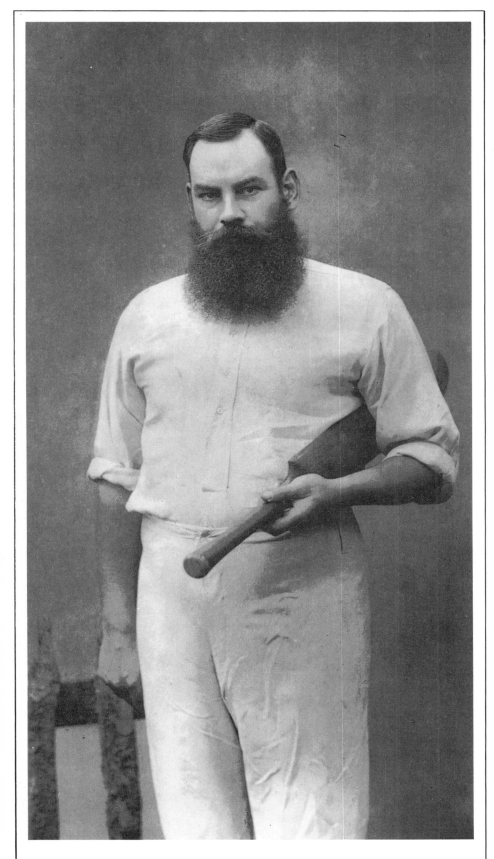

Grace, William Gilbert

Grace was born on 18 July 1848 at Downend, Bristol. Taught cricket by his mother, he was an opening right-hand batsman, a medium-pace round-arm bowler and excellent field. He made his debut for Gloucestershire in 1870 and for England in 1880. He became the most famous cricketer of all time, and, with his black beard, the most recognizable. Two of his brothers, E.M. and G.F., also played for England and all three played in the first Test in England in 1880.

Grace created most of the first-class cricket records, but as he went to Australia only once, he appeared in only 22 Tests, in 13 of which he was captain. He scored 1,098 runs, average 32.29, and took nine wickets, average 26.22. He died at Mottingham, Kent, on 23 October 1915.

finger. Fifteen players made their Test debuts in this match, eight of them for England. W.G. Grace made his Test debut, as did his two brothers E.M. and G.F., to provide the first instance of three brothers playing in the same Test (equalled only 12 years later by the Hearnes, who did not play all the same side, however).

England, captained by Lord Harris, batted first and W.G. scored the first English Test century. His 152 helped England to a total of 420, and with A.P. Lucas he added 120 for the second wicket, thus also establishing the first Test century partnership. Fred Morley of Notts took five Australian wickets for 56, and Australia, all out 149, were forced to follow on.

Murdoch, who had opened and scored a duck in the first innings, batted at number three and made 152 not out in the second. He became the first Test captain to score a century. Even so, with the eighth wicket down, Australia still needed 84 to avoid an innings defeat. However the last two wickets added 140, leaving England to get 57, and at 31 for 5 there might have been the makings of the first amazing reversal of fortunes in a Test match, but England had altered the batting order, and now W.G. came in to see them home. His brother, G.F., who scored a pair but took a brilliant catch, caught a chill and died at Basingstoke exactly a fortnight after the match.

1880   3rd Series   Eng 1, Aus 0
THE OVAL   **England won by 5 wkts**
England 420 (W G Grace 152, A P Lucas 55, Lord Harris 52) and 57–5
Australia 149 (F Morley 5–56) and 327 (W L Murdoch 153)

1881–82: More betting problems and another beating-up

In contrast to the previous tour, the 1881–82 English party to Australia was all-professional, and much stronger. The tour was still privately organized, with the Nottinghamshire professionals Alfred Shaw and Arthur Shrewsbury joining James Lillywhite of Sussex in a venture which arrived in Australia after touring America. The remaining players came from only four counties – two-thirds of the players came from Notts and Yorkshire.

Crowds were large, and 20,000 were at the second day of the second first-class game. This was against Victoria at Melbourne, and the home side had much the better of it for three innings, so that they needed only 94 to win when they began the fourth. At this stage, most of the tourists had £1 each on themselves at 30–1, and when Ted Peate took 6–30 to dismiss Victoria for 75, they collected. It then appeared that two English players, who had fielded badly (one dropped a catch) had been bribed with £100 to throw the match. Midwinter, who had been asked to join them, reported the matter and was later beaten up for his honesty.

The first Test was at Melbourne, beginning on 31 December 1881. Lillywhite, who had captained England in the first Test of all, was the English umpire. Alfred Shaw captained England, and Midwinter was in the side. Midwinter had played for Australia in the two Tests of 1876–77 and thus became the only player to play for both countries in Australia v England matches. Murdoch continued to captain Australia.

England made 294, with George Ulyett (87) and John Selby (55) adding 137 for the second wicket, a Test record stand. Australia passed this score by making 320, Tom Horan making 124. England batted solidly in the second innings for 308 leaving Australia to make 279 to win.

The match went into a fourth day (this was the first Test in which over 1,000 runs were scored) and the steamship waiting to take the tourists to New Zealand delayed its departure, but there was not time for a finish and the match was drawn at 127 for 3.

After playing various sides of 22 and 15 players, the tourists returned to Sydney for the second Test, this being the first Test to be played at Sydney. England fell before the bowling of George Palmer and Ted Evans, who bowled all through the innings (58 and 57 four-ball overs respectively) to take 7–68 and 3–64. England were out for 133, but fought back to dismiss Australia for 197 and go ahead with all second innings wickets intact when Ulyett (67) and R.G. Barlow

1881–82 4th Series Aus 2, Eng 0, Drawn 2
1 MELBOURNE **Match Drawn**
England 294 (G Ulyett 87, W Bates 58, J Selby 55) and 308 (J Selby 70, W H Scotton 50, W H Cooper 6–120)
Australia 320 (T P Horan 124) and 127–3
2 SYDNEY **Australia won by 5 wkts**
England 133 (G E Palmer 7–68) and 232 (G Ulyett 67, R G Barlow 62, T W Garrett 4–62, G E Palmer 4–97)
Australia 197 (W Bates 4–52) and 169–5
3 SYDNEY **Australia won by 6 wkts**
England 188 (A Shrewsbury 82, G E Palmer 5–46) and 134 (T W Garrett 6–78, G E Palmer 4–44)
Australia 260 (P S McDonnell 147, A C Bannerman 70, E Peate 5–43) and 66–4
4 MELBOURNE **Match Drawn**
England 309 (G Ulyett 149, T W Garrett 5–80) and 234–2 (G Ulyett 64, R G Barlow 56, W Bates 50)
Australia 300 (W L Murdoch 85, P S McDonnell 52, W E Midwinter 4–81)

England v Australia
1881–82 Averages

Batting	I	No	Runs	HS	Avge
G. Ulyett (E)	8	0	438	149	54.75
P.S. McDonnell (A)	7	1	302	147	50.33
W.L. Murdoch (A)	7	1	215	85	35.83
T.P. Horan (A)	7	1	212	124	35.33
R.G. Barlow (E)	7	0	210	62	30.00
J. Selby (E)	8	1	202	70	28.85

Bowling	O	M	Runs	W	Avge	BB
T.W. Garrett (A)	213.3	76	367	18	20.38	6–78
W. Bates (E)	240.2	121	334	16	20.87	4–52
G.E. Palmer (A)	365.2	145	522	24	21.75	7–68
E. Peate (E)	232	117	256	11	23.37	5–43
W. Midwinter (E)	194	79	272	10	27.20	4–81

(62) made the first Test opening stand of a century (122). The later batting failed, however, and Australia needed only 168, which they scored for the loss of five wickets.

In the third Test, also at Sydney, England were dismissed for 188, despite Shrewsbury's 82. A.C. Bannerman (70) and Percy McDonnell (147) added a record Test stand of 199 for Australia's fourth wicket. The other nine batsmen managed only 29 between them. England failed again with 134, and Australia won comfortably by six wickets.

In the fourth and final Test at Melbourne Ulyett opened and scored 149 on the first day to record England's first century in Australia. The first innings scores were very even at 309 and 300, and England had made 234 for 2 in the second innings when the match was left drawn, there being no play on the fourth day. Strangely this was the last drawn Test match in Australia for over 60 years.

1882: The Ashes of English cricket taken to Australia

The only Test match played by the visiting Australians in 1882 provided England with the greatest cricketing shock in her history, and set up the Ashes series which has enthralled cricketers until this day.

Murdoch beat Hornby in the toss at the Oval, and Australia batted. Heavy rain had made the pitch difficult, and they were rapidly 30 for six, and twenty minutes after lunch all out for 63, Peate and Barlow being the destroyers. The England batting was extremely strong, with only one player averaging less than 24, but Spofforth's dismissal of W.G. Grace for 4 gave the Aussies encouragement, and at the end of the day they had dismissed England for 101, with Spofforth taking seven for 46.

It poured overnight, to such an extent that when play resumed late next day, the conditions and wet ball were against the bowlers. Hugh Massie made the most of it by hitting out, scoring 55 runs in as many minutes in an opening stand of 66. When his brilliant

1882 5th Series Aus 1, Eng 0
1 THE OVAL **Australia won by 7 runs**
Australia 63 (R G Barlow 5–19, E Peate 4–31) and 112 (H H Massie 55, E Peate 4–40)
England 101 (F R Spofforth 7–46) and 77 (F R Spofforth 7–44)

innings was over, Australia slumped to 79 for five, but Murdoch held firm and by scoring 29 helped raise the total to 122. England needed just 85 to win.

Hornby and Barlow (of Francis Thompson's famous poem 'At Lord's') were dismissed by Spofforth with successive balls at 15, but Grace and Ulyett took the score past 50 and all seemed well. Then both were out: 53 for four.

Spofforth and Boyle continued to bowl splendidly, and wickets continued to fall: four fell between 70 and 75, leaving the last pair, Studd and Peate, to get ten to win. They could manage only two, and Australia won by seven runs. Spofforth's seven for 44 gave him match figures of 14 for 90 – he was truly the 'Demon' bowler. Grace described Blackham's wicket-keeping as perfection.

But the most famous comment has been credited to Reginald Shirley Brooks and appeared in the *Sporting Times* as an obituary notice, shown below.

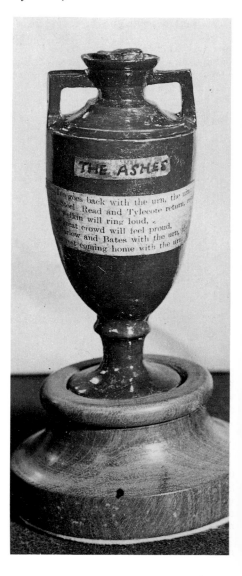

IN AFFECTIONATE REMEMBRANCE

OF

ENGLISH CRICKET

WHICH DIED AT THE OVAL

ON

29th August 1882,

Deeply lamented by a large circle of sorrowing friends and acquaintances.

R. I. P.

N.B.—The body will be cremated, and the ashes taken to Australia.

1882–83: The Ashes assume substance and return to England

The 1882–83 tour of Australia was organized and managed by the Melbourne Cricket Club. The Hon Ivo Bligh, the Kent batsman, captained the party of eight amateurs and four professionals.

At a dinner before departure Bligh promised to bring back to England 'the Ashes of English cricket' of the famous obituary notice.

On the way out on the boat the team played a match at Colombo in Ceylon, which was to become a tradition lasting until air travel for Test teams replaced the steamer. Unfortunately 360 miles out of Colombo the boat collided with a sailing ship, and both returned to port. The party's only fast bowler, the Notts professional Fred Morley, broke a rib and was not much use on tour.

Having easily beaten Victoria and New South Wales, the tourists arrived at Sydney to begin the first of three matches billed as 'Mr Murdoch's XI v The Hon Ivo F.W. Bligh's Team'. Murdoch's XI was in effect the side which had won at the Oval, and this was the first 'Test' of the series.

With Morley in bed, the England team was the remainder. Australia scored 291, George Bonnor's hard-hitting 85 being the highlight, while the best bowler was the seventh tried, the debutant C.F.H. Leslie, whose 3–31 remained his best effort in all first-class cricket. England could muster only 177, with Palmer taking seven for 65, and under the rules of the day were asked to follow on, making 169. Needing only 57 to win, Australia scored them easily. The match aroused great excitement and 54,000 watched the three days play.

The visitors played much better at Melbourne, and established some new Test records. Batting first, they made 294, and in Australia's innings Willie Bates of Yorkshire took England's first hat-trick in dismissing McDonnell, Giffen and Bonnor. He finished with seven for 28 as Australia were dismissed for 114 and made to follow on. Bates then returned 7–74 as Australia were put out again for 153. England thus achieved the first innings victory in Test cricket, while Bates, who scored 55 in England's knock, became the first player to score a half-century and take ten or more wickets in a match.

Both teams travelled straight to Sydney for the third and deciding match of the rubber. Bligh again won the toss and batted, and 20,000 spectators saw the beginning of play. England, at 75 for five, were not batting well, but E.F.S. Tylecote, the Kent wicket-keeper, scored 66, the first Test half-century by a keeper, and England reached 247. The opening batsman A.C. Bannerman did well for Australia, scoring 94, and at the end of the first day Australia were 133 for one, but on the second day they collapsed for 218. England then made only 123, with Spofforth taking seven for 44. Australia needed only 153 to win, but Dick Barlow returned even better figures of 7–40 as the home side were shot out for 83.

A curiosity of this match was that two pitches were prepared with the captains

being able to choose on which pitch to bat. There was some criticism of Barlow from the Australians, who accused him of running on the pitch and spoiling it with his spikes. Bligh's defence was that Spofforth was in the habit of doing exactly the same.

England had thus won the series 2–1, and some Melbourne ladies burned a bail, placed the ashes in a small urn and presented them to Bligh, as 'the Ashes of English cricket' which he had won back. The urn, with the embroidered velvet bag in which it was presented, remains in the Memorial Gallery at Lord's and is not sent back and forth between England and Australia, although the ownership of the Ashes has been hotly contested ever since.

Although England won the Ashes, a fourth match now designated a Test match was played at Sydney, between the tourists and a 'Combined Australian XI'. By now the small party was suffering further handicaps in the form of injuries and Australia won an interesting match by four wickets. There were some good performances, notably from Steel, who made 135 not out, and Blackham, who became the first wicket-keeper to score two half-centuries in a Test.

Two oddities in this match concerned the pitch, or rather pitches, because four were prepared, one for each innings, and Midwinter, who after two appearances for Australia and four for England, now reverted to Australia for the first of another six matches.

So Australia levelled the series and the

tourists, nursing their aches and pains, finished with an innings defeat by Victoria. But by reclaiming the Ashes they had added interest to the whole series of England-Australia matches.

ENGLAND V AUSTRALIA 1882
Only Test, The Oval: Australia won by seven runs

AUSTRALIA

A.C. Bannerman	c Grace b Peate	9	c Studd b Barnes	13
H.H. Massie	b Ulyett	1	b Steel	55
W.L. Murdoch*	b Peate	13	(4) run out	29
G.J. Bonnor	b Barlow	1	(3) b Ulyett	2
T.P. Horan	b Barlow	3	c Grace b Peate	2
G. Giffen	b Peate	2	c Grace b Peate	0
J.M. Blackham†	c Grace b Barlow	17	c Lyttelton b Peate	7
T.W. Garrett	c Read b Peate	10	(10) not out	2
H.F. Boyle	b Barlow	2	(11) b Steel	0
S.P. Jones	c Barnes b Barlow	0	(8) run out	6
F.R. Spofforth	not out	4	(9) b Peate	0
Extras	(B 1)	1	(B 6)	6
Total		**63**		**122**

ENGLAND

R.G. Barlow	c Bannerman b Spofforth	11	(3) b Spofforth	0
W.G. Grace	b Spofforth	4	(1) c Bannerman b Boyle	32
G. Ulyett	st Blackham b Spofforth	26	(4) c Blackham b Spofforth	11
A.P. Lucas	c Blackham b Boyle	9	(5) b Spofforth	5
Hon A. Lyttelton†	c Blackham b Spofforth	2	(6) b Spofforth	12
C.T. Studd	b Spofforth	0	(10) not out	0
J.M. Read	not out	19	(8) b Spofforth	0
W. Barnes	b Boyle	5	(9) c Murdoch b Boyle	2
A.G. Steel	b Garrett	14	(7) c and b Spofforth	0
A.N. Hornby*	b Spofforth	2	(2) b Spofforth	9
E. Peate	c Boyle b Spofforth	0	b Boyle	2
Extras	(B 6, LB 2, NB 1)	9	(B 3, NB 1)	4
Total		**101**		**77**

ENGLAND	O	M	R	W	O	M	R	W	FALL OF WICKETS				
Peate	38	24	31	4	21	9	40	4		A	E	A	E
Ulyett	9	5	11	1	6	2	10	1	Wkt	1st	1st	2nd	2nd
Barlow	31	22	19	5	13	5	27	0	1st	6	13	66	15
Steel	2	1	1	0	7	0	15	2	2nd	21	18	70	15
Barnes					12	5	15	1	3rd	22	57	70	51
Studd					4	1	9	0	4th	26	59	79	53
									5th	30	60	79	66
AUSTRALIA									6th	30	63	99	70
Spofforth	36.3	18	46	7	28	15	44	7	7th	48	70	114	70
Garrett	16	7	22	1	7	2	10	0	8th	53	96	117	75
Boyle	19	7	24	2	20	11	19	3	9th	59	101	122	75
									10th	63	101	122	77

1882–83 6th Series Aus 2, Eng 2

1 MELBOURNE   Australia won by 9 wkts
Australia 291 (G J Bonnor 85) and 58–1
England 177 (G E Palmer 7–65) and 169 (G Giffen 4–38)

2 MELBOURNE   England won by an innings and 27 runs
England 294 (W W Read 75, W Bates 55, C F H Leslie 54, G E Palmer 5–103, G Giffen 4–89)
Australia 114 (W Bates 7–28) and 153 (W Bates 7–74)
W Bates performed the hat-trick in the first innings

3 SYDNEY   England won by 69 runs
England 247 (W W Read 66, E F S Tylecote 66, F R Spofforth 4–73) and 123 (F R Spofforth 7–44)
Australia 218 (A C Bannerman 94, F Morley 4–47) and 83 (R G Barlow 7–40)

4 SYDNEY   Australia won by 4 wkts
England 263 (A G Steel 135) and 197
Australia 262 (G J Bonnor 87, J McC Blackham 57) and 199–6 (A C Bannerman 63, J McC Blackham 58)

1882–83 Averages

Batting	I	No	Runs	HS	Avge
A.G. Steel (E)	7	1	274	135	45.66
A.C. Bannerman (A)	8	1	255	94	36.42
J.M. Blackham (A)	7	1	204	58	34.00
W.W. Read (E)	7	0	228	75	32.57
G.J. Bonnor (A)	7	0	217	87	31.00

Bowling	O	M	Runs	W	Avge	BB
W. Bates (E)	192.3	87	286	18	15.88	7–28
A.G. Steel (E)	130	49	195	11	17.72	3–27
G.E. Palmer (A)	270.1	114	397	21	18.90	7–65
R.G. Barlow (E)	244	124	343	16	21.43	7–40
F.R. Spofforth (A)	244.1	93	408	18	22.66	7–44

1884: 'No play—rain' at Old Trafford and Lord's first Test

The Australian party which came to England in 1884 was a strong one, and for the first series of Tests in England the home country also put out strong teams – only three players made their Test debuts during the series.

Old Trafford staged the first Test on 10, 11 and 12 July, and amazingly there was no play on the first day because of rain. Old Trafford thereby began as it often seemed to continue in future years.

When play started, England batted first and were rapidly put out for 95, Spofforth and Boyle taking four for 42 and six for 42 respectively. Australia nearly doubled this with 182, but there was not quite time to complete a third innings by the end of the match, England being 180 for 9 at the close.

The second Test, on 21, 22 and 23 July was the first to be at Lord's, which thus became the third Test ground in England and the fifth in the world. At this stage England teams were picked by the authorities at the ground staging the match. There were four changes between Old Trafford and Lord's, and it is interesting to note that the captain and wicket-keeper at Old Trafford, the Lancashire players Hornby and Dick Pilling, were replaced at Lord's by Lord Harris and the Hon A. Lyttelton.

Australia batted first at Lord's and made 229, an odd feature being that the top scorer, H.J.H. Scott, was caught by his captain, Murdoch. W.G. Grace had injured a finger, and Murdoch, who had already been dismissed, fielded as substitute for him. Peate clean bowled four of the top five batsmen, establishing an English superiority early in the match. Steel scored 148 for England, and Ulyett took seven for 36 when Australia batted again, giving England victory by an innings and five runs.

Records were established at the Oval. Australia made 551, easily the highest innings total to date, and Murdoch, with 211, scored the first double century. Three of the first four' Australians made centuries, and Murdoch and Scott's stand of 207 for the third wicket was a Test match record. Australia reached 432, higher than any previous Test innings, before the fourth wicket fell.

The laws did not allow declarations in 1884, and Murdoch was forced to bat on. All eleven England players bowled (the first instance of such in a Test) and the most successful was the wicket-keeper, Alfred Lyttelton, who took four for 19 with lobs, claiming Midwinter caught behind the wicket by his substitute, W.G. Grace. England followed on, but there was no time for a result, and at 85 for two forced the draw. So England retained the hard-won Ashes in a strange and in many ways unsatisfactory first rubber in England.

1884 7th Series Eng 1, Aus 0, Drawn 2

1 OLD TRAFFORD Match Drawn
England 95 (H F Boyle 6–42, F R Spofforth 4–42) and 180–9 (G E Palmer 4–47)
Australia 182

2 LORD'S England won by an innings and 5 runs
Australia 229 (H J H Scott 75, G Giffen 63, E Peate 6–85) and 145 (G Ulyett 7–36)
England 379 (A G Steel 148, G E Palmer 6–111)

3 THE OVAL Match Drawn
Australia 551 (W L Murdoch 211, P S McDonnell 103, H J H Scott 102, A Lyttelton 4–19)
England 346 (W W Read 117, W H Scotton 90, G E Palmer 4–90) and 85–2

All eleven of England bowled in Australia's innings – Lyttelton, the wicket-keeper, bowling under-arm, had the best figures

---

1884 Averages

Batting	I	No	Runs	HS	Avge
H.J.H. Scott (A)	4	1	220	102	73.33
W.L. Murdoch (A)	4	0	266	211	66.50
A.G. Steel (E)	4	0	212	148	53.00

Bowling	O	M	Runs	W	Avge	BB
G. Ulyett (E)	136.1	67	194	11	17.63	7–36
G.E. Palmer (A)	173	65	260	14	18.57	6–111
E. Peate (E)	168	68	280	11	25.45	6–85
F.R. Spofforth (A)	192.1	82	301	10	30.10	4–42

1884–85: Captains, bowlers and umpires rebel, but an exciting series

The entrepreneurial team of Lillywhite, Shaw and Shrewsbury arranged their second tour to Australia in 1884–85, Lillywhite confining himself solely to umpiring this time, and Shaw being manager and occasional player in minor games. Shrewsbury was captain. It was the strongest side sent to Australia to date, with six of the players coming from Notts, four from Yorkshire, and one each from Lancashire and Surrey.

On the way, the team played a match in Suez, and on arrival at Adelaide learned that Fred Morley, the main victim of the boating accident off Ceylon on their previous tour, had died.

The eighth match played in Australia added the Adelaide Oval to the list of Test grounds. This first Test was labelled 'Murdoch's Australian Team v Alfred Shaw's Team', although in fact Shaw did not play and Shrewsbury was captain. The Australian team represented the 1884 tourists to England, although there were two enforced changes from the team at the Oval. There was no change in the excellence of McDonnell's batting, however, as he made 124 to register his second century in successive Test innings to become the first to achieve this feat. Australia's total of 243 was not good enough, however, England passing it with only two men out. Barnes' 134 was top score in a total of 369.

McDonnell was run out for 83 in Australia's second knock, but a total of 191 left only 65 for England to get. They got them for the loss of two wickets, the four batsmen to appear all being from Nottinghamshire.

Adelaide is regarded as one of the more beautiful Australian grounds, but this match, arranged by the South Australian Cricket Association, did not augur well. A violent dust storm on the second day caused the players to lie down to avoid suffocation, and the next day, luckily a Sunday, the ground was flooded.

There was an unfortunate squabble about money, too. The English organizers, who were, it must be remembered, speculators hoping to make a profit, objected to the Australian players being paid the same fee as the English, this not having been the case in 1884, when the English had played for £10 a man and the Australian tourists had made a good profit. Murdoch, however, insisted that his team should receive the same as the English tourists, but most of the rest of Australia agreed with the tourists' view, with the result that when the second Test was played at Melbourne, none of the Australian 1884 tourists was picked. Nine of the team were making their Test debuts, one of the exceptions being the captain, Tom Horan. The changes meant that the wicket-keeper, Blackham, missed his first Test, having played in the first 17, the longest run of the 22 players who had played in the very first Test.

England were not surprisingly too strong for the Australians, scoring 401 (Briggs 121), forcing the follow-on, and needing to score only six runs for a ten-wicket victory.

For the third Test at Sydney, four of the 1884 Australians agreed to play, including Spofforth, who took ten wickets. H.H. Massie was the captain. England this time had the troubles, their best bowler Barnes, who had taken nine wickets in the previous Test, having an argument with Shrewsbury and refusing to bowl. It undoubtedly cost England the match. In a low-scoring game England needed 214 in the fourth innings, and despite a century stand for the seventh wicket between Flowers and Read, who each scored 56, they fell seven short.

Barnes bowled for England in the fourth Test, also at Sydney, when Blackham returned and captained the Australian side. England, having scored 269, were having the best of it until George Bonnor came to the wicket with Australia 119 for six. He scored the fastest Test century to date (100 minutes) and his 128 gave Australia a lead of 40. England were caught on a drying pitch and Palmer and Spofforth, bowling unchanged, dismissed them for 77, leading to an eight-wicket win for Australia.

This was the first Test series of five Tests, and the fifth assumed great significance as it would decide the rubber. It followed directly the Sydney Test and was played at Melbourne. Australia's captain changed for every Test in this series, Horan now being reinstated as skipper. In contrast, England played all five Tests with an unchanged side.

Australia's first-innings total of 163 would have been worse without a last-wicket stand of 64 between Trumble and Spofforth, who scored 50 at number eleven. Shrewsbury then made 105 not out as England compiled 386, and the match was virtually settled. Australia were hurried out for 125 and England won the series with an emphatic innings victory. An oddity was that Jarvis, the wicket-keeper, became the second Australian to field as a substitute for England and hold a catch (Spofforth). There were umpiring problems with umpire Hodges refusing to stand after tea on the third day because of the English players' criticism of him.

The tourists played a final match at Adelaide, and again were interrupted by a duststorm and violent rain. Other perils of touring were brought home when Briggs was reported killed after an accident when he was thrown from a horse and his pipe was rammed into the roof of his mouth – luckily he regained consciousness after four hours.

1884–85 8th Series Eng 3, Aus 2

1 ADELAIDE England won by 8 wkts
Australia 243 (P S McDonnell 124, J McC Blackham 66, W Bates 5–31) and 191 (P S McDonnell 83, R Peel 5–51)
England 369 (W Barnes 134, W H Scotton 82, G Ulyett 68, G E Palmer 5–81) and 67–2

2 MELBOURNE England won by 10 wkts
England 401 (J Briggs 121, A Shrewsbury 72, W Barnes 58, S P Jones 4–47) and 7–0
Australia 279 (A H Jarvis 82, T P Horan 63, J W Trumble 59) and 126 (W Barnes 6–31)

3 SYDNEY Australia won by 6 runs
Australia 181 (T W Garrett 51, W Flowers 5–46, W Attewell 4–53) and 165 (W Bates 5–24)
England 133 (T P Horan 6–40, F R Spofforth 4–54) and 207 (W Flowers 56, J M Read 56, F R Spofforth 6–90)

4 SYDNEY Australia won by 8 wkts
England 269 (W Bates 64, W Barnes 50, G Giffen 7–117) and 77 (F R Spofforth 5–30, G E Palmer 4–32)
Australia 309 (G J Bonnor 128, A C Bannerman 51, W Barnes 4–61) and 40–2

5 MELBOURNE England won by an innings and 98 runs
Australia 163 (F R Spofforth 50, G Ulyett 4–52) and 125
England 386 (A Shrewsbury 105, W Barnes 74, W Bates 61)

1884–85 Averages

Batting	I	No	Runs	HS	Avge	
W. Barnes (E)	8	1	369	134	52.71	
A. Shrewsbury (E)	9	3	301	105*	50.20	

Bowling	O	M	Runs	W	Avge	BB
W. Barnes (E)	206.2	97	292	19	15.36	6–31
F.R. Spofforth (A)	194.1	84	306	19	16.10	6–90
G. Ulyett (E)	178.2	86	295	14	21.07	4–52
R. Peel (E)	390.2	193	451	21	21.47	5–51
W. Attewell (E)	325.1	190	310	13	23.00	4–53

The Adelaide Oval became a Test match ground in 1884, joining Melbourne and Sydney in Australia and the Oval, Old Trafford and Lord's in England. This is the scene during the Test in January 1937.

1886: Arthur Shrewsbury and W.G. swop the English innings record

It was a weak Australian party which toured England and played three Tests in 1886. Spofforth, Palmer and Garrett were all nearing the ends of their Test careers. H.J.H. Scott captained the tourists, and A.G. Steel led England in all three Tests.

In the first Test at Old Trafford, Hornby and Pilling were recalled to the colours, but in the event Hornby could not play – he and Barnes, another who cried off, were replaced by Barlow and Briggs, two other Lancastrians. Australia made 205, of which Sam Jones made 87, a total England bettered by only 18. Barlow took seven for 44 in helping dismiss Australia a second time for only 123, but England did not find the 106 runs needed easy to get, winning only by four wickets.

At Lord's Briggs and Barlow retained their places, but Pilling was replaced by Tylecote. Shrewsbury batted brilliantly on a wicket made awkward by rain, and compiled England's highest score to date with 164. The total of 353 was too much for Australia, who were dismissed for 121, Briggs taking five for 29, and forced to follow on. Briggs did even better this time with six for 45, and Australia were beaten by an innings and 106 runs.

W.G. Grace opened the England innings at the Oval and soon regained his highest Test score for England record, making 170, which was also the size of the opening partnership between him and W.H. Scotton, a record opening for either side. Scotton made only 34 of them, having spent over an hour on 24. George Lohmann, in his first series, took seven Australian wickets for 36, bowling throughout the innings with Briggs, and Australia made only 68. The batting order was revised for the follow-on, and 149 was a more respectable score, but not enough to avoid defeat by an innings and 217. Lohmann and Briggs took eight wickets between them in this innings. It was an easy retention of the Ashes for England.

1886   9th Series   Eng 3, Aus 0
1 OLD TRAFFORD   **England won by 4 wkts**
Australia 205 (S P Jones 87, G Ulyett 4–46) and 123 (R G Barlow 7–44)
England 223 (W W Read 51, F R Spofforth 4–82) and 107–6
2 LORD'S   **England won by an innings and 106 runs**
England 353 (A Shrewsbury 164, W Barnes 58, F R Spofforth 4–73)
England 121 (J Briggs 5–29) and 126 (J Briggs 6–45)
3 THE OVAL   **England won by an innings and 217 runs**
England 434 (W G Grace 170, W W Read 94, J Briggs 53, F R Spofforth 4–65)
Australia 68 (G A Lohmann 7–36) and 149 (G A Lohmann 5–68)

1886 Averages

Batting	I	No	Runs	HS	Avge
A. Shrewsbury (E)	4	0	243	164	60.75
W.G. Grace (E)	4	0	200	170	50.00

Bowling	O	M	Runs	W	Avge	BB
J. Briggs (E)	134.1	75	132	17	7.76	6–45
R.G. Barlow (E)	120	70	95	10	9.50	7–44
G.A. Lohmann (E)	116.2	55	191	13	14.69	7–36
F.R. Spofforth (A)	168.3	73	260	14	18.57	4–65

1886–87: England win again, but Australia's new boys shine

The third Lillywhite/Shaw/Shrewsbury party to tour Australia, with its usual dependence on Nottinghamshire, included only eleven players.

Australia produced two brilliant new Test bowlers for the combined Australia XI which played Shaw's Team in the first Test at Sydney, J.J. Ferris and C.T.B. Turner. They were the only bowlers required for the first innings. Percy McDonnell, captaining Australia for the first time, put England in – the first occasion this happened in a Test – and with such spectacular results that England were shot out for what remains their lowest Test total, 45. It might have been worse – Lohmann made 17 at number eight, coming in at 17 for six.

Australia did not bat too well in their turn, making only 119. England made good the arrears with only one man out but then lost six wickets in adding 23, only a wagging tail bringing their score to 184 in a fluctuating match. Australia sadly fell 14 runs short of their target, being out for 97, Barnes taking six for 28. McDonnell's brave decision had not paid.

McDonnell and Barnes, both argumentative characters came to blows and Barnes got the worst of it, for a punch intended for the Aussie skipper's face missed and hit a brick wall, putting Barnes out of action for most of the rest of the tour. While mentioning law and order, a curiosity of the match was that Charles Bannerman, who played in the first Test of all, made his Test umpiring debut in a match in which his brother, A.C., was playing.

When the Second Test came round, also

at Sydney, Reg Wood, born in Cheshire but living in Australia and working on the Melbourne ground, was co-opted to take Barnes' place in what for him was, not surprisingly, his only Test.

England batted first again, and were again dismissed for a low score, 151, with Turner and Ferris sharing the wickets. Lohmann, however, bowled brilliantly and took eight wickets for 35, the most wickets anybody had taken in a Test innings to date. Australia were out for 84. Australia, following England's 154, needed 222 in the fourth innings, but fell 72 short. Wood, England's 'substitute', scored six in each innings.

England had retained the Ashes, and had now won six Tests consecutively, but Turner and Ferris, the Australian bowlers in their debut series, had taken 35 of the 40 English wickets.

Above: The 1886–87 English tourists in Australia.

The Australian tourists in 1886. Left to right, back: McIlwraith, Trumble, Jarvis, Bruce, Jones, Palmer, Spofforth. Front: Major B.J. Wardill (manager), Blackham, Evans, Scott, Bonnor, Garrett, Giffen.

1886–87   10th Series   Eng 2, Aus 0
1 SYDNEY   **England won by 13 runs**
England 45 (C T B Turner 6–15, J J Ferris 4–27) and 184 (J J Ferris 5–76)
Australia 119 and 97 (W Barnes 6–28)
2 SYDNEY   **England won by 71 runs**
England 151 (J J Ferris 5–71, C T B Turner 5–41) and 154 (J J Ferris 4–69, C T B Turner 4–52)
Australia 84 (G A Lohmann 8–35) and 150 (W Bates 4–26)

1887–88: Discord as two parties tour Australia

The manager of the 1886 Australian tourists to England, Major Wardill, indicated that the Melbourne Club would invite a team to Australia in 1887–88. The Hon M.B. Hawke (later Lord Hawke) captained a party raised by G.F. Vernon, consisting of six professionals from Yorkshire, Surrey and Notts, and seven amateurs, including Hawke and Vernon. The Lillywhite, Shaw and Shrewsbury combination would not give up their by now established tour and organized a rival party. Supported by the New South Wales Association and captained by C.A. Smith (later C. Aubrey Smith, the Hollywood film actor) it consisted of eight professionals (another five from Yorkshire, Surrey and Notts) and four amateurs.

The parties arrived at Adelaide on the same boat, but went their different ways, only to join together when Vernon's team had played 21 games and Shrewsbury's 16. The occasion was the Combined England Team v Combined Australia, at Sydney, now regarded as the only Test of the tour.

The England side contained seven of Shrewsbury's men (six professional) and four of Vernon's (two professional), one of whom, W.W. Read, was captain.

It should have been the most representative match to date between the countries, but several Australians refused to play, and the England bowlers, in particular, were too good. Put in by McDonnell on a dead pitch, England made 113, but Lohmann and Peel bowled throughout to dismiss Australia for

42. Set a target of 209, Australia were dismissed largely by the same bowlers for 82. Turner and Ferris took 18 wickets for Australia to maintain their run.

1887–88 11th Series Eng 1, Aus 0
1 SYDNEY England won by 126 runs
England 113 (C T B Turner 5–44, J J Ferris 4–60) and 137 (C T B Turner 7–43)
Australia 42 (R Peel 5–18, G A Lohmann 5–17) and 82 (R Peel 5–40, G A Lohmann 4–35)

1888: Rain causes collapses for both sides

The 1888 Australians had played a match against Vernon's side and two against Shrewsbury's side in Australia, losing them all, so prospects did not look good when P.S. McDonnell opened his side's batting at Lord's. England had now won seven Tests consecutively.

Play began late because of heavy rain. Australia were dismissed for 116, but this turned out to be a winning score. They captured three England wickets overnight, and then on a muddy pitch the next day 27 wickets fell for 157 in little more than three hours: England 53, Australia 60, England 62. Australia won by 61 runs, Turner and Ferris doing the damage.

At the Oval, the Surrey selectors chose five Surrey men (two more than at Lord's), and Grace took over the captaincy from Steel. Australia made only 80, and when England replied with 317, were dismissed again for 100 and an innings defeat.

All was to play for at Old Trafford, hosting the final Test. True to tradition, Pilling was back as wicket-keeper and there was a downpour before the start.

England made 172, and like Australia's 116 in the first Test it proved to be a big score. Two Australian wickets were down overnight, but the remaining 18 fell before lunch on the second day, setting up several records: the most wickets to fall before lunch in a Test, the shortest innings in a Test (69 minutes) and the shortest Test in England (6 hours, 34 minutes of play). Peel did most damage with nine pre-lunch wickets (11 in all).

The figures of Turner and Ferris remained astonishing – since their joint debuts in Test cricket they had taken 85 of 96 wickets taken by Australian bowlers.

1888 12th Series Eng 2, Aus 1
1 LORD'S Australia won by 61 runs
Australia 116 (R Peel 4–36) and 60 (R Peel 4–14, G A Lohmann 4–33)
England 53 (C T B Turner 5–27) and 62 (C T B Turner 5–36, J J Ferris 5–26)
2 THE OVAL England won by an innings and 137 runs
Australia 80 (J Briggs 5–25) and 100 (W Barnes 5–32, R Peel 4–49)
England 317 (R Abel 70, W Barnes 62, G A Lohmann 62, C T B Turner 6–112)
3 OLD TRAFFORD England won by an innings and 21 runs
England 172 (C T B Turner 5–86)
Australia 81 (R Peel 7–31) and 70 (R Peel 4–37)

1888 Averages
Batting: No one qualifies

Bowling	O	M	Runs	W	Avge	BB
R. Peel (E)	110.2	48	181	24	7.54	7–31
J. Briggs (E)	84.1	42	94	12	7.83	5–25
C.T.B. Turner (A)	164	62	261	21	12.42	6–112
G.A. Lohmann (E)	94.3	50	144	11	13.09	4–33
J.J. Ferris (A)	119.2	59	167	11	15.18	5–26

1890: Records for debutants beginning short careers

Australia brought a strong team to England under Murdoch in 1890, and John Lyons began the tour confidently enough by having his half-century on the board only 36 minutes after the start of the first Test at Lord's. Australia, however, subsided to 132. England began much worse, with W.G. Grace out without a run on the board, but prospered to 174 despite Lyons claiming five wickets – the first Australian bowler other than Turner or Ferris to obtain more than two for six Tests. A debutant, John Barrett, opened in Australia's second knock and carried his bat for 67 not out, the first instance in Test matches. Australia's 176 left England to get 136, and W.G. was still there when the seven-wicket win was achieved.

The second Test was at the Oval, and Yorkshire refused to release Peel and Ulyett, two stalwarts, for the match, so Stoddart decided he, too, would miss the Test to play against them for Middlesex.

Rain delayed the start, and Australia were soon out for 92 on a difficult wicket, Fred Martin of Kent, making his debut, taking six for 50. England did little better with only 100, and Australia lost two more quick second-innings wickets on the first day. Australia did reach 102, the highest innings of the match, on the second day, however, and Turner and Ferris caused England to struggle to get the 95 needed, taking eight wickets in the process. The match was won on an overthrow by Barrett, the record-maker of the first Test. Sadly, because of his profession as a doctor, he did not play Test cricket again. Martin took six wickets in the second innings – his 12 in a match on his debut was a record which lasted for 82 years, but strangely he, too, was to play in only two Tests. Even more oddly, his record was beaten by Bob Massie in 1972, with 16 wickets on his debut at Lord's – he, too, had a very short Test career, appearing in only two series.

The third Test at Old Trafford was washed out without a ball being bowled. Barrett was thus deprived of another Test, but not Martin – after his 12-wicket debut he was not picked.

1890 13th Series Eng 2, Aus 0
1 LORD'S England won by 7 wkts
Australia 132 (J J Lyons 55, W Attewell 4–42) and 176 (J E Barrett 67)
England 173 (G Ulyett 74, J J Lyons 5–30) and 137–3 (W G Grace 75)
2 THE OVAL England won by 2 wkts
Australia 92 (F Martin 6–50) and 102 (F Martin 6–52)
England 100 (J J Ferris 4–25) and 95–8 (J J Ferris 5–49)
(The match arranged to be played at Old Trafford was abandoned without a ball being bowled)

Turner, Charles Thomas Biass

Turner was born at Bathurst, NSW, on 16 November 1862, appearing first for New South Wales in 1882–83. He was a right-arm medium fast bowler, and made his debut for Australia in 1886–87. His Test career was highly successful, and he led the Australian bowling on his three tours to England. In 17 Tests he took 101 wickets, average 16.53. All his wickets were against England, and of those with 100 wickets in Ashes Tests, his average is the best. He died on 1 January 1944 at Manly, NSW.

1891–92: The recovery of Australia and Australian cricket

Because the dual tour of Australia in 1887–88 had been disastrous financially, nobody cared to risk another. Cricket began to fall in popularity in Australia. Lord Sheffield, a great patron of Sussex cricket, then came to the rescue by organizing a tour for 1891–92, with W.G. Grace as captain. (Sheffield later presented the Sheffield Shield for inter-state cricket in Australia.) Shrewsbury and Gunn of the old order declined the terms, but it was a strong side which included four Surrey professionals.

Blackham, the wicket-keeper, captained the Combined Australia side which began the first of three Tests by batting at Melbourne on New Year's Day. Australia's 240 was passed by England's 264, Grace scoring 50 in his first Test in Australia. Over 20,000 watched the first two days and over 10,000 the next two in what was a good match. Scoring 286, Australia left England needing 213. Grace and Stoddart soon had 60 on the board, but then both were out, and England collapsed, to manage only 158.

England were unlucky in the second Test at Sydney. Lohmann captured eight Australian wickets for the second time in his career as the home team were dismissed for 145. Bobby Abel then became the first English batsman to carry his bat through a Test innings with 132 not out in a total of 307. But excellent batting by Lyons (134) and a stubborn innings by Bannerman (91 in 448 minutes) turned certain defeat into chance of victory, with England set 230 to win. Rain did not help the cause, and Australia were victorious amid enthusiastic scenes at a great recovery.

A perfect wicket at the Adelaide Oval enabled England to reach 490 for 9 on the second day before a rainstorm stopped play for the day. Australia had no chance on the damaged pitch, especially against Briggs, who took 12 wickets, and were beaten by an innings.

1891–92 14th Series Aus 2, Eng 1
1 MELBOURNE Australia won by 54 runs
Australia 240 (W Bruce 57, J W Sharpe 6–84) and 236 (J J Lyons 51)
England 264 (W G Grace 50, G Bean 50, R W McLeod 5–55) and 158 (C T B Turner 5–51)
2 SYDNEY Australia won by 72 runs
Australia 145 (G A Lohman 8–58) and 391 (J J Lyons 134, A C Bannerman, W Bruce 72, J Briggs 4–69)
England 307 (R Abel 132, G Giffen 4–88) and 156 (A E Stoddart 69, G Giffen 6–72, C T B Turner 4–46)
3 ADELAIDE England won by an innings and 230 runs
England 499 (A E Stoddart 134, R Peel 83, W G Grace 58, J M Read 57)
Australia 100 (J Briggs 6–49) and 169 (J Briggs 6–87)

1891–92 Averages

Batting	I	No	Runs	HS	Avge
R. Abel (E)	5	1	217	132*	54.25
A.E. Stoddart (E)	5	0	565	134	53.00
J.J. Lyons (A)	6	0	287	134	47.83
W. Bruce (A)	6	0	226	72	37.66
A.C. Bannerman (A)	6	0	202	91	33.66

Bowling	O	M	Runs	W	Avge	BB
J. Briggs (E)	116.3	31	268	17	15.76	6–49
G.A. Lohmann (E)	188.3	71	289	16	18.06	8–58
C.T.B. Turner (A)	155.2	52	338	16	21.12	5–51
R.W. McLeod (A)	110.4	37	227	10	22.70	5–55
G.Giffen (A)	130.3	35	397	15	26.46	6–72

1893: Newcomers appear with centuries and wickets

Debutants and an old-stager made the biggest impressions on the first Test at Lord's. Arthur Shrewsbury, opening for England, made 106 in the first innings and 81 in the second, passing 1,000 runs in Tests, the first player to achieve this aggregate. F.S. Jackson, one of four English debutants, made 91, helping Shrewsbury to add 137 in the first innings, in which England totalled 334.

When Australia batted, it was the turn of another England debutant to make a name for himself, Bill Lockwood, with six for 101. Australia's only newcomer, Harry Graham, did best of all, making his maiden first-class century when coming in at 75 for five. The match petered out as rain interfered, but Stoddart, captain because Grace was unavailable through injury, did just have time to become the first captain to use the Law allowing declarations in a Test match.

The Surrey player, J.M. Read, who retired early for professional reasons, was awarded the Oval Test as a benefit match, although his Test career had ended with the previous Test. Jackson made a century with the last man at the wicket, and England batted solidly for 483. Australia collapsed before Lockwood and Briggs, who repeated their nine wickets in the second innings, but this time Australia batted with determination to 349. It did not avoid the innings defeat, but A.C. Bannerman had the consolation of becoming the second player, and first Australian, to 1,000 Test runs.

At Old Trafford, Tom Richardson, the Surrey fast bowler, was a notable newcomer, and he took ten wickets, five in each innings. With a deficit of 37 on first innings, Australia were heading for defeat at 200 for nine, but Turner and Blackham put on 36 and used up time for the last wicket, which

Peel, Robert

Peel was born on 12 February 1857 at Cherwell, Leeds, and first played for Yorkshire in 1882. He was a slow left-arm bowler, whose success quickly led to an England place in 1884–85. He played in 20 Tests, 14 of them on his four tours to Australia. His Test career was cut short when Lord Hawke sacked him from the Yorkshire side in 1897 for his inebriate habits. All his 102 Test wickets were Australian, taken at an average of 16.81, the best average of any Englishman with 100 Australian wickets. He died on 12 August 1941 at Leeds, Yorkshire.

saved the game, England, with the series won, not attempting the eventual target of 198 in 135 minutes. Dr Grace belied his reputation for bad sportsmanship by putting back Turner's dislocated finger during the match-saving stand.

1893 15th Series Eng 1, Aus 0, Drawn 2
1 LORD'S Match Drawn
England 334 (A Shrewsbury 106, F S Jackson 91, C T B Turner 6–67) and 234–8 dec (A Shrewsbury 81, W Gunn 77, G Giffen 5–43)
Australia 269 (H Graham 107, S E Gregory 57, W H Lockwood 6–101)
2 THE OVAL England won by an innings and 43 runs
England 483 (F S Jackson 103, A E Stoddart 83, W G Grace 68, A Shrewsbury 66, A Ward 55, W W Read 52, G Giffen 7–128)
Australia 91 (J Briggs 5–34, W H Lockwood 4–37) and 349 (G H S Trott 92, A C Bannerman 55, G Giffen 53, J Briggs 5–114, W H Lockwood 4–96)
3 OLD TRAFFORD Match Drawn
Australia 204 (W Bruce 68, T Richardson 5–49, J Briggs 4–81) and 236 (A C Bannerman 60, T Richardson 5–107)
England 243 (W Gunn 102, G Giffen 4–113) and 118–4

1893 Averages

Batting	I	No	Runs	HS	Avge
A. Shrewsbury (E)	5	1	284	106	71.00
W. Gunn (E)	5	1	208	102*	52.00

Bowling	O	M	Runs	W	Avge	BB
W.H. Lockwood (E)	93	27	234	14	15.28	6–101
T. Richardson (E)	57.4	20	156	10	15.60	5–49
J. Briggs (E)	120.1	40	293	16	18.31	5–34
G. Giffen (A)	171.4	59	342	16	21.37	7–128
C.T.B. Turner (A)	170	72	315	11	28.63	6–67

1894–95: Twists of fortune finally point England's way in five exciting Tests

The growing importance of Test cricket was evidenced by the fact that in 1894–95 the Melbourne and Sydney authorities agreed to promote jointly an English touring team. The opposite side of the coin was that five of England's best players declined the tour, so the side was not representative, particularly in batting.

At Sydney, Australia were 21 for three, but climbed to 586, with Giffen making 161 and Syd George 201, while captain Blackham, far from declaring, made 74 at number ten, helping Gregory add 154. England batted well without a really big individual effort, and compiled 325, being forced to follow on. This time Albert Ward added 117 to his first-innings 75 (top scorer in each innings) and 437 was amassed. Australia needed only 177 to win and at the end of the fifth day were 113 for two. For the first time a Test went into a sixth day, and it was a fatal day for Australia. The rains came after the fifth day, and on the last morning Peel and Briggs wrapped up eight wickets for 53, the last five falling for only eight runs. England had won an exciting, if lucky, victory after following on 261 behind – the next Test victory after a follow-on would not occur for about 87 years.

Giffen, George

Born on 27 March 1859 at Adelaide, Giffen was the nearest Australian counterpart to W.G. Grace. He was a hard-hitting right-hand middle-order batsman and a medium-slow bowler. He first appeared for South Australia in 1877–78 and for Australia in 1881–82. He made five tours to England. In 31 Tests, in four of which he was captain, he scored 1,238 runs, average 23.35, and took 103 wickets, average 27.09. He died on 29 November 1927 at Adelaide.

The next Test, at Melbourne, was almost as remarkable. The only debutant was Arthur Coningham, whose first ball in Test cricket dismissed A.C. MacLaren. It was also the first ball of the Test – registering two 'firsts' in Test match history. This, oddly, was Coningham's only Test.

England stumbled on an awkward wicket to 75 all out, fought back to dismiss Australia for 123, then, as the wicket eased, scored 475, with every batsman reaching double figures and Stoddart getting an English record Test score of 173. Australia began well, with 191 on the board before the second wicket fell, but reached only 333 to lose by 94. Giffen, who had taken over the captaincy from Blackham, had scored 277 and taken 14 wickets in the first two Tests without being on the winning side. Giffen's time came in the third Test at Adelaide. First he scored 58 to help Australia to 238, then took five wickets as England were put out for 124. Iredale made 140 in Australia's second knock and Albert Trott took eight for 43 to give Australia a big win by 382 runs. Trott, whose first Test this was, also took part in last-wicket stands of 81 and 64, scoring 110 runs without being out. One excuse given for the poor English performance was the extraordinary heat, which reached 155F.

At Sydney, Stoddart put Australia in on a glue pot, and they were soon 51 for six, but then Graham, brought back into the side, scored a century which won the match. He thus made a century on his first appearance in both England and Australia, but he only played in two more Tests. He was helped in this match by Trott, who, promoted to number nine, helped add 112, and made 85, again not out. England were dismissed rapidly for an overwhelming Australian win which levelled the rubber.

During this match Johnny Briggs became the first to take 100 Test wickets, but only because Australia batted first. Turner achieved the feat in the English first innings.

All was to be decided at Melbourne, and public interest was at its greatest for the big match. Australia batted solidly all down the order on a good wicket to total 414, the England bowlers at last dismissing A.E. Trott. MacLaren made 120 for England before being out 'hit wicket' – at 385 England were 29 behind. Richardson (6–104) bowled well when Australia went in again, but everybody got double figures except A.E. Trott (0), and 267 left England needing 297 for the Ashes.

Two men were out for 28, but John Brown then played an exhilarating innings, passing 50 in 28 minutes and 100 in 95, both new Test records, and adding 210 with Ward before being out for 140. Ward was out for 93 but England won a famous victory by six wickets. Giffen scored 573 runs and took 34 wickets in the series – a great all-round performance in a series-losing team. It was A.E. Trott's third and last match for Australia – he later played twice for England against South Africa.

1894–95 16th Series Eng 3, Aus 2

1 SYDNEY England won by 10 runs
Australia 586 (S E Gregory 201, G Giffen 161, F A Iredale 81, J McC Blackham 74, T Richardson 5–181) and 166 (J Darling 53, R Peel 6–67)
England 325 (A Ward 75, J Briggs 57, G Giffen 4–75) and 437 (A Ward 117, J T Brown 53, G Giffen 4–164)

2 MELBOURNE England won by 94 runs
England 75 (C T B Turner 5–32) and 475 (A E Stoddart 173, R Peel 53, G Giffen 6–15)
Australia 123 (T Richardson 5–57) and 333 (F A Iredale 68, G H S Trott 95, W Bruce 54, R Peel 4–77)

3 ADELAIDE Australia won by 382 runs
Australia 238 (G Giffen 58, T Richardson 5–75) and 411 (F A Iredale 140, W Bruce 80, A E Trott 72, R Peel 4–96)
England 124 (G Giffen 5–76, S T Callaway 5–37) and 143 (A E Trott 8–43)

4 SYDNEY Australia won by an innings and 147 runs
Australia 284 (H Graham 105, A E Trott 85, J Briggs 4–65)
England 65 and 72 (G Giffen 5–26, C T B Turner 4–33)

5 MELBOURNE England won by 6 wkts
Australia 414 (J Darling 74, S E Gregory 70, G Giffen 57, J J Lyons 55, R Peel 4–114) and 267 (G Giffen 51, J Darling 50, T Richardson 6–104)
England 385 (A C MacLaren 120, R Peel 73, A E Stoddart 68, G H S Trott 4–71, G Giffen 4–130) and 298–4 (J T Brown 140, A Ward 93)

1894–95 Averages

Batting

	I	No	Runs	HS	Avge
G. Giffen (A)	9	0	475	161	52.88
J.T. Brown (E)	10	2	343	140	42.87
A. Ward (E)	10	0	419	117	41.00
S.E. Gregory (A)	9	0	362	201	40.22
A.E. Stoddart (E)	10	1	352	173	39.11
F.A. Iredale (A)	9	0	337	140	38.44
G.H.S. Trott (A)	9	0	264	95	29.33
J. Darling (A)	9	0	258	74	28.66

Bowling

	O	M	Runs	W	Avge	BB
C.T.B. Turner (A)	187.1	76	349	18	19.38	5–32
G. Giffen (A)	343.2	111	820	34	24.11	6–155
G.H.S. Trott (A)	102.4	17	296	12	24.66	4–71
T. Richardson (E)	309.1	63	849	32	26.53	6–104
R. Peel (E)	325.1	77	721	27	26.70	6–67
J. Briggs (E)	150.3	29	435	15	29.00	4–65

AUSTRALIA V ENGLAND 1894–95
1st Test, Sydney: England won by ten runs

AUSTRALIA

J.J. Lyons	b Richardson	1	b Richardson		25
G.H.S. Trott	b Richardson	12	c Gay b Peel		8
G. Giffen	c Ford b Brockwell	161	lbw b Briggs		41
J. Darling	b Richardson	0	c Brockwell b Peel		53
F.A. Iredale	c Stoddart b Ford	81	(6) c and b Briggs		5
S.E. Gregory	c Peel b Stoddart	201	(5) c Gay b Peel		16
J.C. Reedman	c Ford b Peel	17	st Gay b Peel		4
C.E. McLeod	b Richardson	15	not out		2
C.T.B. Turner	c Gay b Peel	1	c Briggs b Peel		2
J.M. Blackham*†	b Richardson	74	(11) c and b Peel		2
E. Jones	not out	11	(10) c MacLaren b Briggs		1
Extras	(B 8, LB 3, W 1)	12	(B 2, LB 1, NB 4)		7
Total		**586**			**166**

ENGLAND

A.C. MacLaren	c Reedman b Turner	4	b Giffen		20
A. Ward	c Iredale b Turner	75	b Giffen		117
A.E. Stoddart*	c Jones b Giffen	12	c Giffen b Turner		36
J.T. Brown	run out	22	c Jones b Giffen		53
W. Brockwell	c Blackham b Jones	49	b Jones		37
R. Peel	c Gregory b Giffen	4	b Giffen		17
F.G.J. Ford	st Blackham b Giffen	30	c and b McLeod		48
J. Briggs	b Giffen	57	b McLeod		42
W.H. Lockwood	c Giffen b Trott	18	b Trott		29
L.H. Gay†	c Gregory b Reedman	33	b Trott		4
T. Richardson	not out	0	not out		12
Extras	(B 17, LB 3, W 1)	21	(B 14, LB 8)		22
Total		**325**			**437**

ENGLAND	O	M	R	W	O	M	R	W
Richardson	55.3	13	181	5	11	3	27	1
Peel	53	14	140	2	30	9	67	6
Briggs	25	4	96	0	11	2	25	3
Brockwell	22	7	78	1				
Lockwood	3	2	1	0	16	3	40	0
Ford	11	2	47	1				
Stoddart	3	0	31	1				

AUSTRALIA	O	M	R	W	O	M	R	W
Turner	44	16	89	2	35	14	78	1
Jones	18	6	44	1	19	0	57	1
Giffen	43	17	75	4	75	25	164	4
McLeod	14	2	25	0	30	6	67	2
Trott	15	4	59	1	12.4	3	22	2
Reedman	3.3	1	12	1	6	1	12	0
Lyons	2	2	0	0	2	0	12	0
Iredale					2	1	3	0

FALL OF WICKETS

	A	E	E	A
Wkt	1st	1st	2nd	2nd
1st	10	14	44	26
2nd	21	43	115	45
3rd	21	78	217	130
4th	192	149	245	135
5th	331	155	290	147
6th	379	211	296	158
7th	400	211	385	159
8th	409	252	398	161
9th	563	325	420	162
10th	586	325	437	166

1896: Clem Hill and Ranji enter the lists

Australia took a strong team under G.H.S. Trott to England for the 1896 series. Clem Hill made his debut in the first Test at Lord's, as did two outstanding wicket-keepers, A.F.A. Lilley for England and J.J. Kelly for Australia.

Australia were dismissed by the Surrey pair of Richardson and Lohmann, playing his last Test, for 53. A huge crowd of 30,000 saw England take a big lead on the first day, with captain Grace completing his 1,000 runs in Tests. However, Trott and Gregory fought back and added a record Test partnership of 221 after three second-innings wickets had fallen for 62.

Australia had 347, but England needed only 109 to win by six wickets.

Old Trafford witnessed a very exciting match. Australia made 412, with Iredale making a century, and then removed England for 231, forcing the follow-on. Ranjitsinhji, making his debut, followed his first innings 62 with a brilliant 154 not out, scoring the last 113 before lunch on the third day. With 305, England set Australia to get 125 to win, which they achieved, but only after losing seven wickets for 100. Richardson took 13 of the 17 Australian wickets. George Giffen became the first to 1,000 runs and 100 wickets in Tests.

Five players, four of them from Surrey, disputed the fees for the deciding match at the Oval, and Gunn and Lohmann refused to play. Rain prevented play for most of the first day, and gave the spinners the opportunity to skittle the opposition from the second. England made 145, and Australia collapsed from 75 without loss to 119 all out. England then made only 84, but Australia made their lowest total in England to date with 44, a score which relied on 16 from number eleven McKibbin. In fact at 25 for nine, Australia had lost 19 wickets while scoring 69. Peel, in his last Test, and J.T. Hearne, did the damage, while Trumble took 12 wickets for Australia.

1896 17th Series Eng 2, Aus 1

1 LORD'S **England won by 6 wkts**
Australia 53 (T Richardson 6–39) and 347 (G H S Trott 143, S E Gregory 103, J T Hearne 5–76, T Richardson 5–134)
England 292 (R Abel 94, W G Grace 66) and 111–4

2 OLD TRAFFORD **Australia won by 3 wkts**
Australia 412 (F A Iredale 108, G Giffen 80, G H S Trott 53, T Richardson 7–168) and 125–7 (T Richardson 6–76)
England 231 (A F A Lilley 65, K. S. Ranjitsinhji 62) and 305 (K S Ranjitsinhji 154)

3 THE OVAL **England won by 66 runs**
England 145 (H Trumble 6–59) and 84 (H Trumble 6–30)
Australia 119 (J T Hearne 6–41) and 44 (R Peel 6–32, J T Hearne 4–19)

1896 Averages

Batting	I	No	Runs	HS	Avge	
K.S. Ranjitsinhji (E)	4	1	235	154*	78.33	
G.H.S. Trott (A)	6	0	206	143	34.33	

Bowling	O	M	Runs	W	Avge	BB
J.T. Hearne (E)	127.1	56	211	15	14.06	6–41
T.R. McKibbin (E)	69.3	20	162	11	14.72	3–35
T. Richardson (E)	175	58	439	24	18.29	7–168
H. Trumble (A)	170.1	58	339	18	18.38	6–30

1897–98: Australia regain Ashes with convincing win over Stoddart's team

After the great success of the previous tour, A.E. Stoddart took another side to Australia at the invitation of the Sydney and Melbourne authorities.

Stoddart did not play in the first Test at Sydney because his mother had died, and MacLaren was the England captain. The Sydney authorities put the match back by a day because they considered the pitch unfit, which caused controversy. It helped England because it gave Ranjitsinhji, who had been ill, time to recover. Coming in at number seven, he scored a rapid 175, England's highest so far, and England reached 551. MacLaren also scored a century. Australia were dismissed for 237 and then 408, despite Darling's century. Charles McLeod,

Trumble, Hugh

Trumble was born on 12 May 1867 at Abbotsford, Victoria, and played for Victoria from 1887–88. A tall off-break bowler, he bowled at medium pace and with such control that he gave the batsman no rest. He made his Test debut in 1890 in England, and made five tours to England. All his 141 Test wickets were English, a record number for the Ashes series until passed by Lillee. His wickets cost 21.78 runs each. He also scored 851 runs, average 19.79. He became secretary of Melbourne Cricket Club. He died on 14 August 1938 at Hawthorn, Victoria.

the Australian all-rounder batting at number three in the second innings, was run out by Derbyshire's wicket-keeper, Bill Storer, when he left his crease after being bowled by a no-ball, his deafness having led him not to hear the call. England easily scored the 95 needed to win.

At Melbourne, McLeod, who opened, scored 112, and was then bowled ironically by Storer, forced into use as England's seventh bowler as Australia compiled 520. England got the worst of the wicket in this match and were beaten by an innings and 55. Monty Noble made his debut for Australia and took six second-innings wickets. Ernest Jones, Australia's fast bowler, was the first player to be no-balled for throwing in a Test match.

The wicket was perfect at Adelaide but England, with Stoddart returned as captain, were again outplayed. Darling made 178,

and Australia's total was higher than at Melbourne: 573. England followed on nearly 300 behind, and when a second-wicket stand of 142 between MacLaren, like Darling scoring his second century of the series, and Ranjitsinhji was broken, England collapsed to another innings defeat.

England, and especially Hearne, began well at Melbourne in the fourth Test, where they needed a win to even the rubber, and Australia were reduced to 58 for six. But Clem Hill, still two months short of 21, with tail-end support played one of the great Test innings of 188, hoisting Australia's total to 323. For the third time running, at 174, England followed on, but at least this time set Australia a target: 115. Australia won by eight wickets.

With the Ashes lost, Stoddart dropped himself from the fifth Test at Sydney, and MacLaren once more took over. England batted well to make 335, and Richardson, in his last Test, bowled superbly for his best analysis, 8–94, and England led by 96. The second-innings batting was poor, however, and Australia were given a chance with a target of 275. Darling then made his third hundred of the series in only 91 minutes and went on to 160, helping Australia to win by six wickets.

It was an emphatic series win and led to a period of Australian excellence.

1897–98 18th Series Aus 4, Eng 1

1 SYDNEY **England won by 9 wkts**
England 551 (K S Ranjitsinhji 175, A C MacLaren 109, T W Hayward 72, G H Hirst 62) and 96–1 (A C MacLaren 50)
Australia 237 (H Trumble 70, C E McLeod 50, J T Hearne 5–42) and 408 (J Darling 101, C Hill 96, J T Hearne 4–99)

2 MELBOURNE **Australia won by an innings and 55 runs**
Australia 520 (C E McLeod 112, F A Iredale 89, G H S Trott 79, S E Gregory 71, C Hill 58)
England 315 (K S Ranjitsinhji 71, W Storer 51, H Trumble 4–54) and 150 (M A Noble 6–49) H Trumble 4–53)

3 ADELAIDE **Australia won by an innings and 13 runs**
Australia 573 (J Darling 178, F A Iredale 84, C Hill 81, S E Gregory 52, T Richardson 4–164)
England 278 (G H Hirst 85, T W Hayward 70, W P Howell 4–70) and 282 (A C MacLaren 124, K S Ranjitsinhji 77, C E McLeod 5–65, M A Noble 5–84)

4 MELBOURNE **Australia won by 8 wkts**
Australia 323 (C Hill 188, J T Hearne 6–98) and 115–2 (C E McLeod 64)
England 174 (E Jones 4–56) and 263 (K S Ranjitsinhji 55)

5 SYDNEY **Australia won by 6 wkts**
England 335 (A C Maclaren 65, N F Druce 64, E Jones 6–82) and 178 (H Trumble 4–37)
Australia 239 (C E McLeod 64, T Richardson 8–94) and 276–4 (J Darling 160, J Worrall 62)

1897–98 Averages

Batting	I	No	Runs	HS	Avge	
J. Darling (A)	8	0	537	178	67.12	
C.E. McLeod (A)	8	2	352	112	58.66	
C. Hill (A)	8	0	452	188	56.50	
A.C. MacLaren (E)	10	1	488	124	54.22	
K.S. Ranjitsinhji (E)	10	1	457	175	50.77	
S.E. Gregory (A)	8	2	264	71	44.00	
T.W. Hayward (E)	9	0	336	72	37.33	
N.F. Druce (E)	9	0	252	64	28.00	

Bowling	O	M	Runs	W	Avge	BB
M.A. Noble (A)	150.5	33	385	19	20.29	6–49
E. Jones (A)	198.2	32	553	22	25.13	6–82
J.T. Hearne (E)	217	66	538	20	26.90	6–98
H. Trumble (A)	232.3	57	535	19	28.15	4–37
T. Richardson (E)	255.3	50	776	22	35.27	8–94

1899: Australia have Trumper and the luck and register a narrow victory

The side which Australia sent to England in 1899 under Joe Darling was regarded as one of the strongest seen, and is still acknowledged as outstanding. England, too, had some good players, and the series of the 'Golden Age' of cricket were brilliantly fought.

The first Test was the first at Trent Bridge, England's fourth Test ground, and Wilfred Rhodes made his debut. He was to become the oldest player in Test cricket, and by coincidence this match was the last of W.G. Grace, who, at nearly 51, established the record Rhodes was to beat. Australia, too, had a great debutant: Victor Trumper. Australia made 252 (Trumper b Hearne 0), but England could manage only 193. Australia declared their second innings at 230 for eight, setting England 290, and captured four quick wickets, but 93 not out from Ranjitsinhji ensured the draw.

At Lord's England, with MacLaren back as captain, were restricted to 206, thanks to Jones, who took seven for 88, and Australia took a big lead by scoring 421. Trumper, who was only 21, made 135 not out, and Hill, now just turned 22, also scored 135. England were dismissed for 240 and Australia won by ten wickets.

Headingley joined the Test match circuit for the third Test, and Australia were dismissed for 172. Johnny Briggs, who took three wickets, had an epileptic fit on the first night and was sent to Cheadle Asylum. He returned to cricket, but not to Tests, but was to die in the Asylum less than three years later. England established a lead of 48, and dismissing Australia for 224 were on the way to victory at 19 without loss at the end of the second day, but rain washed out the last day, and Australia's 1–0 lead was preserved.

At Old Trafford, 130 from Tom Hayward helped England to 372, and then good bowling by Walter Bradley, in his first Test, and H.I. Young, in his second, dismissed Australia for 196, forcing them to follow on. Noble, 60 not out in the first innings, continued batting and made 89, thus uniquely scoring two separate 50s on the same day. Altogether he batted 510 minutes, saving the match. Australia made a declaration and the match was drawn. MacLaren had not wished to enforce the follow-on, which at that time was compulsory when a side was 120 behind, and the match provoked the change whereby the follow-on is at the discretion of the side in the lead.

England's last chance to level the series was at the Oval, and Hayward and Jackson began with a record Test opening stand of 185. England went impressively on to 576. Lockwood took seven for 71 as Australia were finally got out for 352, but McLeod, Worrall and Noble made sure there would be no quick dismissal in the second innings and the match was drawn.

1899 19th Series   Aus 1, Eng 0, Drawn 4

1 TRENT BRIDGE   Match drawn
Australia 252 (C Hill 52, W Rhodes 4–58, J T Hearne 4–71) and 230–8 dec (C Hill 80)
England 193 (C B Fry 50, E Jones 5–88) and 155–7 (K S Ranjitsinhji 93)

2 LORD'S   Australia won by 10 wkts
England 206 (F S Jackson 73, G L Jessop 51, E Jones 7–88) and 240 (A C MacLaren 88, T W Hayward 77)
Australia 421 (C Hill 135, V T Trumper 135, M A Noble 54) and 28–0

3 HEADINGLEY   Match Drawn
Australia 172 (J Worrall 76, H I Young 4–30) and 224 (H Trumble 56, J T Hearne 4–50)
England 220 (A F A Lilley 55, H Trumble 5–60) and 19–0

4 OLD TRAFFORD   Match Drawn
England 372 (T W Hayward 130, A F A Lilley 58) and 94–3
Australia 196 (M A Noble 60, W M Bradley 5–67, H I Young 4–79) and 346–7 dec (M A Noble 89, V T Trumper 63, J Worrall 53)

5 THE OVAL   Match Drawn
England 576 (T W Hayward 137, F S Jackson 118, C B Fry 60, K S Ranjitsinhji 54, E Jones 4–164)
Australia 352 (S E Gregory 117, J Worrall 55, J Darling 71, W H Lockwood 7–71) and 254–5 (C E McLeod 77, J Worrall 75, M A Noble 69)

1899 Averages

Batting	I	No	Runs	HS	Avge
T.W. Hayward (E)	7	1	413	137	68.83
C. Hill (A)	5	0	301	135	60.20
M.A. Noble (A)	9	2	367	89	52.42
K.S. Ranjitsinhji (E)	8	2	278	93	46.33
J. Worrall (A)	8	1	318	76	45.42
Hon F.S. Jackson (E)	8	1	303	118	43.28

Bowling	O	M	Runs	W	Avge	BB
H.I. Young (Eng)	110.1	39	262	12	21.83	4–30
J.T. Hearne (E)	199.3	87	321	13	24.69	4–50
H. Trumble (A)	192.3	78	375	15	25.00	5–60
E. Jones (A)	255.1	73	657	26	25.26	7–88
W. Rhodes (E)	146.2	41	341	13	26.23	4–56
M.A. Noble (A)	170	73	406	13	31.23	3–82

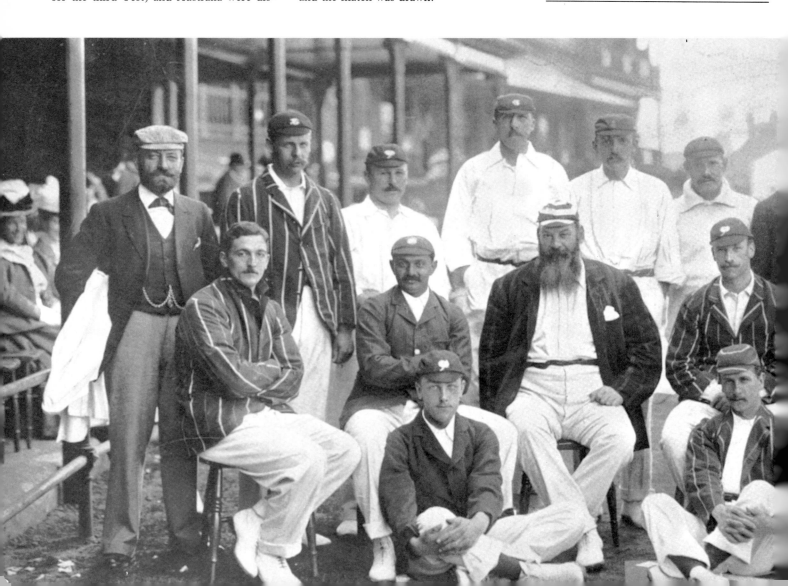

1901–02: Barnes makes an impact, but Australia win well

The MCC agreed to make the arrangements to send a side to Australia in 1901–02, but then withdrew, finding it impossible to raise a representative side. The Yorkshire committee refused to allow Rhodes and Hirst, the best bowlers of the summer, to go. A.C. MacLaren was asked to get a side together, and although he took some good players, it was clear that the side would struggle against the strong Australians.

As it happened, England began well, MacLaren, who went on to his fourth Test century, and Hayward scoring 154 for the first wicket at Sydney. The revelation of the match, was, however, Sydney Barnes, most of whose cricket had been for Rishton and Burnley in the Lancashire League. The unknown bowler took five wickets and Australia were dismissed for 168, followed on nearly 300 behind and were finally beaten by an innings and 124 runs.

At Melbourne MacLaren won the toss and put Australia in on a sticky wicket. Barnes took Trumper's wicket with the second ball, and he and Blythe shot out Australia for 112. However Noble (7–17) and Trumble did better, and England were dismissed for 61. But the first day was still possibly England's as Barnes had four more wickets as Australia collapsed again to 48 for five. However the best batsmen had been held back. Clem Hill

The England team at Trent Bridge in 1899. Left to right, back: Barlow (umpire), Hayward, Hirst, Gunn, Hearne, Storer, Brockwell, Titchmarsh (umpire). Seated: Fry, Ranjitsinhji, Grace, Jackson. Front: Rhodes, Tyldesley.

The Australians in England in 1899. Left to right, back: Trumper, Laver, Trumble, Howell, McLeod, Noble. Seated: Johns, Jones, Darling, Kelly, Worrall, Iredale. Front: Hill, Gregory.

made 99, and became the first to be dismissed at this score, and Reg Duff, batting number ten, made a century on his debut. He and Warwick Armstrong, also playing his first Test, added 120 for the tenth wicket, the first century last-wicket stand. Australia reached 353 and dismissed England for 175, Trumble's hat-trick at the end restricting Noble to 13 wickets in the match.

England were unlucky to lose the third Test at Adelaide. They made 388 with Braund getting a century, and dismissed Australia for 321, despite Barnes, who had taken 19 wickets in the first two Tests, having to retire with an injured knee after only seven overs. He took no further part in the series. Trumble bowled well in the second innings but Australia needed 315 to win. Unfortunately, with Barnes in bed, Blythe injured his finger, and Australia became the first side to score 300 in the fourth innings to win a Test. A curiosity was that Hill followed his 99 on the previous Test with innings of 98 and 97.

After one innings each at Sydney, England had a lead of 18 runs, but their batting in the second innings against Noble and J.V. Sanders, making his debut, was appalling and they were dismissed for 99. Australia clinched the rubber with a seven-wicket win.

The fifth Test at Melbourne was evenly fought. England led again on first innings, and needing 211 were 87 for three overnight, and they fell 33 short of their target.

23

Noble and Trumble took 60 wickets between them in the series, exploiting their new mastery of swing bowling. Trumble captained Australia in the last two Tests.

1901-02 20th Series Aus 4, Eng 1

1 SYDNEY **England won by an innings and 124 runs**
England 464 (A C MacLaren 116, A F A Lilley 84, T W Hayward 69, L C Braund 58, C E McLeod 4–84)
Australia 168 (S F Barnes 5–65) and 172 (L C Braund 5–61, C Blythe 4–30)

2 MELBOURNE **Australia won by 229 runs**
Australia 112 (S F Barnes 6–42, C Blythe 4–64) and 353 (R A Duff 104, S F Barnes 7–121)
England 61 (M A Noble 7–17) and 175 (J T Tyldesley 66, M A Noble 6–60, H Trumble 4–49)

3 ADELAIDE **Australia won by 4 wkts**
England 388 (L C Braund 103, T W Hayward 90, W G Quaife 68, A C MacLaren 67) and 247 (H Trumble 6–74)
Australia 321 (C Hill 98, V T Trumper 65, S E Gregory 55, J R Gunn 5–76) and 315–6 (C Hill 97, J Darling 69, H Trumble 62)

4 SYDNEY **Australia won by 7 wkts**
England 317 (A C MacLaren 92, J T Tyldesley 79, J V Saunders 4–119) and 99 (M A Noble 5–54, J V Saunders 5–43)
Australia 299 (M A Noble 56, W W Armstrong 55, G L Jessop 4–68, L C Braund 4–118) and 121–3 (R A Duff 51)

5 MELBOURNE **Australia won by 32 runs**
Australia 144 (T W Hayward 4–22, J R Gunn 4–38) and 255 (C Hill 87, L C Braund 5–95)
England 189 (H Trumble 5–62) and 178 (M A Noble 6–98)

1901–2 Averages

Batting	I	No	Runs	HS	Avge
C. Hill (A)	10	0	521	99	52.10
A.C. MacLaren (E)	9	0	412	116	45.77
R.A. Duff (A)	8	1	311	104	44.42
L.C. Braund (E)	9	2	256	103*	36.57
T.W. Hayward (E)	9	0	305	90	33.88
S.E. Gregory (A)	10	1	269	55	29.88

Bowling	O	M	Runs	W	Avge	BB
S.F. Barnes (E)	138.2	33	323	19	17.00	7–21
M.A. Noble (A)	230	68	608	32	19.00	7–17
H. Trumble (A)	267.2	93	561	28	20.03	6–74
J.R. Gunn (E)	144.3	52	360	17	21.17	5–76
C. Blythe (E)	175	63	470	18	26.11	4–30
L.C. Braund (E)	258.1	76	738	21	35.14	5–61

Trumper, Victor Thomas

Trumper was born on 2 November 1877 at Darlinghurst, NSW. He was a brilliant opening right-hand batsman, and a medium-pace bowler. He played for New South Wales from 1894–95 and Australia from 1899. Trumper was a natural batsman, who played with such grace and artistry combined with a modesty and lack of concern for statistics that he became a legendary figure even among the giants of the 'golden age'. In 48 Tests he scored 3,163 runs, average 39.04. He also took eight wickets at 39.62. He died young, at Darlinghurst on 28 June 1915, of Bright's disease.

1902: Australia win the battle of the two great sides

The 1902 season is often thought of as one where each country had one of its strongest sides. It produced some exhilarating cricket and two of the closest finishes in Tests.

Unfortunately the first two Tests were spoiled by rain. At Edgbaston, which joined the list of Test grounds, Australia were caught on a sticky wicket and dismissed for their record low score, 36 (Rhodes 7–17) after a big England score, but the rain prevented a finish.

At Lord's there was only 105 minutes play, but Hopkins caused a flutter by removing Fry and Ranjitsinhji before a run was on the board.

The third Test was at Bramall Lane, Sheffield, a new Test venue staging its only Test. Barnes returned to the England attack for his only Test of the series and took six for 49, but Australia gained a lead of 49, and then Trumper hit a rapid 62 and Hill 119 to set England 339 to win, but Trumble and Noble shared the wickets as Australia won by 143.

Old Trafford proved to be a decisive match, and poor Fred Tate is famous for his part in it. On the first morning MacLaren asked his bowlers to keep Trumper quiet till lunch, by when the sun would have had time to work on the rain-affected wicket. But Trumper was 103 not out at lunch and Australia 173–1. It was the first of only three centuries scored before lunch on the first day in Tests. Jackson (128) and Braund (65) added 141 for England's sixth wicket, but at 262 all out England trailed by 37.

Australia were then out for 86, but Fred Tate dropped Darling at a crucial stage, and Darling made top score of 37. England required 124 and were proceeding satisfactorily at 92 for three, but then wickets began to fall to Trumble and Saunders. Hill made a wondrous running and diving catch on the boundary to dismiss Lilley and when Tate joined Rhodes for the last wicket eight were still required. Tate scored four and was bowled. It was his one and only Test. Later his son Maurice retrieved the family reputation.

The fifth Test at the Oval saw one of the great recoveries and innings of Test cricket. Australia batted and reached 324, thanks to some strong lower-order run-making, and then Trumble, who had made 64 not out at number nine, took eight for 65 to dismiss England for 183. As the wicket began to deteriorate, Australia made 121, and England, needing 263, were 48 for five when Gilbert Jessop joined Jackson.

Jessop then played perhaps the most exciting innings in Test cricket, scoring a century in 75 minutes. Only one Test century has been scored faster, and in much

ENGLAND V AUSTRALIA 1902
4th Test, Old Trafford: Australia won by three runs

AUSTRALIA

V.T. Trumper	c Lilley b Rhodes	104	c Braund b Lockwood		4
R.A. Duff	c Lilley b Lockwood	54	b Lockwood		3
C. Hill	c Rhodes b Lockwood	65	b Lockwood		0
M.A. Noble	c and b Rhodes	2	(6) c Lilley b Lockwood		4
S.E. Gregory	c Lilley b Rhodes	3	lbw b Tate		24
J. Darling*	c MacLaren b Rhodes	51	(4) c Palairet b Rhodes		37
A.J.Y. Hopkins	c Palairet b Lockwood	0	c Tate b Lockwood		2
W.W. Armstrong	b Lockwood	5	b Rhodes		3
J.J. Kelly†	not out	4	not out		2
H. Trumble	c Tate b Lockwood	0	lbw b Tate		4
J.V. Saunders	b Lockwood	3	c Tyldesley b Rhodes		0
Extras	(B 5, LB 2, W 1)	8	(B 1, LB 1, NB 1)		3
Total		**299**			**86**

ENGLAND

L.C.H. Palairet	c Noble b Saunders	6	b Saunders		17
R. Abel	c Armstrong b Saunders	6	(5) b Trumble		21
J.T. Tyldesley	c Hopkins b Saunders	22	c Armstrong b Saunders		16
A.C. MacLaren*	b Trumble	1	(2) c Duff b Trumble		35
K.S. Ranjitsinhji	lbw b Trumble	2	(4) lbw b Trumble		4
Hon F.S. Jackson	c Duff b Trumble	128	c Gregory b Saunders		7
L.C. Braund	b Noble	65	st Kelly b Trumble		3
A.F.A. Lilley†	b Noble	7	c Hill b Trumble		4
W.H. Lockwood	run out	7	b Trumble		0
W. Rhodes	c and b Trumble	5	not out		4
F.W. Tate	not out	5	b Saunders		4
Extras	(B 6, LB 2)	8	(B 5)		5
Total		**262**			**120**

ENGLAND	O	M	R	W	O	M	R	W	FALL OF WICKETS				
Rhodes	25	3	104	4	14.4	5	26	3		A	E	A	E
Jackson	11	0	58	0					Wkt	1st	1st	2nd	2nd
Tate	11	1	44	0	5	3	7	2	1st	135	12	7	44
Braund	9	0	37	0	11	3	22	0	2nd	175	13	9	68
Lockwood	20.1	5	48	6	17	5	28	5	3rd	179	14	10	72
									4th	183	30	64	92
AUSTRALIA									5th	256	44	74	97
Trumble	43	16	75	4	25	9	53	6	6th	256	185	76	107
Saunders	34	5	104	3	19.4	4	52	4	7th	288	203	77	109
Noble	24	8	47	2	5	3	10	0	8th	292	214	79	109
Trumper	6	4	6	0					9th	292	235	85	116
Armstrong	5	2	19	0					10th	299	262	86	120
Hopkins	2	0	3	0									

The Australians of 1902. Left to right, back: Howell, Armstrong, Jones, Trumble, Major B.J. Wardill (manager), Hopkins, Gregory, Hill. Seated: Trumper, Saunders, Darling, Noble, Kelly. Front: Carter, Duff.

different circumstances. Jackson, then Hirst, supported him, and when he was dismissed for 104 out of 139, England were 187 for 7.

There was still a long way to go for victory but Hirst kept going, and 15 were needed when Rhodes joined him for the last wicket. According to one of Neville Cardus' romances, they decided to 'make them in singles'. Although this was invention, make them they did for a legendary win.

1902 21st Series Aus 2, Eng 1, Drawn 2

1 EDGBASTON Match Drawn
England 376–9 dec (J T Tyldesley 138, F S Jackson 53, W H Lockwood 52)
Australia 36 (W Rhodes 7–17) and 46–2

2 LORD'S Match Drawn
England 102–2 (F S Jackson 55)
Australia did not bat

3 BRAMALL LANE, SHEFFIELD Australia won by 143 runs
Australia 194 (S F Barnes 6–49) and 289 (C Hill 119, V T Trumper 62, W Rhodes 5–63)
England 145 (J V Saunders 5–50, M A Noble 5–51) and 195 (A C MacLaren 63, G L Jessop 55, M A Noble 6–52, H Trumble 4–49)

4 OLD TRAFFORD Australia won by 3 runs
Australia 299 (V T Trumper 104, C Hill 65, R A Duff 54, J Darling 51, W H Lockwood 6–48, W Rhodes 4–104) and 86 (W H Lockwood 5–28)
England 262 (F S Jackson 128, L C Braund 65, H Trumble 4–75) and 120 (H Trumble 6–53, J V Saunders 4–52)

5 THE OVAL England won by 1 wkt
Australia 324 (H Trumble 64, M A Noble 52, G H Hirst 5–77) and 121 (W H Lockwood 5–45)
England 183 (H Trumble 8–65) and 263–9 G L Jessop 104, G H Hirst 58, H Trumble 4–108, J V Saunders 4–105)

1902 Averages

Batting	I	No	Runs	HS	Avge	
Hon F.S. Jackson	8	1	308	128	44.42	
C. Hill (A)	8	1	258	119	36.85	

Bowling	O	M	Runs	W	Avge	BB
W.H. Lockwood (E)	81.1	18	206	17	12.11	6–48
H. Trumble (A)	172.4	55	371	26	14.26	8–65
W. Rhodes (E)	140.5	38	336	22	15.27	7–17
M.A. Noble (A)	127	41	307	14	21.92	6–52
J.V. Saunders (A)	131.1	23	473	18	26.27	5–50

ENGLAND V AUSTRALIA 1902
5th Test, The Oval: England won by one wicket

AUSTRALIA

V.T. Trumper	b Hirst	42	run out	2
R.A. Duff	c Lilley b Hirst	23	b Lockwood	6
C. Hill	b Hirst	11	c MacLaren b Hirst	34
J. Darling*	c Lilley b Hirst	3	c MacLaren b Lockwood	15
M.A. Noble	c and b Jackson	52	b Braund	13
S.E. Gregory	b Hirst	23	b Braund	9
W.W. Armstrong	b Jackson	17	b Lockwood	21
A.J.Y. Hopkins	c MacLaren b Lockwood	40	c Lilley b Lockwood	3
H. Trumble	not out	64	(10) not out	7
J.J. Kelly†	c Rhodes b Braund	39	(11) lbw b Lockwood	0
J.V. Saunders	lbw b Braund	0	(9) c Tyldesley b Rhodes	2
Extras	(B 5, LB 3, NB 2)	10	(B 7, LB 2)	9
Total		**324**		**121**

ENGLAND

A.C. MacLaren*	c Armstrong b Trumble	10	b Saunders	2
L.C.H. Palairet	b Trumble	20	b Saunders	6
J.T. Tyldesley	b Trumble	33	b Saunders	0
T.W. Hayward	b Trumble	0	c Kelly b Saunders	7
Hon F.S. Jackson	c Armstrong b Saunders	2	c and b Trumble	49
L.C. Braund	c Hill b Trumble	22	c Kelly b Trumble	2
G.L. Jessop	b Trumble	13	c Noble b Armstrong	104
G.H. Hirst	c and b Trumble	43	not out	58
W.H. Lockwood	c Noble b Saunders	25	lbw b Trumble	2
A.F.A. Lilley†	c Trumper b Trumble	0	c Darling b Trumble	16
W. Rhodes	not out	0	not out	6
Extras	(B 13, LB 2)	15	(B 5, LB 6)	11
Total		**183**	(9 wickets)	**263**

ENGLAND	O	M	R	W	O	M	R	W
Lockwood	24	2	85	1	20	6	45	5
Rhodes	28	9	46	0	22	7	38	1
Hirst	29	5	77	5	5	1	7	1
Braund	16.5	5	29	2	9	1	15	2
Jackson	20	4	66	2	4	3	7	0
Jessop	6	2	11	0				

AUSTRALIA	O	M	R	W	O	M	R	W
Trumble	31	13	65	8	33.5	4	108	4
Saunders	23	7	79	2	24	3	105	4
Noble	7	3	24	0	5	0	11	0
Armstrong					4	0	28	1

FALL OF WICKETS

	A	E	A	E
Wkt	1st	1st	2nd	2nd
1st	47	31	6	5
2nd	63	36	9	5
3rd	69	62	31	10
4th	82	67	71	31
5th	126	67	75	48
6th	174	83	91	157
7th	175	137	99	187
8th	256	179	114	214
9th	324	183	115	248
10th	324	183	121	—

1903–04: Foster's great innings and the new Bosies regain the Ashes

MacLaren was asked by the Australian authorities to bring a team in 1903–04 but declined when Barnes and Lockwood refused to go. MCC stepped in and for the first time were responsible for the touring side. They announced Pelham Warner as captain. Most of the best English amateur batsmen declined to go. Noble captained Australia.

Noble made 133 on the first Test at Sydney, but was eclipsed by R.E. Foster, whose 287 was the highest Test score to date. It remains the highest English Test innings in Australia, and the highest score by a Test batsman on his debut. He added 130 with Rhodes for the last wicket, the highest last-wicket Ashes stand. England led by nearly 300, but Trumper, too, played a magnificent innings, reaching 100 in 94 minutes, and continuing to 185 not out. England needed 194 and got them for five wickets. A total of 1,541 runs were scored, but E.G. Arnold bowled the great Trumper with his first ball in Test cricket.

Foster retired ill on 49 not out in the second Test at Melbourne, but England were then 221 for two, runs which proved doubly valuable when rain interfered on the second day. The last three innings only just

passed 100, and England were fortunate winners. The catching on both sides was described as appalling, and Rhodes is said to have had eight catches dropped despite ending with figures of 15 for 124.

Australia won the third Test at Adelaide when Trumper, Hill and Gregory all mastered the faster wicket better than the English and Australia won by 216. Hill passed 2,000 runs in Tests and Trumper scored his fourth century against England – both records.

The fourth Test at Sydney was again several times interrupted by rain, and on the second day, with about 30,000 present, the crowd began some intensive barracking and bottle-throwing. There had earlier been trouble at Sydney in the first Test when Hill had been adjudged run out and Warner had considered withdrawing his team from the match.

Knight made 70 in 260 minutes in a low-scoring match and Bosanquet, in his first series, sealed England's Ashes-winning victory with a spell of five for 12 with his googlies in the second innings. Rain spoiled the fifth Test at Melbourne, where this time Australia had the same luck that England had had two months earlier. Batting first they made 247, while neither side could make more than 133 after the rains came. Trumble, in his last first-class match, took his second Test hat-trick.

Right: A page from the scorebook of the 1905 Test at Trent Bridge.

Below right: The 1905 Australians. Left to right, top: Newland, Duff, Hill, Cotter, Laver. Middle: Gregory, Gehrs, Darling, Noble, Kelly. Bottom: Armstrong, Hopkins, McLeod, Trumper, Howell.

1905: England keep the Ashes without alarms

Jackson was captain for the Australian tour of 1905, winning all five tosses, while Darling once again led the visitors.

The first Test was at Trent Bridge, and although Jackson reduced Australia from 129 for one to 130 for four in one over, Australia passed England's 196 to lead by 25. Then MacLaren made a record fifth Test century and England could declare at 426 for five. Trumper was unable to bat because of a back strain, and Bosanquet took eight for 105, England winning by 213 runs.

Prolonged rain ruined the second Test at Lord's (as it had in 1902), England having the better of draws here and at Headingley, where Jackson and Tyldesley made centuries and Arnold Warren of Derbyshire took six wickets, including Trumper twice, in his only Test.

At Old Trafford England made 446 by solid batting, including another century from Jackson, and won by an innings when Walter Brearley, on his debut, took four wickets in each innings.

Centuries from Fry, Tyldesley and Duff and fine bowling from Cotter could not produce a result at the Oval, and England retained the Ashes 2–0. The disappointing form of Hill, Trumper and Noble and the return of the best English batsmen made the series a little one-sided.

Barnes, Sydney Francis

Regarded by his contemporaries as the greatest of all bowlers, he bowled right-arm, varied his pace each side of medium and could turn the ball both ways. He was a master on any type of wicket. Born on 19 April 1873 in Smethwick, Staffordshire, he was an aloof character and did not care for county cricket, preferring League cricket, although he did play for Lancashire and Warwickshire. However, he was chosen by MacLaren to tour Australia in 1901–02, when he made his Test debut. He played in 27 Tests, although only ten at home, where those in authority were wary of his forbidding ways. He took 189 wickets, then a record, at only 16.43 each. On the South African tour of 1913–14 he took 49 wickets, still a record for one series, in only four Tests. He died on Boxing Day 1967.

1903-04 22nd Series Eng 3, Aus 2

1 SYDNEY England won by 5 wkts
Australia 285 (M A Noble 133, E G Arnold 4–76) and 485 (V T Trumper 185, R A Duff 84, C Hill 51, W Rhodes 5–94)
England 577 (R E Foster 287, L C Braund 102, J T Tyldesley 53) and 194–5 (T W Hayward 91, G H Hirst 60)

2 MELBOURNE England won by 185 runs
England 315 (J T Tyldesley 97, P F Warner 68, T W Hayward 58, H Trumble 4–107) and 103 (J T Tyldesley 62, H Trumble 5–34)
Australia 122 (V T Trumper 74, W Rhodes 7–56) and 111 (W Rhodes 8–68)

3 ADELAIDE Australia won by 216 runs
Australia 388 (V T Trumper 113, C Hill 88, R A Duff 79, M A Noble 59) and 351 (S E Gregory 112, M A Noble 65, V T Trumper 59, B J T Bosanquet 4–73)
England 245 (G H Hirst 58) and 278 (P F Warner 79, T W Hayward 67, A J Hopkins 4–81)

4 SYDNEY England won by 157 runs
England 249 (A E Knight 70, M A Noble 7–100) and 210 (T W Hayward 54)
Australia 131 (E G Arnold 4–28, W Rhodes 4–33) and 171 (M A Noble 53, B J T Bosanquet 6–51)

5 MELBOURNE Australia won by 218 runs
Australia 247 (V T Trumper 88, L C Braund 8–81) and 133 (G H Hirst 5–48)
England 61 (A Cotter 6–40, M A Noble 4–19) and 101 (H Trumble 7–28)

1903-4 Averages

Batting	I	No	Runs	HS	Avge
V.T. Trumper (A)	10	1	574	185*	63.77
R.E. Foster (E)	9	1	486	287	60.75
M.A. Noble (A)	10	3	417	133	59.57
T.W. Hayward (E)	9	0	321	91	36.66
R.A. Duff (A)	10	0	277	97	27.70
J.T. Tyldesley (E)	10	0	277	97	27.70
C. Hill (A)	10	0	276	88	27.60

Bowling	O	M	Runs	W	Avge	BB
W. Rhodes (E)	172	36	488	31	15.74	8–68
H. Trumble (A)	199.4	60	398	24	16.58	7–28
M.A. Noble (A)	136.1	41	330	16	20.62	7–100
W.P. Howell (A)	137.5	51	296	14	21.14	4–43
B.J.T. Bosanquet (E)	104.1	7	403	16	25.18	6–51
E.G. Arnold (E)	158.3	32	475	18	26.38	4–28
L.C. Braund (E)	129.3	30	359	13	27.61	8–81
G.H. Hirst (E)	163.2	29	451	15	30.06	5–48

1905 23rd Series Eng 2, Aus 0, Drawn 3

1 TRENT BRIDGE England won by 213 runs
England 196 (J T Tyldesley 56, F Laver 7–64) and 426–5 dec (A C MacLaren 140, F S Jackson 82, J T Tyldesley 61)
Australia 221 (C Hill 54, M A Noble 50, F S Jackson 5–52) and 188 (S E Gregory 51, B J T Bosanquet 8–107)

2 LORD'S Match Drawn
England 282 (C B Fry 73, A C MacLaren 56) and 151–5 (A C MacLaren 79)
Australia 181 (F S Jackson 4–50)

3 HEADINGLEY Match Drawn
England 301 (F S Jackson 144, and 295–5 dec (J T Tyldesley 100, T W Hayward 60, W W Armstrong 5–122)
Australia 195 (W W Armstrong 66, A Warren 5–57) and 224–7 (M A Noble 62)

4 OLD TRAFFORD England won by an innings and 80 runs
England 446 (F S Jackson 113, T W Hayward 82, R H Spooner 52, C E McLeod 5–125)
Australia 197 (J Darling 73, W Brearley 4–72) and 169 (R A Duff 60, W Brearley 4–54)

5 THE OVAL Match Drawn
England 430 (C B Fry 144, F S Jackson 76, T W Hayward 59, A Cotter 7–148) and 261–6 dec (J T Tyldesley 112, R H Spooner 79)
Australia 363 (R A Duff 146, J Darling 57, W Brearley 5–110) and 124–4

1905 Averages

Batting	I	No	Runs	HS	Avge
Hon F.S. Jackson (E)	9	2	492	144*	70.28
C.B. Fry (E)	7	1	348	144	58.00
J.T. Tyldesley (E)	9	1	424	112*	53.00
A.C. MacLaren (E)	7	0	303	140	43.28
R.A. Duff (A)	8	0	335	146	41.87
T.W. Hayward (E)	9	0	305	82	33.88
W.W. Armstrong (A)	9	1	252	66	31.50

Bowling	O	M	Runs	W	Avge	BB
Hon F.S. Jackson (E)	67.5	8	201	13	15.46	5–52
W. Brearley (E)	73.1	16	277	14	19.78	5–110
F. Laver (A)	189.3	55	510	16	31.87	7–64
A. Cotter (A)	127	13	427	13	32.84	7–148
W.W. Armstrong (A)	280.3	94	538	16	33.62	5–122

Cricket Match.
Played at Trent Bridge Ground **Date** May 29.30.31. 1905

England – VERSUS Australia. (First Test Match)

First INNINGS OF England

ORDER OF GOING IN	BATSMAN'S NAME	RUNS AS SCORED	HOW OUT	BOWLER'S NAME	TOTAL RUNS
1	T. W. Hayward (Surrey)			Laver	4
2	Hayward (Surrey)			Cotter	5
3	J. T. Tyldesley (Lancashire)		c Duff	Laver	56
4	A. C. Maclaren Esq (Lancashire)		c Kelly	Laver	2
5	Hon P. S. Jackson (Yorkshire) (Captain)			Cotter	0
6	R. S. Bosanquet Esq (Middlesex)			Laver	27
7	J. Gunn (Nottinghamshire)			Cotter	8
8	G. L. Jessop (Gloucestershire)			Laver	0
9	A. A. Lilley (Warwickshire)		c + b	Laver	37
10	W. Rhodes (Yorkshire)		c Noble	Laver	29
11	C. Arnold (Worcestershire)		not out		2

BYES 6   LEG BYES 1   WIDE BALLS   NO BALLS   **26**

| RUNS AT THE FALL of each wicket | 1 for 6 | 2 for 24 | 3 for 40 | 4 for 49 | 5 for 98 | 6 for 119 | 7 for 119 | 8 for 139 | 9 for 189 | 10 for 196 | TOTAL | 196 |

1905 — The Australian Cricket Team.

P. M. NEWLAND.   R. A. DUFF.   C. HILL.   A. COTTER.   F. LAVER.

S. E. GREGORY.   D. R. A. GEHRS.   J. DARLING.   M. A. NOBLE.   J. J. KELLY.

W. W. ARMSTRONG.   A. J. HOPKINS.   C. E. McLEOD.   V. TRUMPER.   W. P. HOWELL.

Hill, Clement

Hill was born on 18 March 1877 at Adelaide, South Australia, and made his debut for his state in 1892–93. A brilliant left-hand middle-order batsman, he made his first Test appearance in England on the 1896 tour. He was one of Australia's leading players of the 'golden age', playing in 49 Tests and scoring 3,412 runs, average 39.21. He is also remembered for a famous diving catch in front of the pavilion at Old Trafford in 1902 which helped win the match for Australia by three runs. He died on 5 September 1945 in Melbourne.

Armstrong, Warwick Windridge

Born in Kyneton, Victoria, on 22 May 1879, Armstrong was a good right-hand batsman and a bowler who began for Victoria in 1895–99 at fast-medium but in 1905 switched to leg-breaks. He played 50 times for Australia from 1901–02, captaining them from 1920–21. As captain he led his country to eight successive wins over England. He scored 2,863 Test runs, average 38.66, and took 87 wickets at 33.59. Always tall, by the end of his career he weighed over 20 stone and was known as 'The Big Ship'. He died on 13 July 1947 at Darling Point, NSW.

1907–08: The third innings provides the big totals throughout

Squabbles among the Australian authorities made a 1906–07 tour of Australia difficult to arrange – when they were settled MCC said it was too late and sent a team to New Zealand instead.

The Australian tour took place in 1907–08 under A.O. Jones of Notts, but many players declined the invitation, and it was not a representative side which sailed.

Jones was taken ill early in the tour and F.L. Fane of Essex captained the side in the first Test at Sydney. Noble captained Australia. Jack Hobbs, on his first tour, was England's 12th man.

George Gunn of Notts, who was not a member of the party but in Australia for his health, played for England and made 119 on his debut. Australia, scoring 300, led by 27 on the first innings, and when England also scored exactly 300 on their second knock, with Gunn again top scorer, Australia needed 274 to win, a hard task. At 124 for six they faced defeat, but wicket-keeper Hanson Carter (born in Halifax, Yorkshire) came in and made 61. An unbroken ninth-wicket stand of 56 by Hazlitt and Cotter then saw Australia home by two wickets.

Rolls were reversed in the second Test at Melbourne. Australia made 266, but Hobbs, on his debut, made 83 and K.L. Hutchings, in his second Test, 126, and England reached 382. Australia batted better to make

397, setting England to make 282. At 209 for eight it seemed lost, but Barnes added 34 with Humphries and 39 unbeaten with Fielder to win by one wicket. Hazlitt's throw missed the wicket as the winning single was made.

There was a dramatic change of fortune in the third Test at Adelaide. England led by 78 on the first innings, and with Australia at 180 for seven in the second, appeared to have the match won. But Hill, who had flu and was unable to field, then came in at number nine in very severe heat to join debutant Roger Hartigan. They were both dropped early on, but added 243, Hill getting 160 and Hartigan 116. Saunders and O'Connor then shared the wickets as England were beaten by 183.

It was England's last chance of retaining the Ashes, as rain conspired against them at Melbourne. Jones returned as captain, and Fielder and Crawford did well to dismiss Australia for 214. England then batted on a pitch ruined by rain, and could make only 105, with Hobbs making a brilliant 57. The England bowlers did not take full advantage of the pitch. Australia were 77 for five, but as conditions improved went on to 385, with Warwick Armstrong getting 133 not out.

Needing 495, England were well beaten by 308 runs.

The fifth Test followed a similar course to the third. England, with Gunn making 122 not out, established a lead of 144, but Australia again made a big score in the third innings. This time it was Trumper who turned the match with 166 in 241 minutes. England fell 50 runs short of the 279 needed and Australia regained the Ashes 4–1.

1907–08   24th Series   Aus 4, Eng 1

1 SYDNEY   Australia won by 2 wkts
England 273 (G Gunn 119, A Cotter 6–101) and 300 (G Gunn 74, J Hardstaff 63, J V Saunders 4–68)
Australia 300 (C Hill 87, A Fielder 6–82) and 275–8 (H Carter 61)

2 MELBOURNE   England won by 1 wkt
Australia 266 (M A Noble 61, J N Crawford 5–79) and 397 (W W Armstrong 77, C G Macartney 54, M A Noble 64, V T Trumper 63, H Carter 53, S F Barnes 5–72)
England 382 (K L Hutchings 126, J B Hobbs 83, A Cotter 5–142) and 282–9 (F L Fane 50)

3 ADELAIDE   Australia won by 245 runs
Australia 285 (C G Macartney 75, A Fielder 4–80) and 506 (C Hill 160, R J Hartigan 116, M A Noble 65)
England 363 (G Gunn 65, J N Crawford 62, J Hardstaff 61) and 183 (J Hardstaff 72, J V Saunders 5–65, J D A O'Connor 5–40)

4 MELBOURNE   Australia won by 308 runs
Australia 214 (V S Ransford 51, J N Crawford 5–48, A Fielder 4–54) and 385 (W W Armstrong 133, H Carter 66, V S Ransford 54, A Fielder 4–91)
England 105 (J B Hobbs 57, J V Saunders 5–28) and 186 (J V Saunders 4–76)

5 SYDNEY   Australia won by 49 runs
Australia 137 (S F Barnes 7–60) and 422 (V T Trumper 166, S E Gregory 56, J N Crawford 5–141, W Rhodes 4–102)
England 281 (G Gunn 122, J B Hobbs 72) and 229 (W Rhodes 69, J V Saunders 5–82)

1907–8 Averages

Batting	I	No	Runs	HS	Avge	
G. Gunn (E)	10	1	462	122*	51.33	
W.W. Armstrong (A)	10	1	410	133*	45.55	
J.B. Hobbs (E)	8	1	302	83	43.14	
H. Carter (A)	10	3	300	66	42.85	
M.A. Noble (A)	10	0	396	65	39.60	
C. Hill (A)	10	0	360	160	36.00	
V.T. Trumper (A)	10	0	338	166	33.80	
V.S. Ransford (A)	10	1	288	54	32.00	
J. Hardstaff, sr (E)	10	0	311	72	31.10	
C.G. Macartney (A)	10	0	273	75	27.30	
K.L. Hutchings (E)	10	0	273	126	27.30	

Bowling	O	M	Runs	W	Avge	BB
J.V. Saunders (A)	267.1	52	716	31	23.09	5–28
J.N. Crawford (E)	237.4	36	742	30	24.73	5–48
J.D.A. O'Connor (A)	107	21	300	12	25.00	5–40
A. Fielder (E)	218.3	31	627	25	25.08	6–82
W.W. Armstrong (A)	180.1	63	361	14	25.78	3–53
S.F. Barnes (E)	273.2	74	626	24	26.08	6–82
A. Cotter (A)	108.5	8	426	14	30.42	6–101

1909: Australia retain the Ashes after losing first Test

Noble led Australia to England in 1909, and met a much stronger England side led by MacLaren.

The first Test at Edgbaston was a fairly short affair, the left-arm bowlers Hirst and Blythe getting all the Australian wickets as they were shot out for 74 and 151. England needed 105 to win, and Hobbs and Fry, both out first ball in the first innings, knocked them off without loss.

An innings of 143 not out by Ransford, who was dropped three times, established an Australian lead of 81 at Lord's, and then excellent bowling by Armstrong meant that only 41 were required to win.

Ranjitsinhji, Kumar Shri

Ranji, as he was popularly known, was born at Sarodar, India, on 10 September 1872. Later he was to become His Highness Shri Sir Ranjitsinhji Vibhaji, Jam Sahib of Nawanagar. He studied at Cambridge University and played for Sussex from 1895. He was a magical right-hand batsman who revolutionized techniques, developing the leg-glance into an art in an age of front-foot driving. The most prolific batsman of his day, he made his debut for England in 1896, and in 15 Tests scored 989 runs, average 44.95. He died on 2 April 1933 at Jamnagar, India.

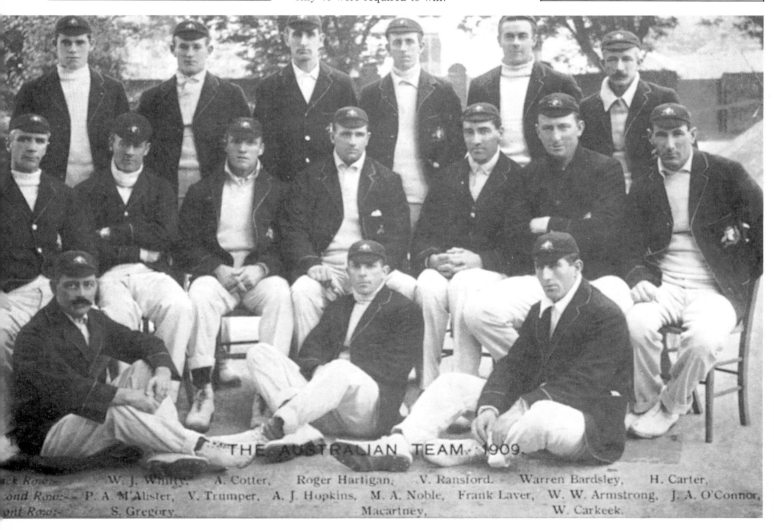

THE AUSTRALIAN TEAM. 1909.

W. J. Whitty,   A. Cotter,   Roger Hartigan,   V. Ransford   Warren Bardsley,   H. Carter.
P. A. M'Alister,   V. Trumper,   A. J. Hopkins,   M. A. Noble,   Frank Laver,   W. W. Armstrong,   J. A. O'Connor.
S. Gregory,   Macartney,   W. Carkeek.

Barnes returned to the England side at Headingley, but Macartney, with 11 wickets, was the dominant bowler of the match. Jessop was unfit to bat for England in either innings, and after a level first innings England collapsed for 87 in the second to lose by 126 runs.

Barnes and Blythe did well to dismiss Australia for 147 at Old Trafford, but Frank Laver produced what remains the best analysis by a tourist in a Test in England: eight for 31 as England were out for 119. Australia declared on the second innings, but there was no prospect of a result.

The feature of the Oval Test was the batting of Warren Bardsley, who scored 136 and 130 to become the first to score a century in each innings of a Test. Jack Sharp, the Everton footballer, scored a century for England but a high-scoring match was drawn and Australia kept the Ashes 2–1. Noble won the toss in all five Tests.

1909 Averages

Batting	I	No	Runs	HS	Avge	
V.S. Ransford (A)	9	3	353	143*	58.83	
W. Bardsley (A)	10	0	396	136	39.60	

Bowling	O	M	Runs	W	Avge	BB
C. Blythe (E)	91.3	19	242	18	13.44	6–44
F. Laver (A)	108.2	38	189	14	13.50	8–31
C.G. Macartney (A)	127.2	33	258	16	16.12	7–58
S.F. Barnes (E)	155.3	52	340	17	20.00	6–63
W.W. Armstrong (A)	140.2	51	293	14	20.92	6–35
A. Cotter (A)	122.4	10	365	17	21.47	6–95
G.H. Hirst (E)	143.4	27	348	16	21.75	5–58

1911–12: Hill and Trumper retire in a losing series; Hobbs takes over

A strong team went to Australia in 1911–12, captained again by Warner, after Fry had finally declined to go. In the event Warner became ill before the first Test, and J.W.H.T. Douglas was captain in all five.

In the first at Sydney, he was criticized for not opening the bowling with Barnes. Australia made 447 (Trumper 113) and led by 129, eventually winning a high-scoring game by 146 runs, the googly bowler H.V. Hordern taking 12 wickets.

The Test at Melbourne opened sensationally, with Barnes, given the new ball, having four wickets for one run after five overs, and five for six after 11. Australia recovered to 184, but J.W. Hearne scored a century (at just under 21 the youngest Englishman to do so until Compton). England needed 219 and scored them easily with Hobbs making his first hundred against Australia.

Australia were shot out for 133 at Adelaide by Foster and Barnes, and Hobbs and Rhodes put on 147 for England's first wicket, Hobbs going on to 187, and England to 501. Although Australia made 476 in the second innings, with Hill making 98 (his fifth Test score between 96 and 99), England won easily.

Australia were put in at Melbourne, and Barnes and Foster dismissed them for 191. Hobbs and Rhodes scored 323 for the first wicket, still a record in Ashes history. England scored 589 and won easily by an innings.

At Sydney England batted first and Woolley made 133 not out from 324. Australia needed 363 in the second innings to win but fell 71 short.

Barnes' 34 wickets in the rubber was an English record but Foster (32 wickets and 226 runs) did even better. The last Test marked the end of the Test careers of Hill and Trumper, the only cricketers at the time to have scored over 3,000 Test runs.

Left, below: The 1909 Australians. Left to right, back: Whitty, Cotter, Hartigan, Ransford, Bardsley, Carter. Middle: McAlister, Trumper, Hopkins, Noble, Laver, Armstrong, O'Connor. Front: Gregory, Macartney, Carkeek.

Below: A menu decoration for a celebration dinner given to the England touring team on their return from Australia in 1912.

1911–12 Averages

Batting	I	No	Runs	HS	Avge
J.B. Hobbs (E)	9	1	662	187	82.75
W. Rhodes (E)	9	1	463	179	57.87
F.E. Woolley (E)	7	1	289	133*	48.16
G. Gunn (E)	9	0	381	75	42.33
J.W. Hearne (E)	9	1	281	114	35.12
W.W. Armstrong (A)	10	0	324	90	32.40
V.S. Ransford (A)	10	2	252	43	31.50
R.B. Minnett (A)	10	0	305	90	30.50
V.T. Trumper (A)	10	1	269	113	29.88
C. Hill (A)	10	0	274	98	27.40

Bowling	O	M	Runs	W	Avge	BB
F.R. Foster (E)	275.4	58	692	32	21.62	6–91
S.F. Barnes (E)	297	64	778	34	22.88	5–44
J.W.H.T. Douglas (E)	139.5	30	355	15	23.66	5–46
Dr H.V. Hordern (A)	277.2	43	780	32	24.37	7–90
A. Cotter (A)	166	26	548	12	45.66	4–73

1912: A disappointing Triangular Tournament is won by England and the rain

In 1912 a triangular tournament was played in England in which Australia and South Africa played the host country and each other three times each. The whole project was ruined by rain.

Bitter squabbles between players, selectors and the Australian Board were weakening Australian cricket at this time. Jealousies had led to a fist fight between Peter McAlister, a selector, and Clem Hill, captain and selector in 1911–12. The two had already been appointed selectors for the 1912 party, where the biggest problem concerned whether the players would be allowed their own manager, Frank Laver. The Board, apparently not satisfied with the book-keeping of the 1905 tour, when Laver kept an account book for the players but vice-captain McAlister had failed to do so for the Board, decreed they would not. Hill, Trumper, Armstrong, Cotter, Carter and Ransford declined to tour. The 1912 Australian party was thus something of a second eleven.

In the first England v Australia Test, at Lord's, England declared after Hobbs had made a century, but Australia could not complete an innings – Macartney made 99.

It was worse at Old Trafford, only five hours play being possible.

Before the ninth and final match of the tournament it was decided that the winners would be champions and the match would be played to a finish. England, after Hobbs and Rhodes had put on 107, made only 245, but Barnes and Woolley dismissed Australia for 111. G.R. Hazlitt got seven English second-innings wickets for 25, but the wicket by now was so bad that there was no chance of Australia scoring 310, and Woolley for the second time took five wickets as they were dismissed for 65.

England were thus Champions of a tournament so disappointing that nothing like it was attempted again until the World Cup was instituted in 1975.

1912 27th Series Eng 1, Aus 0, Drawn 2
1 LORD'S **Match Drawn**
England 310–7 dec (J B Hobbs 107, W Rhodes 59)
Australia 282–7 (C G Macartney 99, C Kelleway 61)
2 OLD TRAFFORD **Match Drawn**
England 203 (W Rhodes 92, G R Hazlitt 4–77, W J Whitty 4–43)
Australia 14–0
3 THE OVAL **England won by 244 runs**
England 245 (J B Hobbs 66, F E Woolley 62, R B Minnett 4–34, W J Whitty 4–69) and 175 (C B Fry 79, G R Hazlitt 7–25)
Australia 111 (S F Barnes 5–30, F E Woolley 5–29) and 65 (H . Dean 4–19, F E Woolley 5–20)

1912 Averages

Batting	I	No	Runs	HS	Avge	
J.B. Hobbs (E)	4	0	224	107	56.00	
W. Rhodes (E)	4	0	204	92	51.00	
Bowling	O	M	Runs	W	Avge	BB
F.E. Wolley (E)	23.2	7	55	10	5.50	5–20
G.R. Hazlitt (A)	113.3	36	218	12	18.16	7–25
W.J. Whitty (A)	110	42	252	12	21.00	4–43

Noble, Montague Alfred
Noble was born on 28 January 1873 in Sydney, NSW, and made his debut for that state in 1893–94. A defensive middle-order right-hand batsman, and medium-paced off-break bowler, he was also a brilliant field at point. He first appeared for Australia in 1897–98, and became captain in 1903–04. In 42 Tests he scored 1,997 runs, average 30.25 and took 121 wickets, average 25.00. On retirement he wrote some notable books on cricket. He died on 22 June 1940 at Randwick, NSW.

Tate, Maurice William
Born on 30 May 1895 at Brighton, Tate was the son of a Test cricketer. He made his debut for Sussex in 1912 as an off-break bowler. Ten years later he changed to right-arm fast-medium and became one of the best bowlers in the world. He was a pioneer of the use of the seam. He was also a hard-hitting middle-order batsman. He first played for England in 1924, and in 39 Tests scored 1,198 runs, average 25.48, and took 155 wickets, average 26.16. He achieved 1,000 runs and 200 wickets in a season three times, a record, and is one of nine players with 2,000 wickets and 20,000 runs in a career. He died on 18 May 1956 at Wadhurst.

1920–21: Australia win all five Tests in a series of 14 centuries

Exactly half of the players in the first post-war Ashes match were making their debuts. MCC had declined to tour the previous year, but this time sent a party under Douglas, Spooner having been forced to drop out.

England did well to dismiss Australia for 267 at Sydney but then collapsed to 190 all out themselves. Centuries by Herbie Collins, in his first Test, and captain Armstrong, paved the way for an Australian total of 581, and England were heavily beaten by 377.

At Melbourne, it was the turn of C.E. Pellew and J.M. Gregory to score centuries, and Australia totalled 499. Gregory then took seven English wickets, and despite Hobbs' 122, England were made to follow-on on a rain-ruined pitch, and lost by an innings and 91.

Collins scored his second century at Adelaide, 162 out of 354, but C.A.G. Russell made 135 not out and England led by 92. Australia then made the highest score to date, 582, with Kelleway, Armstrong and Pellew making hundreds. Hobbs scored the sixth century of the match, but England, despite scoring 370, were beaten by 119. The 1,753 runs scored remains an Ashes record; 302 were scored off Arthur Mailey, who took five wickets in each innings.

J.W.H. Makepeace, the second Everton footballer to score a century against Australia, made 117 out of 284 in the fourth Test, but Armstrong made his third century of the series and Australia led by 105. Mailey's nine wickets (9–121) in the second innings remains an Australian record in

Tests. Australia needed 211 and scored them for the loss of two wickets.

Macartney made his highest Test score at Sydney of 170 in 244 minutes, giving Australia a lead which left them only 93 to get in the second innings and complete the only

Woolley, Frank Edward
Born in Tonbridge, Kent, on 27 May 1887, Woolley first played for the county in 1906. A tall and graceful middle-order left-hand batsman, he was also a left-arm medium, and later slow, bowler, and a brilliant slip fielder. In a long career he was one of nine players to take 2,000 wickets and score 20,000 runs (he had nearly 60,000). He also took 1,018 catches, a record except for wicket-keepers. He first played for England in 1909, and in 64 Tests scored 3,283 runs, average 36.07, and took 83 wickets, average 33.91. He died on 18 October 1978 at Halifax, Nova Scotia.

5–0 'whitewash' between the two countries. Mailey's 39 wickets in the series remains an Australian record for a five-Test rubber.

1920–21 28th Series Aus 5, Eng 0

1 SYDNEY Australia won by 377 runs
Australia 267 (H L Collins 70) and 581 (W W Armstrong 158, H L Collins 104, C Kelleway 78, C G Macartney 69, W Bardsley 57, J M Taylor 51)
England 190 (F E Woolley 52) and 281 (J B Hobbs 59, J W Hearne 57, E H Hendren 56)

2 MELBOURNE Australia won by an innings and 91 runs
Australia 499 (C E Pellew 116, J M Gregory 100, J M Taylor 68, H L Collins 64, W Bardsley 51)
England 251 (J B Hobbs 122, E H Hendren 67, J M Gregory 7–69) and 157 (F E Woolley 50, W W Armstrong 4–26)

3 ADELAIDE Australia won by 119 runs
Australia 453 (H L Collins 162, W A S Oldfield 50, C H Parkin 5–60) and 582 (C Kelleway 147, W W Armstrong 121, C E Pellew 104, J M Gregory 78, H Howell 4–115)
England 447 (C A G Russell 135, F E Woolley 79, J W H Makepeace 60, J W H T Douglas 60, A A Mailey 5–160) and 370 (J B Hobbs 123, C A G Russell 59, E H Hendren 51, A A Mailey 5–142)

4 MELBOURNE Australia won by 8 wkts
England 284 (J W H Makepeace 117, J W H T Douglas 50, A A Mailey 4–115) and 315 (W Rhodes 73, J W H T Douglas 60, P G H Fender 59, J W H Makepeace 54, A A Mailey 9–121)
Australia 389 (W W Armstrong 123, J M Gregory 77, H L Collins 59, W Bardsley 56, P G H Fender 5–122) and 211–2 (J M Gregory 76, J Ryder 52)

5 SYDNEY Australia won by 9 wkts
England 204 (F E Woolley 53, C Kelleway 4–27) and 280 (J W H T Douglas 68, A A Mailey 5–119)
Australia 392 (C G Macartney 170, J M Gregory 93, P G H Fender 5–90) and 93–1 (W Bardsley 50)

1920–21 Averages

Batting	I	No	Runs	HS	Avge
C.G. Macartney (A)	4	1	260	170	86.66
W.W. Armstrong (A)	7	1	464	158	77.33
J.M. Gregory (A)	8	2	442	100	73.66
H.L. Collins (A)	9	0	557	162	61.88
C.E. Pellew (A)	6	0	319	116	53.16
J.B. Hobbs (E)	10	0	505	123	50.50
C. Kelleway (A)	7	0	330	147	47.14
J.W.H.T. Douglas (E)	10	1	354	68	39.33
W. Bardsley (A)	9	1	311	57	38.87
C.A.G. Russell (E)	8	1	258	135*	36.85
J.W.H. Makepeace (E)	8	0	279	117	34.87
E.H. Hendren (E)	10	0	319	67	31.90
F.E. Woolley (E)	10	0	285	79	28.50

Bowling	O	M	Runs	W	Avge	BB
C. Kelleway (A)	146.5	32	315	15	21.00	4–27
J.M. Gregory (A)	208.1	30	556	23	24.17	7–69
A.A. Mailey (A)	243.5	27	946	36	26.27	9–121
P.G.H. Fender (E)	100.2	7	410	12	34.16	5–90
C.H. Parkin (E)	212.2	28	670	16	41.87	5–60

Hobbs, John Berry

Hobbs was born in Cambridge on 16 December 1882, and played for Surrey from 1905. He was a brilliant opening right-hand batsman, and an excellent field, especially at cover. He was called 'The Master', and is regarded by some as the world's greatest batsman, although his figures were later well beaten by Bradman. Hobbs was an attractive, artistic batsman, whose best innings were often played on difficult wickets. He was highly admired in Australia, where he made five successful tours. His totals of first-class runs, 61,760, and centuries, 199, are unsurpassed. His Test debut was in 1907–08, and he played in 61 Tests, scoring 5,410 runs, average 56.95. With Sutcliffe, he made 15 opening stands of 100 for England. He was knighted in 1953, and died on 21 December 1963 at Brighton.

The Australians in 1921. Left to right, standing: Bardsley, Ryder, Hendry, Gregory, Mayne, Andrews, S. Smith jun (manager). Seated: Mailey, MacDonald, Collins, Armstrong, Macartney, Carter, Taylor. Front: Pellew, Oldfield.

1921: Armstrong reads a paper to see who is playing for England

Armstrong captained the party to England in 1921. Hobbs was injured or ill for the whole series; although he appeared at Headingley he retired with appendicitis while fielding and did not bat. England were still in a state of post-war flux and no fewer than 16 players made their debuts during the series.

At Headingley, Gregory and McDonald, Australia's fast-bowling partnership, captured nine wickets as England were dismissed for 112, and seven more in the second innings, when Ernest Tyldesley played a bumper from Gregory onto his wicket via his face. Australia won by 10 wickets.

The treatment continued at Lord's. Thirteen wickets for the fast-bowling pair led to a comfortable eight-wicket victory for Australia.

Australia batted first at Headingley and Macartney made the first century of the series. Australia totalled 407. The Hon

31

Lionel Tennyson captained England, Douglas having led the side to seven successive defeats against Australia. He kept his place, and took over the captaincy when Tennyson injured his hand fielding. Tennyson showed spirit in scoring 63 virtually one-handed in England's 259. He also made 36 in the second innings but could not prevent a 219-run defeat.

Rain washed out the first day at Old Trafford, a Test interesting mostly for a breach in the rules. With Russell scoring 101, Tennyson attempted to declare on the second day, but Armstrong pointed out that under two-day rules this was not permissible unless 100 minutes batting were possible for the other side. After a 25-minute delay England resumed and Armstrong bowled consecutive overs; having bowled the last before the break, he bowled the first afterwards. England were well on top but the match was destined to be a draw.

At the Oval, Sandham was England's 30th player of the rubber, a record. Mead scored 182 not out, including 109 before lunch on the second day. England declared, led by 14, but could only bat out time. Armstrong read a paper in the outfield to demonstrate the pointlessness of it.

1921 29th Series   Aus 3, Eng 0, Drawn 2
1 TRENT BRIDGE   Australia won by 10 wkts
England 112 (J M Gregory 6–58) and 147 (E A McDonald 5–32)
Australia 232 (W Bardsley 66) and 30–0
2 LORD'S   Australia won by 8 wkts
England 187 (F E Woolley 95, A A Mailey 4–55) and 283 (F E Woolley 93, L H Tennyson 74, J M Gregory 4–76, E A McDonald 4–89)
Australia 342 (W Bardsley 88, J M Gregory 52, F J Durston 4–102) and 131–2 (W Bardsley 63)

3 HEADINGLEY   Australia won by 219 runs
Australia 407 (C G Macartney 115, W W Armstrong 77, C E Pellew 52, J M Taylor 50, C H Parkin 4–106) and 273–7 dec (T J E Andrews 92)
England 259 (J W H T Douglas 75, L H Tennyson 63, G Brown 57, E A McDonald 4–105) and 202
4 OLD TRAFFORD   Match Drawn
England 362–4 dec (C A G Russell 101, G E Tyldesley 78) and 44–1
Australia 175 (C H Parkin 5–38)
5 THE OVAL   Match Drawn
England 403–8 dec (C P Mead 182, L H Tennyson 51, E A McDonald 5–143) and 244–2 (C A G Russell 102, G Brown 84, J W Hitch 51)
Australia 389 (T J E Andrews 94, J M Taylor 75, C G Macartney 61)

1921 Averages

Batting	I	No	Runs	HS	Avge
G. Brown (E)	5	0	250	84	50.00
W. Bardsley (A)	8	2	281	88	46.83
F.E. Woolley (E)	8	0	343	95	42.87
C.G. Macartney (A)	8	1	300	115	42.85
T.J.E. Andrews (A)	7	0	275	94	39.28

Bowling	O	M	Runs	W	Avge	BB
E.A. McDonald (A)	205.5	32	668	27	24.74	5–32
C.H. Parkin (E)	131.5	21	420	16	26.25	5–38
J.M. Gregory (A)	182.2	35	552	19	29.05	6–58
A.A. Mailey (A)	124.4	18	398	12	33.16	4–55

1924–25: Hobbs and Sutcliffe join forces, but Australia win again

The England party under A.E.R. Gilligan included seven of the players who had lost 5–0 four years earlier.

Centuries by the captain, H.L. Collins, and W.H. Ponsford, on his debut, got Australia away to a good start of 450 in the first Test at Sydney. Hobbs and Sutcliffe opened the England innings for the first time

together, and put on 157, but the rest of the side, except Hendren, batted poorly. With a lead of 152, Australia added 452, J.M. Taylor scoring a century and adding 127 for the last wicket with Mailey, still Australia's highest against England. Hobbs and Sutcliffe opened with another three-figure stand (each scored a century and a fifty in the match), Woolley scored 123, and England's 411 was a fourth-innings record, but they lost by 193.

At Melbourne Ponsford became the first to score a century in each of his first two Tests; V.Y. Richardson scored another, and Australia made a record Test score of 600. Hobbs (154) and Sutcliffe (176) then batted all the third day, the first such instance in Tests, and put on 283, but again the rest of the batting failed and England made 479. Set to get 372 they fell 82 short, despite a third century in three innings by Sutcliffe. Tate had 20 wickets in the first two Tests.

Injuries possibly cost England the third Test. With Australia 22 for three, Tate and Gilligan had to retire, and at 119 for six Freeman followed. Ryder then made 201 not out and Australia recovered to 489. England kept Hobbs (119) and Sutcliffe back to numbers five and six and made 365. Having dismissed Australia for 250 with the help of a little rain, England needed 375 and made a great effort, finishing only 12 short of victory.

At Melbourne, England won the toss for the only time in the series. Hobbs and Sutcliffe opened with 126, Sutcliffe became the first batsman to score four centuries in a series and England made 548. Australia were beaten by an innings and 29 runs, their first defeat in 17 Tests.

Clarrie Grimmett made his debut for Australia at Sydney, and took 11 wickets in a 307-run Australian victory. Sutcliffe's and Tate's aggregates of 734 runs and 38 wickets were records for a series.

The England tourists in Australia, 1924–25. Left to right, back: Bryan, Tyldesley, Tate, F.C. Toone (manager), Whysall, Chapman, Sandham. Middle: Hearne, Strudwick, Douglas, Gilligan, Hobbs, Woolley. Front: Kilner, Hendren, Freeman, Sutcliffe, Howell.

1924–25 30th Series Aus 4, Eng 1

1 SYDNEY Australia won by 195 runs

Australia 450 (H L Collins 114, W H Ponsford 110, M W Tate 6–130) and 452 (J M Taylor 108, A J Richardson 98, H L Collins 60, M W Tate 5–98)

England 298 (J B Hobbs 115, H Sutcliffe 59, E H Hendren 74, J M Gregory 5–115, A A Mailey 4–129) and 411 (F E Woolley 123, H Sutcliffe 115, J B Hobbs 57, A P Freeman 50)

2 MELBOURNE Australia won by 81 runs

Australia 600 (V Y Richardson 138, W H Ponsford 128, A E V Hartkopf 80, J M Taylor 72) and 250 (J M Taylor 90, M W Tate 6–99, F E Woolley 4–84)

England 479 (H Sutcliffe 176, J B Hobbs 154) and 290 (H Sutcliffe 127, F E Woolley 50, A A Mailey 5–92, J M Gregory 4–87)

3 ADELAIDE Australia won by 11 runs

Australia 489 (J Ryder 201, A J Richardson 69, T J E Andrews 72, R Kilner 4–127) and 250 (J Ryder 88, R Kilner 4–51, F E Woolley 4–77)

England 365 (J B Hobbs 119, E H Hendren 92) and 363 (W W Whysall 75, H Sutcliffe 59, A P F Chapman 58)

4 MELBOURNE England won by an innings and 29 runs

England 548 (H Sutcliffe 143, W W Whysall 76, R Kilner 74, J B Hobbs 66, E H Hendren 65, A A Mailey 4–186)

Australia 269 (J M Taylor 86) and 250 (J M Taylor 68, M W Tate 5–75)

5 SYDNEY Australia won by 307 runs

Australia 295 (W H Ponsford 80, M W Tate 4–92, R Kilner 4–97) and 325 (T J E Andrews 80, C Kelleway 73, W A S Oldfield 65, M W Tate 5–115)

England 167 (C V Grimmett 5–45) and 146 (C V Grimmett 6–37)

1924–25 Averages

Batting	I	No	Runs	HS	Avge
H. Sutcliffe (E)	9	0	734	176	81.55
J. Ryder (A)	6	1	363	201*	72.60
J.B. Hobbs (E)	9	0	573	154	63.66
J.M. Taylor (A)	10	0	541	108	54.10
W.H. Ponsford (A)	10	0	468	128	46.80
W.A.S. Oldfield (A)	10	3	291	65	41.57
E.H. Hendren (E)	9	1	314	92*	39.25
F.E. Woolley (E)	9	0	325	123	36.11
H.L. Collins (A)	10	0	294	114	29.40
C. Kelleway (A)	10	1	252	73	28.00

Bowling	O	M	Runs	W	Avge	BB
M.W. Tate (E)	315	62	881	38	23.18	6–99
R. Kilner (E)	179.1	35	399	17	23.47	4–51
C. Kelleway (A)	171	39	413	14	29.50	3–57
J.M. Gregory (A)	207.5	22	816	22	37.09	5–111
A.A. Mailey (A)	239	21	999	24	41.62	5–92

1926: England regain the Ashes at last

Collins led the Australians to England in 1926, but was not called upon for many decisions in the first Test at Trent Bridge, only 50 minutes play being possible.

At Lord's Bardsley carried his bat through the Australian innings of 383, making 193 not out. Hobbs (119) and Sutcliffe (82) put on 182, Hendren made 127 not out, and England captain A.W. Carr declared at 475 for three. But Macartney made 133 not out and the match was drawn. Hobbs became the first to pass 4,000 runs in Tests.

Bardsley captained Australia at Headingley because Collins was ill, but was out without a run on the board. Macartney then arrived to make a century before lunch. With Woodfull and A.J. Richardson also scoring centuries Australia reached 494, and dismissed England for 294. Hobbs and Sutcliffe, with a 156 opening stand, ensured the draw.

At Old Trafford, rain ruined the first day, and then Macartney and Woodfull scored their third and second centuries of the series respectively, but there was no time for England to complete their innings.

The Oval Test was to be played to a finish, and England replaced Carr as captain with A.P.F. Chapman. Rhodes was recalled at 45 years old after a five-year break, and

Woolley was chosen for his 52nd consecutive Test match, dating back to 1909.

England made 298, Maily claiming six for 138, and Australia recovered from 122 for six to 302, a lead of 22. England were ahead by the end of the second day, but then came a storm. The batting of Hobbs and Sutcliff on a sticky wicket on the third day has become legendary. Their first-wicket stand realized 172; both made centuries and Sutcliffe went on to 161. The partnership won the match. Australia were set 415 and were shot out for 125.

1926 31st Series Eng 1, Aus 0, Drawn 4

1 TRENT BRIDGE Match Drawn

England 32–0 Australia did not bat

2 LORD'S Match Drawn

Australia 383 (W Bardsley 193, R Kilner 4–70) and 194–5 (C G Macartney 133)

England 475–3 dec (E H Hendren 127, J B Hobbs 119, F E Woolley 87, H Sutcliffe 82, A P F Chapman 50)

3 HEADINGLEY Match Drawn

Australia 494 (C G Macartney 151, W M Woodfull 141, A J Richardson 100, M W Tate 4–99)

England 294 (G G Macaulay 76, C V Grimmett 5–88) and 254–3 (H Sutcliffe 94, J B Hobbs 88)

4 OLD TRAFFORD Match Drawn

Australia 335 (W M Woodfull 117, C G Macartney 109, C F Root 4–84)

England 305–5 (G E Tyldesley 81, J B Hobbs 74, F E Woolley 58)

5 THE OVAL England won by 289 runs

England 280 (H Sutcliffe 76, A A Mailey 6–138) and 436 (H Sutcliffe 161, J B Hobbs 100)

Australia 302 (J M Gregory 73, H L Collins 61) and 125 (W Rhodes 4–44)

1926 Averages

Batting	I	No	Runs	HS	Avge
C.G. Macartney (A)	6	1	473	151	94.60
J.B. Hobbs (E)	7	1	486	119	81.00
H. Sutcliffe (E)	7	1	472	161	78.66
W.M. Woodfull (A)	6	0	306	141	51.00

Bowling	O	M	Runs	W	Avge	BB
M.W. Tate (E)	208.3	64	388	13	29.84	5–88
C.V. Grimmett (A)	204	59	414	13	31.84	5–88
A.A. Mailey (A)	172.4	25	592	14	42.28	6–138

The most successful of all Test opening partnerships, Jack Hobbs and Herbert Sutcliffe. In the 1924–25 and 1926 series, Hobbs averaged 63.66 and 81.00, Sutcliffe 81.55 and 78.66.

1928–29: Hammond's triumphant tour and England win easily

Chapman continued as England captain for the tour to Australia in 1928–29. Ryder captained Australia.

Brisbane made its debut as a Test venue for the first Test, and Bradman made his first appearance for Australia. Most of the English players scored runs, Hendren's 169 being the main score of the side's 521. Larwood, on his first visit to Australia, then achieved his best Test analysis, 6–32, on a perfect batting pitch. Australia made 122. England declared at 342 for eight (Oldfield did not allow a bye in 863 runs). It was a wise decision not to enforce the follow-on, because after Larwood had taken two quick wickets in the fourth innings, overnight rain led Australia to be dismissed for 66, and a record victory for England in terms of runs alone by 675 runs.

Bradman was dropped for the second Test at Sydney, where Australia made 253. A record crowd of 58,456 turned up to watch Hobbs bat on the second day, and they gave him a tremendous ovation. It was Hammond who scored most of England's runs, however, in a record Test total of 636: he made 251. Woodfull and Hendry made centuries second time round for Australia, but England needed only 15 to win, and the bowlers were sent in to get them.

Australia needed to win at Melbourne, and began with 397, with Ryder and Kippax scoring centuries and adding 161 together. Hammond, however, became the first player to score a double-century in successive Test innings, and England led by 20 runs. Australia set a target of 332, with Woodfull and Bradman (at 20 years 129 days old) getting centuries. The odds were heavily in Australia's favour when England began, for rain had made the wicket almost unplayable, but Hobbs and Sutcliffe produced some of the best batting ever seen in the circumstances. Playing a dead bat to everything that needed to be played, they put on 105 and stayed while the wicket eased. Sutcliffe completed his

fourth century at Melbourne and England won by three wickets.

At Adelaide Hammond scored 119 not out and England reached 334. Then Archie Jackson, opening for Australia on his debut, scored 164 at 19 years 152 days old, the youngest to score an Ashes century. It helped Australia to a 35-run lead. Hammond (177) then completed his second century of the match and his fourth of the rubber (equalling Sutcliffe's record), and with Jardine (98) put on 262 for the third wicket. Australia needed 349 to win, and batting solidly, failed by only 13 runs. J.C. White took eight for 126.

In the last Test at Melbourne, Hobbs, at 46 years 82 days, became the oldest to score a Test century (142), and Leyland scored 137 in his first match against Australia. England, without Sutcliffe, made 519. Woodfull and Bradman made centuries for Australia, who ended only 28 behind. Good bowling by T.W. Wall, on his debut, helped get England out for 257, and, needing 286, Australia won by five wickets. Hammond's aggregate of 905 runs (av 113.12) for the series was a record, and in his second innings Hobbs became the first to pass 5,000 runs in Tests.

1928–29 32nd Series Eng 4, Aus 1
1 BRISBANE England won by 675 runs
England 521 (E H Hendren 169, H Larwood 70, A P F Chapman 50) and 342–8 dec (C P Mead 73, D R Jardine 65, C V Grimmett 6–131)
Australia 122 (H Larwood 6–32) and 66 (J C White 4–7)
2 SYDNEY England won by 8 wkts
Australia 253 (W M Woodfull 68, G Geary 5–35) and 397 (H S T L Hendry 112, W M Woodfull 111, J Ryder 79, M W Tate 4–99)
England 636 (W R Hammond 251, E H Hendren 74, G Geary 66, D D Blackie 4–148) and 16–2

The England tourists in Australia, 1928–29. Left to right, back: Duckworth, Ames, Mead, Tate, Hendren, Geary. Middle: Leyland, Staples, Hammond, F.C. Toone (manager), Sutcliffe, Larwood, Freeman. Front: Tyldesley, White, Chapman, Jardine, Hobbs.

3 MELBOURNE England won by 3 wkts
Australia 397 (J Ryder 112, A F Kippax 100, D G Bradman 79) and 351 (D G Bradman 112, W M Woodfull 107, J C White 5–107)
England 417 (W R Hammond 200, D R Jardine 62, H Sutcliffe 58, D D Blackie 6–94) and 332–7 (H Sutcliffe 135)
4 ADELAIDE England won by 12 runs
England 334 (W R Hammond 119, J B Hobbs 74, H Sutcliffe 64, C V Grimmett 5–102) and 383 (W R Hammond 177, D R Jardine 98, R K Oxenham 4–67)
Australia 369 (A Jackson 164, J Ryder 63, J C White 5–130, M W Tate 4–77) and 336 (J Ryder 87, D G Bradman 58, A F Kippax 51, J C White 8–126)
5 MELBOURNE Australia won by 5 wkts
England 519 (J B Hobbs 142, M Leyland 137, E H Hendren 95) and 257 (J B Hobbs 65, M W Tate 54, M Leyland 53, T W Wall 5–66)
Australia 491 (D G Bradman 123, W M Woodfull 102, A G Fairfax 65, G Geary 5–105) and 287–5 (J Ryder 57)

1928–29 Averages

Batting	I	No	Runs	HS	Avge
W. R. Hammond (E)	9	1	905	251	113.12
A. Jackson (A)	4	0	276	164	69.00
D.G. Bradman (A)	8	1	468	123	66.85
J. Ryder (A)	10	1	492	112	54.66
W.M. Woodfull (A)	10	1	491	111	54.55
E.H. Hendren (E)	9	0	472	169	52.44
H. Sutcliffe (E)	7	0	355	135	50.71
J.B. Hobbs (E)	9	0	451	142	50.11
D.R. Jardine (E)	9	1	341	98	42.62
A.F. Kippax (A)	10	1	311	100	31.10

Bowling	O	M	Runs	W	Avge	BB
G. Geary (E)	240.3	70	477	19	25.10	5–35
J.C. White (E)	405.5	134	760	25	30.10	5–35
D.D. Blackie (A)	210	52	444	14	31.71	6–94
H. Larwood (E)	258.7	41	728	18	40.44	6–32
M.W. Tate (E)	371	122	693	17	40.76	4–77
C.V. Grimmett (A)	398.2	95	1024	23	44.52	6–131

1930: Farewell to Hobbs, and the rise of Bradman

Chapman retained the captaincy of England when W.M. Woodfull's Australians arrived in England in 1930. At Trent Bridge England led by 126 in a low-scoring first innings, and then, thanks to Hobbs' second 70, made 302, setting Australia 429 to win. With Bradman and McCabe batting well at 229 for three, a Notts groundstaff substitute, S.H. Copley, made a brilliant catch to dismiss McCabe for 49. Bradman made 131 in his first Test in England but England won by 93.

At Lord's Duleepsinhji's 173 helped England to 425, but Australia replied with 729 for six declared, the highest score made at Lord's. Bradman contributed 254 (the highest Test score at Lord's) and Kippax 155. Chapman's century could not save England from a seven-wicket defeat.

Bradman broke more records at Headingley. He made 309 on the first day (still a record for one day in a Test), including 105 before lunch. His final score of 334 was the highest individual Test score. Australia made 566, but Hammond scored a century and the match was drawn.

There was little play at Old Trafford after the first two days. Hobbs and Sutcliffe made their last (eleventh) century opening stand against Australia.

The final Test at the Oval was a timeless Test to decide the rubber. R.E.S. Wyatt took over the England captaincy and helped Sutcliffe (161) add 170 for the sixth wicket. England made 405, but Australia passed this total with only three wickets down, Bradman (232) and Ponsford (110) doing most damage. With a deficit of 290, England made only 251 (Hornibrook 7–92), and Australia won back the Ashes.

Hobbs' Test career ended with a record

5,410 runs, while Bradman's stormed ahead with a record series aggregate of 974, average 139.14.

1930 33rd Series Aus 2, Eng 1, Drawn 2

1 TRENT BRIDGE England won by 93 runs
England 270 (J B Hobbs 78, A P F Chapman 52, R W V Robins 50, C V Grimmett 5–107) and 302 (J B Hobbs 74, E H Hendren 72, H Sutcliffe 58, C V Grimmett 5–94)
Australia 144 (A F Kippax 64, R W V Robins 4–51) and 335 (D G Bradman 131)

2 LORD'S Australia won by 7 wkts
England 425 (K S Duleepsinhji 173, M W Tate 54, A G Fairfax 4–101) and 375 (A P F Chapman 121, G O B Allen 57, C V Grimmett 6–167)
Australia 729–6 dec (D G Bradman 254, W M Woodfull 155, A F Kippax 83, W H Ponsford 81) and 72–3

3 HEADINGLEY Match Drawn
Australia 566 (D G Bradman 334, A F Kippax 77, W M Woodfull 50, M W Tate 5–124)
England 391 (W R Hammond 113, C V Grimmett 5–135) and 95–3

4 OLD TRAFFORD Match Drawn
Australia 345 (W H Ponsford 83, W M Woodfull 54, A F Kippax 51, C V Grimmett 50)
England 251–8 (H Sutcliffe 74, K S Duleepsinhji 54, S J McCabe 4–41)

5 THE OVAL Australia won by an innings and 39 runs
England 405 (H Sutcliffe 161, R E S Wyatt 64, K S Duleepsinhji 50, C V Grimmett 4–135) and 251 (W R Hammond 60, H Sutcliffe 54, P M Hornibrook 7–92)
Australia 695 (D G Bradman 232, W H Ponsford 110, A Jackson 73, W M Woodfull 54, S J McCabe 54, A G Fairfax 53, I A R Peebles 6–204)

1930 Averages

Batting

	I	No	Runs	HS	Avge
D.G. Bradman (A)	7	0	974	334	139.14
H. Sutcliffe (E)	7	2	436	161	87.20
K.S. Duleepsinhji (E)	7	0	416	173	59.42
W.M. Woodfull (A)	7	1	345	155	57.50
W.H. Ponsford (A)	6	0	330	110	55.00
A.F. Kippax (A)	7	1	329	83	54.83
A.P.F. Chapman (E)	6	0	259	1231	43.16
W.R. Hammond (E)	9	0	306	113	34.00
J.B. Hobbs (E)	9	0	301	78	33.44

Bowling

	O	M	Runs	W	Avge	BB
A.G. Fairfax (A)	134.2	34	335	12	27.91	4–101
C.V. Grimmett (A)	349.4	78	925	29	31.89	6–167
P.M. Hornibrook (A)	196.1	50	471	13	36.23	7–92
M.W. Tate (E)	280.1	82	574	15	38.26	5–124
T.W. Wall (A)	229.4	44	593	13	45.61	3–67

ENGLAND V AUSTRALIA 1930
3rd Test, Headingley: Match Drawn

AUSTRALIA

W.M. Woodfull*	b Hammond	50			
A.A. Jackson	c Larwood b Tate	1			
D.G. Bradman	c Duckworth b Tate	334			
A.F. Kippax	c Chapman b Tate	77			
S.J. McCabe	b Larwood	30			
V.Y. Richardson	c Larwood b Tate	1			
E.L. a'Beckett	c Chapman b Geary	29			
W.A.S. Oldfield†	c Hobbs b Tate	2			
C.V. Grimmett	c Duckworth b Tyldesley	24			
T.W. Wall	b Tyldesley	3			
P.M. Hornibrook	not out	1			
Extras	(B 5, LB 8, W 1)	14			
Total		**566**			

ENGLAND

J.B. Hobbs	c A'Beckett b Grimmett	29	run out	13
H. Sutcliffe	c Hornibrook b Grimmett	32	not out	28
W.R. Hammond	c Oldfield b McCabe	113	c Oldfield b Grimmett	35
K.S. Duleepsinhji	b Hornibrook	35	c Grimmett b Hornibrook	10
M. Leyland	c Kippax b Wall	44	not out	1
G. Geary	run out	0		
G. Duckworth†	c Oldfield b A'Beckett	33		
A.P.F. Chapman*	b Grimmett	45		
M.W. Tate	c Jackson b Grimmett	22		
H. Larwood	not out	10		
R.K. Tyldesley	c Hornibrook b Grimmett	6		
Extras	(B 9, LB 10, NB 3)	22	(LB 8)	8
Total		**391**	**(3 wickets)**	**95**

ENGLAND	O	M	R	W	O	M	R	W
Larwood	33	3	139	1				
Tate	39	9	124	5				
Geary	35	10	95	1				
Tyldesley	33	5	104	2				
Hammond	17	3	46	1				
Leyland	11	0	44	0				
AUSTRALIA								
Wall	40	12	70	1	10	3	20	0
A'Beckett	28	8	47	1	11	4	19	0
Grimmett	56.2	16	135	5	17	3	33	1
Hornibrook	41	7	94	1	11.5	5	14	1
McCabe	10	4	23	1	2	1	1	0

FALL OF WICKETS

	A	E	E
Wkt	1st	1st	2nd
1st	2	53	24
2nd	194	64	72
3rd	423	123	94
4th	486	206	—
5th	491	206	—
6th	508	289	—
7th	519	319	—
8th	544	370	—
9th	565	375	—
10th	566	391	—

Jack Hobbs sweeps high to leg in the Test at Trent Bridge in 1930. Hobbs made 78 and 74.

The Australian tourists in 1930. Left to right, back: McCabe, Hurwood, Wall, Hornibrook, A'Beckett, Kippax, Grimmett, Oldfield. Front: Bradman, Ponsford, Richardson, Woodfull, Walker, Jackson, Fairfax.

Douglas Jardine, the controversial England captain on the 1932–33 tour of Australia, whose fast leg-theory tactics earned the name 'bodyline' and sparked off a famous row between the countries.

1932–33: Bodyline causes bitterness and injury

The 1932–33 Test series in Australia was to become the most famous in cricket history, and its 50th anniversary saw books, films and a television series made about it.

The controversy it inspired centred on the England tactics employed by their stern captain, D.R. Jardine, and dubbed by the Australian press as 'bodyline', to subdue the prolific scoring of Bradman.

Ironically, Bradman was unfit for the first Test at Sydney. The bodyline tactics, which consisted of fast, short-pitched bowling to a string of close leg-side catchers, were used, but not exclusively, in Australia's innings. McCabe played what is regarded as the best innings against bodyline – a dashing, hooking 187 not out, including 51 of a last-wicket stand of 55. Australia totalled 360. Centuries from Sutcliffe (194), Hammond and the Nawab of Pataudi, on his Test debut, gave England a lead of 164, and they required only one second-innings run for a ten-wicket victory. The fast bowler Larwood, on whom bodyline was based, took ten wickets.

At Melbourne, on a pitch suited to leg-breaker W.J. O'Reilly, who took ten wickets, Australia levelled the series by a

111-run victory. Bradman, on his return, was bowled first ball by Bowes, but made 103 not out in the second innings.

The bodyline argument came to a head at Adelaide, a Test watched by a record 172,926 spectators, including 50,962 on the fateful second day. After England recovered from 30 for four to 341, Australian captain Woodfull was struck over the heart by Larwood and there were angry crowd scenes. After play Woodfull made a much-publicized remark to the England manager that only one side was playing cricket. After a rest day filled with heated comments from the Australian press, Jardine continued his tactics and Oldfield's skull was fractured by another ball from Larwood. The deliveries causing the main injuries were not strictly bodyline, but were pitched on the off, and Oldfield sportingly admitted later that he had ducked into his, but opinion now was such that the Australian Board of Control sent a cable to MCC which read:

'Bodyline bowling has assumed such proportions as to menace the best interests of the game, making protection of the body by the batsman the main consideration. This is causing intensely bitter feeling between the players as well as injury. In our opinion it is unsportsmanlike. Unless stopped at once it is likely to upset the friendly relations existing between Australia and England.'

That put the majority Australian view clearly. The MCC view was that leg-theory bowling was quite legal and long-established, that the Australian batsmen made difficulties for themselves with their style of moving across the wicket, that 'unsportsmanlike' was not a term they could countenance and that if the Australian authorities so wished they would abandon the tour.

Eventually the two Governments were drawn into the dispute, but after much diplomacy and cabling the tour continued, with the England tactics unchanged. England won the Adelaide match by 338 runs.

At Brisbane, where England regained the Ashes with a six-wicket win, there were no serious incidents, the batsman Paynter being the hero with a fine four-hour innings after being summoned from a hospital bed where he was being treated for acute tonsillitis. Sadly the brilliant young batsman Archie Jackson died aged 23 on the day Paynter's six settled the series.

At Sydney, England emphasized their superiority with an eight-wicket win, largely due to Verity's bowling; Larwood, who injured his foot, nevertheless getting 98 runs as night-watchman. His 33 wickets at 19.51 won the series, but he did not play another Test, and was the principal sufferer of the bitterness aroused by bodyline.

Larwood, Harold

Larwood was born on 14 November 1904 at Nuncargate, Nottinghamshire. He first appeared for Notts in 1924 and for England two years later. He was a devastating right-arm fast bowler, whose name will always be linked with the 'bodyline' series of 1932–33. He was the ideal fast bowler to implement the English captain's policy of leg-theory bowling, which was calculated to neutralize Bradman. England won the series 4–1, amid tremendous controversy, but for one reason or another Larwood did not play for England again. In 21 Tests from 1926 he took 78 wickets at 28.35 each. He scored valuable Test runs, averaging 19.40. He emigrated to Australia in 1949.

Larwood bowling to Australian captain Woodfull at Brisbane in 1932–33. Woodfull ducks under a bouncer. Notice the ring of six close in on the leg side, the 'bodyline' field.

1932–33 34th Series Eng 4, Aus 1

1 SYDNEY   England won by 10 wkts
Australia 360 (S J McCabe 187, H Larwood 5–96, W Voce 4–110) and 164 (H Larwood 5–28)
England 524 (H Sutcliffe 194, W R Hammond 112, Nawab of Pataudi 102) and 1–0

2 MELBOURNE   Australia won by 111 runs
Australia 228 (J H W Fingleton 83) and 191 (D G Bradman 103)
England 169 (H Sutcliffe 52, W J O'Reilly 5–63, T W Wall 4–52) and 139 (W J O'Reilly 5–66, H Ironmonger 4–26)

3 ADELAIDE   England won by 338 runs
England 341 (M Leyland 83, R E S Wyatt 78, E Paynter 77, T W Wall 5–72) and 412 (W R Hammond 85, L E G Ames 69, D R Jardine 56, W J O'Reilly 4–79)
Australia 222 (W H Ponsford 85, G O B Allen 4–71) and 193 (W M Woodfull 73, D G Bradman 66, G O B Allen 4–50, H Larwood 4–71)

4 BRISBANE   England won by 6 wkts
Australia 340 (V Y Richardson 83, D G Bradman 76, W M Woodfull 67, H Larwood 4–101) and 175
England 356 (H Sutcliffe 86, E Paynter 83, W J O'Reilly 4–120) and 162–4 (M Leyland 86)

5 SYDNEY   England won by 8 wkts
Australia 435 (L S Darling 85, S J McCabe 73, L P J O'Brien 61, W A S Oldfield 52, H Larwood 4–98) and 182 (D G Bradman 71, W M Woodfull 67, H Verity 5–33)
England 454 (W R Hammond 101, H Larwood 98, H Sutcliffe 56, R E S Wyatt 51, P K Lee 4–111) and 168–2 (W R Hammond 75, R E S Wyatt 61)

1932–33 Averages

Batting	I	No	Runs	HS	Avge
D.G. Bradman (A)	8	1	396	103*	56.57
H. Sutcliffe (E)	9	1	440	194	55.00
W.R. Hammond (E)	9	1	440	112	55.00
R.E.S. Wyatt (E)	9	2	327	78	46.71
S.J. McCabe (A)	10	1	385	187*	42.77
M. Leyland (E)	9	0	306	86	34.00
W.M. Woodfull (A)	10	1	305	73*	33.88
V. Richardson (A)	10	0	279	83	27.90

Bowling	O	M	Runs	W	Avge	BB
H. Larwood (E)	220.1	42	644	33	19.51	5–28
T.W. Wall (A)	160.1	33	409	16	25.56	5–72
W.J. O'Reilly (A)	383.4	144	724	27	26.81	5–63
H. Ironmonger (A)	245.3	96	405	15	27.00	4–26
W. Voce (E)	133.3	23	407	15	27.13	4–110
G.O.B. Allen (E)	170.6	29	593	21	28.23	4–50

1934: Ponsford and Bradman make big partnerships

Many behind-the-scenes meetings had been held as a result of the bodyline tour, and one result was the absence from the England team of the three major bodyline figures: Jardine, the captain, and Larwood and Voce, the fast bowlers. MCC opinion was now firmly against its use.

C.F. Walters captained England at Trent Bridge as Wyatt was injured. A.G. Chipperfield lunched at 99 not out in his first Test, but failed to get the vital run. Australia won with ten minutes to spare, after O'Reilly had taken 11 wickets in the match.

Fortune favoured England at Lord's where Wyatt returned. England reached 440, during which innings Oldfield became the first wicket-keeper to achieve 100 Test dismissals. Rain made the wicket on the third day a paradise for Hedley Verity, who caused the Australian first innings to collapse and then dismissed the side a second time, taking 14 wickets in the day – a Test record. England won by an innings.

O'Reilly caused England to collapse from 68 without loss to 72 for three at Old Trafford, with three wickets in four balls, but Hendren (132) and Leyland (153) repaired the damage.

G.O.B. Allen's first over included three wides and four no-balls. McCabe made 137 and the match was destined to be a draw.

After England had been dismissed for 200 at Headingley, Bradman scored his second successive triple-century there. With Ponsford (181) he added 388 for the fourth wicket, to create a new record for Ashes matches. Rain on the last day saved England from probable defeat.

The final Test at the Oval was again the decisive match, played to a finish. Australia batted and Ponsford (266) and Bradman (244) broke all Test partnership records with 451 for the second wicket, which remains a record. Australia made 701 and Woodfull batted again with a lead of 380. England finally needed 708 to win and were beaten by 562. The spin bowlers Grimmett and O'Reilly took 53 wickets in the series.

1934 35th Series   Aus 2, Eng 1, Drawn 2
1 TRENT BRIDGE   Australia won by 238 runs
Australia 374 (A G Chipperfield 99, S J McCabe 65, W H Ponsford 53, K Farnes 5–102) and 273–8 dec (S J McCabe 88, W A Brown 73, K Farnes 5–77)
England 268 (E H Hendren 79, H Sutcliffe 62, G Geary 53, C V Grimmett 5–81, W J O'Reilly 4–75) and 141 (W J O'Reilly 7–54)

2 LORD'S   England won by an innings and 38 runs
England 440 (L E G Ames 120, M Leyland 109, C F Walters 82, T W Wall 4–108)
Australia 284 (W A Brown 105, H Verity 7–61) and 118 (H Verity 8–43)

3 OLD TRAFFORD   Match Drawn
England 627–9 dec (M Leyland 153, E H Hendren 132, L E G Ames 72, H Sutcliffe 63, G O B Allen 61, H Verity 60, C F Walters 52, W J O'Reilly 7–189) and 123–0 (H Sutcliffe 69, C F Walters 50)
Australia 491 (S J McCabe 137, W M Woodfull 73, W A Brown 72, H Verity 4–78) and 66–1

4 HEADINGLEY   Match Drawn
England 200 (C V Grimmett 4–57) and 229–6
Australia 584 (D G Bradman 304, W H Ponsford 181, W E Bowes 6–142)

5 THE OVAL   Australia won by 562 runs
Australia 701 (W H Ponsford 266, D G Bradman 244, W E Bowes 4–164, G O B Allen 4–170) and 327 (D G Bradman 77, S J McCabe 70, W E Bowes 5–55, E W Clark 5–98)
England 321 (M Leyland 110, C F Walters 64) and 145 (C V Grimmett 5–64)

McCabe, Stanley Joseph

McCabe, born on 16 July 1910 at Grenfell, NSW, played two of the most famous Test innings of all time. After making his debut for New South Wales in 1928–29, he made his Test appearance on the tour of England in 1930. He was a brilliant middle-order right-hand batsman, and a medium-paced bowler. He was very strong against fast bowling and could cut and hook powerfully. This helped him to make 187 not out at Sydney in 1932–33, often described as the best innings against bodyline. At Trent Bridge in 1938 he made 232 out of 411, including 72 out of 77 for the last wicket, an innings singled out by Bradman as the best he'd seen. In 39 Tests McCabe scored 2,748 runs, average 48.21, and took 36 wickets at 42.86 each. He died at Mosman, NSW, on 25 August 1968.

1934 Averages					
Batting	I	No	Runs	HS	Avge
W.H. Ponsford (A)	7	1	569	266	94.83
D.G. Bradman (A)	8	0	758	304	94.75
M. Leyland (E)	8	1	478	153	68.28
S.J. McCabe (A)	9	1	483	137	60.37
H. Sutcliffe (E)	7	1	304	69*	50.66
C.F. Walters (E)	9	1	401	82	50.12
E.H. Hendren (E)	6	0	298	132	49.66
L.E.G. Ames (E)	7	1	261	120	43.50
W.A. Brown (A)	9	0	300	105	33.33
Bowling	O	M	Runs	W	Avge BB
H. Verity (E)	271.2	93	576	24	24.00 8–43
W.J. O'Reilly (A)	333.4	128	698	28	24.92 7–54
W.E. Bowes (E)	144.3	27	483	19	25.42 6–142
C.V. Grimmett (A)	396.3	148	668	25	26.72 5–64

Maurice Tate bowling at Old Trafford in 1935 in his last Test match. He was England's most successful bowler in Australia in the 1920s.

1936–37: Thanks to Bradman Australia recover from 2–0 down

G.O.B. Allen, who had declined to bowl bodyline on the previous tour, was captain of the next England party to Australia, which included Voce, who had come to terms with the authorities.

Bradman captained Australia for the first time at Brisbane. McCormick claimed Worthington with the first ball of the first Test and reduced England to 20 for three, but lumbago prevented him playing much further part, and England recovered, thanks

to Leyland (126), to 358. Fingleton became the first to score centuries in four successive Test innings. But Australia trailed, and, dismissed on a rain-affected pitch for 58 second time round, were beaten by 322 runs.

At Sydney Hammond made his third double-century against Australia and was 231 not out at the end of a rain-affected second day. Allen then declared at 426 for six, the rain came again, and Australia were shot out for 80. Following on, they did better as the pitch improved, but were beaten by an innings.

1936–37 36th Series   Aus 3, Eng 2
1 BRISBANE   England won by 322 runs
England 358 (M Leyland 126, C J Barnett 69, W J O'Reilly 5–102) and 256 (G O B Allen 68, F A Ward 6–102)
Australia 234 (J H W Fingleton 100, S J McCabe 51, W Voce 6–41) and 58 (G O B Allen 5–36, W Voce 4–16)

2 SYDNEY   England won by an innings and 22 runs
England 426–6 dec (W R Hammond 231, C J Barnett 57)
Australia 80 (W Voce 4–10) and 324 (S J McCabe 93, D G Bradman 82, J H W Fingleton 73)

3 MELBOURNE   Australia won by 365 runs
Australia 200–9 dec (S J McCabe 63) and 564 (D G Bradman 270, J H W Fingleton 136)
England 76–9 dec (M W Sievers 5–21) and 323 (M Leyland 111, R W V Robins 61, W R Hammond 51, L O'B Fleetwood-Smith 5–124)

4 ADELAIDE   Australia won by 148 runs
Australia 288 (S J McCabe 88, A G Chipperfield 57) and 433 (D G Bradman 212, S J McCabe 55, R G Gregory 50, W R Hammond 5–57)
England 330 (C J Barnett 129, L E G Ames 52, W J O'Reilly 4–51, L O'B Fleetwood-Smith 4–129) and 243 (R E S Wyatt 50, L O'B Fleetwood-Smith 6–110)

5 MELBOURNE   Australia won by an innings and 200 runs
Australia 604 (D G Bradman 169, C L Badcock 118, S J McCabe 112, R G Gregory 80, K Farnes 6–96)
England 239 (J Hardstaff jun 83, W J O'Reilly 5–51, L J Nash 4–70) and 165 (W R Hammond 56)

1936–37 Averages					
Batting	I	No	Runs	HS	Avge
D.G. Bradman (A)	9	0	810	270	90.00
W.R. Hammond (E)	9	1	468	231*	58.00
M. Leyland (E)	9	1	441	126	55.12
S.J. McCabe (A)	9	0	491	112	54.55
J.H.W. Fingleton (A)	9	0	398	136	44.22
C.J. Barnett (E)	9	0	395	129	43.88
J. Hardstaff, jr (E)	9	0	256	83	28.44
Bowling	O	M	Runs	W	Avge BB
W. Voce (E)	162.1	20	560	26	21.53 6–41
W.J. O'Reilly (A)	247.6	89	555	25	22.20 5–51
L.O'B.Fleetwood-Smith (A)	131.4	20	463	19	24.36 6–110
W.R. Hammond (E)	88.4	8	301	12	25.08 5–57
G.O.B. Allen (E)	128.7	12	526	17	30.94 5–36

A record crowd for any match of 350,534 watched the third Test, in which it was Australia's turn for the luck. They reached 200 for nine, rain again played a part and, with the wicket worsening, Bradman declared. England were reduced to 76 for nine, and also declared. Bradman reversed his batting order, sending in his tail-enders and holding back Fingleton, McCabe and himself. He joined Fingleton at 97 for five, with the wicket easing, and they added a record Test sixth-wicket partnership of 346. Bradman made 270. Leyland's unbeaten century in a total of 323 left England still 365 short.

Australia batted first on a good wicket at Adelaide, and were out for 288, England passing this with only five wickets down, thanks to Barnett's century. But the lead was to be only 42, Bradman scored 212 in the second innings and Australia won by 148 runs.

In the Ashes decider at Melbourne, Australia again won the toss, Bradman, McCabe and Badcock scored centuries, and the total of 604 was enough for an innings victory. For the first time a side had won a series from 2–0 down.

Bradman (right) and Fingleton in 1938. Bradman had just completed 1,000 runs before the end of May, the only batsman to achieve this feat twice.

Woodfull, William Maldon

Woodfull was born at Maldon, Victoria, on 22 August 1897, and first played for Victoria in 1921–22. He was a sound defensive opening right-hand batsman. He made his debut for Australia in 1926, and became captain in 1930. He was captain during the controversial bodyline tour of 1932–33, in which he was a central figure. In 35 Tests he scored 2,300 runs, average 46.00. He died while playing golf at Tweed Heads, NSW, on 11 August 1965.

1938: Records tumble at the Oval

Two strong batting sides met in the first Test at Trent Bridge, with Bradman and Hammond the two captains.

Barnett reached 98 by lunch, completing his century off the first ball afterwards. He and Hutton put on 219 for the first wicket, and this set the pattern: there were two double centuries (Paynter and McCabe) and five other centuries in the match.

Compton, at 20 years 19 days, became England's youngest Test century-maker. McCabe's innings was possibly the best, Bradman regarding it as the best he'd seen. He batted 235 minutes for 232, gave no chance, and scored 72 of 77 added for the last wicket. Australia followed on, but the match was drawn.

Hammond made 240 at Lord's, and W.A. Brown carried his bat through the Australian innings for 206 not out. A Bradman century in the second innings ensured the draw for Australia.

Not a ball was bowled at Old Trafford, the second instance in history, both at the same ground.

At Headingley, England made 223, and, in bad light and on a difficult pitch, Bradman made a century for the sixth consecutive Test, a record. Australia led by 19, and they required only 105 in the fourth innings. Even so, it needed a firm innings of 33 out of 41 by Hassett to get them home by five wickets. O'Reilly's ten wickets were decisive.

The Oval Test was played to a finish.

England won the toss and Hutton batted for 13 hours and 17 minutes, stayed while 770 runs were added and made 364, all Test records. England's total of 903 for seven declared remains a record as does Fleetwood-Smith's concession of 298 runs (he took one wicket). With Bradman and Fingleton unable to bat because of injury, Australia were beaten by an innings and 579 runs – another record as the biggest victory in Test cricket.

1938 37th Series Aus 1, Eng 1, Drawn 2
1 TRENT BRIDGE Match Drawn
England 658–8 dec (E Paynter 216, C J Barnett 126, D C S Compton 102, L Hutton 100, L O'B Fleetwood-Smith 4–153)
Australia 411 (S J McCabe 232, D G Bradman 51, K Farnes 4–106, D V P Wright 4–153) and 427–6 (D G Bradman 144, W A Brown 133)
2 LORD'S Match Drawn
England 494 (W R Hammond 240, E Paynter 99, L E G Ames 83, W J O'Reilly 4–93, E L McCormick 4–101) and 242–8 dec (D C S Compton 76)
Australia 422 (W A Brown 206, A L Hassett 56, H Verity 4–103) and 204–6 (D G Bradman 102)
3 HEADINGLEY Australia won by 5 wkts
England 223 (W R Hammond 76, W J O'Reilly 5–66) and 123 (W J O'Reilly 5–56) L O'B Fleetwood-Smith 4–34)
Australia 242 (D G Bradman 103, B A Barnett 57, K Farnes 4–77) and 107–5
4 THE OVAL England won by an innings and 579 runs
England 903–7 dec (L Hutton 364, M Leyland 187, J Hardstaff jun 169, W R Hammond 59, A Wood 53)
Australia 201 (W A Brown 69, W E Bowes 5–49) and 123 (K Farnes 4–63)
D G Bradman and J H W Fingleton were absent injured in both innings
(The match arranged to be played at Old Trafford was abandoned without a ball being bowled)

Grimmett, Clarence Victor

Grimmett started his Test career astonishingly late for one who accomplished so much. He was born on Christmas Day, 1891, at Dunedin, New Zealand. He played for Wellington in 1911–12, but after the First World War turned out for Victoria in 1918–19, and switched to South Australia in 1924–25. He was a brilliant leg-break and googly bowler, bowling with a low arm action after a trundle to the wicket. He made his Test debut in 1924–25 aged 33. Short and balding, he did not look dangerous, but he took 11 English wickets in his first Test. Carrying on from there he played in 37 Tests, becoming the first to take 200 Test wickets. He ended with 216, average 24.21. He died on 2 May 1980 in Adelaide.

Oldfield, William Albert Stanley

Oldfield was born on 9 September 1894 at Alexandria, NSW. He began playing for his state in 1919–20, and became the leading wicket-keeper of his time. He made his Test debut in 1920–21 and from 1924–25 was Australia's first-choice keeper for 13 years. It was his being struck and laid out by a delivery from Larwood which climaxed the bodyline argument. In 54 Tests he made 78 catches and 52 stumpings, the aggregate of 130 being a record. He made 1,427 Test runs, average 22.65. He died on 10 August 1976 at Killara, NSW.

Paynter, Edward

Paynter was born at Oswaldtwistle, Lancashire, on 5 November 1901. He made his debut for Lancashire in 1926, but was not a regular until 1931. He was an attacking middle-order left-hand batsman, and although lacking the top joints of two fingers after an early accident he was a brilliant deep fieldsman. He first played for England in 1931, and was not always in favour although he seldom failed in Tests. In 20 matches he scored 1,540 runs, average 59.23, bettered by only four batsmen in the whole history of Tests. In seven Tests against Australia, easily the strongest opposition of the 1930s, his average was a remarkable 84.42. He died in Keighley, Yorkshire, on 5 February 1979.

Verity, Hedley

Verity was born at Headingley, Leeds, on 18 May 1905, and in 1930 made his debut for Yorkshire. He was a slow left-arm bowler, but not of classic mould. He was tall and made the ball turn and lift from little short of medium pace. He became the most successful slow bowler of the 1930s, and achieved the best analysis in first-class cricket, ten for ten for Yorkshire against Notts in 1932. He first appeared in a Test in 1931, and he took 14 wickets in a day against Australia at Lord's in 1934. In 40 Tests he took 144 wickets at 24.37 each. He batted right-hand and once opened in a Test in Australia. His Test average was 20.90. He died of wounds in a prisoner-of-war camp at Casate, Italy, on 31 July 1943.

O'Reilly, William Joseph

O'Reilly was born on 20 December 1905 at White Cliffs, NSW, and played for his state from 1927–28. He was a tall leg-break and googly bowler, who bowled quicker than most of that type, with a flurry of whirling arms designed to get maximum life from the pitch. His aggressive style led to the nickname 'Tiger'. He made his Test debut in 1931–32, and in 27 matches took 144 wickets, average 22.59. Some would say he was the best bowler of his era. On retirement he became a distinguished cricket writer.

1938 Averages

Batting	I	No	Runs	HS	Avge
L. Hutton (E)	4	0	473	364	118.25
D.G. Bradman (A)	6	2	434	144*	108.50
E. Paynter (E)	6	2	407	216*	101.75
W.A. Brown (A)	8	1	512	206*	73.14
W.R. Hammond (E)	6	0	403	240	67.16
S.J. McCabe (A)	8	0	362	232	45.25

Bowling	O	M	Runs	W	Avge	BB
H. Verity (E)	154.1	53	354	14	25.28	4–103
W.J. O'Reilly (A)	263	78	610	22	27.72	5–66
K. Farnes (E)	179.4	32	581	17	34.17	4–63
D.V.P. Wright (E)	120	20	426	12	35.50	4–153
L.O'B. Fleetwood-Smith (A)	217.5	34	727	14	51.92	4–34

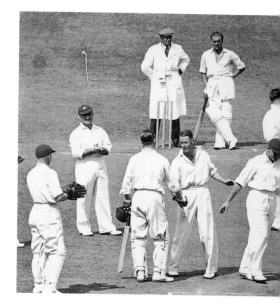

Above: Hutton receiving congratulations after breaking the Test innings record at the Oval in 1938. W.A. Brown is shaking his hand. Hardstaff is the non-striker.

Below left: The England team at the Oval in 1938.

Below: The Australians in 1938.

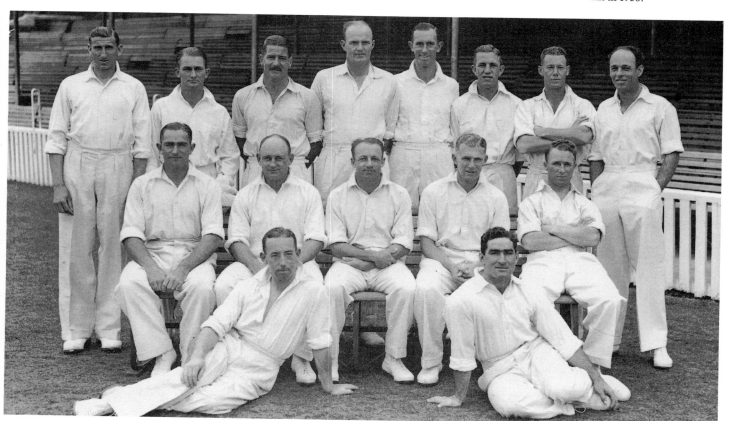

1946–47: Bradman returns with lucky decision

Bradman and Hammond were rival captains again when Ashes cricket resumed after the Second World War.

An umpiring decision concerning Bradman in the first Test was to have a lasting effect on cricket history. Bradman was not sure if he was fit enough for Test cricket, and might have retired had he been given out after what seemed a legitimate catch in the gully when 28. He went on to 187, adding 276 with Hassett (128) for the third wicket. Australia made 645, and England were forced to bat twice after thunderstorms. Australia's win by an innings and 332 was the largest over England, each side's biggest win having come in successive Tests. Tests in Australia were now limited to 30 hours play, as in England, and Australia's win came in the final session.

England batted first at Sydney, but batted badly and were out for 255. Bradman, coming in at number six, and S.G. Barnes, who opened, both scored 234, and shared a partnership of 405 for the fifth wicket, still a Test record. Evans conceded no byes in Australia's 659 for eight declared, and despite a century by Edrich, England lost by an innings.

There was little in the Melbourne Test until Tallon and Lindwall added 154 in 88 minutes for Australia's eighth wicket in the second innings. England held on for a draw, the first draw in a Test in Australia for 65 years.

The fourth Test at Adelaide was even closer. Australia led by 27 on a high-scoring first innings, and England declared at 340 for eight in the second, but the match was destined to be another draw. A feature of the match was that Denis Compton and Arthur Morris each scored a century in each innings – the only occasion opposing batsmen have done this in a Test. An oddity was Godfrey Evans batting for 97 minutes in the second innings before scoring.

Yardley took over the England captaincy in the final Test, Hammond having fibrositis. Hutton, 122 not out overnight, took no further part in the match, contracting tonsillitis. Even so England gained a lead of 27, Wright taking seven wickets, but their second innings effort was poor, and Australia won by five wickets.

1946–47 Averages

Batting	I	No	Runs	HS	Avge
D.G. Bradman (A)	8	1	680	234	97.14
K.R. Miller (A)	7	2	384	141*	76.80
S.G. Barnes (A)	6	0	443	234	73.83
A.R. Morris (A)	8	1	503	155	71.85
C.L. McCool (A)	7	2	272	104*	54.40
L. Hutton (E)	9	1	417	122*	52.12
D.C.S. Compton (E)	10	1	459	147	51.00
A.L. Hassett (A)	7	0	332	128	47.42
W.J. Edrich (E)	10	0	462	119	46.20
C. Washbrook (E)	10	0	363	112	36.30
N.W.D. Yardley (E)	10	2	252	61	31.50

Bowling	O	M	Runs	W	Avge	BB
R.R. Lindwall (A)	122.1	20	367	18	20.38	7–63
K.R. Miller (A)	122.3	15	334	16	20.87	7–60
E.R.H. Toshack (A)	178.4	49	437	17	25.70	6–82
C.L. McCool (A)	182	27	491	18	27.27	5–54
D.V.P. Wright (E)	240.2	23	990	23	43.04	7–105
A.V. Bedser (E)	246.3	37	876	16	54.75	3–97

1946–47   38th Series   Aus 3, Eng 0, Drawn 2

1 BRISBANE   Australia won by an innings and 332 runs
Australia 645 (D G Bradman 187, A L Hassett 128, C L McCool 95, K R Miller 79, D V P Wright 5–167)
England 141 (K R Miller 7–60) and 172 (E R H Toshack 6–82)

2 SYDNEY   Australia won by an innings and 33 runs
England 255 (W J Edrich 71, J T Ikin 60, I W Johnson 6–42) and 371 (W J Edrich 119, D C S Compton 54, C L McCool 5–109)
Australia 659–8 dec (S G Barnes 234, D G Bradman 234)

3 MELBOURNE   Match Drawn
Australia 365 (C L McCool 104, D G Bradman 79) and 536 (A R Morris 155, R R Lindwall 100, D Tallon 92)
England 351 (W J Edrich 89, C Washbrook 62, N W D Yardley 61, B Dooland 4–69) and 310–7 (C Washbrook 112, N W D Yardley 53)

4 ADELAIDE   Match Drawn
England 460 (D C S Compton 147, L Hutton 94, J Hardstaff jun 67, C Washbrook 65, R R Windwall 4–52) and 340–8 dec (D C S Compton 103, L Hutton 76, E R H Toshack 4–76)
Australia 487 (K R Miller 141, A R Morris 122, A L Hassett 78, I W Johnson 52) and 215–1 (A R Morris 124, D G Bradman 56)

5 SYDNEY   Australia won by 5 wkts
England 280 (L Hutton 122, W J Edrich 60, R R Lindwall 7–63) and 186 (D C S Compton 76, C L McCool 5–44)
Australia 253 (S G Barnes 71, A R Morris 57, D V P Wright 7–105) and 214–5 (D G Bradman 63)

1948: A great Australian victory at Leeds

The 1948 Australian touring party under Bradman is regarded by common consent as the best of modern times. Based on a fast attack of Lindwall, Miller and Johnston, an experimental rule allowing a new ball every 55 overs considerably helped the tourists.

At Trent Bridge, England were quickly removed for 165 and Australia built up a big lead at 509, Bradman and Hassett scoring centuries. A brilliant innings by Compton, who scored 184, forced Australia to bat again, but they won by eight wickets.

Australia batted first at Lord's and made 350, enough for a lead of 135. With Barnes scoring 141, England were set 596 to win, and failed by 410 runs.

Hardstaff gets the ball away between Lindwall and McCool at Adelaide in 1946–47.

Bradman, Donald George

Bradman was born on 27 August 1908 at Cootamundra, NSW. He made his debut for NSW in 1927–28, changing to South Australia in 1935–36. He was an outstanding batsman from the start and made his Test debut in 1928–29. He dominated all bowlers from the late 1920s, and his prowess was the reason for England's 'bodyline' tactics in 1932–33. His career averages are about 50 per cent better than those of any other player in history. On his four visits to England he averaged over 84 each time, his 115.66 in 1938 being the highest ever for an English season. In the Test match at Leeds in 1930 he scored 309 on the first day, and his final 334 was at the time a Test record. He played in 52 Tests, captaining Australia in 24. He scored 6,996 runs for an average of 99.94. In his last Test at the Oval in 1948, he was applauded all the way to the wicket, and bowled for a duck, when four runs would have given him an average of 100. He became a leading administrator in Australia and was knighted in 1949.

Top: Dooland dismisses Hammond caught and bowled for nine in the third Test at Melbourne on the 1946–47 England tour of Australia.

Above: The 1948 Australian team at Worcester. Left to right, back: Johnson, Morris, Toshack, Miller, Tallon, Lindwall, Harvey. Front: Brown, Hassett, Bradman, McCool, Barnes.

Hutton was dropped for the Old Trafford Test, where Compton played another great innings. After hooking a bouncer onto his forehead, he retired hurt but later resumed to score 145 not out in a total of 363. Pollard pulled a ball into Barnes' midriff, who, after attempting to carry on, spent 10 days in hospital. Australia made only 221, but a day was lost and, after England declared, Morris and Bradman carefully played out time.

The Headingley Test was remarkable for the fourth innings. England won the toss, and passed 400 with only two wickets down, but eventually made only 496. R.N. Harvey made 112 in his first match against England, but England led by 38 and on the last morning declared, setting Australia 404 to win in 344 minutes. Morris and Bradman added 301 in 217 minutes for the second wicket and Australia reached the target to win by seven wickets.

Lindwall breezed through England at the Oval, taking six for 20 in a total of 52. Hutton batted throughout for 30, and was on the field for all but the last 57 minutes. Morris made 196 for Australia, who won by an innings and 149 runs. Bradman, in his last Test, was cheered all the way to the wicket, and bowled by Hollies second ball, needing only four runs for a Test match average of 100.

1948 39th Series Aus 4, Eng 0, Drawn 1

1 TRENT BRIDGE Australia won by 8 wkts
England 165 (J C Laker 63, W A Johnston 5–36) and 441 (D C S Compton 184, L Hutton 74, T G Evans 50, K R Miller 4–125, W A Johnston 4–147)
Australia 509 (D G Bradman 138, A L Hassett 137, S G Barnes 62, J Laker 4–138) and 98–2 (S G Barnes 64)

2 LORD'S Australia won by 409 runs
Australia 350 (A R Morris 105, D Tallon 53, A V Bedser 4–100) and 460–7 dec (S G Barnes 141, D G Bradman 89, K R Miller 74, A R Morris 62)
England 215 (D C S Compton 53, R R Lindwall 5–70) and 186 (E R H Toshack 5–40)

3 OLD TRAFFORD Match Drawn
England 363 (D C S Compton 145, R R Lindwall 4–99) and 174–3 dec (C Washbrook 85, W J Edrich 53)
Australia 221 (A R Morris 51, A V Bedser 4–81) and 92–1 (A R Morris 54)

4 HEADINGLEY Australia won by 7 wkts
England 496 (C Washbrook 143, W J Edrich 111, L Hutton 81, A V Bedser 79) and 365–8 dec (D C S Compton 66, C Washbrook 65, L Hutton 57, W J Edrich 54, W A Johnston 4–95)
Australia 458 (R N Harvey 112, S J E Loxton 93, R R Lindwall 77, K R Miller 58) and 404–3 (A R Morris 182, D G Bradman 173)

5 THE OVAL Australia won by an innings and 149 runs
England 52 (R R Lindwall 6–20) and 188 (L Hutton 64, W A Johnston 4–40)
Australia 389 (A R Morris 196, S G Barnes 61, W E Hollies 5–131)

1948 Averages

Batting	I	No	Runs	HS	Avge
A.R. Morris (A)	9	1	696	196	87.00
S.G. Barnes (A)	6	2	329	141	82.25
D.G. Bradman (A)	9	2	508	173	72.57
D.C.S. Compton (E)	10	1	562	184	62.44
C. Washbrook (E)	8	1	356	143	50.85
A.L. Hassett (E)	8	1	310	137	44.28
L. Hutton (E)	8	0	342	81	42.75
W.J. Edrich (E)	10	0	319	111	31.90

Bowling	O	M	Runs	W	Avge	BB
R.R. Lindwall (A)	222.5	57	530	27	19.62	6–20
K.R. Miller (A)	138.1	43	301	13	23.15	4–125
W.A. Johnston (A)	309.2	92	630	27	23.33	5–36
A.V. Bedser (E)	274.3	75	688	18	38.22	4–81

Lindwall, Raymond Russell

Lindwall, born on 3 October 1921 at Mascot, NSW, played for New South Wales from 1941–42, switching to Queensland in 1954–55. A right-arm fast bowler, he was, like Larwood, not tall, but he had a perfect action and became the leading fast bowler of the immediate post-war period. He made his Test debut in 1945–46 and in 61 matches took 228 wickets, average 23.03. He also made two Test centuries and had an average of 21.15.

Above: Bradman's reception when he came out to bat at the Oval in 1948 for his last Test innings. He was given three cheers by the England team, but was then dismissed for a duck.

Left: The 1948 Australians at Balmoral, where they were visiting King George VI.

Right: Denis Compton unluckily dismissed at Trent Bridge in 1948, stumbling and falling on his wicket after playing a ball from Miller. He made 184.

1950–51: Australia have the luck and win easily

F.R. Brown was third choice captain for the tourists, who included many young and inexperienced players. Hassett was Australia's captain.

England began very unluckily at Brisbane. After a good performance in dismissing Australia for 228, they found a rain-damaged pitch unplayable and declared at 68 for seven. Australia did worse, declaring at 32 for seven. England were all but beaten at close of play on the third day, during which 20 wickets fell while 102 runs were being scored. Hutton, held back to number eight, completed 62 not out of the last 92 runs in a remarkable innings, but could only reduce the deficit to 70.

Harvey, Robert Neil

Born on 8 October 1928 at Fitzroy, Victoria, Harvey and his three brothers all played for Victoria. Neil made his debut in 1946–47 and switched to New South Wales in 1958–59. A small man, he was a brilliant middle-order left-hand batsman, noted for his footwork. He was a dynamic fielder, usually at cover point. He made his first appearance for Australia in 1947–48 and played in 79 Tests, at the time an Australian record. His run aggregate was second to Bradman's. He scored 6,419, average 48.41.

In a low-scoring match at Melbourne, England, without Compton, led by three runs on first innings and required only 179 to win in the fourth, but tried to make them with extreme caution and fell 29 runs short.

After making 290 at Sydney, England had to bowl on a good pitch with only three bowlers, two having been injured batting. Australia took a lead of 136, and won by an innings when England collapsed to the new 'mystery' spin bowler Jack Iverson, who took six for 27.

There were some remarkable centuries at Adelaide. Morris scored 206 for Australia, who totalled 371. Hutton then demonstrated once more how much the England batting depended on him this tour by carrying his bat for 156 not out from a total of only 272. Hutton's 57 per cent of his side's total was slightly higher than Morris's. J.W. Burke made a century in his first Test and Australia won by 274 runs.

In the final Test Australia were out for 217, and a fine innings by R.T. Simpson of 156 not out, including 64 in a last-wicket stand of 74, gave England a lead of 103. Five wickets for A.V. Bedser for the second time in the match left England needing only 95, of which Hutton scored 60 not out. It was England's first win over Australia since his big innings at the Oval in 1938.

The England touring party on board ship for Australia in 1950, captain Brown making a farewell speech. On his left is Brian Close, England's youngest Test player.

1950–51 40th Series Aus 4, Eng 1

1 BRISBANE Australia won by 70 runs
Australia 228 (R N Harvey 74, A V Bedser 4–45) and 32–7 dec (T E Bailey 4–22)
England 68–7 dec (W A Johnston 5–35) and 122 (L Hutton 62, J B Iverson 4–43)

2 MELBOURNE Australia won by 28 runs
Australia 194 (A L Hassett 52, A V Bedser 4–37, T E Bailey 4–40) and 181 (F R Brown 4–26)
England 197 (F R Brown 62, J B Iverson 4–37) and 150 (W A Johnston 4–26)

3 SYDNEY Australia won by an innings and 13 runs
England 290 (F R Brown 79, L Hutton 62, K R Miller 4–37) and 123 (J B Iverson 6–27)
Australia 426 (K R Miller 145, I W Johnson 77, A L Hassett 70, A V Bedser 4–107, F R Brown 4–153)

4 ADELAIDE Australia won by 274 runs
Australia 371 (A R Morris 206, D V P Wright 4–99) and 403–8 dec (J W Burke 101, K R Miller 99, R N Harvey 68)
England 272 (L Hutton 156) and 228 (R T Simpson 61, W A Johnston 4–73)

5 MELBOURNE England won by 8 wkts
Australia 217 (A L Hassett 92, A R Morris 50, A V Bedser 5–46, F R Brown 5–49) and 197 (G B Hole 63, R N Harvey 52, A V Bedser 5–59)
England 320 (R T Simpson 156, L Hutton 79, K R Miller 4–76) and 95–2 (L Hutton 60)

1950–51 Averages

Batting	I	No	Runs	HS	Avge
L. Hutton (E)	10	4	533	156*	88.83
K.R. Miller (A)	9	1	350	145*	43.75
A.L. Hassett (A)	9	0	366	92	40.66
R.N. Harvey (A)	9	0	362	74	40.22
R.T. Simpson (E)	10	1	349	156*	38.77
A.R. Morris (A)	9	0	321	206	35.66

Bowling	O	M	Runs	W	Avge	BB
T.E. Bailey (E)	75.1	18	198	14	14.14	4–22
J.B. Iverson (A)	138.2	29	320	21	15.23	6–27
A.V. Bedser (E)	195	34	482	30	16.06	5–46
K.R. Miller (A)	106.6	23	301	17	17.70	4–37
W.A. Johnston (A)	153.7	28	422	22	19.18	5–35
F.R. Brown (E)	109	12	389	18	21.61	5–49
R.R. Lindwall (A)	98.3	11	344	15	22.93	3–29

Miller, Keith Ross

Born in Sunshine, Victoria, on 28 November 1919, Miller was given the name of the two airmen who made the first flight from England to Australia, Keith Smith and Ross Smith. After playing for Victoria from 1937–38, he became a wartime pilot, and played for the Australian services team in the Victory Tests in England. After the war he switched to New South Wales. He made his Test debut in 1945–46. He was an attacking middle-order right-hand batsman and fast bowler, whose partnership with Lindwall carried all before it. He was an inspirational cricketer, altering his run up and style of bowling as the whim took him, and would play his best when it most mattered. In 55 Tests, he scored 2,958 runs, average 36.97, and took 170 wickets, average 22.97.

1953: England regain the Ashes after Watson saves them

Hutton had become England's captain by the time Hassett led the Australian tourists to England in 1953.

After Hassett had made 115 at Trent Bridge, Australia collapsed from 237 for three to 249 all out, Bedser taking seven wickets. England, however, batted poorly and finished 145 behind. Another seven wickets for Bedser shot Australia out for 123, and at the end of the third day England were 42 for one, but rain prevented much more play and the match was drawn.

At Lord's, another century for Hassett saw Australia reach 346, but Hutton (145) and Graveney (78) batted beautifully and England led by 26. With Miller making a century, Australia seemed to have the match won overnight on the fourth day with England, needing 343, already reduced to 20 for three. But Willie Watson played a memorable defensive innings of 109. With Bailey (71) he added 163 in 248 minutes on the last day and saved the game.

Rain ruined the Old Trafford match, with Australia's second-innings 35 for eight (Wardle 4–7) being not too significant.

Australia put England in at Headingley and out again for 167. Australia led by 99, Bedser's sixth wicket taking him past Grimmett's record Test haul of 216. Bailey played another long innings in England's 275: 262 minutes for 38. Australia needed only 177 to win in 115 minutes. They began quickly enough but Bailey again saved the match with legside bowling off a long run – tactics not universally approved but effective.

All was to play for at the Oval, a Test extended to six days. Australia made 275, thanks to a recovery led by Lindwall. England lost nine wickets before passing this total, but managed to gain a valuable lead of 31. Laker and Lock then removed Australia for 162, and England knocked off the runs for the loss of two wickets to regain the Ashes after nearly 19 years. Bedser's 39 wickets was a new Ashes record for England.

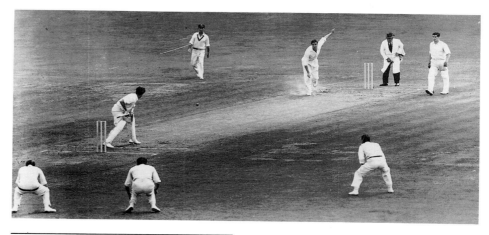

1953 41st Series Eng 1, Aus 0, Drawn 4
1 TRENT BRIDGE Match drawn
Australia 249 (A L Hassett 115, A R Morris 67, K R Miller 55, A V Bedser 7–55) and 123 (A R Morris 67, A V Bedser 7–44)
England 144 (R R Lindwall 5–57) and 120–1 (L Hutton 60)
2 LORD'S Match Drawn
Australia 346 (A L Hassett 104, A K Davidson 76, R N Harvey 59, J H Wardle 4–77, A V Bedser 5–105) and 368 (K R Miller 109, A R Morris 89, R R Lindwall 50, F R Brown 4–82)
England 372 (L Hutton 145, T W Graveney 78, D C S Compton 57, R R Lindwall 5–66) and 282–7 (W Watson 109, T E Bailey 71)
3 OLD TRAFFORD Match Drawn
Australia 318 (R N Harvey 122, G B Hole 66, A V Bedser 5–115) and 35–8 (J H Wardle 4–7)
England 276 (L Hutton 66)
4 HEADINGLEY Match Drawn
England 167 (T W Graveney 55, R R Lindwall 5–54) and 275 (W J Edrich 64, D C S Compton 61, K R Miller 4–63)
Australia 266 (R N Harvey 71, G B Hole 53, A V Bedser 6–95) and 147–4
5 THE OVAL England won by 8 wkts
Australia 275 (R R Lindwall 62, A L Hassett 53, F S Trueman 4–86) and 162 (G A R Lock 5–45, J C Laker 4–75)
England 306 (L Hutton 82, T E Bailey 64, R R Lindwall 4–70) and 132–2 (W J Edrich 55)

1953 Averages

Batting	I	No	Runs	HS	Avge	
L. Hutton (E)	9	1	443	145	55.37	
A.L. Hassett (A)	10	0	365	115	36.50	
R.N. Harvey (A)	10	0	346	122	34.60	
A.R. Morris (A)	10	0	337	89	33.70	
G.B. Hole (A)	10	0	273	66	27.30	
Bowling	O	M	Runs	W	Avge	BB
A.V. Bedser (E)	265.1	58	682	39	17.48	7–44
R.R. Lindwall (A)	240.4	62	490	26	18.84	5–54
J.H. Wardle (E)	155.3	57	344	13	26.46	4–7

Edrich and Compton (ducking) race for the pavilion after England's Ashes win in 1953.

Top left: High jinks on board the SS *Stratheden* in 1950. From left: Bailey, Simpson, Parkhouse, Compton, McIntyre, Hutton.

Top right: Hassett caught by Evans off Bedser for 53 at the Oval in 1953. Edrich is the slip.

Above: Miller, in a cloud of dust, bowls to Bailey at the Oval in 1953. Trueman is the non-striker.

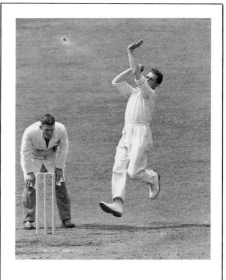

Laker, James Charles

Laker was a Yorkshireman, born on 9 February 1922 in Bradford, but after war service he settled in Surrey and played for them from 1946. He became one of cricket's greatest off-break bowlers, and was one of the principal reasons for Surrey's seven successive Championships in the 1950s. He made his Test debut in 1947–48 on a Tour to West Indies. He did not always have the confidence of the selectors, but in an amazing season in 1956 he twice took all ten Australian wickets in an innings, once for Surrey and once for England. At Old Trafford he set a first-class and Test record with 19 wickets in a match. His 46 wickets in that series is an Ashes record. In 46 Tests he took 193 wickets, average 21.24. He became a television commentator and died on 23 April 1986.

Left: Arthur Morris skies the ball at Trent Bridge in 1953. The ball fell safe and Morris reached 60 in each innings.

Below: Edrich clips the ball to leg at the Oval.

1954–55: Fast bowling by Tyson and Statham wins the rubber

Hutton led England to Australia for the only time in 1954–55, and in the first Test at Brisbane put Australia in, having selected a fast seam attack. Australia survived the early liveliness of the wicket and went on to 601 for eight declared (Morris 153, Harvey 162). Compton had fractured his hand on the fence and England made little show, losing by an innings and 154 runs.

Morris, deputizing for Ian Johnson, put England in at Sydney, and his fast bowlers did better in dismissing England for 154. Australia in return were restricted to 228, which seemed to be enough when England were 55 for three. But May (104) and Cowdrey (54) made a stand of 116, and Australia were eventually set 223. Tyson, who had been knocked unconscious by a Lindwall bouncer when batting, and Statham then bowled with exceptional speed and venom to bowl Australia out for 184, a victory for England by 38. Statham had previously scored 25 in a last-wicket stand of 46. Harvey, undefeated, scored half of Australia's runs. Bedser had been omitted from this Test, to great surprise.

At level pegging, there was great interest in the Melbourne Test. Miller, bowling with great fire, dismissed Hutton, Edrich and Compton for five runs, and England were 41 for four, and reached 191 only because Cowdrey made a splendid 102. However it still needed the last two Australian wickets to add 80 to give Australia a lead of 40. May's 91 helped England to 279, leaving Australia 240 to win. Tyson (7–27) and Statham swept through them again and they made only 111.

In great heat at Adelaide, Australia scored 323 and England plodded to 341 in 541 minutes, the match then looking to be a draw. But Appleyard claimed three quick second-innings wickets and Australia were again all out on their 'unlucky' score of 111. England needed only 94, lost three wickets scoring 18 (to Miller again) but won comfortably by five wickets.

With the Ashes retained, England were unable to start batting until after lunch on the fourth day at Sydney, because of the worst storms seen there in 50 years. They declared at 371 for seven after a Graveney century, forced the follow-on and were four wickets short of another win when play ended.

1954-55   42nd Series   Eng 3, Aus 1, Drawn 1
1 BRISBANE   **Australia won by an innings and 154 runs**
Australia 601–8 dec (R N Harvey 162, A R Morris 153, R R
  Lindwall 64, G B Hole 57)
England 190 (T E Bailey 88) and 257 (W J Edrich 88)
2 SYDNEY   **England won by 38 runs**
England 154 and 296 (P B H May 104, M C Cowdrey 54)
Australia 228 (F H Tyson 4–45, T E Bailey 4–59) and 184 (R N
  Harvey 92, F H Tyson 6–85)
3 MELBOURNE   **England won by 128 runs**
England 191 (M C Cowdrey 102, R G Archer 4–33) and 279 (P B
  H May 91, W A Johnston 5–85)
Australia 231 (J B Statham 5–60) and 111 (F H Tyson 7–27)
4 ADELAIDE   **England won by 5 wkts**
Australia 323 (L V Maddocks 69) and 111
England 341 (L Hutton 80, M C Cowdrey 79, R Benaud 4–120)
  and 97–5
5 SYDNEY   **Match Drawn**
England 371–7 dec (T W Graveney 111, D C S Compton 84, P B
  H May 79, T E Bailey 72)
Australia 221 (C C McDonald 72, J H Wardle 5–79) and 118–6

Top: Denis Compton swings the ball to leg at the Oval in 1953 to win the match and bring back the Ashes to England for the first time since the war.

Above: Ray Lindwall bowling at the Oval in 1953. Trevor Bailey is the non-striking batsman. Bailey played a match-saving innings at Lord's in this series.

1954–55 Averages

Batting	I	No	Runs	HS	Avge
R.N. Harvey (A)	9	1	354	162	44.25
P.B.H. May (E)	9	0	351	104	39.00
T.E. Bailey (E)	9	1	296	88	37.00
M.C. Cowdrey (E)	9	0	319	102	35.44

Bowling	O	M	Runs	W	Avge	BB
R.G. Archer (A)	97.6	32	215	13	16.53	4–33
F.H. Tyson (E)	151	16	583	28	20.82	7–27
W.A. Johnston (A)	141.4	37	423	19	22.26	5–85
R.R. Lindwall (A)	130.6	28	381	14	27.21	3–27
J.B. Statham (E)	143.3	16	499	18	27.72	5–60

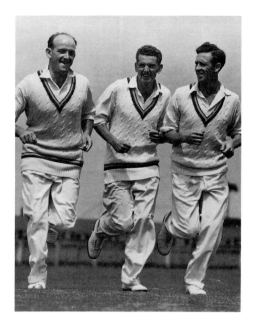

Left: Three happy England pace bowlers in 1954–55 in Australia, Frank Tyson, Peter Loader, who was not in the Test team, and Brian Statham.

Above: Frank Tyson bowling in the fourth Test at Adelaide in 1954–55. Tyson was the main destroyer of the Australian batting during the series.

Evans, Thomas Godfrey

Born on 18 August 1920 at Finchley, Middlesex, Evans made his debut for Kent in 1939 and took over as Kent and England wicket-keeper from L.E.G. Ames immediately after the war. A brilliant, acrobatic keeper, he was also a hard-hitting lower-order batsman. In Tests he stood up to A.V. Bedser, forming an effective partnership with the medium-paced bowler. In his 91 Tests he caught 173 batsmen and stumped 46, the aggregate of 219 being a record at the time. He also scored 2,439 runs, average 20.49.

1956: Laker breaks the bowling records at Old Trafford

Peter May was captain of England when Ian Johnson's tourists arrived in 1956.

Peter Richardson made his debut in the first Test at Trent Bridge and made 81 and 73. The second day was washed out, and although England declared twice they could not achieve a result.

At Lord's Australia made 285, after McDonald and Burke had started with 130 for the first wicket. England were then put out for 171, despite Australia's new bowler, W.P.A. Crawford, breaking down in his fifth over. Miller took five for 72. Australia recovered from 112 for six when Benaud made a dashing 97. A total of 257 left England needing 372, and Australia won easily by 185 runs. Miller took ten wickets in the match for the only time in his career, and Gil Langley established a Test record with nine dismissals behind the stumps.

At Headingley England recalled a selector, Washbrook, whose last Test had been five years earlier. Washbrook joined May after Archer had reduced England to 17 for three on the first morning. The two added 157, with May scoring a century and Washbrook being lbw for 98. With the wicket taking spin, Laker and Lock ran through Australia twice, taking 11 and 7 wickets respectively. Only Harvey provided much resistance as England levelled the series with victory by an innings and 42 runs.

The Old Trafford Test will never be forgotten because of the astonishing bowling of Jim Laker. The Rev David Sheppard was recalled and made 113. Richardson and

Cowdrey also scored well and England reached 459. On a pitch becoming dusty, Laker then went through the Australian first innings, taking nine for 37, finishing it off with a spell of seven for eight in 22 balls. At the close of the second day he had captured Harvey's wicket for his second duck of the day. A storm then allowed less than two hours play on the third and fourth days. On the fifth Laker completed his amazing analysis: 10 for 53, 19 for 90 in the match. McDonald resisted for 337 minutes over five sessions for 89 and held out until after tea on the fifth day, but England won by an innings and 170 with only an hour to spare.

England recalled Compton for the Oval Test and completed a hat-trick of inspired selections. Compton, minus a knee-cap after an operation, made 94, rescuing England from 66 for three to 222 for four in company with May. England got a lead, declared, but could not force a result. Laker took seven wickets, establishing an Ashes record of 46 for the series, second only in all Tests to Barnes' 49 in South Africa in 1913–14.

1956 43rd Series Eng 2, Aus 1, Drawn 2
1 TRENT BRIDGE Match Drawn
England 217–8 dec (P E Richardson 81, P B H May 73, K R Miller 4–69) and 188–3 dec (M C Cowdrey 81, P E Richardson 73)
Australia 148 (R N Harvey 64, J C Laker 4–58) and 120–3 (J W Burke 58)
2 LORD'S Australia won by 185 runs
Australia 285 (C C McDonald 78, J W Burke 65) and 257 (R Benaud 97, F S Trueman 5–90, T E Bailey 4–64)
England 171 (P B H May 63, K R Miller 5–72) and 186 (P B H May 53, K R Miller 5–80, R G Archer 4–71)
3 HEADINGLEY England won by an innings and 42 runs
England 325 (P B H May 101, C Washbrook 98)
Australia 143 (J C Laker 5–58, G A R Lock 4–41) and 140 (R N Harvey 69, J C Laker 6–55)

4 OLD TRAFFORD   England won by an innings and 170 runs
England 459 (D S Sheppard 113, P E Richardson 104, M C Cowdrey 80, I W Johnson 4–151)
Australia 84 (J C Laker 9–37) and 205 (C C McDonald 89, J C Laker 10–53)

5 THE OVAL   Match Drawn
England 247 (D C S Compton 94, P B H May 83, R G Archer 5–53, K R Miller 4–91) and 182–3 dec (D S Sheppard 62)
Australia 202 (K R Miller 61, J C Laker 4–80) and 27–5

1956 Averages

Batting	I	No	Runs	HS	Avge
P.B.H. May (E)	7	2	453	101	90.60
P.E. Richardson (E)	8	0	364	104	45.50
J.W. Burke (A)	10	1	271	65	30.11

Bowling	O	M	Runs	W	Avge	BB
J.C. Laker (E)	283.5	127	442	46	9.60	10.53
K.R. Miller (A)	205.1	44	467	21	22.23	5–72
G.A.R. Lock (E)	237.2	115	337	15	22.46	4–41
R.G. Archer (A)	207.4	67	451	18	25.05	5–53

The 1956 Australians about to leave for England. Left to right, standing: Wilson, Mackay, Davidson, Burge, Crawford, Benaud, Archer, Harvey. Sitting: Langley, Miller, Johnson, Lindwall, McDonald, Burke. Front: Craig, Maddocks, Rutherford.

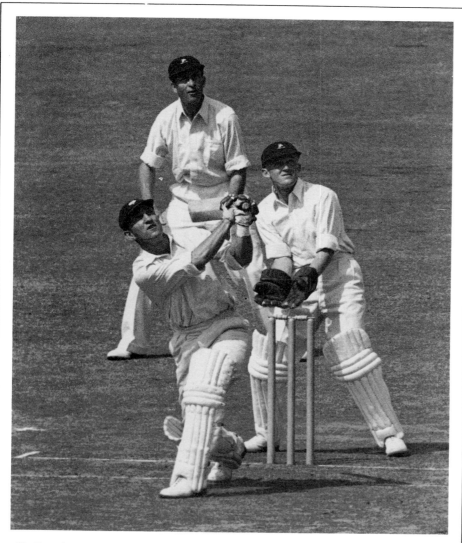

Hutton, Leonard

Hutton was born in Pudsey, Yorkshire, on 23 June 1916. A stylish right-hand opening batsman, he made his Yorkshire debut in 1934, and his Test debut three years later. He made a worldwide impact on cricket at the Oval in 1938, when, just 22, he broke the Test innings record with 364 against Australia. An accident during the war left him with a shortened left arm, but he overcame this handicap and played as brilliantly as ever. He had all the strokes but for England was often forced to play in a restrained manner. In 1952 he became the first professional to be selected to captain England. In 79 Tests he scored 6,971 runs, average 56.67. He was knighted in 1956.

1958–59: England well-beaten amid complaints of chucking

England took what was regarded as a strong side to Australia in 1958–59, but met an Australian side in which Benaud and Davidson realized their potential as all-rounders and Norman O'Neill made his debut as a Test batsman. But the story of the series was one of bitterness over the Australian bowling actions. Four bowlers – Meckiff, Slater, Rorke and Burke – were considered to throw, and in addition the giant Rorke had a drag which took him well past the bowling crease before he released the ball.

For the first time Australians saw a Test live on television, but ironically Brisbane provided some of the slowest scoring ever. England were out for 134 and Australia for 186 before Bailey made 68 second innings runs in over 7½ overs. Australia needed only 147 to win, and on the last day opener Jack Burke took over four hours making 28 of them. Australia won by eight wickets.

At Melbourne, Davidson took three wickets in his second over: England were seven for three. They totalled 259 thanks to a century from May, Davidson finishing with six for 64. Statham then took seven for 57 for England, but Harvey made a brilliant 167 and Australia led by 49. Meckiff played his biggest role of the series by taking six for 38 as England collapsed for only 87. Australia won again by eight wickets.

Benaud was the destructive bowler at Sydney. England were dismissed for 219 and Australia led by 138. A third-wicket stand of 182 between May (92) and Cowdrey (100 not out) saved England.

May put Australia in at Adelaide, which was generally regarded as a mistake. Australia had 276 on the board before the second wicket fell and totalled 476, thanks mainly to McDonald (170), who was almost bowled by the first ball of the match from Statham. During this innings there were a number of umpiring mistakes.

Lindwall was recalled by Australia and Rorke made his debut. Benaud bowled best, however, as England were put out for 240 and asked to follow on. They did little better second time, making 270, and Australia scored the 35 needed without loss to re-capture the Ashes.

Benaud put England in at Melbourne in the last Test, and helped dismiss them for 205. McDonald then made his second successive century (133) and Australia built a lead of 146. England failed again second time round and Australia made the 69 needed for the loss of one wicket. Lindwall passed Grimmett's Australian record of 216 Test wickets.

1958–59 44th Series Aus 4, Eng 0, Drawn 1

1 BRISBANE   Australia won by 8 wkts
England 134 and 198 (T E Bailey 68, R Benaud 4–66)
Australia 186 (P J Loader 4–56) and 147–2 (N C O'Neill 71)

2 MELBOURNE   Australia won by 8 wkts
England 259 (P B H May 113, A K Davidson 6–64) and 87 (I Meckiff 6–38)
Australia 308 (R N Harvey 167, J B Statham 7–57) and 42–2

3 SYDNEY   Match Drawn
England 219 (R Benaud 5–83) and 287–7 dec (M C Cowdrey 100, P B H May 92, R Benaud 4–94)
Australia 357 (N C O'Neill 77, A K Davidson 71, K D Mackay 57, L E Favell 54, J C Laker 5–107, G A R Lock 4–130) and 54–2

4 ADELAIDE   Australia won by 10 wkts
Australia 476 (C C McDonald 170, J W Burke 66, N C O'Neill 56, F S Trueman 4–90) and 36–0
England 240 (M C Cowdrey 84, R Benaud 5–91) and 270 (P B H May 59, T W Graveney 53, R Benaud 4–82)

5 MELBOURNE   Australia won by 9 wkts
England 205 (P E Richardson 68, R Benaud 4–43) and 214 (T W Graveney 54)
Australia 351 (C C McDonald 133, A T W Grout 74, R Benaud 64, F S Trueman 4–92) and 69–1 (C C McDonald 51)

1958–59 Averages

Batting	I	No	Runs	HS	Avge
C.C. McDonald (A)	9	1	520	170	65.00
N.C. O'Neill (A)	7	2	282	77	56.40
R.N. Harvey (A)	9	3	291	167	48.50
M.C. Cowdrey (E)	10	1	391	100*	43.44
P.B.H. May (E)	10	0	405	113	40.50
T.W. Graveney (E)	10	1	280	54	31.11

Bowling	O	M	Runs	W	Avge	BB
I. Meckiff (A)	112.2	24	292	17	17.17	6–38
R. Benaud (A)	233.2	65	584	31	18.83	5–83
A.K. Davidson (A)	183.5	45	456	24	19.00	6–64
J.C. Laker (E)	127.6	24	318	15	21.20	5–107
J.B. Statham (E)	104	12	286	12	23.83	7–57

Benaud, Richard

Benaud, known throughout his cricket career as 'Richie', was born on 6 November 1930 at Penrith, NSW. Beginning as a right-hand batsman for New South Wales in 1948–49, he developed great skill as a leg-break and googly bowler and with his catching and captaincy he was an excellent Test all-rounder. He made his Test debut in 1951–52 and captained Australia 28 times from 1958–59. He was captain in the first tied Test against West Indies in 1960–61. In 63 Tests he scored 2,201 runs, average 24.45, and took 248 wickets, average 27.03. He was the first to score 2,000 runs and take 200 wickets. He is now a respected cricket writer and TV commentator.

1961: Australia's great win at Old Trafford

By 1961 Australia had eliminated the chuckers. The main bowler in the first Test at Edgbaston was, surprisingly, all-rounder Ken Mackay, who broke the back of England's batting with three wickets in four balls, making the score 122 for six. England made 195. Bill Lawry made 57 in his first Test innings and, with Harvey's 114 the best of other good scores, Australia were able to declare at 516 for nine. Dexter's brilliant innings of 180 on the last day, with support from Subba Row's 112, ensured the draw.

Cowdrey set a Test record by winning his ninth successive toss at Lord's, but good bowling by Davidson removed England for 206. Lawry made 130 on a lively pitch (the Lord's ridge was discovered) with the tail-enders helping him retrieve a poor start, and Australia to reached 340. Graham McKenzie, making his debut, took five wickets in England's second-innings 202, and Australia were left with only 69 to get. They lost five wickets to Trueman and Statham, but made the runs. Harvey captained Australia for the only time, because of Benaud's injury.

Benaud and May were back as captains at Headingley and after 12 successful English tosses, May lost. Australia, however, made only 237, thanks mainly to Trueman. England led with only four men out, but collapsed, and the lead was only 62. Australia then collapsed even more dramatically, with Trueman enjoying a spell of five for nothing as they subsided from 99 for two to 120 all out. England won by eight wickets.

The Old Trafford Test, although it did not start until 2.40 on the first day, proved to be one of the most exciting for years. Australia were rapidly dismissed for 190, despite Lawry's gritty 74, Statham taking five wickets. England passed this with only three wickets down, and reached 358 for six, but Bobby Simpson then took the last four wickets, including Barrington, for two runs and England's lead was kept to 177. Australia, in turn, knocked these off with only two men out, Lawry making a century, but wickets fell and nine were out for 334, a lead of only 157. On the last morning McKenzie joined Davidson, who suddenly hit Allen, who had taken four wickets, for 20 in an

The 1961 Australians in England. Left to right, back: Booth, Lawry, Misson, Gaunt, McKenzie. Middle row: A. James (physiotherapist), J. Cameron (scorer), Jarman, Quick, R. Steele (treasurer), Kline, O'Neill, Burge, Simpson. Front: Grout, Davidson, Benaud, S.G. Webb (manager), Harvey, McDonald, Mackay.

over. The two added 98 for the last wicket before McKenzie was bowled, leaving Davidson 77 not out. England needed 256 to win at 67 an hour.

When Pullar was out, Dexter played what Benaud described as the finest innings he

Peter Burge sweeps in the fifth Test at the Oval in 1961. Murray is the wicket-keeper. Burge scored 181 to end a successful series.

had seen in a Test match. But after he had scored 76 in 84 minutes he was caught behind off Benaud. The score was 150 for two, but Benaud, bowling round the wicket, then bowled May round his legs for a duck, and went on to a spell of five for 12 in 25 balls. Suddenly, after England had looked sure to win, the pendulum had tipped Australia's way. With 20 minutes remaining Davidson bowled Statham, and Australia had won by 54 runs to keep the Ashes.

At the Oval, England made 256, but any hopes they had of squaring the rubber disappeared with a chanceless innings by Peter Burge of 181. With O'Neill (117) and Booth (71) he helped add 308 runs for the fourth and fifth wickets. Australia made 494. There was rain on the third and fourth days, and England had made 370 for eight (Subba Row 137) by the close. It was May's last Test match.

1961 45th Series   Aus 2, Eng 1, Drawn 2

1 EDGBASTON   Match Drawn
England 195 (R Subba Row 59, K D Mackay 4–57) and 401–4 (E R Dexter 180, R Subba Row 112;
Australia 516 (R N Harvey 114, N C O'Neill 82, R B Simpson 76, K D Mackay 64, W M Lawry 57)

2 LORD'S   Australia won by 5 wkts
England 206 (A K Davidson 5–42) and 202 (K F Barrington 66, G D McKenzie 5–37)
Australia 340 (W M Lawry 130, K D Mackay 54, F S Trueman 4–118) and 71–5

3 HEADINGLEY   England won by 8 wkts
Australia 237 (R N Harvey 73, C C McDonald 54, F S Truman 5–58) and 120 (R N Harvey 53, F S Trueman 6–30)
England 299 (M C Cowdrey 93, G Pullar 53, A K Davidson 5–63) and 62–2

4 OLD TRAFFORD   Australia won by 54 runs
Australia 190 (W M Lawry 74, J B Statham 5–53) and 432 (W M Lawry 102, A K Davidson 77, N C O'Neill 67, R B Simpson 51, D A Allen 4–58)
England 367 (P B H May 95, K F Barrington 78, G Pullar 63, R B Simpson 4–23) and 201 (E R Dexter 76, R Benaud 6–70)

5 THE OVAL   Match Drawn
England 256 (P B H May 71, K F Barrington 53, A K Davidson 4–83) and 370–8 (R Subba Row 137, K F Barrington 83, K D Mackay 5–121)
Australia 494 (P J P Burge 181, N C O'Neill 117, B C Booth 71, D A Allen 4–133)

1961 Averages

Batting	I	No	Runs	HS	Avge
W.M. Lawry (A)	8	0	420	130	52.50
P.J.P. Burge (A)	8	1	332	181†	47.42
R. Subba Row (E)	10	0	468	137	46.80
K.F. Barrington (E)	9	1	364	83	45.50
R.N. Harvey (A)	8	0	338	114	42.25
E.R. Dexter (E)	9	0	378	180	42.00
N.C. O'Neill (A)	8	0	324	117	40.50
P.B.H. May (E)	8	1	272	95	38.85
G. Pullar (E)	10	1	287	63	31.88

Bowling	O	M	Runs	W	Avge	BB
A.K. Davidson (A)	280.2	86	572	23	24.86	5–42
F.S. Trueman (E)	164.4	21	529	20	26.45	6–30
D.A. Allen (E)	134	53	354	13	27.23	4–58
J.B. Statham (E)	201.4	41	501	17	29.47	5–53
R. Benaud (A)	214.3	76	488	15	32.53	6–70
K.D. Mackay (A)	273	87	525	16	32.81	5–121

Subba Row, batting with a runner, sweeps a boundary at the Oval.

1962–63: A disappointing finale to a drawn series

Ted Dexter captained England in Australia in 1962–63. The first Test at Brisbane was a high-scoring match with 14 innings passing 50, although only Brian Booth went on to a century. After an Australian second-innings declaration, England needed 378 in a day to win – long before the end the match was clearly destined to be a draw.

At Melbourne each team used seven bowlers. A third-wicket stand of 175 by Dexter (93) and Cowdrey (113) enabled England to pass Australia's 316 by 15. Booth's second century of the series left England needing 234. Sheppard, who had made a

A turning point in 1961. Dexter is caught by Grout off Benaud for a brilliant 76 at Old Trafford.

duck and dropped some vital catches, now scored 113 as Australia dropped catches. Sheppard was run out going for the winning run, but England won by seven wickets. Trueman took eight wickets.

England were dismissed for 279 at Sydney, with Bobby Simpson taking five wickets. That Australia led by only 40 was due to Titmus, who took seven for 79 after Simpson and Harvey had added 160 for Australia's second wicket. Davidson struck early with three quick wickets in England's second innings and they never recovered, being out for 104. Davidson had nine wickets in the match. Australia won comfortably by eight wickets to level the series.

At Adelaide, both sides seemed frightened of defeat. Harvey and O'Neill made centuries for Australia, Harvey's 154 being the last of his 21 Test centuries. England batted steadily to reach 331, 62 behind. Davidson broke down in his fourth over. In Australia's second-innings 293, Statham passed Bedser's Test record of 236 wickets. Needing 356 at 89 an hour, England easily drew, with Barrington scoring an unbeaten century.

With everything to play for at Sydney, the fifth Test was a disappointment. With Barrington's second century, England spent the first day reaching 195 for five. The final total of 321 was passed by Australia's 349, Burge making a century. England then declared with eight wickets down, setting Australia a reasonable target of 241 in 240 minutes, but Lawry batted out time amid much barracking.

This was the last Test for Harvey, whose 79 Tests were an Australian record, and Davidson.

1962–63 46th Series Eng 1, Aus 1, Drawn 3

1 BRISBANE Match Drawn
Australia 404 (B C Booth 112, K D Mackay 86, R Benaud 51, R B Simpson 50) and 362–4 dec (W M Lawry 98, R B Simpson 71, R N Harvey 57, N C O'Neill 56)
England 389 (P H Parfitt 80, K F Barrington 78, E R Dexter 70, R Benaud 6–115) and 278–6 (E R Dexter 99, G Pullar 56, D S Sheppard 53)

2 MELBOURNE England won by 7 wkts
Australia 316 (W M Lawry 52, F J Titmus 4–43) and 248 (B C Booth 103, W M Lawry 57, F S Trueman 5–62)
England 331 (M C Cowdrey 113, E R Dexter 93, A K Davidson 6–75) and 237–3 (D S Sheppard 113, M C Cowdrey 58, E R Dexter 52)

3 SYDNEY Australia won by 8 wkts
England 279 (M C Cowdrey 85, G Pullar 53, R B Simpson 5–57, A K Davidson 4–54) and 104 (A K Davidson 5–25)
Australia 319 (R B Simpson 91, B K Shepherd 71, R N Harvey 64, F J Titmus 7–79) and 67–2

4 ADELAIDE Match Drawn
Australia 393 (R N Harvey 154, N C O'Neill 100) and 293 (B C Booth 77, R B Simpson 71, F S Trueman 4–60)
England 331 (K F Barrington 63, E R Dexter 61, F J Titmus 59, G D McKenzie 5–89) and 223–4 (K F Barrington 132)

5 SYDNEY Match Drawn
England 321 (K F Barrington 101) and 268–8 dec (K F Barrington 94, D S Sheppard 68, M C Cowdrey 53)
Australia 349 (P J P Burge 103, N C O'Neill 73, R Benaud 57, F J Titmus 5–103) and 152–4 (P J P Burge 52)

1962–1963 Averages

Batting	I	No	Runs	HS	Avge
K.F. Barrington (E)	10	2	582	132*	72.75
B.C. Booth (A)	10	2	404	112	50.50
E.R. Dexter (E)	10	0	481	99	48.10
R.B. Simpson (A)	10	1	401	91	44.55
M.C. Cowdrey (E)	10	1	394	113	43.77
R.N. Harvey (A)	10	0	395	154	39.50
W.M. Lawry (A)	10	1	310	98	34.44
N.C. O'Neill (A)	9	0	310	100	34.44
D.S. Sheppard (E)	10	0	330	113	33.00

Bowling	O	M	Runs	W	Avge	BB
A.K. Davidson (A)	176.2	30	480	24	20.00	6–75
F.S. Trueman (E)	158.3	9	521	20	26.05	5–62
F.J. Titmus (E)	236.3	54	616	21	29.33	7–79
G.D. McKenzie (A)	205.3	25	619	20	30.95	5–89
R. Benaud (A)	228	56	688	17	40.47	6–115
J.B. Statham (E)	165.2	16	580	13	44.61	3–66

1964: Rain the winner as Australia retain Ashes

Bobby Simpson led the 1964 tourists to England, when the series was spoilt by the weather.

At Trent Bridge, where Geoff Boycott made his Test debut, England declared at 216 for eight after rain had interrupted the play. Australia were dismissed for only 164, and England declared their second innings at 193 for nine, but rain, which had allowed only one full day, had the last word.

Rain prevented play until the third day at Lord's. Australia were put in by Dexter and again dismissed cheaply, for 176, Trueman taking five wickets, and with John Edrich making a century England took a lead of 70. But rain again ended the match soon after lunch on the last day.

Norman O'Neill was one of the most exciting Australian batsmen throughout the 1960s.

A result was achieved at Headingley. England made 268, Neil Hawke and McKenzie getting the wickets. The match turned with Australia struggling against the off-spin of Titmus at 187 for seven. Dexter took the new ball, and Peter Burge played a magnificent innings of 160, hoisting Australia to 389. England were restricted to 229 and Australia scored the 109 needed to win by seven wickets.

Australia won the toss on a perfect Old Trafford wicket, and Lawry and Simpson began with a stand of 201. Simpson went on to 311. He batted 762 minutes, the third longest in first-class cricket. Australia declared at 656 for eight. England replied with 611, Barrington (256) and Dexter (174) putting on 246 for the third wicket. There was time for two overs in the second innings.

At the Oval, England made 182, Hawke taking six for 47. Hawke achieved more fame in this match, however, by becoming Trueman's 300th Test victim, the first time this figure had been reached. Australia reached 379, and England 381 for four, with Boycott making his first Test century, before rain wiped out the last day of a frustrating series.

Barrington, Kenneth Frank

Barrington was born on 24 November 1930 at Reading, and made his debut for Surrey in 1953. He was initially a brilliant attacking batsman but made a false start in Tests in 1955. He was dropped after two matches, and restyled his game, eliminating risk and becoming an on-side player. Regaining his Test place four years later, he became the most reliable batsman in the team. In 82 Tests he scored 6,806 runs, average 58.67. He also took 29 wickets with his leg-break mixture. He retired in 1968 after a mild heart attack, but he died of a second heart attack while assistant manager of the touring party in West Indies, at Bridgetown on 14 March 1981.

1964 47th series   Aus 1, Eng 0, Drawn 4

1 TRENT BRIDGE   Match Drawn

England 216–8 and 193–9 dec (E R Dexter 68, G D McKenzie 5–53)

Australia 168 (R B Simpson 50) and 40–2

2 LORD'S   Match Drawn

Australia 176 (T R Veivers 54, F S Trueman 5–48) and 168–4 (P J P Burge 59)

England 246 (J H Edrich 120, G E Corling 4–60)

3 HEADINGLEY   Australia won by 7 wkts

England 268 (J M Parks 68, E R Dexter 66, N J N Hawke 5–75, G D McKenzie 4–74) and 229 (K F Barrington 85)

Australia 389 (P J P Burge 160, W M Lawry 78, F J Titmus 4–69) and 111–3 (I R Redpath 58)

4 OLD TRAFFORD   Match Drawn

Australia 656–8 dec (R B Simpson 311, W M Lawry 106, B C Booth 98) and 4–0

England 611 (K F Barrington 256, E R Dexter 174, J M Parks 60, G Boycott 58, G D McKenzie 7–153)

5 THE OVAL   Match Drawn

England 182 (N J N Hawke 6–47) and 381–4 (G Boycott 113, M C Cowdrey 93, F J Titmus 56, K F Barrington 54)

Australia 379 (W M Lawry 94, B C Booth 74, T R Veivers 67, F S Trueman 4–87)

1964 Averages

Batting	I	No	Runs	HS	Avge
R.B. Simpson (A)	8	2	458	311	76.33
K.F. Barrington (E)	8	1	531	256	75.85
G. Boycott (E)	6	0	291	113	48.50
E.R. Dexter (E)	8	0	384	174	48.00
P.J.P. Burge (A)	8	1	322	160	46.00
W.M. Lawry (A)	9	1	317	106	39.62

Bowling	O	M	Runs	W	Avge	BB
G.D. McKenzie (A)	256	61	654	29	22.55	7–153
F.S. Trueman (E)	133.3	25	399	*17	23.47	5–48
N.J.N. Hawke (A)	242.1	80	496	18	27.55	6–47
G.E. Corling (A)	193.1	50	447	12	37.25	4–60

A record for Fred Trueman. Cowdrey at first slip grabs a snick from Neil Hawke and Trueman becomes the first player to take 300 wickets in Test matches. Peter Parfitt is the other slip and Jim Parks the wicket-keeper.

1965–66: Nothing between the sides in another drawn series

M.J.K. Smith was England's captain on the 1965–66 tour. In the first and third Tests his opposite number was Brian Booth, standing in for an injured or ill Bobby Simpson.

Booth won the toss at Brisbane, where Doug Walters made his debut with 155. Lawry batted 419 minutes for 166 after rain had washed out 1½ days, and although England followed on the match was clearly going to be drawn.

There were big scores at Melbourne, where Australia's 358 was overshadowed by England's 558, John Edrich and Cowdrey making centuries. In Australia's second innings Parks missed a stumping of Burge with Australia 204 for four, and Burge and Walters took the score to 374, both topping the hundred to ensure the draw.

England made a great start at Sydney, Boycott (84) and Barber (185) putting on 234 for the first wicket in 242 minutes. Barber's score is the highest by an Englishman on the first day of a Test in Australia. With Edrich making his second successive century, England made 488, despite Hawke's seven for 105. David Brown then took five wickets to help force Australia to follow on at 221, and with the wicket taking spin David Allen and Titmus took four wickets each as Australia were dismissed again for 174, leaving England winners by an innings and 93.

McKenzie removed Barber and Edrich with only 25 on the board at Adelaide, and

England could make only 241, McKenzie finishing with six for 48. Australia passed this without loss, Simpson (225) and Lawry (119) putting on 244, an Australian first wicket record in Ashes matches. Australia scored 516, Jeff Jones taking six for 118. Barrington made 102, his tenth score over 50

in ten innings at Adelaide, but at 266 England were beaten by an innings and 9.

In the decider at Melbourne, Barrington made another century, taking only 122 balls, but the momentum was not maintained. England declared at 485 for nine, but Australia made 543 for eight declared, with Bob Cowper scoring the only triple century made by an Australian at home. It took 727 minutes, the longest first-class innings in Australia. Lawry too made a century, but for the second consecutive Ashes series, the deciding Test at Melbourne ended in a disappointing stalemate.

Wally Grout ended his Test career with 187 dismissals, at the time an Australian wicket-keeping record.

1965–66   48th Series   Eng 1, Aus 1, Drawn 3

1 BRISBANE   Match Drawn

Australia 443–6 dec (W M Lawry 166, K D Walters 155, T R Veivers 46)

England 280 (F J Titmus 60, K F Barrington 53, J M Parks 52, P I Philpott 5–90) and 186–3 (G Boycott 63)

2 MELBOURNE   Match Drawn

Australia 358 (R M Cowper 99, W M Lawry 88, R B Simpson 59, B R Knight 4–84) and 426 (P J P Burge 120, K D Walters 115, W M Lawry 78, R B Simpson 67)

England 558 (J H Edrich 109, M C Cowdrey 104, J M Parks 71, K F Barrington 63, F J Titmus 56, G Boycott 51, G D McKenzie 5–134) and 5–0

3 SYDNEY   England won by an innings and 93 runs

England 488 (R W Barber 185, J H Edrich 103, G Boycott 84, D A Allen 50, N J N Hawke 7–105)

Australia 221 (R M Cowper 60, G Thomas 51, D J Brown 5–63) and 174 (F J Titmus 4–40, D A Allen 4–47)

4 ADELAIDE   Australia won by an innings and 9 runs

England 241 (K F Barrington 60, G D McKenzie 6–48) and 266 (K F Barrington 102, F J Titmus 53, N J N Hawke 5–54)

Australia 516 (R B Simpson 225, W M Lawry 119, G Thomas 52, I J Jones 6–118)

5 MELBOURNE   Match Drawn

England 485–9 dec (K F Barrington 115, J M Parks 89, J H Edrich 85, M C Cowdrey 79, K D Walters 4–53) and 69–3

Australia 543–8 dec (R M Cowper 307, W M Lawry 108, K D Walters 60)

1965–66 Averages

Batting	I	No	Runs	HS	Avge
R.B. Simpson (A)	4	0	355	225	88.75
W.M. Lawry (A)	7	0	592	166	84.57
R.M. Cowper (A)	6	0	493	307	82.16
K.D. Walters (A)	7	1	410	155	68.33
K.F. Barrington (E)	8	1	464	115	66.28
F.J. Titmus (E)	6	2	258	60	64.50
M.C. Cowdrey (E)	6	1	267	104	53.40
J.M. Parks (E)	6	0	290	89	48.38
J.H. Edrich (E)	8	0	375	109	46.87
G. Boycott (E)	9	2	300	84	42.85
R.W. Barber (E)	9	1	328	185	41.00

Bowling	O	M	Runs	W	Avge	BB
N.J.N. Hawke (A)	142.7	29	419	16	26.18	7–105
G.D. McKenzie (A)	133.4	20	467	16	29.18	6–48
I.J. Jones (E)	129	15	533	15	35.53	6–118

1968: Mopping up at the Oval saves the rubber

Bill Lawry and Colin Cowdrey were the captains in the 1968 series in England. At Old Trafford Australia made 357, and England unaccountably collapsed after Edrich and Boycott had put on 86 for the first wicket. The score became 97 for five, and eventually 165 all out. Pocock (6–79) bowled well to dismiss Australia for 220 second time, but England's 253 meant defeat by 159 runs.

Strangely Pocock and D'Oliveira, England's top scorer at Old Trafford, were both omitted at Lord's where England batted solidly down the order to declare at 351 for seven. Australia were then shot out for 78, with Brown taking five for 42, but rain had interrupted throughout and Australia, following on, saved the match at 127 for four.

The first day's play was lost to rain at Edgbaston, where Cowdrey celebrated his 100th Test (a record) with a century, and became the second player after Hammond to score 7,000 Test runs. Other good scores took England to 409, and Australia were dismissed for 222. England declared at 143 for three, leaving Australia to score 530 in just over a day, but rain washed out play at 12.30 with the score 68 for one.

Cowdrey and Lawry were injured at Edgbaston, and at Headingley Graveney and Jarman captained their countries for the only time. Keith Fletcher and John Inverarity were among the debutants. Australia made 315, and England 302 (Connolly 5–72), thanks partly to Underwood scoring 45 not out at number eleven. Illingworth took six for 87 in Australia's 312, setting England 326 in 295 minutes, but they made only 230 for four.

At the Oval, D'Oliveira was recalled when Prideaux was injured, and made 158. With Edrich making 164, England scored 494. Lawry replied with 135, but at 324 Australia trailed by 170. They bowled well in the second innings on a wearing wicket to dismiss England for 181, leaving themselves 352 to win. At lunch on the final day they appeared

well beaten at 85 for five, but in the interval a freak storm left much of the ground covered in water. The sun came out, and spectators helped the ground staff to mop up to such effect that play resumed at 4.45, with 75 minutes remaining. Thirty-nine minutes were safely negotiated before D'Oliveira bowled Jarman. Underwood then came on and took the last four wickets, the last being Inverarity, who batted throughout the innings for 56 out of 124. England levelled the series with five minutes to spare, Underwood recording seven for 50.

1968 49th Series Aus 1, Eng 1, Drawn 3
1 OLD TRAFFORD Australia won by 159 runs
Australia 357 (A P Sheahan 88, W M Lawry 81, K D Walters 81, I M Chappell 73, J A Snow 4–97) and 220 (K D Walters 86, P I Pocock 6–79)
England 165 (R M Cowper 4–48) and 253 (B L D'Oliveira 87)
2 LORD'S Match Drawn
England 351–7 dec (C Milburn 83, K F Barrington 75)
Australia 78 (D J Brown 5–42) and 127–4 (I R Redpath 53)
3 EDGBASTON Match Drawn
England 409 (M C Cowdrey 104, T W Graveney 96, J H Edrich 88, E W Freeman 4–78) and 142–3 dec (J H Edrich 64)
Australia 222 (I M Chappell 71, R M Cowper 57) and 68–1
4 HEADINGLEY Match Drawn
Australia 315 (I R Redpath 92, I M Chappell 65, D L Underwood 4–41) and 312 (I M Chappell 81, K D Walters 56, R Illingworth 6–87)
England 302 (R M Prideaux 64, J H Edrich 62, A N Connolly 5–72) and 230–4 (J H Edrich 65)
5 THE OVAL England won by 226 runs
England 494 (J H Edrich 164, B L D'Oliveira 158, T W Graveney 63) and 81 (A N Connolly 4–65)
Australia 324 (W M Lawry 135, I R Redpath 67) and 125 (R J Inverarity 56, D L Underwood 7–50)

1968 Averages

Batting	I	No	Runs	HS	Avge
B.L. D'Oliveira (E)	4	1	263	158	87.66
J.H. Edrich (E)	9	0	554	164	61.55
W.M. Lawry (A)	7	1	270	135	45.00
I.M. Chappell (A)	10	2	348	81₄	43.50
T.W. Graveney (E)	9	1	337	96	41.12
K.D. Walters (A)	9	0	343	86	38.11
I.R. Redpath (A)	10	0	310	92	31.00

Bowling	O	M	Runs	W	Avge	BB
D.L. Underwood (E)	209.5	103	302	20	15.10	7–50
R. Illingworth (E)	183.2	82	291	13	22.39	6–87
A.N. Connolly (A)	267.1	75	591	23	25.69	5–72
J.A. Snow (E)	203	44	508	17	29.88	4–97
D.J. Brown (E)	144	34	401	12	33.41	5–42
J.W. Gleeson (A)	193.5	65	417	12	34.75	3–44
G.D. McKenzie (A)	264	77	595	13	45.76	3–33

Simpson, Robert Baddeley
Born on 3 February 1936 at Marrickville, NSW, Simpson played for his native state from 1952–53 to 1977–78, with a spell for Western Australia in the middle. He was an attractive right-hand opening batsman, a leg-break and googly bowler and a brilliant slip fieldsman. He made his debut for Australia in 1957–58 and became captain in 1963–64. He retired from Test cricket in 1967–68 but when Australia's leading players signed for the 'rebel' WSC in 1977–78 he was brought back as captain in two series. In all he played in 62 Tests, 39 as captain, scoring 4,869 runs, average 46.81. He also took 71 wickets at 42.26 each. He equalled Hammond's record of 110 Test catches, a figure since passed.

Left: The incredible scene as Inverarity is out lbw to Underwood and England win the final Test at the Oval with five minutes to spare. All the England players are in the picture.

1970–71: Snow helps England regain Ashes after 16 years

Illingworth was preferred to Cowdrey as England captain in Australia in 1970–71. Lawry continued to lead Australia. Rodney Marsh was the most notable debutant at Brisbane, where Keith Stackpole hit 207 after Boycott had clearly indicated he thought he had run him out at 18. With Walters making 112, the score reached 418 for three, but an astonishing collapse saw the side out for 433, Snow taking six for 114. England, with all the batsmen contributing, made 464, Cowdrey establishing a new Test record aggregate by passing Hammond's 7,249. Australia were then dismissed for 214, but there was not time to force a win.

The second Test was the first played at the WACA ground at Perth. Greg Chappell made his debut, but had to wait to bat as Lawry put England in. Boycott (70) and Brian Luckhurst (131 in his second Test) put on 171 for the first wicket, and England totalled 397. Redpath made 171, and Greg Chappell, on his debut, 108 (batting number seven) and Australia reached 440. Edrich then made a century and an England declaration at 287 for six left Australia to make 245 in 145 minutes. Lawry did not accept the challenge, taking over an hour for six and the match was drawn.

The third Test at Melbourne was abandoned on the third day without a ball being bowled. A one-day game played on what would have been the final day established the current enthusiasm for one-day internationals.

At Sydney Bob Willis made his Test debut after being flown out to Australia when Alan Ward was injured. England made 332 and led by 96 when Australia were dismissed for 236. Boycott made 142 not out as England reached 319 for five before declaring, setting Australia 416 to win. Lawry was the only batsman to withstand Snow, who took seven for 40, as Australia were beaten by 299 runs. Lawry carried his bat for 60 not out. McKenzie, hit by a ball from Snow, retired hurt in his last Test match.

A fifth Test at Melbourne was an additional Test arranged to replace the washed-out third Test. It was an unsatisfactory match. Amid many missed catches, particularly by Cowdrey, Ian Chappell made a century, at which the crowd invaded the pitch and retired with a stump and two players' caps. Lawry declared at 493 for nine. England made 392, with Luckhurst, despite a broken finger, and D'Oliveira scoring centuries. Lawry declared but there was no chance of a result, and the crowd demonstrated against the pointlessness of the last day.

The sixth Test at Adelaide saw the first appearance of Dennis Lillee. He took five for 84 when England batted, but Edrich made 130 and England 470. Australia could manage only 235, but Illingworth did not enforce the follow-on. Instead he declared at

233 for four. Boycott made a century and he and Edrich opened each innings with a century stand. The pitch was easing and with Stackpole and Ian Chappell making centuries, Australia easily saved the match.

Lawry's Test career ended when he was dropped for the seventh Test at Sydney, which Australia had to win, and Ian Chappell preferred as captain. Chappell put England in, and achieved success by dismissing them for 184. When Australia batted, at 195 for seven, a ball from Snow hit Jenner on the head, Jenner being taken to hospital. Snow was warned about bouncers, and the crowd threw a few beer cans. When Snow went to field near the fence, a drunken spectator grabbed his shirt, and more cans were thrown. Illingworth led the team off the field, but returned when the umpires threatened to award the match to Australia. Australia led by 80, but determined batting by England accrued 302 runs, and Australia were set 223 to win. Snow bowled Eastwood without a run on the board, but injured his hand on the fence attempting to catch Stackpole, and retired. Nevertheless steady bowling by the other bowlers (six England bowlers took a wicket) saw Australia dismissed for 160, and England regained the Ashes by 2–0.

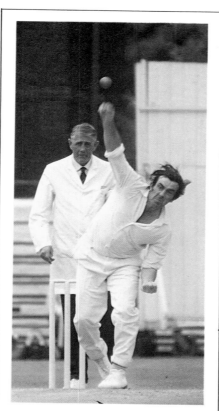

Trueman, Frederick Sewards

Born on 6 February 1931 at Stainton, Yorkshire, Trueman first appeared for the county in 1949. He was a strong, aggressive right-arm fast bowler, with a classical action and a belligerent fiery nature. His debut for England in 1952 was sensational, for he took three quick wickets in the second innings. With Bedser getting one, India were nought for four. A tendency to air his views might have cost him a few Test appearances, but he made 67, and was the first player to take 300 Test wickets. He ended with 307, average 21.57. He became a radio commentator.

1970–71   50th Series   Eng 2, Aus 0, Drawn 4

1 BRISBANE   Match Drawn
Australia 433 (K R Stackpole 207, K D Walters 112, I M Chappell 59, J A Snow 6–114) and 214 (W M Lawry 84, K Shuttleworth 5–47)
England 464 (J H Edrich 79, B W Luckhurst 74, A P E Knott 73, B L D'Oliveira 57) and 39–1

2 PERTH   Match Drawn
England 397 (B W Luckhurst 131, G Boycott 70, G D McKenzie 4–66) and 287–6 dec (J H Edrich 115, G Boycott 50)
Australia 440 (I R Redpath 171, G S Chappell 108, I M Chappell 50, J A Snow 4–143) and 100–3

3 SYDNEY   England won by 299 runs
England 332 (G Boycott 77, J H Edrich 55, A A Mallett 4–40, J W Gleeson 4–83) and 319–5 dec (G Boycott 142, B L D'Oliveira 56, R Illingworth 53)
Australia 236 (I R Redpath 64, K D Walters 55, D L Underwood 4–66) and 116 (W M Lawry 60, J A Snow 7–40)

4 MELBOURNE   Match Drawn
Australia 493–9 dec (I M Chappell 111, R W Marsh 92, W M Lawry 56, I R Redpath 72, K D Walters 55) and 169–4 dec
England 392 (B W Luckhurst 109, B L D'Oliveira 117) and 161–0 (G Boycott 76, J H Edrich 74)

5 ADELAIDE   Match Drawn
England 470 (J H Edrich 130, K W R Fletcher 80, G Boycott 58, J H Hampshire 55, D K Lillee 5–84) and 233–4 dec (G Boycott 119)
Australia 235 (K R Stackpole 87, P Lever 4–49) and 328–3 (K R Stackpole 136, I M Chappell 104)

6 SYDNEY   England won by 62 runs
England 184 and 302 (B W Luckhurst 59, J H Edrich 57)
Australia 264 (G S Chappell 65, I R Redpath 59) and 160 (K R Stackpole 67)

After the match at Perth, the next Test should have been played at Melbourne, but bad weather prevented a ball being bowled and the match was re-arranged

1970–71 Averages

Batting	I	No	Runs	HS	Avge
G. Boycott (E)	10	3	657	142*	93.85
J.H. Edrich (E)	11	2	648	130	72.00
B.W. Luckhurst (E)	9	1	455	131	56.87
K.R. Stackpole (A)	12	0	627	207	52.25
I.R. Redpath (A)	12	2	497	171	49.70
W.M. Lawry (A)	10	2	324	84	40.50
I.M. Chappell (A)	12	0	452	111	37.66
K.D. Walters (A)	12	2	373	112	37.30
R. Illingworth (E)	10	1	333	53	37.00
B.L. D'Oliveira (E)	10	0	369	117	36.90

Bowling	O	M	Runs	W	Avge	BB
J.A. Snow (E)	225.5	47	708	31	22·83	7–40
R.G.D. Willis (E)	88	16	329	12	27.41	3–58
D.L. Underwood (E)	194.6	50	520	16	32.50	4–66
P. Lever (E)	143.5	25	439	13	33.76	4–49
A.L. Thomson (A)	189.7	33	654	12	54.50	3–79

1972: Problems over the pitch at Headingley

Illingworth and Ian Chappell remained captains for the 1972 series, when Tony Greig made his debut in the first Test at Old Trafford, and was England's top scorer in each innings. England made 249 in the first, and good bowling by Snow and Arnold removed Australia for 142. Lillee took six for 66 in the second innings, England making 234, but a target of 342 was too much for Australia. Snow took four wickets for the second time and although Marsh hit a defiant 91 England won by 89 runs.

The Lord's Test provided one of the most amazing performances of modern cricket. Bob Massie, making his debut, so bamboozled England with his swing that he took eight for 84 as England crashed to 272. Australia made 308 thanks mainly to Greg Chappell's 131, whereupon Massie again went through England with eight for 53. Australia required only 81 to win by eight wickets. Massie's 16 wickets is easily the most by a bowler in his first Test, and only two players have achieved more in the whole of Test cricket.

Snow took five wickets again in Australia's first innings at Trent Bridge, but, helped by dropped catches, Stackpole made 114 and Australia 315. Lillee and Massie dismissed England for 189, allowing Chappell to declare at 324 for four, with Ross Edwards 170 not out. England easily saved the game at 290 for four.

The Headingley pitch for the fourth Test caused great controversy. It took spin from the first day, when Australia were dismissed for 146, Underwood getting four wickets. Underwood had been recalled for this match, which caused many Australians to become suspicious. England did a little better against Mallett and Inverarity, reaching 263 mainly through Illingworth and Snow adding 104 for the eighth wicket. It was a decisive stand, as Underwood's six for 46 meant Australia made only 136, leaving England only 20 to get for a three- day victory. The explanation for the grassless and uneven wicket was freak weather conditions (storm and sunshine) which caused an outbreak of a fungus called *Fusarium oxysporum*. As John Snow pointed out to disgruntled Australians, by batting first they should have won.

It meant England retained the Ashes but Australia fought well to level the rubber at the Oval. England were all out for 284, thanks to five wickets for Lillee, three of them in four balls. Then 201 runs were added for Australia's third wicket by Ian Chappell (118) and Greg Chappell (113), the first instance of brothers scoring centuries in the same Test innings. Australia made 399. Lillee took another five wickets in the second innings, but England batted well to get 356. Australia were set to get 242, and when Illingworth, Snow and D'Oliveira were unfit to bowl, they made them for the loss of five wickets. Lillee's 31 wickets and Marsh's 23 behind the stumps were Australian records for a tour of England.

Above: Greg Chappell caught by Peter Parfitt at Trent Bridge in 1972. John Snow is the bowler. Chappell was second in the batting averages in a drawn series.

Below: The victorious England team at Old Trafford in 1972. Left to right, back: Luckhurst, Arnold, Greig, Smith, Gifford, Knott. Front: Snow, Boycott, Illingworth, Edrich, D'Oliveira.

1972 51st Series Eng 2, Aus 2, Drawn 1

1 OLD TRAFFORD England won by 89 runs
England 249 (A W Greig 57) and 234 (A W Greig 62, D K Lillee 6–66)
Australia 142 (K R Stackpole 53, J A Snow 4–41, G G Arnold 4–62) and 252 (R W Marsh 91, K R Stackpole 67, A W Greig 4–53, J A Snow 4–87)

2 LORD'S Australia won by 8 wkts
England 272 (A W Greig 54, R A L Massie 8–84) and 116 (R A L Massie 8–53)
Australia 308 (G S Chappell 131, I M Chappell 56, R W Marsh 50, J A Snow 5–57) and 81–2 (K R Stackpole 57)

3 TRENT BRIDGE Match Drawn
Australia 315 (K R Stackpole 114, D J Colley 54, J A Snow 5–92) and 324–4 dec (R Edwards 170, G S Chappell 72, I M Chappell 50)
England 189 (D K Lillee 4–35, R A L Massie 4–43) and 290–4 (B W Luckhurst 96, B L d'Oliveira 50)

4 HEADINGLEY England won by 9 wkts
Australia 146 (K R Stackpole 52, D L Underwood 4–37) and 136 (D L Underwood 6–45)
England 263 (R Illingworth 57, A A Mallett 5–114) and 21–1

5 THE OVAL Australia won by 5 wkts
England 284 (A P E Knott 92, P H Parfitt 51, D K Lillee 5–58) and 356 (B Wood 90, A P E Knott 63, D K Lillee 5–123)
Australia 399 (I M Chappell 118, G S Chappell 113, R Edwards 79, D L Underwood 4–90) and 242–5 (K R Stackpole 79)

1972 Averages

Batting	I	No	Runs	HS	Avge
K.R. Stackpole (A)	10	1	485	114	53.88
G.S. Chappell (A)	10	1	437	131	48.55
R. Edwards (A)	7	1	291	170*	48.50
A.W. Greig (E)	9	1	288	62	36.00
I.M. Chappell (A)	10	0	334	118	33.40

Bowling	O	M	Runs	W	Avge	BB
D.L. Underwood (E)	125	49	266	16	16.62	6–45
D.K. Lillee (E)	249.5	83	548	31	17.67	6–66
R.A.L. Massie (A)	199.1	58	409	23	17.78	8–53
G.G. Arnold (E)	110.5	25	279	13	21.46	4–62
J.A. Snow (E)	205.5	46	555	24	23.12	5–57

Bob Massie made the most sensational debut in modern Test history at Lord's in 1972, taking 16 wickets in his first Test, a record.

1974–75: Lillee and Thomson come together to defeat England

Mike Denness had taken Illingworth's place as captain when England toured Australia in 1974–75. Boycott, whom some thought might have succeeded Illingworth, withdrew from the party for personal reasons.

At Brisbane, the pitch was prepared by the Lord Mayor, who did not like the way the curator was preparing it and, as he was also a member of the cricket ground trust, dismissed him. Australia had first use of it and made 309. Despite Greig's 110, England finished 44 behind. Chappell's declaration at 288 for five set England a task of scoring 333 in 400 minutes, but Jeff Thomson, whom they were meeting for the first time, took six for 46 (nine in the match) and their score of 166 meant defeat by the same amount. Amiss batted in the second innings with a broken thumb and Edrich with a broken hand, and Cowdrey was flown out to reinforce the batting.

At Perth, Titmus reappeared for the first time since losing four toes in an accident in the West Indies in 1968. Chappell put England in, and rapidly out again for 208. Ross Edwards and Walters made centuries for Australia, Walters between tea and the close on the second day. Australia led by 272 and needed only 21 in the fourth innings to win by nine wickets.

England were put in again at Melbourne, and made 242. Five wickets for Willis helped England to dismiss Australia for 241. They then made 244, with Amiss scoring 90, and a very close match was finally drawn with Australia eight runs short of victory with two wickets left.

Denness dropped himself for the fourth Test at Sydney, where Australia won the toss again, but this time batted. Australia made 405, and led by 110 on first innings, then declared at 289 for four with Redpath

and Greg Chappell each getting centuries and adding 220 for the second wicket. England made 228, Australia winning with just over 10 overs left. Edrich captained England but was forced to go to hospital when hit in the ribs by Lillee when facing his first ball in the second innings. He suffered his second fracture of the series, but returned to be 33 not out at the end of the innings.

At Adelaide, Denness returned as captain and put Australia in on a damp pitch after the first day was lost to rain. Underwood reduced Australia to 84 for five, but the tail wagged and 304 was too many against Lillee and Thomson. England were out for 172, and Australia declared at 272 for five, Underwood having taken 11 of the 15 Australian wickets to fall. Thomson could not bowl in the second innings, having injured his shoulder playing tennis on the rest day, but England still fell 164 short of the target of 405.

Peter Lever replaced the injured Willis for the sixth Test at Melbourne and took six for 38 as Australia were rushed out for 152. Lillee bruised his foot after six overs and retired. Without Lillee or Thomson bowling England prospered, Denness (188) and Fletcher (146), two disappointments of the tour, adding 192 for the fourth wicket. England reached 529, with Max Walker

Jeff Thomson was the outstanding bowler in the 1974–75 series. This catch at Melbourne shows one wicket-keeper dismissing another: Knott caught Marsh bowled Thomson for four.

taking eight for 143, his best Test figures. Despite Greg Chappell's century, Australia were beaten by an innings and four runs.

1974–75   52nd Series   Aus 4, Eng 1, Drawn 1

1 BRISBANE   Australia won by 166 runs
Australia 309 (I M Chappell 90, G S Chappell 58, R G D Willis 4–56) and 288–5 dec (G S Chappell 71, K D Walters 62, R Edwards 53)
England 265 (A W Greig 110, M H N Walker 4–73) and 166 (J R Thomson 6–46)

2 PERTH   Australia won by 9 wkts
England 208 (A P E Knott 51) and 293 (F J Titmus 61, J R Thomson 5–93)
Australia 481 (R Edwards 115, K D Walters 103, G S Chappell 62) and 23–1

3 MELBOURNE   Match Drawn
England 242 (A P E Knott 52, J R Thomson 4–72) and 244 (D L Amiss 90, A W Greig 60, A A Mallett 4–60, J R Thomson 4–72)
Australia 241 (I R Redpath 55, R G D Willis 5–61) and 238–8 (G S Chappell 61, A W Greig 4–56)

4 SYDNEY   Australia won by 171 runs
Australia 405 (G S Chappell 84, R B McCosker 80, I M Chappell 53, G G Arnold 5–86, A W Greig 4–104) and 289–4 dec (G S Chappell 144, I R Redpath 105)
England 295 (A P E Knott 82, J H Edrich 50, J R Thomson 4–74) and 228 (A W Greig 54, A A Mallett 4–21)

5 ADELAIDE   Australia won by 163 runs
Australia 304 (T J Jenner 74, K D Walters 55, D L Underwood 7–113) and 273–5 dec (K D Walters 71, R W Marsh 55, I R Redpath 52, D L Underwood 4–102)
England 172 (M H Denness 51, D K Lillee 4–49) and 241 (A P E Knott 106, K W R Fletcher 63, D K Lillee 4–69)

6 MELBOURNE   England won by an innings and 4 runs
Australia 152 (I M Chappell 65, P Lever 6–38) and 373 (G S Chappell 102, I R Redpath 83, R B McCosker 76, I M Chappell 50, A W Greig 4–88)
England 529 (M H Denness 188, K W R Fletcher 146, A W Greig 89, J H Edrich 70, M H N Walker 8–143)

1974–75 Averages

Batting

	I	No	Runs	HS	Avge
G.S. Chappell (A)	11	0	608	144	55.27
J.H. Edrich (E)	7	1	260	70	43.33
I.R. Redpath (A)	12	1	472	105	42.90
K.D. Walters (A)	11	2	383	103	42.55
A.W. Greig (E)	11	0	446	110	40.54
A.P.E. Knott (E)	11	1	364	106*	36.40
K.W.R. Fletcher (E)	9	0	324	146	36.00
M.H. Denness (E)	9	0	318	188	35.33
I.M. Chappell (A)	12	1	387	90	35.18
R.W. Marsh (A)	11	2	313	55	34.77
R. Edwards (A)	9	1	261	115	32.62

Bowling

	O	M	Runs	W	Avge	BB
J.R. Thomson (A)	175.1	34	592	33	17.93	6–46
A.A. Mallett (A)	140.6	47	339	17	19.94	4–21
D.K. Lillee (A)	182.6	36	596	25	23.84	4–49
M.H.N. Walker (A)	218.7	46	684	23	29.73	8–143

Right: Tony Greig driving at Sydney in the fourth Test, where he was top scorer in England's second innings. Greig was defiant in a losing side.

Far right: Rodney Marsh, whose total dismissals in Tests is a record for a wicket-keeper. Marsh's career was almost exactly contemporary with Lillee's, and each achieved a record number of Test victims.

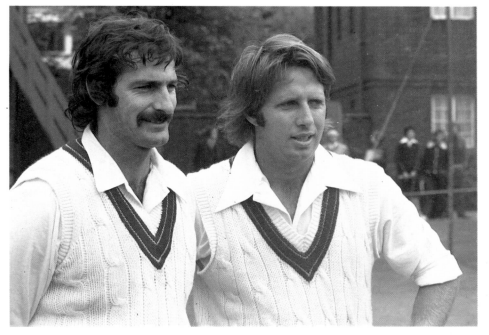

Left: In 1974–75 the Australian fast bowlers, Dennis Lillee (left) and Jeff Thomson, routed the English tourists and became known collectively as 'Lillian Thomson'. Between them they took 58 wickets.

Left: The Australian team at Sydney in 1974–75. Left to right, back: Walters, Thomson, Lillee, Walker, Mallett, McCosker, Jenner. Front: Marsh, Redpath, Ian Chappell, Edwards, Greg Chappell. Australia won by 171 runs, and took the series by four matches to one.

Knott, Alan Philip Eric

Born in Belvedere, Kent, on 9 April 1946, Knott made his debut for the county in 1964. He became the third in a line of Kent wicket-keepers (Ames, Evans, Knott) who kept for England for most of 50 years. A fitness fanatic, he frequently performed his callisthenics at the wicket. Small and agile, he batted in the same darting and quick-footed manner as he kept wicket. He made his Test debut in 1967, and in 95 Tests he caught 250 and stumped 19 batsmen, at the time a record. He also scored 4,389 runs, average 32.75, making him a genuine all-rounder. His Test career was cut short by a combination of World Series Cricket, a 'rebel' South African tour and a final distaste for touring every winter.

1975: Australia win a short series

England played a four-match series with Australia after the first Prudential World Cup in 1975. At Edgbaston, Denness put Australia in, who went on to make 359. After one over of England's reply, a thunderstorm wrecked the wicket and England were shot out for 101 by Lillee and Walker. Following on they made 173, Thomson this time getting five wickets, and lost by an innings and 85. Graham Gooch, in his first Test, bagged a pair. Denness was much criticized for his decision to field, and was dropped for the second Test.

Greig assumed the captaincy at Lord's and prudently batted. He also scored 96, helping England recover from a bad start to 315. David Steele made 50 in his first Test. Australia made 268, recovering from 133 for eight thanks to 99 from Ross Edwards and a career first-class best score from Lillee of 73 not out. Edrich made 175, enabling England to declare at 436 for seven, but Australia easily batted out time for a draw.

The prospect of an exciting finish at Headingley was ruined by vandals. England made 288 and rushed through Australia, who could manage only 135, with Phil Edmonds, in his first Test, taking five for 28. In the second knock England made 291 (Steele top-scored in each innings) and set Australia to get 445 to win. At the end of the fourth day they were making a good attempt at 220 for three, with McCosker 95 not out. Overnight, however, vandals protesting the innocence of a man serving a prison sentence, damaged the pitch with knives and oil, ending the play. Rain for most of the afternoon might well have meant a draw in any case.

In the fourth and last Test at the Oval, Australia made 532 for nine declared, with McCosker (127) and Ian Chappell (192) making centuries. England could manage only 191 and followed on. They recovered well, however, saving the match with 538 in the second innings, Bob Woolmer, in only his second Test, making 149 in 499 minutes. This was the longest first-class match played in England, covering six days with just over three hours for stoppages.

1975 53rd Series Aus 1, Eng 0, Drawn 3

1 EDGBASTON Australia won by an innings and 85 runs

Australia 359 (R W Marsh 61, R B McCosker 59, R Edwards 56, I M Chappell 52)

England 101 (D K Lillee 5–15, M H N Walker 5–48) and 173 (K W R Fletcher 51, J R Thomson 5–38)

2 LORD'S Match Drawn

England 315 (A W Greig 96, A P E Knott 69, D S Steele 50, D K Lillee 4–84) and 436–7 dec (J H Edrich 175, B Wood 52)

Australia 268 (R Edwards 99, J A Snow 4–66) and 329–3 (I M Chappell 86, R B McCosker 79, G S Chappell 73, R Edwards 52)

3 HEADINGLEY Match Drawn

England 288 (D S Steele 73, J H Edrich 62, A W Greig 51, G J Gilmour 6–85) and 291 (D S Steele 92)

Australia 135 (P H Edmonds 5–28) and 220–3 (R B McCosker 95, I M Chappell 62)

4 THE OVAL Match Drawn

Australia 532–9 dec (I M Chappell 192, R B McCosker 127, K D Walters 65) and 40–2

England 191 (J R Thomson 4–50, M H N Walker 4–63) and 538 (R A Woolmer 149, J H Edrich 96, G R J Roope 77, D S Steele 66, A P E Knott 64, K D Walters 4–34, D K Lillee 4–91)

1975 Averages

Batting	I	No	Runs	HS	Avge
R.B. McCosker (A)	7	2	414	127	82.80
I.M. Chappell (A)	6	0	429	192	71.50
D.S. Steele (E)	6	0	365	92	60.83
R.A. Woolmer (E)	4	0	218	149	54.50
J.H. Edrich (E)	8	0	428	175	53.50
R. Edwards (A)	6	1	253	99	50.60
A.P.E. Knott (E)	8	1	261	69	37.28
A.W. Greig (E)	8	0	284	96	35.50

Bowling	O	M	Runs	W	Avge	BB
D.K. Lillee (A)	207	72	460	21	21.90	5–15
J.R. Thomson (A)	175.1	56	457	16	28.56	5–38
J.A. Snow (E)	135.5	31	355	11	32.27	4–66
M.H.N. Walker (A)	204.1	59	486	14	34.71	5–48

Below left: Ian Chappell, captain of the 1975 Australians to England, driving at the Oval, and *below right* Max Walker bowling to John Edrich at Lord's. Walker and Edrich were the consistent players who did not always attract the headlines, but were vital to their sides.

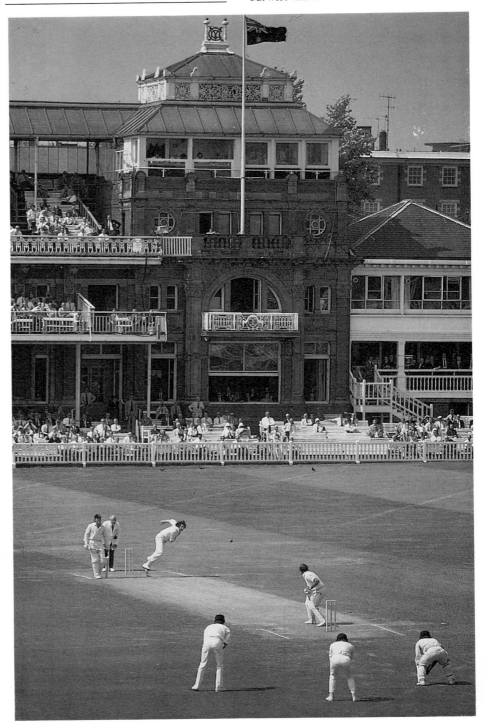

1976–77: The Centenary Test provides exciting match

On their way home from a tour of India and Sri Lanka, England called in at Melbourne to play a match there to celebrate the first Test at Melbourne 100 years earlier.

All past Ashes cricketers were invited to what was an outstanding cricket and social occasion.

Greig and Greg Chappell were captains, and England put Australia in, performing well to dismiss them for 138. However Australia, particularly Lillee (6–26) and Walker (4–54), did even better and England were shot out for 95. Sanity returned to the batting in the second innings, and Marsh became the first Australian wicket-keeper to score a century against England. Australia declared at 419 for nine, setting England to get 463 to win. Lillee took five wickets again, but for 139, and England made a great attempt, getting to 346 for four at one stage. Derek Randall batted brilliantly for 174, but the tail-enders could not quite sustain the effort, and the innings closed at 417. Australia's winning margin, 45 runs, was by coincidence the same as that in the first Test 100 years before.

The two teams for the Centenary Test Match at Melbourne on 12–17 March 1977. *Left to right, back*: D.L. Amiss, D.W. Hookes, R.A. Woolmer, G.J. Gilmour, J.K. Lever, K.J. O'Keeffe, R.G.D. Willis, G.J. Cosier, C.M. Old, S.J. Rixon, G.D. Barlow, R.J. Bright, I.C. Davis, D.W. Randall. *Front*: K.W.R. Fletcher, M.H.N. Walker, A.P.E. Knott, R.W. Marsh, A.W. Greig, G.S. Chappell, J.M. Brearley, K.D. Walters, D.L. Underwood, D.K. Lillee. Another

player, R.B. McCosker, was absent with a broken jaw.

Below: The Centenary Test at Melbourne in 1977 was a splendid occasion attended by many old Test cricketers. Derek Randall was the man of the match for his second-innings 174, and is shown staring belligerently at the most successful bowler, Dennis Lillee.

1976–77   54th Series (Centenary Test)   Aus 1, Eng 0
MELBOURNE   **Australia won by 45 runs**
Australia 138 and 419–9 dec (R W Marsh 110, I C Davis 68, K
   D Walters 66, D W Hookes 56, C M Old 4–104)
England 95 (D K Lillee 6–26, M H N Walker 4–54) and 417 (D W
   Randall 174, D L Amiss 64, D K Lillee 5–139)

1977: Botham arrives and Boycott returns in triumph

The 1977 tour to England came after the revelation that Kerry Packer had signed up many of the world's leading cricketers for World Series Cricket. Greig lost the England captaincy (but not his place), through his part in the operation, Brearley taking over. Lillee did not tour.

The first Test at Lord's was staged as a Jubilee Test, celebrating 25 years of Queen Elizabeth's reign. England batted and made only 216. Willis then bowled well, taking seven for 78, but Australia took a first-innings lead of 80. In the second innings Woolmer made 120, but England lost four wickets at 286, and totalled only 305. The England bowlers were on top in the final innings, but because nearly a day had been lost to rain, Australia held out for a draw at 114 for six.

At Old Trafford, all six England bowlers got at least one wicket, but Australia made a respectable 297. Woolmer's 137, made in partnerships with Randall and Greig, led to England getting 437 and leading by 140. Greg Chappell made an elegant 112 in Australia's second knock, but he was one of Underwood's victims in his six for 66, and he had little support, scoring over half Australia's 218. England needed only 79 and won by nine wickets.

At Trent Bridge Ian Botham made his debut and took five for 74 as Australia were dismissed for 243. Boycott returned to Test cricket after missing 30 matches and in an eventful innings ran out Randall, made 20 in his first three hours and was dropped in the slips by McCosker. England were 82 for five when Knott joined him. The two added 215, Boycott making 107 and Knott 135, the highest by a wicket-keeper in Ashes matches. England made 364. McCosker made a century in 309, but England needed only 189 to win, and won by seven wickets. Boycott (80 not out) became the second batsman (after M.L. Jaisimha) to bat on all five days of a Test.

At Headingley Boycott was centre stage again, becoming the first batsman to score his hundredth century in a Test match. He went on to 191 in a total of 436. Australia fell to some excellent swing bowling by Hendrick (4–41) and Botham (5–21). All out 103, they followed on and were dismissed again for 248, Randall performing a somersault after catching Marsh to retain the Ashes. Boycott who batted throughout England's innings, was on the field for the whole of the match.

Australia put England in at the Oval and out again for 214, by courtesy of M.F. Malone (5–63 in his first Test) and Thomson. After a shaky start Australia made 385; but nearly 12 hours, including the whole of the first day, had been lost to rain, and a draw was obvious from early in the game.

Greig, Malone and Walker ended their Test careers, largely because of WSC. Boycott averaged 147.33, a record for Ashes matches.

1977 55th Series Eng 3, Aus 0, Drawn 2

1 LORD'S **Match Drawn**
England 216 (R A Woolmer 79, D W Randall 53, J R Thomson 4–41) and 305 (R A Woolmer 120, A W Greig 91, J R Thomson 4–86)
Australia 296 (C S Serjeant 81, G S Chappell 66, K D Walters 53, R G D Willis 7–78) and 114–6 (D W Hookes 50)

2 OLD TRAFFORD **England won by 9 wkts**
Australia 297 (K D Walters 88) and 218 (G S Chappell 112, D L Underwood 6–66)
England 437 (R A Woolmer 137, D W Randall 79, A W Greig 76) and 82–1

3 TRENT BRIDGE **England won by 7 wkts**
Australia 243 (R B McCosker 51, I T Botham 5–74) and 309 (R B McCosker 107, R G D Willis 5–88)
England 364 (A P E Knott 135, G Boycott 107, L S Pascoe 4–80) and 189–3 (J M Brearley 81, G Boycott 80)

4 HEADINGLEY **England won by an innings and 85 runs**
England 436 (G Boycott 191, A P E Knott 57, L S Pascoe 4–91, J R Thomson 4–113)
Australia 103 (I T Botham 5–21, M Hendrick 4–41) and 248 (R W Marsh 63, M Hendrick 4–54)

5 THE OVAL **Match Drawn**
England 214 (M F Malone 5–63, J R Thomson 4–87) and 57–2
Australia 385 (D W Hookes 85, M H N Walker 78, R W Marsh 57, R G D Willis 5–102)

1977 Averages

Batting
	I	No	Runs	HS	Avge
G. Boycott (E)	5	2	442	191	147.33
R.A. Woolmer (E)	8	1	394	137	56.28
G.S. Chappell (A)	9	0	371	112	41.22
A.P.E. Knott (E)	7	0	255	135	36.42
D.W. Hookes (A)	9	0	283	85	31.44
R.B. McCosker (A)	9	0	255	107	28.33

Bowling
	O	M	Runs	W	Avge	BB
R.G.D. Willis (E)	166.4	36	534	27	19.77	7–78
M. Hendrick (E)	128.4	33	290	14	20.71	4–41
J.R. Thomson (A)	200.5	44	583	23	25.34	4–41
D.L. Underwood (E)	169.1	61	362	13	27.84	6–66
L.S. Pascoe (A)	137.4	35	363	13	27.92	4–80
M.H.N. Walker (A)	273.2	88	551	14	39.35	3–40

Left: A shot that was a landmark in Test history. Geoff Boycott drives Greg Chappell for four runs and becomes the first player to score his 100th century in a Test match.

1978–79: England much too good for a Packer-depleted Australia

The 1978–79 series in Australia was played in opposition to the World Series Cricket matches. Those players who had signed for Kerry Packer's rival to Test cricket were not considered. Australia suffered most. While England lost four of her best players, Australia had to find almost a whole new team.

Brearley, although not considered worthy of a Test place as a batsman, retained the England captaincy, while Graeme Yallop led Australia.

In the first Test, England's fast bowlers reduced Australia to 26 for six, which became 116 all out. England took a first-innings lead of 170, despite Rodney Hogg taking six for 74 in his first Test. Hughes and Yallop both made centuries, but Randall ensured England's seven-wicket victory.

At Perth, Yallop put England in, but after three quick wickets had fallen Gower made a century and England reached 309. Good bowling by Willis then helped put out Australia for 190. England set Australia to score 328 and won easily by 166 runs. Hogg took five wickets in each innings. There was criticism of some umpiring decisions, and on the last day umpire Tom Brookes announced his retirement.

The Melbourne pitch had numerous bare patches, and Australia were lucky enough to win the toss and bat. Allan Border made his debut and a determined century by Graeme

Wood was the foundation of a score of 258. Fourteen wickets tumbled on a second day in which only 122 runs were scored. England were out for 143, and after Australia's 167 needed 283 to win. They made just 179, Wood's being the only innings over 50. Hogg again took five wickets in each innings to have 26 in his first three Tests.

England were dismissed for 152 at Sydney in temperatures so hot that Australia's wicket-keeper John Maclean retired with heat exhaustion. When Australia scored 294 they looked likely to level the series; Randall, batting very slowly in the tremendous heat, scored 150, allowing England to set a reasonable target of 203. Australia then collapsed before the off-spin of Emburey and Miller for 111, and were defeated by 93. Border was not out in each innings.

Put in at Adelaide, England were 27 for five, but thanks to Botham reached 169. Botham was also prominent in dismissing Australia for five fewer. They weren't helped by an accident to Darling, who was struck on the heart by a ball from Willis in the first over, and was given the kiss of life by Emburey and umpire O'Connell before being stretchered off. He resumed later. Bob Taylor made 97, his highest Test score, in the second innings, and Australia, needing 366, lost by 205.

At Sydney, Yallop, coming in at 19 for two, scored 121 of the last 179 runs. His share of the whole Australian innings of 198 was 61.11 per cent. England made 308, and with Miller and Emburey again getting to work on a wearing wicket, England were set only 44 to get, and won the series by 5–1. Hogg, however, with 41 wickets, set a new series record for Australia against England.

1978–79   56th Series   Eng 5, Aus 1

1 BRISBANE   England won by 7 wkts
Australia 116 (R G D Willis 4–44) and 339 (K J Hughes 129, G N Yallop 102)
England 286 (D W Randall, 75, R M Hogg 6–74, A G Hurst 4–93) and 170–3 (D W Randall 74)

2 PERTH   England won by 166 runs
England 309 (D I Gower 102, G Boycott 77, R M Hogg 5–65) and 208 (R M Hogg 5–57)
Australia 190 (P M Toohey 81, R G D Willis 5–44) and 161 (G M Wood 64, J K Lever 4–28)

3 MELBOURNE   Australia won by 103 runs
Australia 258 (G M Wood 100) and 167
England 143 (R M Hogg 5–30) and 179 (R M Hogg 5–36)

4 SYDNEY   England won by 93 runs
England 152 (I T Botham 5–28, A G Hurst 5–28) and 346 (D W Randall 150, J M Brearley 53, J D Higgs 5–148, R M Hogg 4–67)
Australia 294 (W M Darling 91, A R Border 60) and 111 (J E Emburey 4–46)

5 ADELAIDE   England won by 205 runs
England 169 (I T Botham 74, R M Hogg 4–26) and 360 (R W Taylor 97, G Miller 64, A G Hurst 4–97)
Australia 164 (I T Botham 4–42) and 160

6 SYDNEY   England won by 9 wkts
Australia 198 (G N Yallop 121, I T Botham 4–57) and 143 (B Yardley 61, G Miller 5–44, J E Emburey 4–52)
England 308 (G A Gooch 74, D I Gower 65, J D Higgs 4–69) and 35–1

1978–79 Averages

Batting	I	No	Runs	HS	Avge
D.I. Gower (E)	11	1	420	102	42.00
D.W. Randall (E)	12	2	385	150	38.50
G.N. Yallop (A)	12	0	391	121	32.58
I.T. Botham (E)	10	0	291	74	29.10
K.J. Hughes (A)	12	0	345	129	28.75
G.M. Wood (A)	12	0	344	100	28.66
G. Boycott (E)	12	0	263	77	21.91

Bowling	O	M	Runs	W	Avge	BB
R.M. Hogg (A)	217.4	60	527	41	12.85	6–74
G. Miller (E)	177.1	54	346	23	15.04	5–44
M. Hendrick (E)	145	30	299	19	15.73	3–19
J.E. Emburey (E)	144.4	49	306	16	19.12	4–46
R.G.D. Willis (E)	140.3	23	461	20	23.05	5–44
A.G. Hurst (A)	204.2	44	577	25	23.08	5–28
J.D. Higgs (A)	196.6	47	468	19	24.63	5–148
I.I. Botham (E)	158.4	25	567	23	24.65	4–42

Above: England easily won the 1978–79 series played without the WSC players. Gooch catches Maclean off Miller in the second Test at Perth.

Below: Ray Illingworth was a successful English captain in the 1970s, whose main achievement was the winning of the Ashes in 1970–71.

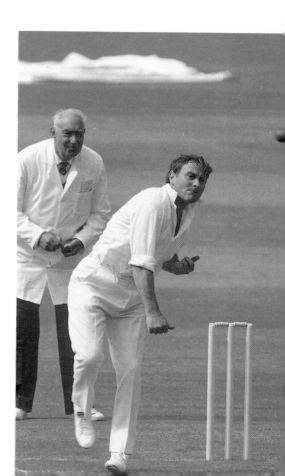

1979–80: Post-Packer Australians take their revenge for the previous season

When the rift between 'establishment' cricket and WSC was healed, part of the deal involved the cancellation of the Indian tour to Australia in 1979–80, with both England and West Indies touring and playing three-match series against the home side. England claimed the Ashes were not at stake, but Australia reckoned they were.

All the WSC cricketers returned to the Australian side, captained by Greg Chappell, but England took only Underwood of the Packer players.

Brearley put Australia in at Perth, but early success was cancelled by 99 from Kim Hughes, Australia getting 244 (Botham 6–78). Lillee began to bat with a bat made of aluminium, and held up play with a ten-minute tantrum when asked to change it for a wooden one. A century by Border helped Australia to 337 in the second innings, when the score-card entry everybody had been waiting for appeared: Lillee c Willey b Dilley. Botham took 11 wickets in the match. Boycott batted throughout England's second innings, but was left on 99 not out when the innings closed at 215. Dymock took six for 34.

The pitch at Sydney was left exposed to a pre-match storm, and when Chappell won the toss the match was virtually settled on the shortened first day, when England were 90 for seven. Australia also had difficulty on the second day, but established a lead of 22. Gower, batting at number seven, made 98 not out as the pitch began to ease, but Greg Chappell made an identical score as Australia won an unsatisfactory match by six wickets.

England began well at Melbourne, collapsed, and then rallied to reach 306. Gooch was run out attempting a silly run when 99, and Lillee (6–60) passed 200 Test wickets. Solid batting by Australia, highlighted by Greg Chappell's century, took them to 477, and England were still well behind at 92 for six in the second innings. Botham then made a magnificent 119 not out, but Australia still had a target of only 103 and made a clean sweep of the three matches.

1979–80   57th Series   Aus 3, Eng 0
1 PERTH   Australia won by 138 runs
Australia 244 (K J Hughes 99, I T Botham 6–78) and 337 (A R Border 115, J M Wiener 58, I T Botham 5–98)
England 228 (J M Brearley 64, D K Lillee 4–73) and 215 (G Boycott 99, G Dymock 6–34)
2 SYDNEY   Australia won by 6 wkts
England 123 (D K Lillee 4–40, G Dymock 4–42) and 237 (D I Gower 98)
Australia 145 (I T Botham 4–29) and 219–4 (G S Chappell 98)
3 MELBOURNE   Australia won by 8 wkts
England 306 (G A Gooch 99, J M Brearley 60, D K Lillee 6–60) and 273 (I T Botham 119, G A Gooch 51, D K Lillee 5–78, L S Pascoe 4–80)
Australia 477 (G S Chappell 114, I M Chappell 75, B M Laird 74, A R Border 63, J K Lever 4–111) and 103–2

1979–80 Averages

Batting	I	No	Runs	HS	Avge
G.S. Chappell (A)	6	2	317	114	79.25

Bowling	O	M	Runs	W	Avge	BB
G. Dymock (A)	130.3	40	260	17	15.29	6–34
D.K. Lillee (A)	155.1	41	388	23	16.86	6–34
I.T. Botham (E)	173.1	62	371	19	19.52	6–78
L.S. Pascoe (A)	93.5	17	241	10	24.10	4–80
D.L. Underwood (E)	160.2	48	405	13	31.15	3–71

Above: Australian jubilation as Miller is caught by Maclean off Hurst in the fourth Test at Sydney in 1978–79.

Underwood, Derek Leslie
Underwood was born on 8 June 1945 at Bromley, Kent, and first appeared for Kent in 1963. He was a left-arm slow or slow-medium bowler, devastating on damaged pitches. He first played for England in 1966 and played in 86 Tests, taking 297 wickets, average 25.83. Had he not joined WSC and then the 'rebel' tour to South Africa, which virtually ended his Test career, he would probably have become the leading wicket-taker in Tests.

1980: The second Centenary Test Match

The 1980 match at Lord's was to celebrate the centenary of the first Test in England, in 1880 at the Oval. Botham led England.

The match was marred by rain, and will be remembered for its off-the-pitch incidents more than the play. Chappell batted, and centuries by Wood and Hughes allowed a declaration at 385 for five. But play had been lost on the first two days, and when the umpires returned from a pitch inspection on Saturday afternoon they and Botham were jostled by MCC members when entering the pavilion. There was little hope of a result, despite a second Australian declaration which set England 370 in 350 minutes. Boycott made a not-out century as a sad match fizzled out into a draw.

1980   58th Series (Centenary Test)   Drawn 1
LORD'S   Match Drawn
Australia 385–5 dec (K J Hughes 117, G M Wood 112, A R Border 56) and 189–4 dec (K J Hughes 84, G S Chappell 59)
England 205 (G Boycott 62, L S Pascoe 5–59, D K Lillee 4–43) and 244–3 (G Boycott 128, M W Gatting 51)

1981: Botham's magnificent season as he and England recover

The 1981 series was one of the most exciting of modern times, rivalling 1902 in its twists, and in dramatic finishes.

Ian Botham and Kim Hughes led their countries in the first Test at Trent Bridge, the first Test match in England in which cricket was played on Sunday – there was no rest day in the middle. Terry Alderman and Trevor Chappell made debuts for Australia – Chappell being the brother of Ian and Greg, the first instance of three brothers all playing for Australia.

Kim Hughes in the Centenary match at Lord's in 1980, when between the showers he made 117 and 84.

the Monday evening was magical – he reached his century in 87 balls, having scored 62 of the last 64 in boundaries. The pair added 117 for the eighth wicket, when Old (29) provided further support in a stand of 67 for the ninth. Willis helped add a last-wicket 37, leaving Botham not out 149 and England 129 ahead. Botham scored 106 in the final session on Monday.

The last wicket fell very early on the last day – it still seemed a formality for Australia. But Willis began to take wickets with regularity after Botham had got the first, and in a remarkable spell the score slid from 56 for one to 75 for eight. A mini-stand of 35 between Bright and Lillee threatened the story-book ending but both fell to Willis and England won by 18 runs. Willis took eight for 43 on the last day. It was only the second time in Test cricket that a side had won after following on, and this was a much more incredible fight-back. Two Australians, however, had something to celebrate: Alderman again had nine wickets in the match, and Marsh passed Knott's wicket-keeping record of 263 dismissals in Tests.

In the fourth Test, England were dismissed for 189, Alderman getting five wickets. Australia took a lead of 69 (with the help of 44 extras) and having put England out again for 219 needed only 151 to win. Forty-six

were needed with five wickets left when Botham came into the attack. Botham claimed them all for 11 runs and England won by 29. No batsman reached 50 – the first such occurrence for 46 years.

At Old Trafford, England reached 231, of which 92 came from the last two wickets. Australia, however, could do no better than 130. England then batted so slowly that in the Saturday pre-lunch session only 29 runs were scored in the 28 overs bowled. Tavare, the principal reason, eventually scored 78 in 423 minutes, including the slowest-ever first-class 50 in England. Botham, coming in at 104 for five, despite first playing himself in, then reached 100 in 86 balls, batting with controlled power and brilliance. Some thought it his best innings. When Lillee and Alderman took the new ball he scored 66 in eight overs. Knott and Emburey consolidated, and England reached 404.

Yallop and Border, who batted with a broken finger, each made centuries, Yallop stylishly and Border grittily and Australia reached 402, but lost by 103. Botham, for the third match running, was chosen Man of the Match. Whitney played the first of his

The two England captains of 1981, Ian Botham, left, and Mike Brearley. The series was a triumph for both.

England were put in in conditions favouring swing bowling, and Alderman (4–68), supported by Lillee and Hogg, dismissed them for 185. Australia however fared no better against England's seamers and were removed for 179. At the end of three days interrupted by rain and bad light, England were 94 for six. Sunday was at last a sunny day, and Australia, needing 132 to win, made them for a four-wicket victory. Alderman took nine wickets.

There were more interruptions at Lord's, and more scenes of crowd dissatisfaction when the sun shone brightly after play had been abandoned on the second day. England were put in again but the match was destined for a draw when they compiled a slow 311, Lawson taking seven for 81. Play was well into the fourth day when Australia were dismissed for 345 (of which 32 were no-balls). An England declaration was no more than a formality. Botham made a pair and resigned as England captain while the selectors were considering his sacking. Brearley was appointed captain for the rest of the series.

The third Test at Headingley was one of the most extraordinary in the series, and was a great personal triumph for Ian Botham. Australia batted first and a century by Dyson was the basis of a good score of 401 for nine declared. Botham took six for 95, and when England batted was the only player to reach 50, the side being all out for 174. The follow-on was enforced and Gooch was out for the second time in one day. Botham came in at 105 for five, which soon became 135 for seven. At this stage, with 92 still required to avoid the innings defeat, England were quoted in the betting tent at 500–1, odds which Lillee and Marsh actually took for a small amount. With Dilley (56) in support, Botham's batting on

two Tests, having been summoned from Gloucestershire when about to play only his seventh first-class match (Hogg and Lawson were injured).

At the Oval, Australia led on the first innings after centuries by Border and Boycott and Dirk Wellham made a century in his first Test in the second innings. England saved the game with three wickets to spare. Botham took 10 wickets in the match and Lillee 11, but Alderman's five made him the leading bowler of the series. His 42 wickets remain second to Grimmett's 44 against South Africa among Australians.

1981   59th Series   Eng 3, Aus 1, Drawn 2

1 TRENT BRIDGE   **Australia won by 4 wkts**
England 185 (M W Gatting 52, T M Alderman 4–68) and 125 (D K Lillee 5–46, T M Alderman 5–62)
Australia 179 (A R Border 63) and 132–6 (G R Dilley 4–24)

2 LORD'S   **Match Drawn**
England 311 (P Willey 82, M W Gatting 59, G F Lawson 7–81) and 265–8 dec (D I Gower 89, G Boycott 60)
Australia 345 (A R Border 64) and 90–4 (G M Wood 62)

3 HEADINGLEY   **England won by 18 runs**
Australia 401–9 dec (J Dyson 102, K J Hughes 89, G N Yallop 58, I T Botham 6–95) and 111 (R G D Willis 8–43)
England 174 (I T Botham 50, D K Lillee 4–49) and 356 (I T Botham 149, G R Dilley 56, T M Alderman 6–135)

4 EDGBASTON   **England won by 29 runs**
England 189 (T M Alderman 5–42) and 219 (R J Bright 5–68)
Australia 258 (J E Emburey 4–43) and 121 (I T Botham 5–11)

5 OLD TRAFFORD   **England won by 103 runs**
England 231 (C J Tavare 69, P J W Allott 52, D K Lillee 4–55, T M Alderman 4–88) and 404 (I T Botham 118, C J Tavare 78, A P E Knott 59, J E Emburey 57, T M Alderman 5–109)
Australia 130 (M F Kent 52, R G D Willis 4–63) and 402 (A R Border 123, G N Yallop 114)

6 THE OVAL   **Match Drawn**
Australia 352 (A R Border 106, G M Wood 66, M F Kent 54, I T Botham 6–125, R G D Willis 4–91) and 344–9 dec (D M Wellham 103, A R Border 84, R W Marsh 52, M Hendrick 4–82, I T Botham 4–128)
England 314 (G Boycott 137, M W Gatting 53, D K Lillee 7–89) and 261–7 (A P E Knott 70, M W Gatting 56, J M Brearley 51, D K Lillee 4–70)

Boycott lbw to Lillee in 1981.

| 1981 Averages | | | | | |
Batting	I	No	Runs	HS	Avge
A.R. Border (A)	12	3	533	123*	59.22
I.T. Botham (E)	12	1	399	149*	36.27
G. Boycott (E)	12	0	392	137	32.66
M.W. Gatting (E)	12	0	370	59	30.83
G.M. Wood (A)	12	1	310	66	28.18
G.N. Yallop (A)	12	0	316	114	26.33
D.I. Gower (E)	10	0	250	89	25.00
K.J. Hughes (A)	12	0	300	89	25.00

Bowling	O	M	Runs	W	Avge	BB
G.R. Dilley (E)	98	24	275	14	19.64	4–24
I.T. Botham (E)	272.3	81	700	34	20.58	6–95
T.M. Alderman (A)	325	76	893	42	21.26	6–135
D.K. Lillee (A)	311.4	81	870	39	22.30	7–89
R.G.D. Willis (E)	252.4	56	666	29	22.96	8–43
G.F. Lawson (A)	106.1	30	285	12	23.75	7–81
R.J. Bright (A)	191.4	82	390	12	32.50	5–68
J.E. Emburey (E)	193.5	58	399	12	33.25	4–43

Border, Allan Robert

Born on 27 July 1955 at Cremorne, NSW, Border became an all-rounder whose bowling declined as his stubborn left-handed batting developed. He played for New South Wales from 1976–77 before joining Queensland and becoming captain. He made his Test debut in 1978–79 and took over the captaincy in 1984–85. He has the useful habit of playing his best innings when his side is up against it. At Lahore against Pakistan in 1979–80 he became the first to score 150 in each innings of a Test. By the end of the 1986–87 season he had played in 89 Tests, scoring 6,917 runs, average 52.80.

Botham and Taylor after the sensational English victory at Headingley in 1981, 'Botham's Match'.

1982–83: Captains put in opposition and Australia regain Ashes

A 'rebel' tour of South Africa, which was estranged from cricket because of its racial policies, by an English side of Test match strength, and the subsequent three-year ban on those players, weakened the England party to Australia in 1982–83.

At Perth, however, England batted solidly to reach 411 after being put in by Chappell. When the 400 was reached, some drunken supporters of England ran on to the field, and a skirmish developed. Alderman tackled one but so damaged a shoulder that he missed the rest of the season. Greg Chappell scored a century to give Australia a small lead, but Randall replied with another on an easy wicket and the match was drawn.

England were put in again at Brisbane, and were dismissed for 216 by Lawson, who took six for 47. South African-born Kepler Wessels, making his debut as one of five Queensland players in the side, was dropped at 15, and then went on to 162, giving Australia a lead of 122. The England captain Willis took five wickets. England batted better in the second innings, although the total of 309 owed much to an Australian record of 52 extras. Lawson and a restored Thomson shared the wickets equally, Lawson totalling 11 for the match, while Marsh equalled Langley's record of nine catches in a match. Australia won by seven wickets.

Willis made the mistake of putting Australia in at Adelaide. His opposing captain Chappell scored a century in a total of 438. England collapsed from 181 for three to 216 all out, and followed on. This time they reached 247 for three, but collapsed again to 304. Only Gower and Botham batted well in each innings. Lawson took nine wickets in the match, and Australia won comfortably.

England needed to win the last two Tests to square the series. At Melbourne they were put in again. This Test was remarkable in that all four innings were within ten runs of each other. Once again the last seven wickets crashed, 217 for three becoming 284 all out. Australia achieved a lead of three. After England made 294, with the lower order at last contributing well, excellent bowling by Norman Cowans reduced Australia to 218 for nine. Needing 74 more to win, Border and Thomson made half of them by the close on the fourth day, and 18,000 watched free as they attempted the last 37 on the last day. When three short of the England total, Thomson snicked Botham to Tavare at second slip. He could only knock the ball over his head, but Miller came behind him from first slip to catch the ball low down. During the match Marsh claimed his 27th victim of the series, beating the record of J.H.B. Waite of South Africa, which he had equalled seven years earlier.

For the first time in the series, the captain winning the toss batted at Sydney. Australia had a big slice of luck in the first over when Dyson was shown by TV replays to be run out by a very long way. He was allowed to stay (for over five hours), and made 79 out of 314. England, pressing, made 237, but a century from Hughes made a win impossible. Night-watchman Hemmings made 95

on the last day, but the match was drawn, Australia regaining the Ashes. Marsh's record of 28 dismissals remains a series record.

1982–83 60th Series Aus 2, Eng 1, Drawn 2

1 PERTH Match Drawn
England 411 (C J Tavare 89, D W Randall 78, D I Gower 72, B Yardley 5–107) and 358 (D W Randall 115, A J Lamb 56, G F Lawson 5–108)
Australia 424–9 dec (G S Chappell 117, K J Hughes 62, D W Hookes 56, J Dyson 52, G F Lawson 50, G Miller 4–70) and 73–2

2 BRISBANE Australia won by 7 wkts
England 219 (A J Lamb 72, G F Lawson 6–47) and 309 (G Fowler 83, G Miller 60, J R Thomson 5–73, G F Lawson 5–87)
Australia 341 (K C Wessels 162, G S Chappell 53, B Yardley 53, R G D Willis 5–66) and 190–3 (D W Hookes 66)

3 ADELAIDE Australia won by 8 wkts
Australia 438 (G S Chappell 115, K J Hughes 88, I T Botham 4–112) and 83–2
England 216 (A J Lamb 82, D I Gower 60, G F Lawson 4–56) and 304 (D I Gower 114, I T Botham 58, G F Lawson 5–66)

4 MELBOURNE England won by 3 runs
England 284 (C J Tavare 89, A J Lamb 83, R M Hogg 4–69, B Yardley 4–89) and 294 (G Fowler 65, G F Lawson 4–66)
Australia 287 (K J Hughes 66, D W Hookes 53, R W Marsh 53) and 288 (D W Hookes 68, A R Border 62, N G Cowans 6–77)

5 SYDNEY Match Drawn
Australia 314 (A R Border 89, J Dyson 79, I T Botham 4–75) and 382 (K J Hughes 137, A R Border 83, K C Wessels 53)
England 237 (D I Gower 70, D W Randall 70, J R Thomson 5–50) and 314–7 (E E Hemmings 95, B Yardley 4–139)

1982–83 Averages

Batting	I	No	Runs	HS	Avge
K.J. Hughes (A)	8	1	469	137	67.00
D.W. Hookes (A)	8	1	344	68	49.14
G.S. Chappell (A)	10	2	389	117	48.62
K.C. Wessels (A)	8	0	386	162	48.25
D.W. Randall (E)	8	0	365	115	45.62
A.R. Border (A)	9	2	317	89	45.28
D.I. Gower (E)	10	0	441	114	44.10
A.J. Lamb (E)	10	0	414	83	41.40
J. Dyson (A)	10	2	283	79	35.37
I.T. Botham (E)	10	0	270	58	27.00

Bowling	O	M	Runs	W	Avge	BB
J.R. Thomson (A)	128.4	22	411	22	18.68	5–50
G.F. Lawson (A)	230.4	51	687	34	20.20	6–47
R.G.D. Willis (E)	166.3	28	486	18	27.00	5–66
G. Miller (E)	171	50	397	13	30.53	4–70
B. Yardley (A)	292.2	91	793	22	36.04	5–107
I.T. Botham (E)	213.5	35	729	18	40.50	4–75

Graham Gooch, who returned to the England colours in 1985 and made 196 at the Oval.

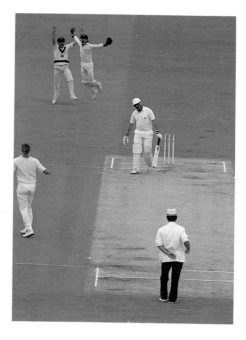

Gooch is caught by Phillips at Edgbaston in 1985 and Jeff Thomson claims his 200th Test wicket.

1985: A day at Edgbaston turns the series England's way

Allan Border was captain of Australia when the 1985 tourists arrived in England. His counterpart was David Gower. The South African 'rebels' were now eligible again.

At Headingley, Andy Hilditch made 119 for Australia, who passed 200 with only two men out but then collapsed to 331. Opener Tim Robinson then made 175, and with good support helped the England total to 533. With rain and bad light playing a part, there was a rush to get Australia out again in time to win. England finally needed 123 in 200 minutes and won by five wickets.

Border put England in at Lord's – and out again for 290 (McDermott 6–70). He then scored an impressive 196, adding 216 for the fifth wicket with Ritchie (94). Australia reached 451, and dismissing England for 261 (Holland 5–68), needed only 127 to win. Five wickets were down for 65, including a run-out by Gower of Wessels from silly point off a defensive stroke. Australia held together, however, to win by four wickets.

At Trent Bridge Gower made 166 on a good pitch, adding 187 with Gatting for the third wicket, which fell at 358. England's 456 was passed by Australia who made 539, with Wood making 172 and Greg Ritchie 146, the pair adding 161 for the sixth wicket. Breaks for rain ensured the match was a high-scoring draw.

Rain also affected the Old Trafford Test, where Gower successfully put Australia in – they made only 257. Gatting made his first Test century in England (160), and with most of the batsmen scoring well, England declared at 482 for nine. Craig McDermott was the only bowler to get a wicket – he took eight for 148 and there was a run-out. On the last day England needed six Australian wickets, but play started late, Border was missed in the first over (he went on to 146 not out) and the match was drawn.

The 1985 Australian party in England. Left to right, back: G.R. Mackay (physiotherapist), R.B. Phillips, Ritchie, Gilbert, McDermott, O'Donnell, Bennett, Holland, Matthews, Wellham, M.P. Ringham (scorer). Front: Wood, Wessels, Thomson, Border, R.F. Merriman (manager), G. Dymock (assistant manager), Hilditch, Lawson, W.B. Phillips, Boon.

There was plenty of rain at Edgbaston, where Australia, put in, had scored 335 for eight, apparently safe from defeat. But Saturday's exciting play determined the series. The last two wickets were taken in the first over, Richard Ellison finishing with six for 77. By close of play England were ahead at 355 for one. Robinson (148) and Gower (215) played brilliantly, eventually adding 331 for the second wicket. Gatting scored a century, and England declared at 595 for five. The only bright spot for Australia was the 200th Test wicket for the recalled Jeff Thomson. Rain seemed the only hope for Australia after they finished the fourth day at 35 for five (Ellison having claimed four for one), and indeed play did not start till 2.30, when Wayne Phillips and Ritchie batted till tea. The break-through was controversial. Phillips, on 59, slashed Edmonds square, and Lamb at silly point, jumped to avoid injury. The ball hit his foot in mid-air and was caught by Gower. The incident occurred so fast that umpire Shepherd and most of the players were unsure of what happened, but square-leg umpire Constant confirmed that Phillips was out. England won with 14 overs to spare. It was the first Ashes Test to be won with the loss of no more than five wickets.

Australia needed to win at the Oval to save the series and the Ashes, but on a fast pitch this seemed unlikely after the first day, when England were 376 for three. This state of affairs arose from a stand of 351 for the second wicket between Gooch (196) and Gower (157). The innings subsided somewhat to 464, but Australia could manage only 241, and then, following on, they batted feebly (apart from Border) before Ellison, who took five for 46, and were out for 129. England thus regained the Ashes 3–1.

1985   61st Series   Eng 3, Aus 1, Drawn 2

1 HEADINGLEY   England won by 5 wkts

Australia 331 (A M J Hilditch 119) and 324 (W B Phillips 91, A M J Hilditch 80, K C Wessels 64, J E Emburey 5–82, I T Botham 4–107)

England 533 (R T Robinson 175, I T Botham 60, P R Downton 54, M W Gatting 53, C J McDermott 4–134) and 123–5

2 LORD'S   Australia won by 4 wkts

England 290 (D I Gower 86, C J McDermott 6–70) and 261 (I T Botham 85, M W Gatting 75, R G Holland 5–68)

Australia 425 (A R Border 196, G M Ritchie 94, I T Botham 5–109) and 127–6

3 TRENT BRIDGE   Match Drawn

England 456 (D I Gower 166, G A Gooch 76, M W Gatting 74, G F Lawson 5–103) and 196–2 (R T Robinson 77)

Australia 539 (G M Wood 172, G M Ritchie 146)

4 OLD TRAFFORD   Match Drawn

Australia 257 (D C Boon 61, P H Edmonds 4–40, I T Botham 4–79) and 340–5 (A R Border 146, K C Wessels 50, J E Emburey 4–99)

England 482–9 dec (M W Gatting 160, G A Gooch 74, A J Lamb 67, C J McDermott 8–141)

5 EDGBASTON   England won by an innings and 118 runs

Australia 335 (K C Wessels 83, G F Lawson 53, R M Ellison 6–77) and 142 (W B Phillips 59, R M Ellison 4–27)

England 595–5 dec (D I Gower 215, R T Robinson 148, M W Gatting 100)

6 THE OVAL   England won by an innings and 94 runs

England 464 (G A Gooch 196, D I Gower 157, G F Lawson 4–101)

Australia 241 (G M Ritchie 64) and 129 (A R Border 58, R M Ellison 5–46)

1985 Averages

Batting	I	No	Runs	HS	Avge
M.W. Gatting (E)	9	3	527	160	87.83
D.I. Gower (E)	9	0	732	215	81.33
A.R. Border (A)	11	2	597	196	66.33
R.T. Robinson (E)	9	1	490	175	61.25
G.A. Gooch (E)	9	0	487	196	54.11
G.M. Ritchie (A)	11	1	422	146	42.20
A.M.J. Hilditch (A)	11	0	424	119	38.54
A.J. Lamb (E)	8	1	256	67	36.57
W.B. Phillips (A)	11	1	350	91	35.00
K.C. Wessels (A)	11	0	368	83	33.45
G.M. Wood (A)	9	0	260	172	28.88

Bowling	O	M	Runs	W	Avge	BB
R.M. Ellison (E)	75.5	20	185	17	10.88	6–77
I.T. Botham (E)	251.4	36	855	31	27.58	5–109
J.E. Emburey (E)	248.4	75	544	19	28.63	5–82
C.J. McDermott (A)	234.2	21	901	30	30.03	8–141
P.H. Edmonds (E)	225.5	59	549	15	36.60	4–40
G.F. Lawson (A)	246	38	830	22	37.72	5–103

Boycott, Geoffrey

Born on 21 October 1940 at Fitzwilliam, Yorkshire, Boycott made his debut for Yorkshire in 1962. He was a very sound and correct opening batsman. He wore spectacles when making his first appearance for England in 1964. Later he changed to contact lenses. He played in 108 Test matches, scoring 8,114 runs, average 47.72. His aggregate was a record until passed by Gavaskar. The highlight of his career was the scoring of his 100th century in a Test match at Headingley in 1977.

1986–87: England keep Ashes with all-round performance

Gatting was Border's opposing captain when England visited Australia in 1986–87. England's form had been wretched in the games before the first Test, in which Border put them in, but the early batsmen applied themselves well, and then Botham came in to play a commanding innings of 138. He hit 22 in an over from Merv Hughes, equalling the 22 he and Tavare (3) had taken from Lillee in 1981. Dilley took five for 68 to help dismiss Australia for 248 and just enforce the follow-on. Geoff Marsh batted the whole of the fourth day for Australia, but nobody stayed with him long enough. Emburey took five for 80 in nearly 43 overs and England needed just 75, winning by eight wickets. DeFreitas, making his debut, was given out, caught, but reinstated after non-striker Botham had intervened and the umpires had conferred.

At Perth, England chose to bat and never looked back after Broad (162) and Athey (96) had put on 223 for the first wicket. Gower added 136 and Jack Richards 133 in his second Test, England declaring at 592 for eight. Border, with 125, led a rearguard action which this time just avoided the follow-on. England declared at 199 for eight, but the Australians found plenty of determination to bat out time.

All the Australian batsmen, led by David Boon (103), got runs at Adelaide, allowing Border to declare at 514 for five. Board and Gatting also scored centuries, however, and England's 455 doomed the match to another draw. Border declared on reaching his hundred on a rain-affected last day, but it was a formality.

At Melbourne, Gatting put Australia in on a true pitch and hustled them out for 141, excellent bowling by Botham and Gladstone Small allowing them to share the wickets. Broad then scored his third century in consecutive Ashes Tests, Hobbs and Hammond having previously achieved this feat. Few Australian batsmen offered much resistance in the second innings, and 194 all out meant an innings defeat in three days and England retaining the Ashes.

In the last Test at Sydney, Dean Jones made a splendid 184 not out for Australia, more than half the team's total of 343. Small again took five wickets. England began badly but recovered somewhat to 275. Peter Taylor, an off-spinner making his Test debut, took six of the last seven wickets for 78. He had played only six first-class matches, and his selection was so surprising that Australian commentators only half-jokingly suggested his selection was a case of mistaken identity.

At 145 for seven, Australia faced defeat again, but Taylor scored 42, helping Waugh set a target of 320 to win. Emburey took seven for 78. When the final 20 overs began, England needed 90 with five wickets left, but when Gatting was out for 96 it became a question of saving the game. Peter Sleep, however, took his fifth wicket with the last ball of the penultimate over to end Australia's record sequence of 15 Tests without a win.

1986–87 62nd Series   Eng 2, Aus 1, Drawn 2

1 BRISBANE   England won by 7 wkts
England 456 (I T Botham 138, C W J Athey 76, M W Gatting 61, D I Gower 51) and 77–3
Australia 248 (G R Marsh 56, G R J Matthews 56, G R Dilley 5–68) and 282 (G R Marsh 110, J E Emburey 5–80)

2 PERTH   Match Drawn
England 592–8 dec (B C Broad 162, D I Gower 136, C J Richards 133, C W J Athey 96, B A Reid 4–115) and 199–8 dec (M W Gatting 70, S R Waugh 5–69)
Australia 401 (A R Border 125, S R Waugh 71, G R Dilley 4–79) and 197–4 (D M Jones 69)

3 ADELAIDE   Match Drawn
Australia 514–5 dec (D C Boon 103, D M Jones 93, S R Waugh 79, G R Matthews 73, A R Border 70) and 201–3 dec (A R Border 100)
England 455 (B C Broad 116, M W Gatting 100, C W J Athey 55, B A Reid 4–64, P R Sleep 4–132) and 39–2

4 MELBOURNE   England won by an innings and 14 runs
Australia 141 (D M Jones 59, I T Botham 5–41, G C Small 5–48) and 194 (G R Marsh 60)
England 349 (B C Broad 112, B A Reid 4–78, C J McDermott 4–83)

5 SYDNEY   Australia won by 55 runs
Australia 343 (D M Jones 184, G C Small 5–75) and 251 (S R Waugh 73, J E Emburey 7–78)
England 275 (D I Gower 72, J E Emburey 69, P L Taylor 6–78) and 264 (M W Gatting 96, P R Sleep 5–72)

1986–87 Averages

Batting	I	No	Runs	HS	Avge
B.C. Broad (E)	9	2	487	162	69.57
D.I. Gower (E)	8	1	404	136	57.71
D.M. Jones (A)	10	1	511	184*	56.78
A.R. Border (A)	10	1	473	125	52.56
S.R. Waugh (A)	8	1	310	79	44.29
M.W. Gatting (E)	9	0	393	100	43.67
G.R. Marsh (A)	10	0	429	110	42.90
C.J. Richardson (E)	7	0	264	133	37.71
C.W.J. Athey (E)	9	0	303	96	33.67

Bowling	O	M	Runs	W	Avge	BB
G.C. Small (E)	78.4	23	180	12	15.00	5–48
B.A. Reid (A)	198.4	44	527	20	26.35	4–64
G.R. Dilley (E)	176.1	38	511	16	31.94	5–68
P.H. Edmonds (E)	261.4	78	538	15	35.87	3–45
J.E. Emburey (E)	315.5	86	663	18	36.83	7–78

Botham, Ian Terence

Botham was born on 24 November 1955 at Heswall, Cheshire, and made his debut for Somerset, to where his family moved, in 1974. His Test debut came in 1977. He became a very hard-hitting right-hand middle-order batsman, a fast-medium swing bowler and an outstanding close fielder. Among his all-round achievements, he became the first to score a century and take ten wickets in a Test match, against India in 1979–80. He became the first player to pass 3,000 runs and 300 wickets in Tests. He captained England in 12 Tests, but was unfortunate to meet the strong West Indian side in nine of those, and lost the job. His most famous match followed immediately, when an innings of 149 not out at Headingley against Australia in 1981 won the match from an almost impossible position. In 94 Tests to the end of 1987 he had scored 5,057 runs, average 34.87, and taken 373 wickets, average 27.86. His aggregate of wickets is the world record. Always in the news, he has occasional brushes with the law and the authorities, makes charity walks, and left Somerset for Worcestershire amid much publicity in 1987. He is cricket's biggest box-office attraction of the 1980s.

Above: Emburey bowls McDermott at Melbourne in 1986–87 and England retain the Ashes with an innings victory and with one match to come. Emburey's 18 wickets were the most by an England bowler in the series.

Far Left: David Boon batting at Adelaide in 1986–87 where he scored a century and saved his Test place which was in danger after two disappointing Tests.

Left: The Adelaide ground during the Australia v England third Test in 1986–87. Adelaide is one of the most beautiful and peaceful of Australian grounds, although some of the most tense cricket has been played there.

England v South Africa

1888–89: South Africa well beaten by England in first Test series

Major R. Gardner Warton, on retiring from service in South Africa, decided to take a touring party there in 1888–89. It contained seven regular first-class cricketers, one of whom, C.A. Smith, was captain. He later became more famous as Sir C. Aubrey Smith, a Hollywood film actor. Sixteen matches were played against teams of 15, 18 and 22 players before an 11-a-side match with South Africa, which is now regarded as the first Test match between the two countries.

The match was at Port Elizabeth. England included five players who had already played against Australia, the other 16 in the match making their Test debuts. This was the first first-class match in South Africa, and for two England players the two Tests represented their only two appearances in first-class cricket. O.R. Dunell captained South Africa, who won the toss, decided to bat on a green matting wicket, and lost their first two wickets to Briggs without a run on the board.

South Africa eventually reached 84, the captain making 26 not out, while the English captain, Smith, took five for 19. England scored 148, but needed 32 from number eleven, A.J. Fothergill, after Bobby Abel had opened with 46. A. Rose-Innes took five wickets. In their second knock South Africa made 129, and, needing 66, England won by eight wickets. The match lasted two days.

In the second Test at Cape Town, Smith was unable to play because of fever, and another player, J.E.P. McMaster, made his only first-class appearance in a Test match, scoring a duck, not bowling and not taking a catch. Smith's place as captain was taken by M.P. Bowden, of Surrey, who was to stay on in South Africa and play for Transvaal, but who died three years later. South Africa had three new players, and W.H. Milton captained the side.

England batted, and made 292, Abel scoring the first first-class century in South Africa. W.H. Ashley took seven wickets in his only Test. On the second day South Africa were dismissed twice for 47 and 43, Briggs taking seven for 17 and eight for 11, his 15 wickets in a day being a Test record. Briggs' eight second-innings wickets were all clean bowled. In South Africa's first innings 47, opener A.B. Tancred carried his bat for 26 not out.

C. Aubrey Smith, like Bowden, also stayed in South Africa, setting up a business there before he gained fame as an actor, appearing in many films in the 1930s as a typical Englishman. He founded a cricket club in Hollywood.

1888–89 1st Series Eng 2, SA 0
1 PORT ELIZABETH **England won by 8 wkts**
South Africa 84 (C A Smith 5–19, J Briggs 4–39) and 129 (A J Fothergill 4–19)
England 148 (A Rose-Innes 5–43) and 67–2
2 CAPE TOWN **England won by an innings and 202 runs**
England 292 (R Abel 120, H Wood 59, W H Ashley 7–95)
South Africa 47 (J Briggs 7–17) and 43 (J Briggs 8–11)

1891–92: South Africa lose only Test by an innings

The English party which toured South Africa in 1891–92, playing 21 matches, was much stronger than Major Warton's despite the fact that another side was touring Australia at the same time. It was led by W.W. Read, and included J.J. Ferris and W.L. Murdoch, both of whom had played for Australia. Ferris was to play for Gloucestershire and Murdoch for Sussex.

Both Australians played in the only first-class match of the tour, the Test match at Cape Town, thus becoming two of the first three players to play for two countries in Tests. The other was Frank Hearne, who after playing for England on the earlier tour, had emigrated to South Africa and opened a sports outfitters. He was now in the South African team. Two of Hearne's brothers, Alec and George Gibbons Hearne (all three played for Kent) were making their debuts for England, thus providing the second of three instances (after the Graces) of three brothers playing in a Test. Their cousin, J.T. Hearne, was also in the England side.

South Africa batted, and were out for 97. England then compiled 369, H. Wood making his only first-class century. South Africa were then dismissed for 83, leaving England easy winners by an innings. Ferris took 13 wickets in the match.

1891–92 2nd Series Eng 1, SA 0
1 CAPE TOWN **England won by an innings and 189 runs**
England 369 (H Wood 134)
South Africa 97 (J J Ferris 6–54) and 83 (J J Ferris 7–37)

1895–96: A strong England side again win easily

A strong side went to South Africa in 1895–96, under Lord Hawke. There were political problems on the tour, the Jameson Raid postponing one fixture and a terrific explosion causing another to be abandoned.

Three Test matches were played. In the first at Port Elizabeth there were seven debutants for South Africa and nine for England. One of the nine was S.M.J. Woods, another who had already played for Australia. Two others were T.W. Hayward and C.B. Fry.

South Africa, led by E.A. Halliwell, the wicket-keeper, put England in, and with J. Middleton taking five wickets on his debut, England were out for only 185. However George Lohmann was too strong for their batsmen, and they were out themselves for 93. By making 226, England set South Africa over 300, but removed them for 30, Lohmann, finishing with a hat-trick, having the astonishing analysis of eight for seven. Of his 15 wickets in the match, 12 were clean bowled.

The second Test was at Johannesburg, where the Old Wanderers ground was being used to house the injured from the recent explosion. England made 482, Tom Hayward making a century, and then South Africa were put out for 151. Lohmann beat his previous figures with nine for 28, the second best analysis in Test cricket. Following on, South Africa made 134, and lost by an innings and 197.

The final Test was at Cape Town, and England put in South Africa, now led by A.R. Richards in his only Test. Lohmann was as devastating as before, taking seven for 42, and South Africa were out for 115. A.J.L. Hill made a century as England reached 265, and South Africa (117) were beaten by an innings. Lohmann's 35 wickets in the series cost 5.80 each.

1895–96 3rd Series Eng 3, SA 0
1 PORT ELIZABETH **England won by 288 runs**
England 185 (J Middleton 5–64) and 226 (S M J Woods 53, J Middleton 4–66)
South Africa 93 (G A Lohmann 7–38) and 30 (G A Lohmann 8–7)
2 JOHANNESBURG **England won by an innings and 197 runs**
South Africa 151 (G A Lohmann 9–28) and 134 (C Heseltine 5–38)
England 482 (T W Hayward 122, H R Bromley-Davenport 84, C W Wright 71, A J L Hill 65, C B Fry 64, G A Rowe 5–115, J H Sinclair 4–118)
3 CAPE TOWN **England won by an innings and 32 runs**
South Africa 115 (G A Lohmann 7–42) and 117 (A J L Hill 4–8)
England 265 (A J L Hill 124)

1895–96 Averages

Batting	I	No	Runs	HS	Avge
A.J.L. Hill (E)	4	0	251	124	62.75

Bowling	O	M	Runs	W	Avge	BB
G.A. Lohmann (E)	103.4	38	203	35	5.80	9–28
J. Middleton (SA)	85.3	24	180	12	15.00	5–64

1898–99: South Africa fail to press home first-innings advantage

The Hon J.D. Logan promoted another tour led by Lord Hawke in 1898–99. The side was not as strong as the previous ones. M. Bisset captained South Africa.

Fourteen players made their Test debuts at Johannesburg, where A.E. Trott was the, by now, almost obligatory Australian Test player now playing for England. England won the toss, batted, and were dismissed by sound bowling for 145. J.H. Sinclair then made 86 for South Africa before being run out, and at 251 the home side led by 106. At the end of the second day the tourists were 173 for seven, and defeat seemed likely. But P.F. Warner, who had opened, was still there, and he carried his bat for 132 not out. England reached 237, setting South Africa 132 to win. Good bowling by Trott (5–49) dismissed them for 99, England winning by 32.

Before the second and final Test at Cape Town the team was involved in a railway

1898–99 4th Series Eng 2, SA 0
1 JOHANNESBURG **England won by 32 runs**
England 145 and 237 (P F Warner 132, J Middleton 5–51)
South Africa 251 (J H Sinclair 86, A E Trott 4–61) and 99 (A E Trott 5–49)
2 CAPE TOWN **England won by 210 runs**
England 92 (J H Sinclair 6–26, J Middleton 4–18) and 330 (J T Tyldesley 112)
South Africa 177 (J H Sinclair 106, A E Trott 4–69) and 35 (S Haigh 6–11, A E Trott 4–19)

accident, but escaped with minor injuries. England were dismissed for 92, J.H. Sinclair taking six for 26. The last nine wickets fell for 31. Sinclair then made the century he missed in the previous Test, his 106 being South Africa's first Test century. But he was poorly supported, the whole side making only 177. J.T. Tyldesley made a century in England's second-innings 330, but Trott and S. Haigh proved unplayable in the fourth innings, which lasted only 114 balls. South Africa scored 35, losing both matches after leading on the first innings.

1905–06: South Africa win their first Test and Series

England's next tour of South Africa was after the Boer War. The team, led by P.F. Warner, was regarded as only moderate county standard, although there were only four English Test debutants in the first Test at Johannesburg, to South Africa's six.

England, winning the toss, batted and made 184. Good bowling, mainly by W.S. Lees, removed South Africa for 91, and a second innings total of 190 meant South Africa needed 284 to win. At 105 for six the match looked as good as over, but G.C. White (81) and A.W. Nourse (usually known as Dave) added 121 for the sixth wicket, giving South Africa a chance at 226 for six. However, 45 were still required when the last man, P.W. Sherwell, the captain and wicket-keeper, joined Nourse. In great excitement the two scored the runs and recorded South Africa's first Test victory.

The second Test, also at Johannesburg two months later, saw England bat first again, and make only 148. South Africa made 277, and, dismissing England for 160, required only 32 this time, and lost only one wicket in scoring them.

The Tests continued at Johannesburg with only a day's break between second and third. South Africa batted first. With Hathorn leading the way with a century, all the players reached double figures, and South Africa got 385. Lees took six for 78. England managed 295, F.L. Fane getting 143. Eight South Africans bowled, Snooke and Schwarz getting four wickets each. G.C. White scored 147 for South Africa second

1905–06 5th Series SA 4, Eng 1

1 JOHANNESBURG   South Africa won by 1 wkt
England 184 and 190 (P F Warner 51, G A Faulkner 4–26)
South Africa 91 (W S Lees 5–34) and 287–9 (A W Nourse 93, G C White 81)

2 JOHANNESBURG   South Africa won by 9 wkts
England 148 and 160 (F L Fane 65, R O Schwarz 4–30)
South Africa 277 (J H Sinclair 66, S Haigh 4–64) and 33–1

3 JOHANNESBURG   South Africa won by 243 runs
South Africa 385 (C M H Hathorn 102, A W Nourse 61, W S Lees 6–78) and 349–5 dec (G C White 147, L J Tancred 73, A W Nourse 61)
England 295 (F L Fane 143, S J Snooke 4–57, R O Schwarz 4–67) and 196 (D Denton 61, S J Snooke 8–70)

4 CAPE TOWN   England won by 4 wkts
South Africa 218 (C Blythe 6–68) and 138 (G C White 73, C Blythe 5–50, W S Lees 4–27)
England 198 (J H Sinclair 4–41, G A Faulkner 4–49) and 160–6 (F L Fane 66)

5 CAPE TOWN   South Africa won by an innings and 16 runs
England 187 (J N Crawford 74, J H Sinclair 4–45) and 130 (A W Nourse 4–25)
South Africa 333 (A E E Vogler 62, S J Snooke 60)

time round, allowing a declaration at 349 for five, setting England 440. England collapsed to S.J. Snooke (8–70) and lost by 243.

At Cape Town Blythe bowled well for England, taking six for 68 as South Africa were all out for 218, but England could manage only 198. Blythe took five second-innings wickets for 50 in South Africa's 138,

and England at 160 for six won by four wickets.

The final Test followed on at Cape Town, and the England batting was once again poor, the side being out for 187. South Africa's last three wickets added 151, A.E.E. Vogler scoring 62 not out at number eleven, a Test record which lasted 65 years. England were rushed out for 130, South Africa winning by an innings and 16.

Throughout the series, South Africa's bowlers were too good for the English batsmen. Snooke was fast-medium and Sinclair medium, but R.O. Schwarz, G.A. Faulkner, G.C. White and A.E.E. Vogler, all of whom got wickets, were leg-break and googly bowlers, googlies being a new invention and apparently well-suited to the matting wickets.

1905–06 Averages

Batting	I	No	Runs	HS	Avge
G.C. White (SA)	9	1	437	147	54.62
A.W. Nourse (SA)	8	2	290	93*	48.33
F.L. Fane (E)	10	1	342	143	38.00
J.N. Crawford (E)	10	1	281	74	31.22

Bowling	O	M	Runs	W	Avge	BB
S.J. Snooke (SA)	145	36	369	24	15.37	8–70
R.O. Schwarz (SA)	113.3	21	310	18	17.22	4–30
W.S. Lees (E)	209.2	69	467	26	17.96	6–78
G.A. Faulkner (SA)	119.4	34	272	14	19.42	4–26
J.H. Sinclair (SA)	177.3	49	418	21	19.90	4–41
C. Blythe (E)	226.4	74	548	21	26.09	6–68

1907: South Africa's first overseas series is narrowly lost

South Africa played their first Tests abroad in 1907, the team which had done so well at home being the basis of the touring party under P.W. Sherwell which played three Tests in England.

The first was at Lord's, where L.C. Braund (104) and G.L. Jessop (93) added 145 in 75 minutes for the sixth wicket, England totalling 428. Vogler, nevertheless, claimed seven for 128. E.G. Arnold took five for 37 in dismissing South Africa for 140, of which 98 came from the fourth wicket stand of Nourse and Faulkner. South Africa followed on, but rain washed out the last day with the score 185 for three.

At Headingley, rain and bad light made batting difficult, and Faulkner took six for 17, England being out for only 76. Blythe was England's destroyer, taking eight for 59, but South Africa reached 110 and a lead of

1907 6th Series Eng 1, SA 0, Drawn 2

1 LORD'S   Match Drawn
England 428 (L C Braund 104, G L Jessop 93, J T Tyldesley 52, A E E Vogler 7–128)
South Africa 140 (A W Nourse 62, E G Arnold 5–37) and 185–3 (P W Sherwell 115)

2 HEADINGLEY   England won by 53 runs
England 76 (G A Faulkner 6–17) and 162 (C B Fry 54, G C White 4–47)
South Africa 110 (C Blythe 8–59) and 75 (C Blythe 7–40)

3 THE OVAL   Match Drawn
England 295 (C B Fry 129, R E Foster 51) and 138 (A E E Vogler 4–49)
South Africa 178 (S J Snooke 63, C Blythe 5–61) and 159–5

34. Fry batted well to score 54 in the second innings, allowing England to set a target of 129. It proved too difficult against Blythe, who took seven for 40 (15 in the match) to

remove the tourists for 75 and give England victory by 53.

At the Oval, Fry made a century and England 295, enough for a lead of 117 as Blythe again took five wickets. England could make only 138 in the second innings, setting South Africa 256 in 150 minutes. They made a gallant try, but the light deteriorated and they had to settle for a draw, losing the series 1–0.

1907 Averages

Batting	I	No	Runs	HS	Avge
C.B. Fry (E)	5	0	221	129	44.20

Bowling	O	M	Runs	W	Avge	BB
C. Blythe (E)	100.3	26	270	26	10.38	8–59
G.A. Faulkner (SA)	73	11	218	12	18.16	6–17
G.H. Hirst (E)	87	28	185	10	18.50	3–39
A.E.E. Vogler (SA)	104.5	24	295	15	19.66	7–128

1909–10: Faulkner's all-round skills tilt the scales for South Africa

Despite the presence of J.B. Hobbs, the side that H.D.G. Leveson Gower took to South Africa in 1909–10 was not representative in batting strength. S.J. Snooke led South Africa, and decided to bat in the first Test at Johannesburg. An under-arm bowler, G.H.T. Simpson-Hayward, by taking six for 43, helped limit them to 208. Hobbs and Rhodes put on 159 for England's first wicket, and England built a lead of 102. Faulkner, who had made 78 in the first innings, was top scorer again in the second with 123. A total of 345 meant England needed 244, but Vogler and Faulkner, who had taken all the wickets in the first innings, did so again in the second and England were beaten by 19. Faulkner had a brilliant match, and was carried shoulder-high round the ground.

The second Test was the first to be held at Durban, and the first innings was tied at 199. South Africa made 357, White scoring 118, and England could not equal this against Faulkner, who took six for 87.

At Johannesburg South Africa made a good start with 305, but D. Denton's only Test century helped England to a lead of 17. Simpson-Hayward struck again with five wickets, and England wanted 221 to win. Hobbs, who batted at number seven and number five, scored 93 not out to see England home by three wickets.

Hobbs scored only one run in the fourth Test at Cape Town, where South Africa took a first innings lead of four at 207. Good bowling by Vogler then got out England for 178. South Africa lost five wickets for 91 before winning at 175 for six, Faulkner again steadying the ship.

After a day's rest the fifth Test began on the same Newlands ground. Hobbs, going from one extreme to the other, scored 187, and England were in control from the time he and Rhodes put on 221 for the opening stand. South Africa used eight bowlers as England made 417. They themselves scored only 103, with J.W. Zulch carrying his bat for 43 not out. They made 327 following on, with Faulkner getting 99. Hobbs took his only Test wicket. England needed 14 and won. Simpson-Hayward took 23 wickets, the last time an under-arm bowler played a significant part in a Test series.

1909–10 7th Series SA 3, Eng 2
1 JOHANNESBURG **South Africa won by 19 runs**
South Africa 208 (G A Faulkner 78, A W Nourse 53, G H T Simpson-Hayward 6–43) and 345 (A W Nourse 123, C P Buckenham 4–110)
England 310 (J B Hobbs 89, W Rhodes 66, A E E Vogler 5–87, G A Faulkner 5–120) and 224 '(G J Thompson 63, A E E Vogler 7–94)
2 DURBAN **South Africa won by 95 runs**
South Africa 199 (G H T Simpson-Hayward 4–42) and 347 (G C White 118, A W Nourse 69, S J Snooke 53)
England 199 (J B Hobbs 53, A E E Vogler 5–83) and 252 (J B Hobbs 70, G A Faulkner 6–87)
3 JOHANNESBURG **England won by 3 wkts**
South Africa 305 (G A Faulkner 76, G C White 72, A E E Vogler 65, C P Buckenham 5–115) and 237 (S J Snooke 52, G H T Simpson-Hayward 5–69)
England 322 (D Denton 104, F E Woolley 58, G A Faulkner 4–89, A E E Vogler 4–98) and 221–7 (J B Hobbs 93, A E E Vogler 4–109)
4 CAPE TOWN **South Africa won by 4 wkts**
England 203 (F E Woolley 69, M C Bird 57) and 178 (F E Woolley 64, A E E Vogler 5–72)
South Africa 207 (G J Thompson 4–50) and 175–6
5 CAPE TOWN **England won by 9 wkts**
England 417 (J B Hobbs 187, W Rhodes 77, G J Thompson 51, N O Norton 4–47) and 16–1
South Africa 103 (C Blythe 7–46) and 327 (G A Faulkner 99)

1909–10 Averages

Batting	I	No	Runs	HS	Avge
J.B. Hobbs (E)	9	1	539	187	67.37
G.A. Faulkner (SA)	10	1	545	123	60.55
G.C. White (SA)	8	0	284	118	35.50
G.J. Thompson (E)	9	1	267	63	33.37
F.E. Woolley (E)	9	1	256	69	32.00
S.J. Snooke (SA)	10	0	259	53	25.90

Bowling	O	M	Runs	W	Avge	BB
C. Blythe (E)	83	32	168	12	14.00	7–46
G.H. Simpson-Hayward (E)	149.4	18	420	23	18.26	6–43
A.E.E. Vogler (SA)	224.5	33	783	36	21.75	7–94
G.A. Faulkner (SA)	209.1	45	635	29	21.89	6–87
G.J. Thompson (E)	233.5	66	619	23	26.91	4–50
C.P. Buckenham (E)	197	25	593	21	28.23	5–115

1912: Barnes takes over half the wickets for England

South Africa played three Tests against England in the Triangular Tournament of 1912, Australia also taking part. The tournament was ruined by rain.

F. Mitchell led South Africa while C.B. Fry captained England. At Lord's F.R. Foster and S.F. Barnes proved almost unplayable, bowling throughout and sharing the wickets as South Africa scored 58, extras making the biggest contribution of 17. S.J. Pegler took seven for 65 for South Africa but Spooner made a century in 337. South Africa were then bowled out for 217, largely by Barnes (6–85) and England scored an innings victory.

England also batted first at Headingley, making 242. Barnes bowled well again (6–52) to give England a lead of 95 to which England added 238. Barnes completed ten wickets in the match as England won by 174.

Barnes and Woolley shared the wickets as South Africa were dismissed for 95 at the Oval on a wet pitch. Faulkner fought back with seven for 84, but England gained a lead of 81, and in miserable conditions Barnes took eight for 29 as South Africa scored 98. England won before lunch on the second day. Barnes took 34 wickets in the three matches.

1912 8th Series Eng 3, SA 0
1 LORD'S **England won by an innings and 62 runs**
South Africa 58 (F R Foster 5–16, S F Barnes 5–25) and 217 (C B Llewellyn 75, S F Barnes 6–85)
England 337 (R H Spooner 119, F E Woolley 73, S J Pegler 7–65)
2 HEADINGLEY **England won by 174 runs**
England 242 (F E Woolley 57, A W Nourse 4–52) and 238 (R H Spooner 82, J B Hobbs 55, G A Faulkner 4–50)
South Africa 147 (S F Barnes 6–52) and 159 (S F Barnes 4–63)
3 THE OVAL **England won by 10 wkts**
South Africa 95 (S F Barnes 5–28, F E Woolley 5–41) and 93 (S F Barnes 8–29)
England 176 (J B Hobbs 68, G A Faulkner 7–84) and 14–0

1912 Averages

Batting	I	No	Runs	HS	Avge
R.H. Spooner (E)	4	0	248	119	62.00

Bowling	O	M	Runs	W	Avge	BB
S.F. Barnes (E)	128	38	282	34	8.29	8–29
A.W. Nourse (SA)	74.4	24	160	10	16.00	4–52
F.R. Foster (E)	92.1	32	184	11	16.72	5–16
G.A. Faulkner (SA)	95.3	14	260	13	20.00	7–84
S.J. Pegler (SA)	116	17	340	15	22.66	7–65

1913–14: Barnes breaks records in his last series

After the defeat of the previous tour, MCC sent a much stronger side under J.W.H.T. Douglas to South Africa in 1913–14. H.W. Taylor led the South Africans, who included seven newcomers in the side for the first Test at Durban. Taylor batted brilliantly to make 109 out of 182, Barnes claiming five for 57. Douglas copied his opposing captain by scoring a century, but in a different context, as England made 450. Another five-wicket haul by Barnes meant an innings victory for England.

At Johannesburg Barnes' figures kept getting better. He took eight for 56 as South Africa scored 160, a total England left well behind with Rhodes and Mead making centuries in 403. Barnes then took nine for 103 in another innings victory. His 17 wickets in the match established a Test record which is still second to Laker's 1956 haul of 19 at Old Trafford. Rhodes, in capturing one of the other three, became the first Englishman to claim 100 Test wickets and 1,000 Test runs.

After a day's interval, the third Test began on the same ground. England made 238, and South Africa 151, J.W. Hearne this time getting five wickets, but Barnes got five in the second innings, when South Africa, set 396, scored 304 after Taylor and Zulch had begun with 153 for the first wicket.

Barnes, in the last of his 27 Tests, took seven for 56 as South Africa made 170 at Durban. Then C.P. Carter, bowling left-arm round-the-wicket into a strong wind, took six for 50 and England failed by seven to equal South Africa. The home team, with Taylor getting 93, declared at 305 for seven second time. Hobbs (97) and Rhodes began well, but the match petered out into a draw.

The last Test at Port Elizabeth began immediately. Barnes declined to play, either because of an argument or illness, but South Africa made only 193. Mead made a century in England's 411 and despite another fine opening of 129 by Taylor and Zulch, South Africa made only 228 and England needed 11 to win, all scored by Hobbs.

Barnes took 49 wickets in the series, average 10.93. This aggregate remains a record for a series, despite his playing in only four Tests on this tour.

1913–14 9th Series Eng 4, SA 0, Drawn 1
1 DURBAN **England won by an innings and 157 runs**
South Africa 182 (H W Taylor 109, S F Barnes 5–57) and 111 (S F Barnes 5–48)
England 450 (J W H T Douglas 119, J B Hobbs 82, M C Bird 61, L H Tennyson 52)
2 JOHANNESBURG **England won by an innings and 12 runs**
South Africa 160 (G P D Hartigan 51, S F Barnes 8–56) and 231 (A W Nourse 56, S F Barnes 9–103)
England 403 (W Rhodes 152, C P Mead 102, A E Relf 63, J M Blanckenberg 5–83)
3 JOHANNESBURG **England won by 91 runs**
England 238 (J B Hobbs 92) and 308 (C P Mead 86, J W H T Douglas 77, C Newberry 4–72)
South Africa 151 (J W Hearne 5–49) and 304 (J W Zulch 82, H W Taylor 70, J M Blanckenberg 59, S F Barnes 5–102)
4 DURBAN **Match Drawn**
South Africa 170 (P A M Hands 51, S F Barnes 7–56) and 305–9 dec (H W Taylor 93, S F Barnes 7'–88)
England 163 (J B Hobbs 64, C P Carter 6–50) and 154–5 (J B Hobbs 97)
5 PORT ELIZABETH **England won by 10 wkts**
South Africa 193 (P A M Hands 83, J W H T Douglas 4–14) and 228 (H W Taylor 87, J W Zulch 60, M W Booth 4–49)
England 411 (C P Mead 117, F E Woolley 54, E B Lundie 4–101) and 11–0

1913–14 Averages

Batting	I	No	Runs	HS	Avge
J.B. Hobbs (E)	8	1	443	97	63.28
C.P. Mead (E)	7	0	378	117	54.00
H.W. Taylor (SA)	10	0	508	109	50.80
W. Rhodes (E)	8	1	289	152	41.28
J.W.H.T. Douglas (E)	7	0	266	119	38.00
P.A.M. Hands (SA)	10	0	281	83	28.10

Bowling	O	M	Runs	W	Avge	BB
S.F. Barnes (E)	226	56	536	49	10.93	9–103
J.M. Blanckenberg (SA)	171.4	44	428	19	22.52	5–83

1922–23: England narrowly win the series thanks to Russell

F.T. Mann's touring side in 1922–23 was without several notable players, but was considered reasonably strong.

The two first innings at Johannesburg were low: South Africa 148, England 182. J.M. Blanckenburg took six for 76 for the home team. South Africa then made 420, their highest against England, with captain Taylor making a superb 176. Nupen and Blanckenburg made sure of a home victory by 168 runs.

The second Test at Cape Town followed after a couple of days and for a while took a similar course to the first. South Africa were skittled for 113, and England took a lead of 70, restricted by Blanckenburg's five for 61. Taylor again followed with a good second innings, and helped by Catterall carried South Africa to 242. G.G. Macaulay, on his debut, took five wickets, having taken one with his first ball in Test cricket. England struggled against another newcomer, A.E. Hall, who took seven for 63, and when the last man, Macaulay, came to the wicket at 168 for nine, five more runs were still required. Macaulay made the winning hit, thus distinguishing himself at first and last.

At the Kingsmead ground at Durban, staging its first Test, Mead made 181 and England 428. South Africa replied with 368, but it rained and there was little time for more cricket.

With the series still level, a record crowd watched South Africa get a first-innings lead at Johannesburg. Hall's six for 82 restricted England to 244, South Africa getting 51 in front. Woolley, who survived when Hall's first ball to him apparently brushed a bail without removing it, made a century in the second innings and England declared at 376 for six. Taylor also scored a century but time ran out.

The fifth Test at Durban was to be played to a finish. England won a valuable toss, and C.A.G. Russell, despite not feeling well, made 140 out of England's 281. South Africa could manage only 179. In the second innings Russell batted at number six, coming in at 26 for four. He scored 111, helping Gilligan add 92 for the last wicket in a score

---

1922–23   10th Series   Eng 2, SA 1, Drawn 2

1 JOHANNESBURG   South Africa won by 168 runs
South Africa 148 (A S Kennedy 4–37, V W C Jupp 4–59) and 420 (H W Taylor 176, W H Brann 50, A S Kennedy 4–132)
England 182 (J M Blanckenberg 6–76) and 218 (E P Nupen 5–53)

2 CAPE TOWN   England won by 1 wkt
South Africa 113 (P G H Fender 4–29) and 242 (R H Catterall 76, H W Taylor 68, G G Macaulay 5–64, A S Kennedy 4–58)
England 183 (J M Blanckenberg 5–61, A E Hall 4–49) and 173–9 (A E Hall 7–63)

3 DURBAN   Match Drawn
England 428 (C P Mead 181, F T Mann 84, P G H Fender 60, A E Hall 4–105) and 11–1
South Africa 368 (H W Taylor 91, C M Francois 72, A W Nourse 52, R H Catterall 52, A S Kennedy 5–88)

4 JOHANNESBURG
England 244 (A W Carr 63, A E Hall 6–82) and 376–6 dec (F E Woolley 115, C A G Russell 96, F T Mann 59, A Sandham 58)
South Africa 295 (T A Ward 64, A W Nourse 51, L E Tapscott 50) and 247–4 (H W Taylor 101, A W Nourse 63)

5 DURBAN   England won by 109 runs
England 281 (C A G Russell 140, C P Mead 66) and 241 (C A G Russell 111)
South Africa 179 and 234 (H W Taylor 102, A S Kennedy 5–76)

---

of 241. Needing 344, South Africa reached 111 for three at the end of the fourth day, but lost three wickets in a rain-curtailed fifth day, and lost by 109 on the sixth, when Taylor was out for 102.

A collection was made on the ground for Russell, who pocketed over £90 for his great effort. He was the first Englishman to score a century in each innings of a Test. Strangely, it was his last.

1922–23 Averages

Batting	I	No	Runs	HS	Avge
H.W. Taylor (SA)	9	0	582	176	64.66
C.A.G. Russell (E)	7	0	437	140	62.42
C.P. Mead (E)	9	0	392	181	43.55
F.T. Mann (E)	9	1	281	84	35.12
A.W. Nourse (SA)	9	0	304	63	33.77
C.M. Francois (SA)	9	1	252	72	31.50
R.H. Catterall (SA)	9	0	272	76	30.22

Bowling	O	M	Runs	W	Avge	BB
A.E. Hall (SA)	250.5	82	501	27	18.55	7–63
A.S. Kennedy (E)	280.3	91	599	31	19.32	5–76
G.G. Macauley (E)	161	46	326	16	20.37	5–64
V.W.C. Jupp (E)	121.4	33	332	14	23.71	4–59
J.M. Blanckenberg(SA)	251.4	60	613	25	24.52	6–76

1924: Rain spoils a disappointing series after Edgbaston sensations

A.E.R. Gilligan was England's captain when Herbie Taylor's side toured England in 1924, and had a hand in sensational events in the first Test at Edgbaston. South Africa summoned G.M. Parker from the Bradford League to open their bowling, and he took six wickets. England had some more distinguished debutants, including Herbert Sutcliffe, who joined Hobbs in the first of their century opening stands in Tests. But South Africa's was the most astonishing innings. Maurice Tate, another newcomer, took a wicket with his first ball. He took four for 12, but Gilligan took six for seven, and South Africa were out for 30 in 48 minutes, equalling the lowest score in Tests, also theirs. In the second innings they made 390, with Catterall scoring 120, but they lost by an innings. Gilligan (11) and Tate (8) took all the wickets apart from a run-out.

At Lord's, Catterall made another 120, and South Africa made 273. But Hobbs (211) and Sutcliffe (122) nearly reached this, putting on 268, Woolley scored 134 not out and England reached 531 for two declared, 503 being made on the second day. When South Africa were out for 240, the margin of victory, an innings and 18, was the same as the first Test.

At Headingley, Hendren made his first Test hundred in England's 396. Tate's six for 42 was his best for England as South Africa failed again in the first innings. Following on 264 behind, they made 323, but lost by nine wickets.

The Old Trafford Test was washed out at 4 o'clock on the first day, and is notable perhaps for being the only Test of J.C.W. MacBryan, who did not bat, bowl, or make a catch.

Rain also wrecked the last Test after England had reached 421 for eight in reply to South Africa's 342. Hendren made his second century but Catterall missed his third by five runs.

1924   11th Series   Eng 3, SA 0, Drawn 2

1 EDGBASTON   England won by an innings and 18 runs
England 438 (J B Hobbs 76, E H Hendren 74, H Sutcliffe 64, F E Woolley 64, R Kilner 59, G M Parker 6–152)
South Africa 30 (A E R Gilligan 6–7, M W Tate 4–12) and 390 (R H Catterall 120, J M Blanckenberg 56, M J Susskind 51, A E R Gilligan 5–83, M W Tate 4–103)

2 LORD'S   England won by an innings and 18 runs
South Africa 273 (R H Catterall 120, M J Susskind 64) and 240 (M J Susskind 53)
England 531–2 dec (J B Hobbs 211, F E Woolley 134, H Sutcliffe 122, E H Hendren 50)

3 HEADINGLEY   England won by 9 wkts
England 396 (E H Hendren 132, H Sutcliffe 83, S J Pegler 4–116) and 60–1
South Africa 132 (H W Taylor 59, M W Tate 6–42) and 323 (H W Taylor 56, R H Catterall 56)

4 OLD TRAFFORD   Match Drawn
South Africa 116–4 (T A Ward 50)
England did not bat

5 THE OVAL   Match Drawn
South Africa 342 (R H Catterall 95, M J Susskind 65)
England 421–8 (E H Hendren 142, F E Woolley 51, M W Tate 51)

1924 Averages

Batting	I	No	Runs	HS	Avge
E.H. Hendren (E)	4	1	398	142	132.66
F.E. Woolley (E)	4	1	249	134*	83.00
H. Sutcliffe (E)	5	1	303	122*	75.75
J.B. Hobbs (E)	5	0	355	211	71.00
R.H. Catterall (SA)	8	1	471	120	67.28
M.J. Susskind (SA)	8	0	268	65	33.50

Bowling	O	M	Runs	W	Avge	BB
M.W. Tate (E)	217.2	68	424	27	15.70	6–42
A.E.R. Gilligan (E)	133.3	38	322	17	18.94	6–7
R.K. Tyldesley (E)	130.5	50	249	12	20.75	3–50

1927–28: South Africa come back from two down to level

A weak, much criticized team toured South Africa in 1927–28. It was led by Captain R.T. Stanyforth, an Army cricketer who had not played county cricket. South Africa were captained by H.G. Deane, although Taylor still played.

At Johannesburg South Africa made 196, Catterall's 86 being highest. England's innings was strange. Sutcliffe made 102, G.E. Tyldesley 122 (they added 230 for the second wicket) and newcomer W.R. Hammond 51, but the other eight batsmen made only 13 between them. England made 313.

Only three reached double figures in South Africa's second innings, Nupen (53) and Coen (41 not out) being highest, batting at numbers nine and ten. England needed only 54 for a ten-wicket win. G. Geary took 12 wickets with his spinners.

At Cape Town, England were limited to 133, newcomer G.F. Bissett getting the first five wickets. South Africa led by 117, but Holmes (88) and Sutcliffe (99) passed this without being parted in the second innings. England made 428 and won by 87 runs.

South Africa made 246 at Durban, where R.E.S. Wyatt had an odd analysis. After a new ball spell of 11 overs and 10 maidens, in which he bowled Herbie Taylor in conceding one run, he was brought back when the eighth wicket had added 95, and claimed both batsmen in his first over, finishing with three for four. England scored 430, Vincent

Deane, who won all five tosses, put England in again at Durban, where G.T.S. Stevens captained England because of Stanyforth's injury. Rain washed out the first day, and G.E. Tyldesley made 100 on the second, England reaching 282 (Nupen 5–83). Catterall scored 119, and Deane declared at 332 for seven, only 50 ahead, in an effort to win. Bissett, with the help of a strong wind, was fiery in the second innings. He claimed Holmes for a pair and forced Wyatt to retire hurt for a while. He claimed seven for 29 and South Africa wanting only 69 to win, deservedly squared the series.

1927–28 Averages

Batting	I	No	Runs	HS	Avge
G.E. Tyldesley (E)	9	1	520	122	65.00
H. Sutcliffe (E)	10	1	418	102	46.44
R.H. Catterall (SA)	10	1	379	119	42.11
H.W. Taylor (SA)	10	0	412	101	41.20
W.R. Hammond (E)	9	1	321	90	40.12
H.G. Deane (SA)	9	1	277	73	34.62
P. Holmes (SA)	10	1	302	88	33.55

Bowling	O	M	Runs	W	Avge	BB
G. Geary (E)	77.3	18	180	12	15.00	7–70
G.F. Bissett (SA)	164.5	29	469	25	18.76	7–29
C.L. Vincent (SA)	222.4	43	517	23	22.47	6–131
W.R. Hammond (E)	161.2	44	399	15	26.60	5–36
W.E. Astill (E)	130.2	33	330	12	27.50	3–48
A.P. Freeman (E)	132.3	29	399	14	28.50	4–58
S.J. Staples (E)	191.3	50	435	15	29.00	3–50
E.P. Nupen (SA)	245.4	55	551	14	39.35	5–83

1929: Ten England centuries in winning series

Deane's young side to England in 1929 included Bruce Mitchell, whose 88 in his first Test innings at Edgbaston helped South Africa to a total of 250 and a first innings lead of five. Larwood took five wickets. With Sutcliffe and Hammond making centuries, South Africa were set an impossible target and the match was drawn. Mitchell in all batted 575 minutes, helping Catterall in opening stands of 119 and 171.

A.J. Bell, on his debut, took the last six England wickets at Lord's, where Sutcliffe scored 100 in England's 302. South Africa (322) again took a narrow lead, England declared after two centuries, this time by Leyland and Tate, but South Africa had difficulty in saving the game. Bad light rescued them at 90 for five.

South Africa batted first at Headingley, making 236, Freeman, on his recall, getting seven for 115. England passed this by 92, N.A. Quinn getting six for 92. H.G. Owen-Smith, who was to captain England at rugby, scored a forceful 129, including 100 before lunch, setting England a target by adding 103 for the last wicket with Bell, a South African Test record. However, England scored the 184 needed for a five-wicket win.

Wyatt (113) and Woolley (154) added 245 for England's third wicket at Old Trafford, where A.W. Carr took over from J.C. White as England captain. Freeman (7–71) then bowled South Africa out for 130, and they followed on nearly 300 behind. Five more wickets for Freeman in the second innings and England had won the rubber with an innings victory.

South Africa put England in at the Oval and, thanks to Vincent, got them out for 258 (Sutcliffe 104). A century by Taylor and other good scores allowed Deane to declare at 492 for eight, but hopes of a win dis-

Hammond, Walter Reginald

Hammond was born on 19 June 1903 at Dover, Kent, but played for Gloucestershire, making his debut in 1920. He became the leading English batsman of his day, particularly strong on the off-side. He was also a right-arm medium-pace bowler and a brilliant specialist slip fielder. He headed the English batting averages for eight successive seasons from 1933, a record. He made his Test debut in 1927–28. In 85 Tests he scored 7,249 runs, average 58.45, and took 83 wickets at 37.80. He also held 110 catches, at the time a record. In 1932–33 he scored 336 not out at Auckland against New Zealand, which set a new Test record. He turned amateur in 1938 and captained England in his last 20 Tests, but he was not the same player in his three post-war series. Had he not played after the war, his Test average would have been over 60. He died in Durban, South Africa, on 1 July 1965.

appeared with a second century of the match from Sutcliffe and another from Hammond. The match ended with England 264 for one.

1929 13th Series   Eng 2, SA 0, Drawn 3

1 EDGBASTON   Match Drawn
England 245 (E H Hendren 70, A L Ochse 4–79) and 308–4 dec (W R Hammond 138, H Sutcliffe 114)
South Africa 250 (B Mitchell 88, R H Catterall 67, H Larwood 5–57) and 171–1 (R H Catterall 98, B Mitchell 61)

2 LORD'S   Match Drawn
England 302 (H Sutcliffe 100, M Leyland 73, A J Bell 6–99, D P B Morkel 4–93) and 312–8 dec (M Leyland 102, M W Tate 100, A L Ochse 4–99)
South Africa 322 (D P B Morkel 88, J A J Christy 70, H G Owen-Smith 52) and 90–5

3 HEADINGLEY   England won by 5 wkts
South Africa 236 (R H Catterall 74, C L Vincent 60, A P Freeman 7–115) and 275 (H G Owen-Smith 129)
England 328 (F E Woolley 83, W R Hammond 65, N A Quinn 6–92) and 186–5 (F E Woolley 95)

4 OLD TRAFFORD   England won by an innings and 32 runs
England 427–7 dec (F E Woolley 154, R E S Wyatt 113, M Leyland 55)
South Africa 130 (D P B Morkel 63, A P Freeman 7–71) and 265 (H B Cameron 83, H W Taylor 70, A P Freeman 5–100)

5 THE OVAL   Match Drawn
England 258 (H Sutcliffe 104, C L Vincent 5–105) and 264–1 (H Sutcliffe 109, W R Hammond 101, J B Hobbs 52)
South Africa 492–8 dec (H W Taylor 121, H G Deane 93, D P B Morkel 81, H B Cameron 62, Q McMillan 50)

1927–28 12th Series   Eng 2, SA 2, Drawn 1

1 JOHANNESBURG   England won by 10 wkts
South Africa 196 (R H Catterall 86, G Geary 7–70) and 170 (C L Vincent 53, W R Hammond 5–36, G Geary 5–60)
England 313 (G E Tyldesley 122, H Sutcliffe 102, W R Hammond 51, H L E Promnitz 5–58) and 57–0

2 CAPE TOWN   England won by 87 runs
England 133 (G F Bissett 5–37, C L Vincent 4–22) and 428 (H Sutcliffe 99, R E S Wyatt 91, P Holmes 88, G E Tyldesley 87)
South Africa 250 (H W Taylor 68, A P Freeman 4–58) and 224 (H W Taylor 71)

3 DURBAN   Match Drawn
South Africa 246 (H G Deane 77, E P Nupen 51) and 464–8 dec (J F W Nicolson 78, R H Catterall 76, H G Deane 73, E P Nupen 69, H W Taylor 60)
England 430 (W R Hammond 90, G E Tyldesley 78, G T S Stevens 69, C L Vincent 6–131, E P Nupen 4–94) and 132–2 (G E Tyldesley 62, P Holmes 56)

4 JOHANNESBURG   South Africa won by 4 wkts
England 265 (R E S Wyatt 58, A E Hall 6–100, G F Bissett 4–43) and 215 (P Holmes 63, G F Bissett 4–70)
South Africa 328 (H W Taylor 101, H B Cameron 64) and 156–6

5 DURBAN   South Africa won by 8 wkts
England 282 (G E Tyldesley 100, W R Hammond 66, H Sutcliffe 51, E P Nupen 5–83) and 118 (G F Bissett 7–29)
South Africa 332–7 dec (R H Catterall 119, H B Cameron 53) and 69–2

(6–131) and Nupen (4–94) sharing the wickets, and led by 184, but South Africa's 464 for eight declared meant a draw.

At Johannesburg, England were put in, and fast right-arm Bissett (4–43) and medium-fast left-arm Hall, who was recalled, (6–100) got them out for 265. Taylor then made 101 in South Africa's 328. Good home bowling got England out for 215, and South Africa kept the series alive by winning by four wickets.

Left: The South African party in England in 1924. Left to right, standing: Deane, Hands, Dixon, Susskind, Bissett, Nupen, Nourse, G. Allsop (manager). Sitting: Blanckenberg, Conmaille, Taylor, Pegler, Ward. Front: Catterall, Carter, Hearne, Meintjes.

1929 Averages

Batting	I	No	Runs	HS	Avge
F.E. Woolley (E)	4	1	378	154	126.00
H. Sutcliffe (E)	9	1	513	114	64.12
W.R. Hammond (E)	8	2	352	138*	58.66
D.P.B. Morkel (SA)	8	1	321	74*	45.85
H.G. Owen-Smith (SA)	8	2	252	129	42.00
M. Leyland (E)	7	0	294	102	42.00
B. Mitchell (SA)	9	1	251	88	31.37
R.H. Catterall (SA)	9	0	256	98	28.44

Bowling	O	M	Runs	W	Avge	BB
A.P. Freeman (E)	188.1	47	547	22	24.86	7–71
D.P.B. Morkel (SA)	173	41	458	14	32.71	4–93
N.A. Quinn (SA)	164.2	27	441	13	33.92	6–92
C.L. Vincent (SA)	154	25	475	13	36.53	5–105

1930–31: South Africa take the lead and resist strong challenges

Sutcliffe was surprisingly omitted from A.P.F. Chapman's touring party in 1930–31, but the side was otherwise a good one.

Nupen captained South Africa in the first Test, only being selected because Deane was unavailable. He lost the toss, and his side were shot out for 126, largely by Voce and Peebles with four wickets each. But Nupen's five for 63 restricted England's lead to 67, and the batsmen fought back in the second innings to total 306. England were never happy against Nupen, whose six for 87 allowed him to lead his team to victory by 28 runs in his only Test as captain. He had lost an eye in an accident when four years old.

Deane was back at Cape Town, where for the first time in South Africa a Test was played on turf. Mitchell (123) and I.J. Siedle (141) put on 260 for the first wicket, Taylor made 117, and South Africa declared at 513 for eight. England made 350, and following on, 252, but used up all the time for a draw.

Rain saved South Africa at Durban, where England declared 46 ahead at 223 for one (Hammond 136 not out) after a day was washed out, and then took eight second-innings wickets. Taylor's 64 not out saved the day.

Injury-hit England incorporated H.W. Lee, who was coaching in South Africa, for his only Test at Johannesburg. H.B. Cameron took over as captain of South Africa from Deane, who wished to retire. England made 442, and thanks to Peebles (six for 63) dismissed South Africa for 295.

1930–31 14th Series SA 1, Eng 0, Drawn 4
1 JOHANNESBURG **South Africa won by 28 runs**
South Africa 126 (I A R Peebles 4–43, W Voce 4–45) and 306 (B Mitchell 72, R H Catterall 54, H B Cameron 51, W Voce 4–59, W R Hammond 4–63)
England 193 (E P Nupen 5–63) and 211 (W R Hammond 63, M J L Turnbull 61, E P Nupen 6–87)
2 CAPE TOWN **Match Drawn**
South Africa 513–8 dec (I J Siedle 141, B Mitchell 123, H W Taylor 117, R H Catterall 56)
England 350 (E H Hendren 93, W R Hammond 57, M Leyland 52) and 252 (E H Hendren 86, W R Hammond 65)
3 DURBAN **Match Drawn**
South Africa 177 (W Voce 5–58) and 145–8 (H W Taylor 64)
England 223–1 dec (W R Hammond 136, R E S Wyatt 54)
4 JOHANNESBURG **Match Drawn**
England 442 (M Leyland 91, W R Hammond 75, E H Hendren 64, A E Hall 4–105) and 169–9 (E P Nupen 6–46)
South Africa 295 (H W Taylor 72, B Mitchell 68, I J Siedle 62, I A R Peebles 6–63) and 280–7 (B Mitchell 74, H B Cameron 69, W Voce 4–87)
5 DURBAN **Match Drawn**
South Africa 252 (B Mitchell 73, I J Siedle 57, I A R Peebles 4–67) and 219–7 dec
England 230 (M W Tate 50, C L Vincent 6–51) and 72–4

Quick runs on the last day, when Nupen took six for 46, enabled Chapman to set South Africa 317 in four hours. England got on top at 153 for five, but 69 not out from Cameron forced another draw.

Chapman put in South Africa on a drying pitch at Durban, and complained when 20 minutes were lost because of the absence of bails. Rain ended play after 70 minutes. South Africa made 252, and England 230 (Vincent 6–51). More time was lost on the third day, and South Africa's declaration was not intended to be a serious challenge. So South Africa won the series. The fourth Test was the last on matting in South Africa.

1930–1 Averages

Batting	I	No	Runs	HS	Avge
W.R. Hammond (E)	9	1	517	136*	64.62
B. Mitchell (SA)	9	0	455	123	50.55
H.W. Taylor (SA)	7	1	299	117	49.83
E.H. Hendren (E)	7	0	329	93	47.00
M. Leyland (E)	8	1	300	91	42.85
I.J. Siedle (SA)	9	0	384	141	42.66

Bowling	O	M	Runs	W	Avge	BB
E.P. Nupen (SA)	157.5	21	413	21	19.66	6–46
C.L. Vincent (SA)	169	47	374	18	20.79	6–63
M.W. Tate (E)	193 2	56	341	14	24.35·	3–79
W. Voce (E)	250.4	65	561	23	24.39	5–58
I.A.R. Peebles (E)	167.3	27	466	18	25.88	6–63

1935: South Africa win their first series in England

H.F. Wade brought a side to England in 1935, and made his debut in the first Test at Trent Bridge, as did, among others, Dudley Nourse and Eric Rowan. Wyatt captained England and made his highest Test score, 149, England declaring at 384 for seven. M.S. Nichols (6–35) dismissed the tourists for 220, forcing a follow-on, but rain washed out the last day and saved the match for South Africa.

At Lord's South Africa made only 228, but X.C. Balaskas, a googly bowler of Greek ancestry, took five for 49 and England fell 30 behind. South Africa declared at 278 for seven after Mitchell's 164 not out, and won by 157 runs by dismissing England for 151, Balaskas getting four more wickets.

England scored 216 at Headingley, and removed South Africa for 171. A declaration at 294 for seven set South Africa 340 in 4½ hours, but despite using eight bowlers England could capture no more than five wickets for 194.

The Old Trafford Test took a not dissimilar course. R.W.V. Robins' 108 helped England to 357 (R.J. Crisp 5–99) and K.G. Viljoen's 124 kept the deficit down to 39, with Bowes getting five for 100. England's declaration at 231 for six left South Africa to get 271 in 225 minutes, but Mitchell, who batted throughout that time for 48, protected the tourists' one-match lead.

A desperate Wyatt put South Africa in on a perfect wicket at the Oval, but centuries from Mitchell and E.L. Dalton allowed them to compile a safe-from-defeat 476. England declared at 534 for six, Leyland (161) and Ames (148) scoring rapidly, but South Africa batted out time at 287 for six.

South Africa thus won their first series in England. Their former captain, Jock Cameron, who on the tour had hit Verity for 30 in an over, inspiring the famous story: 'You had him in two minds – he didn't know

whether to hit you for six or four', contracted fever on the boat home and died aged only 30.

1935 15th Series SA 1 Eng 0, Drawn 4
1 TRENT BRIDGE **Match Drawn**
England 384–7 dec (R E S Wyatt 149, M Leyland 69, H Sutcliffe 61)
South Africa 220 (I J Siedle 59, H B Cameron 52, M S Nichols 6–35) and 17–1
2 LORD'S **South Africa won by 157 runs**
South Africa 228 (H B Cameron 90) and 278–7 dec (B Mitchell 164)
England 198 (R E S Wyatt, 53, X C Balaskas 5–49) and 151 (A B C Langton 4–31, X C Balaskas 4–54)
3 HEADINGLEY **Match Drawn**
England 216 (W R Hammond 63, A Mitchell 58, C L Vincent 4–45, A B C Langton 4–59) and 294–7 dec (W R Hammond 87, A Mitchell 72, D Smith 57, C L Vincent 4–104)
South Africa 171 (E A B Rowan 62) and 194–5 (B Mitchell 58)
4 OLD TRAFFORD **Match Drawn**
England 357 (R W V Robins 108, A H Bakewell 63, M Leyland 53, R J Crisp 5–99) and 231–6 dec (W R Hammond 63, A H Bakewell 54, C L Vincent 4–78)
South Africa 318 (K G Viljoen 124, H B Cameron 53, W E Bowes 5–100) and 169–2 (A D Nourse 53)
5 THE OVAL **Match Drawn**
South Africa 476 (B Mitchell 128, E L Dalton 117, A B C Langton 73, K G Viljoen 60, H D Read 4–136) and 287–6 (E L Dalton 57)
England 534–6 dec (M Leyland 161, L E G Ames 148, W R Hammond 65)

1935 Averages

Batting	I	No	Runs	HS	Avge
B. Mitchell (SA)	10	3	488	164*	69.71
W.R. Hammond (E)	8	2	389	87*	64.83
M. Leyland (E)	6	0	342	161	57.00
R.E.S. Wyatt (E)	8	1	317	149	45.28
K.G. Viljoen (SA)	7	0	280	124	40.00
H.B. Cameron (SA)	8	0	306	90	38.25

Bowling	O	M	Runs	W	Avge	BB
H. Verity (E)	172	78	250	12	20.83	3–52
M.S. Nichols (E)	139.3	32	382	13	29.38	6–35
W.E. Bowes (E)	178.4	43	412	14	29.42	5–100
C.L. Vincent (SA)	194.3	39	601	18	33.38	4–45
R.J. Crisp (SA)	131	14	444	13	34.15	5–99
A.B.C. Langton (SA)	202.3	29	623	15	41.53	4–31

1938–39: Edrich comes good in timeless Test

W.R. Hammond, having become an amateur, led England's party in 1938–39, while Alan Melville captained South Africa. In the first Test in Johannesburg, Eddie Paynter scored a century in England's 422, with N. Gordon, on his Test debut, getting five wickets. South Africa made 390, despite a hat-trick by T.W.J. Goddard. E.L. Dalton made 102, and in fact all but four of the runs off the bat were scored by five batsmen – there were also five ducks. England declared after Paynter had completed a century in each innings, while P.A. Gibb, preferred to Hutton, almost did the same (93 and 106). The match was drawn.

Rain delayed the second Test at Cape Town and an easy wicket ensured the draw. Hammond, Ames and Valentine scored centuries for England, as did Dudley Nourse for South Africa.

The English run-feast continued at Durban, with Paynter making 243, the highest score in matches between the countries. Hammond made 120 in 469 for four declared. South Africa collapsed to 103 all out, followed on, and although Mitchell made a century, a score of 353 was still 13 runs short.

Hammond won his eighth successive toss at Johannesburg, but England were removed amid showers for 215, A.B.C. Langton getting five for 58. South Africa declared 134 ahead but the third day was washed out and the match drawn.

With England only one up, the fifth Test was to be played to a finish. It became one of the most famous of Test matches, the longest and highest scoring. P.G.V. van der Bijl and Dudley Nourse made centuries as South Africa began strongly enough with 530 in 2½ days. R.T.D. Perks, in his first Test took five for 100. England made only 316, and appeared in trouble. Melville did not enforce the follow on, and by the end of the sixth day had made a second innings century himself and South Africa had added 481 to their lead. England were set to get 696 to win. On the seventh day they made 253 for one. Rain washed out the Saturday play, and on Monday, the ninth day, England moved to 496 for three, needing 200. On the tenth day they began slowly, but with more rain in the air, began to hit out. A thunderstorm stopped play at 4 o'clock with the score 654 for five, and only 42 more runs wanted. But England had a two-day rail journey to their ship, and the match was left drawn. Gibb and Hammond made centuries, but the backbone of the innings was 219 from W.J. Edrich, who had been persevered with and was playing his ninth successive Test match, although before this innings he had scored only 88 runs, average 8.00.

Alan Melville, the South African captain, batting at Trent Bridge in 1947, where he made 189.

1938–39   16th Series   Eng 1, SA 0, Drawn 4
1 JOHANNESBURG   Match Drawn
England 422 (E Paynter 117, B H Valentine 97, P A Gibb 93, N Gordon 5–103) and 291–4 dec (P A Gibb 106, E Paynter 100, W R Hammond 58)
South Africa 390 (E L Dalton 102, B Mitchell 73, A D Nourse 73, A B C Langton 64, K G Viljoen 50, H Verity 4–61) and 108–1

2 CAPE TOWN   Match Drawn
England 449–9 dec (W R Hammond 181, L E G Ames 115, B H Valentine 112, P A Gibb 58, N Gordon 5–157)
South Africa 286 (A D Nourse 120, H Verity 5–70) and 201–2 (E A B Rowan 89, P G V van der Bijl 87)

3 DURBAN   England won by an innings and 13 runs
England 469–4 dec (E Paynter 243, W R Hammond 120)
South Africa 103 (K Farnes 4–29) and 353 (B Mitchell 109, E A B Rowan 67, K G Viljoen 61)

4 JOHANNESBURG   Match Drawn
England 215 (L Hutton 92, A B C Langton 5–58) and 203–4 (W R Hammond 61)
South Africa 349–8 dec (E A B Rowan 85, A Melville 67, B Mitchell 63)

5 DURBAN   Match Drawn
South Africa 530 (P G V van der Bijl 125, A D Nourse 103, A Melville 78, R E Grieveson 75, E L Dalton 57, R T D Perks 5–100) and 481 (A Melville 103, P G V van der Bijl 97, B Mitchell 89, K G Viljoen 74, K Farnes 4–74)
England 316 (L E G Ames 84, E Paynter 62, E L Dalton 4–59) and 654–5 (W J Edrich 219, W R Hammond 140, P A Gibb 120, E Paynter 75, L Hutton 55)

1938–39 Averages

Batting	I	No	Runs	HS	Avge
W.R. Hammond (E)	8	1	609	181	87.00
E. Paynter (E)	8	0	653	243	81.63
B.H. Valentine (E)	6	2	275	112	68.75
L.E.G. Ames (E)	8	3	339	115	67.80
A.D. Nourse (SA)	9	2	422	120	60.29
P.A. Gibb (E)	8	0	473	120	59.13
B. Mitchell (SA)	9	1	466	109	58.25
P.G.V. van der Bijl (SA)	9	0	460	125	51.11
A. Melville (SA)	7	1	286	103	47.67
E.A.B. Rowan (SA)	7	1	284	89	47.33
L. Hutton (E)	6	0	265	92	44.17

Bowling	O	M	Runs	W	Avge	BB
H. Verity (E)	283.2	85	552	19	29.05	5–70
K. Farnes (E)	186.3	35	519	16	32.44	4–29
N. Gordon (SA)	245.6	28	807	20	40.35	5–103
A.B.C. Langton (SA)	219.6	37	672	13	51.69	5–58

1947: Run-feast for Compton, Edrich, Melville, Nourse, Mitchell

The glorious English summer of 1947 saw Denis Compton and Bill Edrich both pass the 40-year-old record of most runs in a season. The South African tourists, led by Alan Melville, were on the receiving end of many of these runs.

Despite this, South Africa had the better of the first Test at Trent Bridge, scoring 533, with centuries from Melville (189) and Dudley Nourse (149), who added 319 for the third wicket, a new South African Test record. England were out for 208 (L. Tuckett 5–68) and followed on, but with Compton making 163 and adding 237 for the fifth wicket with Yardley (99), made 551. This was enough to draw, although the tourists were only 61 short of winning at 166 for one, with Melville becoming the first South African to score a century in each innings.

At Lord's Edrich (189) and Compton (208) set a world Test record for the third wicket with a stand of 370. England declared at 554 for eight (Tuckett 5–115) and dismissed South Africa for 327, with D.V.P. Wright getting five wickets with his leg breaks and Melville scoring his third successive century of the series (fourth in all). Wright got five more wickets in the follow-on and England won by ten wickets.

At Old Trafford, South Africa scored 339, and then Edrich (191) and Compton (115, his third successive century) added 228 in England's 478. Nourse made a hundred in reply, but England emerged seven-wicket winners.

In the fourth Test, South Africa could make only 175. England declared at 317 for seven (Hutton 100), and needed only 47 for a ten-wicket win.

At the Oval, England batted right down

1947   17th Series   Eng 3, SA 0, Drawn 2
1 TRENT BRIDGE   Match Drawn
South Africa 533 (A Melville 189, A D Nourse 149, T A Harris 60, W E Hollies 5–123) and 166–1 (A Melville 104, K G Viljoen 51)
England 208 (D C S Compton 65, W J Edrich 57, L Tuckett 5–68) and 551 (D C S Compton 163, N W D Yardley 99, T G Evans 74, C Washbrook 59, W J Edrich 50, V I Smith 4–143)

2 LORD'S   England won by 10 wkts
England 554–8 dec (D C S Compton 208, W J Edrich 189, C Washbrook 65, L Tuckett 5–115) and 26–0
South Africa 327 (A Melville 117, A D Nourse 61, D V P Wright 5–95) and 252 (B Mitchell 80, A D Nourse 58, D V P Wright 5–80)

3 OLD TRAFFORD   England won by 7 wkts
South Africa 339 (K G Viljoen 93, B Mitchell 80, D V Dyer 62, W J Edrich 4–95) and 267 (A D Nourse 115, A Melville 59, W J Edrich 4–77)
England 478 (W J Edrich 191, D C S Compton 115, L Tuckett 4–108) and 130–3

4 HEADINGLEY   England won by 10 wkts
South Africa 175 (B Mitchell 53, A D Nourse 51, H J Butler 4–34) and 184 (A D Nourse 57, K Cranston 4–12)
England 317–7 dec (L Hutton 100, C Washbrook 75, N B F Mann 4–68) and 47–0

5 THE OVAL   Match Drawn
England 427 (L Hutton 83, N W D Yardley 59, D C S Compton 53, C Gladwin 51, N B F Mann 4–93) and 325 (D C S Compton 113)
South Africa 302 (B Mitchell 120, O C Dawson 55) and 423–7 (B Mitchell 189, A D Nourse 97)

the order for 427, while South Africa's 302 was dependent on Bruce Mitchell's 120. After a Compton century England declared at 325 for six, setting South Africa 451 to win. With Mitchell as sheet-anchor, they made a good attempt, ending at 423 for seven. With 189 not out, Mitchell made a century in each innings, and was on the field for all but eight minutes of the full five days.

1947 Averages

Batting	I	No	Runs	HS	Avge
W.J. Edrich (E)	6	1	552	191	110.40
D.C.S. Compton (E)	8	0	753	208	94.12
A.D. Nourse (SA)	9	0	621	149	69.00
B. Mitchell (SA)	10	1	597	189*	66.33
A. Melville (SA)	10	1	569	189*	63.22
C. Washbrook (E)	10	2	396	75	49.50
L. Hutton (E)	10	2	344	100	43.00
N.W.D. Yardley (E)	7	0	273	99	39.00
K.G. Viljoen (SA)	10	1	270	93	30.00

Bowling	O	M	Runs	W	Avge	BB
W.J. Edrich (E)	134.5	33	370	16	23.12	4–77
D.V.P. Wright (E)	183.2	50	484	19	25.47	5–80
N.B.F. Mann (SA)	329.5	127	603	15	40.20	4–68
L. Tuckett (SA)	252	44	644	15	44.26	5–68
A.M.B. Rowan (SA)	274.2	48	671	12	55.91	3–92

Compton, Denis Charles Scott

Born on 23 May 1918, Compton became a leading cricketer and footballer, although his soccer caps were unofficial war-time ones. He was a brilliant right-hand batsman and occasional left-arm slow bowler. He made his debut for Middlesex in 1936, and his Test debut in 1937 as a 19-year-old. His cavalier style, and his speciality, the leg sweep, made him the most popular English batsman of the immediate post-war years. In the 1947 season he established a new record aggregate of runs (3,816) and centuries (18). His later career was handicapped by a knee injury. In 78 Tests he made 5,807 runs, average 50.06. He also took 25 wickets, average 56.40.

Top: The South African tourists in 1947. Left to right, back: Harris, Ovenstone, Begbie, Smith, Tuckett, Plimsoll, Payn, Lindsay, Fullerton. Front: Dawson, Dyer, Mitchell, Melville, A.S. Frames (manager), Nourse, Viljoen, Mann, Rowan.

Compton sweeping at Old Trafford in 1947. Compton enjoyed a record-breaking season in 1947, taking over 750 runs off the South African tourists in Test matches alone, including four centuries, highest 208.

1948–49: Two narrow wins for England settle the series

After a disastrous tour by a weak side in the West Indies in 1947–48, MCC laid down conditions under which official tours would take place. One result was that the party to South Africa the following winter under F.G. Mann was the strongest available, given the continuing 'need' for an amateur captain.

The first Test at Durban was one of the most exciting between the countries. South Africa made only 161, but excellent spin bowling by N.B.F. Mann (6–59) and Athol Rowan (4–108) kept England to 253. South Africa's 219 left England only 128 to win. However, some superb bowling by C.N. McCarthy on his debut (6–43) brought about a situation where, with three balls left, England needed two to win with two wickets left. C. Gladwin 'scored' the winning run off the last ball with a leg-bye.

At Ellis Park, Johannesburg, before a record crowd of 35,000, the bat ruled, with Hutton (158) and Washbrook (195) establishing a new Test record opening partnership of 359. Compton also scored a century in a total of 608. A rear-guard action by South Africa (315 and 270 for two) saved the match, Eric Rowan getting 156 not out.

At Cape Town, Athol Rowan's five for 80 kept England down to 308 and old-stagers Mitchell (120) and Nourse (112) added 190 and get South Africa to 298 before the third wicket fell, but the last eight wickets added only 58. England's declaration set a target of 229 in 125 minutes, and the match was drawn.

England made 379 at Johannesburg, with A.J. Watkins scoring 111, and South Africa declared at 257 for nine, with Nourse 129 not out. Hutton made a century, and a declaration set South Africa 376 to win in 270 minutes. There was no attempt to score them.

At Port Elizabeth, South Africa made 379, with W.W. Wade getting a century after Mitchell had missed what would have been his last by one run. With Mann scoring his only Test century England took a lead of 16. Nourse, in a last desperate attempt to square the series, declared, setting a realistic target of 172 in 95 minutes. Hutton and Washbrook, each hitting their first balls to the boundary, raced to 58, but wickets then tumbled regularly. England won with three wickets and one minute left.

1948–49 18th Series   Eng 2, SA 0, Drawn 3

1 DURBAN   England won by 2 wkts
South Africa 161 (A V Bedser 4–39) and 219 (W W Wade 63, D V P Wright 4–72)
England 253 (L Hutton 83, D C S Compton 72, N B F Mann 6–59, A M B Rowan 4–108) and 128–8 (C N McCarthy 6–43)

2 JOHANNESBURG   Match Drawn
England 608 (C Washbrook 195, L Hutton 158, D C S Compton 114, J F Crapp 56)
South Africa 315 (B Mitchell 86, W W Wade 85) and 270–2 (E A B Rowan 156, A D Nourse 56)

3 CAPE TOWN
England 308 (C Washbrook 74, A M B Rowan 5–80) and 276–3 dec (L Hutton 87, A J Watkins 64, J F Crapp 54, D C S Compton 51)
South Africa 356 (B Mitchell 120, A D Nourse 112, O E Wynne 50 (D C S Compton 5–70) and 142–4 (R O Jenkins 4–48)

4 JOHANNESBURG   Match Drawn
England 379 (A J Watkins 111, C Washbrook 97, J F Crapp 51, C N McCarthy 5–114) and 253–7 dec (L Hutton 123, A M B Rowan 4–69)
South Africa 257–9 dec (A D Nourse 129, W W Wade 54) and 194–4 (E A B Rowan 86, K G Viljoen 63)

5 PORT ELIZABETH   England won by 3 wkts
South Africa 379 (W W Wade 125, B Mitchell 99, A D Nourse 73, A V Bedser 4–61) and 187–3 dec (B Mitchell 56)
England 395 (F G Mann 136, A M B Rowan 5–167) and 174–7 (N B F Mann 4–65)

1948–49 Averages

Batting

	I	No	Runs	HS	Avge
A.D. Nourse (SA)	10	3	536	129*	76.57
L. Hutton (E)	9	0	577	158	64.11
C. Washbrook (E)	9	0	542	195	60.22
E.A.B. Rowan (SA)	8	2	319	156	53.16
B. Mitchell (SA)	10	1	475	120	52.77
W.W. Wade (SA)	9	1	407	125	50.87
D.C.S. Compton (E)	9	1	406	114	50.75
F.G. Mann (E)	8	1	254	136	36.28
A.J. Watkins (E)	9	2	251	111	35.85

Bowling

	O	M	Runs	W	Avge	BB
N.B.F. Mann (SA)	165.3	42	430	17	25.29	6–59
C.N. McCarthy (SA)	160.5	15	561	21	26.71	6–43
R.O. Jenkins (E)	132.7	21	495	16	30.93	4–48
A.M.B. Rowan (SA)	277.2	40	794	24	33.08	5–80
A.V. Bedser (E)	206.5	37	554	16	34.62	4–39

1951: South Africa win first Test but England come back to take series

Nourse led a strong side to England in 1951, and was himself the hero of the first Test at Trent Bridge. Batting in pain from a thumb fractured three weeks earlier, he made 208 before declaring at 483 for nine. Eric Rowan then took over the captaincy. Centuries by R.T. Simpson and Compton brought England to 419 for nine, when F.R. Brown declared. South Africa made only 121 on a now tricky wicket, A.V. Bedser getting six for 37, but excellent bowling by Athol Rowan (5–68) and Mann (4–24) got England out for 114 and South Africa won their first Test for 16 years by 71 runs.

At Lord's, rain after England scored 311 made South Africa's task very difficult. Off-spinner R. Tattersall, with 12 wickets in the match, dismissed them for 115 and 211, and England won by 10 wickets on the third afternoon.

At Old Trafford each side had a distinguished newcomer: T.W. Graveney for England and R.A. McLean for South Africa. On a rain-affected pitch Bedser took seven for 58, South Africa making 158. G.W.A. Chubb, in his only Test series, replied with six for 51 as England struggled after more rain to 211. Bedser (5–54) got South Africa out for 191 and England made the 139 needed, losing only one wicket. Hutton made 98 not out, just missing becoming the first to score his hundredth

Above: Dudley Nourse batting in 1951. Nourse, the South African captain, played a gallant innings in the first Test, scoring a double century despite a fractured thumb. South Africa won the match, but eventually lost the series.

Below: Cliff Gladwin bowled by Cuan McCarthy in the fourth Test at Johannesburg in 1948–49. In the first Test Gladwin had won the match with a leg-bye off the last ball, and England won the series.

century in a Test match, leaving this distinction for Boycott to achieve 26 years later.

A high-scoring Headingley Test was drawn, Eric Rowan making South Africa's top score against England (236) in 538, adding 198 with C.B. van Ryneveld for the second wicket. Hutton and P.B.H. May (on his debut) made centuries in 505 and the match was drawn.

South Africa made a great effort to tie the series at the Oval. On a pitch taking spin they made 202 and, by dismissing England for 194, led by eight. Laker then got six for 55 (ten in the match) to get South Africa out for 154, England needing only 163 to win. Hutton then became the first batsman in Test history to be out 'obstructing the field'. In preventing a ball from Rowan from dropping onto his wicket, the umpire ruled that he prevented Endean from catching it. England eventually got home by four wickets.

1955: Five results in splendid series

Jack Cheetham captained the South African party in 1955, and a future captain, Trevor Goddard made his debut in the first Test, together with another notable player, Ken Barrington. Hutton was picked as England captain for the series but did not play because of lumbago, and P.B.H. May began his long sequence of matches as England captain.

England began well at Trent Bridge, scoring 334, although Barrington made a duck. Wardle (4–24) bowled well to help dismiss the tourists for 181, and following on they could manage only 148, Tyson (6–28) finishing the innings with five for five. 'Sticky' McGlew top-scored in both innings, batting over nine hours for 68 and 51.

At Lord's, P.S. Heine (5–60), on his debut, and Goddard (4–59) skittled England for 133, and then Roy McLean played a brilliant innings of 142, helping South Africa to a lead of 171. But May made 112, allowing England to set a target of 183. Statham then bowled brilliantly, taking seven for 39, and causing Cheetham to retire with a chipped bone in the elbow. South Africa made only 111 and lost by 71.

Compton made 158 at Old Trafford, but England only 284. McGlew, who was captain, and Goddard put on 147, but Goddard was out and McGlew hurt his hand. He returned later to complete his century, and Waite and Winslow made hundreds, adding 171 for the sixth wicket. May made a century second time, and Evans, with a broken finger (Graveney kept wicket), scored 36 at number eleven. Heine took five wickets and South Africa needed 145. It was not easy, but they won by three wickets. It was Bedser's last Test.

South Africa began badly at Headingley, being 34 for five and 98 for seven before struggling to 171. England did little better, collapsing from 152 for four to 191 all out, despite Adcock injuring a foot. A South African record opening stand of 176 between McGlew (133) and Goddard (74) turned the game. Endean scored 116 not out and the score reached 500. Tayfield and Goddard took five wickets each as South Africa won by 224 to square the series.

With all to play for at the Oval, where Cheetham returned, England could make only 151, Goddard again taking five wickets. But Laker and Lock got South Africa out for 112, and another Surrey player, May, made 89 not out in England's 204. May had the benefit of a close lbw decision when four, which might have swayed the match. A total of 244 was too much for South Africa against Laker (5–56) and Lock (4–62) and they lost by 92.

his was one of the best series in England, the first in which a result was reached in all five games. It was ironic for captain Cheetham that the two South African wins were in the matches he missed.

May, Peter Barker Howard
Born on 31 December 1929 at Reading, May was a brilliant schoolboy batsman and made his debut for Surrey on vacation from Cambridge University in 1950. He made his Test debut the following year. He was a correct and polished right-hand bat, the most talented English batsman of the 1950s. He played for Surrey throughout their seven successive championships. He played in 66 Tests, captaining England 41 times, an English record. He scored 4,537 runs, average 46.77. Ill-health caused him to give up Test cricket in 1961.

Above: Peter Heine throws up his hands in disappointment as a chance is spilled at short leg in the first Test at Johannesburg in 1956–57.

The South African team in the last Test at the Oval in 1955. Left to right, back: Fuller, Mansell, Goddard, Heine, Keith, Waite. Front: McLean, McGlew, Cheetham, Endean, Tayfield. South Africa lost a very exciting series by three matches to two, having levelled the series with wins in the third and fourth test.

Below: Taylor lbw to Tayfield when MCC lost to a South African XI during the 1956–57 tour. MCC lost their first match in South Africa for 26 years. Tayfield took 37 wickets in the drawn Test series.

1956–57: South Africa draw series of slow, cautious batting

May took a strong team to South Africa in 1956–57. McGlew was appointed South African captain, but played in only the second Test because of a shoulder injury, C.B. van Ryneveld captaining in four matches.

May won the first toss at Johannesburg, where over 100,000 watched the five days' play. England made only 45 for two in two hours before lunch. Peter Richardson eventually scored 117 in 488 minutes (including the slowest Test hundred) and England 268. This earned a lead of 53, to which England could add only 150, setting the home side 204 to win. Bailey took five for 20 and South Africa collapsed for 72.

England batted again at Cape Town, where Cowdrey scored a century in 368 (Tayfield 5–130). South Africa scored only 205 (Wardle 5–53), and an England declaration set them 385 to win. Endean, involved in Test cricket's first 'obstructing the field' dismissal, now found himself the first batsman to be out 'handled the ball' in Tests. He padded a ball from Laker and stopped it hitting the stumps with his hand. For the second match in succession South Africa were dismissed for 72. Wardle took seven for 36 (12 in the match).

Richardson and Bailey put on 115 for England's first wicket at Durban, but the side were out for 218. McLean scored 100 and South Africa led by 65. Bailey fractured a bone in the second innings but returned to hold up South Africa (three runs in 55 minutes), helping his Essex colleague Insole (110 not out) to prolong the innings. Even

so, with Tayfield taking eight for 69, South Africa needed only 190 in 250 minutes, but could not get them, the match being drawn at 142 for six.

South Africa won the toss and batted at Johannesburg, and a lively 93 from McLean helped them to 340, good enough for a lead of 89. They made only 142 second time, England needing 232 to win the series. Tayfield bowled magnificently, and England, needing only 56 with five wickets left, crashed to 214 all out and defeat by 17 runs. It was South Africa's first home defeat of England on turf. Tayfield bowled non-stop for nearly five hours on the last day, and became the only South African to take nine wickets in a Test innings. The last was caught by his brother, fielding as a substitute.

On a recently relaid pitch at St George's Park, Port Elizabeth, the ball frequently shot along the ground. South Africa made only 164, but England scored a mere 110. Tyson took six for 40 in getting the home team out again for 134, but 189 to win was difficult in the circumstances and Tayfield's six for 78 levelled the series and gave him 37 wickets in the rubber. Only 122 runs were scored on the third day.

1956–57   21st Series   Eng 2, SA 2, Drawn 1

1 JOHANNESBURG   **England won by 131 runs**
England 268 (P E Richardson 117, M C Cowdrey 59, N A T Adcock 4–36) and 150
South Africa 215 and 72 (T E Bailey 5–20)

2 CAPE TOWN   **England won by 312 runs**
England 369 (M C Cowdrey 101, T G Evans 62, D C S Compton 58, H J Tayfield 5–130) and 220–6 dec (D C S Compton 64, M C Cowdrey 61)
South Africa 205 (J H Wardle 5–53 and 72 (J H Wardle 7–36)

3 DURBAN   **Match Drawn**
England 218 (T E Bailey 80, P E Richardson 68, N A T Adcock 4–39) and 254 (D J Insole 110, H J Tayfield 8–69)
South Africa 283 (R A McLean 100, T L Goddard 69, J H Wardle 5–61) and 142–6

4 JOHANNESBURG   **South Africa won by 17 runs**
South Africa 340 (R A McLean 93, T L Goddard 67, J H B Waite 61) and 142
England 251 (P B H May 61, H J Tayfield 4–79) and 214 (D J Insole 68, M C Cowdrey 55, H J Tayfield 9–113)

5 PORT ELIZABETH   **South Africa won by 58 runs**
South Africa 164 (W R Endean 70) and 134 (F H Tyson 6–40)
England 110 (P S Heine 4–22, N A T Adcock 4–20) and 130 (H J Tayfield 6–78)

1956–57 Averages

Batting	I	No	Runs	HS	Avge
D.J. Insole (E)	10	2	312	110*	39.00
P.E. Richardson (E)	10	0	369	117	36.90
T.L. Goddard (SA)	10	0	333	69	33.30
M.C. Cowdrey (E)	10	0	331	101	33.10
R.A. McLean (SA)	10	0	309	100	30.90
T.E. Bailey (E)	10	0	259	80	25.90

Bowling	O	M	Runs	W	Avge	BB
T.E. Bailey (E)	142.3	43	232	19	12.21	5–20
J.H. Wardle (E)	139.6	37	359	26	13.80	7–36
N.A.T. Adcock (SA)	142	31	313	21	14.90	4–20
H.J. Tayfield (SA)	285	105	636	37	17.18	9–113
T.L. Goddard (SA)	210.7	81	370	15	24.66	3–51
J.B. Statham (E)	130.1	20	349	14	24.92	3–37
P.S. Heine (SA)	185	34	517	18	28.72	4–22

1960: No-balling of Griffin caps a bad tour for South Africa

A young South African side under McGlew had a miserable tour in a damp summer. Cowdrey won the toss for England at Edgbaston and the home side made 292 (Adcock 5–62). South Africa finished 106 behind and needed 310 to win in the fourth innings. They lost by 100.

The South African twelve for the first Test at Edgbaston in 1960. Left to right, back: Griffin, Pithey, Carlstein, Adcock, Fellows-Smith, O'Linn, Wesley (12th man). front: Tayfield, Waite, McGlew, Goddard, McLean. England won despite Waite passing 50 in each innings.

Cowdrey, Michael Colin

Cowdrey was born on Christmas Eve, 1932, at Ootacamund, India. A schoolboy prodigy, he played for Tonbridge School at Lord's when he was 13, and made his debut for Kent in 1950. A middle-order right-hand batsman, his solid strength and timing sent the ball to the boundary effortlessly. He played for England from 1954–55. His total of 114 Test appearances was a world record until passed by Gavaskar. On 27 of these he was captain. He scored 7,624 runs, average 44.06. He usually fielded at slip, and his 120 catches was also a Test record.

At Lord's, England made 362 for eight declared, and the innings was remarkable for the no-balling of fast bowler Geoff Griffin, playing in his second Test. He became the only South African to take a Test hat-trick. But he was no-balled for throwing 11 times during the innings (after being no-balled in previous games). It ended his Test career and his bowling on the tour, and his career lasted only three more years. South Africa collapsed twice before Statham (6–63 and 5–34) and lost by an innings and 73.

England batted again at Trent Bridge, made 287 (Goddard 5–80) and enforced the follow-on by dismissing South Africa for 88 (Trueman 5–27). Despite Syd O'Linn's 98, England needed only 49 to win.

There was no play for the first two days at Old Trafford, where England again batted and led on the first innings by 31, despite McLean's 109. England declared and set South Africa 185 in 105 minutes, but there was no attempt to get them.

At the Oval, Neil Adcock (6–65) and Jim Pothecary (4–58) removed England for 155 after Cowdrey had completed a nap hand of all five tosses. South Africa made 419. Pullar (175) and Cowdrey (155) put on 290 for England's opening wicket. A declaration at 479 for nine set South Africa 216 in three hours, but rain washed out a dreary season.

1960   22nd Series   Eng 3, SA 0, Drawn 2

1 EDGBASTON   England won by 100 runs
England 292 (R Subba Row 56, M J K Smith 54, E R Dexter 52, N A T Adcock 5–62) and 203 (H J Tayfield 4–62)
South Africa 186 (J H B Waite 58, F S Trueman 4–58) and 209 (R A McLean 68, J H B Waite 56)

2 LORD'S   England won by an innings and 73 runs
England 362–8 dec (M J K Smith 99, R Subba Row 90, E R Dexter 56, P M Walker 52, G M Griffin 4–87)
South Africa 152 (J B Statham 6–63, A E Moss 4–35) and 137 (J B Statham 5–34)

3 TRENT BRIDGE   England won by 8 wkts
England 287 (K F Barrington 80, M C Cowdrey 67, T L Goddard 5–80) and 49–2
South Africa 88 (F S Trueman 5–27) and 247 (S O'Linn 98, J H B Waite 60, F S Trueman 4–77)

4 OLD TRAFFORD   Match Drawn
England 260 (K F Barrington 76, N A T Adcock 4–66) and 153–7 dec
South Africa 229 (R A McLean 109, D A Allen 4–58) and 46–0

5 THE OVAL   Match Drawn
England 155 (G Pullar 59, N A T Adcock 6–65, J E Pothecary 4–58) and 479–9 dec (G Pullar 175, M C Cowdrey 155)
South Africa 419 (T L Goddard 99, J H B Waite 77, S O'Linn 55) and 97–4

1960 Averages

Batting

	I	No	Runs	HS	Avge
G. Pullar (E)	6	1	293	175	58.60
R. Subba Row (E)	6	1	251	90	50.20
J.H.B. Waite (SA)	9	2	267	77*	38.14
M.C. Cowdrey (E)	9	0	312	155	34.66
R.A. McLean (SA)	9	1	269	109	33.62
S. O'Linn (SA)	8	0	261	98	32.62

Bowling

	O	M	Runs	W	Avge	BB
J.B. Statham (E)	203	54	491	27	18.18	6–63
F.S. Trueman (E)	180.3	31	508	25	20.32	5–27
N.A.T. Adcock (SA)	263	69	587	26	22.57	6–65
T.L. Goddard (SA)	202	80	414	17	24.35	5–80
H.J. Tayfield (SA)	187.3	68	454	12	37.83	4–62

Ken Barrington during his innings of 76 at Old Trafford in 1960. Barrington played well after missing the first Test.

Below left: Pithey caught by Parks behind the wicket off the bowling of Statham at Old Trafford in 1960. Statham took most wickets and headed the averages in the series.

1964–65: England win the first Test and hold on

M.J.K. Smith led the touring party in 1964–65, Dexter and Cowdrey being unavailable. Goddard captained South Africa. Smith won the toss at Durban and declared at 485 for five, when Barrington (148 not out) and Jim Parks (108 not out) had added 206. With the wicket taking spin, first Allen and then Titmus, two off-spinners, dismissed South Africa for an innings win. Barrington became the first player to score a century in all seven Test-playing countries.

Another century from Barrington, plus 172 from Dexter, helped England to 531 at Johannesburg and South Africa were again forced to follow on. Allen and Titmus again bowled well, but South Africa easily saved the match, with Colin Bland making a second-innings 144 not out.

It was South Africa's turn at Cape Town to win the toss and bat. Positions were reversed as Barlow (138) and Pithey (154) took the home side to 501 for seven declared. But the follow-on could not be enforced; despite H.O. Bromfield's five for 88, Smith scored 121 and the match was drawn. Barrington 'walked' after being given not out caught behind on 49. Barlow had decided not to in his innings, and the gesture caused much comment. A feature of the match was that twenty players bowled, the exceptions being the wicket-keepers.

England asked South Africa to bat in the fourth Test, but despite rain interruptions the ploy was a failure. South Africa declared at 390 for six, and removed England for 384, despite Peter Parfitt's 122 not out. Smith was recalled after being run out while 'gardening' by Van der Merwe, who had received the ball from the wicket-keeper. Goddard 'over-ruled' the appeal. He then scored a second-innings century, declared,

and had six English wickets down at the close, a stubborn 76 not out by Boycott being necessary to save the game.

South Africa needed to win the last Test and began well by winning the toss and scoring 502 in under two days. Graeme Pollock made 137. But Boycott (117) and Barrington (72) played the defensive innings their side needed. Goddard declared and set England a sporting 246 in 233 minutes, but rain washed out most of the last day.

1964–65 23rd Series Eng 1, SA 0, Drawn 4
1 DURBAN England won by an innings and 104 runs
England 485–5 dec (K F Barrington 148, J M Parks 108, R W Barber 74, G Boycott 73)
South Africa 155 (D A Allen 5–41) and 226 (K C Bland 68, F J Titmus 5–66)
2 JOHANNESBURG Match Drawn
England 531 (E R Dexter 172, K F Barrington 121, R W Barber 97, P H Parfitt 52, P M Pollock 5–129)
South Africa 317 (A J Pithey 85, E J Barlow 71, F J Titmus 4–73) and 336–6 (K C Bland 144, R G Pollock 55, T L Goddard 50, D A Allen 4–87)
3 CAPE TOWN Match Drawn
South Africa 501–7 dec (A J Pithey 154, E J Barlow 138, K C Bland 78) and 346 (E J Barlow 78, R G Pollock 73, K C Bland 64, D T Lindsay 50)
England 442 (M J K Smith 121, E R Dexter 61, R W Barber 58, J M Parks 59, H D Bromfield 5–88) and 15–0
4 JOHANNESBURG Match Drawn
South Africa 390–6 dec (E J Barlow 96, A J Pithey 95, J H B Waite 64, T L Goddard 60, K C Bland 55) and 307–3 dec (T L Goddard 112, R G Pollock 65)
England 384 (P H Parfitt 122, K F Barrington 93, R W Barber 61, A H McKinnon 4–128) and 153–6 (G Boycott 76)
5 PORT ELIZABETH Match Drawn
South Africa 502 (R G Pollock 137, E J Barlow 69, P L van der Merwe 66, T L Goddard 61) and 178–4 dec (R G Pollock 77)
England 435 (G Boycott 117, K F Barrington 72) and 29–1

1964–65 Averages

Batting	I	No	Runs	HS	Avge
K.F. Barrington (E)	7	2	508	148*	101.60
R.W. Barber (E)	4	0	290	97	72.50
K.C. Bland (SA)	10	2	572	144*	71.50
R.G. Pollock (SA)	10	2	459	137	57.37
E.R. Dexter (E)	7	1	344	172	57.33
E.J. Barlow (SA)	10	0	558	138	55.80
A.J. Pithey (SA)	9	0	462	154	51.33
G. Boycott (E)	8	2	298	117	49.66
M.J.K. Smith (E)	6	0	257	121	42.83
T.L. Goddard (SA)	10	0	405	112	40.50

Bowling	O	M	Runs	W	Avge	BB
D.A. Allen (E)	254.5	87	458	17	26.94	5–41
P.M. Pollock (SA)	169.5	51	445	12	37.08	5–129
F.J. Titmus (E)	312.1	88	694	18	38.55	5–66

1965: The last series before 'D'Oliveira Affair'

South Africa came to England in 1965 under Van de Merwe determined to do better in a three-Test series, but at Lord's they could manage only 280, and England took a lead of 58, excellent fielding by Bland resulting in two run-outs to keep the lead down. England needed 191 in 235 minutes to win, but after John Edrich had retired after being hit on the head by a ball from Peter Pollock, were never up with the clock and the match was drawn.

At Trent Bridge a dazzling 125 out of 160 by Graeme Pollock in damp conditions took South Africa to 269 (Cartwright 6–94) and Cowdrey's century could not prevent the tourists gaining a lead of 29. With Cartwright unable to bowl, a second-innings 289 left England needing 319, but after 13 for four they fell 95 short of victory. Peter Pollock took five wickets in each innings, so it was something of a family triumph.

At the Oval, England needed to win, and put South Africa in. Five wickets for a re-called Statham in his last Test helped get them out for 208. But Peter Pollock also took five wickets and England were out for

202. Bland made a century as South Africa scored 392, setting England 399 to save the series. At 308 for four England were well on the way but, with 70 minutes left, heavy rain prevented a result.

This was the last Test between the two countries. The English team to tour South Africa in 1968–69 included as a late replacement Basil d'Oliveira, a Cape Coloured cricketer who had qualified for England. The South African Prime Minister, Mr Vorster, announced that South Africa would not accept a team picked with political considerations, and subsequently MCC cancelled after protests in England over South African *apartheid* policies.

1965 24th Series SA 1, Eng 0, Drawn 2
1 LORD'S Match Drawn
South Africa 280 (R G Pollock 56) and 248 (K C Bland 70, E J Barlow 52)
England 338 (K F Barrington 91, R W Barber 56, F J Titmus 59) and 145–7 (R Dumbrill 4–30)

2 TRENT BRIDGE South Africa won by 94 runs
South Africa 269 (R G Pollock 125, T W Cartwright 6–94) and 289 (E J Barlow 76, A Bacher 67, R G Pollock 59, J D F Larter 5–68)
England 240 (M C Cowdrey 105, P M Pollock 5–53) and 224 (P H Parfitt 86, P M Pollock 5–34)
3 THE OVAL Match Drawn
South Africa 208 (H R Lance 69, J B Statham 5–40, K Higgs 4–47) and 392 (K C Bland 127, A Bacher 70, H R Lance 53, K Higgs 4–96)
England 202 (M C Cowdrey 58, P M Pollock 5–43) and 308–4 (M C Cowdrey 78, K F Barrington 73, W E Russell 70)

1965 Averages

Batting	I	No	Runs	HS	Avge
M.C. Cowdrey (E)	6	1	327	105	65.40
R.G. Pollock (SA)	6	0	291	125	48.50
K.C. Bland (SA)	6	0	286	127	47.66
A. Bacher (SA)	6	0	218	70	36.33
K.F. Barrington (E)	6	0	202	91	33.66

Bowling	O	M	Runs	W	Avge	BB
P.M. Pollock (SA)	164.2	55	366	20	18.30	5–34

1970 25th Series
Five Tests were arranged – at Lord's, Trent Bridge, Edgbaston, Headingley and The Oval – but the visit was cancelled at the request of the British Government

Statham's 250th Test wicket came in the last match with South Africa, in 1965. Tiger Lance, South Africa's top scorer in the first innings at the Oval, is lbw for 69.

Australia v South Africa

1902–03: Darling's Australians give boost to South Africa

After the Boer War, South Africa were anxious to resume top-class international cricket, and invited the Australians touring England in 1902 to return home via South Africa and play three Tests there. The invitation was accepted, so J. Darling and H.M. Taberer, in his only Test, captained the two sides in the first Test between the countries. A.W. 'Dave' Nourse also made his Test debut.

South Africa made 454 on matting at Johannesburg against the newly arrived Australians, and then dismissed them for 296, C.B. Llewellyn, a slow left-arm bowler, following an innings of 90 with six for 92. In the follow-on Australia did better, declaring at 372 for seven after Hill had scored 142, including 116 before lunch on the third day. The match was drawn.

A second match at Johannesburg four days later saw Australia out for 175 (Llewellyn 5–43) and South Africa, captained by J.H. Anderson, reached 240. Armstrong came to the rescue this time with 150 not out, and with Saunders taking seven for 34 South Africa were out for 85, Australia winning by 159.

At Cape Town Llewellyn again bowled well with six for 97, but South Africa, captained now by E.A. Halliwell, could make only 85 and trailed by 167. They batted better in the follow-on, particularly J.H. Sinclair, whose century in 80 minutes remains South Africa's fastest in Tests. But Australia needed only 59 and won by 10 wickets.

Australia v South Africa
1902–03 1st Series Aus 2, SA 0, Drawn 1
1 JOHANNESBURG Match Drawn
South Africa 454 (L J Tancred 97, C B Llewellyn 90, A W Nourse 72, E A Halliwell 57) and 101–4
Australia 296 (R A Duff 82, C Hill 76, V T Trumper 63, C B Llewellyn 6–92, J H Sinclair 4–129) and 372–7 dec (C Hill 142, W W Armstrong 59, M A Noble 53)
2 JOHANNESBURG Australia won by 159 runs
Australia 175 (C B Llewellyn 5–43) and 309 (W W Armstrong 159, C B Llewellyn 5–73)
South Africa 240 (J H Sinclair 101) and 85 (J V Saunders 7–34)
3 CAPE TOWN Australia won by 10 wkts
Australia 252 (C Hill 91, V T Trumper 70, C B Llewellyn 6–97) and 59–0
South Africa 85 (W P Howell 4–18, J V Saunders 4–37) and 225 (J H Sinclair 104, W P Howell 5–81)

Australia v South Africa
1902–3 Averages
Batting	I	No	Runs	HS	Avge
C. Hill (A)	5	1	327	142	81.75
W.W. Armstrong (A)	5	1	281	159*	70.25
R.A. Duff (A)	6	2	238	82*	59.50
V.T. Trumper (A)	6	1	239	70	47.80
J.H. Sinclair (SA)	6	0	286	104	47.66

Bowling	O	M	Runs	W	Avge	BB
J.V. Saunders (A)	49.3	8	176	15	11.73	7–34
W.P. Howell (A)	64	·16	174	14	12.42	5–81
C.B. Llewellyn (SA)	132.4	23	484	25	17.92	6–92

1910–11: South African tourists lose 4–1 in Australia

P.W. Sherwell captained South Africa's tourists to Australia in 1910–11. Clem Hill won the toss in the first Test at Sydney, and

made 191, helping Bardsley (132) to add 224 for the second wicket. Australia made 494 for six on the first day, still a first-day Test record. South Africa followed on and were beaten by an innings and 114, A. Cotter and W.J. Whitty each taking eight wickets in the match.

At Melbourne, Australia made 348, but Faulkner played a magnificent innings of 204 to gain South Africa a lead of 158. Trumper then made 159, and Australia set South Africa 170 to win. Whitty, with the help of a strong wind, took six for 17 as South Africa collapsed to 80 and a second defeat.

If this was discouraging, winning the toss and batting was what was needed at Adelaide, and J.W. Zulch (105) and S.J. Snooke (103) helped them to 482. Trumper then

1910–11 2nd Series Aus 4, SA 1
1 SYDNEY Australia won by an innings and 114 runs
Australia 528 (C Hill 191, W Bardsley 132, D R A Gehrs 67, R O Schwarz 5–102)
South Africa 174 (G Faulkner 62, R O Schwarz 61, A Cotter 6–69, W J Whitty 4–75) and 240 (A W Nourse 64, P W Sherwell 60, W J Whitty 4–75)
2 MELBOURNE Australia won by 89 runs
Australia 348 (W Bardsley 85, W W Armstrong 75, V S Ransford 58) and 327 (V T Trumper 159, R O Schwarz 4–76, C B Llewellyn 4–81)
South Africa 506 (G A Faulkner 204, S J Snooke 77, J H Sinclair 58, W W Armstrong 4–134) and 80 (W J Whitty 6–17, A Cotter 4–47)
3 ADELAIDE South Africa won by 38 runs
South Africa 482 (J W Zulch 105, S J Snooke 103, G A Faulkner 56, W W Armstrong 4–103) and 360 (G A Faulkner 115, C B Llewellyn 80, W J Whitty 6–104)
Australia 465 (V T Trumper 214, W Bardsley 54, V S Ransford 50, C B Llewellyn 4–107) and 339 (C Kelleway 65, W Bardsley 58, C Hill 55, R O Schwarz 4–48)
4 MELBOURNE Australia won by 530 runs
Australia 328 (W Bardsley 82, V S Ransford 75, C Kelleway 59) and 578 (W W Armstrong 132, C Hill 100, V S Ransford 95, V T Trumper 87, D R A Gehrs 58)
South Africa 205 (A W Nourse 92, W J Whitty 4–78) and 171 (G A Faulkner 80, H V Hordern 5–66)
5 SYDNEY Australia won by 7 wkts
Australia 364 (C G Macartney 137, W Bardsley 94, H V Hordern 50, R O Schwarz 6–47) and 198–3 (V T Trumper 74, C G Macartney 56)
South Africa 160 (G A Faulkner 52, H V Hordern 4–73) and 401 (J W Zulch 150, G A Faulkner 92, W J Whitty 4–66)

1910–11 Averages
Batting	I	No	Runs	HS	Avge
V.T. Trumper (A)	9	2	661	214*	94.42
G.A. Faulkner (SA)	10	0	732	204	73.20
W. Bardsley (A)	9	0	573	132	63.66
C. Hill (A)	8	0	425	191	53.12
W.W. Armstrong (A)	8	0	410	132	51.25
C. Kelleway (A)	9	2	295	65	42.14
J.W. Zulch (SA)	10	1	354	150	39.33
A.W. Nourse (SA)	10	2	304	92*	38.00
V.S. Ransford (A)	9	0	318	95	35.33
S.J. Snooke (SA)	10	0	259	103	25.90

Bowling	O	M	Runs	W	Avge	BB
W.J. Whitty (A) ，	233.3	55	632	37	17.08	6–17
Dr. H.V. Hordern (A)	80.3	7	295	14	21.07	5–66
R.O. Schwarz (SA)	167.4	19	651	25	26.04	6–47
A. Cotter (A)	194.5	23	633	22	28.77	6–69
C.B. Llewellyn (SA)	131	6	559	14	39.92	4–18

demonstrated his skill with 214 not out, and Australia finished only 17 behind. Faulkner scored another century and Australia were set 378 to win. They reached 339, but South Africa won their first overseas Test.

At Melbourne, Australia took a first innings lead of 123, then scored 578 with Hill and Armstrong again making centuries. H.V. Hordern, on his debut, took five for 66 (eight in the match) and South Africa were out for 171. The victory margin of 530 runs was a Test record.

In the last Test R.O. Schwarz took six for 47 for South Africa, but Macartney had made 137 and Australia reached 364. South Africa followed on 204 behind but made 401, with Zulch getting 150. Australia won by seven wickets, Whitty claiming 37 wickets in the series.

1912: Australia maintain easy mastery in Triangular Tournament

Australia, led by S.E. Gregory, and South Africa, led by F. Mitchell, played three matches in the Triangular Tournament in England in 1912. Mitchell was making his South African debut, having played for England in South Africa. H.W. Taylor made his debut for South Africa in the first Test at Old Trafford, where Australia, with centuries from Kelleway and Bardsley, made 448 (Pegler 6–105). Despite Faulkner's not out century in the first innings, Australia won by an innings. T.J. Matthews performed the unique feat of a hat-trick in each innings of a Test. Both came on the second and last day, and T.A. Ward was the third victim of each.

At Lord's South Africa made 263, but Kelleway and Bardsley again made centuries and Australia won by ten wickets.

In the third match at Trent Bridge, South Africa, led by L.J. Tancred, made 329 and established a lead of 110, but rain washed out the last day.

1912 3rd Series Aus 2, SA 0, Drawn 1
1 OLD TRAFFORD Australia won by an innings and 88 runs
Australia 448 (W Bardsley 121, C Kelleway 114, S J Pegler 6–105)
South Africa 265 (G A Faulkner 122, W J Whitty 5–55) and 95 (C Kelleway 5–33)
2 LORD'S Australia won by 10 wkts
South Africa (H W Taylor 93, W J Whitty 4–68) and 173 (C B Llewellyn 59, T J Matthews 4–29)
Australia 390 (W Bardsley 164, C Kelleway 102, S J Pegler 4–79) and 48–0
3 TRENT BRIDGE Match Drawn
South Africa 329 (A W Nourse 64, G C White 59)
Australia 219 (W Bardsley 56, S J Pegler 4–80)

1912 Averages
Batting	I	No	Runs	HS	Avge
W. Bardsley (A)	3	0	341	164	113.66
C. Kelleway (A)	3	0	253	114	84.33

Bowling	O	M	Runs	W	Avge	BB
T.J. Matthews (A)	66.5	18	142	13	10.92	4–29
W.J. Whitty (A)	110	34	243	13	18.69	5–55
S.J. Pegler (SA)	115.2	23	279	14	19.92	6–105

1921–22: The strong Aussies win the last Test for the series

After the Australian Imperial Forces side had played in South Africa on their way home from England after the war, Warwick Armstrong's victorious Test side did the same in 1921, although H.L. Collins captained the visitors because Armstrong had suffered injury on the boat.

At Durban, Australia made 299 (Blanckenburg 5–90) and then the fast bowler J.M. Gregory took six for 77 to give Australia a 67-run lead. Macartney made a century as this was extended by 324 before a cautious declaration. South Africa drew at 184 at seven.

Collins scored 203 at Johannesburg, and

Gregory made the fastest Test century (to this day) in 70 minutes. C.P. Carter, who claimed them both, bravely took six for 91. Australia made 450, enforced the follow-on, but found a defiant South Africa declaring at 472 for eight, C.N. Frank and 'Dave' Nourse scoring centuries. It was a token declaration in another draw.

South Africa, batting first at Cape Town, could manage only 180. Jack Ryder scored a century in 396, and South Africa avoided an innings defeat by only one run, which was scored by number eleven Arthur Mailey.

1921–22 4th Series Aus 1, SA 0, Drawn 2
1 DURBAN Match Drawn
Australia 299 (J Ryder 78, C G Macartney 59, J M Gregory 51, J M Blanckenberg 5–78) and 324–7 dec (C G Macartney 116, J Ryder 58)
South Africa 000 (J W Zulch 80, J M Gregory 6–77) and 184–7
2 JOHANNESBURG Match Drawn
Australia 450 (H L Collins 203, J M Gregory 119, J Ryder 56, C P Carter 6–91) and 7–0
South Africa 243 (A W Nourse 64, J M Gregory 4–71) and 472–8 dec (C N Frank 152, A W Nourse 111, H W Taylor 80)
3 CAPE TOWN Australia won by 10 wkts
South Africa 180 (J W Zulch 50, A A Mailey 4–40) and 216 (C G Macartney 5–44)
Australia 396 (J Ryder 142, H L Collins 54, J M Blanckenberg 4–82) and 1–0

1921–22 Averages

Batting	I	No	Runs	HS	Avge
J.S. Ryder (A)	4	1	334	142	111.33
H.L. Collins (A)	5	1	340	203	85.00
C.G. Macartney (A)	3	0	219	116	73.00
A.W. Nourse (SA)	6	1	280	111	56.00
J.M. Gregory (A)	4	0	205	119	51.25
C.N. Frank (SA)	6	0	236	152	39.33
H.W. Taylor (SA)	6	0	200	80	33.33

Bowling	O	M	Runs	W	Avge	BB
J.M. Gregory (A)	115.4	29	284	15	18.93	6–77
C.P. Carter (SA)	96.5	13	329	15	21.93	6–91
J.M. Blanckenberg (SA)	107.4	17	365	12	30.41	5–78
A.A. Mailey (A)	153	25	423	13	32.53	4–40
E.A. MacDonald (A)	149	48	371	10	37.10	3–53

1931–32: South Africa annihilated by Grimmett and Bradman

H.W. Taylor was the only survivor of the previous Test when cricket between the countries resumed in Australia in 1931–32. W.M. Woodfull (Australia) and H.B. Cameron were the captains.

Australia won the toss in the first Test to be played at the Woolloongabba ground, Brisbane. Don Bradman, missed at 11 and 15, made 226 of Australia's 450. South Africa, at 126 for three at the close of the second day, then had to bat on a rain-affected pitch and collapsed twice to lose by an innings, T.W. Wall and H. Ironmonger doing the damage.

South Africa also lost by an innings at Sydney, after batting first. Grimmett took four wickets in each innings and K.E. Rigg and Bradman each made centuries.

At Melbourne, A.J. Bell and N.A. Quinn got Australia out for only 198, and then every South African player reached double figures, and led by K.G. Viljoen's 111, the total reached 358, a lead of 160. Alas for South Africa, Woodfull (161) and Bradman (167) added 274 for the second wicket, and Grimmett and Ironmonger took the wickets as Australia won in the end by 169 runs.

Grimmett took seven for 116 at Adelaide but 308 was a respectable total until Bradman got going. He ran out Thurlow when going for his 300th run, and finished on 299 not out. Bell, bowling with pain-killing injections for a

foot injury, took five wickets for the third successive match. Grimmett took seven for 83 in South Africa's second innings. The match was W.J. O'Reilly's debut – he and Grimmett shared 18 wickets. Australia won by ten wickets.

The fifth Test was played on one of Melbourne's notorious sticky wickets, and although play ended on the third day, the total playing time of 5 hours 53 minutes is the shortest of all Tests. South Africa were dismissed for 36 and 45, Ironmonger taking five for six and six for 18. In between Australia made 153 for an innings win. Curiously Grimmett, the series' most successful bowler, was not required to bowl, and Bradman, whose series average was 201.50, twisted his ankle and did not bat.

1931–32 5th Series Aus 5, SA 0
1 BRISBANE Australia won by an innings and 163 runs
Australia 450 (D G Bradman 226, W M Woodfull 76, W A S Oldfield 56, A J Bell 4–120)
South Africa 170 (B Mitchell 58, H Ironmonger 5–42) and 117 (T W Wall 5–14, H Ironmonger 4–44)
2 SYDNEY Australia won by an innings and 155 runs
South Africa 153 (S J McCabe 4–13, C V Grimmett 4–28) and 161 (C V Grimmett 4–44)
Australia 469 (K E Rigg 127, D G Bradman 112, S J McCabe 79, W M Woodfull 58, A J Bell 5–140)
3 MELBOURNE Australia won by 169 runs
Australia 198 (K E Rigg 68, A F Kippax 52, A J Bell 5–69, N A Quinn 4–42) and 554 (D G Bradman 167, W M Woodfull 161, S J McCabe 71, A F Kippax 67, Q McMillan 4–150, C L Vincent 4–154)
South Africa 358 (K G Viljoen 111) and 225 (J A J Christy 63, C V Grimmett 6–92, H Ironmonger 4–54)
4 ADELAIDE Australia won by 10 wkts
South Africa 308 (H W Taylor 78, B Mitchell 75, H B Cameron 52, C V Grimmett 7–116) and 274 (B Mitchell 95, H W Taylor 84, J A J Christy 51, C V Grimmett 7–83)
Australia 513 (D G Bradman 299, W M Woodfull 82, A J Bell 5–142) and 73–0
5 MELBOURNE Australia won by an innings and 72 runs
South Africa 36 (H Ironmonger 5–6, L J Nash 4–18) and 45 (H Ironmonger 6–18)
Australia 153

1931–32 Averages

Batting	I	No	Runs	HS	Avge
D.G. Bradman (A)	5	1	806	299*	201.50
W.M. Woodfull (A)	7	1	421	161	70.16
K.E. Rigg (A)	5	0	253	127	50.60
B. Mitchell (SA)	10	0	322	97	32.20
H.W. Taylor (SA)	10	0	314	84	31.40

Bowling	O	M	Runs	W	Avge	BB
H. Ironmonger (A)	221.5	112	300	31	9.67	6–18
C.V. Grimmett (A)	306	108	557	33	16.87	7–83
T.W. Wall (A)	129.1	38	266	13	20.46	5–14
A.J. Bell (SA)	207	28	627	23	27.26	5–69
N.A. Quinn (SA)	207.4	44	512	13	39.38	4–42

1935–36: Grimmett breaks records as Australia win 4–0

V.Y. Richardson led the Australian tourists to meet H.F. Wade's team which had just won a series in England, although their spirits were dampened by the death of their wicket-keeper H.B. Cameron. Bradman was unavailable for Australia.

Taylor, Herbert Wilfred

Taylor was born in Durban on 5 May 1889, and made his debut for Natal in 1909–10. He also played for Transvaal. He was a stylish right-hand opening batsman and an excellent fielder. He first played for South Africa in England against Australia, in the 1912 Triangular Tournament. He was a stalwart of South African cricket until 1931–32. In 42 Tests, he was captain in 18. He scored 2,936 runs, average 40.77. He died on 8 February 1973 at Cape Town.

South Africa batted first at Durban and made 248, but with S.J. McCabe and A.G. Chipperfield making centuries, Australia reached 429, enough for a 10-wicket victory. The spinners O'Reilly, Grimmett and L. O'B. Fleetwood-Smith (on his debut) took all but one of the wickets.

At Johannesburg, South Africa made only 157, but kept Australia's lead to 93. Then Dudley Nourse made 231, a new South African record, and South Africa set Australia 399 to win. Even so, at 274 for two, with McCabe 189 not out, Australia were well on the way when a storm ended the match on the last afternoon.

Rain washed out the first day at Cape Town, but W.A. Brown (121) and J.H.W. Fingleton (112) then made a decisive 233 for Australia's first wicket. Australia declared at 362 for eight and won by an innings with spinners O'Reilly, Grimmett and Fleetwood-Smith again taking all but one of the wickets in conditions made for them.

Grimmett and O'Reilly were mainly responsible for South Africa's poor score of 157 at Johannesburg, and Fingleton's second successive century ensured a big lead for Australia. Grimmett then took seven for 40 as South Africa collapsed to 98 to lose by an innings.

At Durban, Grimmett took seven for 100 in South Africa's 222, and Fingleton scored his third century in successive innings in Australia's 455 (Mitchell 5–87). Australia just won by an innings with Grimmett ending his Test career with six for 73. In his last series he established an Australian record of 44 wickets in a series, and a world record of 216 in a career.

1935–36 6th Series Aus 4, SA 0, Drawn 1
1 DURBAN Australia won by 9 wkts
South Africa 248 (E A B Rowan 66, L O'B Fleetwood-Smith 4–64) and 282 (I J Siedle 59, W J O'Reilly 5–49)
Australia 429 (S J McCabe 149, A G Chipperfield 109, W A Brown 66, L S Darling 60, A B C Langton 4–113) and 102–1 (W A Brown 55)
2 JOHANNESBURG Match Drawn
South Africa 157 (W J O'Reilly 4–54) and 491 (A D Nourse 231)
Australia 250 (J H W Fingleton 62, W A Brown 51, B Mitchell 4–26, A B C Langton 4–85) and 274–2 (S J McCabe 189)
3 CAPE TOWN Australia won by an innings and 78 runs
Australia 362–8 dec (W A Brown 121, J H W Fingleton 112, X C Balaskas 4–126)
South Africa 102 (C V Grimmett 5–32) and 182 (I J Siedle 59, C V Grimmett 5–56, W J O'Reilly 4–35)
4 JOHANNESBURG Australia won by an innings and 184 runs
South Africa 157 (W J O'Reilly 5–20) and 98 (C V Grimmett 7–40)
Australia 439 (J H W Fingleton 108, L P J O'Brien 59, W J O'Reilly 56, E Q Davies 4–75, X C Balaskas 4–165)
5 DURBAN Australia won by an innings and 6 runs
South Africa 222 (K G Viljoen 56, A D Nourse 50, C V Grimmett 7–100) and 227 (B Mitchell 72, C V Grimmett 6–73, W J O'Reilly 4–47)
Australia 455 (J H W Fingleton 118, W A Brown 84, L S Darling 62, B Mitchell 5–87)

1934–36 Averages

Batting	I	No	Runs	HS	Avge
S.J. McCabe (A)	7	2	420	189*	84.00
J.H.W. Fingleton (A)	7	1	478	118	79.66
W.A. Brown (A)	7	0	417	121	59.57
A.D. Nourse (SA)	10	1	518	231	57.55
I.J. Siedle (SA)	10	0	332	59	33.20
B. Mitchell (SA)	10	2	251	72*	31.37

Bowling	O	M	Runs	W	Avge	BB
C.V. Grimmett (A)	346.1	140	642	44	14.59	7–40
W.J. O'Reilly (A)	250.2	112	460	27	17.03	5–20
E.L. McCormick (A)	125.1	24	418	15	27.86	3–28
A.B.C. Langton (SA)	204.2	32	532	12	44.33	4–85

1949–50: Another 4–0 win for Australia in South Africa

A.L. Hassett's was the first Australian side to visit South Africa after the Second World War. Dudley Nourse was South Africa's captain.

Hassett and S.J.E. Loxton both made centuries in the first Test at Johannesburg after openers A.R. Morris and J. Moroney had both made ducks. Australia enforced the follow-on and won by an innings, fast bowlers K.R. Miller and W.A. Johnston and off-spinner I.W. Johnson getting the wickets.

1949–50 7th Series   Aus 4, SA 0, Darwn 1

1 JOHANNESBURG   Australia won by an innings and 85 runs
Australia 413 (A L Hassett 112, S J E Loxton 101, I W Johnson 66)
South Africa 137 (E A B Rowan 60, K R Miller 5–40) and 191 (W A Johnston 6–44)

2 CAPE TOWN   Australia won by 8 wkts
Australia 526–7 dec (R N Harvey 178, J R Moroney 87, K R Miller 58, A L Hassett 57, N B F Mann 4–105) and 87–2
South Africa 278 (E A B Rowan 67, A D Nourse 65, C L McCool 5–41) and 333 (A D Nourse 114, H J Tayfield 75, R R Lindwall 5–32)

3 DURBAN   Australia won by 5 wkts
South Africa 311 (E A B Rowan 143, A D Nourse 66, W A Johnston 4–75) and 99 (I W Johnson 5–34, W A Johnston 4–39)
Australia 75 (H J Tayfield 7–23) and 336–5 (R N Harvey 151, S J E Loxton 54)

4 JOHANNESBURG   Match Drawn
Australia 465–8 dec (J R Moroney 118, A R Morris 111, K R Miller 84, R N Harvey 56, A L Hassett 53, M G Melle 5–113) and 259–2 (J R Moroney 101, R N Harvey 100)
South Africa 352 (G M Fullerton 88, E A B Rowan 55, N B F Mann 52)

5 PORT ELIZABETH   Australia won by an innings and 259 runs
Australia 549–7 dec (A L Hassett 167, A R Morris 157, R N Harvey 116)
South Africa 158 (K R Miller 4–42) and 132 (A D Nourse 55)

1949–50 Averages

Batting

	I	No	Runs	HS	Avge
R.N. Harvey (A)	8	3	660	178	132.00
A.L. Hassett (A)	6	0	402	167	67.00
A.R. Morris (A)	8	0	422	157	52.75
J.R. Moroney (A)	8	1	352	118	50.28
A.D. Nourse (SA)	9	0	405	114	45.00
E.A.B. Rowan (SA)	9	0	404	143	44.88
S.J. Loxton (A)	6	0	255	101	42.50

Bowling

	O	M	Runs	W	Avge	BB
W.A. Johnston (A)	160.5	31	392	23	17.04	6–44
R.R. Lindwall (A)	94	13	248	12	20.66	5–32
C.L. McCool (A)	83	14	272	13	20.92	5–41
K.R. Miller (A)	135	17	390	17	22.94	5–40
I.W. Johnston (A)	135.2	24	432	18	24.00	5–34
N.B. F. Mann (SA)	194.2	29	623	16	38.93	4–105
H.J. Tayfield (SA)	198.4	21	726	17	42.70	7–23

At Cape Town other Australians shone. R.N. Harvey made 178 out of 526 for seven declared, and South Africa, made to follow on, set Australia only 86 to win. R.R. Lindwall and C.L. McCool took most wickets. Dudley Nourse made a captain's 114 in the second innings.

In an extraordinary match at Durban, Eric Rowan scored 143 of South Africa's 311, and then remarkable bowling in his third Test by H.J. Tayfield (7–23) removed Australia for 75. With the weekend to ponder his tactics, Nourse decided not to enforce the follow-on on a wicket already showing wear. Johnston and Johnson then removed South Africa for 99, leaving Australia 336 to win. In a superb innings Harvey made a patient 151 not out in 5½ hours to get Australia home with 25 minutes to spare.

In the fourth Test Morris and Moroney began with 214 and Australia declared at 465 for eight. M.G. Melle took five for 113 on his debut. South Africa scored 352 and the

match was drawn, but not before Moroney scored his second century of the match and Harvey his third of the series.

At Port Elizabeth, Morris, Harvey and Hassett all scored centuries (Australia made 11 in the series) and Australia lost only seven wickets in winning by an innings and 259 runs.

1952–53: South Africa announce their revival by tying series

Jack Cheetham led a young touring side to Australia in 1952–53. With the retirements of Nourse and the Rowan brothers, the team was expected to be too weak for Australia.

At Brisbane, Australia, led by Hassett, made 280, Harvey's 109 being his fifth century in successive matches against South Africa. Melle and J.C. Watkins shared the wickets. South Africa made 221 (Ring 6–72). Australia's 277 set the tourists 337, and Lindwall's five for 60 ensured a home win by 96 runs. A feature of the match was the brilliant fielding of South Africa.

South Africa batted at Melbourne and struggled to 227. Tayfield took six for 84 to restrict Australia's lead to only 16, and with Endean scoring 162 not out in the second innings Australia were set 373 to win. With Tayfield again bowling brilliantly (7–81), South Africa won by 82 runs. It was only their second win in 31 Tests against Australia.

However, at Sydney South Africa could make only 173, and Harvey returned to his old ways with 190 in Australia's 443. He

Jack Cheetham batting. His young side in Australia in 1952–53 shocked the Aussies by drawing the series.

SOUTH AFRICA V AUSTRALIA 1949-50
3rd Test, Durban: Australia won by five wickets

SOUTH AFRICA

E.A.B Rowan	c Johnston b Miller	143	c Saggers b Lindwall	4
O.E. Wynne	b Johnston	18	b Johnson	29
J.D. Nel	c and b Johnson	14	lbw b Johnston	20
A.D. Nourse*	c Saggers b Johnston	66	c McCool b Johnson	27
W.W. Wade†	b Lindwall	24	b Johnston	0
N.B.F. Mann	b Johnston	9	(9) lbw b Johnson	0
J.E. Cheetham	c Hassett b Johnston	4	(6) c Hassett b Johnson	1
J.C. Watkins	b Lindwall	5	(7) st Saggers b Johnson	2
H.J. Tayfield	run out	15	(8) b Johnston	4
V.I. Smith	b Lindwall	1	not out	2
C.N. McCarthy	not out	0	(B 2, LB 1, NB 1)	7
Extras	(B 3, LB 7, NB 2)	12		
Total		**311**		**99**

AUSTRALIA

A.R. Morris	c Smith b Tayfield	25	hit wkt b Tayfield	44
J. Moroney	b Tayfield	10	lbw b Tayfield	10
I.W. Johnson	lbw b Tayfield	2		
K.R. Miller	b Tayfield	2	(3) lbw b Mann	10
A.L. Hassett*	lbw b Tayfield	2	(4) lbw b Mann	11
R.A. Saggers†	c Cheetham b Mann	2		
C.L. McCool	lbw b Mann	1	not out	39
R.R. Lindwall	b Mann	7		
R.N. Harvey	c and b Tayfield	2	(5) not out	151
S.J.E. Loxton	c Cheetham b Tayfield	16	(6) b Mann	54
W.A. Johnston	not out	2		
Extras	(B 3, LB 1)	4	(B 7, LB 9, NB 1)	17
Total		**75**	(5 wickets)	**336**

AUSTRALIA	O	M	R	W	O	M	R	W
Lindwall	19	3	47	3	4	1	7	1
Miller	24	5	73	1	7	0	12	0
McCool	13	3	35	0				
Johnston	31.2	5	75	4	18.2	6	39	4
Loxton	6	1	31	0				
Johnson	16	5	38	1	17	2	34	5
SOUTH AFRICA								
McCarthy	6	2	8	0	12	3	32	0
Watkins	4	1	9	0	6	2	10	0
Mann	10	1	31	3	51.6	13	101	3
Tayfield	8.4	1	23	7	49	5	144	2
Smith					5	0	32	0

FALL OF WICKETS

Wkt	SA 1st	A 1st	SA 2nd	A 2nd
1st	32	31	9	14
2nd	75	51	33	
3rd	242	37	85	59
4th	264	39	85	95
5th	283	42	88	230
6th	289	45	90	—
7th	293	46	93	—
8th	304	53	93	—
9th	308	63	93	—
10th	311	75	99	—

completed 1,000 runs against South Africa in only eight Tests. Australia won by an innings.

Colin McDonald (154) and Hassett (163) added 275 for the second wicket at Adelaide, and Australia totalled 530. South Africa, 387, avoided the follow-on by seven runs, which probably saved them the match. Australia declared after another Harvey hundred, but South Africa held on with four wickets left.

Ian Craig, at 17 years 239 days, became Australia's youngest Test player at Melbourne in the fifth Test. Harvey continued his amazing run against South Africa with 205 out of 520. South Africa batted solidly all the way down for 435 (Johnston 6–152). E.R.H. Fuller, in his second Test, took five for 66 in helping dismiss Australia for 209, leaving the tourists 295 to win. At 191 for four, McLean came in and was dropped first ball. He celebrated by smashing 76 in 80 minutes and South Africa levelled the series with a six-wicket victory.

1952–53   8th Series   Aus 2, SA 2, Drawn 1

1 BRISBANE   Australia won by 96 runs
Australia 280 (R N Harvey 109, A L Hassett 55, M G Melle 6–71, J C Watkins 4–41) and 277 (A R Morris 58, R N Harvey 52, H J Tayfield 4–116)
South Africa 221 (D T Ring 6–72) and 240 (D J McGlew 69, K J Funston 65, R R Lindwall 5–60)

2 MELBOURNE   South Africa won by 82 runs
South Africa 227 (A R A Murray 51, K R Miller 4–62) and 388 (W R Endean 162, J H B Waite 62)
Australia 243 (C C McDonald 82, K R Miller 52, H J Tayfield 6–84) and 290 (R N Harvey 60, D T Ring 53, H J Tayfield 7–81)

3 SYDNEY   Australia won by an innings and 38 runs
South Africa 173 (K J Funston 56, R R Lindwall 4–40) and 232 (W R Endean 71, R A McLean 65, R R Lindwall 4–72)
Australia 443 (R N Harvey 190, C C McDonald 67, D T Ring 58, K R Miller 55, A R A Murray 4–169)

4 ADELAIDE   Match Drawn
Australia 530 (A L Hassett 163, C C McDonald 154, R N Harvey 84, G B Hole 59, H J Tayfield 4–142) and 233–3 dec (R N Harvey 116, A R Morris 77)
South Africa 387 (K J Funston 92, J C Watkins 76, W R Endean 56, W A Johnston 5–110, R Benaud 4–118) and 177–6 (D J McGlew 54)

5 MELBOURNE   South Africa won by 6 wkts
Australia 520 (R N Harvey 205, A R Morris 99, I D Craig 53) and 209 (E R H Fuller 5–66)
South Africa 435 (J W Watkins 92, R A McLean 81, J E Cheetham 66, J H B Waite 64, P N F Mansell 52, W A Johnston 6–152) and 297–4 (R A McLean 76, W R Endean 70, J C Watkins 50)

1952–53 Averages

Batting	I	No	Runs	HS	Avge
R.N. Harvey (A)	9	0	834	205	92.66
W.R. Endean (SA)	10	1	438	162*	48.66
C.C. McDonald (A)	9	0	437	154	48.55
A.L. Hassett (A)	8	0	346	163	43.25
R.A. McLean (SA)	10	1	370	81	41.11
A.R. Morris (A)	9	0	370	99	41.11
K.J. Funston (SA)	10	0	365	92	36.50
J.C. Watkins (SA)	10	0	352	92	35.20
D.J. McGlew (SA)	8	0	250	69	31.25
J.H.B. Waite (SA)	10	0	293	64	29.30

Bowling	O	M	Runs	W	Avge	BB
K.R. Miller (A)	91	17	241	13	18.53	4–62
R.R. Lindwall (A)	137.7	18	383	19	20.15	5–60
H.J. Tayfield (SA)	278.4	58	843	30	28.10	7–81
W.A. Johnston (A)	266.7	59	737	21	35.09	6–152
M.G. Melle (SA)	130.5	9	531	14	37.92	6–71
D.T. Ring (A)	184.1	30	624	13	48.00	6–72

1957–58: Ian Craig's side easily win series

Ian Craig was captain of Australia when they toured South Africa in 1957–58, the youngest Test captain at the time. C.B. van Ryneveld captained South Africa, but McGlew deputized in the first Test.

AUSTRALIA V SOUTH AFRICA 1952–53
5th Test, Melbourne: South Africa won by six wickets

AUSTRALIA

C.C. McDonald	c McLean b Mansell	41	c Watkins b Fuller	11
A.R. Morris	run out	99	lbw b Tayfield	44
R.N. Harvey	c Cheetham b Fuller	205	b Fuller	7
A.L. Hassett*	run out	40	c Endean b Mansell	30
I.D. Craig	c Keith b Fuller	53	c Endean b Tayfield	47
R.G. Archer	c Waite b Fuller	18	c Watkins b Fuller	30
R. Benaud	c and b Tayfield	20	c Endean b Mansell	0
D.T. Ring	b Tayfield	14	not out	26
G.R.A. Langley†	b Murray	2	c Cheetham b Fuller	5
W.A. Johnston	c Endean b Tayfield	12	b Fuller	1
G. Noblet	not out	13	(B 7, LB 1)	8
Extras	(LB 3)	3		
Total		**520**		**209**

SOUTH AFRICA

W.R. Endean	c Langley b Johnston	16	b Johnston	70
J.H.B. Waite†	run out	64	c Archer b Noblet	18
J.C. Watkins	b Archer	92	b Ring	50
K.J. Funston	lbw b Johnston	16	b Benaud	35
H.J. Keith	b Johnston	10	not out	40
R.A. McLean	lbw b Noblet	81	not out	76
J.E. Cheetham*	c McDonald b Johnston	66		
P.N.F. Mansell	lbw b Johnston	52		
A.R.A. Murray	c and b Johnston	17		
H.J. Tayfield	c Benaud b Ring	17		
E.R.H. Fuller	not out	0		
Extras	(B 1, LB 3)	4	(B 2, LB 6)	8
Total		**435**	(4 wickets)	**297**

SOUTH AFRICA	O	M	R	W	O	M	R	W
Fuller	19	4	74	3	30.2	4	66	5
Watkins	23	3	72	0	14	4	33	0
Tayfield	35.4	4	129	3	32	8	73	3
Murray	25	3	84	1				
Mansell	22	0	114	1	8	3	29	2
Keith	9	0	44	0				

AUSTRALIA	O	M	R	W	O	M	R	W
Noblet	30	6	65	1	24	9	44	1
Archer	33	4	97	1	5	0	23	0
Johnston	46	8	152	6	38	7	114	1
Ring	19.1	1	62	1	13	2	55	1
Benaud	15	3	55	0	15	4	41	1
Hassett					0.5	0	12	0

FALL OF WICKETS

	A	SA	A	SA
Wkt	1st	1st	2nd	2nd
1st	122	31	36	42
2nd	166	129	44	124
3rd	269	189	70	174
4th	417	189	128	191
5th	450	239	129	–
6th	459	290	152	–
7th	490	401	152	–
8th	493	402	187	–
9th	495	435	193	–
10th	520	435	209	–

Grout and Simpson were distinguished debutants for Australia, and Meckiff, whose career was to spark a throwing controversy, was another. McGlew and J.H.B. Waite made centuries in South Africa's 470 and Benaud made 122 in Australia's 368 (Heine 6–58). Davidson's six for 34 dismissed South Africa for 201, but the match was drawn. A record 36,057 watched the third day (Boxing Day). Meckiff, with eight wickets, was the most successful bowler.

J.W. Burke made 189 at Cape Town, and South Africa were forced to follow on. They were then dismissed for 99 to lose by an innings and 141 runs. Goddard carried his bat for 56 not out. Benaud took nine wickets in the match, which L.F. Kline, in his second Test, ended with a hat-trick.

At Durban, South Africa removed Australia for 160, thanks to Adcock, who took six for 43. McGlew and Waite then made their second centuries of the series, and gave South Africa a lead of 221. But McGlew took nine hours and 35 minutes for 105, the slowest Test century at the time, and at 292 for seven Australia saved the match.

Heine took six for 96 at Johannesburg, but Australia reached 401 (Benaud 100). Benaud then took nine wickets as South Africa

Trevor Goddard made his first tour of Australia in 1957–58 and captained the South Africans there in 1963–64.

were forced to follow on, and for the second time against Australia avoided an innings defeat by one run. In the second innings McGlew made the slowest Test 50 (313 minutes).

At Port Elizabeth, Burke and Benaud were both hit by bouncers which Adcock and Heine bowled in an attempt to soften up the Australian batsmen. Australia's 291 passed South Africa's 214 by 77 and when Davidson and Benaud removed the home side for 144 an Australian win was a formality.

1957–58 9th Series Aus 3, SA 0, Drawn 2

1 JOHANNESBURG Match Drawn
South Africa 470–9 dec (J H B Waite 115, D J McGlew 108, T L Goddard 90, W R Endean 50, R A McLean 50, I Meckiff 5–125) and 201 (W R Endean 77, J H B Waite 59, A K Davidson 6–34)
Australia 368 (R Benaud 122, C C McDonald 75, R B Simpson 60, P S Heine 6–58) and 162–3 (K D Mackay 65)

2 CAPE TOWN Australia won by an innings and 141 runs
Australia 449 (J W Burke 189, C C McDonald 99, K D Mackay 63, H J Tayfield 5–120)
South Africa 209 (R Benaud 4–95) and 99 (T L Goddard 56, R Benaud 5–49)

3 DURBAN Match Drawn
Australia 163 (I D Craig 52, N A T Adcock 6–43) and 292–7 (J W Burke 83, R N Harvey 68, K D Mackay 52)
South Africa 384 (J H B Waite 134, D J McGlew 105, R Benaud 5–114)

4 JOHANNESBURG Australia won by 10 wkts
Australia 401 (R Benaud 100, K D Mackay 83, J W Burke 81, A K Davidson 62, P S Heine 6–96) and 1–0
South Africa 203 (K J Funston 70, R Benaud 4–70) and 198 (D J McGlew 70, K J Funston 64, R Benaud 5–84)

5 PORT ELIZABETH Australia won by 8 wkts
South Africa 214 (H J Tayfield 66, A K Davidson 4–44, L F Kline 4–33) and 144 (A K Davidson 5–38, R Benaud 5–82)
Australia 291 (K D Mackay 77, C C McDonald 58) and 68–2

1957–58 Averages

Batting	I	No	Runs	HS	Avge
K.D. MacKay (A)	7	4	375	83	125.00
J.W. Burke (A)	8	2	389	189	64.00
R. Benaud (A)	7	1	329	122	54.83
C.C. McDonald (A)	9	1	349	99	43.62
J.H.B. Waite (SA)	9	0	362	134	40.22
D.J. McGlew (SA)	9	0	354	108	39.11
T.L. Goddard (SA)	9	1	284	90	35.50
W.R. Endean (SA)	9	0	253	77	28.11

Bowling	O	M	Runs	W	Avge	BB
L.F. Kline (A)	113.3	31	245	15	16.33	4–33
A.K. Davison (A)	201.5	47	425	25	17.00	6–34
P.S. Heine (SA)	126.3	20	321	17	18.88	6–58
R. Benaud (A)	242.1	55	658	30	21.93	5–49
H.J. Tayfield (SA)	276.3	102	639	17	37.58	5–120

1963–64: South Africa narrowly fail to win series in Australia

South Africa's party under T.L. Goddard were not expected to do well in Australia in 1963–64, but again they caused a surprise. Two outstanding debutants for them at Brisbane were D.T. Lindsay and R.G. Pollock. R. Benaud was the captain of Australia, and won the toss. Peter Pollock (6–95) was the only bowler to make an impression on the Aussies, who made 435, with 169 coming from B.C. Booth. Barlow scored a century for South Africa, who made 346. Benaud then took five wickets, but the most notable event was the no-balling for throwing of Meckiff by umpire C.J. Egar. Four calls in his first and only over meant the end of his Test career, and he announced his complete retirement during the match. Rain washed out the third day and most of the last and the match was drawn.

Benaud was injured for the second Test at Melbourne, R.B. Simpson taking over. He

Top left: Goddard caught by Grout off Vievers for 93 in the Final Test in 1963–64, which was drawn with South Africa on top. *Top right*: Simpson takes a low catch to dismiss Graeme Pollock in his second Test at Melbourne. *Above*: Peter Pollock gets a wicket as Brian Booth is caught by Barlow for 169 in the first Test at Brisbane. *Left*: Grout dives to catch Pithey off Hawke during the fourth Test, giving him a record 131 Test victims for Australia.

put South Africa in; Barlow made another century, but the tourists made only 274. Lawry (157) and I.R. Redpath (97 in his first Test) scored 219 for Australia's first wicket, and Australia gained a lead of 173. Although South Africa made 301, they lost by eight wickets.

On Benaud's return, Simpson retained the Australian captaincy, Benaud announcing he was to retire at the end of the series. Australia scored 260, Peter Pollock getting five for 83, and South Africa 302, Graeme Pollock getting a rapid 122. At just under 20 years old, he remains South Africa's youngest centurion. Australia's declaration at 240 for nine set South Africa 409 in 430 minutes and they had reached 326 for five by the close.

After Australia had made 345 at Adelaide (Goddard 5–60), Barlow (201) and Graeme Pollock (175) added 341 in 283 minutes for South Africa's third wicket. At 595 (Hawke 6–139) the lead was exactly 250, and although Australia scored 331 there was ample time for South Africa to win by ten wickets.

South Africa put Australia in at Sydney and got them out for 311, Booth making 102 not out. J.T. Partridge took seven for 91, taking the seventh, eighth and ninth wickets for no runs, but the last wicket added 46. Bland made 126 and South Africa gained a vital lead of exactly 100. With Australia 225 for nine, South Africa had almost won, but again the last wicket was troublesome. By adding 45 in 75 minutes Vievers and Hawke saved the rubber. South Africa were left to score 171 in 85 minutes, but with Pollock injured they could not make them.

Eddie Barlow and wicket-keeper Denis Lindsay celebrating a catch by the keeper. These players were very prominent in South Africa's series wins against Australia in the 1960s.

1963–64 10th Series Aus 1, SA 1, Drawn 3

1 BRISBANE **Match Drawn**
Australia 435 (B C Booth 169, N C O'Neill 82, P M Pollock 6–95) and 144–1 dec (W M Lawry 87)
South Africa 346 (E J Barlow 114, J H B Waite 66, T L Goddard 52, R Benaud 5–68) and 13–1

2 MELBOURNE **Australia won by 8 wkts**
South Africa 274 (E J Barlow 109, K C Bland 50, G D McKenzie 4–82) and 306 (J H B Waite 77, A J Pithey 76, E J Barlow 54)
Australia 447 (W M Lawry 157, I R Redpath 97, B K Shepherd 96, J T Partridge 4–108) and 136–2 (R B Simpson 55)

3 SYDNEY **Match Drawn**
Australia 260 (B C Booth 75, R B Simpson 58, P M Pollock 5–83, J T Partridge 4–88) and 450–9 dec (R Benaud 90, W M Lawry 89, N C O'Neill 88, G D McKenzie 76, J T Partridge 5–123)
South Africa 302 (R G Pollock 122, T L Goddard 80, K C Bland 51) and 326–5 (K C Bland 85, T L Goddard 84, A J Pithey 53)

4 ADELAIDE **South Africa won by 10 wkts**
Australia 345 (P J P Burge 91, R B Simpson 78, B K Shepherd 70, B C Booth 58, T L Goddard 5–60) and 331 (B K Shepherd 78, N C O'Neill 66)
South Africa 595 (E J Barlow 201, R G Pollock 175, N J N Hawke 6–139) and 82–0

5 SYDNEY **Match Drawn**
Australia 311 (B C Booth 102, P J P Burge 56, J T Partridge 7–91) and 270 (B C Booth 87)
South Africa 411 (K C Bland 126, T L Goddard 93, D T Lindsay 65, R Benaud 4–118) and 76–0

1963–64 Averages

Batting	I	No	Runs	HS	Avge
B.C. Booth (A)	7	1	531	169	88.50
E.J. Barlow (SA)	10	2	603	201	75.37
T.L. Goddard (SA)	10	3	454	93	64.85
K.C. Bland (SA)	6	0	367	126	61.16
R.G. Pollock (SA)	7	0	399	175	57.00
W.M. Lawry (A)	10	1	496	157	55.11
N.C. O'Neill (A)	8	1	285	88	40.71
R.B. Simpson (A)	10	1	361	78	40.11
P.J.P. Burge (A)	9	1	317	91	39.62
B.K. Shepherd (A)	7	0	268	96	38.28

Bowling	O	M	Runs	W	Avge	BB
P.M. Pollock (SA)	159.3	11	710	25	28.40	6–95
J.T. Partridge (SA)	247.4	33	833	25	33.32	7–91
N.J.N. Hawke (A)	147	18·	473	14	33.78	6–139
R. Benaud (A)	169.1	37	449	12	37.41	5–68
G.D. McKenzie (A)	168.4	14	689	16	43.06	4–82

1966–67: Lindsay's records as South Africa win at last

South Africa, under P.A. van der Merwe, had a strong side in 1966–67 and had great hopes of beating R.B. Simpson's visiting Australians. But, batting at Johannesburg, they made only 199, G.D. McKenzie taking five for 46. Australia passed this with one wicket down, and made 325. Lindsay took

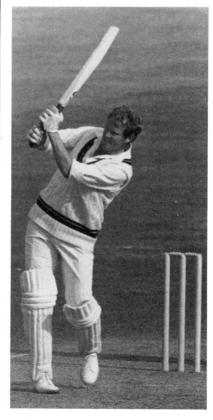

Pollock, Robert Graeme

Pollock was born on 27 February 1944 in Durban. His older brother was Peter, who also became a Test cricketer. Graeme made his debut for Eastern Province in 1961–62. He was an attacking middle-order left-hand batsman, a tall, strong man who used a heavy bat and hit the ball very hard. He first appeared for South Africa in 1963–64 and had time for 23 Tests before his country's ostracism from international cricket. He scored 2,256 runs, average 60.97. This average is second only to Bradman's.

six catches, and then scored 182 as South Africa made their highest Test score of 620. H.B. Taber, in his first Test claimed eight wicket-keeping victims. Goddard took six for 53 to ensure South Africa's victory, which came by 233 runs.

At Cape Town, Simpson scored 153, and Stackpole, batting number seven, 134 as Australia reached 542 (Barlow 5–85). Graeme Pollock made 209 in 350 minutes, but his team could reach only 353 (McKenzie 5–65) and followed on. A second-innings 367 set a

1966–67 11th Series SA 3, Aus 1, Drawn 1

1 JOHANNESBURG **South Africa won by 233 runs**
South Africa 199 (D T Lindsay 69, G D McKenzie 5–46) and 620 (D T Lindsay 182, R G Pollock 90, P L van der Merwe 76, H R Lance 70, A Bacher 63, E J Barlow 50)
Australia 325 (W M Lawry 98, R B Simpson 65) and 261 (T R Veivers 55, T L Goddard 6–53)

2 CAPE TOWN **Australia won by 6 wkts**
Australia 542 (R B Simpson 153, K R Stackpole 134, I R Redpath 54, G D Watson 50, E J Barlow 5–85) and 180–4 (I R Redpath 69)
South Africa 353 (R G Pollock 209, P L van der Merwe 50, G D McKenzie 5–65) and 367 (D T Lindsay 81, P M Pollock 75, D B Pithey 55, H R Lance 53)

3 DURBAN **South Africa won by 8 wkts**
South Africa 300 (D T Lindsay 137) and 185–2 (R G Pollock 67, A Bacher 60)
Australia 147 and 334 (R B Simpson 94, I R Redpath 80, M J Procter 4–71)

4 JOHANNESBURG **Match Drawn**
Australia 143 (M J Procter 4–32) and 148–8
South Africa 332–9 dec (D T Lindsay 131, D A Renneberg 5–97)

5 PORT ELIZABETH **South Africa won by 7 wkts**
Australia 173 (R M Cowper 60) and 278 (R M Cowper 54)
South Africa 276 (R G Pollock 105, T L Goddard 74, G D McKenzie 5–65) and 179–3 (T L Goddard 59)

1966–67 Averages

Batting	I	No	Runs	HS	Avge
J.D. Lindsay (SA)	7	0	606	182	86.57
R.G. Pollock (SA)	9	2	537	209	76.71
R.B. Simpson (A)	10	0	483	153	48.30
I.R. Redpath (A)	10	1	386	80	42.88
H.R. Lance (SA)	8	1	261	70	37.28
T.L. Goddard (SA)	9	0	294	74	32.66
W.M. Lawry (A)	10	0	296	98	29.60
K.R. Stackpole (A)	9	0	254	134	28.22
R.M. Cowper (A)	10	0	255	60	25.50

Bowling	O	M	Runs	W	Avge	BB
T.L. Goddard (SA)	255.3	101	422	26	16.23	6–53
M.J. Procter (SA)	109.2	30	263	15	17.53	4–32
E.J. Barlow (SA)	129.3	37	324	15	21.60	5–85
G.D. McKenzie (A)	275.2	69	624	24	26.00	5–46
P.M. Pollock (SA)	167.1	35	470	12	39.16	2–42

target, but Australia won with 25 minutes in hand.

Simpson put South Africa in at Durban but Lindsay's 137 led to a respectable score of 300. Australia made only 147, top scorer Lawry (44) completing his innings with 10 stitches in his hand after being hit by a Pollock delivery. Following on, Australia made 334, but South Africa won to regain the lead in the series.

At Johannesburg, Australia were shot out for 143, Lindsay scored 131 in 332 for nine declared, and Australia were 148 for eight when rain, which had washed out the fourth day, came to their rescue again just after tea on the fifth, saving them from certain defeat.

Australia were put in at Port Elizabeth and removed cheaply again for 173. South Africa made 276, with Pollock scoring a century and McKenzie claiming five wickets. Australia made the highest score, 278, but South Africa easily won by seven wickets to take their first rubber against Australia by a decisive 3–1. Lindsay, clapped to the wicket, took 24 catches, a record for a Test series, and scored 606, a record for a wicket-keeper in a Test rubber.

1969–70: South Africa's best-ever Test team crush Australia

Lawry's Australians in South Africa in 1969–70 played the last four Tests in South Africa's Test history before the *apartheid* policies of the government isolated South Africa from international sporting competition.

A. Bacher captained a home team in which Barry Richards made his debut. Bacher won all four tosses. At Cape Town South Africa made 382, Barlow's 127 being the foundation. Mallett took five for 126. Australia made only 164, and after 232 (Connolly 5–47) from the home side needed 451 to win. South Africa won by 170.

At Durban, Richards made 140 in 164 balls, but was over-shadowed by Pollock whose 274 remains South Africa's highest in Test matches. The total of 622 for nine declared is also South Africa's highest. With Australia dismissed for 157 and 336, South Africa won by an innings and 129 with over a day left.

South Africa were contained to only 279 at Johannesburg, but five for 39 by Peter Pollock assured a lead of 77. Barlow scored 110 in a second-innings 408 (J.W. Gleeson 5–125) and Australia's dismissal for 178 meant an overwhelming win by 307 runs.

Australia's chance of salvaging a little pride from the series lessened when South Africa won the toss again at Port Elizabeth. Good bowling by Connolly, who took six for 47, held them to 311, but this was good enough for a lead of 99. Centuries from Richards and B.L. Irvine allowed a declaration at 470 for eight, and M.J. Procter's six for 73 meant Australia could not get beyond 246. 'suth Africa won by 323 runs.

So South Africa won all the Tests in their last series by huge margins. It was a pity for them that their last team was arguably one of the strongest Test teams ever: Richards, Barlow, the two Pollocks, Lindsay and Procter in particular being among the best players of the day.

1969–70 12th Series SA 4, Aus 0
1 CAPE TOWN   South Africa won by 170 runs
South Africa 382 (E J Barlow 127, A Bacher 57, A A Mallett 5–126) and 232 (R G Pollock 50, A N Connolly 5–47, J W Gleeson 4–70)
Australia 164 (K D Walters 73, P M Pollock 4–20) and 280 (W M Lawry 83, M J Procter 4–47)
2 DURBAN   South Africa won by an innings and 129 runs
South Africa 622–9 dec (R G Pollock 274, B A Richards 140, H R Lance 61)
Australia 157 (A P Sheahan 62) and 336 (I R Redpath 74, K D Walters 74, K R Stackpole 71)
3 JOHANNESBURG   South Africa won by 307 runs
South Africa 279 (B L Irvine 79, B A Richards 65, R G Pollock 52) and 408 (E J Barlow 110, B L Irvine 73, R G Pollock 87, J W Gleeson 5–127)
Australia 202 (K D Walters 64, P M Pollock 5–39) and 178 (I R Redpath 66)
4 PORT ELIZABETH   South Africa won by 323 runs
South Africa 311 (B A Richards 81, E J Barlow, A N Connolly 6–47) and 470–8 dec (B A Richards 126, B L Irvine 102, A Bacher 73, D T Lindsay 60)
Australia 212 (A P Sheahan 67, I R Redpath 55) and 246 (M J Procter 6–73)

1969–70 Averages

Batting	I	No	Runs	HS	Avge
R.G. Pollock (SA)	7	0	517	274	73.85
B.A. Richards (SA)	7	0	508	140	72.57
E.J. Barlow (SA)	7	0	360	127	51.42
B.L. Irvine (SA)	7	0	353	102	50.42
I.R. Redpath (A)	8	2	283	47*	50.42
M.J. Procter (SA)	7	1	209	48	34.83
K.D. Walters (A)	8	0	258	74	32.25
A.Bacher (SA)	7	0	217	73	31.00
A.P. Sheahan (A)	8	0	247	67	30.87

Bowling	O	M	Runs	W	Avge	BB
M.J. Procter (SA)	143	50	353	26	13.57	6–73
P.M. Pollock (SA)	115	39	258	15	17.20	5–39
E.J. Barlow (SA)	94	27	257	11	23.36	3–24
A.N. Connolly (A)	214.2	27	257	11	23.36	3–24
J.W. Gleeson (A)	255	68	740	19	38.94	5–125

The West Indian party which toured England in 1928, when their country played its first Test matches.
Left to right, back: J. Scheult (assistant manager), St Hill, Rae, Hoad, Small, Martin, Constantine, Griffith, Scott. Front: Bartlett, Fernands, Wright, Nunes, Challenor, Browne. Three players, Francis, Roach and Neblett, all of whom played in Tests, were absent from the group.

England v West Indies

1928: Three heavy defeats for West Indies in first series

Cricket tours between England and the West Indies date back to the 19th century, but it was not until 1928 that the West Indies were awarded Test status. Their first Test was at

England v West Indies
1928 1st Series Eng 3, W I 0
1 LORD'S   England won by an innings and 58 runs
England 401 (G E Tyldesley 122, A P F Chapman 50, L N Constantine 4–82)
West Indies 177 (V W C Jupp 4–37) and 166 (J A Small 52, A P Freeman 4–37)
2 OLD TRAFFORD   England won by an innings and 30 runs
West Indies 206 (C A Roach 50, A P Freeman 5–54) and 115 (A P Freeman 5–39)
England 351 (D R Jardine 83, W R Hammond 63, H Sutcliffe 54, J B Hobbs 53)
3 THE OVAL   England won by an innings and 71 runs
West Indies 238 (C A Roach 52, M W Tate 4–59) and 129 (A P Freeman 4–47)
England 438 (J B Hobbs 159, G E Tyldesley 73, H Sutcliffe 63, M W Tate 54, H C Griffith 6–103, G N Francis 4–112)

England v West Indies
1928 Averages

Batting	I	No	Runs	HS	Avge
J.B. Hobbs (E)	2	0	212	159	106.00

Bowling	O	M	Runs	W	Avge	BB
A.P. Freeman (E)	140	50	302	22	13.72	5–39
M.W. Tate (E)	127	43	246	13	18.92	4–59
H.C. Griffith (WI)	79.5	20	250	11	22.72	6–103

Lord's in 1928. R.K. Nunes, the wicket-keeper, led the side, of which the most famous players entering Test cricket were probably G. Challenor, W.H. St Hill and L.N. Constantine. England, for whom D.R. Jardine made his debut, were led by A.P.F. Chapman. England batted and made 401, of which 382 came on the first day. G.E. Tyldesley made a century. West Indies made 177 and 166 and lost by an innings.

West Indies batted first at Old Trafford, and made 206. Hobbs and Sutcliffe made a century opening stand and England reached 351, enough to win by an innings when West Indies were dismissed for 115. A.P. Freeman's leg-breaks and googlies took five wickets in each innings.

At the Oval, West Indies made 238, but England exactly 200 more, Hobbs scoring 159. H.C. Griffith took six for 103 with his fast-medium bowling. England completed a clean sweep of three innings victories.

W. RHODES.
(YORKSHIRE)
Copyright
PHOTO HAWKINS BRIGH
R.P. 1381.

Rhodes, Wilfred

Rhodes was born on 29 October 1877 at Kirkheaton, Yorkshire, and first played for the county in 1898. He was a slow left-arm bowler and made such a quick impact that he played for England in 1899. During his career, his right-hand batting developed to such an extent that after beginning at number eleven for England he eventually opened with Hobbs and in 1911–12 at Melbourne they made the highest opening stand in Ashes Tests of 323. As a bowler, Rhodes took more first-class wickets than anybody else: 4,204. He is the only man over 4,000. His Test career lasted to 1929–30, when he played in the West Indies aged 52 years, 165 days, the oldest Test player. His Test career spanned 30 years, another record. In 58 Tests he scored 2,325 runs, average 30.19, and took 127 wickets, average 26.96. He died in Branksome, Dorset, on 8 July 1973, aged 95.

1929–30: Records fall in 'timeless' Test in West Indies

England toured West Indies in 1929–30, while another side toured New Zealand. Nevertheless, the touring side was quite strong, probably the strongest to tour West Indies till then. The Hon F.S.G. Calthorpe, making his debut, was captain, while E.L.G. Hoad captained West Indies. W. Voce made his debut for England in the first Test at Bridgetown, while among West Indies' newcomers G.A. Headley was the most significant, while J.E.D. Sealy, who had made a century against the tourists for Barbados, at 17 years and 122 days, was the youngest Test player. George Gunn, recalled by England at the age of 50, had played his previous Test before Sealy was born.

West Indies made 369, C.A. Roach being their first century-maker. Sandham made 152 in England's reply of 467. Headley made 176 in West Indies' second-innings 384, G.T.S. Stevens taking five wickets for the second time in the match. Set 287 in 165 minutes, England drew at 167 for three. Sealy made 58 and 15, Gunn 35 and 29. Gunn's tactic of walking down the wicket to the fast bowlers and playing a dead bat led to 'bodyline' bowling from the West Indies, particularly by Constantine.

England were 12 fo three at Port-of-Spain, but reached 208 (H.C. Griffith 5–63). West Indies led with 254. Hendren followed up a first-innings 70 with 205 not out, England declaring at 425 for eight. Voce (7–70) was too good for the West Indian batsmen, and England won by 167 runs.

At Georgetown, Roach made 209 and Headley 114 in a West Indies total of 471.

1929–30 2nd Series Eng 1 W I 1, Drawn 2
1 BRIDGETOWN Match Drawn
West Indies 369 (C A Roach 122, F I de Caires 80, J E D Sealey 58, G T S Stevens 5–105) and 384 (G A Headley 176, C A Roach 77, F I de Caires 70, G T S Stevens 5–90)
England 467 (A Sandham 152, E H Hendren 80) and 167–3 (A Sandham 51)
2 PORT OF SPAIN England won by 167 runs
England 208 (E H Hendren 77, H C Griffith 5–63) and 425–8 dec (E H Hendren 205, L E G Ames 105, L N Constantine 4–165)
West Indies 254 (E A C Hunte 58, L N Constantine 52, W E Astill 4–58, W Voce 4–79) and 212 (W Voce 7–70)
3 GEORGETOWN West Indies won by 289 runs
West Indies 471 (C A Roach 209, G A Headley 114, E A C Hunte 53) and 290 (G A Headley 112, C R Browne 70, W E Astill 4–70)
England 145 (E H Hendren 56, L N Constantine 4–35, G N Francis 4–40) and 327 (E H Hendren 123, L N Constantine 5–87)
4 KINGSTON Match Drawn
England 849 (A Sandham 325, L E G Ames 149, G Gunn 85, E H Hendren 61, R E S Wyatt 58, J O'Connor 51, O C Scott 5–266) and 272–9 dec (E H Hendren 55, A Sandham 50, O C Scott 4–108)
West Indies 286 (R K Nunes 66) and 408–5 (G A Headley 223, R K Nunes 92)

1929–30 Averages

Batting	I	No	Runs	HS	Avge
E.H. Hendren (E)	8	2	693	205	115.50
G.A. Headley (WI)	8	0	703	223	87.87
A. Sandham (E)	8	0	592	325	74.00
L.E.G. Ames (E)	8	1	417	149	59.57
C.A. Roach (WI)	8	0	467	209	58.37
F.I. de Caires (WI)	6	0	232	70	38.66
G. Gunn (E)	8	0	276	85	34.50

Bowling	O	M	Runs	W	Avge	BB
G.T.S. Stevens (E)	68.4	9	241	11	21.91	5–90
L.N. Constantine (WI)	163.4	42	497	18	27.61	5–87
H.C. Griffith (WI)	190.1	38	508	16	31.75	5–63
W. Voce (E)	188.2	34	584	17	34.35	7–70
W.E. Astill (E)	233.1	65	526	13	40.46	4–58
W. Rhodes (E)	246	92	453	10	45.30	3–110

Francis and Constantine did not allow a recovery and England were out for 145. West Indies batted again and Headley completed a century in each innings – he was the youngest batsman to score three Test hundreds. England were set 617 and made 327 (Hendren 123). Constantine's five wickets gave him nine in the match. M.P. Fernandez captained West Indies in their first Test win.

R.K. Nunes captained West Indies in the deciding Test at Kingston, which was 'timeless'. England made 849, a record Test score, of which Andy Sandham's 325 was a record individual score. Ames also made a century, while O.C. Scott took five wickets for 266. West Indies made only 286, but Calthorpe did not enforce the follow-on, preferring to declare at 272 for nine, setting West Indies 836 to win. Scott took four for 108, his concession of 374 runs remaining a Test record. Headley made 223, and became the youngest to score a Test double-century. West Indies reached 408 for five at the end of the seventh day, but rain then washed out two days, and the match was drawn as England had to catch the boat home.

In this match England had two players over 50: Gunn and Rhodes. It was the last Test for both, with Rhodes, at 52 years and 165 days, remaining the oldest to play in Tests.

Constantine, Mr. L. N. (Trinidad).

Constantine, Learie Nicholas

Constantine was born on 21 September 1901 in Diego Martin, Trinidad. He made his debut for Trinidad in 1921–22. He toured England from 1923, and played for West Indies in their first Test match in 1928. He was a fast bowler, a hard-hitting middle-order batsman and an outstanding fielder. He played in 18 Tests, scoring 635 runs, average 19.24, and taking 58 wickets, average 30.10. Not world-beating figures, but his electric presence was inspirational. He became High Commissioner for Trinidad and Tobago and became a life peer in 1969. He died on 1 July 1971 in Hampstead, London.

1933: West Indies well beaten in England

G.C. Grant led the West Indian party to England in 1933, where Jardine captained the home team after his 'bodyline' success in Australia.

Constantine was not released by Lancashire League club Nelson for the first Test at Lord's, where England made 296. R.W.V. Robins took six for 32 with his leg-breaks and West Indies, out for 97, followed on. They did better second time with 172 but lost by an innings.

Constantine played at Old Trafford, where West Indies made 375, based on a second-wicket stand of 200 by I. Barrow (105) and Headley (169). When England batted, Constantine and E.A. Martindale bowled 'bodyline'. Hammond was hit on the chin. Jardine made a typically dogged 127 but Martindale took five for 73 and West Indies got a lead of one run. James Langridge, in his first Test, then took seven for 56 with his left-arm slows and West Indies were out for 225, but there was no time for England to bat.

Martindale took five wickets again at the Oval, where R.E.S. Wyatt captained the home side, but England scored 312, A.H. Bakewell making 107. West Indies subsided to 100 and 195 before the leg-breaks and googlies of C.S. Marriott, who took 11 wickets in his only Test.

Hammond batting in 1934. In the tour of West Indies in the winter his two innings won the first Test.

Grant, Wyatt reversed his order, opening with his fast bowlers. Hammond came in at number six, with the score 29 for four, and Wyatt himself at eight, with the score 48 for six – 25 still needed. But there the mayhem stopped, and England crept home by four wickets. Martindale had five for 22. Hammond described his two innings of 43 and 29 not out as the hardest he'd played.

At Port-of-Spain West Indies made 302 after Wyatt had put them in, and England 258, J. Iddon (73) and E.R.T. Holmes (85 not out) rescuing them from 23 for five. West Indies declared at 280 for six and England scored only 107, Wyatt again sending in the bowlers to keep the batsmen from the new ball. West Indies levelled the series with a win by 217 runs.

After a late start the third Test was a dull match, except for W.E. Hollies, whose seven for 50 was his best Test analysis. West Indies were set 203 at about two-a-minute and the match was drawn.

The fourth Test at Kingston was the decider, and Headley made a record score

---

1933 3rd Series Eng 2, W I 0, Drawn 1

1 LORD'S England won by an innings and 27 runs

England 296 (L E G Ames 83, C F Walters 51, E A Martindale 4–85)

West Indies 97 (R W V Robins 6–32) and 172 (G A Headley 50, H Verity 4–45, G G Macaulay 4–57)

2 OLD TRAFFORD Match Drawn

West Indies 375 (G A Headley 169, I Barrow 105, E W Clark 4–99) and 225 (C A Roach 64, L N Constantine 64, Jas Langridge 7–56)

England 374 (D R Jardine 127, R W V Robins 55, E A Martindale 5–73)

3 THE OVAL England won by an innings and 17 runs

England 312 (A H Bakewell 107, C J Barnett 52, E A Martindale 5–93)

West Indies 100 (C S Marriott 5–37) and 195 (C A Roach 56, C S Marriott 6–59)

1933 Averages

Batting	I	No	Runs	HS	Avge
G.A. Headley (WI)	6	1	227	169	55.40

Bowling	O	M	Runs	W	Avge	BB
C.S. Marriott (E)	41.1	8	96	11	8.72	6–59
E.A Martindale (WI)	72.3	9	251	14	17.92	5–73
R.W.V. Robins (E)	63.4	5	220	11	20.00	6–32
E.W. Clark (E)	84	22	233	11	21.18	4–99

1934–35: Odd batting orders as West Indies break their duck

The first Test between R.E.S. Wyatt's weakish tourists and G.C. Grant's West Indians was a remarkable match. Wyatt put the opposition in on a sticky pitch at Bridgetown, and West Indies were all out for 102, and then Wyatt declared at 81 for seven to get West Indies in again on the bad pitch. Grant opened with his bowlers, hoping the pitch would ease, but when Headley came in at number seven and was out for a duck, he, too, declared – at 51 for six (C.I.J. Smith, on his debut, five for 16). It was now, because of stoppages, after tea on the third day, so England were given, in theory, over a day to make 73 to win! Like

---

WEST INDIES V ENGLAND 1934-35
1st Test, Bridgetown: England won by four wickets

WEST INDIES

C.A. Roach	c Paine b Farnes	9	(6) not out		10
G.M. Carew	c Holmes b Farnes	0			
G.A. Headley	run out	44	(7) c Paine b Farnes		0
C.M. Jones	c Leyland b Farnes	3			
J.E.D. Sealy	c Paine b Farnes	0			
G.C. Grant*	c Hendren b Hollies	4	(8) not out		0
R.S. Grant	c Hammond b Hollies	5	(2) c Paine b Smith		0
L.G. Hylton	st Ames b Paine	15	(1) lbw b Smith		19
C.M. Christiani	not out	9	(5) b Smith		11
E.F. Achong	st Ames b Paine	0	(4) b Smith		0
E.A. Martindale	c Leyland b Paine	9	(3) lbw b Smith		0
Extras	(LB 2, NB 2)	4	(B 4, LB 4, NB 3)		11
Total		**102**	(6 wickets declared)		**51**

ENGLAND

R.E.S. Wyatt*	c R.S. Grant b Martindale	8	(8) not out		6
M. Leyland	c and b Martindale	3	(5) c R.S. Grant b Martindale		2
W.R. Hammond	c R.S. Grant b Hylton	43	(6) not out		29
E.H. Hendren	c R.S. Grant b Martindale	3	(4) b Martindale		20
L.E.G. Ames†	lbw b R.S. Grant	8			
C.I.J. Smith	c Jones b Hylton	0	(2) c Christiani b Martindale		0
J. Iddon	not out	14			
E.R.T. Holmes	c Achong b Hylton	0	(3) c G.C. Grant b Martindale		6
K. Farnes	)		(1) c G.C. Grant b Hylton		5
G.A.E. Paine	) did not bat		(7) c R.S. Grant b Martindale		2
W.E. Hollies	)				
Extras	(B 1, NB 1)	2	(B 2, NB 3)		5
Total	(7 wickets declared)	**81**	(6 wickets)		**75**

ENGLAND	O	M	R	W	O	M	R	W	FALL OF WICKETS				
										WI	E	WI	E
Farnes	15	4	40	4	9	2	23	1	Wkt	1st	1st	2nd	2nd
Smith	7	3	8	0	8	4	16	5	1st	1	12	4	3
Hollies	16	4	36	2					2nd	11	14	4	7
Paine	9	3	14	3	1	1	0	0	3rd	20	28	4	25
Hammond					1	0	1	0	4th	20	52	40	29
									5th	31	54	47	43
WEST INDIES									6th	49	81	51	48
Martindale	9	0	39	3	8.3	1	22	5	7th	81	81	–	–
Hylton	7.3	3	8	3	8	0	48	1	8th	86	–	–	–
Achong	6	1	14	0					9th	88	–	–	–
R.S. Grant	7	0	18	1					10th	102	–	–	–

for West Indies of 270 not out. He and Sealy (91) added 202 for the third wicket. West Indies declared at 535 for seven. Wyatt was taken to hospital unconscious with a fractured jaw after being struck by a ball from Constantine when one, and England never recovered, despite Ames scoring 126. Following on, they lost by an innings and 161, West Indies winning their first series.

1934–35 4th Series W I 2, Eng 1, Drawn 1

1 BRIDGETOWN **England won by 4 wkts**
West Indies 102 (K Farnes 4–40) and 51–6 dec (C I J Smith 5–16)
England 81–7 dec and 75–6 (E A Martindale 5–22)

2 PORT OF SPAIN **West Indies won by 217 runs**
West Indies 302 (J E D Sealey 92, L N Constantine 90, C I J Smith 4–100) and 280–6 dec (G A Headley 93)
England 258 (E R T Holmes 85, J Iddon 73) and 107

3 GEORGETOWN **Match Drawn**
England 226 (L G Hylton 4–27) and 160–6 dec (R E S Wyatt 71)
West Indies 184 (G A Headley 53, K L Wishart 52, W E Hollies 7–50) and 104–5

4 KINGSTON **West Indies won by an innings and 161 runs**
West Indies 535–7 dec (G A Headley 270, J E D Sealey 91, R S Grant 77, G A E Paine 5–168)
England 271 (L E G Ames 126, J Iddon 54) and 103 (E A Martindale 4–28)

1934–35 Averages

Batting	I	No	Runs	HS	Avge
G.A. Headley (WI)	6	1	485	270	97.00
J.E.D. Sealey (WI)	6	0	270	92	45.00
E.H. Hendren (E)	8	1	202	41	28.85

Bowling	O	M	Runs	W	Avge	BB
E.A. Martindale (WI)	100.3	23	239	19	12.57	5–22
L.N. Constantine (WI)	109.1	36	197	15	13.13	3–11
L.G. Hylton (WI)	97	23	251	13	19.30	4–27
W.E. Hollies (E)	93	24	217	10	21.70	7–50
G.A.E. Paine (E)	174	43	467	17	27.47	5–168
C.I.J. Smith (E)	119	30	329	11	29.90	5–16

1939: England win final series before the war

R.S. Grant, brother of previous captain G.C., captained the 1939 tourists to England. W.R. Hammond, now an amateur, was the England captain.

Headley scored 106 when West Indies batted at Lord's, but a total of 277 looked small when Hutton (196) and Compton (120) were adding 248 for the fourth wicket in only 140 minutes. England declared at 404 for five. In West Indies' second innings Headley (107) became the first (and so far only) batsman to score a century in each innings of a Test at Lord's. W.H. Copson took four wickets to total nine in his first Test' match. England needed only 99 and won by eight wickets.

In a bleak, rain-shortened Test at Old Trafford, England declared at 164 for seven, dismissed West Indies for 133 (Bowes 6–33) and declared again at 128 for six, but there was no time for a result.

In the final Test at the Oval, England made 352, Constantine getting five for 75. K.H. Weekes, cousin of Everton Weekes, scored a rapid 137, and West Indies led by 146. The match was drawn when Hutton (165) and Hammond (138) added 264 for the third wicket.

J.E.D. Sealy skies a ball at Old Trafford in 1939 in the last Test series to take place before the First World War. England won the series 1–0.

This was the last Test before the Second World War. Among those who did not play Test cricket again were Constantine, Martindale and Sealy.

1939 5th Series Eng 1, W I 0, Drawn 2

1 LORD'S **England won by 8 wkts**
West Indies 277 (G A Headley 106, J B Stollmeyer 59, W H Copson 5–85) and 225 (G A Headley 107, W H Copson 4–67)
England 404–5 dec (L Hutton 196, D C S Compton 120) and 100–2

2 OLD TRAFFORD **Match Drawn**
England 164–7 dec (J Hardstaff jun 76) and 128–6 dec (L N Constantine 4–42)
West Indies 133 (G A Headley 51, W E Bowes 6–33) and 43–4

3 THE OVAL **Match Drawn**
England 352 (J Hardstaff jun 94, N Oldfield 80, L Hutton 73, L N Constantine 5–75) and 366–3 (L Hutton 165, W R Hammond 138)
West Indies 498 (K H Weekes 137, V H Stollmeyer 96, L N Constantine 79, G A Headley 65, J B Stollmeyer 59, R T D Perks 5–156)

1939 Averages

Batting	I	No	Runs	HS	Avge
L. Hutton (E)	6	1	480	196	96.00
G.A. Headley (WI)	5	0	334	107	66.80
W.R. Harmond (E)	6	1	279	138	55.80

Bowling	O	M	Runs	W	Avge	BB
W.H. Copson (E)	52.4	7	185	12	15.41	5–85
W.E. Bowes (E)	70	18	176	11	16.00	6–33
L.N. Constantine (WI)	71.3	8	328	11	29.81	5–75

1947–48: Absences and injuries cause England to be well beaten

MCC sent a very weak side to tour West Indies in 1947–48. The principal players of the 1947 season declined to tour, and G.O.B. Allen was brought out of retirement

to lead the party. J.C. Laker was nevertheless a distinguished debutant in the first Test at Bridgetown, while C.L. Walcott and E. de C. Weekes were to prove the most successful of the West Indian newcomers.

Injuries were another MCC problem, and Allen was an absentee, the Test team being led by K. Cranston. Headley was the home skipper, and he won the toss and batted.

West Indies made 296, Laker taking seven for 103 in his first Test, and led by 43, adding 351 before declaring in the second innings. R. Howorth took six for 124, while R.J. Christiani became the second player to make 99 on his debut. Rain on the last day precluded a result.

With only 12 fit men for the second Test, England brought S.C. Griffith, the Sussex wicket-keeper, into the side as an opening batsman. He rose to the occasion with 140 out of 362, his first first-class century. F.M.M. Worrell also made his first-class debut, and made 97, but the oddity was the 112 of A.G. Ganteaume. This turned out to be his only Test innings, a fact which understandably he viewed with some bitterness. After he and G.M. Carew (107) had put on 173 for the first wicket, West Indies scored 497. In the second innings J.D.B. Robertson made a gritty 133 to stave off defeat. W. Ferguson took 11 wickets for West Indies. G.E. Gomez captained West Indies in Headley's absence, but for the third Test at British Guiana J.D.C. Goddard took over.

G.O.B. Allen, who had broken down in the fifth over of the second innings at Port of Spain, broke down in the third at Georgetown. Rain cut into the first two days, and Goddard declared at 297 for eight. Worrell was 131 not out. L. Hutton had been flown out because of England's plight (Griffith, like Ganteaume, was dropped after his debut century) but England could make only 111 (Goddard 5–31) and followed on. Their 263 (Ferguson eight wickets in the match) left West Indies to get only 78, and they won by seven wickets.

The fourth and final Test was in Kingston, where Hutton and Robertson put on 129 for England's first wicket, only to see the side out for 227. H.H.H. Johnson took five for 41 on his debut. Weekes made 141 to help West Indies get a lead of 263. W. Place scored his only Test century, but Johnson's second five-wicket haul left West Indies to get only 74, and they won the series 2–0.

1947–48 Averages

Batting	I	No	Runs	HS	Avge	
F.M.M. Worrell (WI)	4	2	294	131	147.00	
J.D.B. Robertson (E)	8	1	390	133	55.71	
E. De C. Weekes (WI)	6	0	293	141	48.83	
G.E. Gomez (WI)	6	1	232	75	46.40	
J. Hardstaff, jr (E)	8	0	237	98	39.50	

Bowling	O	M	Runs	W	Avge	BB
H.H.H. Johnson (WI)	65.5	24	96	10	9.60	5–41
W. Ferguson (WI)	214	40	567	23	24.65	6–92
J.D.C. Goddard (WI)	149.5	49	287	11	26.09	5–31
J.C. Laker (E)	186	47	546	18	30.33	7–103
R. Howarth (E)	177.5	33	483	13	37.15	6–124

1950: Calypsos and steel bands for Ramadhin and Valentine

Goddard's team met a representative England side in 1950 led by N.W.D. Yardley.

England batted at Old Trafford, where two young spinners, S. Ramadhin and A.L. Valentine, made their debuts for West Indies. Bespectacled Valentine took the first eight wickets to fall before Ramadhin claimed the last two. Only a first Test century by Evans allowed England to reach 312. It was enough for a lead of 97, as R. Berry, another left-arm spinner, took five for 63 on his debut. England added 288 to this lead and won by 202 runs.

At Lord's A.F. Rae made 106 out of 326 before Ramadhin and Valentine, with nine wickets between them, dismissed England for 151. West Indies added to the lead with 425 for six declared, Walcott smashing 168 not out, and although Washbrook then scored a century West Indies won by 326 runs. Ramadhin had 11 wickets and Valentine seven in the match, and were the main heroes of West Indies' first win in England, as well as providing the chorus of the famous impromptu calypso which celebrates the event:

With those little pals of mine –
Ramadhin and Valentine.

The 1950 West Indians who registered a first success in England. Left to right, back: Williams, Marshall, Valentine, Pierre, Walcott, Johnson, Rae, Testrail, Ferguson (baggage manager). Front: Ramadhin, Jones, Worrell, Palmer, Barnes (assistant manager), Goddard, Gomez, Stollmeyer, Christiani, Weekes.

At Trent Bridge England's 223 was well passed by West Indies 558, Worrell getting 261 and Weekes 129, the pair adding 283 for the fourth wicket. Simpson (94) and Washbrook (102) put on 212 for the first wicket and England fought a long rearguard action, but the two spinners bowled 173.2 overs in the second innings, taking nine wickets, and West Indies won by ten wickets.

Walcott, Clyde Leopold
Born on 17 January 1926 at Bridgetown, Walcott began his career with Barbados in 1941–42, and later played for British Guiana. He was a burly attacking middle-order right-hand batsman who hit the ball very hard, and also kept wicket and occasionally bowled fast-medium. He appeared for West Indies in 1947–48, and with Worrell and Weekes comprised the famous 'three Ws' of West Indian cricket. In 44 Tests he scored 3,798 runs, average 56.68. He also caught 53, stumped 11 and took 11 wickets at 37.09.

1947–48 6th Series W I 2, Eng 0, Drawn 2

1 BRIDGETOWN   Match Drawn
West Indies 296 (G E Gomez 86, J B Stollmeyer 78, J C Laker 7–103) and 351–9 dec (R J Christiani 99, E A V Williams 72, W Ferguson 56, R Howorth 6–124)
England 253 (J Hardstaff jun 98, J D B Robertson 80, P E Jones 4–54) and 86–4 (J D B Robertson 51)

2 PORT OF SPAIN   Match Drawn
England 362 (S C Griffith 140, J C Laker 55, W Ferguson 5–137) and 275 (J D B Robertson 133, W Ferguson 6–892)
West Indies 497 (A G Ganteaume 112, G M Carew 107, F M M Worrell 97, G E Gomez 62) and 72–3

3 GEORGETOWN   West Indies won by 7 wkts
West Indies 297–8 dec (F M M Worrell 131, R J Christiani 51, K Cranston 4–78) and 78–3
England 111 (J D C Goddard 5–31) and 263 (J Hardstaff jun 63, W Ferguson 5–116)

4 KINGSTON   West Indies won by 10 wkts
England 227 (J D B Robertson 64, L Hutton 56, H H H Johnson 5–41) and 336 (W Place 107, J Hardstaff jun 64, L Hutton 60, H H H Johnson 5–55)
West Indies 490 (E de C Weekes 151, W Ferguson 75, K R Rickards 67) and 76–0

Centuries from Rae and Worrell took West Indies to 503 at the Oval. Hutton then played one of the great Test innings, carrying his bat for 202 not out from a total of 344. It was not enough to save the follow-on and England collapsed to 103 and an innings defeat. Valentine's ten wickets took his total in the four matches to 33.

1950   7th Series   W I 3, Eng 1

1 OLD TRAFFORD   England won by 202 runs
England 312 (T G Evans 104, T E Bailey 82, A L Valentine 8–104) and 288 (W J Edrich 71)
West Indies 215 (E de C Weekes 52, R Berry 5–63) and 183 (J B Stollmeyer 78, W E Hollies 5–63, R Berry 4–53)

2 LORD'S   West Indies won by 326 runs
West Indies 326 (A F Rae 106, E de C Worrell 62, F M M Worrell 52, R O Jenkins 5–116) and 425–6 dec (C L Walcott 168, G E Gomez 70, E de C Weekes 63, R O Jenkins 4–174)
England 151 (S Ramadhin 5–66, A L Valentine 4–48) and 274 (C Washbrook 114, S Ramadhin 6–86)

3 TRENT BRIDGE   West Indies won by 10 wkts
England 223 and 436 (C Washbrook 102, R T Simpson 94, W G A Parkhouse 69, J G Dewes 67, T G Evans 63, S Ramadhin 5–135)
West Indies 558 (F M M Worrell 261, E de C Weekes 129, A F Rae 68, A V Bedser 5–127) and 103–0 (J B Stollmeyer 52)

4 THE OVAL   West Indies won by an innings and 56 runs
West Indies 503 (F M M Worrell 138, A F Rae 109, G E Gomez 74, J D C Goddard 58, D V P Wright 5–141)
England 344 (L Hutton 202, J D C Goddard 4–25, A L Valentine 4–121) and 103 (A L Valentine 6–39)

1950 Averages

Batting

	I	No	Runs	HS	Avge
F.M.M. Worrell (WI)	6	0	539	261	89.83
L. Hutton (E)	6	1	333	202*	66.60
C. Washbrook (E)	4	0	255	224	63.75
A.F. Rae (WI)	7	1	377	109	62.83
E. De C. Weekes (WI)	6	0	338	129	56.33
J.B. Stollmeyer (WI)	7	1	305	78	50.83
C.L. Walcott (WI)	6	1	229	168*	45.80
G.E. Gomez (WI)	6	1	207	74	41.40
T.G. Evans (E)	6	0	224	104	37.33

Bowling

	O	M	Runs	W	Avge	BB
A.L. Valentine (WI)	422.3	197	674	33	20.42	8–104
S. Ramadhin (WI)	377.5	170	604	26	23.23	5–66
W.E. Hollies (E)	119	38	268	10	26.80	5–63
A.V. Bedser (E)	181	49	377	11	34.27	5–127
R.O. Jenkins (E)	118.2	20	409	10	40.90	5–116

ENGLAND V WEST INDIES 1950
2nd Test, Lord's: West Indies won by 326

WEST INDIES

A.F. Rae	c and b Jenkins	106	b Jenkins	24
J.B. Stollmeyer	lbw b Wardle	20	b Jenkins	30
F.M.M. Worrell	b Bedser	52	c Doggart b Jenkins	45
E. de C. Weekes	b Bedser	63	run out	63
C.L. Walcott†	st Evans b Jenkins	14	(6) not out	168
G.E. Gomez	st Evans b Jenkins	1	(7) c Edrich b Bedser	70
R.J. Christiani	b Bedser	33	(8) not out	5
J.D.C. Goddard*	b Wardle	14	(5) c Evans b Jenkins	11
P.E. Jones	c Evans b Jenkins	0		
S. Ramadhin	not out	1		
A.L. Valentine	c Hutton b Jenkins	5		
Extras	(B 10, LB 5, W 1, NB 1)	17	(LB 8, NB 1)	9
Total		**326**	**(6 wickets declared)**	**425**

ENGLAND

L. Hutton	st Walcott b Valentine	35	b Valentine	10
C. Washbrook	st Walcott b Ramadhin	36	b Ramadhin	114
W.J. Edrich	c Walcott b Ramadhin	8	c Jones b Ramadhin	8
G.H.G. Doggart	lbw b Ramadhin	0	b Ramadhin	25
W.G.A. Parkhouse	b Valentine	0	c Goddard b Valentine	48
N.W.D. Yardley*	b Valentine	16	c Weekes b Valentine	19
T.G. Evans†	b Ramadhin	8	c Rae b Ramadhin	2
R.O. Jenkins	c Walcott b Valentine	4	b Ramadhin	4
J.H. Wardle	not out	33	lbw b Worrell	21
A.V. Bedser	b Ramadhin	5	b Ramadhin	0
R. Berry	c Goddard b Jones	2	not out	0
Extras	(B 2, LB 1, W 1)	4	(B 16, LB 7)	23
Total		**151**		**274**

ENGLAND	O	M	R	W	O	M	R	W
Bedser	40	14	60	3	44	16	80	1
Edrich	16	4	30	0	13	2	37	0
Jenkins	35.2	6	116	5	59	13	174	4
Wardle	17	6	46	2	30	10	58	0
Berry	19	7	45	0	32	15	67	0
Yardley	4	1	12	0				
WEST INDIES								
Jones	8.4	2	13	1	7	1	22	0
Worrell	10	4	20	0	22.3	9	39	1
Valentine	45	28	48	4	71	47	79	3
Ramadhin	43	27	66	5	72	43	86	6
Gomez					13	1	25	0
Goddard					6	6	0	0

FALL OF WICKETS

	WI	E	WI	E
Wkt	1st	1st	2nd	2nd
1st	37	62	48	28
2nd	128	74	75	57
3rd	233	74	108	140
4th	262	75	146	218
5th	273	86	199	228
6th	274	102	410	238
7th	320	110	–	245
8th	320	113	–	248
9th	320	122	–	258
10th	326	151	–	274

Weekes, Everton de Courcy

Weekes, like Walcott and Worrell of the 'three Ws', was born at Bridgetown. He appeared on 26 February 1925, and made his debut for Barbados in 1944–45. He was an attacking middle-order right-hand batsman, and an excellent field. He holds the record for most centuries in consecutive Test innings: five in England and India in 1947–48 and 1948–49. In the same run he made seven consecutive fifties, also a record. In 48 Tests he scored 4,455 runs, average 58.61. On retiring, he became an international bridge player.

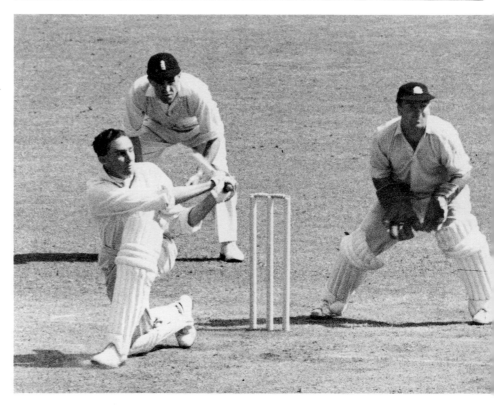

J.B. Stollmeyer batting in the third Test at Trent Bridge in 1950. Stollmeyer was to captain the West Indies in future Tests. He was at the crease when West Indies won this match by ten wickets to take a 2–1 lead in the series.

1953–54: England come back from two down to level

With the previous disastrous tour in mind, MCC sent a strong side to West Indies in 1953–54, Bedser being the most notable absentee. L. Hutton became the first professional to captain an MCC touring side.

England picked a fast attack for the first Test at Kingston, but on a docile pitch West Indies made 417. There were mild attacks on the wife and son of umpire P. Burke after he had given out lbw the local player J.K. Holt jnr, who had scored 94 on his debut. West Indies' spinners did better than the fast men and England were out for 170. The crowd demonstrated when the West Indies captain, J.B. Stollmeyer, did not enforce the follow-on. He declared at 209 for six. During the innings G.A.R. Lock became the second bowler (the first for 56 years) to be no-balled for throwing in a Test match. Set 457, England reached 233 for two by the close of the fifth day, and the crowd was getting restive, but England collapsed on the last day and lost by 140.

At Bridgetown, Walcott scored a swashbuckling 220 in a total of 383, and England were dismissed for 181. Stollmeyer again went in to bat, declaring at 292 for two, with Holt making 166 of them. Again England did much better the second time, but lost by 181. Hutton was disturbed by the crowd's barracking.

England batted first at Georgetown, and despite Ramadhin's six for 113, did much better, reaching 435, of which Hutton contributed a stylish 169. With West Indies 139 for seven, G.A. McWatt and Holt added 99, when McWatt was run out. The crowd rioted and bottles and beer crates were thrown on the pitch. Mounted police and Johnny Wardle with his clowning helped restore order. West Indies followed on and England won by nine wickets.

Port-of-Spain staged a 'three W's' festival: Weekes 206, Worrell 167, Walcott 124, the first two adding 338 for the third wicket. West Indies declared at 681 for eight. But the jute matting wicket was easy for batting, and England made 537, with May (135) and Compton (133) leading the way.

G. St A. Sobers made his debut at Kingston, where Bailey produced his best Test bowling in the first innings, seven for 34, to help dismiss West Indies for 139. Hutton then played another masterly innings of 205, England getting 414. Walcott made 116 in an attempt to save the match, but England needed only 72 and squared the rubber.

On this tour, as well as the sometimes ugly crowd behaviour, there was criticism of the England players' obvious disagreement with many umpiring decisions.

J.K. Holt jun hooks Lock to the boundary at the Kensington Oval, Bridgetown, in 1953–54. He scored 166 in his second Test.

1953–54   8th Series   W I 2, Eng 2, Drawn 1

1 KINGSTON   West Indies won by 140 runs

West Indies 417 (J K Holt 94, C L Walcott 65, J B Stollmeyer 60, E de C Weekes 55, C A McWatt 54, J B Statham 4–90) and 209–6 dec (E de C Weekes 90)

England 170 (S Ramadhin 4–65) and 316 (W Watson 116, P B H May 69, L Hutton 56, E S M Kentish 5–49)

2 BRIDGETOWN   West Indies won by 181 runs

West Indies 383 (C L Walcott 220, B H Pairaudeau 71, D St E Atkinson 53, J C Laker 4–81) and 292–2 dec (J K Holt 166, F M M Worrell 76)

England 181 (L Hutton 72, S Ramadhin 4–50) and 313 (D C S Compton 93, L Hutton 70, T W Graveney 64, P B H May 62)

3 GEORGETOWN   England won by 9 wkts

England 435 (L Hutton 169, D C S Compton 64, S Ramadhin 6–113) and 75–1

West Indies 251 (E de C Weekes 94, C A McWatt 54, J B Statham 4–64) and 256 (J K Holt 64)

4 PORT OF SPAIN   Match Drawn

West Indies 681–8 dec (E de C Weekes 206, F M M Worrell 167, C L Walcott 124, D St E Atkinson 74) and 212–4 dec (F M M Worrell 56, D St E Atkinson 53, C L Walcott 51)

England 537 (P B H May 135, D C S Compton 133, T W Graveney 92) and 98–3

5 KINGSTON   England won by 9 wkts

West Indies 139 (C L Walcott 50, T E Bailey 7–34) and 346 (C L Walcott 116, J B Stollmeyer 64, J C Laker 4–71)

England 414 (L Hutton 205, J H Wardle 66, G St A Sobers 4–75) and 72–1

1953–54 Averages

Batting	I	No	Runs	HS	Avge
L. Hutton (E)	8	1	677	205	96.71
C.L. Walcott (WI)	10	2	698	220	87.25
E. De. C. Weekes (WI)	8	1	487	206	69.57
J.K. Holt (WI)	9	1	432	166	54.00
D.C.S. Compton (E)	7	0	348	133	49.71
F.M.M. Worrell (WI)	8	1	334	167	47.71
P.B.H. May (E)	10	1	414	135	46.00
D. St E. Atkinson (WI)	7	1	259	74	43.16
T.W. Graveney (E)	10	3	265	92	37.85
J.B. Stollmeyer (WI)	9	0	256	64	28.44

Bowling	O	M	Runs	W	Avge	BB
S. Ramadhin (WI)	304.3	133	559	23	24.30	6–113
J.B. Statham (E)	153	24	460	16	28.75	4–64
T.E. Bailey (E)	182	51	459	14	32.78	7–34
J.C. Laker (E)	218.1	84	469	14	33.50	4–71
G.A.R. Lock (E)	292.5	87	718	14	51.28	3–76

1957: England win easily after blunting Ramadhin

The turning point in the series between Goddard's tourists and P.B.H. May's team came as early as the first Test at Edgbaston. England were dismissed for 186, with Ramadhin weaving his old magic with seven for 49. O.G. Smith made a dashing 161 and West Indies led by 288. At 113 for three (two more for Ramadhin), England seemed doomed. But May (285 not out) and Cowdrey (154) then came together and made England's record Test stand of 411. England declared at 583 for four and West Indies nearly lost on the last evening by sliding to 72 for seven. Ramadhin, who bowled the most balls in any Test (774), of which a first-class record of 558 were bowled in the second innings, had finally been tamed.

At Lord's, West Indies batted, and Bailey produced another fine spell against them, taking seven for 44. Cowdrey's 152 was the backbone of England's 424, and they won by an innings and 36. Bailey had 11 wickets in the match.

D.W. Richardson played his only Test at Trent Bridge, he and P.E. being the first brothers to play together for England since the Hearnes in 1891–92. The Test was notable for fine individual batting performances. Graveney made his highest score, 258, and support from P.E. Richardson (126) and May (104) hoisted England to 619 for six declared. Worrell then carried his bat for West Indies at 191 not out from 372. When West Indies followed on, O.G. Smith made 168 and saved the match. Trueman took nine wickets in all. England needed 121 to win, but there was not enough time.

West Indies collapsed at Headingley, losing their last four wickets in consecutive balls. P.J. Loader (6–36) finished the innings with a hat-trick. Despite Worrell's seven for 70, England took a lead of 137, five runs more than West Indies could get in their second innings.

At the Oval, with Richardson scoring 107

and Graveney 164, England reached 412. West Indies were then dismissed for their two lowest totals against England, 89 and 86. Sobers got 39 and 42. Lock took 11 wickets and Laker five to give England a 3–0 win.

1957 9th Series Eng 3, W I 0, Drawn 2

1 EDGBASTON Match Drawn
England 186 (S Ramadhin 7–49) and 583–4 dec (P B H May 285, M C Cowdrey 154)
West Indies 474 (O G Smith 161, C L Walcott 90, F M M Worrell 81, G St A Sobers 53, J C Laker 4–119) and 72–7

2 LORD'S England won by an innings and 36 runs
West Indies 127 (T E Bailey 7–44) and 261 (E de C Weekes 90, G St A Sobers 66, T E Bailey 4–54)
England 424 (M C Cowdrey 152, T G Evans 82, P E Richardson 76, R Gilchrist 4–115)

3 TRENT BRIDGE Match Drawn
England 619–6 dec (T W Graveney 258, P E Richardson 126, P B H May 104, M C Cowdrey 55) and 64–1
West Indies 372 (F M M Worrell 191, F S Trueman 5–63) and 367 (O G Smith 168, J D C Goddard 61, J B Statham 5–118, F S Trueman 4–80)

4 HEADINGLEY England won by an innings and 5 runs
West Indies 142 (P J Loader 6–36) and 132
England 279 (P B H May 69, M C Cowdrey 68, D S Sheppard 68, F M M Worrell 7–70)

5 THE OVAL England won by an innings and 237 runs
England 412 (T W Graveney 164, P E Richardson 107, S Ramadhin 4–107)
West Indies 89 (G A R Lock 5–28) and 86 (G A R Lock 6–20)

1957 Averages

Batting	I	No	Runs	HS	Avge
T.W. Graveney (E)	5	1	472	258	118.00
P.B.H. May (E)	6	1	489	285*	97.80
M.C. Cowdrey (E)	6	0	435	154	72.50
P.E. Richardson (E)	7	0	411	126	58.71
O.G. Smith (WI)	10	0	396	168	39.60
F.M.M. Worrell (WI)	10	1	350	191*	38.88
G.St.A. Sobers (WI)	10	0	320	66	32.00

Bowling	O	M	Runs	W	Avge	BB
G.A.R. Lock (E)	114.2	59	163	15	10.86	6–20
F.S. Trueman (E)	173.3	34	455	22	20.68	5–63
T.E. Bailey (E)	117	37	277	12	23.08	7–44
J.C. Laker (E)	246.2	99	448	18	24.88	4–119
J.B. Statham (E)	158.1	37	433	13	33.30	5–118
S. Ramadhin (WI)	261.3	78	547	14	39.07	7–49

Alf Valentine, the bowling sensation who in his first Test took the first eight wickets to fall at Old Trafford in 1950.

Top: Tom Graveney batting at the Oval in the last Test against West Indies in 1957, when he scored 154.

Above: D.J. Insole pushes away a ball from Gilchrist in the first Test at Edgbaston in 1957.

Above: Sonny Ramadhin bowling to Peter May at Edgbaston in 1957. Both players established records in this match, in which May and Cowdrey (non-striker) finally mastered Ramadhin.

1959–60: England win five tosses and the series

After losing in Australia, England sent a young team to West Indies in 1959–60. May was captain, and F.C.M. 'Gerry' Alexander captained the home team.

May won the toss on a plumb wicket at Bridgetown in the first Test and England made 482, Barrington (128) and Dexter (136 not out) being centurions. West Indies, who began their innings at lunch on the third day, did better. Sobers (226) and Worrell (197 not out) added 399 for the fourth wicket. Theirs was the longest partnership in Test cricket (579 minutes) and lasted from 4.50 on Friday to 11.40 on Tuesday. West Indies made 563 for eight declared and the match was drawn.

The wicket at the Queen's Park Oval, Port-of-Spain, was turf for the first time. Barrington and Smith hit hundreds in 382. During the innings W.W. Hall and C.D. Watson were warned for persistent bouncers. West Indies had reached 98 for seven on the third evening when C.K. Singh, in his first Test, was run out. The record crowd of nearly 30,000 rioted violently. Missiles, then people, poured onto

Collie Smith square driving Trueman in the third Test at Trent Bridge in 1957. Smith's brilliant innings of 168 helped save the match for West Indies after they had followed on nearly 250 behind.

the playing area, and play was suspended for the day while the fire brigade and riot police restored order. Play was normal on the Monday. England batted again and declared at 230 for nine, and despite a brilliant century by R.B. Kanhai, won by 256 runs.

In an exciting match at Kingston, Hall (7–69) was too fast for everybody bar Cowdrey, who made 114 of England's 277. West Indies passed this with only two wickets down, thanks mainly to Sobers' 147, but England fought back to capture the last eight wickets for 54. Pullar and Cowdrey then put on 177 for England's first wicket but they collapsed in turn to 305. But the last wicket had lasted 45 minutes, and West Indies' task was 230 in 245 minutes. May caused controversy by refusing to allow Kanhai to use a runner – it transpired he was in the wrong. When Kanhai was sixth out, West Indies gave up the chase, and drew.

May's health broke down before the Georgetown Test – he had been unwell for some time – and he flew home. Cowdrey deputized as captain. More fiery bowling by Hall (6–90) had England out for 296. With Sobers getting a slow 145 against defensive tactics, West Indies took a long time scoring 402 for eight declared. Subba Row and Dexter scored centuries as the game drifted to a draw.

Statham flew home before the last Test because his son was dangerously ill. J.M. Parks flew out and kept wicket in a Test West Indies had to win to draw the rubber. England won all the tosses in this series, and Cowdrey's opening 119 helped make the game safe. West Indies declared at 338 for eight, 55 behind, but a Parks century removed any hope of a home win. England's declaration did not set a reasonable target.

Pullar cuts Hall at Kingston in the third Test in 1959–60, but straight to Sobers, and England are 29 for one.

1959–60   10th Series   Eng 1, W I 0, Drawn 4

1 BRIDGETOWN   Match Drawn
England 482 (E R Dexter 136, K F Barrington 128, G Pullar 65) and 71–0
West Indies 563–8 dec (G St A Sobers 226, F M M Worrell 197, F S Trueman 4–93)

2 PORT OF SPAIN   England won by 256 runs
England 382 (K F Barrington 121, M J K Smith 108, E R Dexter 77) and 230–9 dec
West Indies 112 (F S Trueman 5–35) and 244 (R B Kanhai 110)

3 KINGSTON   Match Drawn
England 277 (M C Cowdrey 114, W W Hall 7–69) and 305 (M C Cowdrey 97, G Pullar 66, C D Watson 4–62)
West Indies 353 (G St A Sobers 147, E D A St J McMorris 73, S M Nurse 70) and 175–6 (R B Kanhai 57, F S Trueman 4–54)

4 GEORGETOWN   Match Drawn
England 295 (M C Cowdrey 65, D A Allen 55, W W Hall 6–90) and 334–8 (E R Dexter 119, R Subba Row 100, F M M Worrell 4–49)
West Indies 402–8 dec (G St A Sobers 145, R B Kanhai 55)

5 PORT OF SPAIN   Match Drawn
England 393 (M C Cowdrey 119, E R Dexter 76, K F Barrington 69, S Ramadhin 4–73) and 350–7 dec (J M Parks 101, M J K Smith 96, G Pullar 54)
West Indies 338–8 dec (G St A Sobers 92, C C Hunte 72, C L Walcott 53) and 209–5 (F M M Worrell 61)

1959–60 Averages

Batting	I	No	Runs	HS	Avge
G.St.A. Sobers (WI)	8	1	709	226	101.28
E.R. Dexter (E)	9	1	526	136*	65.75
F.M.M. Worrell (WI)	6	1	320	197*	64.00
M.C. Cowdrey (E)	10	1	491	119	54.55
K.F. Barrington (E)	9	0	420	128	46.66
G. Pullar (E)	10	1	385	66	42.77
C.C. Hunte (WI)	8	1	291	72*	41.57
R.B. Kanhai (WI)	8	0	325	110	40.62
M.J.K. Smith (E)	9	0	308	108	34.22

Bowling	O	M	Runs	W	Avge	BB
F.S. Trueman (E)	220.3	62	549	21	26.14	5–35
S. Ramadhin (WI)	248.3	83	491	17	28.88	4–73
W.W. Hall (WI)	236.2	49	679	22	30.86	7–69
C.D. Watson (WI)	199	39	593	16	37.06	4–62

1963: Cowdrey's broken arm fails to save Wisden Trophy

F.M.M. Worrell captained the tourists to England in 1963. The party included many of those who had played in the stirring series in Australia in 1960–61. England were captained by Dexter.

At Old Trafford, Worrell won an important toss and West Indies made 501 for six declared, with C.C. Hunte making 162. L.R. Gibbs took five wickets as England crashed to 205, and six more as they made 296 in the second innings, leaving the tourists to score one run.

The Lord's Test was remarkable in that all four possible results remained until the second last ball. Batting first, West Indies made 301. Trueman took six for 100. C.C. Griffith took five wickets when England batted, and the home side finished four short at 297. Only B.F. Butcher handled Trueman and Shackleton in the second innings, his 133 contributing to a total of 229. England needed 234 to win, but with Cowdrey and Barrington repairing a bad start of 31 for three, Cowdrey's left arm was broken. Barrington and Close batted well, but when Shackleton was run out in the last over England needed six to win with two balls and one wicket left. Cowdrey came out to bat at the non-striker's end, and D.A. Allen negotiated the last two balls and the match was drawn.

At Edgbaston, England won the toss and with the first three days interrupted by rain settled for 216 (Sobers 5–60). West Indies struggled against Trueman and Dexter to get 186. England declared at 278 for nine, setting West Indies 309, but Trueman took their last six wickets for four runs in 24

Barrington clean bowled by Sobers in the second Test at Edgbaston in 1963. This was, however, England's only win in the series.

balls, shooting them out for 91 and claiming 12 wickets in the match.

Fine batting, particularly by Sobers (102), took West Indies to 397 at Headingley, and then Griffith's pace removed England for 174. England were set 453 to win on a pitch taking spin, and Gibbs and Sobers saw that they fell 222 short.

England had to win to square the rubber at the Oval, but Griffith (6–71) kept them to 275. However, England's swing bowling dismissed the tourists for 246. When England were out for 223, West Indies needed 253 to win. With Trueman bowling only one over because of injury, Hunte made 108 not out, seeing West Indies through to an eight-wicket win.

Trueman took 34 wickets and Griffith 32, but Griffith's action was often said to be doubtful, most notably by Trueman in his autobiography.

This series was the first played for the Wisden Trophy, presented for competition between the two countries to commemorate the 100th edition of Wisden Cricketers' Almanack.

1963   11th Series   W I 3, Eng 1, Drawn 1

1 OLD TRAFFORD   West Indies won by 10 wkts
West Indies 501–6 dec (C C Hunte 182, R B Kanhai 90, F M M Worrell 74, G St A Sobers 64) and 1–0
England 205 (E R Dexter 73, L R Gibbs 5–59) and 296 (M J Stewart 87, L R Gibbs 6–98)

2 LORD'S   Match Drawn
West Indies 301 (R B Kanhai 73, J S Solomon 56, F S Trueman 6–100) and 229 (B F Butcher 133, F S Trueman 5–52, D Shackleton 4–72)
England 297 (K F Barrington 80, E R Dexter 70, C C Griffith 5–91) and 228–9 (K F Barrington 60, D B Close 70, W W Hall 4–93)

3 EDGBASTON   England won by 217 runs
England 216 (D B Close 55, G St A Sobers 5–60) and 278–9 dec (P J Sharpe 85, E R Dexter 57, G A R Lock 56, L R Gibbs 4–49)
West Indies 186 (F S Trueman 5–75, E R Dexter 4–38) and 91 (F S Trueman 7–44)

4 HEADINGLEY   West Indies won by 221 runs
West Indies 397 (G St A Sobers 102, R B Kanhai 92, J S Solomon 62, F S Trueman 4–117) and 229 (B F Butcher 78, G St A Sobers 52, F J Titmus 4–44)
England 174 (G A R Lock 53, C C Griffith 6–36) and 231 (J M Parks 57, D B Close 56, L R Gibbs 4–76)

5 THE OVAL   West Indies won by 8 wkts
England 275 (P J Sharpe 63, C C Griffith 6–71) and 223 (P J Sharpe 83, W W Hall 4–39)
West Indies 246 (C C Hunte 80, B F Butcher 53) and 255–2 (C C Hunte 108, R B Kanhai 77)

1963 Averages

Batting	I	No	Runs	HS	Avge
C.C. Hunte (WI)	10	2	471	182	58.87
R.B. Kanhai (WI)	9	0	497	92	55.22
P.J. Sharpe (E)	6	1	267	85*	53.40
B.F. Butcher (WI)	9	1	383	133	47.87
G.St.A. Sobers (WI)	8	0	322	102	40.25
E.R. Dexter (E)	10	0	340	73	34.00
D.B. Close (E)	10	0	315	70	31.50
K.F. Barrington (E)	10	0	275	80	27.50

Bowling	O	M	Runs	W	Avge	BB
C.C. Griffith (WI)	223.5	53	519	32	16.21	6–36
F.S. Trueman (E)	236.4	53	594	34	17.47	7–44
L.R. Gibbs (WI)	249.3	74	554	26	21.30	6–98
G.St.A. Sobers (WI)	231	50	571	20	28.55	5–60
W.W. Hall (WI)	178	26	534	16	33.37	4–39
D. Shackleton (E)	243.2	73	518	15	34.53	4–72

Basil Butcher unluckily run out for 53 in the final Test in 1963. Sobers drove a ball from Lock who deflected it onto the wicket with Butcher out of his ground.

Sobers completed a clean sweep of the toss at the Oval, and batted. He and Kanhai (104) added 122, but a total of 268 was poor. Graveney (165) and J.T. Murray (112) added 217 for the eighth wicket for England, and when both were out Higgs (63) and Snow (59 not out) added 128 for the tenth wicket. All in all it was enough to give England an innings win, but it was Sobers' series.

1966   12th Series   W I 3, Eng 1, Drawn 1

1 OLD TRAFFORD   West Indies won by an innings and 40 runs
West Indies 484 (G St A Sobers 161, C C Hunte 135, F J Titmus 5–83)
England 167 (L R Gibbs 5–37) and 277 (C Milburn 94, M C Cowdrey 69, L R Gibbs 5–69)

2 LORD'S   Match Drawn
West Indies 269 (S M Nurse 64, K Higgs 6–91) and 369–5 dec (G St A Sobers 163, D A J Holford 105)
England 355 (T W Graveney 96, J M Parks 91, G Boycott 60, W W Hall 4–106) and 197–4 (C Milburn 126)

3 TRENT BRIDGE   West Indies won by 139 runs
West Indies 235 (S M Nurse 93, K Higgs 4–71, J A Snow 4–82) and 482–5 dec (B F Butcher 209, G St A Sobers 94, R B Kanhai 63, S M Nurse 53)
England 325 (T W Graveney 109, M C Cowdrey 96, B L d'Oliveira 76, G St A Sobers 4–90, W W Hall 4–105) and 253 (G Boycott 71, B L d'Oliveira 54, C C Griffith 4–34)

4 HEADINGLEY   West Indies won by an innings and 55 runs
West Indies 500–9 dec (G St A Sobers 174, S M Nurse 137, K Higgs 4–94)
England 240 (B L d'Oliveira 88, G St A Sobers 5–41) and 205 (R W Barber 55, L R Gibbs 6–39)

5 THE OVAL   England won by an innings and 34 runs
West Indies 268 (R B Kanhai 104, G St A Sobers 81) and 225 (S M Nurse 70, B F Butcher 60)
England 527 (T W Graveney 165, J T Murray 112, K Higgs 63, J A Snow 59)

1966 Averages

Batting	I	No	Runs	HS	Avge
G.St.A. Sobers (WI)	8	1	722	174	103.14
T.W. Graveney (E)	7	1	459	165	76.50
S.M. Nurse (WI)	8	0	501	137	62.62
B.F. Butcher (WI)	8	1	420	209*	60.00
C. Milburn (E)	8	2	316	126*	52.66
B.L.D'Oliveira (E)	6	0	256	88	42.66
R.B. Kanhai (WI)	8	0	324	104	40.50
M.C. Cowdrey (E)	8	0	252	96	31.50

Bowling	O	M	Runs	W	Avge	BB
L.R. Gibbs (WI)	273.4	103	520	21	24.76	6–39
K. Higgs (E)	236.4	49	611	24	25.45	6–91
G.St.A. Sobers (WI)	269.4	78	545	20	27.25	5–41
W.W. Hall (WI)	175.3	35	555	18	30.83	4–105
C.C. Griffith (WI)	144.3	27	438	14	31.28	4–34
J.A. Snow (E)	138.5	29	451	12	37.58	4–82

1966: Sobers shines as West Indies win series 3–1

Sobers' team in 1966 was not thought to be as strong as the 1963 side. He won the toss in the first Test at Old Trafford, where M.J.K. Smith led England. Hunte scored 135, and Sobers himself a brilliant 161 in West Indies' 484. F.J. Titmus took five wickets and spin played a progressive part as the wicket deteriorated. Gibbs and D.A.J. Holford, Sobers' cousin, removed England for 167, and then Gibbs and Sobers did the trick for 277. Gibbs took ten wickets as West Indies won by an innings.

At Lord's, where B.L. D'Oliveira made his debut, K. Higgs bowled well to get West Indies out for 269. England took a lead of 86, and reduced West Indies to 95 for five. Sobers (163 not out) and Holford (105 not out) then added an unbeaten 274, a stand which swung the series. C. Milburn, in his second Test, made 126 not out as England made a token chase.

West Indies made 235 at Trent Bridge, again passed by England. Graveney's 109 helped to a lead of 90. This time Butcher was the rock on which hopes crashed. His 209 not out allowed West Indies to declare and set a target of 393 in 389 minutes, time enough to get England out for 253 and an easy win.

At Headingley S.M. Nurse (137) helped Sobers (174) in the vital stand: 265 for the fifth wicket. A declaration at 500 for nine set up an innings win. Sobers took eight wickets after his big score.

Top: One captain bowls another. Worrell is bowled by Dexter at Edgbaston in 1963. Both players were outstanding batsmen who could also bowl.

Above: Gary Sobers, the West Indies captain in 1966, with the Wisden Trophy, first presented in 1963 and which his team was defending.

1967–68: Two exciting finishes tip series England's way

The England captain D.B. Close had already been selected to lead the tour to West Indies in 1967–68 when he was censured for 'unfair' time-wasting tactics in a County match and sacked. M.C. Cowdrey led the tourists.

He won the toss at Port-of-Spain and Barrington and Graveney made centuries in a total of 568. Despite a century from C.H. Lloyd, West Indies could not avoid the follow on and faced defeat when they lost three wickets in the over before tea on the last day: at 180 for eight they were still 25 behind. But Sobers and Hall batted out the final session, adding 63, for a draw.

Cowdrey's 101, with support from Edrich and Barrington, led to a total of 376 at Kingston, a total which looked enormous as Snow took seven for 49 and West Indies followed on again, 233 behind. At 204 for five, Butcher was correctly given out caught behind and the crowd rioted. Seventy-five

Above: Palm trees at the Kensington Oval, Bridgetown, Barbados, one of West Indies' most pleasant grounds. This is Lock being bowled by Frank King for a duck.

Left: Geoff Boycott, in his earlier spectacled days, goes down on one knee to sweep at the Queen's Park Oval, Port of Spain, in the first Test 1967–68.

minutes were lost as the bottles were cleared up, and it was agreed that this would be played on an extra sixth day. An undefeated 113 by Sobers saved the match, and he declared, England losing eight wickets for 68 in the last innings.

Titmus lost four toes in a boating accident before the next Test at Bridgetown, P.I. Pocock replacing him for his first Test. West Indies batted and made 349 (Snow 5–86), but Edrich (146) and Boycott (90) put on 172 for the first wicket and England led by 100. Lloyd's unbeaten century saved West Indies.

West Indies' batting at last came good at Port-of-Spain, Nurse (136) and Kanhai (153) putting on 273 for the third wicket, the base for a total of 526 for seven declared. Cowdrey's 148 led England to a respectable 404, Butcher, a very occasional leg-break bowler, getting five for 34. With a dull draw in prospect, Sobers gambled on a win by declaring at 92 for two. England were set

215 runs in 165 minutes and went for them, winning by seven wickets with three minutes to spare. This was the first Test to be lost by a team which declared twice.

Kanhai (150) and Sobers (152) added 250 for West Indies' fourth wicket at Georgetown, in a total of 404. Boycott got a century in England's reply and Lock (89) and Pocock (13) added 109 for the ninth wicket, Pocock defending for 82 minutes before breaking his duck. England reached 371 and West Indies were out for 264, Snow taking ten wickets in the match. England needed 308 to win and slumped to 41 for five. Cowdrey and Knott put on 127 and Knott was still in with last player Jeff Jones when stumps were drawn. England thus won the series with the better of two exciting finishes.

1967–68 13th Series Eng 1, W I 0, Drawn 4

1 PORT OF SPAIN Match Drawn
England 568 (K F Barrington 143, T W Graveney 118, M C Cowdrey 72, G Boycott 68, C C Griffith 5–69)
West Indies 363 (C H Lloyd 118, R B Kanhai 85) and 243–8 (B F Butcher 58)

2 KINGSTON Match Drawn
England 376 (M C Cowdrey 101, J H Edrich 96, K F Barrington 63, W W Hall 4–63) and 68–8
West Indies 143 (J A Snow 7–49) and 391–9 dec (G St A Sobers 113, S M Nurse 73)

3 BRIDGETOWN Match Drawn
West Indies 349 (B F Butcher 85, G St A Sobers 68, G S Camacho 57, J A Snow 5–86) and 284–6 (C H Lloyd 113, B F Butcher 60)
England 449 (J H Edrich 146, G Boycott 90, T W Graveney 55, B L d'Oliveira 51)

4 PORT OF SPAIN England won by 7 wkts
West Indies 526–7 dec (R B Kanhai 153, S M Nurse 136, G S Camacho 87) and 92–2 dec
England 404 (M C Cowdrey 148, A P E Knott 69, G Boycott 62, B F Butcher 5–34) and 215–3 (G Boycott 80, M C Cowdrey 71)

5 GEORGETOWN Match Drawn
West Indies 414 (G St A Sobers 152, R B Kanhai 150, J A Snow 4–82) and 264 (G St A Sobers 95, J A Snow 6–60)
England 371 (G Boycott 116, G A R Lock 89, M C Cowdrey 59) and 206–9 (M C Cowdrey 82, A P E Knott 73, L R Gibbs 6–60)

1967–68 Averages

Batting	I	No	Runs	HS	Avge
G.St.A. Sobers (WI)	9	3	545	152	90.83
M.C. Cowdrey (E)	8	0	534	148	66.75
G. Boycott (E)	8	1	463	116	66.14
R.B. Kanhai (WI)	10	1	535	153	59.44
C.H. Lloyd (WI)	9	2	369	118	52.71
S.M. Nurse (WI)	10	0	434	136	43.40
J.H. Edrich (E)	8	0	340	146	42.50
K.F. Barrington (E)	7	0	288	143	41.14
B.F. Butcher (WI)	9	1	301	86	37.62
G.S. Camacho (WI)	10	0	328	87	32.80
T.W. Graveney (E)	8	0	261	118	32.62

Bowling	O	M	Runs	W	Avge	BB
J.A. Snow (E)	165	29	504	27	18.66	7–49
L.R. Gibbs (WI)	318.3	114	610	20	30.50	6–60
D.J. Brown (E)	162	32	458	14	32.71	3–27
G.St.A. Sobers (WI)	232.5	72	508	13	39.07	3–33
I.J. Jones (E)	198.2	31	656	14	46.84	3–63

1969: Easy England win in three-match series

Sobers brought a side to England in 1969 which lacked the fast bowling strength of earlier and later sides. R. Illingworth, England's new captain, won his first toss and batted at Old Trafford. Five wickets for J.N. Shepherd on his debut were countered by Boycott's century, and West Indies only just avoided an innings defeat after England's 413.

West Indies batted at Lord's and did better, C.A. Davis scoring 103 out of 380 (Snow 5–114). England began badly but

reached 344 thanks to centuries from J.H. Hampshire, on his debut, and Illingworth, who added 83 for the last wicket with Snow. West Indies set England to get 332, and with Boycott scoring a century they ended 37 short with three wickets left.

England's 223 at Headingley earned them a lead of 62, and West Indies were set to get 303 to draw the series. Sobers, who had taken five second-innings wickets, was bowled for a duck, and when Butcher was out to a disputed catch for 91 the task proved too much. England won by 30 to keep the Wisden Trophy.

1969 14th Series Eng 2, W I 0, Drawn 1

1 OLD TRAFFORD England won by 10 wkts
England 413 (G Boycott 128, T W Graveney 75, J H Edrich 58, B L d'Oliveira 57, J N Shepherd 5–104) and 12–0
West Indies 147 (D J Brown 4–39, J A Snow 4–54) and 275 (R C Fredericks 64)

2 LORD'S Match Drawn
West Indies 380 (C A Davis 103, G S Camacho 67, R C Fredericks 63, J A Snow 5–114) and 295–9 dec (C H Lloyd 70, R C Fredericks 60, G St A Sobers 50)
England 344 (R Illingworth 113, J H Hampshire 107, A P E Knott 53) and 295–7 (G Boycott 106, P J Sharpe 86)

3 HEADINGLEY England won by 30 runs
England 223 (J H Edrich 79, V A Holder 4–48) and 240 (G St A Sobers 5–42)
West Indies 161 (B R Knight 4–63) and 272 (B F Butcher 91, G S Camacho 71, D L Underwood 4–55)

1969 Averages

Batting	I	No	Runs	HS	Avge
G. Boycott (E)	6	1	270	125	54.00
B.F. Butcher (WI)	6	0	238	91	39.66
C.A. Davis (WI)	6	0	208	103	34.66
R.C. Fredericks (WI)	6	0	204	64	34.00

Bowling	O	M	Runs	W	Avge	BB
D.J. Brown (E)	110.3	25	288	14	20.57	4–39
J.N. Shepherd (WI)	137.5	44	266	12	22.16	5–104
B.R. Knight (WI)	120.1	29	279	11	25.36	4–63
J.A. Snow (E)	139.3	26	406	15	27.06	5–114
G.St.A. Sobers (WI)	145	47	318	11	28.90	5–42

1973: West Indies reverse 1969 score-line in three-Test series

R.B. Kanhai led the West Indian party to England in 1973. Illingworth was still England's captain. C.H. Lloyd made 132 in the first innings at the Oval, West Indies scoring 415. K.D. Boyce took five wickets and West Indies led by 158. This was the margin of their victory, as both sides scored 255 in the second innings. F.C. Hayes scored 106 not out in his first Test match, while Boyce took 11 for 147 in the match. This was West Indies' first win in 20 matches.

R.C. Fredericks made 150 at Edgbaston, West Indies otherwise struggling to 327. During England's innings, umpire A.E. Fagg refused to carry on because of dissent shown by Kanhai when he turned down an appeal for caught behind with Boycott batting. He resumed after an apology, having missed one over. Boycott was forced to retire and return twice after being hit on the ribs and arm. He was not out 56 when England were dismissed for 305. West Indies were out for 302, leaving England needing 325 in 227 minutes, the match being drawn.

England needed to win at the Oval, a prospect which disappeared with West Indies' first innings of 652 for eight declared. Kanhai (157), Sobers (150 not out) and B.D. Julien (121) all scored centuries. The

seventh wicket added 231, of which 155 were added by Sobers and Julien, the West Indies record for the wicket. Sobers retired with a stomach disorder and resumed later, K.W.R. Fletcher was top-scorer in both England innings, but the match was lost by an innings and 266. There was a bomb scare with England batting and spectators joined the players in the middle. An hour and a half was lost, an hour of which was made up.

1973 15th Series Eng 0, W I 2, Drawn 1

1 THE OVAL West Indies won by 158 runs
West Indies 415 (C H Lloyd 132, A I Kallicharran 80, K D Boyce 72, G G Arnold 5–113) and 255 (A I Kallicharran 80, G St A Sobers 51)
England 257 (G Boycott 97, K D Boyce 5–70) and 255 (F C Hayes 106, K D Boyce 6–77)

2 EDGBASTON Match Drawn
West Indies 327 (R C Fredericks 150, B D Julien 54) and 302 (C H Lloyd 94, G St A Sobers 74, R B Kanhai 54, G G Arnold 4–43)
England 305 (G Boycott 56, D L Amiss 56, K W R Fletcher 52) and 182–2 (D L Amiss 86)

3 LORD'S West Indies won by an innings and 226 runs
West Indies 652–8 dec (R B Kanhai 157, G St A Sobers 150, B D Julien 121, C H Lloyd 63, R C Fredericks 51, R G D Willis 4–118)
England 233 (K W R Fletcher 68, K D Boyce 4–50, V A Holder 4–56) and 193 (K W R Fletcher 86, K D Boyce 4–50)

1973 Averages

Batting	I	No	Runs	HS	Avge
G.St.A. Sobers (WI)	5	1	306	150*	76.50
K.W.R. Fletcher (E)	6	2	266	86*	66.50
C.H. Lloyd (WI)	5	0	318	132*	63.60
G. Boycott (E)	5	1	202	97	50.50
R.C. Fredericks (WI)	5	0	251	150	50.20
D.L. Amiss (E)	6	1	231	86*	46.20
R.B. Kanhai (WI)	5	0	223	157	44.60
B.D. Julien (WI)	5	0	220	121*	44.00
A.I. Kallicharran (WI)	5	0	212	80	42.40

Bowling	O	M	Runs	W	Avge	BB
K.D. Boyce (WI)	98.1	22	294	19	15.47	7–77
G.G. Arnold (E)	149.1	37	390	15	26.00	5–113

1973–74: Greig and Amiss earn England a draw

After the short series in England, an English party with a new captain, M.H. Denness, toured West Indies in the following winter.

Kanhai put England in at Port-of-Spain, and the side was quickly out for 131. After the last ball of the second day, A.I. Kallicharran, on 142, began to walk off before the ball was dead and was run out by A.W. Greig. The appeal was withdrawn overnight to prevent bad feeling and Kallicharran went on to 158 and West Indies to 392. England reached 328 for one, thanks to Boycott (93) and D.L. Amiss (174), but then collapsed to 392 all out before Gibbs (6–108). West Indies won by seven wickets.

England batted at Kingston and made 353. Fredericks (94) and L.G. Rowe (120) then put on 206 for West Indies' first wicket. The score reached 583 for nine declared, a magnificent innings by Amiss saving the match. He batted throughout England's 432 for nine to score 262 not out.

Kanhai put England in again at Bridgetown, where A.M.E. Roberts became the first from Antigua to play Test cricket. Greig's 148, and his sixth-wicket stand of 163 with Knott, took England to 395. L.G. Rowe then scored the first West Indian triple century against England (302). With Kallicharran (119) he added 249 for the second wicket. Greig's six wickets made him the first to score a century and take five wickets in an innings for England. England

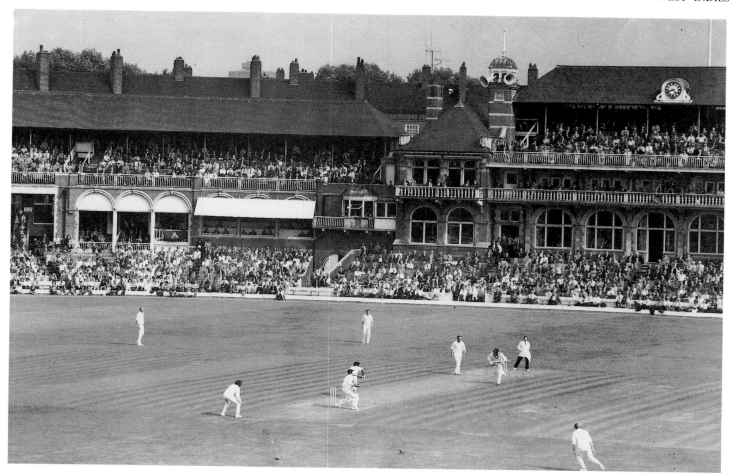

were 201 behind but easily saved the match with Fletcher's 129 not out. There were 99 no balls in the match.

Much of the fourth Test was washed out after Amiss and Greig had continued their successful runs with centuries. Sobers, though picked, did not turn up to play.

At Port-of-Spain England made 267, which West Indies passed by only 38, despite reaching 224 for two, with Rowe scoring 123. Greig took eight for 86. Boycott, who scored 99 in the first innings, made 112 in the second, keeping England in the game. A total of 263 meant West Indies needed 226 to win. Greig, who discovered a new skill with off-breaks in this match, began the last innings bowling them. West Indies, after reaching 63 without loss, then lost five wickets adding 22 and panic set in. Greig took five for 70 (13 in the match) and England won by 26 runs to square the rubber.

This was the last Test of Sobers and Kanhai, and England's last win over West Indies.

1973–74 16th Series W I 1, Eng 1, Drawn 3
1 PORT OF SPAIN West Indies won by 7 wkts
England 131 (K D Boyce 4–42) and 392 (D L Amiss 174, G Boycott 93, L R Gibbs 6–108)
West Indies 392 (A I Kallicharran 158, B D Julien 86, P I Pocock 5–110) and 132–3 (R C Fredericks 65)
2 KINGSTON Match Drawn
England 353 (G Boycott 68, M H Denness 67) and 432–9 (D L Amiss 262)
West Indies 583–9 dec (L G Rowe 120, R C Fredericks 94, A I Kallicharran 93, B D Julien 66, G St A Sobers 57)
3 BRIDGETOWN Match Drawn
England 395 (A W Greig 148, A P E Knott 87, B D Julien 5–57) and 277–7 (K W R Fletcher 129, A P E Knott 67)
West Indies 596–8 dec (L G Rowe 302, A I Kallicharran 119, D L Murray 53, A W Greig 6–164)

4 GEORGETOWN Match Drawn
England 448 (A W Greig 121, D L Amiss 118, A P E Knott 61)
West Indies 198–4 (R C Fredericks 98)
5 PORT OF SPAIN England won by 26 runs
England 267 (G Boycott 99) and 263 (G Boycott 112)
West Indies 305 (L G Rowe 123, R C Fredericks 67, C H Lloyd 52, A W Greig 8–86) and 199 (A W Greig 5–70)

1973–74 Averages

Batting	I	No	Runs	HS	Avge
L.G. Rowe (WI)	7	0	616	302	88.00
D.L. Amiss (E)	9	1	663	262*	82.87
R.C. Fredericks (WI)	7	1	397	98	66.16
A.I. Kallicharran (WI)	7	0	397	158	67.81
A.W. Greig (E)	9	0	430	148	47.77
G. Boycott (E)	9	0	421	112	46.77
A.P.E. Knott (E)	9	1	365	87	45.62
K.W.R. Fletcher (E)	7	1	262	129*	43.66

Bowling	O	M	Runs	W	Avge	BB
A.W. Greig (E)	207.1	46	543	24	22.62	8–86
B.D. Julien (WI)	174	51	378	16	23.62	5–57
G.St.A. Sobers (WI)	223.2	92	421	14	30.07	3–54
L.R. Gibbs (WI)	328	102	661	18	36.72	6–108

1976: Arrogant batting and aggressive bowling destroy England

A side very strong in batting and fast bowling came to England in 1976 under C.H. Lloyd. Greig captained England, and a fairly innocuous remark about making the opposition 'grovel' was blown up by the media and haunted him later in the series.

West Indies batting power was soon in evidence. At Trent Bridge I.V.A. Richards scored 232, adding 303 with Kallicharran (97) for the third wicket. West Indies' 494 was countered by 332 from England, D.S. Steele making 106. West Indies' second-innings declaration set England 339 in 315 minutes but England batted for a draw.

At Lord's, England made 250 and with

Kallicharran batting with Lloyd at the Oval in 1973 when West Indies passed 650.

excellent bowling by Snow and Underwood removed West Indies for 182. Roberts took five wickets for the second time in the match, England's 254 setting West Indies 323 in 294 minutes. At 210 for two, Lloyd claimed the last half-hour, but gave up the chase when he was out at 233 for four Greig, however, now insisted on carrying on with 6.5 overs left. The match was drawn at 241 for six.

At Old Trafford, West Indies were 26 for four, with M.W.W. Selvey, on his debut, taking his first three Test wickets for six runs. The side was out for 211, with C.G. Greenidge scoring 134, 63.5 per cent of the total, a percentage only beaten by Bannerman in the very first Test. But England were shot out for 71, mainly by Holding (5–17). West Indies second-innings batting was more normal at 411 for five declared, with Greenidge scoring his second hundred of the match and Richards another. Roberts then took six for 37 and West Indies won by 425 runs. The England openers, Edrich and Close, were subjected to an attack of bouncers by the West Indian fast bowlers as savage as any seen in England.

West Indies began well at Headingley with Fredericks (109) and Greenidge (115) putting on 192, and the total reached 450. Greig and Knott replied with a stand of 152 for the sixth wicket – each scored 116. England finished 63 behind, and with Willis getting five for 42, bowled out West Indies for 196. But Greig (76 not out) found

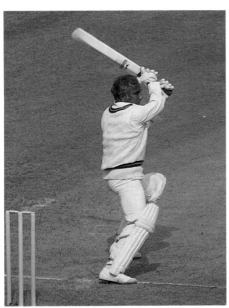

Above: The West Indies tourists in 1973. Left to right, back: L. Pink (scorer), Kallicharran, Inshan Ali, Julien, Boyce, Holder, Shillingford, Headley, Foster, Willett, D.A. Murray. Front: E. Kentish (manager), D.L. Murray, Lloyd, Sobers, Kanhai, Gibbs, Fredericks, G. Gibbs (assistant manager).

Far left: Kanhai batting at Lord's in 1973.

Left: Edrich driving at Trent Bridge in 1976.

Below left: Frank Hayes driving Boyce at the Oval in 1973. Hayes made 106 not out on his Test debut.
Below: England captain Greig bowled by a jubilant Andy Roberts for a duck at Trent Bridge, 1976.

Above: Alan Knott stretches to catch Lloyd off his Kent colleague Underwood at Lord's in 1976. Lloyd made 50.

Below: Fredericks hooks a Willis no-ball at Headingley in 1976. He made 109 in a stand of 192 with Greenidge.

Above: Dennis Amiss acknowledging the applause on reaching 200 at the Oval in 1976. West Indies still won by 231 runs.

nobody to stay with him against the West Indian fast bowling, and England's 204 was 55 runs short of saving the rubber.

At the Oval, Richards made an imperious 291 out of a total of 687 for eight declared. He had 829 in the rubber and a record 1,710 Test runs in a calendar year. Amiss, recalled to the team for his first Test of the series, made what was almost a typical double-century for England, his 203 holding together an innings of 435. Play was suspended when there was a crowd invasion on the dismissal of Greig – his remark being remembered. Holding took eight for 92 in the fun-feast. West Indies batted again, declaring at 182 for none, and dismissed England for 203 to win the series 3–0. Holding bowled magnificently for 14 wickets on a batting pitch.

1976   17th Series   W I 3, Eng 0, Drawn 2
1 TRENT BRIDGE   **Match Drawn**
West Indies 494 (I V A Richards 232, A I Kallicharran 97, D L Underwood 4–82) and 176–5 dec (I V A Richards 63, J A Snow 4–53)
England 332 (D S Steele 106, R A Woolmer 82, W W Daniel 4–53) and 156–2 (J H Edrich 76)
2 LORD'S   **Match Drawn**
England 250 (D B Close 60, A M E Roberts 5–60) and 254 (D S Steele 64, A M E Roberts 5–63)
West Indies 182 (C G Greenidge 84, C H Lloyd 50, J A Snow 4–68, D L Underwood 5–39) and 241–6 (R C Fredericks 138)
3 OLD TRAFFORD   **West Indies won by 425 runs**
West Indies 211 (C G Greenidge 134, M W W Selvey 4–41) and 411–5 dec (I V A Richards 135, C G Greenidge 101, R C Fredericks 50)
England 71 (M A Holding 5–17) and 126 (A M E Roberts 6–37)
4 HEADINGLEY   **West Indies won by 55 runs**
West Indies 450 (C G Greenidge 115, R C Fredericks 109, I V A Richards 66, L G Rowe 50, J A Snow 4–77) and 196 (C L King 58, R G D WIllis 5–42)
England 387 (A W Greig 116, A P E Knott 116) and 204 (A W Greig 76)
5 THE OVAL   **West Indies won by 231 runs**
West Indies 687–8 dec (I V A Richards 291, C H Lloyd 84, R C Fredericks 71, L G Rowe 70, C L King 63) and 182–0 dec (R C Fredericks 86, C G Greenidge 85)
England 435 (D L Amiss 203, A P E Knott 50, M A Holding 8–92) and 203 (A P E Knott 57, M A Holding 6–57)

1976 Averages

Batting	I	No	Runs	HS	Avge
I.V.A. Richards (WI)	7	0	829	291	118.42
C.C. Greenidge (WI)	10	1	592	134	65.77
R.C. Fredericks (WI)	10	1	517	138	57.44
C.H. Lloyd (WI)	9	0	296	84	32.88
D.S. Steele (E)	10	0	308	106	30.80
A.P.E. Knott (E)	9	0	270	116	30.00

Bowling	O	M	Runs	W	Avge	BB
M.A. Holding (WI)	159.3	54	356	28	12.71	8–92
A.M.E. Roberts (WI)	221.4	69	537	28	19.17	6–37
W.W. Daniel (WI)	108	28	317	13	24.38	4–53
V.A. Holder (WI)	158	48	367	15	24.46	3–35
J.A. Snow (E)	106.4	16	423	15	28.20	4–53
D.L. Underwood (E)	224	59	631	17	37.11	5–39

1980: West Indies win 1–0 in very wet summer

I.T. Botham was England's new captain when Lloyd's team arrived in 1980. Against fine bowling by Roberts (5–72) England made 263. The West Indian pace attack established their rate of 14 overs per hour which led to various later agreements and arguments about over rates. West Indies' 308 gave them a lead. Boycott's stubborn 75 could help England set only 208 but Willis (5–65, nine in the match), made West Indies fight all the way for a two-wicket win.

Rain and murky light spoiled the Lord's Test, in which West Indies established a first-innings lead of 249. Gooch, D.L.

Haynes and Richards scored centuries while Holding took six wickets, but there was little play thereafter.

At Old Trafford even more time was lost, including the whole of the third day. England, after being put in, were out on the first afternoon for 150, but fought back to dismiss West Indies for 260 (Lloyd 101) and score 391 for seven by the end.

England scored 370 at the Oval, and led by 105 when dismissing West Indies, for whom Lloyd couldn't bat, for 265. However, with rain again washing out a day, they were reduced to 20 for four by close on the fourth day, and this became 92 for nine soon after lunch on the last. P. Willey was dropped at 111, which might have cost West Indies the match. Willey and Willis added an unbeaten 117 for the last wicket, batting out time.

The England team which played the West Indies at Lord's in 1980. Left to right, back; Gatting, Tavare, Willey, Dilley (12th man), Hendrick, Woolmer, Gooch. Front: Knott, Boycott, Botham, Willis, Underwood. Gooch made a century but West Indies had much the better of a draw.

England had to win at Headingley, but the first and fourth days were washed out. West Indies had the better of the few exchanges there were and retained the Wisden Trophy on the strength of their win in the first Test.

Spain, the first Test began late because vandals had attacked the pitch and covers after local hero Deryck Murray had been omitted from the team. Rain made the delay longer. West Indies, 144 without loss on the first day, declared at 426 for nine (Emburey 5–124). England began their innings on the third day, and were out to C.E.H. Croft (5–40) for 178, and following on made only 169, losing by an innings and 79 runs.

The second Test, scheduled for Guyana, was cancelled for political reasons. R.D. Jackman was the cause. He had been flown out to join the party when Willis broke down and was flown home. Jackman, married to a South African, had played there for 11 years, and was unacceptable to the Guyana authorities. He was served with a deportation order, and the England party declined to play without him.

The third Test at Bridgetown was marred by the death of Ken Barrington, England's assistant manager and coach, from a heart attack on the evening of the second day.

West Indies had been put in, and they made 265, with Lloyd scoring 100. England were out for 122 to the four fast bowlers. Richards made 182 not out and West Indies declared at 379 for seven. Gooch made 116, but he and Gower (54) were the only batsmen to handle the fast battery, and England lost by 298. R.O. Butcher, who had been born in Barbados, was the first black West Indian to play for England.

The fourth Test was the first at St John's, Antigua. Willey made a stubborn 102 not out in England's 271 (Croft 6–74) and then Richards made a careful century on 'his' island. West Indies declared at 468 for nine, when Holding and Croft had added a West Indian record of 67 for the last wicket.

1980–81 19th Series W I 2, Drawn 2
1 PORT OF SPAIN West Indies won by an innings and 79 runs
West Indies 426–9 dec (D L Haynes 96, C G Greenidge 84, C H Lloyd 64, A M E Roberts 50, J M Emburey 5–124)
England 178 (C E H Croft 5–40) and 169 (G Boycott 70)
2 BRIDGETOWN West Indies won by 298 runs
West Indies 265 (C H Lloyd 100, H A Gomes 58, I T Botham 4–77) and 379–7 dec (I V A Richards 182, C H Lloyd 66)
England 122 (C E H Croft 4–39) and 224 (G A Gooch 116, D I Gower 54)
3 ST JOHN'S Match Drawn
England 271 (P Willey 102, C E H Croft 6–74) and 234–3 (G Boycott 104, G A Gooch 83)
West Indies 468–9 dec (I V A Richards 114, E H Mattis 71, C G Greenidge 63, C H Lloyd 58, M A Holding 58, I T Botham 4–127)
4 KINGSTON Match Drawn
England 285 (G A Gooch 153, M A Holding 5–56) and 302–6 (D I Gower 154, P Willey 67)
West Indies 442 (C H Lloyd 95, H A Gomes 90, D L Haynes 84, C G Greenidge 62, G R Dilley 4–116)
The Test arranged for Georgetown was cancelled for political reasons.

1980–81 Averages

Batting	I	No	Runs	HS	Avge
I.V.A. Richards (WI)	5	1	340	182*	85.00
C.H. Lloyd (WI)	5	0	383	100	76.60
G.A. Gooch (E)	8	0	460	153	57.50
D.I. Gower (E)	8	1	376	154*	53.71
P. Willey (E)	8	3	244	102*	48.80
D.L. Haynes (WI)	5	0	234	96	46.80
C.G. Greenidge (WI)	5	0	223	84	44.60
G. Boycott (E)	8	1	295	104*	42.14

Bowling	O	M	Runs	W	Avge	BB
M.A. Holding (WI)	132.3	38	315	17	18.52	5–56
C.E.H. Croft (WI)	157.5	34	455	24	18.95	6–74
J. Garner (WI)	151.2	48	303	10	30.30	2–31
I.T. Botham (E)	145.2	31	492	17	32.80	4–77
G.R. Dilley (E)	129.4	25	450	10	45.00	4–116

1980 18th Series W I 1, Eng 0, Drawn 4
1 TRENT BRIDGE West Indies won by 2 wkts
England 263 (I T Botham 57, A M E Roberts 5–72) and 252 (G Boycott 75, J Garner 4–30)
West Indies 308 (I V A Richards 64, D L Murray 64, C G Greenidge 53, R G D Willis 4–82) and 209–8 (D L Haynes 62, R G D Willis 5–65)
2 LORD'S Match Drawn
England 269 (G A Gooch 123, M A Holding 6–67, J Garner 4–36) and 133–2
West Indies 518 (D L Haynes 184, I V A Richards 145, C H Lloyd 56)
3 OLD TRAFFORD Match Drawn
England 150 (B C Rose 70) and 391–7 (G Boycott 86, P Willey 62, M W Gatting 56)
West Indies 260 (C H Lloyd 101, I V A Richards 65)
4 THE OVAL Match Drawn
England 370 (G A Gooch 83, G Boycott 53, B C Rose 50) and 209–9 dec (P Willey 100, M A Holding 4–79)
West Indies 265 (S F A Bacchus 61, G R Dilley 4–57)
5 HEADINGLEY Match Drawn
England 143 and 227–6 (G A Gooch 55)
West Indies 245 (G R Dilley 4–79)

1980–81: A sad series for England is lost 2–0

Botham and Lloyd soon resumed 'hostilities' in the Caribbean in the winter. At Port-of-

1980 Averages

Batting	I	No	Runs	HS	Avge
I.V.A. Richards (WI)	6	0	379	145	63.16
D.L. Haynes (WI)	6	0	308	184	51.33
G. Boycott (E)	10	1	368	86	40.88
G.A. Gooch (E)	10	0	394	123	39.40
P. Willey (E)	9	2	262	100*	37.42

Bowling	O	M	Runs	W	Avge	BB
J. Garner (WI)	212.4	73	371	26	14.26	4–30
M.D. Marshall (WI)	172.3	42	436	15	29.06	3–36
R.G.D. Willis (E)	110.1	27	407	14	29.07	5–65
I.T. Botham (E)	131	41	385	13	29.61	3–50
M.A. Holding (WI)	230.5	56	632	20	31.60	6–67

There was no play on the fourth day and an unbeaten Boycott century drew the match.

England batted at Lloyd's request in the final Test where Gooch made a dashing 153. But Holding had five for 56 and England's 285 was not enough. West Indies made 442, but a Gower century (154 not out) helped England past 300 for the first time in the series. At 302 for six the match was drawn.

Above: Andy Roberts at Old Trafford in 1976. Roberts took nine wickets in the match and 28 in the series.

Right: Viv Richards hooking Willis for four at the Oval in 1976. Richards made 291 from 386 balls, to complete a record calendar year in which he brought his total number of runs to 1,710.

1984: West Indies win all five Tests in a 'blackwash'

Gower was the new England captain to receive Lloyd's team in 1984. Edgbaston's only debutant, T.A. Lloyd, was struck on the head by a Marshall bouncer and was in hospital for eight days, playing no more that season. England were out for 191, and West Indies, with centuries from H.A. Gomes and Richards and a record West Indian ninth-wicket partnership of 150 between E.A.E. Baptiste (87 not out) and Holding (69), reached 606. They won by an innings when England were out for 235, Garner having nine wickets in the match.

The second Test at Lord's was a remarkable match. Lloyd put England in but Fowler (106) and newcomer Broad (55) had 101 on the board without loss. England only managed 286 facing Marshall (6–85) but it was enough for a lead as Botham took eight for 103 and dismissed West Indies for 245. Good innings from Lamb (110) and Botham (81) allowed Gower to declare on the last morning, setting West Indies 342 to get. A magnificent innings by Greenidge of 214 not out, supported by Gomes (92 not out), had the match won well before the actual end. It was a nine-wicket victory.

At Headingley, Lamb made 100 out of 270, and Gomes made 104 not out for West Indies, having reached his century when Marshall, batting with a fractured thumb, joined him for the last wicket. West Indies led by only 32, but Marshall, despite his injury, took seven for 53 to remove England for 159, West Indies winning by eight wickets.

With the Wisden Trophy retained, West Indies made exactly 500 at Old Trafford, Greenidge scoring 223 to rescue the side from 70 for four when P.J.L. Dujon (101) entered and helped him raise the score to 267. Lamb's 100 not out was his third century in successive Tests, but England followed on and lost by an innings, R.A. Harper getting six second-innings wickets with, for a change, off-breaks.

West Indies made only 190 at the Oval, with Botham getting five wickets, but Marshall did likewise for West Indies and England trailed by 28. Haynes' century set England 375, and West Indies won by 172 to record a 'blackwash', winning all five Tests.

1984 20th Series W I 5, Eng 0

1 EDGBASTON **West Indies won by an innings and 180 runs**
England 191 (I T Botham 64, J Garner 4–53) and 235 (P R Downton 56, J Garner 5–55)
West Indies 606 (H A Gomes 143, I V A Richards 117, E A E Baptiste 87, C H Lloyd 71, M A Holding 69, D R Pringle 5–108)

The England team in the West Indies in 1981. Left to right, back: Bairstow, Jackman, Gatting, Athey, Stevenson, Dilley, Emburey, Willey, Gower, Downton, Butcher, G. Saulez (scorer). Front: B. Thomas (physiotherapist), Gooch, Miller, Botham, A.C. Smith (manager), Boycott, Old, K.F. Barrington (assistant manager).

2 LORD'S   West Indies won by 9 wkts
England 286 (G Fowler 106, B C Broad 55, M D Marshall 6–85) and 300–9 dec (A J Lamb 110, I T Botham 81)
West Indies 245 (I V A Richards 72, I T Botham 8–103) and 344–1 (C G Greenidge 214, H A Gomes 92)

3 HEADINGLEY   West Indies won by 8 wkts
England 270 (A J Lamb 100, M A Holding 4–70) and 159 (G Fowler 50, M D Marshall 7–53)
West Indies 302 (H A Gomes 104, M A Holding 59, P J W Allott 6–61) and 131–2

4 OLD TRAFFORD   West Indies won by an innings and 64 runs
West Indies 500 (C G Greenidge 223, P J Dujon 101, W W Davis 77, P I Pocock 4–121)
England 280 (A J Lamb 100, J Garner 4–51) and 156 (D I Gower 57, R A Harper 6–57)

5 THE OVAL   West Indies won by 172 runs
West Indies 190 (C H Lloyd 60, I T Botham 5–72) and 346 (D L Haynes 125)
England 162 (M D Marshall 5–35) and 202 (I T Botham 54, M A Holding 5–43, J Garner 4–51)

1984 Averages

Batting	I	No	Runs	HS	Avge
C.G. Greenidge (WI)	8	1	572	223	81.71
H.A. Gomez (WI)	8	3	400	143	80.00
C.H. Lloyd (WI)	6	1	255	71	51.00
A.J. Lamb (E)	10	1	386	110	42.88
I.V.A. Richards (WI)	7	1	250	117	41.66
I.T. Botham (E)	10	0	347	81	34.70
G. Fowler (E)	10	0	260	106	26.00

Bowling	O	M	Runs	W	Avge	BB
M.D. Marshall (WI)	167.4	50	437	24	18.20	7–53
J. Garner (WI)	216.5	60	540	29	18.62	5–55
P.J.W. Allott (E)	104.5	26	282	14	20.14	6–61
R.A. Harper (WI)	128.4	47	276	13	21.23	6–57
M.A. Holding (WI)	122.2	24	343	15	22.86	5–43
I.T. Botham (E)	153.2	30	667	19	35.10	8–103

1985–86: Second 'blackwash' won by fast bowlers

Richards had assumed the captaincy of West Indies when Gower's team arrived in 1985–86. Gower decided to bat in the first Test at Kingston, but the side was rushed out for 159 by West Indies' four fast bowlers. West Indies made 357 (Ellison 5–78) and England collapsed again for 152, leaving West Indies to score only five to win. Post-match discussion centred on the intimidatory bowling of West Indies – most of the England players being hit by bouncers.

At Port-of-Spain, Richards put England in, and only Gower (66) and Lamb (62)

Jubilation among the English as Richards is out for 0 at Bridgetown, Barbados in 1980–81.

Richards, Isaac Vivian Alexander

Richards was born on 7 March 1952 at St Johns, Antigua. He played for Leeward Islands from 1971–72, and in England for Somerset from 1974. He became a brilliant middle-order right-hand batsman, and a useful off-break bowler. He was thought by many to be the best batsman of his generation. He loves the big-match atmosphere, and many of his best innings have been played on the big one-day occasions. He first appeared for West Indies in 1974–75, and he took over the captaincy in 1984–85. In 88 Tests to 1986–87 he has scored 6,472 runs, average 52.61, and taken 22 wickets, average 54.90.

reached double figures. England's 176 was 223 behind West Indies' 399, R.B. Richardson scoring 102. Spinner Emburey had five for 78. England batted more solidly in the second innings, reaching 315, but West Indies won easily by seven wickets.

Richardson scored another century (160) at Bridgetown in West Indies' 418. England were forced to follow on and made 189 and 199, to lose by an innings and 30.

It was a similar story at Port-of-Spain, England being dismissed for 200 with the four fast bowlers claiming the wickets. Botham took five for 71 but West Indies reached 312. The quick dose as before removed England for 150, and West Indies needed only 39 to win by ten wickets.

West Indies batted first at Antigua, where Haynes' 131 was backed up by half-centuries from three bowlers, allowing the score to reach 474. England made a good start and Gower's 90 got them to 310. Richards declared second time at 246 for two, with himself at 110 not out. His century came in 56 balls, the fastest in terms of deliveries in Test history. His 110 included seven sixes and seven fours. England were out for 170 and lost by 240 runs.

The West Indian fast bowlers took 94 of the 98 wickets claimed by bowlers: Garner, Marshall, Patterson and Holding had 89 of them. There was criticism of the England party's attitude to training from a battery of 'background' reporters and authors.

1985–86 21st Series W I 5, Eng 0

1 KINGSTON West Indies won by 10 wkts
England 159 (G A Gooch 51, B P Patterson 4–30) and 152 (P Willey 71)
West Indies 307 (C G Greenidge 58, H A Gomes 56, P J L Dujon 54, R M Ellison 5–78) and 5–0

2 PORT OF SPAIN West Indies won by 7 wkts
England 176 (D I Gower 66, A J Lamb 62, M D Marshall 4–38) and 315 (C A Walsh 4–74, M D Marshall 4–94)
West Indies 399 (R B Richardson 102, D L Haynes 67, M D Marshall 62, J E Emburey 5–78) and 95–3

3 BRIDGETOWN West Indies won by an innings and 30 runs
West Indies 418 (R B Richardson 160, D L Haynes 84, I V A Richards 51, J G Thomas 4–70)
England 189 (D I Gower 66, G A Gooch 53, M D Marshall 4–42) and 199 (J Garner 4–69)

4 PORT OF SPAIN West Indies won by 10 wkts
England 200 (J Garner 4–43) and 150
West Indies 312 (I V A Richards 87, I T Botham 5–71) and 39–0

5 ST JOHN'S West Indies won by 240 runs
West Indies 474 (D L Haynes 131, M D Marshall 76, M A Holding 73, R A Harper 60) and 246–2 dec (I V A Richards 110, D L Haynes 70)
England 310 (D I Gower 90, W N Slack 52, G A Gooch 51, J Garner 4–67) and 170 (G A Gooch 51)

1985–86 Averages

Batting

	I	No	Runs	HS	Avge
D.L. Haynes (WI)	9	3	469	131	78.16
I.V.A. Richards (WI)	6	1	331	110*	66.20
R.B. Richardson (WI)	9	2	387	260*	55.28
D.I. Gower (E)	10	0	370	90	37.00
G.A. Gooch (E)	10	0	276	53	27.00

Bowling

	O	M	Runs	W	Avge	BB
J. Garner (WI)	156.1	30	436	27	16.14	4–43
M.D. Marshall (WI)	169.3	36	482	27	17.82	4–38
B.P. Patterson (WI)	118.1	18	426	19	22.42	4–30
M.A. Holding (WI)	102.4	16	385	16	24.06	3–47
J.E. Embury (E)	153	34	448	14	32.00	5–78
I.T. Botham (E)	134.5	16	535	11	48.63	5–71

The West Indians at Worcester in 1984. Left to right, back: Logie, Payne, Gomes, Dujon, Baptiste. Middle row: Hendricks, Marshall, Harper, Walsh, Small, Richardson, Waight. Front: Garner, Richards, Lloyd, Greenidge, Holding.

Above: Ian Botham extremely pleased at taking his 300th Test wicket. Dujon fails to avoid a lifting ball and Tavare takes a slip catch, England v West Indies at the Oval, 1984.

Left: Desmond Haynes on-drives. Haynes topped the batting averages in the 1985–86 series with an average of over 78.

Right: Malcolm Marshall bowling at Headingley in 1984. Marshall topped the series averages with 24 wickets at 18.20 each.

Caribbean cricket. *Top*: Botham hooking at Kingston and *above*: West Indies v England at the Queen's Park Oval, Port of Spain, Trinidad.

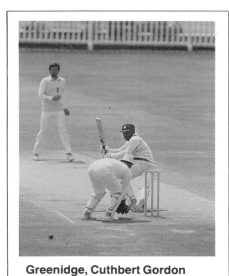

Greenidge, Cuthbert Gordon

Greenidge was born on 1 May 1951 at St Peter, Barbados, and was brought to England as a boy. He made his debut for Hampshire in 1970, and for Barbados in 1972–73. He is a very aggressive opening right-hand batsman. He was eligible for England, but preferred to play for West Indies and made his first appearance for them in 1974–75. In 77 Tests he has scored 5,509 runs, average 48.32.

115

Umbrellas and parasols shading
spectators at Sabina Park, Kingston, Jamaica in
1986.

Garner, Joel

Born in Christchurch, Barbados, on 16
December 1952, the 6ft 8ins tall Garner,
known as 'Big Bird', first played for
Barbados in 1975–76, and made his Test
debut a year later. From 1977 to 1986 he
also played for Somerset. A right-arm fast
bowler he brought the ball down from a
great height and could be at times almost
unplayable. In 58 Tests to the 1986–87
season he had taken 259 wickets at 20.97
each.

Holding, Michael Anthony

Born in Kingston, Jamaica, on 16 February
1954, Holding made his debut for the
island in 1972–73. He was a right-arm fast
bowler. Tall and lithe, he had a long and
graceful run-up, and at his fastest was the
most dangerous bowler in the world. He
first played for West Indies in 1975–76,
and in 60 Tests he took 249 wickets,
average 23.68.

England v New Zealand

1929–30: England win first Test in New Zealand

A.E.R. Gilligan took a party to Australia and New Zealand in 1929–30. It was one of two touring sides that winter (the other was to West Indies) so was not representative of England's strength. Nevertheless when the team reached New Zealand four Tests were played, the first in New Zealand's history. T.C. Lowry captained them.

In the first at Christchurch, New Zealand batted and made 112, M.J.C. Allom getting five wickets, including a hat-trick in his debut. England's 181 was followed by 131 from New Zealand, England getting the 63 needed for two wickets.

At Wellington, J.E. Mills (117 on his debut) and C.S. Dempster (136) put on 276 for New Zealand's first wicket, the side getting to 440. F.E. Woolley took seven for 76. England trailed at 320, and New Zealand declared at 164 for four, but only 110 minutes were left and England easily drew.

Only the last day's play was possible at Auckland because of rain. Lowry put England in so that the crowd could see some of the English batsmen, and K.S. Duleepsinhji's century, in particular, was said to be an exhibition of stroke-play at its best.

An extra Test was played at Auckland and G.B. Legge scored a rapid 196 for England, who led 540 to 387 on first innings, there being little time for much else.

England v New Zealand

1929–30 1st Series Eng 1, NZ 0, Drawn 3
1 CHRISTCHURCH England won by 8 wkts
New Zealand 112 (M J C Allom 5–38, M S Nichols 4–28) and 131
England 181 and 66–2
2 WELLINGTON Match Drawn
New Zealand 440 (C S Dempster 136, J E Mills 117, M L Page 67, F E Woolley 7–76) and 164–4 dec (C S Dempster 80)
England 320 (M S Nichols 78, F E Badcock 4–80) and 107–4 (K S Duleepsinhji 56)
3 AUCKLAND Match Drawn
England 330–4 dec (K S Duleepsinhji 117, E H Bowley 109, F T Woolley 59)
New Zealand 96–1 (C S Dempster 62)
4 AUCKLAND Match Drawn
England 540 (G B Legge 196, M S Nichols 75, K S Duleepsinjhi 63, E W Dawson 55) and 22–3
New Zealand 387 (T C Lowry 80, G L Weir 63, H M McGirr 51, M J C Allom 4–42)

1929–30 Averages

Batting	I	No	Runs	HS	Avge
K.S. Duleepsinhji (E)	6	2	358	117	89.50
C.S. Dempster (NZ)	6	2	341	136	85.25
G.B. Legge (E)	6	1	299	196	59.80

Bowling	O	M	Runs	W	Avge	BB
M.J.C. Allom (E)	99	23	194	13	14.92	5–38
R.C. Blunt (NZ)	65.1	20	171	9	19.00	3–17
F.E. Woolley (E)	101.3	26	261	13	20.07	7–76

1931: New Zealand earn two extra Tests

The tour to England in 1931 included one Test, but the New Zealanders played so well that two more were arranged. Lowry led the party and his opposing captain was D.R. Jardine. At Lord's New Zealand began brightly but collapsed: 132 for two at lunch became 224 all out (Peebles 5–77). At first England failed too, and were 190 for seven at close of play. But on Monday Ames (137) and Allen (122) added 246 for the eighth

New Zealand playing England at Wellington in 1984. Wright has been caught by Cook from the bowling of Botham for 17 in the first Test in 1983–84. The match ended in a draw.

wicket, still a Test record. Dempster and M.L. Page scored centuries for New Zealand, and R.C. Blunt 96, and they declared at 469 for nine. The match was drawn at 146 for five, with honours even.

Rain at the Oval favoured England who batted first, Sutcliffe, Duleepsinhji and Hammond making centuries in 416 for four declared. New Zealand were dismissed on a now awkward pitch for 193 and 197 and lost by an innings.

The Old Trafford Test began only on the last afternoon. E. Paynter made his debut and at least batted when England were put in, but the proceedings were academic.

1931 2nd Series Eng 1, NZ 0, Drawn 2
1 LORD'S Match Drawn
New Zealand 224 (C S Dempster 53, I A R Peebles 5–77) and 469–9 dec (C S Dempster 120, M L Page 104, R C Blunt 96, I A R Peebles 4–150)
England 454 (L E G Ames 137, G O B Allen 122, F E Woolley 80, W E Merritt 4–104) and 146–5
2 THE OVAL England won by an innings and 26 runs
England 416–4 dec (K S Duleepsinhji 109, W R Hammond 100, H Sutcliffe 117)
New Zealand 193 (T C Lowry 62, G O B Allen 5–14) and 197 (H G Vivian 51, I A R Peebles 4–63)
3 OLD TRAFFORD Match Drawn
England 224–3 (H Sutcliffe 109, K S Duleepsinhji 63)
New Zealand did not bat

1931 Averages

Batting	I	No	Runs	HS	Avge
H. Sutcliffe (E)	2	1	226	117	226.00
K.S. Duleepsinhji (E)	4	0	208	109	52.00

Bowling	O	M	Runs	W	Avge	BB
I.A.R. Peebles (E)	102.4	16	325	13	25.00	5–77

1932–33: Rain prevents results but Hammond averages 563

England's victorious 'bodyline' side played two Tests in New Zealand after touring Australia. M.L. Page captained New Zealand against Jardine's team, from which the injured Larwood was missing.

New Zealand began well at Christchurch, Sutcliffe being out to the first ball, and his fellow-opener Paynter also getting a duck. But Hammond made 227 and Ames 103 (they put on 242 in 144 minutes for the fifth wicket) and England declared at 560 for eight. New Zealand followed on at 223 but a dust storm and rain ended the match as a draw.

At Auckland, New Zealand batted but Bowes (6–34) dismissed them for 158. England declared at 548 for seven, when Hammond was 336 not out, a new record score in Test cricket. Rain ended the match and series at the start of the third day. Hammond's series average was 563.00, not unnaturally a record.

1932–33   3rd Series   Drawn 2
1 CHRISTCHURCH   Match Drawn
England 560–8 dec (W R Hammond 227, L E G Ames 103, F R Brown 74, W Voce 66)
New Zealand 223 (G L Weir 66, J L Kerr 59) and 35–0
2 AUCKLAND   Match Drawn
New Zealand 158 (C S Dempster 83, W E Bowes 6–34) and 16–0
England 548–7 dec (W R Hammond 336, R E S Wyatt 60)

1937: Hutton and Compton make their debuts

Page brought a side to England in 1937 for three Tests, R.W.V. Robins leading England. There were notable debutants at Lord's, among them L. Hutton, M.P. Donnelly and W.A. Hadlee.

Hammond, who seemed to like New Zealand bowling, made 140, and with J. Hardstaff, jnr (114) added 245 for England's third wicket. England made 424 and it needed a New Zealand record eighth-wicket stand of 104 between D.A.R. Moloney (64) and A.W. Roberts (66 not out) to avoid having to follow-on at 295. England declared and New Zealand just saved the match with eight wickets down.

1937   4th Series   Eng 1, NZ 0, Drawn 2
1 LORD'S   Match Drawn
England 424 (W R Hammond 140, J Hardstaff jun 114, E Paynter 74, A W Roberts 4–101, J Cowie 4–118) and 226–4 dec (C J Barnett 83, J Hardstaff jun 64)
New Zealand 295 (A W V Roberts 66, D A R Moloney 64, W M Wallace 52) and 175–8 (W M Wallace 56)
2 OLD TRAFFORD   England won by 130 runs
England 358–9 dec (L Hutton 100, C J Barnett 62, J Hardstaff jun 58, J Cowie 4–73) and 187 (F R Brown 57, J Cowie 6–67)
New Zealand 281 (W A Hadlee 93, H G Vivian 58, A W Wellard 4–81) and 134 (H G Vivian 50, T W J Goddard 6–29)
3 THE OVAL   Match Drawn
New Zealand 249 (M P Donnelly 58, M L Page 53, A W Roberts 50, R W V Robins 4–40) and 187 (H G Vivian 57)
England 254–7 dec (J Hardstaff jun 103, D C S Compton 65) and 31–1

1937 Averages					
Batting	I	No	Runs	HS	Avge
J. Hardstaff, jr (E)	5	0	350	114	70.00
W.R. Hammond (E)	4	0	204	140	51.00
Bowling	O	M	Runs	W	Avge BB
J. Cowie (NZ)	139.5	30	395	19	20.78 6–67

At Old Trafford, Hutton, who had made one in two innings at Lord's, scored 100, and England 358. New Zealand made 281 (Hadlee 93) and dismissed England for 187, Cowie, who had Hutton out three times in four innings, taking six for 67. T. W. J. Goddard took six for 29 in New Zealand's second innings and New Zealand were out for 134, England winning by 130 runs.

The last Test at the Oval was spoiled by almost all the first day being lost to rain. D.C.S. Compton and C. Washbrook made their debuts. New Zealand made 249 and England declared at 254 for seven, Hardstaff scoring 103 and Compton 65. New Zealand made 187 but there was no time for much else.

1946–47: Rain ruins only Test

England went by flying boat to New Zealand to play one Test after their first post-war tour of Australia. Bert Sutcliffe made his debut and he and captain Hadlee put on 133 for the first wicket, Hadlee getting a century. New Zealand made 345 for nine declared and England declared at 265 for seven (Cowie six for 83). Rain washed out the third day, and also a fourth which was hastily tacked on.

1946–47   5th Series   Drawn 1
1 CHRISTCHURCH   Match Drawn
New Zealand 345–9 dec (W A Hadlee 116, B Sutcliffe 58, A V Bedser 4–95)
England 265–7 dec (W R Hammond 79, J Cowie 6–83)

H.B. Vivian and W.A. Hadlee at Old Trafford in 1937.

1949: All matches drawn on good pitches

A strong New Zealand side toured England under Hadlee in 1949 and for a change found good weather. F.G. Mann led England.

Hutton and Compton scored centuries at Headingley, while Cowie and T.B. Burtt each took five wickets. England's 372 was nearly matched by New Zealand's 341. T.E. Bailey took six for 118 on his debut. England declared the second innings at 267 for four, but the match was drawn with New Zealand 195 for two.

At Lord's, Mann declared with England 313 for nine (Compton 116), but it was later realized that a first-day declaration was outside the Laws for Tests. Donnelly made a brilliant 206, the highest New Zealand innings against England. New Zealand led with 484 but the match was drawn at 306 for five.

F.R. Brown took over the England captaincy and put New Zealand in at Old Trafford, where future Test captains D.B. Close and J.R. Reid made their debuts. At 18 years, 149 days, D.B. Close was England's youngest Test player. Bailey's six for 84 dismissed the tourists for 293. England passed this and declared at 440 for nine, R.T. Simpson scoring 103. Burtt took six for 162. Sutcliffe made 101 in the second-innings 348 for seven which ended the match.

In the final Test at the Oval, New Zealand's good score of 345 was passed by England's 482, in which Hutton made 206 and W.J. Edrich 100. G.F. Cresswell took six for 168. New Zealand again topped 300 in their second innings, but that was that.

On the good pitches of a dry summer, three days was not long enough to settle the Tests between good batting sides.

Action from the Oval in 1949. W.J. Edrich, who made a century, being missed by Rabone.

1949   6th Series   Drawn 4

1 HEADINGLEY   Match Drawn
England 372 (D C S Compton 114, L Hutton 101, T B Burtt 5–97, J Cowie 5–127) and 267–4 (C Washbrook 103, W J Edrich 70)
New Zealand 341 (F B Smith 96, M P Donnelly 64, T E Bailey 6–118) and 195–2 (B Sutcliffe 82, F B Smith 54)

2 LORD'S   Match Drawn
England 313–9 dec (D C S Compton 116, T E Bailey 93, T B Burtt 4–102) and 306–5 (J D B Robertson 121, L Hutton 66)
New Zealand 484 (M P Donnelly 206, B Sutcliffe 57, W E Hollies 5–133)

3 OLD TRAFFORD   Match Drawn
New Zealand 293 (M P. Donnelly 75, J R Reid 50, T E Bailey 6–84) and 348–7 (B Sutcliffe 101, M P Donnelly 80)
England 440–9 dec (R T Simpson 103, L Hutton 73, W J Edrich 78, T E Bailey 72, T B Burtt 6–162)

4 THE OVAL   Match Drawn
New Zealand 345 (B Sutcliffe 88, V J Scott 60, W M Wallace 55, A V Bedser 4–74) and 308–9 dec (J R Reid 93, W M Wallace 58, B Sutcliffe 54, J C Laker 4–78)
England 484 (L Hutton 206, W J Edrich 100, R T Simpson 68, G F Cresswell 6–168, J Cowie 4–123)

1949 Averages

Batting	I	No	Runs	HS	Avge	
L. Hutton (E)	6	0	469	206	78.16	
M.P. Donnelly (NZ)	6	0	462	206	77.00	
T.E. Bailey (E)	5	2	219	93	73.00	
B. Sutcliffe (NZ)	7	0	423	101	60.42	
W.J. Edrich (E)	6	0	324	100	54.00	
D.C.S. Compton (E)	6	0	300	116	50.00	

Bowling	O	M	Runs	W	Avge	BB
J. Cowie (NZ)	147.1	23	451	14	32.21	5–127
T.B. Burtt (NZ)	195.3	50	568	17	33.41	6–162
T.E. Bailey (E)	158	22	599	16	37.43	6–84
W.E. Hollies (E)	175	54	385	10	38.50	5–133

Above: F.R. Brown tosses and W.A. Hadlee calls before the last Test at the Oval in 1949. Hadlee called correctly and the match and series were drawn.

1950–51: England win as rain gets a result at last

Brown's team in Australia played two Tests in New Zealand in 1950–51. J.B. Statham made his debut in the first at Christchurch, where Hadlee won the toss and batted. Sutcliffe's century helped his team to 417 for eight, but good bowling by A.M. Moir on his debut (6–155) could not prevent England getting 550, Bailey making 134 not out. Washbrook, given out lbw, was recalled when Hadlee said he had played the ball before it hit his pad. There was little second innings action.

At Wellington rain washed out the first day, and there was a mild earthquake on the fourth, but it added up to a result at last. New Zealand made 125 (D.V.P. Wright 5–48) and England took a useful lead with 227. R. Tattersall destroyed New Zealand with six for 44 in the second knock, but England had to work on a deteriorating wicket for the 88 needed, winning by six wickets.

1950–51 7th Series Eng 1, NZ 0, Drawn 1
1 CHRISTCHURCH **Match Drawn**
New Zealand 417–8 dec (B Sutcliffe 116, W M Wallace 66, W A Hadlee 50, J R Reid 50) and 46–3
England 550 (T E Bailey 134, R T Simpson 81, D C S Compton 79, F R Brown 62, C Washbrook 58, A M Moir 6–155)
2 WELLINGTON **England won by 6 wkts**
New Zealand 125 (D V P Wright 5–48) and 189 (V J Scott 60, R Tattersall 6–44)
England 227 (L Hutton 57) and 91–4

1954–55: New Zealand make Test record low

Hutton's successful Ashes-winning side played two Tests in New Zealand against a team led by G.O. Rabone. The first Test ever played in Dunedin saw New Zealand struggle to only 125 runs on the whole of the first day, Sutcliffe getting 74 of them. England did not bat very much better, declaring at 209 for eight. Rain washed out two days but, by dismissing New Zealand for only 132, England had plenty of time to score the 49 necessary for victory.

At Auckland, New Zealand made 200 but England reached only 246. Remarkably this was enough for an innings win as New Zealand were shot out for 26, the lowest score ever made in a Test. Remarkably, four bowlers shared the wickets: Tyson 2–10, Statham 3–9, Appleyard 4–7 and Wardle 1–0.

1954–55 8th Series Eng 2, NZ 0
1 DUNEDIN **England won by 8 wkts**
New Zealand 125 (B Sutcliffe 74, J B Statham 4–24) and 132 (F H Tyson 4–16)
England 209–8 dec (J R Reid 4–36) and 49–2
2 AUCKLAND **England won by an innings and 20 runs**
New Zealand 200 (J R Reid 73, J B Statham 4–28) and 26 (R Appleyard 4–7)
England 246 (L Hutton 53, A M Moir 5–62)

1958: Lock too good for New Zealand on damp pitches

J.R. Reid led the New Zealand tourists in 1958. May was England captain. He and Cowdrey scored most of England's 221 in the first Test at Edgbaston: the second highest stand was 30 for the last wicket. Strangely, New Zealand's biggest stand was 26 for the last wicket – they made only 94 against the pace of Trueman. With Richardson scoring a century, England declared at 215 for six and won by 205 runs.

At Lord's, after England made 269, New Zealand had to bat on a rain-affected pitch. They made only 47 and 74, Lock doing most of the damage, supported by Laker.

Things got worse for them at Headingley, where play started only on the third day. They were out for 67 to Laker (5–17) and Lock (4–14). England opened with two double internationals: C.A. Milton, who played Association football, and who scored 104 not out on his debut, and M.J.K. Smith (rugby). May also scored a century, and declared at 267 for two. Lock (7–51) and Laker (3–27) did the trick again, England winning by an innings and 71.

At Old Trafford, rain came on the third

The England team to play New Zealand at Edgbaston in 1958. Left to right, back: Richardson, Loader, Graveney, Smith, Lock, Cowdrey, Trueman. Front: Evans, May, Bailey, Laker. England won by 205 runs.

and fourth days, after England had established a lead of 98, declaring at 365 for nine (May 101) after getting New Zealand out for 267. It was enough for another innings win as Lock took seven for 35 to dismiss the tourists for 85.

There were only 12 hours play at the Oval, where New Zealand had at least avoided an innings defeat by the close. Lock's 34 wickets in the series cost only 7.47 runs each.

1958   9th Series   Eng 4, NZ 0, Drawn 1

1 EDGBASTON   England won by 205 runs

England 221 (P B H May 84, M C Cowdrey 81, A R MacGibbon 5–64, J C Alabaster 4–46) and 215–6 dec (P E Richardson 100, M C Cowdrey 70)

New Zealand 94 (F S Trueman 5–31) and 137

2 LORD'S   England won by an innings and 148 runs

England 269 (M C Cowdrey 65, J A Hayes 4–36, A R MacGibbon 4–86)

New Zealand 47 (G A R Lock 5–17, J C Laker 4–13) and 74 (G A R Lock 4–12)

3 HEADINGLEY   England won by an innings and 71 runs

New Zealand 67 (J C Laker 5–17, G A R Lock 4–14) and 129 (G A R Lock 7–51)

England 167–2 dec (P B H May 113, C A Milton 104)

4 OLD TRAFFORD   England won by an innings and 13 runs

New Zealand 267 (A R MacGibbon 66, J T Sparling 50, J B Statham 4–71) and 85 (G A R Lock 7–35)

England 365–9 dec (P B H May 101, P E Richardson 74, W Watson 66, E R Dexter 52)

5 THE OVAL   Match Drawn

New Zealand 161 and 91–3 (J R Reid 51)

England 219–9 dec (A R MacGibbon 4–65)

1958 Averages

Batting	I	No	Runs	HS	Avge
P.B.H. May (E)	6	1	337	113*	67.40

Bowling	O	M	Runs	W	Avge	BB
G.A.R. Lock (E)	176	93	254	34	7.47	7–35
J.C. Laker (E)	131	67	173	17	10.17	5–17
F.S. Trueman (E)	131.5	44	256	15	17.06	5–31
A.R. MacGibbon (NZ)	175.4	50	389	20	19.45	5–64

1958–59: Rain has last word again in New Zealand

P.B.H. May's very strong side had lost the Ashes series to Australia's controversial 'chuckers' before going on to New Zealand for two Tests.

At Christchurch, Dexter scored 141 out of 374 and New Zealand were dismissed for 142 and 133 to resume their depressing run against England. Lock took up where he had left off, with 11 wickets for 84 in the match.

What play there was at Auckland was held in very windy conditions. New Zealand made 181 and England 311 for seven, with May being 124 not out. Rain then washed out the last two days.

1958–59   10th Series   Eng 1, NZ 0, Drawn 1

1 CHRISTCHURCH   England won by an innings and 99 runs

England 374 (E R Dexter 141, P B H May 71)

New Zealand 142 (G A R Lock 5–31) and 133 (J W Guy 56, G A R Lock 6–53)

2 AUCKLAND   Match Drawn

New Zealand 181 (B Sutcliffe 61)

England 311–7 (P B H May 124, P E Richardson 67)

1962–63: Three more easy wins for England

Back in New Zealand in 1962–63, Dexter was England captain against Reid's team.

Barrington, Parfitt and Knight all made centuries at Auckland, England declaring at 562 for seven. The stand between Parfitt and Knight of 240 was a new sixth-wicket record for England. J.T. Sparling bowled an 11-ball over, the umpire miscounting. New Zealand made 258 and then, disappointingly, 89 for a defeat by an innings and 215.

At Wellington, New Zealand were put in and scored 194. England made 428 for eight declared, Cowdrey (128 not out) who batted at number eight, adding a new Test record of 163 unbroken for the eighth wicket with A.C. Smith. New Zealand's second-innings 187 did not avoid the customary innings defeat.

At Christchurch, New Zealand made 266 against good fast bowling by Trueman (7–75) and then removed England for 253. Reid made 100 in the second innings, but was so poorly supported that New Zealand made 159, leaving England 173 to get, which they did for three wickets, Knight ending the match in style with strokes for six, four and four. But it was an improvement for the home side.

1962–63   11th Series   Eng 3, NZ 0

1 AUCKLAND   England won by an innings and 215 runs

England 562–7 dec (P H Parfitt 131, K F Barrington 126, B R Knight 125, M C Cowdrey 86, F J Cameron 4–118)

New Zealand 258 (B W Sinclair 66, R C Motz 60, J R Reid 59) and 89 (J D F Larter 4–26, R Illingworth 4–34)

2 WELLINGTON   England won by an innings and 47 runs

New Zealand 194 (R W Blair 64, F S Trueman 4–46) and 187 (W R Playle 65, F J Titmus 4–50)

England 428–8 dec (M C Cowdrey 128, K F Barrington 76, A C Smith 69)

3 CHRISTCHURCH   England won by 7 wkts

New Zealand 266 (J Reid 74, F S Trueman 7–75) and 159 (J R Reid 100, F J Titmus 4–46)

England 253 and 173–3

1962–63 Averages

Batting	I	No	Runs	HS	Avge
M.C. Cowdrey (E)	4	2	292	128*	146.00
K.F. Barrington (E)	4	0	294	126	73.50
B.R. Knight (E)	4	1	208	125	69.33
J.R. Reid (NZ)	6	1	263	100	52.60

Bowling	O	M	Runs	W	Avge	BB
F.S. Trueman (E)	88	29	164	14	11.71	7–75
F.J. Titmus (E)	132	54	227	13	17.46	4–46
J.D.F. Larter (E)	105.1	31	238	10	23.80	4–26

1965: Edrich establishes record after Barrington goes slow

The dogged Reid led his troops into battle again at Edgbaston in 1965, M.J.K. Smith being his new rival captain.

Barrington made 137 in 437 minutes in the first innings and was dropped from the next Test for his slowness. England made 435, R.C. Motz getting five wickets. New Zealand were unlucky to lose Sutcliffe hurt in their innings, but even so 116 was a poor effort, even allowing for the freezing conditions. A much better effort was made in the follow-on, most players contributing to a score of 413, Sutcliffe and V. Pollard adding 104 for the seventh wicket. England won comfortably by nine wickets.

New Zealand made 175 at Lord's, and England 317, Cowdrey getting 119. Another good second-innings effort by New Zealand's top six batsmen allowed them to score 347, and combined with five hours rain it nearly saved the match, but England finally won by seven wickets with 15 minutes to spare. This was Trueman's last Test, and J.A. Snow's first. Trueman retired with a record 307 Test wickets.

At Headingley, Edrich made 310 not out, and his five sixes and 52 fours remain a record number of boundaries in a Test innings. Barrington, restored, supported him with 163, and England declared at 546 for four. New Zealand made 193 and 166 to end

---

the series with another disappointing innings defeat.

1965   12th Series   Eng 3, NZ 0

1 EDGBASTON   England won by 9 wkts

England 435 (K F Barrington 137, M C Cowdrey 85, E R Dexter 57, R C Motz 5–108) and 96–1 (R W Barber 51)

New Zealand 116 (F J Titmus 4–18) and 413 (V Pollard 81, B Sutcliffe 53, R W Barber 4–132)

2 LORD'S   England won by 7 wkts

New Zealand 175 (V Pollard 55, B R Taylor 51, F E Rumsey 4–25) and 347 (B W Sinclair 72, G T Dowling 66, V Pollard 55)

England 307 (M C Cowdrey 119, E R Dexter 62, R O Collinge 4–85) and 218–3 (E R Dexter 80, G Boycott 76)

3 HEADINGLEY   England won by an innings and 187 runs

England 546–4 dec (J H Edrich 310, K F Barrington 163)

New Zealand 193 (J R Reid 54, R Illingworth 4–42, J D F Larter 4–66) and 166 (V Pollard 53, F J Titmus 5–19)

1965 Averages

Batting	I	No	Runs	HS	Avge
J.H. Edrich (E)	1	1	310	310*	—
K.F. Barrington (E)	2	0	300	163	150.00
M.C. Cowdrey (E)	4	1	221	119	73.66
V. Pollard (NZ)	6	1	281	81*	56.20

Bowling	O	M	Runs	W	Avge	BB
F.J. Titmus (E)	171	85	234	15	15.60	5–19
R.C. Motz (NZ)	136	31	389	11	35.36	5–108

1965–66: New Zealand hold on and then miss chance

Matches between the countries again resumed almost immediately, M.J.K. Smith's side, which had drawn in Australia, arriving in New Zealand for three Tests. M.E. Chapple led the home side in the first Test but lost his place through injury, B.W. Sinclair being captain in the next two.

At Christchurch, England made 342 after 47 for four, but New Zealand took a five-run lead thanks to B.E. Congdon (104) and tailenders E.C. Petrie and R.C. Motz. An England declaration set New Zealand 197 in 139 minutes, and they collapsed to 32 for eight, but just held on.

Motz batted well again at Dunedin, hoisting New Zealand to 192 after 100 for seven. England declared at 254 for eight, and reduced New Zealand to 112 for nine with 35 minutes left, but the last pair batted out time.

Sinclair made a century at Auckland, and New Zealand a respectable 296. With Edrich rushed to hospital with appendicitis, England fell behind at 222 all out. New Zealand did not press home the advantage, batting poorly to take six hours for 129 all out. England, needing 204 in 4½ hours reached 159 for four, and New Zealand's best chance to win for many years had gone.

1965–66   13th Series   Drawn 3

1 CHRISTCHURCH   Match Drawn

England 342 (D A Allen 88, P H Parfitt 54, M J K Smith 54) and 201–5 dec (M J K Smith 87)

New Zealand 347 (B E Congdon 104, R C Motz 58, E C Petrie 55, I J Jones 4–71) and 48–8 (K Higgs 4–5)

2 DUNEDIN   Match Drawn

New Zealand 192 (R C Motz 57) and 147–9 (D A Allen 4–46)

England 254–8 dec (M C Cowdrey 89, J T Murray 50)

3 AUCKLAND   Match Drawn

New Zealand 296 (B W Sinclair 114, B E Congdon 64, D A Allen 5–123) and 129

England 222 (M C Cowdrey 59, W E Russell 56) and 159–4

1965–66 Averages

Batting	I	No	Runs	HS	Avge
M.J.K. Smith (E)	5	0	209	87	41.80
B.W. Sinclair (NZ)	6	0	218	114	36.33
B.E. Congdon (NZ)	6	0	214	104	35.67

Bowling	O	M	Runs	W	Avge	BB
K. Higgs (E)	128	50	157	17	9.34	4–5
I.J. Jones (E)	122.3	40	242	14	17.29	4–71
D.A. Allen (E)	190.5	72	359	13	27.62	5–123

1969: Milestones for Turner and Motz, but defeat again for New Zealand

The 1969 New Zealanders were led by G.T. Dowling. R. Illingworth won the toss at Lord's and had to make 53 himself to get the total up to 190. New Zealand were 21 behind at 169. Edrich made a century second time, and a target of 362 was far too many for New Zealand on a wearing wicket. D.L. Underwood took seven for 32, and 131 was all the tourists could muster. However, one had cause for satisfaction: G.M. Turner carried his bat for 43 not out in 253 minutes. At 22 years 63 days he is the youngest player to perform this feat in a Test.

At Trent Bridge, New Zealand got a respectable 294, but Edrich scored 155 and added 249 for the second wicket with P.J. Sharpe. England declared at 451 for eight, but nearly two days was lost to rain, and there was little more action.

Left: Three teenage New Zealand tourists in 1965. From the left, Collinge, Pollard and Vivian, all 19, with skipper Reid.

Below: Pollard in action in the first Test at Edgbaston, where he made 81 not out.

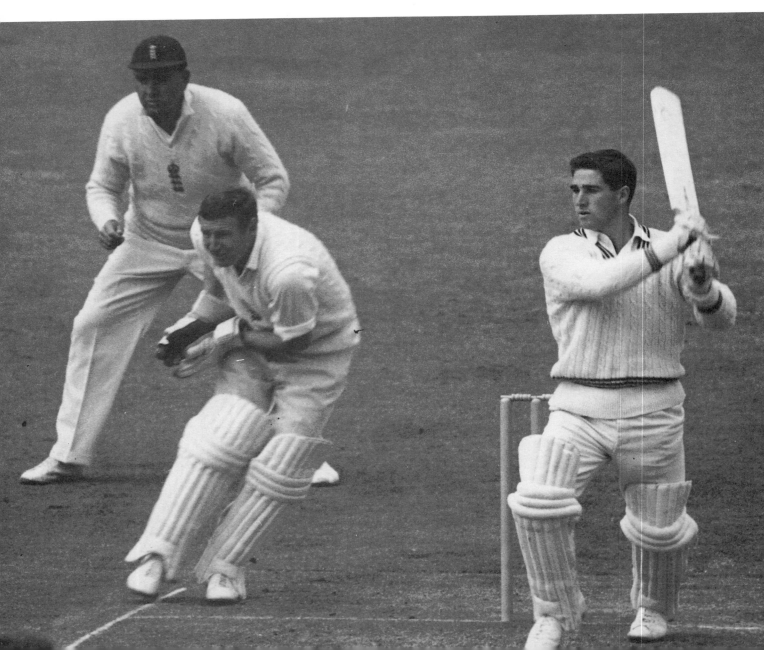

The 1965 New Zealanders. Left to right, back: Motz, Taylor, Collinge, Dick, Congdon, Pollard, Sinclair. Front: Vivian, Yuile, Sutcliffe, Reid, Morgan, Ward, Dowling.

then B. D'Oliveira mastered the pitch with 100 out of 231. Although Underwood took six wickets for the fourth innings running against New Zealand, the home side made 254, forcing England to bat again for 89 runs and an eight-wicket win.

England batted at Auckland and scored 321, Knott scoring a century and R.S. Cunis taking six for 76. New Zealand declared behind, at 313 for seven, M.G. Burgess getting a century. Knott missed the honour of being the first wicket-keeper to score a century in each innings of a Test when out for 96. This was the last point of interest in the match. This Test was continuous, which cost New Zealand B.A.G. Murray and V. Pollard, who were unwilling to play on a Sunday.

1970–71 15th Series Eng 1, NZ 0, Drawn 1
1 CHRISTCHURCH England won by 8 wkts
New Zealand 65 (D L Underwood 6–12) and 254 (G M Turner 76, B E Congdon 55, D L Underwood 6–85)
England 231 (B L d'Oliveira 100, H J Howarth 4–46) and 89–2 (J H Hampshire 51)
2 AUCKLAND Match Drawn
England 321 (A P E Knott 191, P Lever 64, B L d'Oliveira 58, M C Cowdrey 54, R S Cunis 6–76) and 237 (A P E Knott 96, R O Collinge 4–41)
New Zealand 313–7 dec (M G Burgess 104, G M Turner 65, G T Dowling 53, D L Underwood 5–108) and 40–0

Underwood was at his best at the Oval, where six for 41 helped dismiss New Zealand for 150. England made 242, and another six wickets for Underwood left them only 138 to make for an eight-wicket win. Motz, though, had reason to celebrate, becoming the first New Zealander to take 100 Test wickets.

1969 14th Series Eng 2, NZ 0, Drawn 1
1 LORD'S England won by 230 runs
England 190 (R Illingworth 53) and 340 (J H Edrich 115)
New Zealand 169 (R Illingworth 4–37, D L Underwood 4–38) and 131 (D L Underwood 7–32)
2 TRENT BRIDGE Match Drawn
New Zealand 294 (B F Hastings 83, B E Congdon 66, A Ward 4–61) and 66–1
England 451–8 dec (J H Edrich 155, P J Sharpe 111, D R Hadlee 4–88)
3 THE OVAL England won by 8 wkts
New Zealand 150 (G M Turner 53, D L Underwood 6–41) and 229 (B F Hastings 61, D L Underwood 6–60)
England 242 (J H Edrich 68, B R Taylor 4–47) and 138–2 (M H Denness 55)

1969 Averages

Batting	I	No	Runs	HS	Avge	
J.H. Edrich (E)	5	0	376	155	72.20	
P.J. Sharpe (E)	5	1	270	111	67.50	

Bowling	O	M	Runs	W	Avge	BB
D.L. Underwood (E)	150	70	220	24	9.16	7–32
R. Illingworth (E)	101.3	43	154	10	15.40	4–37
B.R. Taylor (NZ)	63.5	17	155	10	15.50	4–47
A. Ward (E)	73.5	15	210	10	21.00	4–61

1970–71: England win but Knott fails to make history

Illingworth took the strong England side which had just regained the Ashes to New Zealand for two Tests in 1970–71. On a bad Christchurch pitch, Dowling's side were rushed out for 65 by Underwood (6–12),

Sharpe lbw to Motz at the Oval in 1969. This was Dick Motz' 100th Test wicket.

1973: Batting successes for New Zealand, but the win eludes them

B.E. Congdon led the New Zealanders who toured England in 1973, playing the first three Tests of the season.

At Trent Bridge, England's first and last wickets produced the highest stands: 92 and 59 out of 250. New Zealand struggled to 97, a total which looked very inadequate as Amiss (138) and Greig (139) allowed Illingworth to declare at 325 for eight. New Zealand's second innings marked the point where their cricket began to improve dramatically. Set 479 to win, they passed 400 with only five wickets down. Congdon (176) and Pollard (116) were responsible, adding 177 for the fifth wicket. They lost the match by 38 runs, being out for 440, but had surprised everybody.

At Lord's, Congdon put England in, and was not disappointed to dismiss them for 253. He then made 175, and with Pollard also making a second successive century, Burgess getting 105 and Hastings 86, New Zealand made 551 for nine declared, their highest Test score. With over an hour and a half left, and England 368 for eight, New Zealand were within two quick wickets of victory, but G.G. Arnold stayed long enough with Fletcher (178) to save the game.

Headingley was disappointing for New Zealand, who made 276 before England, after rain on the second day, made 419 (Boycott 115). Collinge took five for 74. This time there was no fight-back, New Zealand crashing before Snow and Arnold for 142 and an innings defeat, although Turner (81) was last out, nearly carrying his bat for a second time.

The Hadlee brothers Richard (centre) and Dayle (right) with captain Congdon at Lord's in 1973.

1973 16th Series   Eng 2, NZ 0, Drawn 1
1 TRENT BRIDGE   **England won by 38 runs**
England 250 (G Boycott 51, B R Taylor 4–53, D R Hadlee 4–42) and 325–8 dec (A W Greig 139, D L Amiss 138)
New Zealand 97 (A W Greig 4–33) and 440 (B E Congdon 176, V Pollard 116, G G Arnold 5–131)
2 LORD'S   **Match Drawn**
England 253 (A W Greig 63, G R J Roope 56, G Boycott 61) and 463–9 (K W R Fletcher 178, G Boycott 92, D L Amiss 53, G R J Roope 51, H J Howarth 4–144)
New Zealand 551–9 dec (B E Congdon 175, M G Burgess 105, V Pollard 105, B F Hastings 86, C M Old 5–113)
3 HEADINGLEY   **England won by an innings and 1 run**
New Zealand 276 (M G Burgess 87, V Pollard 62, C M Old 4–71) and 142 (G M Turner 81, G G Arnold 5–27)
England 419 (G Boycott 115, K W R Fletcher 81, R Illingworth 65, R O Collinge 5–74)

1973 Averages

Batting	I	No	Runs	HS	Avge
V. Pollard (NZ)	5	2	302	116	100.66
B.E. Congdon (NZ)	5	0	362	176	72.40
G. Boycott (E)	5	0	320	115	64.00
D.L. Amiss (E)	5	1	250	138*	62.50
K.W.R. Fletcher (E)	5	0	309	178	61.80
M.G. Burgess (NZ)	5	0	236	105	47.20
A.W. Greig (E)	5	0	216	139	43.20

Bowling	O	M	Runs	W	Avge	BB
C.M. Old (E)	75.5	12	225	11	20.45	5–113
G.G. Arnold (E)	161	48	351	16	21.93	5–27
R.O. Collinge (NZ)	135	32	289	12	24.08	5–74
J.A. Snow (E)	135.1	27	320	13	24.61	3–21
D.R. Hadlee (NZ)	106.1	16	340	10	34.00	4–42

1974–75: Accident to Chatfield colours series

Two Tests were played in New Zealand by M.H.Denness' side which had been well beaten by Lillee and Thomson in Australia. Congdon captained New Zealand.

At Auckland, Denness (181) and Fletcher (216) added 266 for the fourth wicket, England reaching 593 for six declared. J.M. Parker made 121 in reply, but Greig took five for 98 and New Zealand followed on at 326. They lost by an innings and 83, with Greig again taking five wickets, but the manner of the finish was very disturbing, and almost tragic. New Zealand's number eleven, E.J. Chatfield, making his debut, was struck on the temple by a lifting ball from P. Lever, sustaining a hair-line fracture of the skull. His heart stopped beating for several seconds, and his life was saved only by the prompt action of the MCC physiotherapist Bernard Thomas, who applied heart massage and mouth-to-mouth resuscitation. Chatfield made a complete recovery.

At Christchurch, the first two days and

Turner gets an edge and is caught in the slips off a ball from Geoff Arnold at Trent Bridge in 1973. It was not a successful tour for Turner.

Congdon and Turner going out to bat at Trent Bridge in 1973. Congdon made a second-innings 176 out of 440, New Zealand losing by 38.

1977–78 18th Series Eng 1, NZ 1, Drawn 1

1 WELLINGTON New Zealand won by 72 runs

New Zealand 228 (J G Wright 55, C M Old 6–54) and 123 (R G D Willis 5–32)

England 215 (G Boycott 77, R J Hadlee 4–74) and 64 (R J Hadlee 6–26)

2 CHRISTCHURCH England won by 174 runs

England 418 (I T Botham 103, G Miller 89, G R J Roope 50, P H Edmonds 50, R J Hadlee 4–147) and 96–4 dec

New Zealand 235 (R W Anderson 62, J M Parker 53, I T Botham 5–73, P H Edmonds 4–8) and 105 (R G D Willis 4–14)

3 AUCKLAND Match Drawn

New Zealand 315 (G P Howarth 122, G N Edwards 55, M G Burgess 50, I T Botham 5–109) and 382–8 (G P Howarth 102, R W Anderson 55, G N Edwards 54)

England 429 (C T Radley 158, G R J Roope 68, G Boycott 54, I T Botham 53, S L Boock 5–67, R O Collinge 4–98)

1977–78 Averages

Batting	I	No	Runs	HS	Avge
I.T. Botham (E)	5	1	212	103	53.00
G.P. Howarth (NZ)	6	0	264	122	44.00
R.W. Anderson (NZ)	6	0	203	62	33.83

Bowling	O	M	Runs	W	Avge	BB
R.G.D. Willis (E)	103.6	27	255	14	18.21	5–32
I.T. Botham (E)	101	17	311	17	18.29	5–73
R.O. Collinge (NZ)	104.5	27	293	15	19.53	4–98
R.J. Hadlee (NZ)	121.3	26	371	15	24.73	6–26

---

collapsed completely to Botham (5–39) backed up by Willis (4–16), and England, set 118, won by seven wickets to complete a clean sweep of the series.

1978 19th Series Eng 3, NZ 0

1 THE OVAL England won by 7 wkts

New Zealand 234 (G P Howarth 94, J G Wright 62, R G D Willis 5–42) and 182 (P H Edmonds 4–20)

England 279 (D I Gower 111) and 138–2 (G A Gooch 91)

2 TRENT BRIDGE England won by an innings and 119 runs

England 429 (G Boycott 131, C T Radley 59, G A Gooch 55, J M Brearley 50, R J Hadlee 4–94)

New Zealand 120 (I T Botham 6–34) and 190 (B A Edgar 60, P H Edmonds 4–44)

3 LORD'S England won by 7 wkts

New Zealand 339 (G P Howarth 123, M G Burgess 68, I T Botham 6–101) and 67 (I T Botham 5–39, R G D Willis 4–126)

England 289 (C T Radley 77, D I Gower 71, R J Hadlee 5–84) and 118–3

Geoff Boycott in action against New Zealand in 1978. Boycott was stand-in captain when New Zealand first beat England in the 1977–78 season.

---

the last were lost to rain. Play started (late) on what should have been the rest day. New Zealand's 342 had been countered by Amiss (164 not out) by the close.

1974–75 17th Series Eng 1, NZ 0, Drawn 1

1 AUCKLAND England won by an innings and 83 runs

England 593–6 dec (K W R Fletcher 216, M H Denness 181, J H Edrich 64, A W Greig 51)

New Zealand 326 (J M Parker 121, J F M Morrison 58, K J Wadsworth 58, A W Greig 5–98) and 184 (J F M Morrison 58, G P Howarth 51, A W Greig 5–51)

2 CHRISTCHURCH Match Drawn

New Zealand 342 (G M Turner 98, K J Wadsworth 58)

England 272–2 (D L Amiss 164, M H Denness 59)

1977–78: New Zealand beat England in 48th match

England went to New Zealand after touring Pakistan, where G. Boycott assumed the captaincy when Brearley's arm was broken.

At Wellington, he put New Zealand in, and despite C.M. Old taking six for 54 on a poor wicket, they made 228. England batted very slowly (Boycott 77 in 442 minutes) and failed to get in front at 215. With the pitch worsening, Willis took five for 32 and dismissed New Zealand for 123. England needed 139 but never looked like getting them in the face of strong winds and R.J. Hadlee (brother D.R. was also playing: father W.A. had captained New Zealand). Hadlee took six for 26 (a neat 10 for 100 in the match) and England, 64 all out, lost by 72 runs. It was New Zealand's first win over England in 48 matches spread over 48 years. M.G. Burgess was the successful captain.

At Christchurch, Botham made his first Test century and England made 418. Botham then took five for 73 to help remove New Zealand for 235. Randall, backing up, was run out by Chatfield without warning in the second innings. It hardly mattered as England declared early and won by 174 runs.

The three centuries at Auckland all came from the number three batsmen: G.P. Howarth (122 and 102) and C.T. Radley (158). Botham and S.L. Boock each took five wickets. The batting was too slow for a result and the series was drawn.

1978: England get revenge with a clean sweep

The teams met again in England less than six months after New Zealand's historic first win. Brearley had resumed the England captaincy.

New Zealand began with 234 at the Oval (Willis 5–42) and England took a 45-run lead with Gower making 111. New Zealand did not impress in the second innings and England needed only 138 to win by seven wickets.

At Trent Bridge, England's first five batsmen, led by Boycott (131) scored well and the side totalled 429. Botham's swing then took six for 34 and New Zealand followed on with 120. They did a little better with 190 second time but lost by an innings and 119.

The final Test was at Lord's and New Zealand, with Howarth getting 123, did well to reach 339, Botham again bowling well with six for 101. Hadlee took five for 84, England were out for 289 and New Zealand had a first-innings lead of 50. But they then

1978 Averages

Batting	I	No	Runs	HS	Avge
G.P. Howarth (NZ)	6	2	296	123	74.00
D.I. Gower (E)	5	0	285	111	57.00

Bowling	O	M	Runs	W	Avge	BB
I.T. Botham (E)	142.1	42	337	24	14.04	6–34
P.H. Edmonds (E)	112	48	145	10	14.50	4–20
R.G.D. Willis (E)	99.2	33	229	12	19.08	5–42
R.J. Hadlee (NZ)	121.2	31	270	13	20.76	5–84

1983: New Zealand win a Test in England, but lose series 3–1

There was a gap of five years before the two teams met again, Howarth and Willis being the captains in 1983. The series was of four Tests, the first at the Oval, where England batted.

Hadlee (six for 53) bowled as well as ever to get them out for 209, but this was enough for a lead of 13, although Hadlee, top-scoring with 84, tried hard. He could not maintain his effort, and second-innings centuries by Fowler, Tavare and Lamb

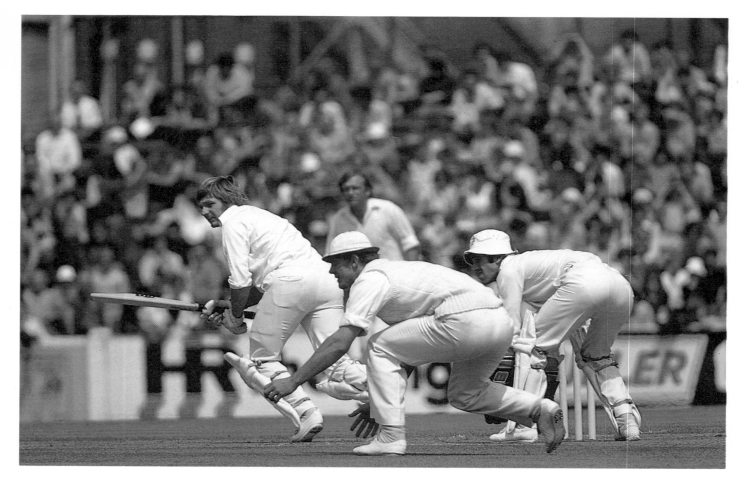

Geoff Howarth gets the ball away during his 94 at the Oval in 1978. Edmonds and Taylor are in the white hats.

allowed a declaration at 446 for six, England winning by 189 when dismissing New Zealand for 270.

At Headingley, England, after being put in by Howarth, made 225, B.L. Cairns recording his best Test analysis with seven for 74. New Zealand made 377 and Chatfield bowled well to get England out again for 252. Gower scored 112 not out. New Zealand needed 101 and got them despite losing five wickets, all to Willis, whose nine wickets for 92 in the match was surprisingly his best Test analysis (it took him past 300 wickets). This was New Zealand's first victory in England in their 29th Test.

England made 326 at Lord's, with Gower getting a second successive century and Hadlee five for 93. New Zealand made only 191 in face of good bowling by Botham and N.G.B. Cook (5–35 on his debut). England's 211 set New Zealand 347 to win. They made 219 and lost by 127.

At Trent Bridge, England's 420 (Botham 103) gave them a lead of 213 when Cook took five for 63. Lamb made 137 not out from 297 in the second innings, which set New Zealand over 500 to win. Hadlee made 92 not out at number eight to get them up to 345.

1983   20th Series   Eng 3, NZ 1
1 THE OVAL   England won by 189 runs
England 209 (D W Randall 75, R J Hadlee 6–53) and 446–6 dec (C J Tavare 109, G Fowler 105, A J Lamb 102)
New Zealand 196 (R J Hadlee 84, R G D Willis 4–43, I T Botham 4–62) and 270 (J G Wright 88, G P Howarth 67)

2 HEADINGLEY   New Zealand won by 5 wkts
England 225 (C J Tavare 69, A J Lamb 58, B L Cairns 7–74) and 252 (D I Gower 112, E J Chatfield 5–95)
New Zealand 377 (J G Wright 93, B A Edgar 84, R J Hadlee 75, R G D Willis 4–57) and 103–5 (R G D Willis 5–35)

3 LORD'S   England won by 127 runs
England 326 (D I Gower 108, M W Gatting 81, C J Tavare 51, R J Hadlee 5–93) and 211 (I T Botham 61)
New Zealand 191 (B A Edgar 191, N G B Cook 5–35, I T Botham 4–50) and 219 (J V Coney 68)

4 TRENT BRIDGE   England won by 165 runs
England 420 (I T Botham 103, D W Randall 83, D I Gower 72, J G Bracewell 4–108) and 297 (A J Lamb 137, R J Hadlee 4–85)
New Zealand 207 (B A Edgar 62, N G B Cook 5–63) and 345 (R J Hadlee 92, B A Edgar 76, J V Coney 68, N G B Cook 4–87)

1983 Averages

Batting	I	No	Runs	HS	Avge
A.J. Lamb (E)	8	2	392	137*	65.33
D.I. Gower (E)	8	1	404	112*	57.71
R.J. Hadlee (NZ)	8	2	301	92*	50.16
B.A. Edgar (NZ)	8	0	336	84	42.00
C.J. Tavaré (E)	8	0	330	109	41.25
J.G. Wright (NZ)	6	0	230	93	38.33
I.T. Botham (E)	8	0	282	103	35.25
J.V. Coney (NZ)	8	1	238	68	34.00

Bowling	O	M	Runs	W	Avge	BB
R.G.D. Willis (E)	123.2	38	273	20	13.65	5–35
N.G.B. Cook (E)	135.2	56	275	17	16.17	5–35
R.J. Hadlee (NZ)	232	65	559	21	26.61	6–53
B.L. Cairns (NZ)	184	52	461	16	28.81	7–74
I.T. Botham (E)	112.5	27	340	10	34.00	4–50
J.G. Bracewell (NZ)	123	28	364	10	36.40	4–108
N.G. Cowans (E)	125	25	447	12	37.25	3–74
E.J. Chatfield (NZ)	153	37	440	11	40.00	5–95

1983–84: New Zealand's first innings victory and series win

Only five months after playing New Zealand at home, England were in New Zealand. Howarth won the toss at Wellington, and for the first time in nine chose to bat. It looked mistaken as they fell for 219, mainly to Botham (5–59). England started badly but

Above: Geoff Howarth well out of his ground at Headingley in 1983. Despite this run-out New Zealand won by five wickets.

Left: Martin Crowe at Trent Bridge in 1983. He became New Zealand's best batsman of the later 1980s.

Botham (138) and Randall (164) added 232 for the sixth wicket in a display of brilliant batting. Cairns took seven for 143 in England's 463. New Zealand saved the match through M.D. Crowe (100) and mainly J.J. Coney (174 not out). He and Cairns added a New Zealand record of 118 for the ninth wicket in a total of 537. The match was drawn.

A.C.S. Pigott was co-opted into the England side at Christchurch because of injuries to fast bowlers. Howarth won the toss and batted again, a crucial choice. They recovered from 137 for five to 307 through Hadlee, who made 99. The wicket cracked, and rain made it treacherous. England were shot out for 82 and followed on for the first time against New Zealand. With Hadlee getting eight wickets in the match, they were out again for 93, New Zealand winning by an innings and 132.

England needed to win at Auckland, but prospects dimmed rapidly as Howarth batted again, rain interrupted the first three days and J.G. Wright, J.J. Crowe and I.O.S. Smith made centuries. New Zealand declared at 496 for nine, and England had only pride to play for. They made 439 (Randall 104) and that was that. New Zealand recorded their first series win over England in the 21st rubber.

Hadlee, Richard John

Hadlee was born on 3 July 1951 at Christchurch, the son of a former New Zealand captain. He first appeared for Canterbury in 1971–72. A genuine right arm-fast bowler, of slim, wiry build, he obtains considerable life from a short run. He also bats very aggressively as a middle-order left-hand batsman. He made his Test debut in 1972–73 and from 1977–78, when he took ten wickets in New Zealand's first-ever defeat of England, he has been at the centre of New Zealand's great revival. In 70 Tests to 1986–87 he has taken 355 wickets (second only to Botham), average 22.46, and scored 2,622 runs, average 27.60.

Above: The Basin Reserve, Wellington, during the first Test against England in 1983–84.

Below: Jubilation among the New Zealanders at Christchurch in 1983–84. Cowans is caught by Smith off Hadlee and New Zealand win by an innings and 132 runs.

1983–84   21st Series   NZ 1, Eng 0, Drawn 2
1 WELLINGTON   **Match Drawn**

New Zealand 219 (J J Crowe 52, I T Botham 5–59) and 537 (J V Coney 174, M D Crowe 100, B L Cairns 64)

England 463 (D W Randall 164, I T Botham 138, B L Cairns 7–143) and 69–0

2 CHRISTCHURCH   **New Zealand won by an innings and 132 runs**

New Zealand 307 (R J Hadlee 99, R G D Willis 4–51)

England 82 and 93 (R J Hadlee 5–28)

3 AUCKLAND   **Match Drawn**

New Zealand 496–9 dec (J G Wright 130, J J Crowe 128, I D S Smith 113) and 16–0

England 439 (D W Randall 104, C L Smith 91, I T Botham 70)

1983–84 Averages

Batting	I	No	Runs	HS	Avge
J.V. Coney (NZ)	4	1	251	174*	83.66
J.J. Crowe (NZ)	4	0	230	128	57.50
J.G. Wright (NZ)	5	1	218	130	54.50

Bowling	O	M	Runs	W	Avge	BB
R.J. Hadlee (NZ)	109.5	33	232	12	19.33	5–28
B.L. Cairns (NZ)	113	37	251	12	20.91	7–143
R.G.D. Willis (E)	115.1	28	306	12	25.50	4–51

1986: The case of the four wicket-keepers

J.V. Coney led the tourists to England in 1986, while M.W. Gatting had succeeded in the first half of the season to the England captaincy.

England v New Zealand at the Oval in 1986. Left to right, back: Athey, Small, Emburey, Edmonds, Dilley, Willey, French. Front: Lamb, Botham, Gatting, Gooch, Gower.

At Lord's, England made 307, in which Hadlee took six for 80. But the match will be remembered for the events after he had knocked out the England wicket-keeper B.N. French. When New Zealand batted, Athey donned the gloves, but after two overs, R.W. Taylor, England's former keeper who had retired two years earlier, took over with Coney's consent. Taylor was at the match as a spectator. The following morning R.J. Parks, whose father J.M. and grandfather J.H. both played for England, was sent for as substitute. On the last day of the New Zealand innings, French returned, so England had uniquely used four wicket-keepers in the innings, two of whom were not in the squad. While this was going, on M.D. Crowe scored 106, he and B.A. Edgar (83) putting on 210 for the third wicket, and New Zealand took a lead of 35. England declared second time at 295 for six after a dashing 183 from Gooch, but by then the match was drifting to a draw.

At Trent Bridge, Coney put England in and Hadlee put them out. His six for 80 kept England to 256. J.G. Bracewell, batting number eight, scored a surprise 110, taking New Zealand past England's score and on to 413. Hadlee pressed home the advantage with four more wickets, and England were out for 230, another number eight, Emburey, top-scoring. New Zealand needed only 74 and won by eight wickets.

Botham returned at the Oval, having been suspended for admitting taking drugs, and with his first ball back he equalled Lillee's record aggregate for Test wickets. In his next over he passed the record. He also scored a rapid 59 not out. Wright, Gower and Gatting scored centuries, but about 2½ days lost to rain and bad light meant a draw and New Zealand's series.

1986 Averages

Batting	I	No	Runs	HS	Avge
M.D. Crowe (NZ)	5	2	206	106	68.66
D.I. Gower (E)	5	0	293	131	58.60
G.A. Gooch (E)	5	0	268	183	53.60

Bowling	O	M	Runs	W	Avge	BB
R.J. Hadlee (NZ)	153.5	42	390	19	20.52	6–80

1986   22nd Series   Eng 0, NZ 1, Drawn 2
1 LORD'S   **Match Drawn**

England 307 (M D Moxon 74, D I Gower 62, R J Hadlee 6–80) and 295–6 dec (G A Gooch 183)

New Zealand 342 (M D Crowe 106, B A Edgar 83, J V Coney 51, G R Dilley 4–82, P H Edmonds 4–97) and 41–2

2 TRENT BRIDGE   **New Zealand won by 8 wkts**

England 256 (D I Gower 71, C W J Athey 55, R J Hadlee 6–80) and 230 (J E Emburey 75, R J Hadlee 4–60)

New Zealand 413 (J G Bracewell 110, R J Hadlee 68, J G Wright 58, E J Gray 50) and 77–2

3 THE OVAL   **Match Drawn**

New Zealand 287 (J G Wright 119, G R Dilley 4–92) and 7–0

England 388–5 dec (D I Gower 131, M W Gatting 121, I T Botham 59)

Australia v West Indies

1930–31: Australia win first series by 4–1

After their Test baptism in England in 1928 and England's return visit, West Indies toured Australia in 1930–31, G.C. Grant captaining the tourists and making his Test debut in the first Test at Adelaide. Woodfull captained Australia.

West Indies reached 296 despite Grimmett's seven for 87. Kippax made 146 of Australia's reply of 376. West Indies set Australia 170 to win, and Ponsford and Jackson got them without loss.

West Indies were unlucky at Sydney, where Australia made 323 for four on the first day, whereupon rain washed out the second day and 20 wickets fell on the awkward pitch on the third. Nobody could match Ponsford's first-innings 183, and West Indies had to face losing by an innings and 172.

Bradman was their downfall at Brisbane. Dropped at four, he made 223, and with Ponsford getting a century the total reached 558. Headley made a brave 102 not out in a total of 193, but West Indies lost again by an innings and 217, Grimmett taking nine wickets.

Ironmonger was the tormentor at Melbourne, taking seven for 23 as West Indies were soon removed for 99. A Bradman century, and a declaration at 328 for eight, allowed Ironmonger to take his match haul to 11 wickets and Australia again won by an innings.

The elements helped West Indies at Sydney when the teams returned there. F.R.

Martin (123) and Headley (105) enabled Grant to declare at 350 for six when rain livened the pitch. Australia made 224. Grant declared again at 124 for five, to get an advantageous wicket for a second time. Although set only 251, Australia lost by 30 runs.

Australia v West Indies

1930–31   1st Series   Aus 4, WI 1

1 ADELAIDE   Australia won by 10 wkts
West Indies 296 (E L Bartlett 84, C A Roach 56, G C Grant 53, C V Grimmett 7–87) and 249 (G C Grant 71, L S Birkett 64, A Hurwood 4–86, C V Grimmett 4–96)
Australia 376 (A F Kippax 146, S J McCabe 90, O C Scott 4–83) and 172–0 (W H Ponsford 92, A Jackson 70)

2 SYDNEY   Australia won by an innings and 172 runs
Australia 369 (W H Ponsford 183, W M Woodfull 58, O C Scott 4–66)
West Indies 107 (C V Grimmett 5–54) and 90 (A Hurwood 4–22)

3 BRISBANE   Australia won by an innings and 217 runs
Australia 558 (D G Bradman 223, W H Ponsford 109, A F Kippax 84, H C Griffith 4–133)
West Indies 193 (G A Headley 102, R K Oxenham 4–39, C V Grimmett 4–95) and 148 (C V Grimmett 5–49)

4 MELBOURNE   Australia won by an innings and 122 runs
West Indies 99 (H Ironmonger 7–23) and 107 (A G Fairfax 4–31, H Ironmonger 4–56)
Australia 328–8 dec (D G Bradman 152, W M Woodfull 83)

5 SYDNEY   West Indies won by 30 runs
West Indies 350–6 dec (F R Martin 123, G A Headley 105, G C Grant 62) and 124–5 dec
Australia 224 (A G Fairfax 54, G N Francis 4–48) and 220 (A G Fairfax 60, H C Griffith 4–50)

1930–31 Averages

Batting	I	No	Runs	HS	Avge
W.H. Ponsford (A)	7	1	467	183	77.83
D.G. Bradman (A)	6	0	447	223	74.50
A.F. Kippax (A)	6	0	277	146	46.16
G.C. Grant (WI)	10	4	255	70*	42.50
G.A. Headley (WI)	10	1	336	105	37.33
F.R. Martin (WI)	10	1	254	123*	28.22

Bowling	O	M	Runs	W	Avge	BB
H. Ironmonger (A)	153	61	323	22	14.68	7–23
C.V. Grimmett (A)	238.4	60	593	33	17.96	7–87
H.C. Griffith (WI)	133.5	20	393	14	28.07	4–50

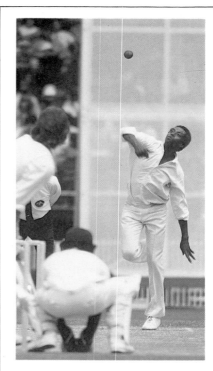

Gibbs, Lancelot Richard

Lance Gibbs was born on 29 September 1934 in Georgetown, in what was then British Guiana. He was an off-break bowler, and made his debut for British Guiana in 1953–54. From 1967 he also played for Warwickshire in England. In 1957–58 he made his first Test appearance. He played 79 Test matches, and in the last set a new record aggregate of Test wickets, ending with 309, average 29.09.

Worrell, Frank Mortimer Maglinne

Worrell was born on 1 August 1924 at Bridgetown, and was thus just the oldest of the 'three Ws' of Barbados and West Indies. He made his debut for the Island in 1941–42, but from 1947–48 played for Jamaica. He was a very stylish opening or middle-order right-hand batsman, and a left-arm medium or slow bowler. He made his first Test appearance in 1947–48. He

became captain in 1960–61, when West Indies had a marvellous tour of Australia. From 1964 the Frank Worrell Trophy has been awarded for competition between the countries. In 51 Tests, he was captain in 15. He scored 3,860 runs, average 49.48. He also took 69 wickets, average 38.72. He was knighted in 1964 and became a senator in the Jamaican parliament. He died of leukaemia on 13 March 1967 at Kingston.

1951–52: Bouncers tame a disappointed West Indies

West Indies returned to Australia 21 years after the first series and a year after their series win in England. Goddard led the tourists and Hassett was the Australian captain.

West Indies batted at Brisbane and made 216. Valentine (5–99) kept Australia's lead down to 10. Ring (6–80) got West Indies out again for 245, leaving Australia needing 236. Despite the efforts of the spinners, particularly Ramadhin (5–90), they made them for the loss of seven wickets.

West Indies were put in at Sydney, but by good middle-order batting they scored 362. Centuries by Hassett (132) and Miller (129), who put on an Australian record stand against West Indies of 235, plus some tail-end hitting, took Australia to 527. Dismissing West Indies for 290, Australia won by seven wickets.

West Indies, who had been troubled by the bouncers of Miller and Lindwall, did better on a damp pitch at Adelaide. Australia made only 82 (Worrell 6–38), and West Indies got a small lead at 105 (Johnston 6–62). Spinners then took over, and Australia's 255 (Valentine 6–102) was not enough, West Indies winning by six wickets.

At Melbourne, Worrell got a century in 272 and, with J. Trim getting five for 34, West Indies led by 56 to which they added 203. Australia needed 260, and Hassett scored 102, but Valentine and Ramadhin reduced them to 222 for nine. West Indies should have levelled the series but Ring (32 not out) and Johnston (7 not out) got the 38 needed for the last wicket.

Goddard stood down at Sydney and J.B. Stollmeyer captained West Indies. Australia, for whom R. Benaud made his debut, were dismissed for 116, largely by Gomez (7–55), but with a barrage of bouncers, particularly from Miller (5–26), West Indies were bundled out for 78. Australia made 377 and, despite Stollmeyer's brave 104, Australia won by 202.

1951–52   2nd Series   Aus 4, WI 1

1 BRISBANE   Australia won by 3 wkts
West Indies 216 (R R Lindwall 4–62) and 245 (E de C Weekes 70, G E Gomez 55, D T Ring 6–80)
Australia 226 (R R Lindwall 61, A L Valentine 5–99) and 236–7 (S Ramadhin 5–90)

2 SYDNEY   Australia won by 7 wkts
West Indies (R J Christiani 76, F M M Worrell 64, C L Walcott 60, G E Gomez 54, R R Lindwall 4–66) and 290 (J D C Goddard 57, E de C Weekes 56)
Australia 517 (A L Hassett 132, K R Miller 129, D T Ring 65, A L Valentine 4–111) and 137–3

3 ADELAIDE   West Indies won by 6 wkts
Australia 82 (F M M Worrell 6–38) and 255 (D T Ring 67, A L Valentine 6–102)
West Indies 105 (W A Johnston 6–62) and 233–4

4 MELBOURNE   Australia won by 1 wkt
West Indies 272 (F M M Worrell 108, K R Miller 5–60) and 203 (J B Stollmeyer 54, G E Gomez 52)
Australia 216 (R N Harvey 83, J Trim 5–34) and 260–9 (A L Hassett 102, A L Valentine 5–88)

5 SYDNEY   Australia won by 202 runs
Australia 116 (G E Gomez 7–55) and 377 (K R Miller 69, A L Hassett 64, C C McDonald 62, G B Hole 62, F M M Worrell 4–95)
West Indies 78 (K R Miller 5–26) and 213 (J B Stollmeyer 104, R R Lindwall 5–52)

1951–52 Averages

Batting	I	No	Runs	HS	Avge
A.L. Hassett (A)	8	1	402	132	57.42
K.R. Miller (A)	10	1	362	129	40.22
G.E. Gomez (WI)	10	1	324	55	36.00
F.M.M. Worrell (WI)	10	0	337	108	33.70
J.B. Stollmeyer (WI)	10	0	328	104	32.80
R.J. Christiani (WI)	10	1	261	76	29.00
R.N. Harvey (A)	10	0	261	61	26.10

Bowling	O	M	Runs	W	Avge	BB
G.E. Gomez (WI)	104.2	23	256	18	14.22	7–55
F.M.M. Worrell (WI)	89.1	10	329	17	19.35	6–38
K.R. Miller (A)	128.3	16	398	20	19.90	5–26
W.A. Johnston (A)	171.4	24	508	23	22.08	6–62
R.R. Lindwall (A)	154	19	484	21	23.04	5–52
A.L. Valentine (WI)	218.1	39	691	24	28.79	6–102
D.T. Ring (A)	99.5	10	390	13	30.00	6–80
S. Ramadhin (WI)	232.3	53	695	14	49.64	5–90

1954–55: Batting records in the West Indies

I.W. Johnson led the first Australian Test team to the West Indies. Stollmeyer captained West Indies, but D. St E. Atkinson deputized in the first and last matches.

At Kingston, centuries from Harvey and Miller allowed Australia to declare at 515 for nine. Despite Walcott's century West Indies followed on at 259, and did little better at 275, O.G. Smith this time getting a century on his Test debut. G.L. Gibbs also made his debut in this match. Australia needed 20, and, when Weekes bowled, all the West Indies players except the wicket-keeper had bowled.

At Port-of-Spain, where the Test for the first time was on a turf wicket, a record crowd saw Walcott (126) and Weekes (139) add 242 for West Indies' third wicket in a total of 382 (Lindwall 6–95). But Australia's first three

batsmen all made centuries, and Johnson declared at 600 for nine. The match was headed for a draw, but Walcott completed a century in each innings while Weekes (87 not out) was left 13 short.

At Georgetown, Australia's bowlers had West Indies out for 182 and the batsmen got a lead of 75. Johnson then took seven for 44 and left his side only 133 to get for an eight-wicket win.

It was a return to big scores at Bridgetown. Australia's opening bowlers, Miller and Lindwall, made hundreds, and first-change Archer 98 as the tourists scored 668. West Indies were 147 for six when Atkinson (219) and C.C. Depeiza (122 in his second Test) added 347, a first-class record for the seventh wicket. They followed Hobbs and Sutcliffe in batting throughout a full day in a Test. Atkinson then took five for 56 in the dismissal of Australia for 249. Atkinson and Depeiza were together again at 234 for six as the match was drawn.

The scoring continued at Kingston. Walcott made his fourth century of the series as West Indies made 357. Miller took six for 107, but Australia, at one time seven for two, produced a record five century-makers headed by Harvey with 204, followed by Archer 128, McDonald 127, Benaud 121 and Miller 109. Australia's 758 for eight remains their highest total. Records did not end there; Walcott, in the second innings, became the only batsman to score a century in each innings twice in a rubber, and to score five centuries in a rubber. Australia won by an innings and 82.

1954–55   3rd Series   Aus 3, WI 0, Drawn 2

1 KINGSTON   Australia won by 9 wkts
Australia 515–9 dec (K R Miller 147, R N Harvey 133, A R Morris 65, C C McDonald 50) and 20–1
West Indies 259 (C L Walcott 108, R R Lindwall 4–61) and 275 (O G Smith 104, J K Holt 60)

2 PORT OF SPAIN   Match Drawn
West Indies 382 (E de C Weekes 139, C L Walcott 126, R R Lindwall 6–95) and 273–4 (C L Walcott 110, E de C Weekes 87)
Australia 600–9 dec (R N Harvey 133, A R Morris 111, C C McDonald 110, R G Archer 84, I W Johnson 66)

3 GEORGETOWN   Australia won by 8 wkts
West Indies 182 (E de C Weekes 81, R Benaud 4–15) and 207 (C L Walcott 73, F M M Worrell 56, I W Johnson 7–44)
Australia 257 (R Benaud 68, C C McDonald 61) and 133–2

4 BRIDGETOWN   Match Drawn
Australia 668 (K R Miller 137, R R Lindwall 118, R G Archer 98, R N Harvey 74, L E Favell 72, G R A Langley 53, D T Dewdney 4–125) and 249 (I W Johnson 57, L E Favell 53, D St E Atkinson 5–56)
West Indies 510 (D St E Atkinson 219, C C Depeiaza 122) and 234–6 (C L Walcott 83)

5 KINGSTON   Australia won by an innings and 82 runs
West Indies 357 (C L Walcott 155, F M M Worrell 61, E de C Weekes 56, K R Miller 6–107) and 319 (C L Walcott 110, G St A Soberts 64)
Australia 758–8 dec (R N Harvey 204, R G Archer 128, C C McDonald 127, R Benaud 121, K R Miller 109)

1954–55 Averages

Batting	I	No	Runs	HS	Avge
R.N. Harvey (A)	7	1	650	204	108.33
C.L. Walcott (WI)	10	0	827	155	82.70
K.R. Miller (A)	6	0	439	147	73.16
C.C. McDonald (A)	8	1	449	127	64.14
R.G. Archer (A)	6	0	364	128	60.66
E.de. C. Weekes (WI)	10	2	469	139	58.62
D.St.E. Atkinson (WI)	8	1	311	219	44.42
A.R. Morris (A)	6	0	266	111	44.33
J.K. Holt (WI)	10	0	251	60	25.10

Bowling	O	M	Runs	W	Avge	BB
R. Benaud (A)	185	49	486	18	27.00	4–15
I.W. Johnson (A)	151.2	51	406	14	29.00	7–44
K.R. Miller (A)	189.2	37	640	20	32.00	6–107
R.R. Lindwall (A)	176	25	643	20	32.15	6–95
D.St.E. Atkinson (WI)	215.1	78	459	13	35.30	5–56

1960–61: The series that had almost everything

Worrell and Benaud were the captains in one of the best Test series since the Second World War. The atmosphere was set by the first match.

West Indies batted first and made 453, Sobers leading some good batting with 132. Davidson bowled well for five for 135. O'Neill scored a dashing 181 and at 505 Australia led by 52. With Davidson taking six for 87 in the second innings, West Indies made 284, leaving Australia 233 to win. Hall reduced Australia to 92 for six, but Benaud joined Davidson and they continued to go for the runs. They added 134 and took Australia to the brink of victory. Then Davidson was run out by Solomon, whose throw hit the wicket. Six were needed off Hall's last over. A leg-bye came off the first ball, and Benaud was caught behind off the second. A bye to the keeper was snatched off the fourth, and another run came off the fifth when Hall dropped a skyer from Grout.

1960–61   4th Series   Aus 2, WI 1, Tied 1, Drawn 1

1 BRISBANE   Match Tied
West Indies 453 (G St A Sobers 132, F M M Worrell 65, J S Solomon 65, F C M Alexander 60, W W Hall 50, A K Davidson 5–135) and 284 (F M M Worrell 65, R B Kanhai 54, A K Davidson 6–87)
Australia 505 (N C O'Neill 181, R B Simpson 92, C C McDonald 57, W W Hall 4–140) and 232 (A K Davidson 80, R Benaud 52, W W Hall 5–63)

2 MELBOURNE   Australia won by 7 wkts
Australia 348 (K D Mackay 74, J W Martin 55, L E Favell 51, W W Hall 4–51) and 70–3
West Indies 181 (R B Kanhai 84, S M Nurse 70, A K Davidson 6–53) and 233 (C C Hunte 110, F C M Alexander 72)

3 SYDNEY   West Indies won by 222 runs
West Indies 339 (G St A Sobers 168, A K Davidson 5–80, R Benaud 4–86) and 326 (F C M Alexander 108, F M M Worrell 82, C W Smith 55, R Benaud 4–113)
Australia 202 (N C O'Neill 71, A L Valentine 4–67) and 241 (R N Harvey 85, N C O'Neill 70, L R Gibbs 5–66, A L Valentine 4–86)

4 ADELAIDE   Match Drawn
West Indies 393 (R B Kanhai 117, F M M Worrell 71, F C M Alexander 63, R Benaud 5–96) and 432–6 dec (R B Kanhai 115, F C M Alexander 87, C L Walcott 110, F M M Worrell 53)
Australia 366 (R B Simpson 85, R Benaud 77, C C McDonald 71, L R Gibbs 5–97) and 273–9 (N C O'Neill 65, K D Mackay 62)

5 MELBOURNE   Australia won by 2 wkts
West Indies 292 (G St A Sobers 64, F M Misson 4–58) and 321 (F C M Alexander 73, C C Hunte 52, A K Davidson 5–84)
Australia 356 (C C McDonald 91, R B Simpson 75, P J P Burge 68, G St A Sobers 5–120, L R Gibbs 4–74) and 258–8 (R B Simpson 92, P J P Burge 53)

1960–1 Averages

Batting	I	No	Runs	HS	Avge
F.C.M. Alexander (WI)	10	2	484	108	60.80
N.C. O'Neill (A)	10	0	522	181	52.20
R.B. Kanhai (WI)	10	0	503	117	50.30
R.B. Simpson (A)	10	1	445	92	49.44
G.St.A. Sobers (WI)	10	0	430	168	43.00
K.D. Mackay (A)	9	2	289	74	41.28
C.C. Hunte (WI)	10	0	377	110	37.70
F.M.M. Worrell (WI)	10	0	375	82	37.50
C.C. McDonald (A)	10	0	337	91	33.70
J.S. Solomon (WI)	10	1	250	65	27.77

Bowling	O	M	Runs	W	Avge	BB
A.K. Davidson (A)	173.7	25	612	33	18.54	6–53
L.R. Gibbs (WI)	192.2	65	395	19	20.78	5–66
W.W. Hall (WI)	144.6	14	616	21	29.33	5–63
R. Benaud (A)	268.1	55	779	23	33.86	5–96
A.L. Valentine (WI)	170.4	42	333	14	38.07	4–67
G.St.A. Sobers (WI)	191	27	588	15	39.20	5–120

Meckiff hit the next ball towards the boundary and Grout was run out by a perfect throw from Hunte when the batsmen went for a third and winning run. Kline, the last man, hit the next ball to square leg, and as

Meckiff for the second time ran for the winning run, Solomon hit the wicket from sideways on and the match was tied. It was the first Test to be tied. The series came alive, and Test cricket was regenerated.

The excitement slackened a little at Melbourne, where Australia made 348 and Davidson (6–53) removed West Indies for 181 (Nurse and Kanhai scoring 154 of them). Hunte made a century in the follow-on, but Australia won by seven wickets.

A brilliant 168 by Sobers at Sydney helped West Indies to 339, which earned them a lead of 137. To this they added 326, Alexander getting a century, and Gibbs and Valentine ensured they won by 222. Davidson took eight wickets in the match.

With the series level, the first innings were almost level at Adelaide. Kanhai made a century, Benaud and Gibbs each took five wickets and West Indies led by 27. Gibbs took a hat-trick. However, Kanhai repeated his century in the second innings and West Indies declared at 432 for six. With 100 minutes left they had practically won, Australia being 207 for nine. But Mackay (62 not out) and Kilne (15 not out) batted out time for a draw.

At Melbourne, West Indies made 292 and Simpson and McDonald had half of these, 146, on the board without loss, but with Sobers getting five for 120 their lead was kept to 64. A world record 90,800 crowd saw the second day. Davidson got five for 84 in the second innings, West Indies' score of 321 leaving Australia to get 258 for the rubber. They got them with two wickets to spare to end an exciting series.

Action from the first tied Test match. O'Neill caught by Alexander off Hall in the final innings.

AUSTRALIA V WEST INDIES 1960–61
1st Test, Brisbane: Match Tied

WEST INDIES

C.C. Hunte	c Benaud b Davidson	24	c Simpson b Mackay	39
C.W. Smith	c Grout b Davidson	7	c O'Neill b Davidson	6
R.B. Kanhai	c Grout b Davidson	15	c Grout b Davidson	54
G. St A. Sobers	c Kline b Meckiff	132	b Davidson	14
F.M.M. Worrell*	c Grout b Davidson	65	c Grout b Davidson	65
J.S. Solomon	hit wkt b Simpson	65	lbw b Simpson	47
P.D. Lashley	c Grout b Kline	19	b Davidson	0
F.C.M. Alexander†	c Davidson b Kline	60	b Benaud	5
S. Ramadhin	c Harvey b Davidson	12	c Harvey b Simpson	6
W.W. Hall	st Grout b Kline	50	b Davidson	18
A.L. Valentine	not out	0	not out	7
Extras	(LB 3, W 1)	4	(B 14, LB 7, W 2)	23
Total		**453**		**284**

AUSTRALIA

C.C. McDonald	c Hunte b Sobers	57	b Worrell	16
R.B. Simpson	b Ramadhin	92	c sub (L.R. Gibbs) b Hall	0
R.N. Harvey	b Valentine	15	c Sobers b Hall	5
N.C. O'Neill	c Valentine b Hall	181	c Alexander b Hall	26
L.E. Favell	run out	45	c Solomon b Hall	7
K.D. Mackay	b Sobers	35	b Ramadhin	28
A.K. Davidson	c Alexander b Hall	44	run out	80
R. Benaud*	lbw b Hall	10	c Alexander b Hall	52
A.T.W. Grout†	lbw b Hall	4	run out	2
I. Meckiff	run out	4	run out	2
L.F. Kline	not out	3	not out	0
Extras	(B 2, LB 8, W 1, NB 4)	15	(B 2, LB 9, NB 3)	14
Total		**505**		**232**

AUSTRALIA	O	M	R	W	O	M	R	W
Davidson	30	2	135	5	24.6	4	87	6
Meckiff	18	0	129	1	4	1	19	0
Mackay	3	0	15	0	21	7	52	1
Benaud	24	3	93	0	31	6	69	1
Simpson	8	0	25	1	7	2	18	2
Kline	17.6	6	52	3	4	0	14	0
O'Neill					1	0	2	0

WEST INDIES	O	M	R	W	O	M	R	W
Hall	29.3	1	140	4	17.7	3	63	5
Worrell	30	0	93	0	16	3	41	1
Sobers	32	0	115	2	8	0	30	0
Valentine	24	6	82	1	10	4	27	0
Ramadhin	15	1	60	1	17	3	57	1

FALL OF WICKETS

Wkt	WI 1st	A 1st	WI 2nd	A 2nd
1st	23	84	13	1
2nd	42	138	88	7
3rd	65	194	114	49
4th	239	278	127	49
5th	243	381	210	57
6th	283	469	210	92
7th	347	484	241	226
8th	366	489	250	228
9th	452	496	253	232
10th	453	505	284	232

Left: Worrell tries to sweep Benaud in the first Test at Brisbane 1960–61. Grout rushes round. Sobers is the non-striker.

Centre left: A part of the huge crowd which turned up to watch the second Test after the first Test had resulted in an exciting tie.

Bottom left: Cammie Smith receives a lifter from Davidson and is about to be caught by Simpson in the third Test at Sydney in 1960–61.

1964–65: West Indies win Frank Worrell Trophy

Sobers and Simpson led the two sides in the West Indies in 1964–65. Many of the Australians of four years earlier had retired. Sobers won the first toss and West Indies made 239. Hall took five for 60 and Australia were dismissed for 22 fewer. West Indies made a solid 373 and their fast bowling did not allow a serious challenge: they won by 179 runs. The Australians were, however, concerned about the action of Griffith, who was alleged to throw. Former captain Benaud was at the front of the criticism.

At Port-of-Spain, Simpson put West Indies in, but led by Butcher (117) they made 429. Cowper (143) and Booth (117) added 225 after O'Neill had retired at 63 for two, hit by a Griffith bouncer. Australia got 516 and did not have time to bat again after West Indies' 386.

1964–65   5th Series   WI 2, Aus 1, Drawn 2

1 KINGSTON   West Indies won by 179 runs
West Indies 239 (W A White 57, L C Mayne 4–43) and 373 (C C Hunte 81, J S Solomon 76, B F Butcher 71, L C Mayne 4–56, P I Philpott 4–109)
Australia 217 (W W Hall 5–60) and 216 (B C Booth 56, W W Hall 4–45)

2 PORT OF SPAIN   Match Drawn
West Indies 429 (B F Butcher 117, C C Hunte 89, G St A Sobers 69, B A Davis 54, N C O'Neill 4–41) and 386 (B A Davis 58, C C Hunte 53, R B Kanhai 53, R B Simpson 4–83)
Australia 516 (R M Cowper 143, B C Booth 117, G Thomas 61)

3 GEORGETOWN   West Indies won by 212 runs
West Indies 355 (R B Kanhai 89, N J N Hawke 6–72) and 180 (N J N Hawke 4–43, P I Philpott 4–49)
Australia 179 and 144 (L R Gibbs 6–29)

4 BRIDGETOWN   Match Drawn
Australia 650–6 dec (W M Lawry 210, R B Simpson 201, R M Cowper 102, N C O'Neill 51) and 175–4 dec (N C O'Neill 74, W M Lawry 58)
West Indies 573 (S M Nurse 201, R B Kanhai 129, C C Hunte 75, G St A Sobers 55, C C Griffith 54, G D McKenzie 4–114) and 242–5 (C C Hunte 81, B A Davis 68)

5 PORT OF SPAIN   Australia won by 10 wkts
West Indies 224 (R B Kanhai 121) and 131 (C C Hunte 60, G D McKenzie 5–33)
Australia 294 (R B Simpson 72, R M Cowper 69, C C Griffith 6–46) and 63–0

1964–65 Averages

Batting	I	No	Runs	HS	Avge
C.C. Hunte (WI)	10	1	550	89	61.11
W.M. Lawry (A)	9	2	386	210	52.57
R.M. Cowper (A)	8	0	417	143	52.12
R.B. Simpson (A)	9	1	399	201	49.87
R.B. Kanhai (WI)	10	0	462	129	46.20
N.C. O'Neill (A)	7	1	266	74*	44.33
B.F. Butcher (WI)	10	0	405	117	40.05
G.St.A. Sobers (WI)	10	1	352	69	39.11
S.M. Nurse (WI)	8	0	291	201	36.27

Bowling	O	M	Runs	W	Avge	BB
N.J.N. Hawke (A)	218.4	52	524	24	21.83	6–72
W.W. Hall (WI)	146	19	454	16	28.37	5–60
L.R. Gibbs (WI)	278.3	87	555	18	30.83	6–29
C.C. Griffith (WI)	154	22	480	15	32.00	6–46
P.I. Philpott (A)	244.3	58	629	18	34.94	4–49
G.D. McKenzie (A)	256	55	677	17	39.82	5–33
G.St.A. Sobers (WI)	192.3	53	492	12	41.00	3–75

West Indies batted first again at Georgetown and made 355, Hawke getting six for 72. After the first day the wicket began to take spin. Australia made 179, West Indies 180, then Gibbs (6–29) spun out Australia for 144.

Australia needed to win at Bridgetown, and Lawry and Simpson batted throughout the first day. Eventually they put on 382 for the first wicket, an Australian record. Both passed 200, and with Cowper scoring a century, the total climbed to 650 for six declared. But the wicket was too good: Nurse also got a double-century and Kanhai passed 100. West Indies made 573. Simpson declared, setting a generous target of 253 in 270 minutes, and West Indies, at 242 for five, nearly reached it. The draw was enough to give them the Frank Worrell Trophy, awarded for competition between the two countries.

Back at Port-of-Spain, except for Kanhai (121), West Indies batted badly to be out for 224. Australia did a little better against Griffith (6–46) to lead by 70. West Indies, perhaps relaxing after the series win, were shot out for 131 (McKenzie 5–33) and Australia won by ten wickets.

1968–69: Australia get on top as series progresses

Sobers and Lawry captained the sides in Australia in 1968–69. At Brisbane, Sobers and Kanhai were the only survivors of the tied first Test eight years earlier. Worrell had died the year before.

Kanhai was top scorer (94) in West Indies' 296. After Australia's first wicket fell without a run on the board, Lawry (105) and I.M.Chappell (117) added 217 for the second wicket, but the team was all out for 284, Gibbs getting five for 88. Lloyd made 129 in West Indies' second knock, which set Australia 366 to win. Sobers, with six for 73 with his finger-spin, made sure they fell 126 short.

The second Test was a turning point for a West Indian team which was growing old. Put in at Melbourne, they capitulated for 200 to McKenzie, who took eight for 71. Lawry then passed this total himself with 205, and he and Ian Chappell (165) beat their stand in the first Test by adding 298. Australia got 510, and won by an innings and 30, Gleeson for the second time in the series getting five second-innings wickets.

The third Test followed a similar pattern – West Indies 264; Australia 547. Walters made a century, and Butcher's in reply could not avoid a ten-wicket defeat.

At Adelaide, the first half of the match was according to formula – West Indies 276; Australia 533. Sobers and Walters each made 110. However, West Indies then batted with great resolution. Butcher scored most with 118, but Holford and Hendricks added 122 for the ninth wicket. West Indies made 616, setting Australia 360 to win. They began well, and reached the final 15 overs needing only 62 with seven wickets left. Then they panicked, and four men were run out, including Redpath backing up, run out by Griffith without the customary warning. In the end West Indies had 26 deliveries to get the last wicket and

win. Sheahan and Connolly held on for the draw.

Having failed to draw level, Sobers put Australia in at Sydney. It was a mistake. Lawry made 151 and Walters 242; they added 336 for the fourth wicket. Australia scored 619, three more than West Indies in the previous Test. Lawry did not enforce the follow-on when dismissing West Indies for 379. He declared at 394 for eight with Walters (103) adding to his aggregate and Redpath also getting a century. Set 735 to win, West Indies made 352, with Sobers and Nurse defiantly getting centuries.

Lloyd, Clive Hubert

Lloyd was born on 31 August 1944 at Georgetown, British Guiana. He is a cousin of Lance Gibbs. He played for British Guiana (which later became Guyana) from 1963–64, and in England played for Lancashire from 1968. A hard-hitting left-hand batsman, a medium-pace right-arm bowler and an outstanding field, especially at cover, Lloyd made his Test debut in 1966–67. He played in spectacles, and with his white sun hat and stooping, prowling gait he was instantly recognized all over the world. He captained West Indies 74 times, a world record. Initially, his captaincy was much admired as he knit players from the West Indian islands into a powerful force, but he was criticized later as more and more of their success was based on intimidatory bowling. In 110 Tests, he scored 7,515 runs, average 46.67, and took ten wickets, average 62.20. He also led West Indies to two World Cup wins.

1968–69 Averages

Batting	I	No	Runs	HS	Avge
K.D. Walters (A)	6	0	699	242	116.50
W.M. Lawry (A)	8	0	667	205	83.37
I.M. Chappell (A)	8	0	548	165	68.50
G.St.A. Sobers (WI)	10	0	497	113	49.70
M.C. Carew (WI)	10	1	427	90	47.44
B.F. Butcher (WI)	10	0	405	118	40.50
C.H. Lloyd (WI)	8	0	315	129	39.37
R.B. Kanhai (WI)	10	0	371	94	37.10
A.P. Sheahan (A)	9	2	257	51	36.71
I.R. Redpath (A)	8	0	291	132	36.37
S.M. Nurse (WI)	10	0	348	137	34.80
R.C. Fredericks (WI)	8	0	271	76	33.87
K.R. Stackpole (A)	9	1	265	62	33.12

Bowling	O	M	Runs	W	Avge	BB
G.D. McKenzie (A)	206.1	27	758	30	25.26	8–71
E.W. Freeman (A)	88.3	11	391	13	30.07	4–52
A.N. Connolly (A)	192	39	628	20	31.40	5–122
J.W. Gleeson (A)	250.6	57	844	26	32.46	5–61
L.R. Gibbs (WI)	292.2	52	923	24	38.45	5–88
G.St.A. Sobers (WI)	206.1	37	733	18	40.72	6–73

1972–73: Australia retain Frank Worrell Trophy against Sobers-less opposition.

Ian Chappell led a young and buoyant Australian side to West Indies in 1972–73, where they met a West Indies, now without Sobers and led by Kanhai, suffering a bad patch.

At Kingston, Australia made a solid 428 for seven declared, most batsmen contributing, and West Indies were out for exactly the same score. M.L.C. Foster made a century, he and Kanhai (84) adding 210 for the fifth wicket, while M.H.N. Walker took six for 114. K.R. Stackpole made a rapid second-innings 142 so that Chappell could declare, but there was no chance of a result.

The second Test was similar. Greg Chappell and Kanhai scored first-innings centuries, West Indies leading by 67. Then not out hundreds by Ian Chappell and Walters preceded a pointless declaration.

The Port-of-Spain Test was very different, and was an exciting match from the time that Walters (112) scored exactly 100 between lunch and tea on the first day with dazzling stroke play. Australia made 332, and led by 52, West Indies being unlucky in that L.G. Rowe damaged an ankle and could not bat in the match. Gibbs (5–102) kept Australia to 281 in the second

West Indies v Australia, Bridgetown, Barbados, 1972–73.

innings, West Indies needing 334. At lunch on the last day they were 268 for five and in control, but Kallicharran (91) was out straight afterwards and Australia won by 44 runs.

At Georgetown, thanks to a brilliant innings by Lloyd (178), West Indies were 269 for three at the end of the first day, but they made only 366, Walters getting five for 66. Ian Chappell made a century, but Australia were 26 behind. However West Indies collapsed for 109 to Walker and J.R. Hammond, and Australia won by ten wickets.

With the rubber decided, the last Test at Port-of-Spain was watched by few spectators, and rain cut into the second and third days. West Indies held on for a draw after being behind all the way.

1972–73   7th Series   Aus 2, WI 0, Drawn 3
1 KINGSTON   Match Drawn
Australia 428–7 dec (R W Marsh 97, K D Walters 72, R Edwards 63, L R Gibbs 4–85) and 260–2 dec (K R Stackpole 142, I R Redpath 60)
West Indies 428 (M L C Foster 125, R B Kanhai 84, L G Rowe 76, A I Kallicharran 50, M H N Walker 6–114, J R Hammond 4–79) and 67 8–3

2 BRIDGETOWN   Match Drawn
Australia 324 (G S Chappell 106, R W Marsh 78, I M Chappell 72) and 300–2 dec (I M Chappell 106, K D Walters 102, K R Stackpole 53)
West Indies 391 (R B Kanhai 105, R C Fredericks 98, D L Murray 90, M H N Walker 5–97) and 36–0

3 PORT OF SPAIN   Australia won by 44 runs
Australia 332 (K D Walters 112, I R Redpath 66, G S Chappell 56) and 281 (I M Chappell 97, L R Gibbs 5–102)
West Indies 280 (R B Kanhai 56, A I Kallicharran 53, T J Jenner 4–98) and 289 (A I Kallicharran 91, R C Fredericks 76, K J O'Keeffe 4–57)

4 GEORGETOWN   Australia won by 10 wkts
West Indies 366 (C H Lloyd 178, R B Kanhai 57, K D Walters 5–66) and 109 (J R Hammond 4–38), M H N Walker 4–45)
Australia 341 (I M Chappell 109, K D Walters 81, G S Chappell 51) and 135–0 (K R Stackpole 76, I R Redpath 57)

5 PORT OF SPAIN   Match Drawn
Australia 419–8 dec (R Edwards 74, K D Walters 70, I M Chappell 56, R W Marsh 56) and 218–7 dec (L R Gibbs 4–66)
West Indies 319 (R C Fredericks 73, C H Lloyd 59, M H N Walker 5–75, T J Jenner 5–90) and 135–5

1972–73 Averages

Batting

	I	No	Runs	HS	Avge
I.M. Chappell (A)	9	2	542	109	77.42
K.D. Walters (A)	8	1	497	112	71.00
C.H. Lloyd (WI)	6	1	297	178	59.40
R.B. Kanhai (WI)	8	1	358	105	51.14
R.W. Marsh (A)	7	1	297	97	49.50
G.S. Chappell (A)	8	1	342	106	48.85
K.R. Stackpole (A)	8	1	335	142	47.85
M.L.C. Foster (WI)	7	1	262	125	43.66
I.R. Redpath (A)	10	1	381	66	42.33
R.C. Fredericks (WI)	10	1	381	98	42.33
A.I. Kallicharran (WI)	9	1	294	91	36.75

Bowling

	O	M	Runs	W	Avge	BB
M.H.N. Walker (A)	271.1	83	539	26	20.73	6–114
T.J. Jenner (A)	137.5	34	347	13	26.69	5–90
L.R. Gibbs (WI)	325	108	696	26	26.76	5–102
J.R. Hammond (A)	171.5	47	488	15	32.53	4–38

1975–76: Australia get on top in unofficial Test championship

Greg Chappell and Clive Lloyd were captains in 1975–76 in a series which was billed as being for the 'world championship', with new World Cup winners West Indies the favourites.

They began very badly at Brisbane, however, losing six wickets for 125 in the first session. They struggled to 214, but Australia, with Greg Chappell scoring 123, cruised past 300 with only four men out.

Their final 366 (Gibbs 5–102) was disappointing. West Indies continued fighting back, Rowe and Kallicharran getting centuries in 370, but it was not enough, and Greg Chappell completed his second century of the match in an eight-wicket win.

At Perth, Ian Chappell made 156 out of 329. Fredericks (156) and Lloyd (149) batted breathtakingly to hoist a total of 585. Penetrating fast bowling by Roberts, who took seven for 54, then removed Australia for 169 and an innings victory.

A crowd of 85,000 turned out at Melbourne to see this exciting cricket, but it was Lillee and Thomson who produced it in the first innings, dismissing West Indies for 224. Redpath and G.J. Cosier, in his first Test, made hundreds and Australia led by 261. They needed only 52 for an eight-wicket win.

At Sydney, three West Indian batsmen retired hurt at various stages, but they made a useful 355. Greg Chappell made 182 not out but Australia's lead was only 50. However, West Indies collapsed before Thomson (6–50) in the second innings, and 128 all out led to an easy seven-wicket win for Australia, who retained the Worrell Trophy.

West Indies lost heart after this and at Adelaide were well beaten. Redpath and A. Turner scored Australian hundreds, and Richards got one for West Indies in a lost cause.

At Melbourne, Australia won by 165 runs after another second-innings declaration. Redpath and McCosker scored centuries, and Lillee took eight wickets in the match.

The late run of form of Viv Richards (50 and 98) was West Indies' only bright spot for the future, while Gibbs took two wickets to end his Test career with a record 309, having equalled Trueman's previous record in the Test at Adelaide.

1975–76 8th Series Aus 5, WI 1

1 BRISBANE Australia won by 8 wkts
West Indies 214 (D L Murray 66, G J Gilmour 4–42) and 370 (L G Rowe 107, A I Kallicharran 101, D L Murray 55)
Australia 366 (G S Chappell 123, A Turner 81, L R Gibbs 5–102) and 219–2 (G S Chappell 109, I M Chappell 74)

2 PERTH West Indies won by an innings and 87 runs
Australia 329 (I M Chappell 156, M A Holding 4–88) and 169 (A M E Roberts 7–54)
West Indies 585 (R C Fredericks 169, C H Lloyd 149, D L Murray 63, A I Kallicharran 57)

3 MELBOURNE Australia won by 8 wkts
West Indies 224 (R C Fredericks 59, J R Thomson 5–62, D K Lillee 4–56) and 312 (C H Lloyd 102)
Australia 485 (G J Cosier 109, I R Redpath 102, R W Marsh 56, G S Chappell 52, A M E Robers 4–126) and 55–2

4 SYDNEY Australia won by 7 wkts
West Indies 355 (L G Rowe 67, C H Lloyd 51, M H N Walker 4–70) and 128 (D L Murray 50, J R Thomson 6–50)
Australia 405 (G S Chappell 182, A Turner 53) and 82–3

5 ADELAIDE Australia won by 190 runs
Australia 418 (I R Redpath 103, G J Gilmour 95, V A Holder 5–108) and 345–7 dec (A Turner 136, I R Redpath 65)
West Indies 274 (K D Boyce 95, A I Kallicharran 76, J R Thomson 4–68) and 299 (I V A Richards 101, K D Boyce 69, A I Kallicharran 67)

6 MELBOURNE Australia won by 165 runs
Australia 351 (I R Redpath 101, G S Chappell 68, G N Yallop 57) and 300–3 dec (R B McCosker 109, I R Redpath 70, G S Chappell 54)
West Indies 160 (I V A Richards 50, G J Gilmour 5–34, D K Lillee 5–63) and 326 (I V A Richards 98, C H Lloyd 91, J R Thomson 4–80)

1975–76 Averages

Batting	I	No	Runs	HS	Avge
G.S. Chappell (A)	11	5	702	182*	117.00
I.R. Redpath (A)	11	0	575	103	52.27
C.H. Lloyd (WI)	11	1	469	149	46.90
I.M. Chappell (A)	12	2	449	156	44.90
I.V.A. Richards (WI)	11	0	426	101	38.72
A.I. Kallicharran (WI)	11	0	421	101	38.27
R.C. Fredericks (WI)	11	0	417	169	37.90
A. Turner (A)	12	0	439	136	36.58
D.L. Murray (WI)	11	0	342	66	31.09
L.G. Rowe (WI)	11	0	270	107	24.54

Bowling	O	M	Runs	W	Avge	BB
G.J. Gilmour (A)	97.6	17	406	20	20.30	5–34
A.M.E. Roberts (WI)	141.6	15	580	22	26.36	7–54
D.K. Lillee (WI)	129.3	7	712	27	26.37	5–63
J.R. Thomson (A)	150.5	15	831	29	28.65	6–50
V.A. Holder (WI)	109	7	513	13	39.46	5–108
L.R. Gibbs (WI)	232.5	48	652	16	40.75	5–102

Jeff Thomson in action in Trinidad in 1977–78.

1977–78: West Indies win series of second elevens

The series in 1977–78 was immediately after World Series Cricket's formation. West Indies retained their 'defaulters' to the pirate organization, but Australia banned their defaulters and picked a completely new team, led by R.B. Simpson, who was brought out of retirement for the purpose. Only Thomson of the established players was available.

At Port-of-Spain, West Indies, led by Lloyd, put Australia in, and the fast bowling battery put them out again for 90. Kallicharran's century led the way to 405, and Australia were beaten by an innings and 106.

Lawrence Rowe batting at Brisbane in 1975–76, when he made 107 in the second innings. Rodney Marsh is the wicket-keeper.

It was closer at Bridgetown, where Thomson (6–77) bowled so well that West Indies overtook Australia's 250 by only 38. But Australia could make only 178 against the fast bowlers second time, and West Indies won by nine wickets. In this match G.N. Yallop wore a version of the now-familiar helmet – the first to do so in a Test.

The position changed in the third Test. The West Indian selectors dropped three WSC players in order to blood players who would be needed for a tour to India, which would clash with World Series Cricket. The captain, Lloyd, resigned in protest, and at the last minute the other WSC players joined him. West Indies, too, had to find a new team – six at Georgetown were making their debuts. Kallicharran took over as captain.

West Indies made 205 and Australia took a lead of 81. However, A.B. Williams, on his debut, and H.A. Gomes made centuries in the second innings, and 439 set Australia 359 to win. G.M. Wood (126) and C.S. Serjeant (124) rose to the challenge, adding 251 after three wickets had fallen for 22, and Australia scraped home by three wickets.

Before small crowds at Port-of-Spain, West Indies took a first-innings lead of two, thanks to Holden who took six for 28. Set 293, Australia collapsed for 94 to the spin of D.R. Parry (5–15) and R.R. Jumadeen (3–34).

West Indies had thus regained the Frank Worrell Trophy in unsatisfactory circumstances, and the last Test was the most unsatisfactory of all. With P.M. Toohey making 122, Australia made 343, and although Gomes made a second century of the series, West Indies trailed by 63, T.J. Laughlin getting five for 101. Australia declared at 305 for three, setting West Indies 369. Kallicharran made 126, but when Holder was given out caught behind with 38 balls remaining, West Indies were 258 for nine. The crowd threw bottles and stopped play in protest at the decision. The West Indian Board wanted to play the 38 balls on an extra day, but one umpire refused and a qualified replacement could not be found.

1 PORT OF SPAIN   West Indies won by an innings and 106 runs

Australia 90 (C E Croft 4–15) and 209 (G N Yallop 81, A M E Roberts 5–56)

West Indies 405 (A I Kallicharran 127, C H Lloyd 86, D L Haynes 61, J D Higgs 4–91)

2 BRIDGETOWN   West Indies won by 9 wkts

Australia 250 (B Yardley 74, G M Wood 69, C E H Croft 4–47, J Garner 4–65) and 178 (G M Wood 56, A M E Roberts 4–50, J Garner 4–56)

West Indies 288 (D L Haynes 66, D L Murray 60, J R Thomson 6–77) and 141–1 (C G Greenidge 80, D L Haynes 55)

3 GEORGETOWN   Australia won by 3 wkts

West Indies 205 (A T Greenidge 56, S Shivnarine 53, J R Thomson 4–56, W M Clark 4–65) and 439 (H A Gomes 101, A B Williams 100, S Shivnarine 63, D R Parry 51, W M Clark 4–124)

Australia 286 (R B Simpson 67, S J Rixon 54, G M Wood 50, N Phillip 4–75) and 362–7 (G M Wood 126, C S Serjeant 124)

4 PORT OF SPAIN   West Indies won by 198 runs

West Indies 292 (A I Kallicharran 92, A B Williams 87) and 290 (A E Greenidge 69, D R Parry 65, B Yardley 4–40)

Australia 290 (G N Yallop 75, V A Holder 6–28) and 94 (D R Parry 5–15)

5 KINGSTON   Match Drawn

Australia 343 (P M Toohey 122, G N Yallop 57, R R Jumadeen 4–72) and 305–3 dec (P M Toohey 97, G M Wood 90)

West Indies 280 (H A Gomes 115, S Shivnarine 53, T J Laughlin 5–101) and 258–9 (A I Kallicharran 126, B Yardley 4–35)

1977–78 Averages

Batting	I	No	Runs	HS	Avge
P.M. Toohey (A)	5	0	296	122	59.20
A.I. Kallicharran (WI)	8	0	408	127	51.00
G.M. Wood (A)	10	0	474	126	47.40
G.N. Yallop (A)	8	1	317	81	45.28
H.A. Gomes (WI)	6	0	265	115	44.16
A.B. Williams (WI)	6	0	257	100	42.83
C.S. Serjeant (A)	10	1	284	124	31.55

Bowling	O	M	Runs	W	Avge	BB
J. Garner (WI)	62.1	16	195	13	15.00	4–56
A.M.E. Roberts (WI)	64.2	14	211	12	17.58	5–56
B. Yardley (A)	153.1	50	377	15	25.13	4–35
J.D. Higgs (A)	139.2	32	384	15	25.60	4–91
J.R. Thomson (A)	151.2	15	577	20	28.85	6–77
D.R. Parry (WI)	124.4	19	360	12	30.00	5–15
W.M. Clark (A)	149.4	26	460	15	30.66	4.64

1979–80: West Indies easily better of full-strength sides

Both England and West Indies toured Australia in 1979–80, in the first series in which Australia reinstated the players who had joined World Series Cricket. Australia played tests against the two visiting sides alternately, beginning with West Indies at Brisbane, where Lloyd was unfit and D.L. Murray captained West Indies for the only time. B.M. Laird, making his debut for Australia, who were put in, scored 92. But at 268 all out, Australia were easily passed by West Indies who reached 441, mainly due to 140 from Viv Richards. Chappell (124) and Hughes (130 not out) took Australia to safety.

Lloyd returned for the second Test at Melbourne, where Australia won the toss and batted but where quickly dismissed by West Indies fast bowlers for 156. Roberts, the only one not to take a wicket, then scored 54, and with Richards earlier having made 96 in 110 balls, West Indies led by 241. With their second knock, Australia could set the tourists only 19 to win, duly accomplished.

At Adelaide, Australia put West Indies in, but Lloyd, who came in at 126 for four, scored 121 and raised West Indies' total to 328. It was too many for Australia, who did not recover from losing Ian and Greg Chappell to successive balls from Roberts at 26, and struggled to 203. Led by Kallicharran's century, the West Indian batsmen piled on the runs, setting Australia 574 to win, and they won by 408.

The pavilion at Sydney, with West Indian batsmen leaving the field in 1975–76.

1 BRISBANE   Match Drawn

Australia 268 (B M Laird 92, G S Chappell 74, J Garner 4–55) and 448–6 dec (K J Hughes 130, G S Chappell 124, B M Laird 75)

West Indies 441 (I V A Richards 140, J Garner 60, L G Rowe 50, D K Lillee 4–104) and 40–3

2 MELBOURNE   West Indies won by 10 wkts

Australia 156 (M A Holding 4–40) and 259 (K J Hughes 70, B M Laird 69)

West Indies 397 (I V A Richards 96, A M E Roberts 54, G Dymock 4–106) and 22–0

3 ADELAIDE   West Indies won by 408 runs

West Indies 328 (C H Lloyd 121, I V A Richards 76, D K Lillee 5–78) and 448 (A I Kallicharran 106, C G Greenidge 76, I V A Richards 74, G Dymock 5–104)

Australia 203 (A R Border 54, B M Laird 52, C E H Croft 4–57) and 165 (M A Holding 4–40)

1979–80 Averages

Batting	I	No	Runs	HS	Avge
I.V.A. Richards (WI)	4	0	386	140	96.50
C.H. Lloyd (WI)	3	0	201	121	67.00
B.M. Laird (A)	6	0	340	92	56.66
A.I. Kallicharran (WI)	5	1	202	106	50.50
K.J. Hughes (A)	6	1	252	130*	50.40
G.S. Chappell (A)	6	0	270	124	45.00

Bowling	O	M	Runs	W	Avge	BB
J. Garner (WI)	127.4	34	301	14	21.50	4–55
M.A. Holding (WI)	111	24	319	14	22.78	4–40
C.E.H. Croft (WI)	121.3	20	378	16	23.62	4–57
G. Dymock (A)	92.5	16	289	11	26.27	5–104
A.M.E. Roberts (WI)	112	20	296	11	26.90	5–78

1981–82: Fast bowlers dominate evenly fought series

Lloyd's post-WSC West Indians were on a 15-Test unbeaten run when they arrived in Australia for a three-match series in 1981–82 against Greg Chappell's team.

At Melbourne, Australia's first four men scored only 11, but Hughes made 100 not out and Australia reached 198 (Holding 5–45). The West Indian innings was remarkably similar, the first four men getting only four, but the side reached 201 (Lillee 7–83). Lillee's haul took him past Gibbs' 309 Test wickets and established a new world record. Australia's second-innings 222 (Holding 6–62) did not seem enough, but West Indies could score only 161 and Australia won by 58, stopping West Indies' run.

Gomes scored a century at Sydney and West Indies led by 117 when Holding took five for 64 in Australia's 267. B. Yardley took the last seven wickets in West Indies' second innings, and Australia had to score 374 for the rubber. Chappell's duck persuaded them not to try, and Dyson batted 377 minutes for 127 not out to save the game.

West Indies, needing to win at Adelaide, put Australia in and Holding and Roberts soon had them 17 for four. There was a recovery, but only to 238 all out. Gomes held the West Indians together with 124 not out, the score reaching 389 (Yardley 5–132). The Australians suffered a few injuries during the match, but Border fought hard to save the game with 126, which helped set West Indies 236 to win. They won by five wickets with 17 balls to spare to retain the Frank Worrell Trophy.

1981–82   11th Series   Aus 1, WI 1, Drawn 1
1 MELBOURNE   Australia won by 58 runs
Australia 198 (K J Hughes 100, M A Holding 5–45) and 222 (A R Border 66, B M Laird 64, M A Holding 6–62)
West Indies 201 (H A Gomes 55, D K Lillee 7–83) and 161 (B Yardley 4–38)
2 SYDNEY   Match Drawn
West Indies 384 (H A Gomes 126, C G Greenidge 66, D K Lillee 4–119) and 255 (C H Lloyd 57, D L Haynes 51, B Yardley 7–98)
Australia 267 (G M Wood 63, A R Border 53, M A Holding 5–64) and 200–4 (J Dyson 127)
3 SYDNEY   West Indies won by 5 wkts
Australia 238 (A R Border 78, G S Chappell 61, M A Holding 5–72, A M E Roberts 4–43) and 386 (A R Border 126, K J Hughes 84, B M Laird 78, J Garner 5–56)
West Indies 389 (H A Gomes 124, C H Lloyd 53, P J Dujon 51, B Yardley 5–132, J R Thomson 4–112) and 239–5 (C H Lloyd 77, C G Greenidge 52, I V A Richards 50)

1981–82 Averages

Batting	I	No	Runs	HS	Avge
H.A. Gomes (WI)	6	1	393	126	78.60
A.R. Border (A)	6	1	336	126	67.20
C.H. Lloyd (WI)	6	1	275	77*	55.00
P.J.L. Dujon (WI)	6	1	227	51	45.40
K.J. Hughes (A)	6	1	226	100*	45.20
B.M. Laird (A)	6	0	200	78	33.33

Bowling	O	M	Runs	W	Avge	BB
M.A. Holding (WI)	140.3	37	344	24	14.33	6–62
D.K. Lillee (A)	121.3	26	317	16	19.81	7–83
B. Yardley (A)	142.5	28	446	20	22.30	7–98
J. Garner (WI)	122	37	275	12	22.91	5–56

1983–84: 'Innings victory' for West Indies in one-sided series

Hughes led Australia in the West Indies in 1983–84 against a strong home side still captained by Lloyd.

At Georgetown the fast Garner (6–75) and off-spinner R.A. Harper (4–56) shared the wickets as Australia made 279, of which Hogg scored 52 at number eleven. Australia's score was enough for a first-innings lead as West Indies made only 230. Hughes declared the second innings at 273 for nine, setting West Indies 323 in 260 minutes. Greenidge and Haynes made centuries and put on 250 for none, at which score the chase was called off. Australia bowled their overs at a slow rate, West Indies having refused a request for a minimum 90 per day.

Garner again struck early at Port-of-Spain after Australia had been put in by Richards, deputizing for the injured Lloyd. Australia were 85 for five before Border (98 not out) got them to 255 (Garner 6–60). West Indies made 468 for eight declared, Dujon scoring 130. Australia saved the game with another long innings by Border of 100 not out. He batted 634 minutes in the match, unbeaten.

Davidson, Alan Keith
Davidson was born in Gosford, NSW, on 14 June 1929. He made his debut for his state as an all-rounder in 1949–50. A middle to lower left-hand batsman, his main value was as a left-arm fast-medium bowler. He was also a brilliant fielder. He made his first Test appearance in England in 1953. In 44 Tests he scored 1,328 runs, average 24.59, and took 186 wickets, average 20.53.

Alderman, the last man, stayed with him for the last 104 minutes to make certain of the draw.

Lloyd himself put Australia in at Bridgetown, but Australia scored 429, W.B. Phillips getting 120 at number eight. Haynes (145) and R.B. Richardson (131) took West Indies to 277 before the second wicket fell. Late wickets for Hogg (6–77) kept them to 509 and a lead of 80. With the pitch deteriorating, Marshall and Holding ran through Australia for 97 and West Indies took a lead in the rubber.

At St John's, Antigua, after Australia had been dismissed for 262, the crowd was delighted to see two Antiguans, Richardson (154) and Richards (178) make a series record by adding 308 for the third wicket. Australia's second-innings 200 (Garner 5–63) was not enough to avoid an innings defeat, West Indies retaining the Frank Worrell Trophy.

Australia were put in and out again for 199 at Kingston. Marshall and Garner were allowed too many bouncers for the Au-

stralians' liking, and Hogg made the point by bowling 12 in two overs to West Indies openers. However they put on 162, Greenidge (127) leading the way. West Indies made 305, dismissed Australia for 160 and won by ten wickets.

West Indies' easy 3–0 win was notable for the fact that they did not lose a second innings wicket in all five matches.

1983–84   12th Series   WI 3, Aus 0, Drawn 2
1 GEORGETOWN   Match Drawn
Australia 279 (K C Wessels 78, R M Hogg 52, J Garner 6–75, R A Harper 4–56) and 273–9 dec (W B Phillips 76, A R Border 54)
West Indies 230 (D L Haynes 60, R L Hogan 4–56) and 250–0 (C G Greenidge 120, D L Haynes 103)
2 PORT OF SPAIN   Match Drawn
Australia 255 (A R Border 98, J Garner 6–60) and 299–9 (A R Border 100)
West Indies 468–8 dec (P J Dujon 130, A L Logie 97, I V A Richards 76, D L Haynes 53)
3 BRIDGETOWN   West Indies won by 10 wkts
Australia 429 (W B Phillips 120, G M Wood 68, G M Ritchie 57) and 97 (M D Marshall 5–42, M A Holding 4–24)
West Indies 509 (D L Haynes 145, R B Richardson 131, C H Lloyd 76, C G Greenidge 64, R M Hogg 6–77) and 21–0

4 ST JOHN'S **West Indies won by an innings and 36 runs**

Australia 262 (A R Border 98, D W Hookes 51) and 200 (J Garner 5–63)

West Indies 498 (I V A Richards 178, R B Richardson 154, C G Rackemann 5–161)

5 KINGSTON **West Indies won by 10 wkts**

Australia 199 and 160 (S B Smith 60, M D Marshall 5–51)

West Indies 305 (C G Greenidge 127, D L Haynes 60, G N Maguire 4–57) and 55–0

1983–84 Averages

Batting	I	No	Runs	HS	Avge
D.L. Haynes (WI)	8	3	468	145	93.60
R.B. Richardson (WI)	5	1	327	154	81.75
C.G. Greenidge (WI)	8	3	393	127	78.60
A.R. Border (A)	10	3	521	100*	74.42
I.V.A. Richards (WI)	5	0	270	178	54.00
W.B. Phillips (A)	10	0	258	120	25.80

Bowling	O	M	Runs	W	Avge	BB
J. Garner (WI)	208.5	53	523	31	16.87	6–60
M.A. Holding (WI)	101.5	20	245	13	18.84	4–24
M.D. Marshall (WI)	158.5	24	480	21	22.85	5–42
G.F. Lawson (A)	170	22	638	12	53.16	3–59

1984–85: West Indies win series but their unbeaten run is finally ended

Lloyd, who kept threatening to retire, was still captain in Australia in 1984–85. Having beaten England 5–0 in 1984, West Indies were thought invincible.

Hughes put them in at Perth, but West Indies recovered from a middling start to 416, thanks to Dujon (139) and Gomes (127). Alderman took six for 128. West Indian power was evident as Australia crashed to 78, Holding taking six for 21. Australia got 228 following on, but lost by an innings.

Australia batted first at Brisbane, but the quick bowlers got them out for 175. Richardson (138) and Lloyd (114) helped West Indies to 424. In Australia's second innings, Lawson twice escaped dismissal

after treading on his stumps. West Indies needed only 23, but lost two wickets getting them – the first second-innings wickets West Indies had lost to Australia in seven Tests. Hughes resigned in tears as Australia's captain after the match. Cricketing politics had apparently squeezed him out.

Border took over as captain at Adelaide, Hughes remaining in the team. West Indies made 356 in a patchy innings. Australia's 284 was not enough. Lloyd declared at 292 for seven with Gomes 120 not out, leaving Australia 365 to win. Marshall completed ten wickets in a Test for the first time and West Indies won by 191 runs.

Richards rescued West Indies with 208 at Melbourne, being last out at 479. Australia's last pair saved the follow-on. Lloyd declared on the last day at 186 for five, leaving Australia 370 to win. During the West Indian innings Lawson, who had annoyed several West Indians, was again in trouble. He was finally fined for his behaviour and language. The 15 minutes Lloyd batted on the last day possibly cost him the match. Australia held out at 198 for eight, Hilditch getting 113. The draw ended a West Indies sequence of eleven wins.

At Sydney, Australia's local spinners, M.J. Bennett and R.G. Holland persuaded Border to bat first. Australia got off to a good start and made 471 for nine declared (Wessels 173). Holland (10 wickets in the match) and Bennett then bowled West Indies to defeat by an innings and 55 runs. There was more abusive language from players on both sides, a sad end to a West Indies run of 27 unbeaten Tests.

1984–85 13th Series WI 3, Aus 1, Drawn 1

1 PERTH **West Indies won by an innings and 112 runs**

West Indies 416 (P J L Dujon 129, H A Gomes 127, D L Haynes 56, T M Alderman 6–128, R M Hogg 4–101)

Australia 76 (M A Holding 6–21) and 228 (G M Wood 56, M D Marshall 4–68)

2 BRISBANE **West Indies won by 8 wkts**

Australia 175 (J Garner 4–67) and 271 (K C Wessels 61, W B Phillips 54, D C Boon 51, M D Marshall 5–82, M A Holding 4–92)

West Indies 424 (R B Robinson 138, C H Lloyd 114, M D Marshall 57, G F Lawson 5–116) and 26–2

3 ADELAIDE **West Indies won by 191 runs**

West Indies 356 (C G Greenidge 95, C H Lloyd 78, P J L Dujon 77, H A Gomes 60, G F Lawson 8–112) and 292–7 dec (H A Gomes 120, D L Haynes 50)

Australia 284 (K C Wessels 98, M D Marshall 5–96) and 173 (K C Wessels 70, M D Marshall 5–38, R A Harper 4–43)

4 MELBOURNE **Match Drawn**

West Indies 479 (I V A Richards 208, H A Gomes 68, M D Marshall 55, R B Richardson 51) and 186–5 dec (D L Haynes 63)

Australia 296 (K C Wessels 90, A M J Hilditch 70, M D Marshall 5–86) and 198–8 (A M J Hilditch 113)

5 SYDNEY **Australia won by an innings and 55 runs**

Australia 471–9 dec (K C Wessels 173, A R Border 69)

West Indies 163 (R G Holland 6–54) and 253 (C H Lloyd 72, I V A Richards 58, R G Holland 4–90)

1984–85 Averages

Batting	I	No	Runs	HS	Avge
H.A. Gomes (WI)	9	2	451	127	64.42
K.C. Wessels (A)	9	0	505	173	56.11
C.H. Lloyd (WI)	8	1	356	114	50.85
P.J.L. Dujon (WI)	8	1	341	139	48.71
I.V.A. Richards (WI)	9	1	342	208	42.75

Bowling	O	M	Runs	W	Avge	BB
M.A. Holding (WI)	88.1	20	249	15	16.60	6–21
M.D. Marshall (WI)	215.2	45	554	28	19.78	5–38
G.F. Lawson (A)	194.4	39	589	23	25.60	8–112
R.G. Holland (A)	130.3	26	404	14	28.85	6–54
J. Garner (WI)	177.4	33	566	19	29.78	4–67
C.A. Walsh (WI)	146.2	29	432	13	33.23	3–55

South Africa v New Zealand

1931–32: South Africa win first two Tests

The first Test match between South Africa and New Zealand took place when H.B. Cameron's tourists to Australia in 1931–32 proceeded to New Zealand for two Tests against a side led by M.L. Page.

The first was at Christchurch, and marked the last Test of the great South African H.W. Taylor. New Zealand batted and made 293. Both South African openers, J.A.J. Christy and B. Mitchell, made centuries and New Zealand eventually needed 158 to avoid an innings defeat. They failed to get them by 12 runs.

At Wellington, New Zealand made 364, with H.G. Vivian scoring his only Test century. At 19 years 121 days he is New Zealand's youngest centurion. South Africa led by 46, X.C. Balaskas getting his only Test century, and won by eight wickets.

1931–32 1st Series SA 2, NZ 0

1 CHRISTCHURCH **South Africa won by an innings and 12 runs**

New Zealand 293 (F T Badcock 64, A W Roberts 54, Q McMillan 4–61) and 146 (G L Weir 74, Q McMillan 5–66)

South Africa 451 (B Mitchell 113, J A J Christy 103, E L Dalton 82, D P B Morkel 51)

2 WELLINGTON **South Africa won by 8 wkts**

New Zealand 364 (H G Vivian 100, C S Dempster 64, F T Badcock 53, I B Cromb 51, Q McMillan 5–125) and 193 (H G Vivian 73, N A Quinn 4–37)

South Africa 410 (X C Balaskas 122, K G Viljoen 81, J A J Christy 62, H G Vivian 4–48) and 150–2 (B Mitchell 53, J A J Christy 53)

1952–53: McGlew sticks to the wicket

Jack Cheetham's side which surprised Australia were next to tour New Zealand, who were led by W.M. Wallace.

D.J. McGlew played a long innings of 255 not out for South Africa and with A.R.A. Murray he added a new world record for the seventh wicket of 246. With New Zealand being dismissed twice for 172, McGlew became the second player to be on the field throughout a completed Test match.

On a difficult Auckland pitch Endean made 116 of South Africa's 377. When New Zealand avoided the follow-on, Cheetham was content to allow the match to peter out to a draw.

1952–53 2nd Series SA 1, NZ 0, Drawn 1

1 WELLINGTON **South Africa won by an innings and 180 runs**

South Africa 524–8 dec (D J McGlew 255, A R A Murray 109, R W Blair 4–98)

New Zealand 172 (B Sutcliffe 62) and 172 (J C Watkins 4–22)

2 AUCKLAND **Match Drawn**

South Africa 377 (W R Endean 116, J H B Waite 72, J E Cheetham 54) and 200–5 dec (D J McGlew 50)

New Zealand 245 (H J Tayfield 5–62) and 31–2

1953–54: Adcock and Tayfield too good for brave New Zealanders

The following season New Zealand, under G.O. Rabone, toured South Africa for a five-match series.

South Africa batted at Durban, and amid dropped catches McLean made 101 and Cheetham declared at 437 for nine. New Zealand were made to follow-on and, despite two fine defensive innings by Rabone (107 and 68), lost by an innings, with Tayfield (nine for 97 in the match) being the best bowler.

At Johannesburg more missed catches allowed South Africa to get 271. In a savage spell of fast bowling in a fiery pitch, Adcock, in his second Test, bowled Chapple and Poore off their chests and sent Sutcliffe and Miller to hospital. Sutcliffe, his head bandaged, returned at 81 for six to play one of cricket's most defiant innings. He hit 80 not out of the last 106, including seven sixes and four fours. R.W. Blair, who on the day before Christmas day had learned of the death of his fiancée in a train crash, helped him add 33 for the last wicket, the crowd standing in silence as he walked to the wicket. Inspired by this bravery, New Zealand dismissed South Africa for 148, but sadly there was no fairy-tale ending. Out for 100, they lost by 132. Adcock and D.E.J.

Ironside, on his debut, had eight wickets each.

At Cape Town, New Zealand made 505, Reid scoring 135 and the 19-year-old Beck 99, and with Rabone taking six for 68 forced South Africa to follow on, but the match was easily drawn.

With Rabone injured, Sutcliffe captained New Zealand in the last two Tests, putting South Africa in at Johannesburg. They made 243, and the 'dismissed' New Zealand registered a nine-wicket win with Adcock getting five second-innings wickets.

At Port Elizabeth, after three fairly level innings, South Africa needed 212 in 225 minutes to win, and scoring faster than at any time in the series, won with 40 minutes to spare for a 4–0 series victory.

1953–54   3rd Series   SA 4, NZ 0, Drawn 1

1 DURBAN   **South Africa won by an innings and 58 runs**
South Africa 437–9 dec (R A McLean 101, D J McGlew 84, C B van Ryneveld 68)
New Zealand 230 (G O Rabone 107, H J Tayfield 6–62) and 149 (G O Rabone 68)

2 JOHANNESBURG   **South Africa won by 132 runs**
South Africa 271 (W R Endean 93, C B van Ryneveld 65) and 148 (J R Reid 4–34, A R MacGibbon 4–62)
New Zealand 187 (B Sutcliffe 80, D E J Ironside 5–51) and 100 (N A T Adcock 5–43)

3 CAPE TOWN   **Match Drawn**
New Zealand 505 (J R Reid 135, J E F Beck 99, M E Chapple 76, B Sutcliffe 66, G O Rabone 56, D E J Ironside 4–117)
South Africa 326 (J E Cheetham 89, D J McGlew 86, G O Rabone 6–68, A R MacGibbon 4–71) and 159–3 (R J Westcott 62)

4 JOHANNESBURG   **South Africa won by 9 wkts**
South Africa 243 (D J McGlew 61, J H B Waite 52) and 25–1
New Zealand 79 (H J Tayfield 6–13) and 188 (N A T Adcock 5–45)

5 PORT ELIZABETH   **South Africa won by 5 wkts**
New Zealand 226 (J C Watkins 4–34, N A T Adcock 4–86) and 222 (J R Reid 73, B Sutcliffe 52, C B van Ryneveld 4–67)
South Africa 237 (J R Reid 4–51) and 215–5 (W R Endean 87)

1955–56 Averages					
Batting	I	No	Runs	HS	Avge
G.O. Rabone (NZ)	5	0	254	107	50.80
D.J. McGlew (SA)	9	1	351	86	43.87
W.R. Endean (SA)	8	1	293	93	41.85
B. Sutcliffe (NZ)	9	1	305	80*	38.12
J.R. Reid (NZ)	9	0	263	135	29.22

Bowling	O	M	Runs	W	Avge	BB
H.J. Tayfield (SA)	192.6	80	377	21	17.95	6–13
D.E.J. Ironside (SA)	123.1	41	275	15	18.33	5–51
N.A.T. Adcock (SA)	174.3	27	485	24	20.20	5–43
A.R. MacGibbon (NZ)	170.1	36	454	22	20.63	4–62
J.R. Reid (NZ)	144	39	384	12	32.00	4–34

1961–62: New Zealand win their first two overseas Tests

J.R. Reid led New Zealand to South Africa in 1961–62, to meet a team led by McGlew which in the first Test at Durban had seven debutants, including E.J. Barlow, K.C. Bland and P.M. Pollock. McGlew carried his bat for 127 not out in a total of 292, which with Pollock's fast bowling earned a win by 30 runs. Pollock took nine wickets, his six for 38 in the second innings remaining his best Test analysis.

Rain, which prevented much play on the first day, ensured a draw at Johannesburg. J.H.B. Waite made a century, and G.B. Lawrence, in his second Test, took eight for 53, the best analysis of a South African fast bowler.

New Zealand made 385 at Cape Town, thanks to 101 from P.G.Z. Harris, and earned a lead of 195, allowing a second-innings declaration and a win by 72 runs.

The most successful bowler in the match was South Africa's S.F. Burke, who took 11 wickets on his debut, and was dropped for the rest of the series on the return of Adcock from injury. He played only one more Test.

On a fast wicket at Johannesburg, South Africa's fast bowlers removed New Zealand for 164, and then McGlew (120) laid the foundations of a South African score of 464, leading to an innings victory. Only Reid mastered the fast bowling, of which Lawrence took nine wickets. Reid was out to a blinding catch by Bland for 60 in the first innings, and scored 142 out of 249 in the second.

At Port Elizabeth, P.T. Barton scored a century in New Zealand's 249, and all the visiting bowlers did well to earn a lead of 85. They set South Africa 314 to win, and got them out for 273 to draw what was, for them, an excellent series.

1961–62   4th Series   SA 2, NZ 2, Drawn 1

1 DURBAN   **South Africa won by 30 runs**
South Africa 292 (D J McGlew 127, R A McLean 63, J C Alabaster 4–59) and 149 (J H B Waite 63)
New Zealand 245 (P G Z Harris 74, P T Barton 54, K A Walter 4–63) and 166 (S N McGregor 55, P M Pollock 6–38)

2 JOHANNESBURG   **Match Drawn**
South Africa 322 (J H B Waite 101, M K Elgie 56, F J Cameron 5–83) and 178–6 dec (R C Motz 4–68)
New Zealand 223 (G T Dowling 74, G B Lawrence 8–53) and 165–4 (J R Reid 75, G T Dowling 58)

---

3 CAPE TOWN   **New Zealand won by 72 runs**
New Zealand 385 (P G Z Harris 101, J R Reid 92, M E Chapple 69, S N McGregor 68, S F Burke 6–128) and 212–9 (A E Dick 50, S F Burke 5–68)
South Africa 190 (E J Barlow 51, F J Cameron 5–48, J C Alabaster 4–61) and 335 (R A McLean 113, D J McGlew 63, J C Alabaster 4–119)

4 JOHANNESBURG   **South Africa won by an innings and 51 runs**
New Zealand 164 (J R Reid 60, G B Lawrence 5–52) and 249 (J R Reid 142, G B Lawrence 4–57)
South Africa 464 (D J McGlew 120, R A McLean 78, E J Barlow 67;

5 PORT ELIZABETH   **New Zealand won by 40 runs**
New Zealand 275 (P T Barton 109) and 228 (G T Dowling 78, J R Reid 69, G B Lawrence 4–85)
South Africa 190 and 273 (E J Barlow 59, P M Pollock 54, J R Reid 4–44)

1961–62 Averages					
Batting	I	No	Runs	HS	Avge
D.J. McGlew (SA)	9	2	426	127*	60.85
J.R. Reid (NZ)	10	1	546	142	60.64
R.A. McLean (SA)	9	0	356	113	39.55
E.J. Barlow (SA)	9	0	330	67	36.66
P.J.Z. Harris (NZ)	10	1	284	101	31.55
J.H.B. Waite (SA)	9	0	263	101	29.22

Bowling	O	M	Runs	W	Avge	BB
P.M. Pollock (SA)	128.4	35	299	17	17.58	6–38
G.B. Lawrence (SA)	222.2	61	512	28	18.28	8–53
F.J. Cameron (NZ)	201.2	54	493	20	24.65	5–48
R.C. Motz (NZ)	182.2	41	505	19	26.57	4–68
J.C. Alabaster (NZ)	224.3	61	617	22	28.04	4–59

Dick Motz in action. He bowled well in South Africa in 1961–62 when New Zealand won two Tests and squared the rubber.

1963–64: The last series drawn

Goddard and Reid were the captains in the last rubber between the countries. The first Test at Wellington was threatened by anti-*apartheid* demonstrators, who damaged the pitch, but it started on time. South Africa batted and were on top throughout, but New Zealand held on for a draw with four wickets standing.

At Dunedin, in miserable conditions which prevented much play on the first two days, bowlers were in control, with Pithey and Reid each gettint six wickets in an innings. South Africa had 27 minutes to score 65 to win, but could not manag it.

At Auckland South Africa's 371 was good enough for a lead of 108, despite Sinclair's 138. P.J. Partridge took six for 86 for South Africa. South Africa set New Zealand 309 in 313 minutes and they were 191 for eight when rain curtailed play by 13 minutes. South Africa drew a series they might have won 3–0.

1963–64 5th Series Drawn 3
1 WELLINGTON **Match Drawn**
South Africa 302 and 218–2 dec (E J Barlow 92)
New Zealand 253 (M E Chapple 59, P M Pollock 6–47) and 138–6 (S G Gedye 52)
2 DUNEDIN **Match Drawn**
New Zealand 149 (B W Sinclair 52, J T Partridge 4–51) and 138 (D B Pithey 6–58)
South Africa 223 (T L Goddard 63, J R Reid 6–60) and 42–3
3 AUCKLAND **Match Drawn**
South Africa 371 (K C Bland 83, T L Goddard 73, E J Barlow 61, R W Blair 4–85) and 200–5 dec (E J Barlow 58)
New Zealand 263 (B W Sinclair 138, S N McGregor 62, J T Partridge 6–86) and 191–8 (S G Gedye 55, T L Goddard 4–18)

1963–64 Averages

Batting	I	No	Runs	HS	Avge
K. C. Bland (SA)	6	3	207	83	69.00
E. J. Barlow (SA)	6	0	295	92	49.16
T. L. Goddard (SA)	5	0	233	73	46.60
B. W. Sinclair (NZ)	6	0	264	138	44.00

Bowling	O	M	Runs	W	Avge	BB
P. M. Pollock (SA)	120	43	258	15	17.20	6–47
D. B. Pithey (SA)	114	42	224	12	18.66	6–58
J. T. Partridge (SA)	162	68	247	13	19.00	6–86
J. R. Reid (NZ)	128.4	49	278	12	23.16	6–60
R. W. Blair (NZ)	115	23	326	12	27.16	4–85

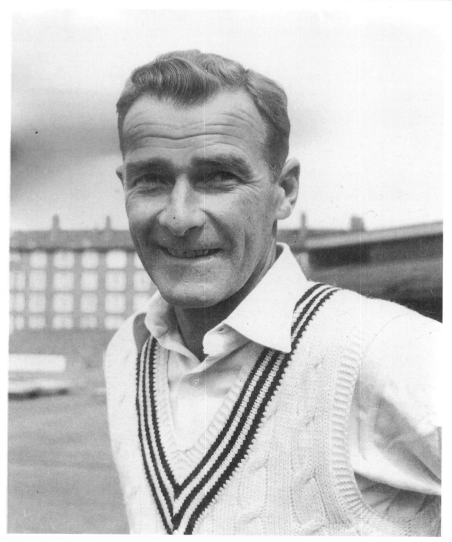

Sutcliffe, Bert
Sutcliffe was born on 17 November 1923 at Auckland and played for Auckland from 1941–42. He also played for Otago and Northern Districts. An excellent opening left-hand batsman, he made his Test debut for New Zealand in 1946–47. He was his country's best player of the 1950s and their batting fortunes often depended upon him. In 42 Tests he scored 2,727 runs, average 40.10. On retiring he became a well-respected coach.

Australia v New Zealand

1945–46: Australia win first Test easily

It is remarkable that Australia and New Zealand did not play each other in Test cricket until 1945–46. Even then the match played at Wellington was granted Test status by the ICC only in retrospect, in 1948.

The side Australia took, under W.A. Brown, was at full strength, except for Bradman, whose health made future cricket uncertain for him. This was the first Test after the Second World War and introduced such Australian stalwarts as I.W. Johnson, R.R. Lindwall, K.R. Miller and D. Tallon.

W.A. Hadlee, leading New Zealand, decided to bat on a wet pitch, and O'Reilly and Toshack dismissed them for 42. Cowie took six for 40 for New Zealand, but Australia declared at 199 for eight, and in getting New Zealand out again for 54, won by an innings and inflicted on New Zealand their lowest Test aggregate.

1945–46 1st Series Aus 1, NZ 0
1 WELLINGTON **Australia won by an innings and 103 runs**
New Zealand 42 (W J O'Reilly 5–14, E R H Toshack 4–12) and 54
Australia 199–8 dec (W A Brown 67, S G Barnes 54, J Cowie 6–40)

1973–74: New Zealand tour Australia and are foiled by rain

Although New Zealand toured Australia in 1967–68, and Australia toured New Zealand in 1969–70, it was not until 1973–74 that Tests were resumed. New Zealand under B.E. Congdon played three Tests against Ian Chappell's side in Australia.

Chappell batted at Melbourne, and Stackpole, dropped in the first over, made 122 in 462 for eight declared. New Zealand, out for 237, were made to follow on and fell 25 short of making Australia bat again.

Australia put New Zealand in at Sydney, and they made 312, with Parker scoring 108. Splendid bowling by the Hadlee brothers (R.J. in particular) got Australia out for 162. The third day's play was lost and New Zealand on the fourth declared at 305 for nine, with Morrison making 117, setting Australia 456 to win. They were 30 for two at the end of the day, but the last day was washed out with New Zealand poised for a morale-boosting win.

The third Test was similar to the first, with Marsh's 132 helping Australia to 477 (O'Sullivan 5–148). New Zealand followed on at 218, and failed by 57 to avoid the innings defeat, Dymock and O'Keeffe getting most wickets.

1973–74 2nd Series Aus 2, NZ 0, Drawn 1
1 MELBOURNE **Australia won by an innings and 25 runs**
Australia 462–8 dec (K R Stackpole 122, K D Walters 79, G S Chappell 60, I M Chappell 54, G J Gilmour 52, D R Hadlee 4–102)
New Zealand 237 (K J Wadsworth 80, G J Gilmour 4–75) and 200 (A A Mallett 4–63)

2 SYDNEY   Match drawn
New Zealand 312 (J M Parker 108, K J Wadsworth 54, K D Walters 4–39) and 305–9 dec (J F M Morrison 117, B F Hastings 83)
Australia 162 (R J Hadlee 4–33) and 30–2
3 ADELAIDE   Australia won by an innings and 57 runs
Australia 477 (R W Marsh 132, K D Walters 94, K J O'Keeffe 85, D R O'Sullivan 5–148)
New Zealand 218 and 203 (B E Congdon 71, G Dymock 5–58)

1973–74 Averages					
Batting	I	No	Runs	HS	Avge
K.D. Walters (A)	3	0	214	94	71.33
J.F.M. Morrison (NZ)	6	0	249	117	38.33
K.J. Wadsworth (NZ)	6	0	230	80	38.33
Bowling	O	M	Runs	W	Avge	BB
K.J. O'Keeffe (A)	114.1	39	255	11	23.18	3–51
A.A. Mallett (A)	106.5	27	297	10	29.70	4–63

Doug Walters, who topped the 1973–74 averages in Australia.

1973–74: New Zealand get first win over Australia in drawn series

A month after the tour in Australia, the teams met again for a three-match series in New Zealand.

Australia batted at Wellington and made 511 for six declared, the third-wicket partnership of Greg Chappell (247) and Ian Chappell (145) adding 264, a record stand for matches between the countries. New Zealand, however, found batting as easy, Congdon (132) and Hastings (101) adding 229 for the fourth wicket. At close Australia were 460 for eight, with the Chappells having scored second centuries. This was the first time in Tests, and the second in first-class cricket, that brothers had each scored a century in each innings. Greg Chappell's aggregate of 380 (247 and 133) established a new Test record.

At Christchurch, Congdon put Australia in and dismissed them for 223. Turner made 101 and New Zealand took a lead of 32. The Hadlee brothers shared eight wickets in removing Australia again for 259, leaving New Zealand 228 to win. Turner completed a magnificent match by scoring 110 not out, steering New Zealand to a five-wicket win, their first against Australia.

A record crowd at Auckland saw Walters score 104 not out and rescue Australia, who were put in, from 37 for four to 221 all out, Collinge and Congdon getting nine wickets between them. Gilmour and Mallett did the same for Australia, and New Zealand were out for 112. Opener Redpath carried his bat

throughout Australia's second innings of 346 for 159 not out, and New Zealand collapsed for 158 after the openers had put on 107.

1973–74   3rd Series   Aus 1, NZ 1, Drawn 1
1 WELLINGTON   Match Drawn
Australia 511–6 dec (G S Chappell 247, I M Chappell 145) and 460–8 (G S Chappell 133, I M Chappell 121, I R Redpath 93)
New Zealand 484 (B E Congdon 132, B F Hastings 101, G M Turner 79, J F M Morrison 66)
2 CHRISTCHURCH   New Zealand won by 5 wkts
Australia 223 (I R Redpath 71) and 259 (K D Walters 65, I R Redpath 58, I C Davis 50, R J Hadlee 4–71, D R Hadlee 4–75)
New Zealand 255 (G M Turner 101, M H N Walter 4–60) and 230–5 (G M Turner 110)
3 AUCKLAND   Australia won by 297 runs
Australia 221 (K D Walters 104, R O Collinge 5–82, B E Congdon 4–46) and 346 (I R Redpath 159, R O Collinge 4–84)
New Zealand 112 (G J Gilmour 5–64, A A Mallett 4–22) and 158 (G M Turner 72, M H N Walker 4–39)

1973–74 Averages					
Batting	I	No	Runs	HS	Avge
G.M. Turner (NZ)	5	1	403	110*	100.75
G.S. Chappell (A)	6	1	449	247*	89.90
I.R. Redpath (A)	6	1	413	159*	82.60
I.M. Chappell (A)	6	0	359	145	59.83
K.D. Walters (A)	6	1	220	104*	44.00
Bowling	O	M	Runs	W	Avge	BB
M.H.N. Walker (A)	117.6	38	267	14	19.07	4–39
R.J. Hadlee (NZ)	52	6	229	10	22.90	4–71
B.E. Congdon (NZ)	74.6	8	285	12	23.75	4–46
R.O. Collinge (NZ)	107.5	14	436	17	25.65	5–82

1976–77: Australia win two-match series 1–0

Greg Chappell and Glen Turner were captains when Australia next visited New Zealand. At Christchurch, New Zealand put Australia in as on the last tour, but this time Walters made his highest Test score of 250, and with Gilmour (101) helping him add 217 for the seventh wicket, Australia made 552. New Zealand just avoided the follow-on, and when Australia declared they were set 350 to win in 390 minutes. Congdon (107 not out) and D.R. Hadlee (8 not out) saved the match by batting for the final 52 minutes.

At Auckland, Australia put New Zealand in, and out again for 229 (Lillee 5–51). New Zealand missed catches as Australia reached 377. A defiant 81 by R.J. Hadlee could not prevent Lillee (6–72) again skittling New Zealand, Australia needing only 28 to win.

1976–77   4th Series   Aus 1, NZ 0, Drawn 1
1 CHRISTCHURCH   Match Drawn
Australia 552 (K D Walters 250, G J Gilmour 101) and 154–4 dec (R B McCosker 77)
New Zealand 357 (M G Burgess 66, H J Howarth 61, K J O'Keeffe 5–101) and 293–8 (B E Congdon 107, M H N Walker 4–65)
2 AUCKLAND   Australia won by 10 wkts
New Zealand 229 (G P Howarth 59, G N Edwards 51, D K Lillee 5–51) and 175 (R J Hadlee 81, D K Lillee 6–72)
Australia 377 (R B McCosker 84, G J Gilmour 64, G S Chappell 58, E J Chatfield 4–100) and 28–0

1980–81: Two easy wins and a draw for Australia.

G.P. Howarth's side went to Australia in 1980–81 after beating West Indies the previous season.

Greg Chappell put them in at Brisbane and they struggled to 225. Wood (111) got Australia off to a good start, Cairns (5–87) fought back, and Australia led by 80. New Zealand collapsed to Lillee (6–53) in the

second innings, only Edgar and Hadlee (both 51) showing resistance. Extras (14) was next best in a total of 142, Australia winning by ten wickets.

Chappell again put New Zealand in at Perth, and Lillee (5–63) again bowled excellently to dismiss them for 196. Hadlee (5–87) restricted Australia to a lead of 59, but New Zealand fell second time for 121, mostly to Higgs (4–25) and Australia had another easy eight-wicket win.

Australia, put in, were saved at Melbourne by Walters (107) who completed his century during a last-wicket stand of 60 in which Higgs was controversially given not out after being caught from a bouncer by medium-paced Cairns. A late call of 'no-ball' was made on the grounds of intimidation. New Zealand made 317 to trail by four, and on a wicket which both captains criticized for uneven bounce dismissed Australia for 188 (Hadlee 6–57). Needing 193, New Zealand slid from 95 for one to 101 for five before batting out time for a draw.

1980–81   5th Series   Aus 2, NZ 0, Drawn 1
1 BRISBANE   Australia won by 10 wkts
New Zealand 225 (G P Howarth 65, J M Parker 52, J D Higgs 4–59) and 142 (B A Edgar 51, R J Hadlee 51, D K Lillee 6–53)
Australia 305 (G M Wood 111, B L Cairns 5–87) and 63–0
2 PERTH   Australia won by 8 wkts
New Zealand 196 (J V Coney 71, D K Lillee 5–63) and 121 (J D Higgs 4–25)
Australia 265 (R W Marsh 91, K D Walters 55, R J Hadlee 5–87, B L Cairns 4–88) and 55–2
3 MELBOURNE   Match Drawn
Australia 321 (K D Walters 107, K J Hughes 51) and 188 (G S Chappell 78, R J Hadlee 6–57)
New Zealand 317 (G P Howarth 65, J M Parker 56, J V Coney 55, R M Hogg 4–60) and 128–6

1980–81 Averages					
Batting – Nil					
Bowling	O	M	Runs	W	Avge	BB
R.M. Hogg (A)	60.2	17	128	10	12.80	4–60
D.K. Lillee (A)	106	27	245	16	15.31	6–53
R.J. Hadlee (NZ)	147.3	35	364	19	19.15	6–57
J.D. Higgs (A)	75.1	17	227	11	20.63	4–25
L.S. Pascoe (A)	99.1	17	272	12	22.66	3–41
B.L. Cairns (NZ)	147.3	42	356	13	27.38	5–87

Turner, Glenn Maitland

Born on 26 May 1946 at Dunedin, Turner first played for Otago in 1964–65. In 1967 he also began a long career with Worcestershire. He was a very sound opening batsman, who changed his style from ultra-defensive to attractive stroke-maker. He made his Test debut in 1968–69. He was the leading New Zealand batsman of his time, and achieved many records. In Test matches he is the youngest to carry his bat through a Test innings (1969) and made the highest score by a player performing this feat (223 in 1971–72). In 41 Tests, of which he was captain in ten, he scored 2,991 runs, average 44.64.

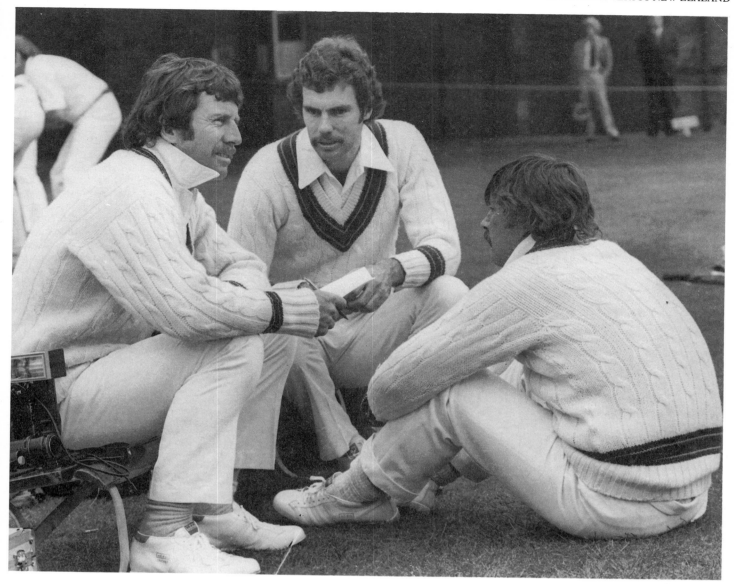

Ian Chappell, Greg Chappell and Rodney Marsh in discussion. These players were Australian stalwarts in the 1970s and 1980s.

1981–82: New Zealand's second win over Australia ties series

Next season the sides were in New Zealand. Less than ten hours play was possible in the first Test at Wellington.

At Auckland, following his normal practice, Howarth put Australia in, and with Chappell and Border run out from successive balls, got them out for 210. Edgar's 161 gave New Zealand a big lead at 387. Australia, largely thanks to Wood (100), cleared this deficit with only two out, but a spell of four for five from Hadlee (5–63) removed the later batting and New Zealand won by five wickets.

At Christchurch, 176 from Greg Chappell, who was twice dropped, spoiled Howarth's ploy of putting Australia in, despite Hadlee's six for 100. Chappell made his last 100 before lunch on the second day. New Zealand were forced to follow on 204 behind Australia's 353, and Wright's 141 in the second innings was the only delay to an Australian victory by eight wickets.

1981–82 6th Series Aus 1, NZ 1, Drawn 1

1 WELLINGTON   **Match Drawn**

New Zealand 266–7 dec (G P Howarth 58, B A Edgar 55)
Australia 85–1

2 AUCKLAND   **New Zealand won by 5 wkts**

Australia 210 (G B Troup 4–82) and 280 (G M Wood 100, R J Hadlee 6–53)
New Zealand 387 (B A Edgar 161, J M Coney 73, G P Howarth 56, B Yardley 4–142) and 109–5

3 CHRISTCHURCH   **Australia won by 8 wkts**

Australia 353 (G S Chappell 176, G M Wood 64, R J Hadlee 6–100) and 63–2
New Zealand 149 (J R Thomson 4–51) and 272 (J G Wright 141, B Yardley 4–80)

1981–82 Averages					
Batting	I	No	Runs	HS	Avge
G.S. Chappell (Aus)	4	1	235	176	78.83
B.A. Edgar (NZ)	5	0	278	161	55.60
G.M. Wood (A)	5	0	229	100	45.80
J.G. Wright (NZ)	5	0	200	141	40.00
Bowling	O	M	Runs	W	Avge	BB
R.J. Hadlee (NZ)	91.5	25	226	14	16.14	6–100
B. Yardley (A)	113.4	41	311	13	23.92	4–80

1985–86: Hadlee's brilliant bowling wins series in Australia

J.V. Coney led a team to meet A.R. Border's Australians in 1985–86. In the first Test at Brisbane, Coney followed Howarth principles and put Australia in. An outstanding bowling performance by Hadlee removed them for 179. Hadlee's nine for 52 was the fourth best Test analysis ever. With J.F. Reid (108) and M.D. Crowe (188) consolidating with a stand of 224, New Zealand led by 374, enough for a win by an innings and 41, despite centuries by Border (152 not out) and Matthews (115). Hadlee took six for 71 to claim 15 for 123 in the match. It was New Zealand's first win in Australia.

Border took the first step to recovery by winning the toss and putting in New Zealand at Brisbane. Holland took six for 106 to get them out for 293, but New Zealand were 169 for nine before Bracewell (83 not out) and Boock (37) added 124 for the last wicket. Hadlee struck again with five for 65 when Australia batted and New Zealand led by 66. Holland took four more wickets as New Zealand were dismissed in the second innings for 193, leaving Australia 260 to get to win. Amid interruptions for rain, dropped catches and a threatened storm, Australia batted with great determination on the last day to win by four wickets and square the series.

Coney put Australia in at Perth, naturally, and with Hadlee getting five for 65 for the second match running, Australia made only 203. New Zealand got a useful lead of 96, and Hadlee, with six for 90, kept New

Zealand's fourth-innings target within bounds at 164. New Zealand got them comfortably for the loss of four wickets.

Hadlee's 33 wickets in three matches was an outstanding performance in New Zealand's first series win against Australia.

1985–86 7th Series NZ 2, Aus 1
1 BRISBANE New Zealand won by an innings and 41 runs
Australia 179 (K C Wessels 70, R J Hadlee 9–52) and 333 (A R Border 152, G R J Matthews 115, R J Hadlee 6–71)
New Zealand 553–7 dec (M D Crowe 188, J F Reid 108, R J Hadlee 54)
2 SYDNEY Australia won by 4 wkts
New Zealand 293 (J G Bracewell 83, B A Edgar 50, R G Holland 6–106) and 193 (B A Edgar 52, R G Holland 4–68)
Australia 227 (G M Ritchie 89, G R J Matthews 50, R J Hadlee 5–65) and 260–6 (D C Boon 81, W B Phillips 63)
3 PERTH New Zealand won by 6 wkts
Australia 203 (R J Hadlee 5–65) and 259 (A R Border 83, D C Boon 50, R J Hadlee 6–90)
New Zealand 299 (B A Edgar 74, M D Crowe 71, G F Lawson 4–79) and 164–4

1985–86 Averages					
Batting	I	No	Runs	HS	Avge
M.D. Crowe (NZ)	5	1	309	188	77.25
A.R. Border (A)	6	1	279	152*	55.80
B.A. Edgar (NZ)	5	0	209	74	41.80
G.R.J. Matthews (A)	6	0	247	115	41.16
Bowling	O	M	Runs	W	Avge	BB
R.J. Hadlee (NZ)	169.3	42	401	33	12.15	9–52
R.G. Holland (A)	158	51	370	15	28.46	6–106

1985–86: New Zealand beat Australia twice in one season

Later in the season of New Zealand's triumph in Australia, the sides met again in a three-match series in New Zealand.

Coney put Australia in at Wellington, but Australia prospered, Matthews making 130 in a total of 435. Coney himself was 101 not out, having added 132 with Hadlee (72 not out) when rain washed out most of the last two days. Hadlee took his 300th Test wicket in this match.

In the second Test at Christchurch, it was Border (140) who foiled Coney's ploy of putting Australia in. They made 364, with Hadlee getting seven for 116. M.D. Crowe made 137 for New Zealand, after retiring hurt at 51, and with Coney (98) kept his team in the game at 334. Border then completed a century in each innings, after rain had again had the last word and sentenced the match to a draw.

Border departed from custom at Auck-

1985–86 8th Series NZ 1, Aus 0, Drawn 2
1 WELLINGTON Match Drawn
Australia 435 (G R J Matthews 130, G M Ritchie 92, D C Boon 70)
New Zealand 379–6 (J V Coney 101, R J Hadlee 72, K R Rutherford 65)
2 CHRISTCHURCH Match Drawn
Australia 364 (A R Border 140, S R Waugh 74, R J Hadlee 7–115) and 219–7 dec (A R Border 114, J G Bracewell 4–77)
New Zealand 339 (M D Crowe 137, J V Coney 98, S R Waugh 4–56, B A Reid 4–90) and 16–1
3 AUCKLAND New Zealand won by 8 wkts
Australia 314 (G R Marsh 118, W B Phillips 62, G M Ritchie 56, J G Bracewell 4–74) and 103 (D C Boon 58, J G Bracewell 6–32)
New Zealand 258 (J V Coney 93, J G Wright 56, G R J Matthews 4–61) and 160–2 (J G Wright 59, K R Rutherford 50)

1985–86 Averages					
Batting	I	No	Runs	HS	Avge
J.V. Coney (NZ)	3	1	292	101*	146.00
A.R. Border (A)	5	1	290	140	72.50
G.M. Marsh (A)	5	0	204	118	40.80
Bowling	O	M	Runs	W	Avge	BB
J.C. Bracewell (NZ)	125.3	48	229	15	15.26	6–32
R.J. Hadlee (NZ)	157.5	36	387	16	24.18	7–116

land and batted. Opener Marsh made 118 and a respectable score of 314 looked even better when New Zealand were out for 258. On the fourth day Australia collapsed to Bracewell, who took six for 32, and were out for 103, Boon carrying his bat for 58 not out. New Zealand batted slowly and sensibly to win by eight wickets. After the umpires had consulted and given Rutherford out caught behind, he was recalled when Zoehrer indicated he had not held the catch.

1987–88: Border and Hadlee break records

After winning the Reliance World Cup in Pakistan and India in 1987, Australia entertained New Zealand to a three-match series. In the first Test at Brisbane, M.R.J. Veletta, on his debut, took a catch with his first touch of the ball. It was the fourth delivery of New Zealand's innings, and they never recovered, being all out for 186. Boon's 143 held the home side together as they reached 305, and as New Zealand could make only 212 in the second knock, Australia needed only 94 and won by nine wickets.

At Adelaide, batsmen dominated as New Zealand reached 485 for nine declared after captain Jeff Crowe had been caught by Veletta from the third ball of the match. Brother Martin made 137 and Andrew Jones made 150. Aussie skipper Border replied, however, with 205, passing on the way Greg Chappell's Australian record of 7,110 Test runs and becoming the seventh highest Test run-getter in history. Australia made 496, and the match was drawn.

New Zealand scored 317 at Melbourne, Wright making 99. There was a great deal of bad feeling between the two camps over the dismissal of New Zealand's Jones by the Australian keeper Dyer, television replays showing that the ball was not held. Australia, led by Sleep (90), recovered from 170 for six to 357. New Zealand made 285, setting Australia 247 to win. In an exciting finish they reached 227 for nine with four overs to play, and the final pair held out for a draw. Hadlee took five wickets in an innings for the 32nd time and ten in a match for the tenth time, both records, and took his total of Test wickets to 373, equalling the world record of Ian Botham.

1987–88 10th Series Aus 1, NZ 0, Drawn 2
1 BRISBANE Australia won by 9 wkts
New Zealand 186 (M D Crowe 67, C J McDermott 4–43) and 212 (D Patel 62, B A Reid 4–53)
Australia 305 (D C Boon 143, D K Morrison 4–86) and 97–2
2 ADELAIDE Match Drawn
New Zealand 485–9 dec (A H Jones 150, M D Crowe 137) and 182–7)
Australia 496 (A R Border 205, P R Sleep 62, S R Waugh 61, G C Dyer 60, R J Hadlee 5–68)
3 MELBOURNE Match Drawn
New Zealand 317 (J G Wright 99, M D Crowe 82, C J McDermott 5–97, M R Whitney 4–92) and 286 (M D Crowe 79, A I C Dodemaide 6–58)
Australia 357 (P R Sleep 90, S R Waugh 55, A I C Dodemaide 50, R J Hadlee 5–109) and 230–9 (D C Boon 54, R J Hadlee 5–67)

1987–88 Averages					
Batting	I	No	Runs	HS	Avge
A.R. Border (A)	4	0	290	205	72.50
M.D. Crowe (NZ)	6	0	396	137	66.00
A.N. Jones (NZ)	6	0	323	150	53.83
D.C. Boon (A)	5	0	237	143	47.40
J.G. Wright (NZ)	6	0	248	99	41.33
Bowling	O	M	Runs	W	Avge	BB
R.J. Hadlee (NZ)	156	44	353	18	19.61	5–61
C.J. McDermott (A)	144.1	30	426	17	25.05	5–97

New Zealand v Pakistan

1955–56: Pakistan too good in first series

New Zealand toured Pakistan and India in 1955–56 under H.B. Cave, playing their first Test match with Pakistan, led by A.H. Kardar, on matting at Karachi. They were baffled by the off-spin of Zulfiqar Ahmed (5–37), and dismissed for 164. Pakistan made 289, which was enough for an innings win, Zulfiqar's six for 42 removing New Zealand for 124 second time.

On turf at Lahore, New Zealand made 348, led by S.N. McGregor's 111. Pakistan, 111 for six, recovered to 561, through Waqar Hassan (189) and Imtiaz Ahmed, who came in at number eight and made 209, a Test record. Their stand of 308 was also a seventh-wicket record for Pakistan. New Zealand made 328 in the second innings and fought hard, Pakistan at 117 for six getting home by only four wickets with 18 minutes to spare.

Rain reduced the match at Dacca, but Hanif's century and Khan Mohammad's bowling nearly won the match for Pakistan.

1955–56 1st Series Pak 2, NZ 0, Drawn 1
1 KARACHI Match Drawn
New Zealand 164 (Zulfiqar Ahmed 5–37) and 124 (Zulfiqar Ahmed 6–42)
Pakistan 289 (Imtiaz Ahmed 64, A R MacGibbon 4–98)
2 LAHORE Pakistan won by 4 wkts
New Zealand 348 (S N McGregor 111, N S Harford 93, A R MacGibbon 61, Khan Mohammad 4–78) and 328 (J R Reid 86, N S Harford 64, Zulfiqar Ahmed 4–114)
Pakistan 561 (Imtiaz Ahmed 209, Waqar Hassan 189, A M Moir 4–114) and 117–6 (J R Reid 4–38)
3 DACCA Match Drawn
New Zealand 70 (Khan Mohammad 6–21) and 69–6
Pakistan 195–6 dec (Hanif Mohammad 103)

1955–56 Averages					
Batting	I	No	Runs	HS	Avge
Imtiaz Ahmed (P)	4	0	284	209	71.00
Waqar Hassan (P)	4	0	231	189	57.75
Bowling	O	M	Runs	W	Avge	BB
A.H. Kardar (P)	138	68	150	10	15.00	3–34
Zulfiqar Ahmed (P)	181.1	78	287	19	15.10	6–42

1964–65: Unenterprising draws in New Zealand

Pakistan under Hanif visited New Zealand to play tests for the first time after touring Australia. J.R. Reid captained New Zealand, who were put in in the first Test at Wellington after a rain-delayed start. They made 266, Asif getting five for 48, but then put Pakistan out for only 187. Reid declared at 179 for seven, setting Pakistan 259 in 188 minutes. They were 64 for six, but Asif, at number eight, saved the match.

At Auckland, Pakistan batted so slowly there were 71 maidens on the first day alone. The match was a low-scoring draw. F.J. Cameron claimed nine wickets.

It was a similar story at Christchurch, where rain interrupted play and New Zealand could not make a fourth-innings target of 314 in 243 minutes.

1964–65 2nd Series Drawn 3
1 WELLINGTON **Match Drawn**
New Zealand 266 (J R Reid 97, B W Sinclair 65, Asif Iqbal 5–48)
and 179–7 dec
Pakistan 187 (R C Motz 4–45) and 140–7 (Asif Iqbal 52)
3 AUCKLAND **Match Drawn**
Pakistan 226 (Javed Burki 63, F J Cameron 4–36, B W Yuile 4–
43) and 207 (Abdul Kadir 58, F J Cameron 5–34)
New Zealand 214 (R W Morgan 66, J R Reid 52, Asif Iqbal 5–52)
and 166–7 (G T Dowling 62, Pervez Sajjad 5–42)
3 CHRISTCHURCH **Match Drawn**
Pakistan 206 (Mohammad Ilyas 88) and 309–8 dec (Hanif
Mohammad 100, Saeed Ahmed 87)
New Zealand 202 (Asif Iqbal 4–46) and 223–5 (R W Morgan 97)

Averages
Batting	I	No	Runs	HS	Avge
J. Reid (NZ)	6	0	229	97	38.16

Bowling	O	M	Runs	W	Avge	BB
Asif Iqbal (P)	131.1	32	248	18	13.77	5–48
F.J. Cameron (NZ)	114	55	203	13	15.61	5–34
R.C. Motz (NZ)	88	31	200	10	20.00	4–45
B.W. Yuile (NZ)	149	83	243	12	20.25	4–43
Pervez Sajjad (P)	130	36	272	12	22·66	5–42
R.O. Collinge (NZ)	109.1	31	265	15	24.33	3–41

1964–65: Pakistan win 2–0 at home

Later in the season, New Zealand toured India and Pakistan. Put in at Rawalpindi, New Zealand made only 175. Pakistan scored 318 and won by an innings by dismissing New Zealand for 79, Pervez Sajjad adding to his first-innings four for 42 with four for five.

Reid asked Pakistan to bat on a rain-affected pitch at Lahore, but Hanif made 203 not out, his highest score at home. He added 217 with Majid for the sixth wicket. Sinclair scored 130 for New Zealand, adding 178 with Reid. New Zealand had the edge at the close.

Reid made 128 out of 285 at Karachi, but Saeed Ahmed replied with 172 in 307. Dismissing New Zealand a second time for 223, Pakistan needed 202 in 330 minutes, and won by eight wickets with Mohammad Ilyas getting 126.

1964–65 3rd Series Pak 2, NZ 0, Drawn 1
1 RAWALPINDI **Pakistan won by an innings and 64 runs**
New Zealand 175 (B R Taylor 76, Pervez Sajjad 4–42) and 79
(Pervez Sajjad 4–5)
Pakistan 318 (Saeed Ahmed 68, Mohammad Ilyas 56, Asif Iqbal
51)
2 LAHORE **Match Drawn**
Pakistan 385–7 dec (Hanif Mohammad 203, Majid Khan 80, F
J Cameron 4–90) and 194–8 dec
New Zealand 482–6 dec (B W Sinclair 130, J R Reid 88, G T
Dowling 83, T W Jarvis 55, R W Morgan 50)
3 KARACHI **Pakistan won by 8 wkts**
New Zealand 285 (J R Reid 128) and 223 (J R Reid 76, B E
Congdon 57, Intikhab Alam 4–39)
Pakistan 307–8 dec (Saeed Ahmed 172) and 202–2
(Mohammad Ilyas 126)

1964–65 Averages
Batting	I	No	Runs	HS	Avge
Hanif Mohammad (P)	3	1	220	203*	110.00
Saeed Ahmed (P)	5	1	286	172	71.50
J.R. Reid (NZ)	5	0	296	128	59.20
Mohammad Ilyas (P)	5	0	223	126	44.60
B.W. Sinclair (NZ)	5	0	211	130	42.20

Bowling	O	M	Runs	W	Avge	BB
Mohammad Farooq (P)	107	28	253	10	25.30	3–25

1969–70: New Zealand win their first Test series

A strong New Zealand side led by G.T. Dowling played Intikhab Alam's side in

Pakistan in 1969–70. Pakistan made 220 at Karachi (H.J. Howarth 5–80) and New Zealand passed it only through an eighth-wicket stand of 100 between B.W. Yuile (47 not out) and D.R. Hadlee (56). Mohammad Nazir took seven for 99 in his first Test. New Zealand were eventually set to score 230 in 195 minutes and made no attempt after being 11 for three. In this match Sadiq Mohammad made his debut in his brother Hanif's last Test. With Mushtaq, they provided the third instance of three brothers playing in a Test match.

At Lahore, Pakistan made only 114, and despite Pervez getting seven for 74, New Zealand led by 127. Pakistan's second-innings 208 meant a target of only 82, but New Zealand lost five wickets in getting them.

At Dacca, Turner's 110 gave New Zealand a presentable score of 273. Pakistan passed it by 17 and declared, and when New Zealand were 101 for eight looked to be about to level the rubber. But Burgess (119 not out) added 96 with Cunis and Pakistan needed a not easy 184 in 2½ hours. At 51 for four bad light stopped play, and then minor rioting led to the match being abandoned with 65 minutes left.

Sadiq Mohammad in action. He made 166 in the first Test in 1972–73.

New Zealand thus won their first Test series 40 years after their first Test.

1969–70 4th Series NZ 1, Pak 0, Drawn 2
1 KARACHI **Match Drawn**
Pakistan 220 (Sadiq Mohammad 69, H J Howarth 5–80) and
283–8 dec (Younis Ahmed 62)
New Zealand 274 (D R Hadlee 56, B A G Murray 50,
Mohammad Nazir 7–99) and 112–5 (Pervez Sajjad 5–33)
2 LAHORE **New Zealand won by 5 wkts**
Pakistan 114 and 208 (Shafqat Rana 95)
New Zealand 241 (B A G Murray 90, B F Hastings 80, Pervez
Sajjad 7–74) and 82–5
3 DACCA **Match Drawn**
New Zealand 273 (G M Turner 110, M G Burgess 59, Intikhab
Alam 5–91) and 200 (M G Burgess 119, Intikhab Alam 5–91,
Pervez Sajjad 4–60)
Pakistan 290–7 dec (Asif Iqbal 92, Shafqat Rana 65, H J
Howarth 4–85) and 51–4 (R S Cunis 4–21)

1969–70 Averages
Batting	I	No	Runs	HS	Avge
M.G. Burgess (NZ)	6	2	273	119*	68.25

Bowling	O	M	Runs	W	Avge	BB
Pervez Sajjad (P)	191	70	344	22	15.63	7–74
H.J. Howarth (NZ)	144.5	51	323	16	20.18	5–80
Mohammad Nazir (P)	126	44	226	10	22.60	7–99
Intikhab Alam (P)	123.5	46	282	10	28.20	5–91

1972–73: Last-wicket record for New Zealand, but Pakistan win

R.J. Hadlee made his debut in the first Test at Wellington when Congdon's side met Intikhab's tourists, who had just lost 3–0 in Australia. Sadiq made 166 in Pakistan's first innings of 357. With J.M. Parker, also making his debut, unable to bat, New Zealand finished 32 behind. Pakistan's second-innings declaration was not meant to produce a result.

At Dunedin, Mushtaq (201) and Asif (175) added 350 for Pakistan's fourth wicket, at the time their highest stand for any wicket. Pakistan lost only six wickets in declaring and winning by an innings and 166 runs. Intikhab and Mushtaq were the successful bowlers, with eleven and seven wickets respectively.

Majid made 110 of 402 at Auckland, where R.E. Redmond made an attractive 107 on his debut for New Zealand. At 251 for nine Collinge (68 not out) joined Hastings (110) and the two added 151 to end the first innings level. The last-wicket stand beat the Test record which had stood for 69 years and Collinge made a record score for a number eleven. The match proceeded to a gentle draw.

1972–73   5th Series   Pak 1, NZ 0, Drawn 2
1 WELLINGTON   **Match Drawn**
Pakistan 357 (Sadiq Mohammad 166, Majid Khan k79, B R Taylor 4–110) and 290–6 dec (Majid Khan 79, Sadiq Mohammad 68, Intikhab Alam 53, H J Howarth 4–99)
New Zealand 325 (M G Burgess 79, B F Hastings 72, Sarfraz Nawaz 4–126) and 78–3
2 DUNEDIN   **Pakistan won by an innings and 166 runs**
Pakistan 507–6 dec (Mushtaq Mohammad 201, Asif Iqbal 175, Sadiq Mohammad 61)
New Zealand 156 (Intikhab Alam 7–52) and 185 (V Pollard 61, Mushtaq Mohammad 5–49, Intikhab Alam 4–78)
3 AUCKLAND   **Match Drawn**
Pakistan 402 (Majid Khan 110, Mushtaq Mohammad 61, Saleem Altaf 53, B R Taylor 4–86) and 271 (Mushtaq Mohammad 52)
New Zealand 402 (B F Hastings 110, R E Redmond 107, R O Collinge 68, G M Turner 58, Intikhab Alam 6–127) and 92–3 (R E Redmond 56)

1972–73 Averages

Batting	I	No	Runs	HS	Avge
Mushtaq Mohammad (P)	3	0	314	201	104.66
Sadiq Mohammad (P)	5	0	366	166	73.20
Majid. J. Khan (P)	5	0	327	110	65.40
Asif Iqbal (P)	5	0	310	175	62.00
G.M. Turner (NZ)	6	1	235	58	47.00

Bowling	O	M	Runs	W	Avge	BB
Intikhab Alam (P)	85.4	10	323	18	17.94	7–52
B.R. Taylor (NZ)	109.4	20	416	13	32.00	4–86
H.J. Howarth (NZ)	148	35	440	10	44.00	4–99

1976–77: Plenty of runs as Pakistan win 2–0

G.M. Turner's side toured Pakistan in 1976–77. Mushtaq won the first toss and batted at Lahore. Javed Miandad (163 on his debut) and Asif (166) rescued the side with a fifth wicket stand of 281 out of 417. New Zealand, 157, followed on and were one for three, but Burgess (111) and R.W. Anderson (92 on his debut) hoisted the final score to 360. Pakistan won by six wickets.

At Hyderabad, Sadiq and Mushtaq emulated the Chappell brothers by scoring a century in the same Test innings. Pakistan

declared at 473 for eight, and dismissing New Zealand twice for 473, needed to bat again for only one run to win.

In the final Test, Majid made 108 before lunch on the first day, the last time this feat was achieved. He set the stage for Javed, who at 19 years 141 days became the youngest to score a Test double-century. Mushtaq made 107 and Pakistan declared at 565 for nine. In New Zealand's innings, Imran was banned for over-use of the bumper. W.K. Lees made 152, and with R.J. Hadlee added 186 for the seventh wicket, the final total being 468. There was time for Pakistan to declare at 290 for five and the match to be drawn with New Zealand 262 for seven. In all, 1,585 runs were scored in five days, exceptional for the sub-continent.

1976–77   6th Series   Pak 2, NZ 0, Drawn 1
1 LAHORE   **Pakistan won by 6 wkts**
Pakistan 417 (Asif Iqbal 166, Javed Miandad 163, R J Hadlee 5–121) and 105–4
New Zealand 157 (Intikhab Alam 4–35) and 360 (M G Burgess 111, R W Anderson 92, Imran Khan 4–59)
2 HYDERABAD   **Pakistan won by 10 wkts**
Pakistan 473–3 dec (Sadiq Mohammad 103, Mushtaq Mohammad 101, Majid Khan 98, Asif Iqbal 73) and 4–0
New Zealand 219 and 254 (J M Parker 82, Intikhab Alam 4–44)
3 KARACHI   **Match Drawn**
Pakistan 565–9 dec (Javed Miandad 206, Majid Khan 112, Mushtaq Mohammad 107, Imran Khan 59, R J Hadlee 4–138) and 290–5 dec (Javed Miandad 85, Mushtaq Mohammad 67, Majid Khan 50)
New Zealand 468 (W K Lees 152, R J Hadlee 87, B L Cairns 52) and 262–7

1976–77 Averages

Batting	I	No	Runs	HS	Avge
Javed Miandad (P)	5	1	504	206	126.00
Mushtaq Mohammad (P)	5	1	284	107	71.00
Asif Iqbal (P)	5	1	282	166	70.50
Majid J. Khan (P)	5	0	304	112	60.80
R.J. Hadlee (NZ)	6	2	214	87	53.50
Sadiq Mohammad (P)	5	1	211	103*	52.75
W.K. Lees (NZ)	6	0	292	152	48.66
M.G. Burgess (NZ)	6	0	226	111	37.66

Bowling	O	M	Runs	W	Avge	BB
Sarfraz Nawaz (P)	79.2	12	283	13	21.76	3–53
Intikhab Alam (P)	120.4	35	331	15	22.06	4–35
Imran Khan (P)	113.4	15	423	14	30.21	4–61
R.J. Hadlee (NZ)	75.2	2	447	10	44.70	5–121

1978–79: Pakistan stay on top in New Zealand

Mushtaq's side in New Zealand in 1978–79 lacked four of their best players, who were engaged in WSC matches, for the first Test at Christchurch, where Burgess won the toss and put Pakistan in. Hadlee (5–62) bowled well and Pakistan were dismissed for 271. B.A. Edgar held the New Zealand batting together with 129, and they led by 19. Javed's 160 not out in the second innings allowed a declaration at 323 for six, and Pakistan won easily, Mushtaq and Wasim dismissing the home side for 176.

Pakistan's regulars returned for the match at the new venue of Napier, and Asif's century helped them to 360. Despite Imran (5–106), Howarth (114) led a spirited reply, adding a New Zealand record for the second wicket of 195 with Wright, and New Zealand led by 142. But it was a draw, with Majid also getting a century.

Putting in New Zealand at Auckland, Pakistan got them out for 254, Wasim Bari catching seven of the first eight batsmen, setting a new Test innings record. Zaheer got a century but New Zealand saved the match, although Pakistan took the series.

1978–79   7th Series   Pak 1, NZ 0, Drawn 2
1 CHRISTCHURCH   **Pakistan won by 128 runs**
Pakistan 271 (Javed Miandad 81, R J Hadlee 5–62) and 323–6 dec (Javed Miandad 160, Talaat Ali 61)
New Zealand 290 (B A Edgar 129, Mushtaq Mohammad 4–60) and 176 (Mushtaq Mohammad 5–59, Wasim Raja 4–68)
2 NAPIER   **Match Drawn**
Pakistan 360 (Asif Iqbal 104, Wasim Raja 74, R J Hadlee 4–101) and 234–3 dec (Majid Khan 119)
New Zealand 401 (G P Howarth 114, J G Wright 88, J V Coney 69, Imran Khan 5–106, Sikander Bakht 4–67)
3 AUCKLAND   **Match Drawn**
New Zealand 254 (J V Coney 82, R J Hadlee 53) and 281–8 dec (M G Burgess 71, Sarfraz Nawaz 4–61)
Pakistan 359 (Zaheer Abbas 135, R J Hadlee 5–104) and 8–0

1978–79 Averages

Batting	I	No	Runs	HS	Avge
Javed Miandad (P)	5	0	297	160*	99.00
J.V. Coney (NZ)	5	0	242	82	48.40

Bowling	O	M	Runs	W	Avge	BB
Mushtaq Mohammad (P)	75.3	11	228	11	20.72	5–59
R.J. Hadlee (NZ)	117.6	13	414	18	23.00	5–62
Sikander Bakht (P)	78	12	301	12	25.08	4–67
Imran Khan (P)	82	17	255	10	25.50	5–106

1984–85: Pakistan win 2–0 at home

J.V. Coney and Zaheer were captains in Pakistan in 1984–85, Coney deciding to bat in the first Test at Lahore. New Zealand were soon out for 157 and Pakistan took a lead of 64. It was enough, as New Zealand in the second innings collapsed after a good start to 241, and Pakistan won by six wickets.

The second Test, at Hyderabad, was the 1,000th. Reid made 106 of 267 when New Zealand batted on a wicket soon taking spin; S.L. Boock took seven for 87 for New Zealand, Javed's century keeping Pakistan in reach at 230. Qadir and Iqbal Qasim then spun the tourists out for 187, leaving Pakistan 227 to get. After the fall of two early wickets Javed and Mudassar mastered the bowling, both getting centuries in another home win. Javed was the second Pakistani to score a century in each innings.

Pakistan's tail-enders rescued their innings in the last Test, raising it to 328 after 124 for five, but Wright (107) led New Zea-

1984–85   8th Series   Pak 2, NZ 0, Drawn 1
1 LAHORE   **Pakistan won by 6 wkts**
New Zealand 157 (M D Crowe 55, Iqbal Qasim 4–41) and 241 (J G Wright 65, Iqbal Qasim 4–65)
Pakistan 221 (Mohsin Khan 58) and 181–4
2 HYDERABAD   **Pakistan won by 7 wkts**
New Zealand 267 (J F Reid 106, Abdul Qadir 5–108) and 189 (J J Crowe 57, Iqbal Qasim 5–79)
Pakistan 230 (Javed Miandad 104, S L Boock 7–87) and 230–3 (Mudassar Nazar 106, Javed Miandad 103)
3 KARACHI   **Match Drawn**
Pakistan 328 (Anil Dalpat 52, Wasim Raja 51, Salim Malik 50, S L Boock 4–83, D A Stirling 4–88) and 308–5 (Salim Malik 119, Wasim Raja 60, Javed Miandad 58)
New Zealand 426 (J G Wright 107, J F Reid 97, J J Crowe 62, Azeem Hafeez 4–132, Iqbal Qasim 4–133)

1984–85 Averages

Batting	I	No	Runs	HS	Avge
Javed Miandad (P)	6	2	337	104	84.24
Salim Malik (P)	5	2	204	119*	68.00
J.F. Reid (NZ)	5	0	232	106	46.40
J.G. Wright (NZ)	5	0	213	107	42.60
J.J. Crowe (NZ)	5	0	201	62	40.20

Bowling	O	M	Runs	W	Avge	BB
Iqbal Qasim (P)	166.5	46	398	18	22.11	5–79
S.L. Boock (NZ)	172.4	54	431	17	25.35	7–87
Abdul Qadir (P)	105.3	24	307	12	25.58	5–108
Azeem Hafeez (P)	103.4	30	271	10	27.10	4–132

land to a lead of 98. With New Zealand pressing, a not-out decision for caught behind against Javed brought disagreements with umpires to a head and Coney almost led the New Zealand team off the field in protest. Thereafter Salim Malik's century soon made the game safe.

1984–85: New Zealand get revenge and win 2–0 at home

A month after the third Test in Pakistan, the teams were meeting again in a series in New Zealand. Howarth returned to lead New Zealand while Javed took over the Pakistan captaincy. At Wellington, Reid made 148 and New Zealand ran up 492. Pakistan just avoided the follow-on and rain then ensured a draw.

Howarth put Pakistan in on a green wicket at Auckland and the seamers shot out the visitors for 169. Reid's second century

(158 not out) was well supported and Howarth declared at 451 for nine. Only Mudassar then offered much resistance as Pakistan were beaten by an innings and 99.

At Dunedin, Pakistan were put in again, and reached 241 for two, but collapsed before Hadlee (6–51) to 274. Wasim Akram took five for 56 in his second Test and New Zealand were out 54 behind. Thanks to Qasim Omar, who made 89 to follow a first-innings 86, Pakistan set New Zealand to get 278, the highest total of the match. They were soon 23 for four but Martin Crowe (84) and Coney (111 not out) began a recovery. But they still needed 50 when the last fit man, Chatfield, came in (Cairns had concussion). He and Coney made the runs for an exciting win.

1984–85 9th Series NZ 2, Pak 0, Drawn 1
1 WELLINGTON **Match Drawn**
New Zealand 492 (J F Reid 148, R J Hadlee 89, I D S Smith 65, Azeem Hafeez 5–127) and 103–4
Pakistan 322 (Salim Malik 66, Abdul Qadir 54, S L Boock 5–117)
2 AUCKLAND **New Zealand won by an innings and 99 runs**
Pakistan 169 (R J Hadlee 4–60) and 183 (Mudassar Nazar 89, B L Cairns 4–49)
New Zealand 451–9 dec (J F Reid 158, M D Crowe 84, J G Wright 66)
3 DUNEDIN **New Zealand won by 2 wkts**
Pakistan 274 (Qasim Omar 96, Javed Miandad 79, R J Hadlee 6–51) and 223 (Qasim Omar 89)
New Zealand 220 (M D Crowe 57, Wasim Akram 5–56) and 278–8 (J V Coney 111, M D Crowe 84, Wasim Akram 5–72)

1984–85 Averages

Batting	I	No	Runs	HS	Avge	
J.F. Reid (NZ)	5	1	333	158*	83.25	
J.V. Coney (NZ)	5	2	226	111*	75.33	
M.D. Crowe (NZ)	5	0	295	84	59.00	
Qasim Omar (P)	5	0	248	96	49.60	
Bowling	O	M	Runs	W	Avge	BB
R.J. Hadlee (NZ)	118.5	29	306	16	19.12	6–51
Wasim Akram (P)	93.4	21	233	12	19.41	5–56
B.L. Cairns (NZ)	120.2	28	305	10	30.50	4–49
Azeem Hafeez (P)	162	40	484	12	40.33	5–127

England v India

1932: England win inaugural Test at Lord's

An England side toured India as early as 1888, but Test matches between the countries have taken place only since 1932, when one Test was played at Lord's.

C.K. Nayudu captained India in the match against Jardine's strong team. S. Nazir Ali, who ended with five for 93, had England at 19 for three, but they recovered to 259. Set 346 to win in the fourth innings, India made 187 and lost by 158, but were not disgraced in their first Test match.

1932 1st Series Eng 1, India 0
1 LORD'S **England won by 158 runs**
England 259 (D R Jardine 79, L E G Ames 65, Mahomed Nissar 5–93) and 275–8 dec (D R Jardine 85, E Paynter 54, M Jahangir Khan 4–60)
India 189 (W E Bowes 4–49) and 187 (L Amar Singh 51)

1933–34: England win first series in India

Jardine's team in 1933–34 was the first to play a Test in India. Nayudu was India's captain.

The first Test was played at the Gymkhana ground in Bombay, and included play on a Sunday, the first in any Test. India made 219, and despite Nissar's five for 90,

The Indian team which toured England in 1932 when India played their first Test. Left to right, standing: Lall Singh, Palia, Jahangir Khan, Mahomed Nizar, Amar Singh, Kapadia, Godambe, Ghulam Mahomed, Navie. *Sitting*: Syed Wazir Ali, Nayudu, H.H. Maharaja Porbandar, Limdi, Syed Nazir Ali, Joginder Singh. On ground: Naoomal Jeoomal, Colah, Marshall.

England made 438 (B.H. Valentine, on his debut, 136). Amarnath (Nanik Shardwaj, known throughout his career as 'Lala') made India's first century in the second innings, but England won by nine wickets.

At Calcutta, England made 403 and made India follow on, but a determined rearguard action left England only half an hour to make 32, ensuring a draw.

At Madras, England made 335 despite Amar Singh taking seven for 86. The wicket took spin after this and Verity (7–49) shot the home side out for 145. C.F. Walters made a second-innings century and Verity and Jas Langridge ensured a 202-run win.

1933–34 2nd Series Eng 2, India 0, Drawn 1
1 BOMBAY **England won by 9 wkts**
India 219 and 258 (L Amarnath 118, C K Nayudu 67, M S Nichols 5–55)
England 438 (B H Valentine 136, C F Walters 78, D R Jardine 60. Mahomed Nissar 5–90) and 40–1

2 CALCUTTA Match Drawn
England 403 (Jas Langridge 70, D R Jardine 61, H Verity 55, L Amar Singh 4–106) and 7–2
India 247 (Dilawar Hussain 59, V M Merchant 54, H Verity 4–64) and 237 (Dilawar Hussain 57, H Verity 4–76)

3 MADRAS England won by 202 runs
England 335 (A H Bakewell 85, D R Jardine 65, C F Walters 59, L Amar Singh 7–86) and 261–7 dec (C F Walters 102, S Nazir Ali 4–83)
India 145 (H Verity 4–49) and 249 (Yuvraj of Patiala 60, Jas Langridge 5–63, H Verity 4–104)

England v India
1933–34 Averages

Batting	I	No	Runs	HS	Avge
D.R. Jardine (E)	4	1	221	65	73.66
C.F. Walters (E)	6	2	284	102	71.00

Bowling	O	M	Runs	W	Avge	BB
H. Verity (E)	157.5	61	387	23	16.83	7–49
J. Langridge (E)	90	30	192	10	19.20	5–63
M.S. Nichols (E)	115.1	31	287	13	22.07	5–55
E.W. Clark (E)	100.3	26	263	10	26.30	3–39

1936: Amarnath sent home and England confirm superiority

The 1936 tour of India to England was marred when, before the first Test and amid dissension in the Indian camp, Amarnath, arguably their best player, was sent home for disciplinary reasons. Amarnath was later to be completely reinstated and captained India, but his absence was a great handicap at the time.

The Maharajkumar of Vizianagram led the tourists, G.O.B. Allen being the England captain. Allen put India in at Lord's, and with five for 35 helped put them out for 147. It was a great shock for England when Amar Singh, with six for 35 tumbled them for 134 for a first-innings lead. However, Allen and Verity got India out for 93 and, Gimblett rapidly knocked off most of the runs needed for a nine-wicket win.

Batsmen were on top at Old Trafford, after India's low first innings. Hammond made a rapid 167, but India saved the day through Merchant and Mushtaq Ali, who made centuries and put on 203 for the first wicket.

In the last Test at the Oval, England batted first and Hammond made a majestic 217, adding 266 for the fourth wicket with Worthington (128). Sims and Allen bowled England to another nine-wicket win, but Nayudu batted bravely after being hit, and averted the innings defeat.

1936 3rd Series Eng 2, India 0, Drawn 1

1 LORD'S England won by 9 wkts
India 147 (G O B Allen 5–35) and 93 (G O B Allen 5–43, H Verity 4–17)
England 134 (M Leyland 60, L Amar Singh 6–35) and 108–1 (H Gimblett 67)

2 OLD TRAFFORD Match Drawn
India 203 (H Verity 4–41) and 390–5 (V M Merchant 114, S Mushtaq Ali 112, C Ramaswami 60)
England 571–8 dec (W R Hammond 167, J Hardstaff jun 94, T S Worthington 87, R W V Robins 76, H Verity 66)

3 THE OVAL England won by 9 wkts
England 471–8 dec (W R Hammond 217, T S Worthington 128, Mahomed Nissar 5–120) and 64–1
India 222 (V M Merchant 52, S Mushtaq Ali 52, J M Sims 5–73) and 312 (C K Nayudu 81, Dilawar Hussain 54, G O B Allen 7–80)

1936 Averages

Batting	I	No	Runs	HS	Avge
W.R. Hammond (E)	3	1	389	217	194.50
T.S. Worthington (E)	2	0	215	128	107.50
V.M. Merchant (I)	6	0	282	114	47.00
Mushtaq Ali (I)	6	0	202	112	33.66

Bowling	O	M	Runs	W	Avge	BB
H. Verity (E)	114	44	228	15	15.20	4–17
G.O.B. Allen (E)	100	19	330	20	16.50	7–80
Mahomed Nissar (I)	84	15	343	12	28.58	5–120
L. Amar Singh (I)	127.4	33	317	10	31.70	6–35

C.K. Nayudu, who captained India in their first Test match.

1946: Bedser takes 22 wickets in first two Tests

Among the Indian party who were England's first post-war tourists were Abdul Hafeez, who later played for Pakistan as A.H. Kardar, A.H. Mankad, always known as 'Vinoo' Mankad, and the captain, the Nawab of Pataudi senior, who had previously played for England, and whose son was also to captain India. A.V. Bedser was England's most notable newcomer.

Bedser took seven for 49 (11 in the match) at Lord's to dismiss India for 200, Hardstaff made 205 (Amarnath 5–118) and England won by ten wickets.

At Old Trafford, rain naturally delayed the start. The two great all-rounders, Amarnath and Mankad, shared England's wickets in both innings. Bedser and R. Pollard, on his debut, took 18 of the 19 Indian wickets to fall. The last wicket held on for 13 minutes and survived two chances to get India a draw.

There was little time for more than one innings at the Oval because of rain, but T.G. Evans made his debut for England and V.M. Merchant made 128 for India.

1946   4th Series   Eng 1, India 0, Drawn 2

1 LORD'S   England won by 10 wkts
India 200 (R S Modi 57, A V Bedser 7–49) and 275 (M H Mankad 63, L Amarnath 50, A V Bedser 4–96)
England 428 (J Hardstaff jun 205, P A Gibb 60, L Amarnath 5–118) and 48–0

2 OLD TRAFFORD   Match Drawn
England 294 (W R Hammond 69, L Hutton 67, C Washbrook 52, D C S Compton 51, L Amarnath 5–96, M H Mankad 5–101) and 153–5 dec (D C S Compton 71)
India 170 (V M Merchant 78, R Pollard 5–24) A V Bedser 4–41) and 152–9 (A V Bedser 7–52)

3 THE OVAL   Match Drawn
India 331 (V M Merchant 128, S Mushtaq Ali 59, W J Edrich 4–68)
England 95–3

1946 Averages

Batting	I	No	Runs	HS	Avge
J. Hardstaff, jr (E)	3	1	210	205*	105.00
V.M. Merchant (I)	5	0	245	128	49.00

Bowling	O	M	Runs	W	Avge	BB
A.V. Bedser (E)	147.2	33	298	24	12.41	7–49
L. Amarnath (I)	137	41	330	13	25.38	5–96
V. Mankad (I)	99.5	40	292	11	26.54	5–101

1951–52: India win their first Test and draw rubber

The England party to India in 1951–52 led by N.D. Howard was not representative of England's full strength. In the first Test S.G. Shinde (6–91) helped bowl England out for 203 and centuries by Merchant (154) and captain V.S. Hazare (164 not out) enabled India to declare at 418 for six. A.J. Watkins saved the match for England with a determined 137 not out.

The second Test at Bombay was a high-scoring match. Pankaj Roy (140) and Hazare (155 not out) allowed India to declare at 485 for nine, and England made 456, thanks to Graveney (175). From then on the match was headed for a draw.

On a slow pitch at Calcutta, England and India laboured to 342 and 344 respectively, D.G. Phadkar making 115 for India, and although England declared the match was a dull draw.

The England team which played India in the final Test at the Oval in 1946. Left to right, back: Evans, Smith, Bedser, Gover, Compton, Langridge. Front: Washbrook, Fishlock, Hammond, Edrich, Hutton. The match was drawn, being cut short by rain.

There was a spinners' pitch at Kanpur, and India were removed for 121 by the Lancashire spinners Tattersall and Hilton. Ghulam Ahmed and Mankad hit back for India, but not quite so successfully, and England led by 82. In the second innings the spinners rubbed the new ball on the ground to open the bowling. England needed just 76 to win by eight wickets.

D.B. Carr captained England in the last Test, when Howard had pleurisy. England made a good start, but Mankad (8–55) got them out eventually for 266. Pankaj Roy (111) and P.R. Umrigar (130 not out) took India to 457 for nine declared. Ghulam Ahmed and Mankad bowled excellently again to get England out for 183 and square the rubber with an innings win. It was India's first Test win in their 25th match.

1951–52 Averages

Batting	I	No	Runs	HS	Avge
A.J. Watkins (E)	8	1	451	138*	64.42
T.W. Graveney (E)	8	2	363	175	60.50
V.S. Hazare (I)	7	1	347	164*	57.83
P. Roy (I)	8	1	387	140	55.28
J.D.B. Robertson (E)	9	1	310	77	38.75
R.T. Spooner (E)	10	1	319	92	35.44

Bowling	O	M	Runs	W	Avge	BB
V. Mankad (I)	370.4	151	571	34	16.97	4–54
R. Tattersall (E)	247.5	65	595	21	28.33	6–48

1951–52 5th Series Eng 1, India 1, Drawn 3

1 NEW DELHI Match Drawn
England 203 (J D B Robertson 50, S G Shinde 6–91) and 368–6 (A J Watkins 138, D B Carr 76, F A Lowson 68, M H Mankad 4–58)
India 418–6 dec (V S Hazare 164, V M Merchant 154)

2 BOMBAY Match Drawn
India 485–9 dec (V S Hazare 155, P Roy 140, C D Gopinath 50, J B Statham 4–96) and 208
England 456 (T W Graveney 175, A J Watkins 80, M H Mankad 4–91) and 5–2

3 CALCUTTA Match Drawn
England 342 (R T Spooner 71, A J Watkins 68, C J Poole 55, M H Mankad 4–89) and 252–5 dec (R T Spooner 92, C J Poole 69)
India 344 (D G Phadkar 115, M H Mankad 59, F Ridgway 4–83, R Tattersall 4–104) and 103–0 (M H Mankad 71)

4 KANPUR England won by 8 wkts
India 121 (R Tattersall 6–48, M J Hilton 4–32) and 157 (H R Adhikari 60, M J Hilton 5–61)
England 203 (A J Watkins 66, Ghulam Ahmed 5–70, M H Mankad 4–54) and 76–2

5 MADRAS India won by an innings and 8 runs
England 266 (J D B Robertson 77, R T Spooner 66, M H Mankad 8–55) and 183 (J D B Robertson 56, M H Mankad 4–53, Ghulam Ahmed 4–77)
India 457–9 dec (P R Umrigar 130, P Roy 111, D G Phadkar 61)

1952: India's efforts ruined by bad starts

After doing so well in India, Hazare brought his team to England, where Hutton became the first professional to lead England in a home series. The home side was very strong, and at Headingley in the first Test included F.S. Trueman on his debut. India batted and made 293, of which V.L. Manjrekar made 133 and with Hazare added 222 for the fourth wicket. England made 334, and then Trueman, helped by Bedser, gave India the worst start in all Test history: 0 for four wickets (Trueman three). Hazare and Phadkar later added 104 for the sixth wicket, but England won by seven wickets.

At Lord's, in reply to India's 235, England made 537, with Hutton (150) and Evans (104) passing 100, but then Mankad, after taking five wickets, scored 184 out of 378. England won by eight wickets, however.

1952 6th Series Eng 3, India 0, Drawn 1

1 HEADINGLEY England won by 7 wkts
India 293 (V L Manjrekar 133, V S Hazare 89, J C Laker 4–39) and 165 (D G Phadkar 64, V S Hazare 56, F S Trueman 4–27, R O Jenkins 4–50)
England 334 (T W Graveney 71, T G Evans 66, Ghulam Ahmed 5–10) and 128–3 (R T Simpson 51)

2 LORD'S England won by 8 wkts
India 235 (M H Mankad 72, V S Hazare 69, F S Trueman 4–72) and 378 (M H Mankad 184, J C Laker 4–102, F S Trueman 4–110)
England 537 (L Hutton 150, T G Evans 104, P B H May 74, T W Graveney 73, R T Simpson 53, M H Mankad 5–196) and 79–2

3 OLD TRAFFORD England won by an innings and 207 runs
England 347–9 dec (L Hutton 104, T G Evans 71, P B H May 69)
India 58 (F S Trueman 8–31) and 82 (A V Bedser 5–27, G A R Lock 4–36)

4 THE OVAL Match Drawn
England 326–6 dec (D S Shepherd 119, L Hutton 86, J T Ikin 53)
India 98 (A V Bedser 5–41, F S Trueman 5–48)

1952 Averages

Batting	I	No	Runs	HS	Avge
L. Hutton (E)	6	1	399	150	79.80
T.G. Evans (E)	4	0	242	104	60.50
V.S. Hazare (I)	7	1	347	164*	57.83
V. Mankad (Ind)	5	0	271	184	54.20
P.B.H. May (E)	6	0	206	74	34.33

Bowling	O	M	Runs	W	Avge	BB
F.S. Trueman (E)	119.4	25	386	29	13.31	8–31
A.V. Bedser (E)	163.5	57	279	20	13.95	5–27
Ghulam Ahmed (E)	185	57	371	15	24.73	5–100

On a greasy pitch at rain-interrupted Old Trafford, England's first innings ended on the third morning at 347 (Hutton 104). Trueman, bowling downwind and with the help of some brilliant catching, then took

The Indian tourists of 1952 at a local match. Left to right, back: J. Scott (umpire), Punkaj Roy, Manjrekar, Sen, Ghulam Ahmed, Gopinath, Ramchand, Gaekwad, A. Banfield (umpire). Front: Phadkar, Adhikari, Hazare, Shinde, Sarwate. In the first Test at Headingley, India found themselves 0–4 in the second innings.

eight for 31, his best analysis, and India were out for 58. They followed on, and Bedser and Lock dismissed them for 82. They were the first Test team to be out twice in a day.

Rain cut play at the Oval in the fourth and final Test to less than two days. Hutton (86) and Sheppard (119) put on 143 for the first wicket, and England declared at 526 for six. India made another terrible start, six for five wickets, and were out for 98, Bedser and Trueman sharing the wickets. There was no time to start the follow-on.

1959: England make their first 5–0 clean sweep

Seven years after the previous series, India toured under D.K. Gaekwad. P.B.H. May captained England and made 106 at Trent Bridge in England's 422. India were dismissed twice, mainly by Statham and Trueman, to lose by an innings.

India batted at Lord's where Pankaj Roy was captain, Gaekwad being ill. Out for 168 (T. Greenhough 5–35), they hit back, mainly through R.B. Desai (5–89) to restrict

Nadkarni passing 50 in the two innings. It was the first time a series had ended 5–0 in England.

Below: Vinoo Mankad plays a ball from Bedser in the third Test at Old Trafford and is about to be caught by Lock at short leg.

Bottom: Hazare batting in 1952. He was one of India's leading batsmen before the Second World War and captained the touring party to England in 1952.

England's lead to 58. However they made only 165 second time and England won by eight wickets.

India's innings were consistent. At Headingley they made 161, only one more than Cowdrey made for England, who declared at 483 for eight. India, 149, lost by an innings and 173.

At Old Trafford, A.A. Baig, an Oxford freshman, earlier co-opted into the party, made his Test debut. Pullar and M.J.K. Smith made centuries in 490, and India were dismissed for 208. Cowdrey, captain in May's absence, did not enforce the follow-on, preferring to declare and set India 548 to win. Baig made a gallant 112, resuming next day after being hit on the head and retiring, and Umrigar made 118, but the target was far too high.

England were attempting a clean sweep at the Oval, and won by an innings, only

1959 7th Series Eng 5, India 0
1 TRENT BRIDGE England won by an innings and 59 runs
England 422 (P B H May 106, T G Evans 73, M J Horton 58, K F Barrington 56, S P Gupte 4–102)
India 206 (P Roy 54, F S Trueman 4–45) and 157 (J B Statham 5–31)
2 LORD'S England won by 8 wkts
India 168 (N J Contractor 81, T Greenhough 5–35) and 165 (V L Manjrekar 61)
England 226 (K F Barrington 80, R B Desai 5–89) and 108–2 (M C Cowdrey 63)
3 HEADINGLEY England won by an innings and 173 runs
India 161 (H J Rhodes 4–50) and 149 (D B Close 4–35)
England 483–8 dec (M C Cowdrey 160, K F Barrington 80, W G A Parkhouse 78, G Pullar 75, S P Gupte 4–111)
4 OLD TRAFFORD England won by 171 runs
England 490 (G Pullar 131, M J K Smith 100, K F Barrington 87, M C Cowdrey 67, R Surendranath 5–115) and 265–8 dec (S P Gupte 4–76)
India 208 (C G Borde 75) and 376 (P R Umrigar 118, A A Baig 112, N J Contractor 56)
5 THE OVAL England won by an innings and 27 runs
India 140 (F S Trueman 4–24) and 194 (R G Nadkarni 76)
England 361 (M J K Smith 98, R Subba Row 94, R Swetman 65, R Illingworth 50, R Surendranath 5–75)

1959 Averages

Batting	I	No	Runs	HS	Avge
K.F. Barrington (E)	6	0	357	87	59.50
M.C. Cowdrey (E)	7	1	344	160	57.33

Bowling	O	M	Runs	W	Avge	BB
J.B. Statham (E)	112.2	44	223	17	13.11	5–31
F.S. Trueman (E)	177.4	53	401	24	16.70	4–24
T. Greenhough (E)	139.41	47	255	14	18.21	5–35
Surendranath (I)	203.4	85	426	16	26.62	5–75
S.P. Gupte (I)	199.4	51	589	17	34.64	4–76
R.B. Desai (I)	189.4	40	602	12	50.16	5–89

The Indian tourists to England in 1967. Left to right, back: Guhar, Saxena, Venkataraghavan, Chandrasekhar, Bedi, Singh, Prasanna. Front: Surti, Borde, the Nawab of Pataudi, Kunderan, Engineer.

1961–62: India win their first series against England

Many of England's top players were not available for the tour to India in 1961–62, and Dexter's party was therefore an unrepresentative side. The five Tests in India were played between the first and second Tests in Pakistan.

N.J. Contractor captained India on an easy Bombay pitch where England made 500 for eight declared in the first Test. Barrington made 151 not out. India avoided the follow-on and the match was drawn. Barrington batted nine hours in the match for 203 unbeaten.

Fines, flashing mirrors and missiles slowed the play at Kanpur, where Umrigar made 147 not out and India declared and enforced the follow-on, with S.P. Gupte getting five wickets. But Pullar, Barrington and Dexter made hundreds, and the match was drawn.

At Delhi, the Nawab of Pataudi junior made his debut. He used the name Mansur Ali Khan when royal titles were abolished in India. India made 466 (Jaisimha 127, Manjrekar 189 not out), and Barrington was 113 not out in England's reply at the end of a match curtailed by rain.

India's 380 at Calcutta (Allen 5–67) was a good score on a wicket that progressively took spin. Durani and Borde dismissed England for 212, and although Lock and Allen fought back, a target of 421 was well beyond England, who lost by 187.

The match at Madras went much the same way. The Indian batsmen, led by Contractor (86) and Pataudi (103) batted fluently to 428. Thereafter Durani (ten wickets in the match) and Lock (6–65 in the second innings) were on top, and India won by 128 runs.

It was India's first series win over England.

1961–62 8th Series India 2, Eng 0, Drawn 3

1 BOMBAY Match Drawn
England 500–8 dec (K F Barrington 151, E R Dexter 85, G Pullar 83, P E Richardson 71, V B Ranjane 4–76) and 184–5 dec (K F Barrington 52)
India 390 (S A Durani 71, C G Borde 69, V L Manjrekar 84, M L Jaisimha 51)

2 KANPUR Match Drawn
India 467–8 dec (P R Umrigar 147, V L Manjrekar 96, M L Jaisimha 70)
England 244 (R W Barber 69, S P Gupte 5–90) and 497–5 (K F Barrington 172, E R Dexter 126, G Pullar 119)

3 NEW DELHI Match Drawn
India 466 (V L Manjrekar 189, M L Jaisimha 127, D A Allen 4–87)
England 256–3 (K F Barrington 113, G Pullar 89)

4 CALCUTTA India won by 187 runs
India 380 (C G Borde 68, M A K Pataudi 64, V L Mehra 62, D A Allen 5–67) and 252 (C G Borde 61, D A Allen 4–95, G A R Lock 4–111)
England 212 (P E Richardson 62, E R Dexter 57, S A Durani 5–47, C G Borde 4–65) and 233 (E R Dexter 62)

5 MADRAS India won by 128 runs
India 428 (M A K Pataudi 103, N J Contractor 86, F M Engineer 65, R G Nadkarni 63) and 190 (V L Manjrekar 85, G A R Lock 6–65)
England 281 (M J K Smith 73, S A Durani 6–105) and 209 (S A Durani 4–72)

1961–62 Averages

Batting	I	No	Runs	HS	Avge
K.F. Barrington (E)	9	3	594	172	99.00
G. Pullar (E)	4	0	337	119	84.25
V.L. Manjrekar (I)	8	1	586	189*	83.71
E.R. Dexter (E)	9	2	409	126*	58.42
P.R. Umrigar (I)	6	1	254	147*	50.80
M.L. Jaisimha (I)	8	0	399	127	49.87
C.G. Borde (I)	8	1	314	69	44.85
P.E. Richardson (E)	9	0	304	71	33.77

Bowling	O	M	Runs	W	Avge	BB
S.A. Durani (I)	249.4	71	622	23	27.04	6–105
D.A. Allen (E)	301.5	121	583	21	27.76	5–67
G.A.R. Lock (E)	306.3	124	628	22	28.04	6–65
C.G. Borde (I)	187.3	55	460	16	28.75	4–65

1963–64: Five draws for injury and sickness-hit England

England undertook a shorter tour of India in 1963–64, and took a stronger team. M.J.K.

Smith was captain, Cowdrey withdrawing through injury, but during the tour, with Barrington injured, Cowdrey and Parfitt were flown out. Pataudi captained India.

After Kunderan (192) and Manjrekar (108) had ensured India a big first-innings score (457 for seven declared), England were battling to save the match, and at the end, set to score 293 on a dusty pitch, were 241 for five, 52 short of victory. Titmus took nine wickets in the match.

At Bombay, England were without four players, played both wicket-keepers, and lost Stewart to dysentery on the first day. The ten fit players in the party did extremely well to get an even draw after losing the toss.

Cowdrey and Parfitt had arrived for the third Test at Calcutta, where India again won the toss and batted, making 241 (Price 5–73). Cowdrey made a century to give England the lead, but rain on the third day meant a draw despite Jaisimha's century.

India batted again at Delhi, and newcomer Hanumant Singh made a century in his first Test innings. However Cowdrey's second successive century put England 107 ahead at 451. Kunderan's 100 ensured the draw and Pataudi's last-day 203 not out was academic.

Pataudi put England in on a dead pitch at Kanpur. Knight and Parfitt scored centuries in 559 for 8 declared. Titmus (6–73) spun out India for 266. India scored only 136 in 5½ hours on the third day, and their run-spree after following on was of little significance. Nadkarni, however, took his aggregate to 294 for the series, average 98, having batted at numbers eight and nine until promoted to number three for the last innings.

1963–64 9th Series Drawn 5

1 MADRAS Match Drawn
India 457–7 dec (B K Kunderan 192, V L Manjrekar 108, D N Sardesai 65, M L Jaisimha 51, F J Titmus 5–116) and 152–9 dec (F J Titmus 4–46)
England 317 (J B Bolus 88, K F Barrington 80, C G Borde 5–88) and 241–5 (J B Mortimore 73, M J K Smith 57)

2 BOMBAY Match Drawn
India 300 (S A Durani 90, C G Borde 84) and 249–8 dec (D N Sardesai 66, M L Jaisimha 66)
England 233 (F J Titmus 84, B S Chandrasekhar 4–67) and 206–3 (J B Bolus 57, J G Binks 55)

3 CALCUTTA Match Drawn
India 241 (D N Sardesai 54, J S E Price 5–73) and 300–7 dec (M L Jaisimha 129)
England 267 (M C Cowdrey 107, R B Desai 4–62) and 145–2 (M J K Smith 75)

4 NEW DELHI Match Drawn
India 344 (Hanumant Singh 105) and 463–4 (M A K Pataudi 203, B K Kunderan 100 C G Borde 67, M L Jaisimha 50)
England 451 (M C Cowdrey 151, P H Parfitt 67, J B Bolus 58)

5 KANPUR Match Drawn
England 559–8 dec (B R Knight 127, P H Parfitt 121, J B Bolus 67, J M Parks 51)
India 266 (D N Sardesai 79, R G Nadkarni 52, F J Titmus 6–73) and 347–3 (R G Nadkarni 122, D N Sardesai 87, S A Durani 61, B K Kunderan 55)

1963–64 Averages

Batting	I	No	Runs	HS	Avge
M.C. Cowdrey (E)	4	1	309	151	103.00
R.G. Nadkarni (I)	8	5	294	122	98.00
B.K. Kunderam (I)	10	0	525	192	52.50
M.J.K. Smith (E)	8	2	306	75*	51.00
J.B. Bolus (E)	8	0	391	88	48.87
D.N. Sardesai (I)	10	0	449	87	44.90
M.L. Jaisimha (I)	10	0	444	129	44.40
Nawab of Pataudi, jr (I)	9	1	308	203*	38.50

Bowling	O	M	Runs	W	Avge	BB
J.S.E. Price (E)	124.1	18	383	14	27.35	5–73
F.J. Titmus (E)	398.5	156	747	27	27.66	6–73

1967: Clean sweep for England in spinners' summer

Pataudi's party to England in 1967 for a three-match series suffered a similar run of injuries to that which had afflicted England in 1963–64. Close was England's captain.

At Headingley, early injuries to R.F. Surti and B.S. Bedi allowed England to get 550 for four against a weakened attack, Boycott making 246 not out and D'Oliveira 109. Boycott's century came in 341 minutes, and he was dropped from the next Test because of his slowness. A demoralized India were dismissed for 164 but fought back splendidly in the follow-on, scoring 510, Pataudi himself getting 148. But England won easily by six wickets.

At Lord's, England dismissed India for 152, and despite the loss of much play to rain on the second and third days made 386, Graveney getting 151 and Chandrasekhar five for 127. Illingworth (6–29) got India out again for 110 and England won by an innings.

Spin ruled at Edgbaston and the England spinners had the edge in a low-scoring match in which Close did not enforce the follow-on. India were set 410 to win and lost by 132.

V.L. Manjrekar batting at Trent Bridge in 1959. He played in 55 Tests in the 1950s and 1960s and scored over 3,000 runs for India at an average of around 40.

1967 10th Series Eng 3, India 0
1 HEADINGLEY   England won by 6 wkts
England 550–4 dec (G Boycott 246, B L d'Oliveira 109, K F Barrington 93, T W Graveney 59) and 126–4
India 164 (M A K Pataudi 64) and 510 (M A K Pataudi 148, A L Wadekar 91, F M Engineer 87, Hanumant Singh 73, R Illingworth 4–100)
2 LORD'S   England won by an innings and 124 runs
India 152 (A L Wadekar 57) and 110 (R Illingworth 6–29)
England 386 (T W Graveney 151, K F Barrington 97, B S Chandrasekhar 5–127)
3 EDGBASTON   England won by 132 runs
England 298 (J T Murray 77, K F Barrington 75) and 203 (E A S Prasanna 4–60)
India 92 and 277 (A L Wadekar 70, D B Close 4–68, R Illingworth 4–92)

1967 Averages

Batting	I	No	Runs	HS	Avge
G. Boycott (E)	3	1	277	246*	138.50
K.F. Barrington (E)	5	0	324	97	64.80
T.W. Graveney (E)	5	0	251	151	50.20
Nawab of Pataudi, jr (Ind)	6	0	269	148	44.83
A.L. Wadekar	6	0	242	91	40.33

Bowling	O	M	Runs	W	Avge	BB
R. Illingworth (E)	154.3	68	266	20	13.30	6–29
J.A. Snow (E)	112.4	29	264	10	26.40	3–49
B.S. Chandrasekhar (I)	169.5	40	435	16	27.18	5–27

1971: India win their first match and series in England

A.L. Wadekar brought an Indian side strong in spin bowling to England in 1971 to face R. Illingworth's team.

There was an exciting first Test at Lord's, where India overtook England's 304 by nine runs and were set to score 183 for victory. In going for a quick single, Gavaskar was knocked over by Snow, attempting a run-out. Snow was later ordered to apologize for the incident, and was omitted from the next Test as a disciplinary measure. Rain prevented play after tea on the last day when India were 38 short of their target with two wickets left.

At Old Trafford, Illingworth made 107 and added a record 168 for the eighth wicket with Lever (88 not out) to rescue England and raise the score to 386. Lever then got five for 70 in India's 212. A Luckhurst century allowed Illingworth to declare, but rain washed out the last day and saved India from probable defeat.

At the Oval, England made 355 and through Illingworth (5–70) dismissed India for 284. Then Chandrasekhar bowled brilliantly, taking six for 38, to remove England for 101 and leave India 173 to win. Careful batting got them home by four wickets.

India thus won their first Test in England after 39 years, and halted England's record run of 26 Tests without defeat.

1971 11th Series India 1, Eng 0, Drawn 2

1 LORD'S Match Drawn
England 304 (J A Snow 73, A P E Knott 67, B S Bedi 4–70) and 191 (J H Edrich 62, S Venkataraghavan 4–52)
India 313 (A L Wadekar 85, G R Viswanath 68, E D Solkar 67, N Gifford 4–84) and 145–8 (S M Gavaskar 53, N Gifford 4–43)

2 OLD TRAFFORD Match Drawn
England 386 (R Illingworth 107, P Lever 88, B W Luckhurst 78, S Abid Ali 4–64) and 245–3 dec (B W Luckhurst 101, J H Edrich 59)
India 212 (S M Gavaskar 57, E D Solkar 50, P Lever 5–70) and 65–3

3 THE OVAL India won by 4 wkts
England 355 (A P E Knott 90, J A Jameson 82, R A Hutton 81) and 101 (B S Chandrasekhar 6–38)
India 284 (F M Engineer 59, D N Sardesai 54, R Illingworth 5–70) and 174–6

1971 Averages

Batting	I	No	Runs	HS	Avge	
A.P.E. Knott (E)	5	0	223	90	44.60	
B.W. Luckhurst (E)	6	0	244	101	40.66	
A.L. Wadekar (I)	6	0	204	85	34.00	

Bowling	O	M	Runs	W	Avge	BB
S. Venkataraghavan (I)	150.3	38	350	13	26.92	4–52
B.S. Chandrasekhar (I)	146.1	32	379	13	29.15	6–38
B.S. Bedi (I)	151.3	46	325	11	29.54	4–70

Wood comprehensively bowled by Bedi during the second Test at Eden Gardens, Calcutta in 1972–73 India won and went on to take the series.

1972–73: India come from behind to win the rubber.

A.R. Lewis led England to India in 1972–73 after Illingworth and M.J.K. Smith had declined. Wadekar won the toss at Delhi and batted, but Arnold (6–45) removed India for 173. Then Chandrasekhar (8–79) bowled so well that England's lead was only 27. England needed 207 to win in the fourth innings and won by six wickets, Greig being the leading batsman.

At Calcutta, India's 210 proved too many as Chandrasekhar (5–65) again bowled well, England this time being 36 behind. Old and Greig got India out for only 155, but England could not get the 192 required, despite Greig's 63, Bedi and Chandrasekhar getting them out for 163.

England batted first at Madras, and made 242, Fletcher being undefeated on 97. Chandrasekhar got six for 90. India batted solidly for 316, got England out for 159, but struggled to get the 86 needed for a four-wicket win.

At Kanpur, India played for a draw. England passed their 357 by 40, with Lewis scoring 125, but the second innings began only on the last day, and although India were 39 for four they saved the situation easily.

At Bombay each side had two century makers, Engineer (121) and Viswanath (113) for India and Fletcher (113) and Greig (148) for England, who led by 32. India made a token declaration, but a draw was certain, India winning the rubber 2–1.

1972–73 12th Series India 2, Eng 1, Drawn 2

1 NEW DELHI England won by 6 wkts
India 173 (S Abid Ali 58, G G Arnold 6–45) and 233 (E D Solkar 75, F M Engineer 63, D L Underwood 4–56)
England 200 (A W Greig 68, B S Chandrasekhar 8–79) and 208–4 (A R Lewis 70)

2 CALCUTTA India won by 28 runs
India 210 (F M Engineer 75) and 155 (S A Durani 53, A W Greig 5–24, C M Old 4–43)
England 174 (B S Chandrasekhar 5–65) and 163 (A W Greig 67, B S Bedi 5–63, B S Chandrasekhar 4–42)

3 MADRAS India won by 4 wkts
England 242 (K W R Fletcher 97, B S Chandrasekhar 6–90) and 159 (M H Denness 76, E A S Prasanna 4–16, B S Bedi 4–38)
India 316 (M A K Pataudi 73, P I Pocock 4–114) and 86–6 (P I Pocock 4–28)

4 KANPUR Match Drawn
India 357 (A L Wadekar 90, S M Gavaskar 69, M A K Pataudi 54, C M Old 4–69) and 186–6 (G R Viswanath 75)
England 397 (A R Lewis 125, J Birkenshaw 64, K W R Fletcher 58, B S Chandrasekhar 4–86)

5 BOMBAY Match Drawn
India 448 (F M Engineer 121, G R Viswanath 113, A L Wadekar 87, S A Durani 73) and 244–5 dec (S M Gavaskar 67, F M Engineer 66)
England 480 (A W Greig 148, K W R Fletcher 113, A P E Knott 56, B S Chandrasekhar 5–135) and 67–2

1972–73 Averages

Batting	I	No	Runs	HS	Avge
A.W. Greig (E)	8	2	382	148	63.66
K.W.R. Fletcher (E)	8	1	312	113	44.57
F.M. Engineer (I)	10	0	415	121	41.50
G.R. Viswanath (I)	10	0	415	121	41.50
A.L. Wadekar (I)	10	1	312	90	34.66
M.H. Denness (E)	8	0	257	76	32.12

Bowling	O	M	Runs	W	Avge	BB
G.G. Arnold (E)	137.3	42	300	17	17.64	6–45
B.S. Chandrasekhar (I)	291.1	83	662	35	18.91	8–79
C.M. Old (E)	135.2	31	371	15	24.73	4–43
B.S. Bedi (I)	372.5	134	632	25	25.28	5–63
P.I. Pocock (E)	177	49	410	14	29.28	4–28
D.L. Underwood (E)	214.4	82	457	15	30.46	4–56

Above: Bishen Bedi, one of India's great slow bowlers of the 1970s.

Right: John Snow removes Gavaskar's middle stump at the Oval in 1971. At Lord's he had been disciplined for knocking over Gavaskar in a run-out attempt.

Below: Sunil Gavaskar square cuts for four at Old Trafford in 1971. Gavaskar became the first Test cricketer to pass 10,000 runs.

1974: India crushed in one-sided series

Wadekar's tourists in 1974 met wet English conditions which favoured the home side. At Old Trafford, Denness won the toss and batted, and England reached 328 (Fletcher 123 not out). Gavaskar was run out for 101

in India's 246. A new regulation allowed an extra hour's play on days where over an hour was lost to the weather, and on the first and third days this regulation was used as rain curtailed the play. Declaring when Edrich reached 100 in the second innings, England won by 113 runs with 15.5 overs left.

At Lord's, Amiss (188), Denness (118)

and Greig (106) made centuries in England's 629. With Chandrasekhar retired hurt, Bedi bore the brunt of the bowling, taking six for 226. India made 302, but followed on in a heavy atmosphere and the swing of Arnold (4–19) and Old (5–21) removed them for 42, their lowest Test score and the lowest ever made at Lord's.

1 OLD TRAFFORD   England won by 113 runs

England 328–9 dec (K W R Fletcher 123, D L Amiss 56, A W Greig 53) and 213–3 dec (J H Edrich 100)

India 246 (S M Gavaskar 101, S Abid Ali 71, R G D Willis 4–64) and 182 (S M Gavaskar 58, G R Viswanath 50, C M Old 4–20)

2 LORD'S   England won by an innings and 285 runs

England 629 (D L Amiss 188, M H Denness 118, A W Greig 106, J H Edrich 96, B S Bedi 6–226)

India 302 (F M Engineer 86, G R Viswanath 52, C M Old 4–67) and 42 (C M Old 5–21, G G Arnold 4–19)

3 EDGBASTON   England won by an innings and 78 runs

India 165 (F M Engineer 64, M Hendrick 4–28) and 216 (S S Naik 77)

England 459–2 dec (D Lloyd 214, M H Denness 100, D L Amiss 79, K W R Fletcher 51)

1974 Averages

Batting	I	No	Runs	HS	Avge
D. Lloyd (E)	2	1	260	214*	260.00
J.H.Edrich (E)	3	1	203	100*	101.50
M.H. Denness (E)	4	1	289	118	96.33
D.L. Amiss (E)	4	0	370	188	92.50
S.M. Gavaskar (I)	6	0	217	101	36.16
G.R. Viswanath (I)	6	0	200	52	33.33

Bowling	O	M	Runs	W	Avge	BB
C.M. Old (E)	89	19	249	18	13.83	5–21
M. Hendrick (E)	85	14	215	14	15.35	4–28
G.G. Arnold (E)	65.5	13	204	10	20.40	4–19
B.S. Bedi (I)	172.2	28	523	10	53.30	6–226

Statham, John Brian

Statham was born on 17 June 1930 at Gorton, Manchester. He got into the Lancashire team in 1950, as an accurate right-arm fast bowler. He was flown out to join the England tour party to Australia in 1950–51 and made his Test debut against New Zealand. He was the most consistent of England's fast bowlers for many years, although sometimes outshone by Trueman or Tyson. In 70 Tests he took 252 wickets, average 24.84, standing second in the all-time aggregates at the time.

With Gavaskar out first ball of the match at Edgbaston, India struggled to 165. Then David Lloyd, in his second Test, made 214 not out, adding 211 with Denness (100), who declared at 459 for two. With India out for 216, England had won while losing only two wickets in the match. The last two matches had brought India two of the biggest defeats in Test history.

Amiss caught by Chandrasekhar at first slip off the bowling of Bedi at Old Trafford in 1974. The wicket-keeper is Engineer and the non-striking batsman is John Edrich, who went on to a not-out century.

1976–77: England win series 3–1 in India

A.W. Greig proved a popular leader in India in 1976–77, where Bedi captained the home side. After four English wickets had gone for 65 in the first Test at Delhi, Amiss (179) led a revival to 381. J.K. Lever, in his first Test innings, took seven for 46, only two bowlers having taken more on their debut. India, 122 all out, followed on and Underwood did the rest, England winning by an innings and 25.

At Calcutta, Willis (5–27) removed India for 155. Greig (103) made a slow century against the wiles of Bedi (5–110), helping England to 321. With India dismissed for 181, England won by ten wickets.

England made 262 at Madras, and Lever (5–59) removed India for 164. There was ill-feeling, however, when the Indian captain thought Lever was using Vaseline on his forehead to shine the ball. Lever was officially cleared of the charge. After a second-innings declaration by England, India were out for 83, England winning by 200.

Willis took six for 53 at Bangalore to help get India out for 253. India relied on the leg-breaks and googlies of Chandrasekhar, and his six for 76 got India a lead of 58. India set England 318 to win, and won by 140 with Bedi (6–71) getting most wickets.

At Bombay, India made 338, Gavaskar getting a century, which gave them a lead of 21. Underwood spun India out in the second innings for 192, England needing 214 to win. They reached 152 for seven by the close.

Gavaskar makes Greig take evasive action at Old Trafford, 1974.

1976–77 14th Series Eng 3, India 1, Drawn 1

1 NEW DELHI England won by an innings and 25 runs
England 381 (D L Amiss 179, A P E Knott 75, J K Lever 53, B S Bedi 4–92)
India 122 (J K Lever 7–46) and 234 (S M Gavaskar 71, D L Underwood 4–78)

2 CALCUTTA England won by 10 wkts
India 155 (R G D Willis 5–27) and 151 (B P Patel 56)
England 321 (A W Greig 103, R W Tolchard 67, C M Old 52, B S Bedi 5–110, E A S Prasanna 4–93) and 16–0

3 MADRAS England won by 200 runs
England 262 (J M Brearley 59, A W Greig 54, B S Bedi 4–72) and 185–9 dec (B S Chandrasekhar 5–50, E A S Prasanna 4–55)
India 163 (J K Lever 5–59) and 83 (D L Underwood 4–28)

4 BANGALORE India won by 140 runs
India 253 (S Amarnath 63, S M H Kirmani 52, R G D Willis 6–53) and 259–9 dec (G R Viswanath 79, S M Gavaskar 50, D L Underwood 4–76)
England 195 (D L Amiss 82, B S Chandrasekhar 6–76) and 177 (A P E Knott 81, B S Bedi 6–71)

5 BOMBAY Match Drawn
India 338 (S M Gavaskar 108, B P Patel 83, D L Underwood 4–89) and 192 (S Amarnath 63, D L Underwood 5–84)
England 317 (J M Brearley 91, A W Greig 76, D L Amiss 50, E A S Prasanna 4–73, B S Bedi 4–109) and 152–7 (K W R Fletcher 58, K D Ghavri 5–33)

1976–77 Averages

Batting	I	No	Runs	HS	Avge
D.L. Amiss (E)	9	1	417	179	52.12
A.W. Greig (E)	8	0	342	103	42.75
S.M. Gavaskar (I)	10	0	394	108	39.40
A.P.E. Knott (E)	8	1	268	81*	38.28
B.P. Patel (I)	10	0	286	83	28.60

Bowling	O	M	Runs	W	Avge	BB
J.K. Lever (E)	149.4	29	380	26	14.61	7–46
R.G.D. Willis (E)	135	25	335	20	16.75	6–53
D.L. Underwood (E)	252.5	95	509	29	17.55	5–84
E.A.S. Prasanna (I)	232.4	79	389	18	21.61	4–55
B.S. Bedi (I)	294	106	574	25	22.96	6–71
B.S. Chandrasekhar (I)	194	40	537	19	28.26	6–76

1979: Gavaskar's great innings consoles India for lost series

The Indians were led in England in 1979 by spinner S. Venkataraghavan while J.M. Brearley had assumed the England captaincy.

Batting first at Edgbaston, Boycott made 155 and Gower 200 not out in a total of 633 for five declared, England's highest total since the war. Kapil Dev took all five wickets. India were forced to follow on and made 297 and 253, Botham being the most successful bowler.

Rain held up play at Lord's and helped India save the game after a first-innings dismissal for 96 (Botham 5–35). England declared 323 ahead, but Vengsarkar (103) and Viswanath (113) saved the match with a stand of 210.

Rain wrecked the Headingley Test, but Botham made a spectacular 137 to keep spectators amused.

The fourth and last Test at the Oval saw England take a lead of 103 and, with Boycott scoring a century, Brearley set India to get 438 runs in over eight hours. Over five of these were used by Gavaskar and C.P.S. Chauhan in scoring 213 for the first wicket. Vengsarkar joined Gavaskar and India entered the last 20 overs at 328 for one. Vengsarkar left at 366 and Kapil Dev at 367, and when Gavaskar was out for a magnificent 221, the innings lost its momentum. India ended at 429 for eight. It was almost a great win, and was a first-class draw.

1979 15th Series Eng 1, India 0, Drawn 3

1 EDGBASTON England won by an innings and 83 runs

England 633–5 dec (D I Gower 200, G Boycott 155, G A Gooch 83, G Miller 63, Kapil Dev 5–146)

India 297 (G R Viswanath 78, S M Gavaskar 61) and 253 (S M Gavaskar 68, C P S Chauhan 56, G R Viswanath 51, I T Botham 4–45)

2 LORD'S Match Drawn

India 96 (I T Botham 5–35) and 318–4 (G R Viswanath 113, D B Vengsarkar 103, S M Gavaskar 59)

England 419–9 dec (D I Gower 82, R W Taylor 64, G Miller 62, D W Randall 57)

3 HEADINGLEY Match Drawn

England 270 (I T Botham 137)

India 223–6 (S M Gavaskar 78, D B Vengsarkar 65)

4 THE OVAL Match Drawn

England 305 (G A Gooch 79, P Willey 52) and 334–8 dec (G Boycott 125, D L Bairstow 59)

India 202 (G R Viswanath 62, I T Botham 4–65) and 429–8 (S M Gavaskar 221, C P S Chauhan 80, D V Vengsarkar 52)

1979 Averages

Batting	I	No	Runs	HS	Avge
S.M. Gavaskar (I)	7	0	542	221	77.42
G. Boycott (E)	5	0	378	155	75.60
D.I. Gower (E)	5	1	289	200*	72.25
I.T. Botham (E)	5	0	244	137	48.80
G.R. Viswanath (I)	7	0	341	113	48.71
D.B. Vengsarkar (I)	7	1	249	103	41.50
G. A. Gooch (E)	5	0	207	83	41.40

Bowling	O	M	Runs	W	Avge	BB
M. Hendrick (E)	129.2	51	218	12	18.16	4–45
I.T. Botham (E)	179	49	472	20	23.60	5–35
R.G.D. Willis (E)	102	23	298	10	29.80	3–53
Kapil Dev (I)	173.5	49	495	16	30.93	5–146

1979–80: Botham and Taylor break records in Golden Jubilee match

After touring Australia, England flew to India to play a Golden Jubilee Test at the Wankhede Stadium, Bombay. Viswanath and Brearley were the captains. India batted first and were out for 242, Botham taking six for 58, and Taylor equalling the world record with seven catches. England were 58 for five, but Botham (114) and Taylor (43) added 171 for the sixth wicket, and England led by 54. During this stand Taylor was given out caught behind, but protested, and Viswanath persuaded the umpire to change his decision. India were out a second time for 149 (Botham 7–48) and England won by ten wickets. Botham became the first player to score a century and take ten wickets in a Test. Taylor took ten catches, a new Test record, eight of them off Botham. The match was truly a triumph for these two players.

1979–80 16th Series (Jubilee Match) Eng 1, India 0

BOMBAY England won by 20 wkts

India 242 (I T Botham 6–58) and 149 (I T Botham 7–48)

England 296 (I T Botham 114, K D Ghavri 5–52) and 98–0

Mankad, Vinoo

Mankad was born on 12 April 1917 at Jamnagar, India. His names were Mulwantrai Himatlal, but he was known as 'Vinoo'. He was an opening right-hand batsman and slow left-arm bowler. He played for many teams in India, beginning with Western India in 1935–36. His Test career did not begin until after the war, in 1946, on the tour to England. He was India's leading all-rounder. In 44 Tests he scored 2,109 runs, average 31.47, and took 162 wickets, average 32.32. He died on 21 August 1978 at Bombay.

1981–82: A quick win and five long draws for India

K.W.R. Fletcher and S.M. Gavaskar were captains when England toured India in 1981–82 with six Tests on the Agenda. The inclusion of G. Boycott and G. Cook in the party caused problems, as they had contacts

Botham being congratulated by his England teammates after removing Viswanath and Sandeep Patil with successive balls in the Golden Jubilee Test at Bombay in 1979–80.

The Indian team for the Golden Jubilee Test match at Bombay in 1979–80. Left to right, back: Hanumant Singh (manager), Shivlal Yadav, Vengsarkar, Sandeep Patil, Binny, Kapil Dev, Dilip Doshi, Yashpal Sharma. Front: Kirmani, Gavaskar, Viswanath, Chetan Chauhan, Ghavri.

with South Africa. The Indian government allowed the tour to go ahead less than a week before the party was due to sail, and Boycott and Cook made anti-*apartheid* observations.

The first Test was at Bombay, where India struggled to 179, but through D.R. Doshi (5–39) removed England for 166. Botham, who took nine wickets in the match, kept England's fourth-innings target to 241, but England surprisingly subsided before the Indian seam attack of Kapil Dev and Madan Lal, who shared the wickets in a total of 102. Botham completed 2,000 runs and 200 wickets in Tests, the third player to do so, but the youngest and quickest.

At Bangalore, England made 400 and Gavaskar, as if batting for the five draws needed to win the series, batted 708 minutes for 172. The match was drawn. There had been complaints from England about the umpiring in the first Test, and these were to persist. The England captain, Fletcher, knocked over his stumps in disgust on being dismissed in the second, and the relationship between England and the umpires continued to be strained. After an objection, one was

replaced for the third Test at Delhi.

This match followed a similar pattern. England made 476 for nine declared, with centuries from Boycott and Tavare, the former becoming the highest Test scorer in history by passing Sobers' record aggregate. But this score took 157 overs, so play went into the third day. India made 487 with Viswanath scoring 107, and the match was drawn.

The Calcutta Test was watched by a world record crowd, estimated at around 400,000. England made 248 (Kapil Dev 6–91) and got India out for 208. They then made 265 for five declared, giving themselves over a day to get India out. However, play started 70 minutes late on the last day, and Gavaskar, 83 not out in 83 overs, did the necessary for the draw.

Boycott had not fielded on the last day of the Test because of ill-health, and there were murmurings when it was learned he had played golf. He shortly left for home 'by mutual agreement', and later left on a 'rebel' tour to South Africa.

For the Madras Test, a desperate Fletcher packed his side with fast bowlers and put India in, only to see Viswanath score 222 and Yashpal Sharma 140. India's fourth wicket added 415, 99 by Vengsarkar and Viswanath, Vengsarkar (71) then retiring hurt, and 316 by Viswanath and Yashpal. England did not take a wicket on the second day. Gooch (127) led England to 328, but the match was clearly a draw. All eleven

England players bowled in the match, ten in the second innings.

In the sixth Test at Kanpur, the all-rounders Botham and Kapil Dev made 142 and 116 respectively, but there was no time to start a second innings with mist and rain taking up nearly ten hours, and India won the series 1–0.

1981–82   17th Series   India 1, Eng 0, Drawn 5

1 BOMBAY   India won by 138 runs
India 179 (S M Gavaskar 55, I T Botham 4–72, G R Dilley 4–47) and 227 (I T Botham)
England 166 (G Boycott 60, C J Tavare 56, D R Doshi 5–39) and 102 (Kapil Dev 5–70, S Madan Lal 5–23)

2 BANGALORE   Match Drawn
England 400 (D I Gower 82, G A Gooch 58, I T Botham 55, G R Dilley 52, R J Shastri 4–83) and 174–3 dec (G Boycott 50)
India 428 (S M Gavaskar 172, K Srikkanth 65, Kapil Dev 59, J K Lever 5–100)

3 NEW DELHI   Match Drawn
England 476–9 dec (C J Tavare 149, G Boycott 105, G A Gooch 71, K W R Fletcher 51, S Madan Lal 5–85) and 68–0
India 487 (G R Viswanath 107, R J Shastri 93, S M H Kirmani 67)

4 CALCUTTA   Match Drawn
England 248 (K W R Fletcher 69, I T Botham 58, Kapil Dev 6–91) and 265–5 dec (D I Gower 74, G A Gooch 63, K W R Fletcher 60)
India 208 (D B Vengsarkar 70) and 170–3 (S M Gavaskar 83)

5 MADRAS   Match Drawn
India 481– dec (G R Viswanath 222, Yashpal Sharma 140) and 160–3 dec (P Roy jun 60)
England 328 (G A Gooch 127, D I Gower 64, I T Botham 52, D R Doshi 4–69)

6 KANPUR   Match Drawn
England 378–9 dec (I T Botham 142, D I Gower 85, G A Gooch 58, D R Doshi 4–81)
India 377–7 (Kapil Dev 116, G R Viswanath 74, Yashpal Sharma 55, S M Gavaskar 52)

1981–82 Averages

Batting

	I	No	Runs	HS	Avge
S.M. Gavaskar (I)	9	1	500	172	62.50
G.R. Viswanath (I)	8	0	466	222	58.25
I.T. Botham (E)	8	0	440	142	55.00
G.A. Gooch (E)	10	1	487	127	54.11
Kapil Dev (I)	8	2	318	116	53.00
D.I. Gower (E)	9	1	375	85	46.87
G. Boycott (E)	8	1	312	105	44.57
C.J. Tavaré (E)	9	0	349	149	38.77
D.B. Vengsarkar (I)	8	0	292	71	36.50

Bowling

	O	M	Runs	W	Avge	BB
D.R. Doshi (I)	267.5	103	468	22	21.27	5–39
Madan Lal (I)	161	34	432	14	30.86	5–23
R.G.D. Willis (E)	129.1	29	381	12	31.75	3–75
Kapil Dev (I)	243.5	40	835	22	37.95	6–91
R.J. Shastri (I)	242	73	462	12	38.50	4–83
I.T. Botham (E)	240.3	52	660	17	38.82	5–61

1982: Much stroke-play in three-match series

The first Test at Lord's in 1982 was celebrated as the golden jubilee of Anglo-Indian Tests. Willis was England's new captain, and he batted. Randall (127) rescued England from a poor start, and they reached 433. Botham's five wickets helped get India out for 128, and they followed on. Vengsarkar's 157 helped avoid the innings defeat, but England won by seven wickets.

Rain cut down the Old Trafford Test, not even the first innings being complete. Despite Doshi's six for 102, the highlights were Botham's 128 and S.M. Patil's 129 not out, which included six fours in one over from Willis (one no-ball), a Test record.

In the third and final Test at the Oval, Botham treated spectators to 200 off 220 balls, going on to 208. Lamb made 107 and England scored 594. Gavaskar at silly point was hit by a Botham drive and retired with a broken ankle. India bravely made 410 and the match was drawn.

1982 18th Series Eng 1, India 0, Drawn 2

1 LORD'S **England won by 7 wkts**

England 455 (D W Randall 126, I T Botham 67, P H Edmonds 64, Kapil Dev 5–125) and 67–3

India 128 (I T Botham 5–46) and 369 (D B Vengsarkar 157, Kapil Dev 89, R G D Willis 6–101)

2 OLD TRAFFORD **Match Drawn**

England 425 (I T Botham 128, G Miller 98, G Cook 66, C J Tavare 57, D R Doshi 6–102)

India 379–8 (S M Patil 129, Kapil Dev 65, S M H Kirmani 58, G R Viswanath 54)

3 THE OVAL **Match Drawn**

England 594 (I T Botham 208, A J Lamb 107, D W Randall 95, G Cook 50) and 191–3 dec (C J Tavare 75)

India 410 (Kapil Dev 97, R J Shastri 66, S M Patil 62, G R Viswanath 56) and 111–3 (G R Viswanath 75)

1982 Averages

Batting

	I	No	Runs	HS	Avge
I.T. Botham (E)	3	0	403	208	134.33
D.W. Randall (E)	3	0	221	126	73.66
Kapil Dev (I)	4	0	292	97	73.00
A.J. Lamb (E)	5	1	207	107	51.75

Bowling

	O	M	Runs	W	Avge	BB
R.G.D. Willis (E)	88	11	330	15	22.00	6–101
D.R. Doshi (I)	157.1	38	445	13	35.00	6–102
Kapil Dev (I)	133	21	439	10	43.90	5–125

Above right: Chandra bowled by Lever at Madras in 1976–77. Lever was the centre of controversy over his alleged use of Vaseline to shine the ball.

Right: Viswanath batting at Lord's in 1979, where he made 113.

1984–85: England master young spinner and recover to win

Tragedy preceded the cricket on this tour. Three hours after the tourists arrived, Mrs Ghandi, the Prime Minister, was assassinated. Rioting and unrest marred the period of mourning and the tourists retired to Sri Lanka for a while. Then, on the eve of the first Test, the British Deputy High Commissioner to Western India, who the previous evening had entertained the tourists, was murdered. The match went ahead, and England collapsed for 195 to an 18-year-old wrist-spinner, L. Sivaramakrishnan, who took six for 64. Shastri and Kirmani made centuries and India declared at 465 for eight. Sivaramakrishnan took six for 117 in the second innings and, despite Gatting's first Test century in his 54th innings, England's 317 could not avoid an eight-wicket defeat.

Above left: Gavaskar turning a ball to leg in the second Test at New Delhi in 1984–85.

Above: Ravi Shastri hitting out at Bombay in 1984–85, when he made 142 and India won to take a lead in the series.

Gavaskar batted at Delhi and India made 307. But R.T. Robinson, in his second Test, made 160, around which England scored 418. Sivaramakrishnan took six for 99. Pocock and Edmonds got India out the second time for 235, the last six wickets falling quickly for 28, surprisingly giving England time to win by eight wickets.

Kapil Dev was dropped at Calcutta for not applying himself at Delhi (he had hit a six and holed out next ball). India batted so slowly that the crowd became restless and threw oranges onto the field. M. Azharuddin, in his first Test, made 110, and Shastri 111, but after 200 rain-interrupted overs India had only 437 for seven, when Gavaskar declared to prevent a riot. The match was a meaningless draw.

With Kapil Dev restored, India went for their shots at Madras but were out for 272 (Foster 6–104). England then at last mastered Sivaramakrishnan. Fowler, dropped early, made 201, and Gatting 207, England declaring at 652 for seven. India fought hard and Azharuddin made another century but Foster bowled well again for five for 95, and there was time for England to get the 33 runs they needed.

India needed to win at Kanpur and batted with more urgency. Azharuddin (122) became the first batsman to score a century in each of his first three Tests. Vengsarkar made 137 and India 553 for eight declared. But England batted steadily for 417 and a hopeful declaration by Gavaskar did not provoke a run-chase.

England were the first side to come from behind to win a series in India.

1984–85   19th Series   Eng 2, India 1, Drawn 2

1 BOMBAY   India won by 8 wkts

England 195 (L Sivaramakrishnan 6–64) and 317 (M W Gatting 136, P R Downton 62, G Fowler 55, L Sivaramakrishnan 6–117)

India 465–8 dec (R J Shastri 142, S M H Kirmani 102) and 51–2

2 DELHI   England won by 8 wkts

India 307 (Kapil Dev 60, R M Ellison 4–66) and 235 (S M Gavaskar 65, M B Amarnath 64, P H Edmonds 4–60, P I Pocock 4–93)

England 418 (R T Robinson 160, P R Downton 74, A J Lamb 52, L Sivaramakrishnan 6–99) and 127–2

3 CALCUTTA   Match Drawn

India 437–7 dec (R J Shastri 111, M Azharuddin 110) and 29–1

England 276 (A J Lamb 67, Chetan Sharma 4–38, Shivlal Yadav 4–86)

4 MADRAS   England won by 9 wkts

India 272 (M B Amarnath 78, Kapil Dev 53, N A Foster 6–104) and 412 (M Azharuddin 105, M B Amarnath 95, S M H Kirmani 75, N A Foster 5–95)

England 652–7 (M W Gatting 207, G Fowler 201, R T Robinson 74, A J Lamb 62) and 35–1

5 KANPUR   Match Drawn

India 553 (D B Vengsarkar 137, M Azharuddin 122, K Srikkanth 84, R J Shastri 59) and 97–1 dec (M Azharuddin 54)

England 417 (R T Robinson 96, D I Gower 78, G Fowler 69, M W Gatting 62, Kapil Dev 4–81) and 91–0

1984–85 Averages

Batting	I	No	Runs	HS	Avge
M. Azharuddin (I)	5	1	439	122	109.75
M.W. Gatting (E)	9	3	575	207	95.83
R.T. Robinson (E)	9	2	444	160	63.43
S.M.H. Kirmani (I)	7	2	291	102	58.20
M. Armanath (I)	8	1	407	95	58.14
G. Fowler (I)	8	0	438	201	54.75
R.J. Shastri (I)	9	2	383	142	54.71
Kapil Dev (I)	6	0	253	60	42.16
D.B. Vengsarkar (I)	8	1	284	137	40.57

Bowling	O	M	Runs	W	Avge	BB
N.A. Foster (E)	87	18	286	14	20.42	6–104
L. Sivaramakrishnan (I)	274.3	63	723	23	31.43	6–64
P.H. Edmonds (E)	276.1	104	584	14	41.71	4–60
Kapil Dev (I)	161.5	33	436	10	43.60	4–81
N.G. Cowans (E)	181.5	41	627	14	44.78	3–103
P.I. Pocock (E)	237.5	53	655	13	50.38	4–93

1986: Vengsarkar's record as India win 2–0

Kapil Dev led the Indian tourists to England in 1986, and in the first Test at Lord's put England in to bat. Chetan Sharma took five for 64, and despite Gooch's 114, England were out for 294. Vengsarkar made 126 not out and became the first overseas player to make three Test centuries at Lord's. India led by 47, and when England batted poorly to make only 180 in the second innings, India won by five wickets. It was only India's second win in England.

Gower was replaced as England captain by Gatting for the second Test at Headingley, where India made 272 and removed England for only 102, R.M.H. Binny taking five for 40. Vengsarkar's 102 not out ensured a high target for England in the fourth innings: 408. But England made only 128 for a humiliating 279-run defeat.

At Edgbaston, Gavaskar made his 115th Test appearance, a new record, passing Cowdrey's. Both sides made 390 in the first innings, England relying on Gatting's 183 not out, but India batting more evenly. England's second-innings 235 (Sharma 6–58) promised a good finish, but drizzle came and India drew at 174 for five, winning the series 2–0.

1986 20th Series India 2, Eng 0, Drawn 2

1 LORD'S India won by 5 wkts
England 294 (G A Gooch 114, D R Pringle 63, Chetan Sharma
5–64) and 180 (Kapil Dev 4–52)
India 341 (D B Vengsarkar 126, M B Amarnath 69, G R Dilley
4–146) and 136–5

2 HEADINGLEY India won by 279 runs
India 272 (D B Vengsarkar 61) and 237 (D B Vengsarkar 102, J
K Lever 4–65, D R Pringle 4–73)
England 101 (R M H Binny 5–40) and 128 (Maninder Singh 4–
26)

3 EDGBASTON Match Drawn
England 380 (M W Gatting 183, Chetan Sharma 4–130) and
235 (Chetan Sharma 6–58)
India 390 (M B Amarnath 79, M Azharuddin 64) and 174–5 (S M
Gavaskar 54, P H Edmonds 4–31)

1986 Averages

Batting	I	No	Runs	HS	Avge
D.B. Vengsarkar (I)	6	2	360	126*	90.00
M.W. Gatting (E)	6	2	293	183*	73.25

Bowling	O	M	Runs	W	Avge	BB
Maninder Singh (I)	114.1	41	187	12	15.58	4–26
Chetan Sharma (I)	102.3	20	300	16	18.75	6–58
R.M.H. Binny (I)	87.2	11	251	12	20.91	5–40
D.R. Pringle (E)	126.3	31	302	13	23.23	4.73
G.R. Dilley (E)	85.2	19	299	10	29.90	4.146
Kapil Dev (I)	128.2	36	306	10	30.60	4.52

Right: Dilip Vengsarkar during his century at Lord's in 1986. He became the first overseas player to score three Test centuries at Lord's.

Below: Mohammad Azharuddin forcing the ball to leg. In 1984–85 against England he became the first player to score centuries in each of his first three Tests.

Above: The Indian tourists in 1986. Left to right, back: Sandeep Patil, Chetan Sharma, Prabhakar, Raman Lamba, Maninder Singh, V.B. Prabhudesai (assistant manager), More, Srikkanth, Azharuddin, Pandit. Front: Binny, Vengsarkar, Amarnath, Kapil Dev, Raj Singh (manager), Shastri, Gavaskar, Yadav.

Left: David Gower scattering the close field at Lord's in 1986. Gower lost his position as England captain after this Test.

Below: Maninder Singh bowling at Edgbaston in 1986, following the fashion for *patkas* made famous by Bedi.

West Indies v India

1948–49: Weekes establishes record in high-scoring series

A West Indies side led by J.D.C. Goddard, which the previous season had beaten the English tourists, visited India in 1948–49 and played the first series of Tests between the two countries. L. Amarnath captained India.

In the first Test at Delhi, four West Indians made centuries: Walcott, Gomez, Weekes and Christiani. Despite Adhikari's 114 not out, India followed on but easily saved the match.

It was a similar story at Bombay; Rae and Weekes made centuries and West Indies declared at 629 for six. India followed on but this time needed stubborn second-innings hundreds from Modi and Hazare to save the game.

West Indies were confined to 366 at Calcutta, with Weekes getting 162. India were out 94 behind, and West Indies added 336 for nine declared to their lead. Walcott and Weekes made centuries. That of Weekes was his fifth in successive Test innings, a world record. Mushtaq Ali made a century for India, who saved the game well.

At Madras, Rae and Stollmeyer began with a West Indies record opening stand of 239. Both hit centuries, but Weekes' run of centuries ended when he was run out for 90. West Indies made 582, but Phadkar salvaged from it his best Test figures of seven for 159. On a pitch faster than the others, the West Indian pace men, P.E. Jones and J. Trim, at last got the batsmen uncomfortable, and India were out twice for 245 and 144.

West Indies won the toss and batted for the fifth time in the last Test at Bombay. They made only 286, Weekes getting a seventh successive 50, another record. India made 193, and West Indies 267, Weekes' run of 50s ending when he was bowled for 48. India needed 361 in 395 minutes. Hazare made 122 and the issue was in doubt almost to the last ball. This was never bowled, for with India needing six more with two wickets left, play ended one ball short, the umpire apparently having miscounted.

1948–49 1st Series WI 1, India 1, Drawn 4
1 NEW DELHI Match Drawn
West Indies 631 (C L Walcott 152, E de C Weekes 128, R J Christiani 107, G E Gomez 101, C R Rangachari 5–107)
India 454 (H R Adhikari 114, K C Ibrahim 85, R S Modi 63, L Amarnath 62) and 220–6

2 BOMBAY Match Drawn
West Indies 629–6 dec (E de C Weekes 194, A F Rae 104, F J Cameron 75, R J Christiani 74, C L Walcott 68, J B Stollmeyer 66)
India 273 (D G Phadkar 74, W Ferguson 4–126) and 333–3 (V S Hazare 134, R S Modi 112, L Amarnath 58)

3 CALCUTTA Match Drawn
West Indies 366 (E de C Weekes 162, C L Walcott 54, Ghulam Ahmed 4–94, S A Banerjee 4–120) and 336–9 dec (C L Walcott 108, E de C Weekes 101)
India 272 (R S Modi 80, V S Hazare 59, S Mushtaq Ali 54) and 325–3 (S Mushtaq Ali 106, R S Modi 87, V S Hazare 58)

4 MADRAS West Indies won by an innings and 193 runs
West Indies 582 (J B Stollmeyer 160, A F Rae 109, E de C Weekes 90, G E Gomez 50, D G Phadkar 7–159)
India 245 (R S Modi 56, J Trim 4–48) and 144 (V S Hazare 52, P E Jones 4–30)

5 BOMBAY Match Drawn
West Indies 286 (J B Stollmeyer 85, E de C Weekes 56, D G Phadkar 4–74) and 267 (A F Rae 97, S N Banerjee 4–54)
India 193 and 355–8 (V S Hazare 122, R S Modi 86, P E Jones 5–85)

West Indies v India 1948–49 Averages Batting	I	No	Runs	HS	Avge
E. De C. Weekes (WI)	7	0	779	194	111.28
J.B. Stollmeyer (WI)	5	0	342	160	68.40
V.S. Hazare (I)	10	2	543	134*	67.57
C.L. Walcott (WI)	7	0	452	152	64.57
R.S. Modi (I)	10	0	560	112	56.00
A.F. Rae (WI)	7	0	374	109	53.42
H.R. Adhikari (I)	8	3	254	114	50.80
R.J. Christiani (WI)	7	0	294	107	42.00
L. Armanath (I)	10	2	294	62	36.75
G.E. Gomez (WI)	7	0	256	101	36.57

Bowling	O	M	Runs	W	Avge	BB
P.E. Jones (WI)	191	44	479	17	28.17	5–85
G.E. Gomez (WI)	257.3	84	454	16	28.37	3–35
D.G. Phadkar (I)	139.5	31	411	14	29.35	7–159
V. Mankad (I)	272.3	52	744	17	43.76	3–54

1952–53: West Indies take home series by a single win

On India's first visit to the West Indies, Stollmeyer and Hazare were the captains.

The wicket was easy at Port-of-Spain where enthusiastic crowds watched the play. India made a steady 417 (Umrigar 130) and West Indies a slightly quicker 438, Weekes getting 207 and B.H. Pairaudeau, on his debut, 115; Gupte took 7 for 162. Set 274 to win, West Indies made no attempt in the time left.

At Bridgetown, the wicket was of uncertain bounce, and suited the spinners. India had to bat last and get 272, but Ramadhin and Valentine got them out for 129.

The third Test was switched to Port-of-Spain because of flooding in Georgetown. A magnificent 161 from Weekes allowed West Indies to get 315 and a lead of 36, but Apte replied with 163 not out for India and the match was another draw, with Stollmeyer's fourth-innings century being academic.

The match at Georgetown was spoiled by rain, water getting under the covers. On the second day play was abandoned, but a hostile crowd persuaded the officials to resume for the final hour, a decision which later drew a critical note from MCC. The match was drawn with Walcott (125) and Valentine (eight wickets) doing best.

There was high scoring at Kingston where Umrigar, in the first innings, and Roy and Manjrekar in the second, made centuries for India, and in West Indies' 576 the 'three Ws', Worrell, Weekes and Walcott, made centuries together for the first time, Worrell's being 237. Gupte and Mankad shared the West Indian wickets, between them taking 10 for 408. Valentine took nine wickets for West Indies. After this run feast, West Indies needed only 181 in 145 minutes, but curiously, after losing the openers for 15, settled for the draw and the series win.

1952–53 2nd Series WI 1, India 0, Drawn 4
1 PORT OF SPAIN Match Drawn
India 417 (P R Umrigar 130, M L Apte 64, G S Ramchand 61) and 294 (P R Umrigar 69, D G Phadkar 65, M L Apte 52)
West Indies 438 (E de C Weekes 207, B H Pairaudeau 115, S F Gupte 7–162) and 142–0 (J B Stollmeyer 76, A F Rae 63)

2 BRIDGETOWN West Indies won by 142 runs
West Indies 296 (C L Walcott 98) and 228 (J B Stollmeyer 54, D G Phadkar 5–64)
India 253 (M L Apte 64, V S Hazare 63, P R Umrigar 56, A L Valentine 4–58) and 129 (S Ramadhin 5–26)

3 PORT OF SPAIN Match Drawn
India 279 (G S Ramchand 62, P R Umrigar 61, F M King 5–74) and 362–7 dec (M L Apte 163, M H Mankad 96, P R Umrigar 67)
West Indies 315 (E de C Weekes 161, S P Gupte 5–107) and 192–2 (J B Stollmeyer 104, E de C Weekes 55)

4 GEORGETOWN Match Drawn
India 262 (M H Mankad 66, C V Gadkari 50, A L Valentine 5–127) and 190–5
West Indies 364 (C L Walcott 125, E de C Weekes 86, F M M Worrell 56, S P Gupte 4–122)

5 KINGSTON Match Drawn
India 312 (P R Umrigar 117, P Roy 85, A L Valentine 5–64) and 444 (P Roy 150, V L Manjrekar 118, G E Gomez 4–72, A L Valentine 4–149)
West Indies 576 (F M M Worrell 237, C L Walcott 118, E de C Weekes 109, B H Pairaudeau 58, S P Gupte 5–180, M H Mankad 5–228) and 92–4

1952–53 Averages Batting	I	No	Runs	HS	Avge
E. De C. Weekes (WI)	8	1	716	207	102.28
C.L. Walcott (WI)	7	1	457	125	76.16
P.R. Umrigar (I)	10	1	560	130	62.22
J.B. Stollmeyer (WI)	9	3	354	104*	59.00
M.L. Apte (I)	10	1	460	163*	51.11
F.M.M. Worrell (WI)	8	0	398	237	49.75
P. Roy (I)	8	0	383	150	47.87
V.L. Manjrekar (I)	8	1	254	118	36.28
B.H. Pairaudeau (WI)	8	0	257	115	32.12

Bowling	O	M	Runs	W	Avge	BB
F.M. King (WI)	238.1	78	480	17	28.23	5–74
S.P. Gupte (WI)	329.3	87	789	27	29.22	7–162
A.L. Valentine (WI)	430	179	828	28	29.57	5–64
S. Ramdhin (WI)	232.4	96	470	13	36.15	5–26
V. Mankad (I)	345	102	796	15	53.06	5–228

Gary Sobers, who made 557 runs against India in the 1958–59 series in India.

Left: Sonny Ramadhin and Alf Valentine, the two spin bowlers who made their Test debuts in England in 1950 and bowled brilliantly during the 1950s for West Indies.

Kapil Dev

Kapil Dev was born in Chandigarh, India, on 6 January 1959 and was close to his 17th birthday when making his first appearance for Haryana in 1975–76. He was a right-arm fast-medium opening bowler, the best in India for a long time, and made his Test debut in 1978–79. He was also a middle-order attacking batsman. In 1980–81 he became the youngest player to take 100 Test wickets,

and two days later the youngest to 1,000 Test runs. In 88 Tests to the end of the 1987 season he had scored 3,668 runs, average 32.17, and taken 311 wickets, average 29.40. He thus became the second player (after Botham) to 3,000 runs and 300 wickets in Tests. He has captained India in 34 Tests, as well as to victory in the World Cup in 1983.

1958–59: West Indies' fast bowlers tip the scales

F.C.M. Alexander and P.R. Umrigar were captains in 1958–59. Butcher and Hall made their debuts for West Indies at Bombay. In a low-scoring match, Sobers' 142 not out allowed West Indies to set India a target of 399 in 9½ hours, but India fought hard for a draw.

At Kanpur, West Indies recovered from a bad start to 222, and India, now led by Ghulam Ahmed, collapsed from a good start to the same score. Gupte (9–102) and Hall (6–50) were the bowlers. Sobers, coming in at nought for two in the second innings, scored 198 and won the match, Hall finishing with 11 wickets.

West Indies made 614 for five declared at Calcutta, Kanhai's first Test century being 256, Butcher and Sobers also passing 100. Hall and Gilchrist dismissed India cheaply twice for an innings win.

At Madras, Umrigar, restored to the Indian captaincy, resigned it and Mankad took over. Butcher's 142 took West Indies to 500. Alexander did not enforce the follow-on, but set India 447. West Indies won by 295.

Adhikari captained India at Delhi, where Borde made a century in 415. But West Indies made a record score in India of 644 for eight declared, with Holt, Smith and Solomon making hundreds. Borde (96) batted stubbornly in the second innings to prevent West Indies batting again – they would have needed only 47.

1958–59 3rd Series WI 3, India 0, Drawn 2

1 BOMBAY Match Drawn
West Indies 227 (R B Kanhai 66, O G Smith 63, S P Gupte 4–86) and 323–4 dec (G St A Sobers 142, B F Butcher 64, O G Smith 58)
India 152 (P R Umrigar 55, R Gilchrist 4–39) and 289–5 (P Roy 90, G S Ramchand 67)

2 KANPUR West Indies won by 203 runs
West Indies 222 (F C M Alexander 70, S P Gupte 9–103) and 443–7 dec (G St A Sobers 198, J S Solomon 86, B F Butcher 60)
India 222 (P R Umrigar 57, W W Hall 6–50) and 240 (N J Contractor 50, W W Hall 5–76)

3 CALCUTTA West Indies won by an Innings and 336 runs
West Indies 614–5 dec (R B Kanhai 256, G St A Sobers 106, B F Butcher 103, J S Solomon 69)
West Indies 124 and 154 (V L Manjrekar 58, R Gilchrist 6–55)

4 MADRAS West Indies won by 295 runs
West Indies 500 (B F Butcher 142, R B Kanhai 99, J K Holt 63, M H Mankad 4–95) and 168–5 dec (J K Holt 81, S P Gupte 4–78)
India 222 (A G Kripal Singh 53, G St A Sobers 4–26) and 151 (C G Borde 56)

5 NEW DELHI Match Drawn
India 415 (C G Borde 109, N J Contractor 92, P R Umrigar 76, H R Adhikari 63, W W Hall 4–66) and 275 (C G Borde 96, P Roy 58, D K Gaekwad 52, O G Smith 5–90)
West Indies 644–8 dec (J K Holt 123, O G Smith 100, J S Solomon 100, C C Hunte 92, B F Butcher 71, R B Desai 4–169)

1958–59 Averages

Batting	I	No	Runs	HS	Avge
J.S. Solomon (WI)	6	3	351	100*	117.00
G. St. A. Sobers (WI)	8	2	557	198	92.83
B.F. Butcher (WI)	8	1	486	142	69.42
R.B. Kanhai (WI)	8	0	538	256	67.25
J.K. Holt (WI)	8	1	343	123	49.00
P.R. Umrigar (I)	9	1	337	76	42.12
C.G. Borde (I)	7	0	281	109	40.14
O.G. Smith (WI)	8	0	287	100	35.87
P. Roy (I)	10	0	334	90	33.40

Bowling	O	M	Runs	W	Avge	BB
R. Gilchrist (WI)	198.1	73	419	26	16.11	6–55
W.W. Hall (WI)	221.4	65	530	30	17.66	6–50
S.P. Gupte (I)	312.3	71	927	22	42.13	9–102

The tour was not a happy one, the West

Indies' fast bowlers, Hall and Gilchrist, being too liberal with bouncers and 'beamers'. Gilchrist, at the end of the tour, was sent home for disciplinary reasons, and missed the tour of Pakistan which followed.

1961–62: West Indies win all five Tests

N.J. Contractor was India's captain in West Indies in 1961–62, having just led India to victory over England. Worrell captained West Indies after his successful tour of Australia.

At Port-of-Spain, West Indies passed India's first-innings 203 by 86, and Hall had India at eight for three in the second innings. They struggled to 98 but West Indies needed only 13.

India made 395 at Kingston, but West Indies replied with 631 for eight declared, McMorris, Kanhai and Sobers scoring centuries. With Hall getting six for 49, India failed by 18 to make West Indies bat again.

Before the third Test, Contractor had had his skull fractured by a ball from C.C. Griffith in a match against Barbados. After an emergency brain operation he recovered, but played no more Test cricket. The Nawab of Pataudi assumed the captaincy, but India, 217 behind on the first innings, were out for 187 in the second, Gibbs' figures of eight for 38 disguising the fact that he took the last eight wickets for six runs.

At Port-of-Spain, India fought hard after following on but still lost by seven wickets. At Kingston, West Indies' new fast bowler, L.A. King, began his Test career by taking five wickets in four overs to reduce India to 26 for five. West Indies won by 123 runs to complete a 5–0 series win.

1961–62 4th Series WI 5, India 0

1 PORT OF SPAIN West Indies won by 10 wkts
India 203 (R F Surit 57, S A Durani 56) and 98 (G St A Sobers 4–22)
West Indies 289 (J L Hendriks 64, C C Hunte 58, S A Durdni 4–82) and 15–0

2 KINGSTON West Indies won by an innings and 18 runs
India 395 (C G Borde 93, R G Nadkarni 78, F M Engineer 53, P R Umrigar 50, G St A Sobers 4–75) and 218 (W W Hall 6–49)
West Indies 631–8 dec (G St A Sobers 153, R B Kanhai 138, E D A St J McMorris 125, I L Mendonca 78, F M M Worrell 58)

3 BRIDGETOWN West Indies won by an innings and 30 runs
India 258 and 187 (D N Sardesai 60, V L Manjrekar 51, L R Gibbs 8–38)
West Indies 475 (J S Solomon 96, R B Kanhai 89, F M M Worrell 77, C C Hunte 59)

4 PORT OF SPAIN West Indies won by 7 wkts
West Indies 444–9 dec (R B Kanhai 139, F M M Worrell 73, E D A St J McMorris 50, V V Rodriguez 50, W W Hall 50, P R Umrigar 5–107) and 176–3 (E D A St J McMorris 56)
India 197 (P R Umrigar 56, W W Hall 5–20) and 422 (P R Umrigar 172, S A Durani 104, V L Mehra 62, L R Gibbs 4–112)

5 KINGSTON West Indies won by 123 runs
West Indies 253 (G St A Sobers, V B Ranjane 4–72) and 283 (F M M Worrell 98, G St A Sobers 50)
India 178 (R G Nadkarni 61, L A King 5–46) and 235 (P R Umrigar 60, G St A Sobers 5–63)

1961–62 Averages

Batting	I	No	Runs	HS	Avge
F.M.M. Worrell (WI)	6	2	332	98*	88.00
R.B. Kanhai (WI)	7	0	495	139	70.71
G. St. A. Sobers (WI)	7	1	424	153	70.66
E.D.A. St J. McMorris (WI)	6	0	439	125	58.16
P.R. Umrigar (I)	10	1	445	172*	49.44
R.G. Nadkarni (I)	10	3	286	78*	3.71
S.A. Durani (I)	10	1	259	104	28.77

Bowling	O	M	Runs	W	Avge	BB
W.W. Hall (WI)	173.4	37	425	27	15.74	6–49
L.R. Gibbs (WI)	264.5	93	490	24	20.41	8–38
G. St. A. Sobers (WI)	218.3	61	473	23	20.56	5–63
S.A. Durani (I)	229	62	600	17	35.29	4–82

1966–67: West Indies win 2–0 on short tour

Pataudi remained India's captain in 1966–67, while Sobers was now captain of West Indies.

At Bombay, Borde's 121 rallied India to 296. West Indies faced Chandrasekhar for the first time, when he took seven for 157, but Hunte hit 101 and West Indies led by 125. India set West Indies 192 and at 90 for four it was even, but Sobers and Lloyd knocked off the runs. It was Clive Lloyd's first Test: he made 82 and 78 not out.

There was no play on the second day at Calcutta, where B.S. Bedi made his debut. There were not enough seats for ticket-holders, resulting in fights, over-zealous police reaction, and stands set on fire. When play resumed, the battered wicket helped the spinners, and West Indies' initial 390 was enough for an innings win, Sobers and Gibbs spinning out India twice.

At Madras, Engineer scored 94 before lunch, and went on to 109. Borde made 125 and India 404, a total West Indies passed by two. Set 322 to win, West Indies were in trouble at 193 for seven, but Griffiths and Sobers, dropped twice early in their innings, lasted out 90 minutes for the draw.

1966–67 5th Series WI 2, India 0, Drawn 1

1 BOMBAY West Indies won by 6 wkts
India 296 (C G Borde 121, S A Durani 55) and 316 (B K Kunderan 79, M A K Pataudi 51, L R Gibbs 4–67)
West Indies 421 (C C Hunte 101, C H Lloyd 82, D A J Holford 80, G St A Sobers 50, B S Chandrasekhar 7–157) and 192–4 (C H Lloyd 78, G St A Sobers 53)

2 CALCUTTA West Indies won by an innings and 45 runs
West Indies 390 (R B Kanhai 90, G St A Sobers 70, S M Nurse 56)
India 167 (L R Gibbs 5–51) and 178 (G St A Sobers 4–56)

3 MADRAS Match Drawn
India 404 (C G Borde 125, F M Engineer 109, R F Surti 50) and 323 (A L Wadekar 67, V Subramanyam 61, Hamumant Singh 50, C C Griffith 4–61, L R Gibbs 4–96)
West Indies 406 (G St A Sobers 95, R B Kanhai 77, B S Chandrasekhar 4–130) and 270–7 (G St A Sobers 74, B S Bedi 4–81)

Bedi, Bishensingh Giansingh

Bedi was born on 25 September 1946 at Amritsar, and became a left-arm slow bowler whose colourful patkas (turbans) made him an easily recognized figure on the Test grounds of the world. He played from 1961–62 for Northern Punjab and Delhi in India and Northants in England. He made his Test debut in 1966–67 and played in 67 Tests, 22 as captain. He took 266 wickets, then India's highest, at 28.71 each.

1966–67 Averages

Batting	I	No	Runs	HS	Avge
G. St. A. Sobers (WI)	5	2	342	95	114.00
C. G. Borde (I)	6	0	346	125	57.66
R. B. Kanhai (WI)	4	0	227	90	56.75
C. H. Lloyd (WI)	5	1	227	82	56.75
C. C. Hunte (WI)	5	0	259	101	51.80

Bowling	O	M	Runs	W	Avge	BB
L. R. Gibbs (WI)	204.5	59	397	18	22.05	5–51
G. St. A. Sobers (WI)	155.1	51	350	14	25.00	4–56
B. S. Chandrasekhar (I)	196.5	52	513	18	28.50	7–157

1970–71: India win first match and first series

Wadekar captained India in 1970–71 against Sobers' side.

The first Test at Kingston started over a day late and India made 387, with Sardesai getting 212. West Indies, 217, followed on, and although they easily saved the match with Kanhai getting 158 not out, it was a promising start for India.

At Port-of-Spain, where S.M. Gavaskar made his debut, West Indies were out for 214, and another century by Sardesai gave India a lead of 138. J.M. Noreiga, in his second Test, took nine for 95 for West Indies. However, their batsmen could make only 216 in the second innings against India's on spinning and India won by seven wickets. Gavaskar made 65 and 67 not out. It was India's first win over West Indies in their 25 meetings.

At Georgetown, 116 by Gavaskar allowed India to pass West Indies' 363 by 13. Second-innings centuries by Davis and Sobers merely ensured a draw.

1970–71   6th Series   India 1, WI 0, Drawn 4

1 KINGSTON   Match Drawn
India 387 (D N Sardesai 212, E D Solkar 61, V A Holder 4–60)
West Indies 217 (R B Kanhai 56, E A S Prasanna 4–65) and 385–5 (R B Kanhai 158, G St A Sobers 93, C H Lloyd 57)

2 PORT OF SPAIN   India won by 7 wkts
West Indies 214 (C A Davis 71, E A Prasanna 4–54) and 261 (R C Fredericks 80, C A Davis 74, S Venkataraghavan 5–95)
India 352 (D N Sardesai 112, S M Gavaskar 65, E D Solkar 55, J M Noreiga 9–95) and 125–3 (S M Gavaskar 67)

3 GEORGETOWN   Match Drawn
West Indies 363 (D M Lewis 81, C H Lloyd 60) and 307–3 dec (C A Davis 125, G St A Sobers 108)
India 376 (S M Gavaskar 116, G R Viswanath 50, S Abid Ali 50) and 123–0 (S M Gavaskar 64, A V Mankad 53)

4 BRIDGETOWN   Match Drawn
West Indies 501–5 dec (G St A Sobers 178, D M Lewis 88, R B Kanhai 85, C A Davis 79) and 180–6 dec
India 347 (D N Sardesai 150, E D Solkar 65, U G Dowe 4–69) and 221–5 (S M Gavaskar 117)

5 PORT OF SPAIN   Match Drawn
India 360 (S M Gavaskar 124, D N Sardesai 75, S Venkataraghavan 51) and 427 (S M Gavaskar 220, A L Wadekar 54, J M Noreiga 5–129)
West Indies 526 (G St A Sobers 132, C A Davis 105, M L C Foster 99, D M Lewis 72, S Venkataraghavan 4–100) and 165–8 (C H Lloyd 64)

Headley, George Alphonso

Headley was born on 30 May 1909 at Colon, Panama, where a number of West Indians were helping build the Canal, but was brought up in Jamaica for whom he had his debut in 1927–28. He was a brilliant middle-order right-hand batsman, sometimes called 'the Black Bradman'. His first Test was in 1929–30. He played in 22, scoring 2,190 runs, at the high average of 60.83. Had he not played three Tests after the war, when he was not so good, his average would have been 66.71, second only to Bradman's. He died on 30 November 1983 in Kingston.

Sobers made another century at Bridgetown, but Sardesai replied with his third of the series. Sobers declared in the second innings but in a high-scoring match Gavaskar's second century of the series ensured the draw.

The last Test at Port-of-Spain was of six days. Gavaskar made 124 as India scored 360. West Indies gave themselves a chance to level the rubber with 526, Davis and Sobers getting centuries. But Gavaskar batted for 505 minutes in the second innings for 220. India made 427 and West Indies needed 262 in 155 minutes. They were hanging on at 165 for eight at the close.

Sobers was the captain of West Indies in 1966–67, and headed the batting averages while being second in the bowling table.

1970–71 Averages

Batting	I	No	Runs	HS	Avge
S. M. Gavaskar (I)	8	3	774	220	154.80
C. A. Davis (WI)	8	4	529	125*	132.25
D. M. Lewis (WI)	5	2	259	88	86.33
D. N. Sardesai (I)	8	0	642	212	80.25
G. St. A. Sobers (WI)	10	2	597	178*	74.62
R. B. Kanhai (WI)	9	1	433	158*	54.12
C. H. Lloyd (WI)	10	0	295	60	29.50

Bowling	O	M	Runs	W	Avge	BB
J. M. Noreiga (WI)	220.2	47	493	17	29.00	9–95
G. St. A. Sobers (WI)	220	70	402	12	33.50	3–72
S. Venkataraghavan (I)	289.3	67	744	22	33.81	5–85
B. S. Bedi (I)	310.4	95	656	15	43.73	3–46

1974–75: West Indies win decider after two wins each

Lloyd and Pataudi, recalled from retirement, were captains in India in 1974–75, Pataudi winning the first toss and putting West Indies in at Bangalore. C.G. Greenidge and I.V.A. Richards made their debuts for West Indies, but Kallicharran was the century-maker in a total of 289. India trailed by 29. Greenidge, run out 93 in his first Test innings, made 107 in the second. Lloyd made 163, declared, and India, minus two batsmen injured, were out for 118 and heavily defeated.

At Delhi, India made 220, and for West Indies Richards made 192 not out in his second Test, out of 493. Gibbs (6–76) spun out India in the second innings, and they just avoided an innings defeat.

Roberts took five for 50 at Calcutta to dismiss India for 233, but, even despite Fredericks' 100, India kept their first-innings deficit to seven. Viswanath then made 139 and India set West Indies to make 310 to win. They failed by 86.

Viswanath ran out of partners on a difficult pitch at Madras, being 97 not out of India's 190, Roberts getting seven for 64. Prasanna and Bedi struck back, and West Indies led by only two. When Roberts completed 12 wickets in the match, West Indies needed 255 to win, but India's spinners won the match by 100 and India levelled the series at 2–2.

In the six-day decider at Bombay, in the new Wankhede Stadium, Fredericks began with 104 for West Indies, and Lloyd made 242 not out. Play was held up for 90 minutes when brutal police treatment of a spectator celebrating Lloyd's 200 caused a riot. West Indies declared at 604 for six. Solkar made 102 for India, but in a long bowl Gibbs took seven for 98 to dismiss them for 406. West Indies then declared and set India 404. They made half of them, Holder's six for 39 winning the match and series for West Indies.

1974–75   7th Series   WI 3, India 2

1 BANGALORE   West Indies won by 267 runs
West Indies 289 (A I Kallicharran 124, C G Greenidge 93, S Venkataraghavan 4–75, B S Chandrasekhar 4–112) and 356–6 dec (C H Lloyd 163, C G Greenidge 107)
India 260 (H S Kanitkar 65) and 118

2 NEW DELHI   West Indies won by an innings and 17 runs
India 220 (P Sharma 54) and 256 (F M Engineer 75, L R Gibbs 6–76)
West Indies 493 (I V A Richards 192, C H Lloyd 71, K D Boyce 68, E A S Prasanna 4–147)

3 CALCUTTA   India won by 85 runs
India 233 (G R Viswanath 52, A M E Roberts 5–50) and 316 (G R Viswanath 139, F M Engineer 61)
West Indies 240 (R C Fredericks 100, S Madan Lal 4–22) and 224 (A I Kallicharran 57, B S Bedi 4–52)

4 MADRAS   India won by 100 runs
India 190 (G R Viswanath 97, A M E Roberts 7–64) and 256 (A D Gaekwad 80, A M E Roberts 5–57)

West Indies 192 (I V A Richards 50, E A S Prasanna 5–70) and 154 (A I Kallicharran 51, E A S Prasanna 4–41)

5 BOMBAY   West Indies won by 201 runs

West Indies 604–6 dec (C H Lloyd 242, R C Fredericks 104, A I Kallicharran 98, D L Murray 91, K D Ghavri 4–140) and 205–3 dec (C G Greenidge 54)

India 406 (E D Solkar 102, G R Viswanath 95, S M Gavaskar 86, A D Gaekwad 51, L R Gibbs 7–98) and 202 (B P Patel 73, V A Holder 6–39)

1974–75 Averages

Batting	I	No	Runs	HS	Avge
C.H. Lloyd (WI)	9	1	636	242*	79.50
A.I. Kallicharran (WI)	9	1	454	124	56.75
G.R. Viswanath (I)	10	1	568	139	53.11
I.V.A. Richards (WI)	9	2	353	192*	50.42
C.G. Greenidge (WI)	9	0	371	107	41.22
R.C. Fredericks (WI)	8	0	323	104	40.37

Bowling	O	M	Runs	W	Avge	BB
A.M.E. Roberts (WI)	200.3	51	585	32	18.28	7–64
V.A. Holder (WI)	150.2	41	315	17	18.52	6–39
L.R. Gibbs (WI)	295.5	103	454	21	21.61	7–98
B.S. Bedi (I)	183.2	55	499	15	33.26	4–52
E.A.S. Prasanna (I)	207.2	49	601	15	40.06	5–70
B.S. Chandrasekhar (I)	157.2	27	579	14	41.35	4–112

Top: G.R. Viswanath, who scored 568 runs and headed the Indian batting averages against the West Indies in 1974–75.

Above: E.A.S. Prasanna, who shared 44 wickets with his fellow-spinners Bedi and Chandrasekhar in 1974–75.

Facing page: Clive Lloyd, West Indies captain, on his way to a century at Bridgetown in 1975–6

Sunil Gavaskar, whose first Test series was in the West Indies where he was sensationally successful.

1975–76: West Indies win series with display of violence

There were four Tests in West Indies in 1975–76, Bedi leading the tourists.

India failed in the first Test at Bridgetown, scoring only 177 (Holford 5–23). Richards and captain Lloyd made centuries and West Indies won by an innings and 17.

Richards made 130 at Port-of-Spain out of only 241, Bedi getting five for 82 after putting West Indies in. Gavaskar (156) and B.P. Patel (115 not out) put on 204 and India declared at 402 for five. West Indies, in their second knock, were 215 for eight at the close, dropped catches and the loss of the first day's play through rain robbing India of victory.

As in 1952–53, the Georgetown Test was moved to Port-of-Spain because of rain. Richards made 177 out of 359, Bedi and Chandrasekhar taking all the wickets. India fell to Holding (6–65) for 228, 131 behind. Kallicharran's century allowed Lloyd to declare at 271 for six. India needed 403 to win, and with Gavaskar and Viswanath making centuries, got them with seven overs to spare. It was the highest score ever made in the fourth innings to win a Test.

The deciding Test at Kingston was very unsatisfactory – the pitch varied in bounce, and at tea on the first day, when India had lost only one wicket, West Indies embarked on a barrage of intimidatory bowling. Viswanath's hand was broken, a battered Gaekwad was eventually hit on the ear and sent to hospital for two days and Patel retired for stitches in a cut mouth. Bedi declared at 306 for six as a protest and to protect from injury himself and Chandrasekhar, the main bowlers but poor batsmen. India's spinners bowled well and at 217 for six looked likely to give their side a lead, but Holding and Holder added 104 and West Indies eventually led by 85. During the match all 17 of India's party fielded. India went through the motions in the second innings, which closed at 97, leaving West Indies to score only 13. Only six men batted and it was assumed that Bedi had declared at 97 for five, carrying his protest further. But he later claimed that he and Chandrasekhar were also injured, as well as the three men clearly hurt.

It was a sorry end to a series, symbolized by the bruised and bandaged party which caught their plane home two days later.

1975–76 8th Series WI 2, India 1, Drawn 1

1 BRIDGETOWN   West Indies won by an innings and 97 runs
India 177 (D A J Holford 5–23) and 214 (G R Viswanath 62, S Madan Lal 55)
West Indies 488–9 dec (I V A Richards 142, C H Lloyd 102, A I Kallicharran 93, R C Fredericks 54,d B S Chandrasekhar 4–163)

2 PORT OF SPAIN   Match Drawn
West Indies 241 (I V A Richards 130), B S Bedi 5–82) and 215–8 (C H Lloyd 70)
India 402–5 dec (S M Gavaskar 156, B P Patel 115)

3 PORT OF SPAIN   India won by 6 wkts
West Indies 359 (I V A Richards 177, C H Lloyd 68, B S Chandrasekhar 6–120, B S Bedi 4–73) and 271–6 dec (A I Kallicharran 103)
India 228 (M A Holding 6–65) and 406–4 (G R Viswanath 112, S M Gavaskar 102, M Amarnath 85)

4 KINGSTON   West Indies won by 10 wkts
India 306–6 dec (A D Gaekwad 81, S M Gavaskar 66, M A Holding 4–82) and 97 (M Amarnath 60)
West Indies 391 (R C Fredericks 82, D L Murray 71, I V A Richards 64, M A Holding 55, B S Chandrasekhar 5–153) and 13–0

1975–76 Averages

Batting	I	No	Runs	HS	Avge
B.P. Patel (I)	4	3	207	115*	207.00
I.V.A. Richards (WI)	6	0	556	177	92.66
S.M. Gavaskar (I)	7	0	390	156	55.71
A.I. Kallicharran (WI)	6	1	237	103*	47.40
C.H. Lloyd (WI)	6	0	283	102	47.16
G.R. Viswanath (I)	6	0	255	112	42.50
M. Armanath (I)	7	0	278	85	39.71
R.C. Fredericks (WI)	7	1	202	82	33.66

Bowling	O	M	Runs	W	Avge	BB
M.A. Holding (WI)	137.5	35	378	19	19.89	6–65
B.S. Bedi (I)	200.5	61	456	18	25.33	5–82
B.S. Chandrasekhar (I)	201.2	43	656	21	31.23	6–120

1978–79: India win their first home series against West Indies

On the tour of India three years later, World Series Cricket had removed many of the top West Indians from the Test scene, and it was a party of very different personnel that Kallicharran led. Gavaskar captained India, and in the first Test at Bombay batted 400 minutes for 205 whenr India had been put in after storms had delayed the start by four hours. India scored 424, and Kallicharran justified his policy by scoring 187 himself and ensuring a lead of 69. The match was drawn.

Gavaskar, Sunil Manohar

Gavaskar was born on 10 July 1949 in Bombay, and played for Bombay from 1967–68. A brilliant opening batsman he had a perfect technique, secure in defence but with all the strokes. Only 5ft 5in tall, he was called the 'Little Master'. His Test debut was made in 1970–71 in the West

Indies, and was astonishing. The 21-year-old made four centuries in four Tests, 774 runs, average 154.80. He continued his prolific run-getting and by the end of the 1986–87 season had played in 125 Tests, a record, and scored 10,122 runs, average 51.12, over 2,000 more than anybody else in the history of Tests.

At Bangalore, West Indies led on first innings by 66 and were 266 ahead with two second-innings wickets left and the last day to come. However, the match ended because of rioting in the city following the arrest of former Prime Minister Mrs Indira Gandhi.

At Calcutta, Gavaskar's 107 from 300 was countered by West Indies' opener A.B. Williams' 111 from 327. But Gavaskar (182 not out) and Vengsarkar (157 not out) added 344 unbeaten for India's second wicket in the second innings. Gavaskar thus became the first player to score a century in each innings of a Test three times. Set 335 to win, West Indies were 197 for nine when bad light ended play 11 balls early.

There was a lively pitch at Madras, where Kallicharran made 98 to take West Indies to 228. Viswanath scored 124 to give India a lead of 27. West Indies made only 151 second time despite Gomes' dogged 91. The match developed into a bumper war, no doubt with its roots in the previous tour. India needed only 125 to win, but lost seven wickets getting them, and at 84 for six West Indies had their chance. They missed catches and over-did the bouncers.

At Delhi, Gavaskar, Vengsarkar and Kapil Dev (with a six) all reached three figures and India declared at 566 for eight. West Indies followed on nearly 400 behind but were saved by rain which washed out most of the last two days.

India's score was their record, but they passed it at Kanpur with 644 for seven declared. There were three different century-makers: Viswanath, Gaekwad and M. Amarnath. Bad light and rain washed out much of the last three days, but there was time for Bacchus to make 250.

India won their first series at home against West Indies.

1978–79 9th Series India 1, WI 0, Drawn 5

1 BOMBAY Match Drawn
India 424 (S M Gavaskar 205, C P S Chauhan 52, G R Viswanath 52, V A Holder 4–94, S T Clarke 4–98) and 224–2 (C P S Chauhan 84, S M Gavaskar 73)
West Indies 493 (A I Kallicharran 187, D A Murray 84, H A Gomes 63, D R Parry 55, B S Chandrasekhar 5–116)

2 BANGALORE Match Drawn
West Indies 437 (S F A Bacchus 96, A I Kallicharran 71, S Shivnarine 62, H A Gomes 51) and 200–8 (H A Gomes 82, K D Ghavri 5–51)
India 371 (A D Gaekwad 87, D B Vengsarkar 73, G R Viswanath 70, S T Clarke 5–126)

3 CALCUTTA Match Drawn
India 300 (S M Gavaskar 107, Kapil Dev 61, N Phillip 4–64) and 361–1 dec (S M Gavaskar 182, D B Vengsarkar 157)
West Indies 327 (A B Williams 111, A I Kallicharran 55, S Venkataraghavan 4–55) and 197–9 (D A Murray 66, K D Ghavri 4–46)

4 MADRAS India won by 3 wkts
West Indies 228 (A I Kallicharran 98, Kapil Dev 4–38) and 151 (H A Gomes 91, S Venkataraghavan 4–43)
India 255 (G R Viswanath 124, N Phillip 4–48, S T Clarke 4–75) and 125–7

5 NEW DELHI Match Drawn
India 566 (Kapil Dev 126, S M Gavaskar 120, D B Vengsarkar 109, C P S Chauhan 60)
West Indies 172 and 179–3 (S F A Baccus 61)

6 KANPUR Match Drawn
India 644–7 dec (G R Viswanath 179, A D Gaekwad 102, M Amarnath 101, C P S Chauhan 79, Kapil Dev 62)
West Indies 452–8 (S F A Bacchus 250, R R Jumadeen 56, K D Ghavri 4–118)

1978–79 Averages

Batting	I	No	Runs	HS	Avge
S.M. Gavaskar (I)	9	1	732	205	91.50
G.R. Viswanath (I)	7	0	497	179	71.00
Kapil Dev (I)	7	2	329	126*	65.80
A.I. Kallicharran (WI)	10	1	538	187	59.77
D.B. Vengsarkar (I)	9	2	417	157*	59.57
S.F.A. Bacchus (WI)	10	0	472	250	47.20
A.D. Gaekwad (I)	7	0	293	102	41.85
C.P.S. Chauhan (I)	8	0	331	84	41.37
H.A. Gomes (WI)	10	0	405	91	40.50
D.A. Murray (WI)	10	1	261	84	29.00

Bowling	O	M	Runs	W	Avge	BB
K.D. Ghavri (I)	205	42	634	27	23.48	5–51
S. Venkataraghavan (I)	262.3	99	495	20	24.75	4–43
Kapil Dev (I)	155.4	27	561	17	33.00	4–38
S.T. Clarke (WI)	233.4	37	711	21	33.85	5–126
N. Phillip (WI)	193.2	38	650	19	34.21	4–48

1982–83: West Indies take four wickets and score 173 after tea to win

Kapil Dev led India to West Indies in 1982–83, Lloyd and his WSC colleagues being restored to West Indies.

India were put in at an overcast Kingston, and two low first-innings scores left West Indies three ahead. The fourth day was washed out and, at tea on the last, India were 164 ahead with four wickets left, with a draw assured. But Roberts took the last four wickets in 20 balls after tea (three in the first over) and West Indies made the 172 needed in 26 overs with four balls to spare, Richards' 61 in 35 balls clinching it.

India were put in again at Port-of-Spain and out for 175 (Marshall 5–37). West Indies were one for three, but then Gomes

(123) and Lloyd (143) added 237. Determined batting by Amarnath (117) and a final fling by Kapil Dev (100 not out in 95 balls) saved the match.

The second and fourth days were completely lost at Georgetown, where centuries by Richards and Gavaskar provided the main interest.

On a lively pitch at Bridgetown, the four West Indies fast bowlers removed India for 209 (Amarnath 91). West Indies got 486 (Logie 130) and needed only one to win when dismissing India for 277. Amarnath got 80 after retiring with a cut lip, being the only batsman to cope with the short-pitching bowling. The first ball in West Indies' innings was a no-ball from wicket-keeper Kirmani which ended the match, and gave him a unique analysis of 0.1–0–0–0.

L. Sivaramakrishnan made his debut at St John's, aged 17 years 118 days, the youngest player for any country except Pakistan. A high-scoring match was drawn with six century-makers, Shastri and Amarnath for India and Greenidge, Haynes, Dujon and Lloyd for West Indies. Greenidge and Haynes made a record West Indian opening partnership of 296. Greenidge, who left the game after three days because his daughter was critically ill, went into the records as 154 retired not out.

1982–83 10th Series WI 2, India 0, Drawn 1

1 KINGSTON West Indies won by 4 wkts
India 251 (B S Sandhu 68, Yashpal Sharma 63, A M E Roberts 4–61) and 174 (A M E Roberts 5–39)
West Indies 254 (C G Greenidge 70, R J Shastri 4–43, Kapil Dev 4–45) and 173–6 (I V A Richards 61, Kapil Dev 4–73)

2 PORT OF SPAIN Match Drawn
India 175 (M Amarnath 58, M D Marshall 5–37) and 469–7 (M Amarnath 117, Kapil Dev 100, Yashpal Sharma 50)
West Indies 394 (C H Lloyd 143, H A Gomes 123)

3 GEORGETOWN Match Drawn
West Indies 470 (I V A Richards 109, C H Lloyd 81, C G Greenidge 70)
India 284–3 (S M Gavaskar 147, D B Vengsarkar 62)

4 BRIDGETOWN West Indies won by 10 wkts
India 209 (M Amarnath 91, A M E Roberts 4–48) and 277 (M Amarnath 80, A D Gaekwad 55, A M E Roberts 4–31)
West Indies 486 (A L Logie 130, D L Haynes 92, I V A Richards 80, C G Greenidge 57, C H Loyd 50) and 1–0

5 ST JOHN'S Match Drawn
India 457 (R J Shastri 102, Kapil Dev 98, D B Vengsarkar 94, M Amarnath 54, M D Marshall 4–87) and 247–5 dec (M Amarnath 116, A D Gaekwad 72)
West Indies 550 (C G Greenidge 154, D L Haynes 136, P J Dujon 110, C H Lloyd 106)

1982–83 Averages

Batting	I	No	Runs	HS	Avge
C.G. Greenidge (WI)	7	2	393	154*	78.60
C.H. Lloyd (WI)	6	0	407	143	67.83
M. Armanath (I)	9	0	598	117	66.44
D.L. Haynes (WI)	7	1	333	136	55.50
P.J. Dujon (WI)	6	1	259	110	51.80
I.V.A. Richards (WI)	6	0	282	109	47.00
Kapil Dev (I)	8	2	254	100*	42.33
D.B. Vengsarkar (I)	9	0	279	94	31.00

Bowling	O	M	Runs	W	Avge	BB
A.M.E. Roberts (WI)	187.5	36	545	24	22.70	5–39
M.D. Marshall (WI)	174.2	39	495	21	23.57	5–37
Kapil Dev (I)	154	32	424	17	24.94	4–45
M.A. Holding (WI)	162	23	500	12	41.66	2–36

1983–84: West Indies win series but Gavaskar breaks records

Lloyd's West Indians played another six-Test tour in India in 1983–84.

At Kanpur, Greenidge's 194 was the

Wayne Daniel, who made his Test debut against India in 1975–76.

backbone of a West Indies total of 454. The West Indian fast bowlers, Marshall, Holding and Davis, proved too good for the Indian batsmen, taking 19 wickets as West Indies won by an innings and 83.

Gavaskar made a century off 94 balls, his fastest in Tests, at Delhi. With Vengsarkar getting 159, India reached 464 and led by 80 when captain Kapil Dev got six for 77. His fellow-captain Lloyd scored 103. There was no time for either side to press for a win.

India put West Indies in at a new Test venue, Ahmedabad, and they struggled before recovering to 281. The pitch was unpredictable and Daniel (5–39) dismissed India for 40 less. However, Gavaskar, who scored 90, passed Boycott's aggregate of Test runs to set a new world record. Kapil Dev bowled manfully in the second innings and took nine for 83, but West Indies had four fast bowlers and India were skittled for 103 and defeat by 138.

India batted at Bombay, and Vengsarkar, returning after illness, made 100 in 463. Despite Richards' 120, West Indies finished 70 behind. Haynes was given out 'handled the ball' when stopping it rolling on to his wicket via a pad. India set West Indies 244 in 156 minutes, but West Indies were happy with the draw.

Both sides began badly and recovered at Calcutta, Lloyd's brilliant 161 not out being the main reason for West Indies' lead of 136. Marshall (6–37) then dismissed India for 90. All 20 Indian wickets were taken by the four fast bowlers. Some of the crowd of 80,000 attacked the Indian team afterwards, injuring Malhotra and the manager.

Demands for sackings, including that of Gavaskar, were ignored by the selectors for the final Test at Madras, which began late after rain. After West Indies made 313,

Gavaskar scored 236 not out, India's highest test score. It was also his 30th Test century, which beat D.G. Bradman's previous world record. There was time for little else.

1983–84 11th Series WI 3, India 0, Drawn 3

1 KANPUR West Indies won by an innings and 83 runs
West Indies 454 (C G Greenidge 194, M D Marshall 92, P J Dujon 81, Kapil Dev 4–99)
India 207 (Madan Lal 63, M D Marshall 4–19) and 164 (D B Vengsarkar 65, M D Marshall 4–47)

2 DELHI Match Drawn
India 464 (D B Vengsarkar 159, S M Gavaskar 121, R M H Binny 52, M A Holding 4–107) and 233 (D B Vengsarkar 63)
West Indies 384 (C H Lloyd 103, I V A Richards 67, A L Logie 63, Kapil Dev 6–77) and 120–2 (C G Greenidge 72)

3 AHMEDABAD West Indies won by 138 runs
West Indies 281 (P J Dujon 98, C H Lloyd 68, Maninder Singh 4–85) and 201 (M A Holding 58, Kapil Dev 9–83)
India 241 (S M Gavaskar 90, W W Daniel 5–39) and 103 (M A Holding 4–30)

4 BOMBAY Match Drawn
India 463 (D B Vengsarkar 100, R J Shastri 77, R M H Binny 65, M A Holding 5–102) and 173–5 (A Malhotra 72)
West Indies 393 (I V A Richards 120, P J Dujon 84, C H Lloyd 67, D L Haynes 55, N S Yadav 5–131) and 104–4

5 CALCUTTA West Indies won by an innings and 46 runs
India 241 (Kapil Dev 69) and 90 (M D Marshall 6–37)
West Indies 377 (C H Lloyd 161, A M E Roberts 68, M D Marshall 54, Kapil Dev 4–91)

6 MADRAS Match drawn
West Indies 313 (P J Dujon 62) and 64–1
India 451 (S M Gavaskar 236, R J Shastri 72, S M H Kirmani 63, M D Marshall 5–72)

1983–84 Averages

Batting	I	No	Runs	HS	Avge
C.H. Lloyd (WI)	8	2	496	161*	82.66
D.B. Vengsarkar (I)	8	0	425	159	53.12
P.J. Dujon (WI)	7	0	367	98	52.42
C.G. Greenidge (WI)	10	2	411	194	51.37
S.M. Gavaskar (I)	11	1	505	236*	50.50
I.V.A. Richards (WI)	9	0	306	120	34.00
R.M.H. Binny (I)	11	0	270	65	24.54

Bowling	O	M	Runs	W	Avge	BB
Kapil Dev (I)	203.5	43	537	29	18.51	9–83
M.D. Mars hall (WI)	221	59	621	33	18.81	6–37
M.A. Holding (WI)	223.4	43	663	30	22.10	5–102
W.W. Daniel (WI)	98	12	332	14	23.71	5–39
W.W. Davis (WI)	178.3	20	562	14	40.14	3–21
R.J. Shastri (I)	211.2	42	567	12	47.25	2–32

India v Pakistan

1952–53: India win first series 2–1

India were Pakistan's first Test opponents after the partition of India in 1947. Pakistan's first captain, A.H. Kardar, had previously played for India as Abdul Hafeez. Amin Elahi had also played for India. India were led by L. Amarnath in the first series.

Hanif Mohammad made his debut for Pakistan aged 17 years 300 days in the first Test at Delhi, where India batted and made 372, Adhikari (81 not out) and Ghulam Ahmed (50) adding 109 for the last wicket, an Indian record. Pakistan were dismissed twice by Mankad (8–52 and 5–79) to lose by an innings and 70.

At Lucknow, India were dismissed by 106 (Fazal Mahmoud 5–52) and Nazar Mohammad carried his bat for Pakistan with 124 not out from a total of 331. As Fazal then took his match wickets to 12 with seven for 42 in dismissing India for 182 and an innings defeat, Nazar was on the pitch for the whole match, the first in Test history.

Pakistan batted first at Bombay but were hustled out for 186. Hazare and Umrigar then made centuries and India declared at 387 for four. Mankad (65 overs, 5–72) and Hanif (6 hours, 96 runs) were the principal figures in a war of attrition in Pakistan's second innings, which closed at 242, India getting the 42 wanted without loss.

The fourth Test was ruined by rain. In the last at Calcutta, R.H. Shodhan made a century on his debut for India, who had the upper hand in a draw.

India v Pakistan

1952–53 1st Series India 2, Pak 1, Drawn 2
1 NEW DELHI India won by an innings and 70 runs
India 372 (H R Adhikari 81, V S Hazare 76, Ghulam Ahmed 50, Amir Elahi 4–134)
Pakistan 150 (Hanif Mohammad 51, M H Mankad 8–52) and 152 (M H Mankad 5–79, Ghulam Ahmed 4–35)

2 LUCKNOW Pakistan won by an innings and 43 runs
India 106 (Fazal Mahmood 5–52) and 182 (L Amarnath 61, Fazal Mahmood 7–42)
Pakistan 331 (Nazar Mohammad 124)

3 BOMBAY India won by 10 wkts
Pakistan 186 (Waqar Hassan 81, L Amarnath 4–40) and 242 (Hanif Mohammad 96, Waqar Hassan 65, M H Mankad 5–72)
India 387–4 dec (V S Hazare 146, P R Umrigar 102) and 45–0

4 MADRAS Match Drawn
Pakistan 344 (A H Kardar 79, Zulfiqar Ahmed 63)
India 175–6 (P R Umrigar 62)

5 CALCUTTA Match Drawn
Pakistan 257 (Imtiaz Ahmed 57, Hanif Mohammad 56, Nazar Mohammad 55, D G Phadkar 5–72) and 236–7 dec (Waqar Hassan 97)
India 397 (R H Shodhan 110, D G Phadkar 57, Fazal Mahmood 4–141) and 28–0

1952 Averages

Batting	I	No	Runs	HS	Avge
Waqar Hassan (P)	8	0	357	97	44.62
P.R. Umrigar (I)	6	0	258	102	43.00
Nazar Mohammad (P)	8	1	277	124*	39.87
Hanif Mohammad (P)	8	0	287	96	35.87

Bowling	O	M	Runs	W	Avge	BB
V. Mankad (I)	265.2	100	514	25	20.56	8–52
Fazal Mahmood (P)	229	74	512	20	25.60	7–42
Ghulam Ahmed (I)	173.3	58	324	12	27.00	4–35
Mahmood Hussain (P)	151	34	418	12	27.00	4–35
Mahmood Hussain (P)	151	34	418	12	34.83	3–35

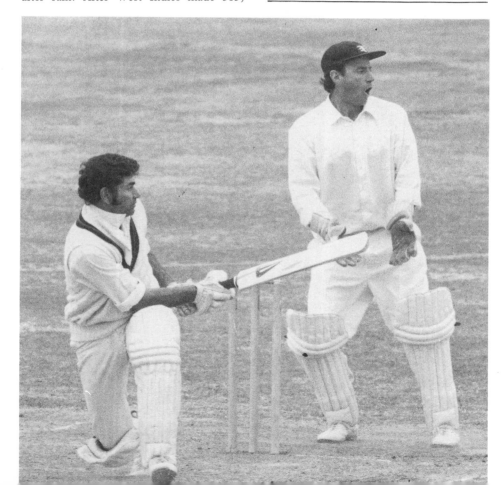

Farokh Engineer batting. He was India's wicket-keeper and opening batsman throughout the 1960s.

1954–55: Stalemate in first series in Pakistan

In Pakistan, with Kardar and Mankad captains, and the Test matches lasting four days, the scoring rate was funereal throughout. Only 710 runs came in 387.3 overs in the drawn first Test at Decca. A similar rate produced another draw at Bahawalpur, where Hanif ground his way to 142.

The story continued at Lahore and Peshawar, where the scoring was the slowest of all, Pakistan's first-innings 188 coming at 1.28 per over, and the rate hardly increasing after that. The final Test at Karachi was interrupted by rain, but followed the same pattern.

This was the first five-Test rubber to produce all draws. The bowling and field-placing was defensive throughout. The fast-medium Khan Mohammad, Fazal Mahmood and Mahmood Hussain took nearly all the wickets for Pakistan, Hanif and Alimuddin scoring the runs. India relied on spinners Gupte and Mankad, and Umrigar and Manjrekar were the main batsmen.

1954–55   2nd Series   Drawn 5

1 DACCA   Match Drawn

India 257 (Imtiaz Ahmed 54, Waqar Hassan 52, Ghulam Ahmed 5–109) and 158 (Alim-ud-Din 51, Waqar Hassan 51, S P Gupte 5–18)

India 148 (Mahmood Hussain 6–67, Khan Mohammad 4–42) and 147–2 (V L Manjrekar 74, P Roy 67)

2 BAHAWALPUR   Match Drawn

India 235 (N S Tamhane 54, G S Ramchand 53, V L Manjrekar 50, Khan Mohammad 5–74, Fazal Mahmood 4–86) and 209–5 (P Roy 77, V L Manjrekar 59)

Pakistan 312–9 dec (Hanif Mohammad 142, Alim-ud-Din 64, P R Umrigar 6–74)

3 LAHORE   Match Drawn

Pakistan 328 (Maqsood Ahmed 99, Wazir Mohammad 55, Imtiaz Ahmed 55, S P Gupte 5–133) and 136–5 (Alim-ud-Din 58)

India 251 (P R Umrigar 78, Mahmood Hussain 4–70) and 74–2

4 PESHAWAR   Match Drawn

Pakistan 188 (S P Gupte 5–63) and 182 (Imtiaz Ahmd 69, M H Mankad 5–64)

India 245 (P R Umrigar 108, Khan Mohammad 4–79) and 23–1

5 KARACHI   Match Drawn

Pakistan 162 (G S Ramchand 6–49) and 241–5 dec (Alim-ud-Din 103, A H Kardar 93)

India 145 (Fazal Mahmood 5–49, Khan Mohammad 5–72) and 69–2

1955 Averages

Batting	I	No	Runs	HS	Avge
P.R. Umrigar (I)	7	2	271	108	54.20
V.L. Manjrekar (I)	8	2	270	74*	45.00
Alimuddin (P)	9	1	273	142	34.12
Hanif Mohammad (P)	9	1	273	77	34.00
P. Roy (I)	10	2	272	77	34.00
Maqsood Ahmed (P)	9	0	250	99	27.77

Bowling	O	M	Runs	W	Avge	BB
Khan Mohammad (P)	170.5	54	349	22	15.86	5–72
Fazal Mahmood (P)	223.2	93	331	15	22.06	5–49
S.P. Gupte (I)	276.5	107	475	21	22.61	5–17
Mahmood Hussain (P)	153.1	37	372	14	26.57	6–67
V. Mankad (I)	263.3	130	399	12	33.25	5–64

1960–61: Five more slow draws in India

In India six years later, with Fazal and N.J. Contractor the captains, Pakistan began at Bombay with a record second-wicket stand of 246 between Hanif (160) and Saeed Ahmed (121). But Pakistan's 350 was passed by India with 449 for nine declared, Joshi and Desai adding the last 149 for India's ninth wicket, still their record. The match subsided to a draw.

At Kanpur, India's first-innings lead of 69

was established by the fifth day – the match was drawn.

Rain took 4½ hours from the Calcutta Test, where Pakistan set India 267 to win in three hours, a rate unheard of in matches between these countries so far.

A batting pitch at Madras saw centuries from Imtiaz Ahmed, Saeed Ahmed, Umrigar and Borde, with time for only 18 second-innings overs.

Umrigar and Mushtaq Mohammad made centuries at Delhi, Mushtaq, at 17 years 72 days, being the youngest Test century-maker. This match came closest to a decision as Pakistan followed on, and at 196 for eight were only 19 ahead, but they just saved the match.

The last 12 matches between the countries were now draws. Pakistan, batting first in the first four Tests, set the slow pattern of scoring, but both sides were too afraid of defeat to go for a win.

1960–61   3rd Series   Drawn 5

1 BOMBAY   Match Drawn

Pakistan 350 (Hanif Mohammad 160, Saeed Ahmed 121, S P Gupte 4–43) and 166–4 (Imtiaz Ahmed 69)

India 449–9 dec (R B Desai 85, V L Manjrekar 73, N J Contractor 62, P G Joshi 52, Mahmood Hussain 5–129, Mohammad Farooq 4–139)

2 KANPUR   Match Drawn

Pakistan 335 (Javed Burki 79, Nasim-ul-Ghani 70, P R Umrigar 4–71) and 140–3

India 404 (P R Umrigar 115, M L Jaisimha 99, V L Manjrekar 52, Haseeb Ahsan 5–121)

3 CALCUTTA   Match Drawn

Pakistan 301 (Mushtaq Mohammad 61, Intikhab Alam 56, Hanif Mohammad 56, C G Borde 4–21, R Surendranath 4–93) and 146–3 dec (Hanif Mohammad 63)

India 180 (Fazal Mahmood 5–26) and 127–4

4 MADRAS   Match Drawn

Pakistan 448–8 dec (Imtiaz Ahmed 135, Saeed Ahmed 103, Hanif Mohammad 62, R B Desai 4–66) and 59–0

India 539–9 dec (C G Borde 177, P R Umrigar 117, N J Contractor 81, Haseeb Ahsan 6–202)

5 NEW DELHI   Match Drawn

India 463 (P R Umrigar 112, N J Contractor 92, R F Surti 64) and 16–0

Pakistan 286 (Mushtaq Mohammad 101, Javed Burki 61, V V Kumar 5–64, R B Desai 4–103) and 250 (Imtiaz Ahmed 53, R G Nadkarni 4–43, R B Desai 4–88)

1960–61 Averages

Batting	I	No	Runs	HS	Avge
C.G. Borde (I)	6	2	330	177*	82.50
P.R. Umrigar (I)	6	0	382	117	63.66
N.J. Contractor (I)	6	0	319	92	56.16
Hanif Mohammad (P)	9	1	410	160	51.25
Saeed Ahmed (P)	10	1	460	121	51.11
Javed Burki (P)	9	2	325	79	46.42
Mushtaq Mohammad (P)	7	1	263	101	43.83
Imtiaz Ahmed (P)	10	1	375	135	41.66

Bowling	O	M	Runs	W	Avge	BB
R.B. Desai (I)	215.5	35	626	21	29.80	4–66
Haseeb Ahsan (P)	210	56	490	15	32.66	6–202
Mahmood Hussain (P)	213.3	59	503	13	38.69	5–129

Zaheer Abbas

Zaheer was born on 24 July 1947 at Sialkot, Pakistan. He made his debut for Karachi in 1965–66, later playing for PWD, PIA and Sind. He also played for Gloucestershire from 1972. He was an attractive middle-order right-hand batsman, who played initially in spectacles and later in contact lenses. He first played for Pakistan in 1969–70, and captained them from 1983–84. In 78 Tests, in 14 of which he was captain, he scored 5,062 runs, average 44.79.

1978–79: Holiday for Pakistan in first win

Wars kept the countries apart for 17 years. Then India, led by Bedi, toured Pakistan, led by Mushtaq, in a three-Test series.

Kapil Dev made his debut in the first Test at Faisalabad, but made no impression on Pakistan, who scored 503 for eight declared with 176 from Zaheer Abbas and 154 from Javed Miandad, their partnership being worth 255. India, too, built a big score of 462 for nine declared, led by Viswanath (145). Asif Iqbal scored a second-innings century in what was clearly a drawn match.

India were dismissed for only 199 on a fast pitch at Lahore, where Zaheer Abbas made 235 not out, allowing Pakistan to declare at 539 for six. India fought a hard rear-guard battle, getting 465, but Pakistan had 100 minutes to get 126, and won with 8.2 overs to spare. This was the first result between the countries for 26 years, and the following day was declared a national holiday in Pakistan.

At Karachi, Gavaskar made 111 from 344, but Pakistan recovered from 187 for five to 481 for nine declared (Javed 100). Gavaskar completed a century in each innings for the second time with 137 out of 300. Set 164 in 26 overs, Pakistan made the runs with seven balls remaining.

Pakistan thus won their first series against India 2–0. With both sides strong in batting, their fast bowlers, Imran Khan and Sarfraz Nawaz, turned the matches on the quicker pitches.

1978–79 4th Series Pak 2, India 0, Drawn 1
1 FAISALABAD Match Drawn
Pakistan 503–8 dec (Javed Miandad 154, Zaheer Abbas 176, B S Chandrasekhar 4–130) and 264–4 dec (Asif Iqbal 104, Zaheer Abbas 96)
India 462–9 dec (G R Viswanath 145, S M Gavaskar 89, D B Vengsarkar 83, Mustaq Mohammad 4–55) and 43–0
2 LAHORE Pakistan won by 8 wkts
India 199 (D B Vengsarkar 76, Sarfraz Nawaz 4–46, Imran Khan 4–54) and 465 (S M Gavaskar 97, C P S Chauhan 93, G R Viswanath 83, S Amarnath 60)
Pakistan 539–6 dec (Zaheer Abbas 235, Wasim Bari 85, Mushtaq Mohammad 67) and 128–2
3 KARACHI Pakistan won by 8 wkts
India 344 (S M Gavaskar 111, Kapil Dev 59, Sarfraz Nawaz 4–89) and 300 (S M Gavaskar 137, M Amarnath 53, Sarfraz Nawaz 5–70)
Pakistan 481–9 dec (Javed Miandad 100, Mushtaq Mohammad 78, Mudassar Nazar 57) and 164–2 (Javed Miandad 62)

1978–79 Averages

Batting	I	No	Runs	HS	Avge
Zaheer Abbas (P)	5	2	583	235*	194.33
Javed Miandad (P)	5	2	357	154*	119.00
S.M. Gavaskar (I)	6	1	447	137	89.40
G.R. Viswanath (I)	5	0	249	145	49.80
C.P.S. Chauhan (I)	6	1	212	93	42.40
Majid. J. Khan (P)	6	0	222	47	37.00

Bowling	O	M	Runs	W	Avge	BB
Sarfraz Nawaz (P)	148.2	27	425	17	25.00	5–70
Imran Khan (P)	162.1	42	441	14	31.50	4–54
B.S. Chandrasekhar (I)	94	13	385	8	48.12	4–130

Right: Mushtaq Mohammad, the Pakistan captain in 1978–79, when Pakistan won the first match not drawn between the countries for 26 years, earning a national holiday for his countrymen.

Below: Gavaskar out, caught Majid bowled Salim at Lahore in 1978–79 and Pakistan are on the way to victory.

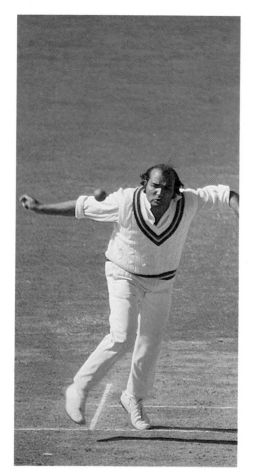

1979–80: India retaliate with 2–0 win in six-match series

The return rubber was played in India next season, with Gavaskar and Asif now the captains. At Bangalore, Mudassar Nazar made a slow 126 from 431, and with India batting solidly for 416, the match was of the familiar drawn kind.

The Delhi match was exciting. Pakistan made 273 (Kapil Dev 5–58), and then Sikander Bakht (8–69) bowled brilliantly for Pakistan to remove India for 126. Pakistan's 242 left India 390 to get in 550 minutes, with Imran injured. Led by Vengsarkar (146 not out in 527 minutes) India slowly advanced to the target. They needed 114 from the last 20 overs, but in the end finished 26 short with four wickets left.

At Bombay, India recovered from a poor start to 334, Sikander again bowling well for five for 55. With the wicket taking spin, Pakistan made 173 and India 160 (Iqbal Qasim 6–40), leaving Pakistan 322 to win. They could manage only 190, so India registered the first win over their rivals for 27 years.

On a bouncy pitch at Kanpur, Sikander and Ehteshamuddin shared India's wickets and removed them for 162. Despite Kapil Dev's six for 63, Pakistan led by 87. Rain ended the fourth day early and penetrated the covers, ending the match, but Sikander provided 'entertainment' when refused an lbw appeal by walking down the wicket and kicking a stump from the ground.

Pakistan made only 272 at Madras. Gavaskar (166 in 593 minutes) made the match safe and Kapil Dev (84 in 98 balls)

gave India the chance to win, and took it himself with seven for 56 in the second innings. Needing 76, India won the series.

Viswanath captained India in the sixth and last Test, Gavaskar having declared himself unavailable to tour (the tour was later cancelled). India made 331, and Pakistan made a determined attempt to win by declaring behind at 272 for four, dismissing India for 205 (Imran 5–63) and going for the 265 needed. However, after two runs-out they called off the chase and drew at 179 for six.

1979–80 5th Series India 2, Pak 0, Drawn 4
1 BANGALORE   Match Drawn
Pakistan 431–9 dec (Mudassar Nazar 126, Javed Miandad 76, Asif Iqbal 55) and 108–2
India 416 (S M Gavaskar 88, G R Viswanath 73, Yashpal Sharma 62, Imran Khan 4–53)
2 NEW DELHI   Match Drawn
Pakistan 273 (Wasim Raja 97, Asif Iqbal 64, Kapil Dev 5–58) and 242 (Wasim Raja 61, Zaheer Abbas 50, Kapil Dev 4–63)
India 126 (Sikander Bakht 8–69) and 364–6 (D B Vengsarkar 146, Yashpal Sharma 60)
3 BOMBAY   India won by 131 runs
India 334 (Kapil Dev 69, D B Vengsarkar 58, Sikander Bakht 5–55, Iqbal Qasim 4–135) and 160 (Iqbal Wasim 6–40)
Pakistan 173 and 190 (Javed Miandad 64, K D Ghavri 4–63)
4 KANPUR   Match Drawn
India 162 (Ehtesham-ud-Din 5–47, Sikander Bakht 5–56) and 193–2 (S M Gavaskar 81, C P S Chauhan 61)
Pakistan 249 (Wasim Raja 94, Kapil Dev 6–63)
5 MADRAS   India won by 10 wkts
Pakistan 272 (Majid Khan 56, Kapil Dev 4–90) and 233 (Wasim Raja 57, Javed Miandad 52, Kapil Dev 7–56)
India 430 (S M Gavaskar 166, Kapil Dev 84, Imran Khan 5–114) and 78–0
6 CALCUTTA   Match Drawn
India 331 (S M Patil 62, Yashpal Sharma 62, Imran Khan 4–67) and 205 (Imran Khan 5–63)
Pakistan 272–4 dec (Taslim Arif 90, Majid Khan 54, Javed Miandad 50, Wasim Raja 50) and 179–6

Above left: B.S. Chandrasekhar, India's outstanding leg-break and googly bowler for over 15 years.

Above centre: Javed Miandad, Pakistan's leading Test run-getter.

Above: Intikhab Alam, Pakistan captain, whose Test career lasted from 1959 to 1977.

1979–80 Averages					
Batting	I	No	Runs	HS	Avge
Wasim Raja (P)	10	2	450	97	56.25
S.M. Gavaskar (I)	11	1	529	166	52.90
D.B. Vengsarkar (I)	8	2	316	146*	52.66
Javed Miandad (P)	11	1	421	76	42.10
Yashpal Sharma (I)	9	1	314	62	39.25
Kapil Dev (I)	9	0	278	84	30.88
Asif Iqbal (P)	10	1	267	64	29.66

Bowling	O	M	Runs	W	Avge	BB
Kapil Dev (I)	211.5	53	566	32	17.68	7–56
Imran Khan (P)	152.2	38	365	19	19.28	5–47
Eteshamuddin (P)	124.4	30	270	14	19.28	5–47
Sikander Bakht (P)	211.3	47	641	24	26.70	8–69
D.R. Doshi (I)	250.3	78	504	18	28.00	3–42
Iqbal Qasim (P)	241.5	80	568	17	33.41	6–40
K.D. Ghavri (I)	182.3	33	616	15	41.06	4–63

1982–83: Triumphs for Pakistan, particularly Mudassar and Imran

Gavaskar and Imran were their countries' captains in Pakistan in 1982–83.

Rain precluded any hope of a result at Lahore, where Zaheer made 215 and became the second player to score his hundredth century in a Test match. M. Amarnath made a century for India, and

Mohsin Khan 94 and 101 not out for Pakistan before play ended.

At Karachi, India were put in on a green wicket and hustled out for 169. Zaheer (186) and Mudassar (119) added 213 for Pakistan's fifth wicket, virtually deciding the match. Fiery bowling by Imran (8–60) dismissed India for 197, giving Pakistan victory by an innings and 86.

On a good pitch at Faisalabad, India made 372 (Imran 6–98). Pakistan's innings included four century-makers: Javed (126), Zaheer (168), Salim Malik (107) and Imran (117). Pakistan made 652, with the indomitable Kapil Dev taking seven for 220. Gavaskar (127 not out) became the first Indian to carry his bat through an innings in India's second knock, and forced Pakistan to bat again, but only for seven runs. Imran's five for 82 gave him 11 wickets in the match, and he became the second to score a century and take 10 wickets in a Test.

At Hyderabad, Mudassar and Javed came together with the score at 60 for two, and equalled the world record stand for all Test cricket with 451. Mudassar made 231 and Javed 280 not out as Pakistan declared at 581 for three. A demoralized India subsided before Imran and Sarfraz for 189 and 273 for an innings defeat.

Mudassar achieved another record at Lahore. In scoring 152 not out from 323, he became the second Pakistani to carry his bat through an innings. The first had been his father, Nazar Mahammad, also against India, 30 years earlier. Kapil Dev took eight for 85. Amarnath made 120 in reply, but rain washed out the last two days.

A high-scoring match at Karachi saw hundreds from Shastri and Amarnath for India and Mudassar for Pakistan. With half a day lost to rioting students, there was little hope of a result.

Pakistan ended the series with three batsmen, Zaheer, Mudassar and Javed averaging over 100, having scored 2,005 runs between them, while Imran had 40 wickets at 14.00 each, plus 247 runs.

1982–83 6th Series   Pak 3, India 0, Drawn 3

1 LAHORE   Match Drawn
Pakistan 485 (Zaheer Abbas 215, Mohsin Khan 94, Mudassar Nazar 50, D R Doshi 5–90) and 135–1 (Mohsin Khan 101)
India 379 (M Amarnath 109, S M Gavaskar 83, S M Patil 68, Arun Lal 51, Sarfraz Nawaz 4–63)

2 KARACHI   Pakistan won by an innings and 86 runs
India 169 (Kapil Dev 73, Qadir 4–67) and 197 (D B Vengsarkar 79, Madan Lal 52, Imran Khan 8–60)
Pakistan 452 (Zaheer Abbas 186, Mudassar Nazar 119, Kapil Dev 5–102)

3 FAISALABAD   Pakistan won by 10 wkts
India 373 (S M Patil 85, S M H Kirmani 66, Madan Lal 54, G R Viswanath 53, Imran Khan 6–99) and 286 (S M Gavaskar 127, M Amarnath 78, Imran Khan 5–82, Sarfraz Nawaz 4–79)
Pakistan 652 (Zaheer Abbas 168, Javed Miandad 126, Imran Khan 117, Salim Malik 107, Kapil Dev 7–220) and 10–0

4 HYDERABAD   Pakistan won by an innings and 119 runs
Pakistan 581–3 dec (Javed Miandad 280, Mudassar Nazar 231)
India 189 (B S Sandhu 71, M Amarnath 61, Imran Khan 6–35) and 273 (M Amarnath 64, S M Gavaskar 60, D B Vengsarkar 58, Sarfraz Nawaz 4–85)

5 LAHORE   Match Drawn
Pakistan 323 (Mudassar Nazar 152, Javed Miandad 85, Kapil Dev 8–85)
India 235–3 (M Amarnath 120, Yashpal Sharma 63)

6 KARACHI   Match Drawn
India 393–8 dec (R J Shastri 128, D B Vengsarkar 89) and 224–2 (M Amarnath 103, S M Gavaskar 67)
Pakistan 420–6 dec (Mudassar Nazar 152, Mohsin Khan 91)

Zaheer Abbas hits Amarnath for four at Lahore in 1978-79, on his way to 235 not out. His average for the series was nearly 200.

1982–83 Averages

Batting	I	No	Runs	HS	Avge
Zaheer Abbas (P)	6	1	650	215	130.00
Mudassar Nazar (P)	8	2	761	231	126.83
Javed Miandad (P)	6	1	594	280*	118.80
M. Amarnath (I)	10	2	584	120	73.00
Mohsin Khan (P)	8	2	341	101*	56.83
S.M. Gavaskar (I)	10	1	434	127*	48.22

Bowling	O	M	Runs	W	Avge	BB
Imran Khan (P)	223.1	69	558	40	13.95	8–60
Sarfraz Nawaz (P)	241.1	62	633	19	33.31	4–63
Kapil Dev (I)	205.2	22	831	24	34.62	8–85

1983–84: Pakistan get three draws in India

Bad feelings, bad weather and bad administration were irritants in a three-match series in India in 1983–84. Kapil Dev and Zaheer were captains.

Bangalore set the tone. India made 275, but there was nearly a riot when play was stopped an hour early on the first day with the sun shining. It later re-started. Altogether seven hours were lost, ensuring the draw. Javed was spoken to by the umpires about his behaviour. After the daily requirement of 77 overs on the final day, Zaheer led Pakistan off the field, but the umpires and batsmen remained, on the grounds that seven of the final 20 overs were left. After much argument, the Pakistanis reappeared 27 minutes later. Gavaskar, 87 at the break, completed his century.

At Jullunder, Pakistan made 337, with Wasim Raja getting 125. India replied with 374, Gaekwad making 201. It took 652 minutes, the slowest double-century in first-class cricket. This might have been deliberate, as Zaheer had caused more controversy by refusing to play on the rest day after the third day had been washed out. Gaekwad's innings occupied most of the last two days. Pakistan had been on top at the time of Zaheer's decision, leading to a suggestion that Pakistan were interested only in three draws, a view given credence by Sarfraz, who claimed he was omitted from the party for not agreeing to such a strategy.

A slow-scoring match at Nagpur was drawn, with Pakistan the only likely winners after leading by 77 on the first innings.

1983–84 7th series Drawn 3

1 BANGALORE Match Drawn

India 275 (R H M Binny 83, Madan Lal 74, Tahir 5–76) and 176–0 (S M Gavaskar 103, A D Gaekwad 66)

Pakistan 288 (Javed Miandad 99, Wasim Bari 64, Kapil Dev 5–68)

2 JULLUNDUR Match Drawn

Pakistan 337 (Wasim Raja 125, Javed Miandad 66, Kapil Dev 4–80) and 16–0

India 374 (A D Gaekwad 201, R M H Binny 54, Wasim Raja 4–50)

3 NAGPUR Match Drawn

India 245 (R J Shastri 52, S M Gavaskar 50, Azim Hafeez 4–58) and 262–8 dec (S M Gavaskar 64, Mohammad Nazir 5–72)

Pakistan 322 (Zaheer Abbas 85, Mudassar Nazar 78, Javed Miandad 60, R J Shastri 5–75) and 42–1

1983–84 Averages

Batting	I	No	Runs	HS	Avge
A.D. Gaekwad (I)	5	1	313	201	78.25
Javed Miandad (P)	3	0	225	99	75.00
S.M. Gavaskar (I)	5	1	264	103*	66.00

Bowling	O	M	Runs	W	Avge	BB
Kapil Dev (I)	91	23	225	12	18.75	5–68
Azeem Hafeez (P)	116	27	312	10	31.20	4–58

Javed Miandad

Javed was born on 12 June 1957 at Karachi, Pakistan, and first played for them in 1973–74. He also played for Sind, Habib Bank, and in England, for Sussex and Glamorgan. He is an aggressive middle-order right-hand batsman, and also bowls leg-breaks and googlies. He first appeared for Pakistan in 1976–77. He is a very combative cricketer, sometimes involved in confrontations with opponents at the wicket. In 86 Tests to the end of 1987 he had scored 6,251 runs, average 54.32. He has also taken 17 wickets at 40.11 each.

1984–85: Arguments over decisions in drawn series in Pakistan

Gavaskar was captain as India played a two-match series in Pakistan. Captain Zaheer rescued the home team from a bad start at Lahore, scoring 168 not in a total of 428 for nine declared. India were rushed out for 156 by Azeem Hafeez (6–46), but saved the match in the follow-on with Amarnath returning to form with 101 not out. Kapil Dev and Gaekwad showed dissent with their dismissals, and Gavaskar later criticized the umpiring.

At Faisalabad, on an easy pitch, Patil and Shastri made centuries while India scored 500. But with Kapil Dev breaking down after five overs, and Gavaskar off the field with 'flu, Pakistan made 674 for six, their highest Test score at the time, batting out the remaining time. Qasim Omar made 210, Mudassar 199 and Salim Malik 122 not out.

1984–85 8th Series Drawn 2

1 LAHORE Match Drawn

Pakistan 428–9 dec (Zaheer Abbas 168, Ashraf Ali 65)

India 156 (Azeem Hafeez 6–46) and 371–6 dec (M B Amarnath 101, R J Shastri 71, A D Gaekwad 60)

2 FAISALABAD Match Drawn

India 500 (R J Shastri 139, S M Patil 127, A D Gaekwad 74, Abdul Qadir 4–104, Azeem Hafeez 4–137)

Pakistan 674–6 (Qasim Omar 210, Mudassar Nazar 199, Salim Malik 102, Mohsin Khan 59)

1986–87: Exciting fifth Test follows four dull draws

Imran Khan led Pakistan on a five-Test series to India in 1986–87, Kapil Dev being his opposite number. There was an incident in Pakistan's first innings at Madras, when Javed survived an appeal for a short-leg catch. Srikkanth threw the ball at the umpire, and conceded two overthrows. Vengsarkar passed an opinion and Shastri, acting captain, had to play diplomat. Shoaib Mohammad and Imran, in a display of hitting, made centuries as Pakistan declared at 487 for nine. India passed this with 527 for nine declared, Srikkanth making an exciting century, and the match could only end in a draw.

Gavaskar, after 106 consecutive Tests, declined to play at Calcutta, where the crowd had barracked him in the past. India were put in but scored 403, Azharuddin making 141. With Binny taking 6 for 56, Pakistan were dismissed for 229 and an Indian declaration set Pakistan 356 to win in 345 minutes. They made no attempt and the 70,000 crowd threw rotten fruit.

In Jaipur's first Test there was no play on the third day, which with high scoring ensured a draw. Azharuddin and Shastri made centuries for India, who were generally on top, Rameez Raja one for Pakistan. Gavaskar was out first ball of the match for the third time in his Test career. Younis Ahmed was recalled by Pakistan after 17 years 111 days – the second longest gap between Tests (George Gunn holding the record).

At Ahmedabad, Pakistan made only 130 for four on the first day. There was bad feeling when Younis and Gavaskar appeared ready for combat after Younis had survived an appeal. Ijaz Faqih, whom Pakistan recalled after 5 years, made 105, but Pakistan's 395 lasted into the third day and was made at exactly two runs per over. On the third day Gavaskar became the first to 10,000 runs in Tests, and there was a 20-minute crowd invasion. On the fourth day, when Vengsarkar passed 100, another crowd invasion led to Pakistani fieldsmen being hit by stones, and Imran led his team off. On the last day, with Pakistan batting out time, Gavaskar and Srikkanth, the opening batsmen, took the new ball, but Pakistan batted even more slowly, scoring 111 in the day. Their 531 runs in the match were scored at 1.79 per over.

There was an exciting match at Bangalore. Batting first, Pakistan fell to Maninder Singh (7–27) for only 116, but after India had passed this total with only four men out, they claimed the last six wickets for 19,

Tauseef Ahmed and Iqbal Qasim taking five wickets each. Pakistan then made 249, with Salim Yousuf and Tauseef adding 51 for the ninth wicket. Pakistan were confident of victory, but Gavaskar played one of his greatest innings. He was eighth out for 96 at 180, scored in 323 minutes. The last wicket fell at 204, Tauseef and Qasim each ending with nine wickets. Pakistan won by 16 runs to take their first series in India.

1986–87   9th Series   Pak 1, India 0, Drawn 4

1 MADRAS   Match Drawn
Pakistan 487–9 dec (Imran Khan 135, Shoaib Mohammad 101, Javed Miandad 94, Wasim Akram 62, Maninder Singh 5–135) and 182–3 (Javed Miandad 54, Rizwan-uz-Zaman 54)
India 527–9 dec (K Srikkanth 123, D B Vengsarkar 96, S M Gavaskar 91, M B Amarnath 89)

2 CALCUTTA   Match Drawn
India 403 (M Azharuddin 141, Kapil Dev 66, R M H Binny 52, J Arun Lal 52, Wasim Akram 5–96) and 181–3 dec (J Arun Lal 70)
Pakistan 229 (Rameez Raja 69, Rizwan-uz-Zaman 60, R M H Binny 6–56) and 179–5 (Javed Minadad 63)

3 JAIPUR   Match drawn
India 465–8 dec (R J Shastri 125, M Azharuddin 110, Kapil Dev 50) and 114–2 (K Srikkanth 51)
Pakistan 341 (Ramez Raja 114, Imran Khan 66, Javed Miandad 50, Gopal Sharma 4–88)

4 AHMEDABAD   Match Drawn
Pakistan 395 (Ijaz Faqih 105, Imran Khan 72, Manzoor Elahi 52, N S Yadav 4–109) and 136–2 (Rizwan-uz-Zaman 58)
India 323 (D B Vengsarkar 109, S M Gavaskar 63, Kapil Dev 50, Wasim Akram 4–60)

5 BANGALORE   Pakistan won by 16 runs
Pakistan 116 (Maninder Singh 7–27) and 249 (R J Shastri 4–69)
India 145 (D B Vengsarkar 50, Iqbal Qasim 5–48, Tauseef Ahmed 5–64) and 204 (S M Gavaskar 96, Iqbal Qasim 4–73, Tauseef Ahmed 4–85)

1986–87 Averages

Batting	I	No	Runs	HS	Avge
D.B. Vengsarkar (I)	8	2	404	109	67.33
Imran Khan (P)	7	2	324	135*	64.80
M. Azharuddin (I)	6	0	315	141	52.50
Javed Miandad (P)	7	1	302	94	50.33
S.M. Gavaskar (I)	6	0	295	96	49.16
Ramiz Raja (P)	9	0	381	114	42.33
K. Srikkanth (I)	8	0	311	123	38.87

Bowling	O	M	Runs	W	Avge	BB
Maninder Singh (I)	260.2	96	478	20	23.90	7–27
Iqbal Qasim (P)	154	46	367	12	30.58	5–48
Wasim Akram (P)	159.2	31	413	13	31.76	5–96
Tausif Ahmed (P)	218.5	34	561	16	36.06	5–54

Bedser, Alec Victor

Bedser is one of twin brothers, born on 4 July 1918 at Reading, who both became part of the Surrey side which won the Championship in seven successive years in the 1950s, having made appearances in 1939. Alec was an outstanding medium-paced bowler who made his Test debut in 1946, taking 11 wickets in each of his first two Tests. He was England's leading bowler for eight years and especially successful against Australia and Bradman. In all he played in 51 Tests and took 236 wickets at 24.89 each. His aggregate was the world record at the time.

England v Pakistan

1954: Pakistan's four bowlers win final Test

Pakistan's first tour of England was in 1954 when A.H. Kardar's team played three Tests against Hutton's Ashes-winning side.

The first Test did not begin until late on the fourth day. Although 22 wickets fell cheaply, a draw was the only possible result.

D.S. Sheppard deputized as captain when Hutton was indisposed at Trent Bridge, where Pakistan were dismissed for 157 (Appleyard 5–51 on his Test debut). England piled on the runs as Simpson made 101 and Compton 278, his highest Test score. England declared at 558 for six and won by an innings when removing Pakistan for 272.

At Old Trafford, England made 359 for eight declared, and Bedser, Wardle and McConnon ran through Pakistan for 90. Rain, which washed out the second, fourth and fifth days, came to Pakistan's rescue at 25 for four in the follow-on.

All this left nobody prepared for the events at the Oval, where Hutton returned. In conditions suitable for swing, Pakistan were out for 133 to Statham, Tyson and Loader, but Fazal's six for 53, supported by Mahmood Hussain's four for 58, dismissed England for 130. Pakistan then recovered from 82 for eight to reach 164 (Wardle 7–56). England needed 168 and passed 100 with only two men out, but Fazal improved on his first innings with six for 48, and England reached only 143. Pakistan thus levelled the series. Fazal Mahmoud was the main hero of this great win, but the other bowlers Shujauddin, Zulfiqar Ahmed and Mahmood Hussain were equally important in a batting role. Pakistan's last two wickets added 56 and 82 in the two innings, England's 15 and 5.

1954   1st Series   Eng 1, Pak 1, Drawn 2
1 LORD'S   Match Drawn
Pakistan 87 (J B Statham 4–18, J H Wardle 4–33) and 121–3 (Waqar Hassan 53)
England 117–9 dec (Khan Mohammad 5–61, Fazal Mahmood 4–54)

2 TRENT BRIDGE   England won by an innings and 129 runs
Pakistan 157 (R Appleyard 5–51) and 272 (Maqsood Ahmed 69, Hanif Mohammad 51)
England 558–6 dec (D C S Compton 278, R T Simpson 101, T W Graveney 84)

3 OLD TRAFFORD   Match Drawn
England 359–8 dec (D C S Compton 93, T W Graveney 65, J H Wardle 54, Fazal Mahmood 4–107)
Pakistan 90 (J H Wardle 4–19) and 25–4

4 THE OVAL   Pakistan won by 24 runs
Pakistan 133 (F H Tyson 4–35) and 164 (J H Wardle 7–56)
England 130 (D C S Compton 53, Fazal Mahmood 6–53, Mahmood Hussain 4–58) and 143 (P B H May 53, Fazal Mahmood 6–46)

Batting	I	No	Runs	HS	Avge
D.C.S. Compton (E)	5	0	453	278	90.60

Bowling	O	M	Runs	W	Avge	BB
J.H. Wardle (E)	142.5	82	176	20	8.80	7–56
A.V. Bedser (E)	74.5	28	158	10	15.50	3–9
J.B. Statham (E)	89	26	213	11	19.36	4–18
Fazal Mahmood (P)	165	50	408	20	20.40	6–46

Right: Len Hutton was England's captain for the first series played against Pakistan. The series was drawn one match each when Pakistan surprisingly won at the Oval.

1961–62: England win first series in Pakistan

Dexter's tourists played Pakistan, led by Imtiaz Ahmed, in three Tests in 1961–62.

England's team was not representative of their strongest, and in the first Test at Lahore Javed Burki made 138 with Pakistan reaching 387 for nine declared. Barrington (139) and M.J.K. Smith (99) rescued England from a bad start, but both were run out and England finished seven short. Pakistan, however, made only 200 second time and England won by five wickets.

England lost a five-Test series in India before returning for the last two Tests. Both were drawn after England had passed Pakistan's first innings score. Hanif (111 and 104) became the first Pakistani to make a century in each innings in the first, while Dexter made a double-century in the second.

1961–62 2nd Series Eng 1, Pak 0, Drawn 0

1 LAHORE **England won by 5 wkts**
Pakistan 387–9 dec (Javed Burki 138, Mushtaq Mohammad 76, Saeed Ahmed 74) and 200
England 380 (K F Barrington 139, M J K Smith 99, Mohammad Munaf 4–42) and 209–5 (E R Dexter 66)

2 DACCA **Match Drawn**
Pakistan 393–9 dec (Javed Burki 140, Hanif Mohammad 111, Saeed Ahmed 69, G A R Lock 4–55) and 216 (Hanif Mohammad 104, Alim-ud-Din 50, D A Allen 5–30, G A R Lock 4–70)
England 439 (G Pullar 165, R W Barber 86, K F Barrington 84, Antao d'Souza 4–94) and 38–0

3 KARACHI **Match Drawn**
Pakistan 253 (Alim-ud-Din 109, Hanif Mohammad 67, B R Knight 4–66) and 404–8 (Hanif Mohammad 89, Imtiaz Ahmed 86, Alim-ud-Din 53)
England 507 (E R Dexter 205, P H Parfitt 111, G Pullar 60, M J K Smith 56, Antao d'Souza 5–112)

1961–62 Averages

Batting	I	No	Runs	HS	Avge
E.R. Dexter (E)	4	1	303	205	101.00
K.F. Barrington (E)	3	0	229	139	76.33
Hanif Mohammed (P)	6	0	407	111	67.83
G. Pullar (E)	5	1	233	165	58.25
J.W. Burki (P)	6	0	340	140	56.66
Alimuddin (P)	4	0	219	109	54.75

Bowling	O	M	Runs	W	Avge	BB
D.A. Allen (E)	180.4	82	334	13	25.69	5–30
G.A.R. Lock (E)	166	71	337	10	33.70	4–70
R.W. Barber (E)	126.5	26	351	10	35.10	3–54

Frank Tyson made his first Test appearance in the fourth Test against Pakistan in 1954.

1962: Pakistan have miserable tour, and lose 4–0

An inexperienced Pakistan led by Javed Burki met a stronger England side in 1962, and also cold English weather, and they could not cope.

England made 544 for five declared at Edgbaston, Cowdrey and Parfitt getting centuries, and dismissed Pakistan for 246 and 274, Statham, Trueman, Allen and Lock getting the wickets.

At Lord's, Trueman's six for 31 removed Pakistan for 100, and England made 370 (Graveney 153). Pakistan did much better in the second innings, Javed Burki and Nasim-ul-Ghani both making 101, the latter as 'night-watchman'. Both fell to L.J. Coldwell, who took six for 85 on his debut. England won by nine wickets.

Pakistan put England in at Headingley, but they made 428 (Parfitt 119). Alimuddin top-scored in both innings for Pakistan, who lost by an innings and 17.

Rain washed out the first day and over half of the fourth at Trent Bridge, where England again made 428 after being put in, Graveney and Parfitt making hundreds before the declaration. Pakistan followed on, but 100 not out from Mushtaq saved the game.

England made 480 for five declared at the Oval, Cowdrey (182) and Dexter (172) adding 248 for the second wicket. Pakistan made 183 and 323, just saving the innings defeat, Imtiaz Ahmed making 98. J.D.F. Larter, in his first Test, took nine wickets.

1962   3rd Series   Eng 4, Pak 0, Drawn 1

1 EDGBASTON   England won by an innings and 24 runs
England 544–5 dec (M C Cowdrey 159, P H Parfitt 101, T W Graveney 97, D A Allen 79, E R Dexter 72)
Pakistan 246 (Mushtaq Mohammad 63, J B Statham 4–54) and 274 (Saeed Ahmed 65)

2 LORD'S   England won by 9 wkts
Pakistan 100 (F S Trueman 6–31) and 355 (Javed Burki 101, Nasim-ul-Ghani 101, L J Coldwell 6–85)
England 370 (T W Graveney 153, E R Dexter 65, Mohammad Farooq 4–70) and 86–1

1 HEADINGLEY   England won by an innings and 117 runs
England 428 (P H Parfitt 119, M J Stewart 86, D A Allen 62, Munir Malik 5–128)
Pakistan 131 (Alim-ud-Din 50, E R Dexter 4–10) and 180 (Alim-lud-Din 60, Saeed Ahmed 54, J B Statham 4–50)

4 TRENT BRIDGE   Match Drawn
England 428–5 dec (T W Graveney 114, P H Parfitt 101, E R Dexter 85, D S Sheppard 83)
Pakistan 219 (Mushtaq Mohammad 55, B R Knight 4–38, F S Trueman 4–71) and 216–6 (Mushtaq Mohammad 100, Saeed Ahmed 64)

5 THE OVAL   England won by 10 wkts
England 480–5 dec (M C Cowdrey 182, E R Dexter 172, D S Sheppard 67, K F Barrington 50) and 27–0
Pakistan 183 (J D F Larter 5–57) and 323 (Imtiaz Ahmed 98, Mushtaq Mohammad 72, J D F Larter 4–88)

1962 Averages

Batting	I	No	Runs	HS	Avge
P.H. Parfitt (E)	5	2	340	119	113.33
T.W. Graveney (E)	4	0	401	153	100.25
E.R. Dexter (E)	6	1	446	172	89.20
M.C. Cowdrey (E)	5	0	409	182	81.80
Mushtaq Mohammed (P)	10	1	401	100*	44.55
Imtiaz Ahmed (P)	8	0	282	98	35.25
Saeed Ahmed (P)	10	0	302	65	30.20
Javed Burki (P)	10	0	252	101	25.20

Bowling	O	M	Runs	W	Avge	BB
L.J. Coldwell (E)	105	30	223	13	17.15	6–85
J.B. Statham (E)	120.1	40	278	16	17.37	4–50
F.S. Trueman (E)	164.5	37	439	22	19.69	6–31

1967: Asif Iqbal's brave innings in defeat

Pakistan sent a stronger and more experienced team, led by Hanif, to England in 1967, but the weather was still against them. Close was England's captain.

At Lord's, Barrington made 148 of England's 369. Hanif made 187 not out in a long innings, putting on a record 130 with Asif for the eighth wicket. Pakistan finished only 15 behind, and in the last innings were set 257 to win in 210 minutes, but were happy to draw at 88 for three.

Storms at Trent Bridge washed out the fourth day. Pakistan made only 140, and Barrington's 109 allowed England to declare with a lead of 112. Pakistan left England to score only three runs, despite Saeed Ahmed's 68. A.P.E. Knott, in his first Test, took seven catches.

The Pakistan touring team in England in 1962. Left to right, back: Saeed Ahmed, Mohammad Farooq, Imtiaz Ahmed, Javed Burki, Alimuddin, Ijaz Butt, Hanif Mohammad, Nasim-ul-Ghani. Front: Intikhab Alam, Wallis Mathias, Mushtaq Mohammad, Asif Ahmed, Munir Malik.

England put Pakistan in at the Oval, and G.G. Arnold (5–58) had them out for 216. Barrington's third century in successive Tests gave England a lead of 214, Barrington becoming the first to score a century on all six of England's current Test grounds. Pakistan were 65 for eight, but Asif then played a typically gallant innings of 146, adding a world Test record of 190 with Intikhab Alam (51) for the ninth wicket. England, however, won by eight wickets.

1967 4th Series Eng 2, Pak 0, Drawn 1

1 LORD'S Match Drawn
England 369 (K F Barrington 148, T W Graveney 81, B L d'Oliveira 59) and 241–9 dec (B L d'Oliveira 81)
Pakistan 354 (Hanif Mohammad 187, Asif Iqbal 76) and 88–3

2 TRENT BRIDGE England won by 10 wkts
Pakistan 140 (K Higgs 4–35) and 114 (Saeed Ahmed 68, D L Underwood 5–52)
England 252–8 dec (K F Barrington 109) and 3–0

3 THE OVAL England won by 8 wkts
Pakistan 216 (Mushtaq Mohammad 66, G G Arnold 5–58) and 255 (Asif Iqbal 146, Intikhab Alam 51, K Higgs 5–58)
England 440 (K F Barrington 142, T W Graveney 77, F J Titmus 65, G G Arnold 59, Mushtaq Mohammad 4–80) and 34–2

1967 Averages

Batting	I	No	Runs	HS	Avge
K.F. Barrington (E)	5	2	426	148	142.00
Hanif Mohammed (P)	5	1	288	187*	57.00
T.W. Graveney (E)	4	0	216	81	54.00
Asif Iqbal (P)	5	0	267	146	53.40

Bowling	O	M	Runs	W	Avge	BB
K. Higgs	119	45	249	17	14.64	5–58
Asif Iqbal (P)	134	45	278	11	25.27	3–66

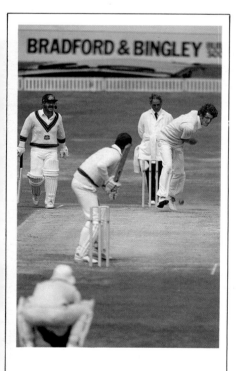

Willis, Robert George Dylan

Willis was born on 30 May 1949 at Sunderland. The Dylan in his name he added himself in admiration of the singer. He first played for Surrey in 1969, but moved to Warwickshire in 1972 for more opportunities. By then he had made his Test debut in 1970–71, when he was flown out as an addition to the party. He was a right-arm fast bowler. He played in 90 Tests, and was captain in 18. His best performance, eight for 43, helped England win the amazing Test match at Headingley in 1981. He took 325 Test wickets, average 25.20.

1968–69: Riots foil Knott and end tour of Pakistan

After the cancellation of MCC's tour to South Africa in 1968–69 because of the 'D'Oliveira affair', a tour of Ceylon and Pakistan was arranged instead. Cowdrey led the tourists, and made his final Test century at Lahore in an England total of 306. Throughout the match a riot was proceeding in the city, and the play was often interrupted. Pakistan were 97 behind on first innings, and were eventually set 323 to win in 295 minutes by England's declaration. They reached 203 for five.

Police had left the rioting students in control at Dacca, which made the atmosphere uncomfortable but led to uninterrupted play. Brown and Snow got Pakistan out for 246 and England were rescued by D'Oliveira, whose 114 not out took them into the lead. On a difficult pitch the match was drawn.

At Karachi, C. Milburn, who had been flown from Australia to join the party, made 139. It was his last Test before losing an eye in a road accident. Graveney also made a century, but, at 502 for seven, hundreds of rioters broke into the ground and covered

Ibadulla caught behind by Knott off Close at Trent Bridge in 1967.

the outfield with banners. The match was abandoned, with Knott four runs short of a first Test century. The tourists shortly afterwards left for home.

1968–69 5th Series Drawn 3

1 LAHORE Match Drawn
England 306 (M C Cowdrey 100, J H Edrich 54, A P E Knott 52, Saeed Ahmed 4–64, Intikhab Alam 4–117) and 225–9 dec (K W R Fletcher 83)
Pakistan 209 (Asif Iqbal 70, R M H Cottam 4–50) and 203–5 (Majid Jahangir Khan 68)

2 DACCA Match Drawn
Pakistan 246 (Mushtaq Mohammad 52, J A Snow 4–70) and 195–6 dec (D L Underwood 5–94)
England 274 (B L d'Oliveira 114, Pervez Sajjad 4–75) and 3–0

3 KARACHI Match Drawn
England 502–7 (C Milburn 139, T W Graveney 105, A P E Knott 96)
Pakistan did not bat

1968–69 Averages

Batting	I	No	Runs	HS	Avge
G. Boycott (E)	3	1	246	121*	123.00
Zaheer Abbas (P)	4	0	386	274	96.50
B.W. Luckhurst (E)	6	2	242	108*	60.50
B.L.D'Oliveira (E)	4	0	241	74	60.25

Bowling	O	M	Runs	W	Avge	BB
Asif Masood (P)	119.5	26	344	13	26.46	5–111

1971: England just win even series

Intikhab Alam led Pakistan in England against Illingworth's Ashes-winning side. They gave England shocks at Edgbaston. Zaheer made 274, Pakistan's highest against England, as was his stand of 291 for the second wicket with Mushtaq (100). Asif made 104 not out, and Pakistan declared at 608 for seven, then their highest against England. Knott's 116 rescued England but at 353 they followed on. Luckhurst (108 not out) and rain, which washed out most of the last day, saved England from probable defeat.

Rain washed out over half the playing time at Lord's, where the only event of note was a century from Boycott.

There was a close match at Headingley. England batted first and made 316, with Boycott getting 112. Pakistan batted solidly and slowly to get 350 and lead by 34. England's 264 left Pakistan to score 231 in plenty of time to win the series. Sadiq Mohammad held firm with 91 while early wickets fell and at 203 for seven it was anybody's match, but Lever then took the last three wickets in four balls. D'Oliveira with 74 and 72 and five wickets did well for England, Wasim Bari with a record-equalling eight catches and 63 did well for Pakistan.

1971 6th Series Eng 1, Pak 0, Drawn 2
1 EDGBASTON **Match Drawn**
Pakistan 608–7 dec (Zaheer Abbas 274, Asif Iqbal 104, Mushtaq Mohammad 10)
England 353 (A P E Knott 116, B L d'Oliveira 73, Asif Masood 5–111) and 229–5 (B W Luckhurst 108, Asif Masood 4–49)
2 LORD'S **Match Drawn**
England 241–2 dec (G Boycott 121) and 117–0 (R A Hutton 58, B W Luckhurst 53)
Pakistan 148
3 HEADINGLEY **England won by 25 runs**
England 316 (G Boycott 112, B L d'Oliveira 74) and 264 (B L d'Oliveira 72, D L Amiss 56, Saleem Altaf 4–11)
Pakistan 350 (Zaheer Abbas 72, Wasim Bari 63, Mushtaq Mohammad 57) and 205 (Sadiq Mohammad 91)

1972–73: Batsmen on top in Pakistan

A.R. Lewis's party played three Tests in Pakistan after a gruelling and losing tour of India and Ceylon. Pakistan, now led by Majid Khan, had toured Australia and New Zealand.

Amiss made his first Test century in Lahore, England getting 355. Sadiq and Asif both made hundreds as Pakistan led by 67. England batted solidly in the second innings to set Pakistan 240 in 145 minutes – they made 124 for three.

In Hyderabad's first Test, Amiss made a second century in 487, passed by Pakistan's 569 for nine declared, Mushtaq and Intikhab scoring centuries. At 77 for five England were in danger of defeat, but Greig and Knott put on 112 to save the match.

The Karachi Test was again interrupted by minor riots and skirmishes. Pakistan declared at 445 for six, with Majid and Mushtaq both scoring 99. Amiss's run ended when he, too, was out for 99, England ending 59 behind. Gifford (5–55) and Birkenshaw (5–57) gave England hope of a win at 108 for seven, but Pakistan soon added enough to save the rubber.

Imran Khan

Born in Lahore on 25 November 1952 Imran made his debut for Lahore in 1969–70. He later played for PIA, and for Worcestershire and Sussex in England. He is a cousin of Majid Khan and Javed Burki, and all three captained Pakistan. An attacking middle-order right-hand batsman, and right-arm fast bowler, he was one of the great all-rounders of the 1980s. He made his Test debut for Pakistan in 1971 but did not become a regular until 1976–77. He became his country's captain in 1982, and in 1987 led Pakistan to their first series win in England. By then he had played in 70 Tests, scoring 2,770 runs, average 32.97, and taking 311 wickets, average 29.40. He was the sixth all-rounder to complete 2,000 runs and 200 wickets in Tests.

1974: Last-day rain twice prevents a result

Pakistan toured England in the second half of 1974, led by Intikhab. Denness was England captain.

Pakistan scored 285 at Headingley and their quick bowlers dismissed England for only 183. The England seamers struck back to remove Pakistan for 179, leaving England 282 to win. At the end of the fourth day they were 238 for six, needing 44, but rain washed out the last day and an exciting finish.

At Lord's, Pakistan batted and declared at 130 for nine after rain had seeped under the covers, Underwood taking five for 20. England made 270, and Underwood then took eight for 51 in removing Pakistan for 226. England needed only 87 to win and were 27 for nought overnight, but then found rain washing out the last day for the second successive Test, this time preventing an easy win.

At the Oval, Pakistan declared at 600 for seven after Zaheer had played one of his big innings: 240. All the other batsmen scored well. Amiss made 183 in reply for England and Fletcher 122, taking 458 minutes to reach 100, an English first-class record. When England saved the follow-on, the match was headed for a draw.

1974 Averages

Batting	I	No	Runs	HS	Avge
K.W.R. Fletcher (E)	4	1	208	122	69.33
Zaheer Abbas (P)	6	0	324	240	54.00
M.J. Khan (P)	6	0	262	98	43.66
Mushtaq Mohammed (P)	6	0	209	76	34.83

Bowling	O	M	Runs	W	Avge	BB
D.L. Underwood (E)	113.5	48	218	17	12.82	8–51
G.G. Arnold (E)	121	28	300	10	30.00	3–36

Two successful batsmen in 1974, Zaheer (top) on his way to 240 at the Oval, and Knott (below) during his 83 at Lord's.

1977–78: Slow batting and three draws in Pakistan

The England side which toured New Zealand and Pakistan under J.M. Brearley was the first to be labelled 'England' rather than 'MCC'. The World Series cricket matches had begun, which in effect meant both sides lost four or five of their 'first teams'. Wasim Bari led Pakistan. At Lahore, there were riots on the second and third days, but the action on the pitch was funereal. Mudassar made the slowest century in first-class cricket (557 minutes). Haroon Rashid scored quicker in Pakistan's 407 for nine declared, but Boycott scored even slower in his 63 for England. The match was a tedious draw.

Haroon made a second century at Hyderabad – it included six sixes. Qadir got six for 44 in England's 191 – 84 behind. Pakistan's declaration was a little too late. The optional half-hour was claimed for Boycott to complete his hundred.

Gatting made his debut for England at Karachi, where Boycott assumed the captaincy, Brearley having broken his arm in a previous match. After England had made 266, Edmonds took seven for 66, but Pakistan led by 15. A slow match petered out into a draw, with all 11 Pakistani players bowling.

1977–78   9th series   Drawn 3

1 LAHORE   Match Drawn
Pakistan 407–9 dec (Haroon Rashid 122, Mudassar Nazar 114, Javed Miandad 71) and 106–3
England 288 (G Miller 98, G Boycott 63, Sarfraz Nawaz 4–68)

2 HYDERABAD   Match Drawn
Pakistan 275 (Haroon Rashid 108, Javed Miandad 88) and 259–4 dec (Mudassar Nazar 66, Javed Miandad 61)
England 191 (G Boycott 79, Abdul Qadir 6–44) and 186–1 (G Boycott 100, J M Brearley 74)

3 KARACHI   Match Drawn
England 266 (G R J Roope 56, Abdul Qadir 4–81) and 222–5 (G Boycott 56, D W Randall 55)
Pakistan 281 (Mudassar Nazar 76, P H Edmonds 7–66)

1977–78 Averages

Batting	I	No	Runs	HS	Avge
Javed Miandad (P)	5	3	262	88*	131.00
Haroon Rashid (P)	5	1	337	122	84.25
G. Boycott (E)	5	1	329	100*	82.25
Mudassar Nazar (P)	5	0	309	114	61.60

Bowling	O	M	Runs	W	Avge	BB
P.H. Edmonds (E)	87	15	236	10	23.60	7–66
Abdul Qadir (P)	132	31	305	12	25.41	6–44
Iqbal Qasim (P)	159.4	60	260	10	26.00	3–56

Above: Sarfraz Nawaz, a Pakistan stalwart in the 1970s and 1980s, bowling Wood in a Prudential Trophy match in 1978.

Below: The third Test at Karachi in 1977–78. Mike Gatting sweeps to leg. All three Tests were drawn.

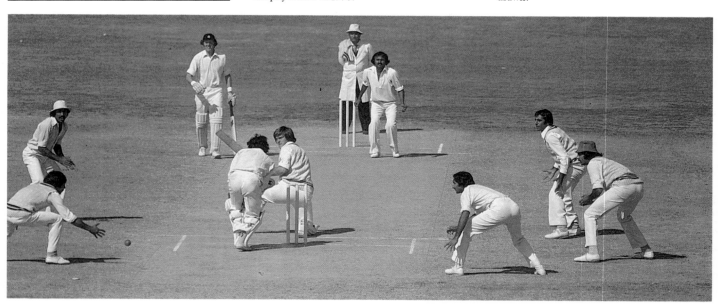

1978: England too good in wet conditions

Test matches in England were sponsored in 1978, in an effort to combat World Series Cricket. Both teams, led again by Brearley and Wasim Bari, remained under strength. Pakistan were dismissed for 164 at Edgbaston, Old, in his seven for 50, taking four wickets in five balls (the odd ball being a no-ball). D.I. Gower made his Test debut, but Radley and Botham were England's century-makers in 452 for eight declared. Pakistan were removed for 231 and lost by an innings.

When play started over a day late at Lord's, Botham made a second century in England's 364. Willis and Edmonds removed Pakistan for 105, then Botham completed a triumphant match with eight for 34 in the follow-on, finishing the innings with six for eight.

Half the match at Headingley was lost through rain and bad covering of the square. Sadiq's innings and Sarfraz's bowling were the highlights of what play there was.

Above: Abdul Qadir bowling at Headingley in 1982. His most successful series was in Pakistan in 1987–88, when he took 30 wickets in a three-match series.

Below: Iqbal Qasim bowling his left-arm spinners at Karachi in 1977–78. He was one of three bowlers to get ten wickets in the three Tests.

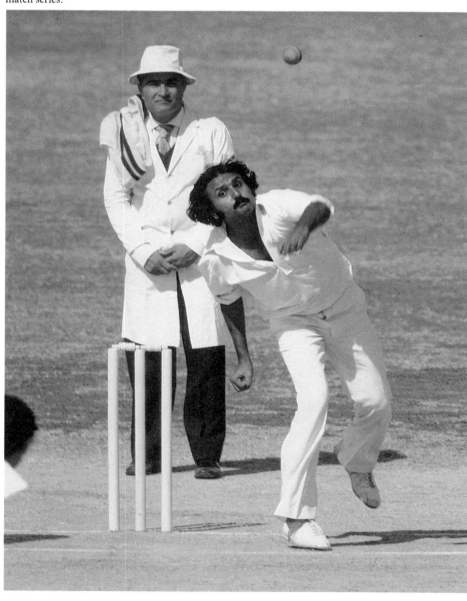

1978 10th Series Eng 2, Pak 0, Drawn 1

1 EDGBASTON **England won by an innings and 57 runs**
Pakistan 164 (C M Old 7–50) and 231 (Sadiq Mohammad 79, P H Edmonds 4–44)
England 452–8 dec (C T Radley 196, I T Botham 100, D I Gower 58, Sikander Bakht 4–132)

2 LORD'S **England won by an innings and 120 runs**
England 364 (I T Botham 108, G R J Roope 69, D I Gower 56, G A Gooch 54)
Pakistan 105 (R G D Willis 5–47, P H Edmonds 4–6) and 139 (I T Botham 8–34)

3 HEADINGLEY **Match Drawn**
Pakistan 201 (Sadiq Mohammad 97, C M Old 4–41, I T Botham 4–59)
England 119–7 (Sarfraz Nawaz 5–39)

1978 Averages

Batting	I	No	Runs	HS	Avge	
I.T. Botham (E)	3	0	212	108	70.66	
Sadiq Mohammed (P)	5	0	210	97	42.00	

Bowling	O	M	Runs	W	Avge	BB
C.M. Old (E)	114.2	47	191	13	14.69	7–50
I.T. Botham (E)	75.5	19	209	13	16.07	8–34
R.G.D. Willis (E)	88.4	16	233	13	17.92	5–47

1982: Extras help England win rubber 2–1

Pakistan, led by Imran Khan, had the second half of the English season for three Tests in 1982. Willis led England.

At Edgbaston, Imran's seven for 52 got England out for 272, but most Pakistan batsmen were out quickly and they finished 21 behind. Randall's 105 runs held England together until the last wicket added 79, Willis's 28 not out being his highest score in 90 Tests. Despite Pakistan's last three wickets adding 101, they lost by 113.

Pakistan fought back at Lord's, where Mohsin Khan's 200 was the first Test double-century there for 33 years. Pakistan declared at 428 for eight. England could make only 227, Qadir bowling well and extras being top scorer. Following on, they found Mudassar (6–32) at his best. Tavare batted 69 minutes before scoring, in all batting 404 minutes for 82. England, 276, set Pakistan only 76 to score for a 10-wicket win.

With all to play for at Headingley, Pakistan made a reasonable 275 against England's swing bowlers. Imran followed his 67 not out with five for 49 to remove England for 256. England's counterpart to Imran, Botham, followed his 57 with five for 74, Pakistan finishing with 199 and setting England 219 to win. They seemed to be cruising at 168 for one but wickets fell to Mudassar and eventually they scraped home by three wickets, G. Fowler scoring 86 on his debut.

An extraordinary statistic was that England's 'top-scorer' in the rubber was Extras with 221, which might have decided the series.

Miller caught by Javed Miandad from Iqbal Qasim's bowling at Lord's in 1978. Mudassar Nazar is slip and Wasim Bari the wicket-keeper. Sadiq Mohammad is in the helmet, the first worn by a Pakistan fielder at Lord's.

1982 11th Series Eng 2, Pak 1

1 EDGBASTON England won by 113 runs
England 272 (D I Gower 74, C J Tavare 54, Imran Khan 7–52) and 291 (D W Randall 105, R W Taylor 54, Tahir Naqqash 5–40)
Pakistan 251 (Mansoor Akhtar 58) and 199 (Imran Khan 65)

2 LORD'S Pakistan won by 10 wkts
Pakistan 428–8 dec (Mohsin Khan 200, Zaheer Abbas 75, Mansoor Akhtar 57) and 77–0
England 227 and 276 (C J Tavare 82, I T Botham 69, Mudassar Nazar 6–32)

3 HEADINGLEY England won by 4 wkts
Pakistan 275 (Imran Khan 67, Mudassar Nazar 65, Javed Miandad 54) and 199 (Javed Miandad 52, I T Botham 5–74)
England 256 (D I Gower 74, I T Botham 57, Imran Khan 5–49) and 190–6 (G Fowler 86)

1982 Averages

Batting	I	No	Runs	HS	Avge	
Mohsin Khan (P)	6	1	310	200	62.00	
Imran Khan (P)	5	1	212	67	53.00	
C.J. Tavaré (E)	6	0	216	82	36.00	

Bowling	O	M	Runs	W	Avge	BB
Mudassar Nazar (P)	54	18	104	10	10.40	6–32
Imran Khan (P)	178.1	48	390	21	18.57	7–52
R.G.D. Willis (E)	74	14	222	10	22.20	3–55
I.T. Botham (E)	150.5	33	478	18	26.55	5–74
Abdul Qadir (P)	160.5	48	406	10	40.60	4–39

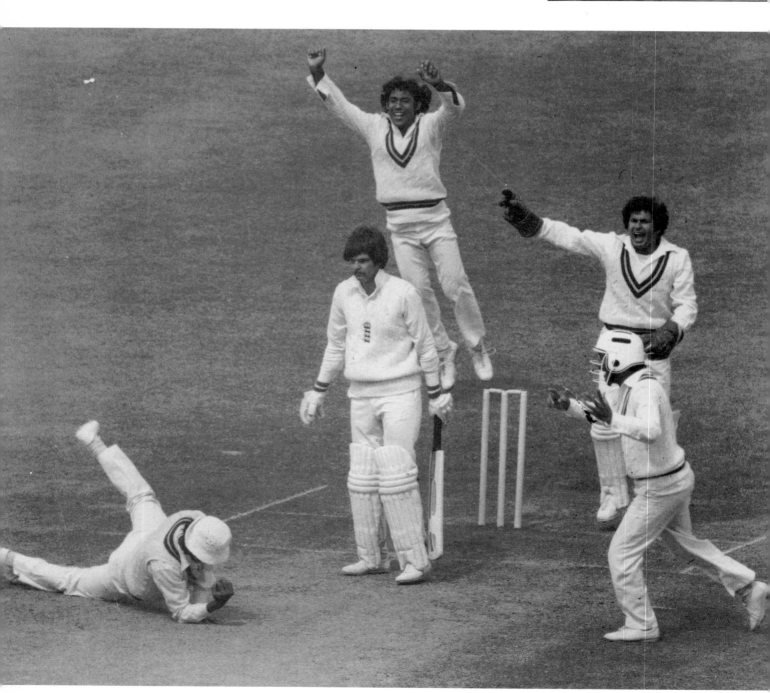

1983–84: Pakistan win first home match and series against England

Willis again captained England in 1983–84, Zaheer being the home skipper.

At Karachi, Sarfraz and Qadir gave Pakistan a good start by dismissing England for 182, their lowest in Pakistan. Cook (6–65) bowled well for England but Pakistan made 277 to lead by 95. England struggled to a new low of 159 in the second innings, leaving Pakistan only 65 to win. This proved surprisingly difficult as Cook took five for 18, and Pakistan won by only three wickets. It was their first home win over England.

England began badly at Faisalabad with Dilley no-balled six times in his first over. Salim Malik and Wasim Raja made centuries in a total of 449 for eight declared. Gower led England in the absence of Willis, who was ill, and who with Botham, injured, returned home. Gower made 152 in England's reply, which reached 546 for eight declared. The match was soon drawn.

Zaheer put England in on a dampish pitch at Lahore, and five wickets were down for 83, but Fowler and V.J. Marks helped the score to 241. At 181 for eight Pakistan were in trouble, but Zaheer (82 not out) and Sarfraz (90) added 161 and Pakistan led by 102. A brilliant 173 not out by Gower allowed him to declare at 344 for nine, Qadir completing ten wickets in the match. Pakistan needed 243, and Mohsin Khan and Shoaib Mohammad put on 173 for the first wicket, but N.G. Cowans then took five wickets in 22 balls as Pakistan slumped to 199 for five, when they decided to bat out time and take the series 1–0.

1983–84 12th Series Pak 1, Eng 0, Drawn 2

1 KARACHI   Pakistan won by 3 wkts
England 182 (D I Gower 58, Abdul Qadir 5–74, Sarfraz Nawaz 4–42) and 159 (D I Gower 57)
Pakistan 277 (Saleem Malik 74, Mohsin Khan 54, N G B Cook 6–65) and 66–7 (N G B Cook 5–18)

2 FAISALABAD   Match Drawn
Pakistan 449–8 dec (Saleem Malik 116, Wasim Raja 112, Zaheer Abbas 68, Abdul Qadir 50) and 137–4 (Saleem Malik 76)
England 546–8 dec (D I Gower 152, M W Gatting 75, C L Smith 66, D W Randall 65, V J Marks 83, G Fowler 57)

3 LAHORE   Match Drawn
England 241 (V J Marks 74, G Fowler 58, Abdul Qadir 5–84) and 344–9 dec (D I Gower 173, V J Marks 55, M W Gatting 53, Abdul Qadir 5–110)
Pakistan 343 (Sarfraz Nawaz 90, Zaheer Abbas 82, Qasim Omar 73, N A Foster 5–67) and 217–6 (Mohsin Khan 104, Shoaib Mohammad 80)

1983–84 Averages

Batting	I	No	Runs	HS	Avge	
D.I. Gower (E)	5	1	449	173	112.25	
Salim Malik (P)	6	0	322	116	35.66	
V.J. Marks (E)	5	0	218	83	43.60	

Bowling	O	M	Runs	W	Avge	BB
Abdul Qadir (P)	185	42	451	19	23.73	5–74
Sarfraz Nawaz (P)	137.2	26	359	14	25.64	4–42
N.G.B. Cook (E)	178.3	54	444	14	31.71	6–56

David Gower sweeping to leg. In the 1983–84 tour of Pakistan he headed the batting table with an average of 112, with the second most successful batsman averaging only 35.

1987: Pakistan win five-match series in England

Imran led Pakistan on a five-match tour in 1987, Gatting being the home captain.

With play beginning late and subject to interruption through rain, progress was painfully slow at Old Trafford. England made 447 (Robinson 166) and with Pakistan 140 for five, the weather closed in to end it.

Three whole days were lost at Lord's. What play there was on the others was enough for one innings and a maiden century for Athey.

England batted on a pitch favouring seam at Headingley, and Pakistan's four swing bowlers had them rapidly out for 136. Foster took eight for 107 for England but was unsupported and Salim Malik (99), supported by the lower order, took the score to 353, a lead of 217. Imran, bowling at his best, then took seven for 40 to dismiss England for 199 and win by an innings and 18.

The Edgbaston Test was a boring affair for a rain-interrupted 4½ days, in which both sides seemed happy to go-slow, and came to life for the last two or three hours. Pakistan were put in and, with Mudassar leading the way with 124 in 416 minutes, reached a comfortable 439 (Dilley 5–92). In longer time but fewer overs, England made 521, Gatting getting 124, and Imran six for 129. On the last day Pakistan began to lose wickets and England pressed to get them out in time to score the runs. In the end, Pakistan were out for 205, and England had 18 overs to score 124. They began well, but eventually had to press too hard and wickets fell. At the end they were 109 for seven.

At the Oval, Pakistan batted and the batsmen gradually got on top. They went on to their highest Test score of 708. Javed made 260, and Salim Malik and Imran Khan also passed 100. Dilley took six for 194. With runs in the bank, Qadir had a long spell of leg-spin and took seven for 96, spinning England out for 232. Gatting (150 not out), supported by Botham, batted with resolution to avoid defeat, but it was Pakistan's second successive series win over England.

1987   13th Series   Pak 1, Eng 0, Drawn 4

1 OLD TRAFFORD   Match Drawn
England 447 (R T Robinson 166, B N French 59, Wasim Akram 4–111, Mohsin Kamal 4–127)
Pakistan 140–5 (Mansoor Akhtar 75)

2 LORD'S   Match Drawn
England 368 (C W J Athey 123, B C Broad 55)

3 HEADINGLEY   Pakistan won by an innings and 18 runs
England 136 (D J Capel 53) and 199 (D I Gower 55, Imran Khan 7–40)
Pakistan 353 (Salim Malik 99, Ijaz Ahmed 50, N A Foster 8–107)

4 EDGBASTON   Match Drawn
Pakistan 439 (Mudassar Nazar 124, Salim Yousuf 91, Javed Miandad 75, G R Dilley 5–92) and 205 (Shoaib Mohammad 50, N A Foster 4–59)
England 521 (M W Gatting 124, R T Robinson 80, D I Gower 61, J E Emburey 58, Imran Khan 6–129) and 109–7

5 THE OVAL   Match Drawn
Pakistan 708 (Javed Miandad 260, Imran Khan 118, Salim Malik 102, Mudassar Nazar 73, Ijaz Ahmed 69, G R Dilley 6–154)
England 232 (M W Gatting 61, J E Emburey 53, Abdul Qadir 7–96) and 315–4 (M W Gatting 150, I T Botham 51)

1987 Averages

Batting	I	No	Runs	HS	Avge
Javed Miandad (P)	5	0	360	260	72.00
M.W. Gatting (E)	8	1	445	150*	63.57
R.T. Robinson (E)	8	0	299	166	37.38

Bowling	O	M	Runs	W	Avge	BB
Imran Khan (P)	168.2	33	455	21	21.67	7–40
N.A. Foster (E)	137.2	35	339	15	22.60	8–107
G.R. Dilley (E)	133.3	26	388	14	27.71	6–154
Wasim Akram (P)	180.4	39	464	16	29.00	4–111

Left: The Pakistan tourists in England in 1987. Left to right, back: Shoaib Mohammad, Asif Mujtaba, Ramiz Raja, Salim Yousef, Mohsin Kamal, Wasim Akram, Salim Jafir, Zakir Khan, Ejaz Ahmed, Mansoor Akhtar, Manzoor Elahi. Front: Salim Malik, Iqbal Qasim, Abdul Qadir, Haseeb Ahsan (manager), Imran Khan, Javed Miandad, Mudassar Nazar, Tauseef Ahmed. Pakistan won the series by 1–0.

Below left: Ian Botham batting against Pakistan at Old Trafford in 1987 in a match spoiled by rain.

Below: A big shout by Imran for lbw against David Gower at Headingley in 1987. Gower scored 55 in the second innings but Imran took seven for 40 and Pakistan won.

1987–88: Umpiring disputes and arguments mar tour

Gatting remained England captain, but Imran had retired and Pakistan were captained by Javed Miandad. The tour, which followed the World Cup, was exceptional for disputes and arguments over umpiring decisions.

The trouble started in the first Test at Lahore, and revolved around one umpire in particular, Shakeel Khan. The worst incident occurred when Chris Broad was given out caught behind and was so reluctant to depart that his partner Gooch was moved to walk down the pitch to usher him away. A decision that Abdul Qadir had been stumped appeared on television replays to be equally suspect, and was vehemently contested by the batsman. However Gatting, after the match, claimed that there were ten bad decisions against England to one against Pakistan. Broad was reprimanded by the tour management for his behaviour, but not fined. The controversy took attention from the outstanding performance of Abdul Qadir. On a wicket ideal for him, he took nine for 56 in dismissing England for 175, and after Mudassar had made 120 in a Pakistan total of 392, took four for 45 as Pakistan won by an innings and 87.

Matters came to a head in the second Test at Faisalabad. After Broad had made a century in England's 292, Pakistan were struggling at the end of the second day at 106 for five. There had already been words between Gatting and umpire Shakoor Rana, notably over what the England players considered an extremely bad decision regarding a disallowed catch. In the penultimate over

of the day, Gatting called in deep square leg to save the single, informing the batsman. However, the adjustment was incomplete when Hemmings began to bowl, the umpire stopped him, and words passed between Gatting and the umpire in which Gatting claimed the umpire called him a cheat and the umpire claimed Gatting had abused him with foul language.

Next day Shakoor Rana refused to continue without an apology in writing; Gatting offered to give one if he received one in return, an arrangement the umpire declined. A whole day's play was thus lost, before the TCCB instructed Gatting to apologise, which he did. When the match eventually resumed on the fourth day (late), it meandered to a draw. The England players issued a statement, in effect backing Gatting and critical of the TCCB's forcing him into unilateral apology. The players were apparently willing to abandon the tour. The chairman and chief executive of the TCCB, Raman Subba Row and Alan Smith, flew to Karachi to sort things out on the spot.

For the final Test at Karachi, the Pakistan board offered to bring in impartial umpires from India, and eventually appointed two experienced local umpires to whom the tourists had no objections. It was a good match. England recovered from 85 for six to 294, and Pakistan from 146 for six to 353. A draw was a fair result. Abdul Qadir took ten wickets in the match, and 30 in the series, the fourth best ever in a three-match series. It was not the end of the unpleasantness. There was overt indignation from Gatting at both umpires being unsighted to judge a caught-behind apopeal, and apparent disagreement from Broad, Athey and Gatting,

the principal 'dissenters', over the decisions which dismissed them in the second innings. The England party declined to attend an end-of-tour dinner.

It became known on the last day through a leak from Lord's that the England players were being given a bonus of £1,000 per man. This surprised many who thought fines might be more appropriate, and it seemed likely that cricket relations between England and Pakistan would be strained for a long time.

1987–88   14th Series   Pak 1, Eng 0, Drawn 2
1 LAHORE   **Pakistan won by an innings and 87 runs**
England 175 (Qadir 9–56) and 130
Pakistan 392 (Mudassar Nazar 120, Javed Miandad 65)
2 FAISALABAD   **Match Drawn**
England 292 (B C Broad 116, M W Gatting 79, Qasim 5–83, Qadir 4–105) and 137–6 dec (G A Gooch 65)
Pakistan 191 (Salim Malik 60, N A Foster 4–42) and 51–1
3 KARACHI   **Match Drawn**
England 294 (D J Capel 98, J E Emburey 70, Qadir 5–88) and 258–9 (G A Gooch 93, J E Emburey 74, Qadir 5–98)
Pakistan 353 (Aamir Malik 98, Qadir 61, Salim Malik 55, Ramiz Raja 50, P A J Defreitas 5–86)

1987–88 Averages

Batting	I	No	Runs	HS	Avge	
J.E. Emburey (E)	6	3	207	74	69.00	
G.A. Gooch (E)	6	0	225	93	37.50	
B.C. Broad (E)	6	0	204	116	34.00	

Bowling	O	M	Runs	W	Avge	BB
Abdul Qadir (P)	234.4	68	437	30	14.56	9–56
Iqbal Qasim (P)	114.2	33	268	10	26.80	5–83

Mike Gatting and Peter Lush of the TCCB in discussion with controversial umpire Shakoor Rana on the third day of the second Test. They failed to reach a compromise and lost a day's play.

Australia v India

1947–48: Three innings defeats for India in first series with Australia

India's first Test series with Australia came in 1947–48. Their they were weakened by some notable absences when Amarnath's side met a team led by Bradman in his last home season.

Bradman batted on a sticky wicket at Brisbane, and declared at 382 for eight, having scored nearly half the runs (185) himself. The second and fourth days were practically wiped out by rain and India found batting very difficult. They were out for 58 in the first innings, Toshack having the astonishing analysis of five for two, and did little better with 98 in the follow-on. Toshack's match figures were eleven for 31.

Three whole days were washed out completely at Sydney, only ten hours play being possible. India made 188, and good bowling by Phadkar and Hazare, plus the running out of Brown by Mankad without warning when backing up, got rid of Australia for 107. India were 61 for seven by the end.

At Melbourne, Bradman made 132 and Australia 394. Mankad made a century and Amarnath declared behind at 291 for nine when it rained overnight. Bradman countered by opening with the bottom three in the order, and when the wicket eased added an unbeaten 223 with Morris for the fifth wicket. Both made centuries, Bradman for the second time in the match. A declaration led to a 233-run win.

Bradman made 201 at Adelaide. Barnes (112) and Hassett (198 not out) also piled on the runs as Australia reached 674. India

made a worthy reply, Hazare and Phadkar getting centuries in 381, but then lost by an innings when Lindwall recorded his best Test analysis of seven for 38. Hazare, however, completed a century in each innings with 145 out of 277.

Bradman won the toss again at Melbourne, but retired hurt with 57. Harvey, at 19 years 121 days, made the first of his Test centuries in another big score of 575 for eight declared. Brown was run out on 99. Mankad opened with a century and India reached 206 for two, but then subsided to 331 and 67, again losing by an innings.

Don Bradman in the nets. He captained Australia in the first series with India.

1956–57: Australia win comfortably in India

Australia played three Tests in India on the way back from England in 1956–57. I.W. Johnson was the Austrálian captain and P.R. Umrigar led India.

India batted first at Madras, but Benaud, with seven for 72, helped dismiss them for 161. Australia were 200 for eight, but reached 319 and won by an innings when Lindwall, recovered from an upset stomach, took seven for 43 to reduce India to 153 all out for the second time.

India reached 251 at Madras, where Ramchand made 109, but Burke (161) and Harvey (140) took Australia past this with

1947–48 1st Series Aus 4, India 0, Drawn 1
1 BRISBANE Australia won by an innings and 226 runs
Australia 382–8 dec (D G Bradman 185, K R Miller 58, L Amarnath 4–84)
India 58 (E R H Toshack 5–2) and 98 (E R H Toshack 6–29)
2 SYDNEY Match Drawn
India 188 (D G Phadkar 51) and 61–7
Australia 107 (V S Hazare 4–29)
3 MELBOURNE Australia won by 233 runs
Australia 394 (D G Bradman 132, A L Hassett 80, L Amarnath 4–78, M H Mankad 4–135) and 255–4 dec (D G Bradman 127, A R Morris 100)
India 291–9 dec (M H Mankad 116, D G Phadkar 55, I W Johnson 4–59) and 125 (I W Johnson 4–35, W A Johnston 4–44)
4 ADELAIDE Australia won by an innings and 16 runs
Australia 674 (D B Bradman 201, A L Hassett 198, S G Barnes 112, K R Miller 67, C R Rangachari 4–141)
India 381 (V S Hazare 116, D G Phadkar 123, I W Johnson 4–64) and 277 (V S Hazare 145, H R Adhikari 51, R R Lindwall 7–38)
5 MELBOURNE Australia won by an innings and 177 runs
Australia 575–8 dec (R N Harvey 153, W A Brown 99, S J E Loxton 80, D G Bradman 57)
India 331 (M H Mankad 111, V S Hazare 74, D G Phadkar 56) and 67

1947–48 Averages

Batting	I	No	Runs	HS	Avge	
D.G. Bradman (A)	6	2	715	201	178.75	
A.L. Hassett (A)	4	1	332	198*	110.66	
D.G. Phadkar (I)	8	2	314	123	52.33	
V.S. Hazare (I)	10	1	429	145	47.66	
V. Mankad (I)	10	0	306	116	30.60	

Bowling	O	M	Runs	W	Avge	BB
W.A. Johnston (A)	84	24	182	16	11.37	4–44
E.R.H. Toshack (A)	62.3	17	170	13	13.07	6–29
I.W. Johnson (A)	93.1	21	261	16	16.31	4–35
R.R. Lindwall (A)	113.4	21	304	18	16.88	7–38
L. Amarnath (I)	126	23	366	13	28.15	4–78
V. Mankad (I)	174	21	630	12	52.50	4–135

only one man out, Johnson eventually declaring at 523 for seven. India defended for a long time to save the match.

Umrigar put Australia in on a spinner's wicket at Calcutta. Ghulam Ahmed was the first to benefit with seven for 49 in Australia's 177. But Benaud (6–52) got out India for 41 fewer, and Australia's 189 for nine declared left India too many to make. Benaud and Burke spun them to defeat by 94 runs.

1956–57 2nd Series Aus 2, India 0, Drawn 1

1 MADRAS Australia won by an innings and 5 runs
India 161 (R Benaud 7–72) and 153 (R R Lindwall 7–43)
Australia 319 (I W Johnson 73, M H Mankad 4–90)

2 BOMBAY Match Drawn
India 251 (G S Ramchand 109, V L Manjrekar 55) and 250–5 (P Roy 79, P R Umrigar 78)
Australia 523–7 dec (J W Burke 161, R N Harvey 140, P J P Burge 83)

3 CALCUTTA Australia won by 94 runs
Australia 177 (P J P Burge 58, Ghulam Ahmed 7–49) and 189–9 dec (R N Harvey 69, M H Mankad 4–49)
India 136 (R Benaud 6–52) and 136 (R Benaud 5–53, J W Burke 4–37)

1956–57 Averages

Batting	I	No	Runs	HS	Avge	
R.N. Harvey (A)	4	0	253	140	63.25	

Bowling	O	M	Runs	W	Avge	BB
Ghulam Ahmed (I)	87.3	28	197	12	16.41	7–49
R.R. Lindwall (A)	114.1	45	199	12	16.58	7–43
R. Benaud (A)	169.5	53	388	23	16.86	7–72
V. Mankad (I)	125.4	29	313	11	28.45	4–49

Above: The Australians in England in 1961 included many of the players that made the first Australian tour of India in 1959–60. Left to right, back: Booth, Lawry, Misson, Gaunt, McKenzie. Middle row: A. James (physiotherapist), J. Cameron (scorer), Jarman, Quick, R. Steele (treasurer), Kline, O'Neill, Burge, Simpson. Front: Grout, Davidson, Benaud, S.G. Webb (manager), Harvey, McDonald, Mackay.

Left: Ian Johnson, the successful Australian captain, in 1956–57 in India.

1959–60: Australia win in first full tour of India

Benaud's successful Ashes-winning side made a full tour of India in 1959–60. Ramchand captained India, and batted in the first Test at Delhi. The fast men were mostly responsible for India's poor total of 135, but Benaud finished with the remarkable analysis of three for nothing. Ten of the Australians made double figures and, led by Harvey's 114, they made 468. Then Benaud and Kline reduced India in the second innings to 206 all out after the openers had put on 121, with Pankaj Roy making 99.

India batted on a newly laid pitch which crumbled at Kanpur, where batting was difficult. Davidson had five for 31 in India's total of 152. J.M. Patel bowled brilliantly to take nine for 69 with his off-spin but could not prevent Australia taking a lead of 67. Contractor then made the highest score of the match, 74, to help India set Australia 225 to win. Patel and Umrigar spun them out for 105. Davidson (12–124) and Patel (14–124) used the conditions expertly.

Patel was ill for Bombay, and his replacement, S.A. Durani, was injured early. Contractor played well again for 108, and India made 289. A stand of 207 by Harvey (102) and O'Neill (163) was the backbone of Australia's 387 for eight declared (Nadkarni 6–105). The match drifted to a draw.

Favell made a century at Madras, and Australia forced the follow-on to win by an innings, with Benaud being the most successful bowler with eight wickets.

It was O'Neill's turn for a century at Calcutta, Australia overtaking India's 194 by 137. Tail-end resistance enabled India to set Australia 203 runs in 150 minutes, but Australia were happy to draw and take the series 2–1.

1959–60 3rd Series Aus 2, India 1, Drawn 2
1 NEW DELHI Australia won by an innings and 127 runs
India 135 and 206 (P Roy 99, R Benaud 5–76, L F Kline 4–42)
Australia 468 (R N Harvey 114, K D Mackay 78, P R Umrigar 4–49)
2 KANPUR India won by 119 runs
India 152 (A K Davidson 5–31, R Benaud 4–63) and 291 (N J Contractor 74, R B Kenny 51, A K Davidson 7–93)
Australia 219 (C C McDonald 53, R N Harvey 51, J M Patel 9–69) and 105 (J M Patel 5–55, P R Umrigar 4–27)
3 BOMBAY Match Drawn
India 289 (N J Contractor 108, A A Baig, A K Davidson 4–62, I Meckiff 4–79) and 226–5 dec (A A Baig 58, P Roy 57, R B Kenny 55)
Australia 387–8 dec (N C O'Neill 163, R N Harvey 102, R G Nadkarni 6–105) and 34–1
4 MADRAS Australia won by an innings and 55 runs
Australia 342 (L E Favell 101, K D Mackay 89, R B Desai 4–93)
India 149 (B K Kunderan 71, R Benaud 5–43) and 138
5 CALCUTTA Match Drawn
India 194 and 339 (M L Jaisimha 74, R B Kenny 62, C G Borde 50, R Benaud 4–103)
Australia 331 (N C O'Neill 113, P J P Burge 60, A T W Grout 50, R B Desai 4–111) and 121–2 (L E Favell 62)

1959–60 Averages					
Batting	I	No	Runs	HS	Avge
N.C. O'Neill (A)	6	0	376	163	62.60
R.N. Harvey (A)	7	0	356	114	50.85
N.J. Contractor (I)	10	0	438	108	43.80
P. Roy (I)	10	0	263	99	26.30
Bowling	O	M	Runs	W	Avge	BB
A.K. Davidson (A)	247.5	85	440	29	15.17	7–93
J.M. Patel (I)	131.3	38	327	19	17.21	9–69
R. Benaud (A)	321.2	147	568	29	19.55	5–43
I. Meckiff (A)	196	50	397	12	33.08	4–79

1964–65: Drawn series finally ends in rain

The 1964–65 three-match series in India was between the Nawab of Pataudi's team and Simpson's England tourists on their way home.

At Madras, Australia made 211, Nadkarni getting five for 31. Despite McKenzie's fine six for 58 for Australia, India took a lead of 65 with the Nawab of Pataudi making 128 not out. Nadkarni took six for 91 in the second innings but could not prevent determined lower-order batting hoisting Australia to 397, setting India a target of 333 in 390 minutes. After losing the openers without a run scored, they could make only 193,

McKenzie taking his match haul to ten wickets.

Good middle-order batting, despite the absence of O'Neill, ill, got Australia to 320 at Bombay, but India, batting lower down, took a lead of 21. Australia collapsed in the second innings from 246 for three to 274 all out. Chandrasekhar and Nadkarni did the damage. A crowd of 42,000 watched the tense last-day finish as India got home with two wickets and half-an-hour to spare.

Australia collapsed again at Calcutta, this time to Durani (6–73), to 174 all out. India took a 61-run lead but rain washed out the last two days.

1964–65 4th Series Aus 1, India 1, Drawn 1
1 MADRAS Australia won by 139 runs
Australia 211 (W M Lawry 62, R G Nadkarni 5–31) and 397 (R B Simpson 77, T R Veivers 74, P J P Burge 60, R G Nadkarni 6–91)
India 276 (M A K Pataudi 128, G D McKenzie 6–58) and 193 (Hanumant Singh 94, G D McKenzie 4–33)
2 BOMBAY India won by 2 wkts
Australia 320 (P J P Burge 80, B N Jarman 78, T R Veivers 67, B S Chandrasekhar 4–50) and 274 (R M Cowper 81, B C Booth 74, W M Lawry 68, R G Nadkarni 4–33, B S Chandrasekhar 4–73)
India 341 (M A K Pataudi 86, M L Jaisimha 66, V L Manjrekar 59, T R Veivers 4–68) and 256–8 (D N Sardesai 56, M A K Pataudi 53)
3 CALCUTTA Match drawn
Australia 174 (R B Simpson 67, W M Lawry 50, S A Durani 6–73) and 143–1 (R B Simpson 71)
India 235 (C G Borde 68, M L Jaisimha 57, R B Simpson 4–45)

1964–65 Averages					
Batting	I	No	Runs	HS	Avge
Nawab of Pataudi, jr (I)	5	1	270	128*	67.50
W.M. Lawry (A)	6	1	284	68	56.80
R.B. Simpson (A)	6	0	292	77	48.66
Bowling	O	M	Runs	W	Avge	BB
R.G. Nadkarni (I)	128.1	49	233	17	13.70	6–91
G.D. McKenzie (A)	108.3	26	214	13	16.46	6–58
T.R. Veivers (A)	163.3	56	268	11	24.45	4–68
S.A. Durani (I)	142	36	428	10	42.80	6–73

Graham McKenzie who took 13 Indian wickets both in 1964–65 in India and in 1967–68 in Australia.

1967–68: Australia win all four Tests

Simpson and Pataudi were captains in Australia in 1967–68, but Borde replaced the injured Pataudi in the first Test at Adelaide, where Simpson decided to bat and Australia made 335, Abid Ali taking six for 55 in his first Test. India reached 250 for three but could total only 307. Simpson and Cowper made second-innings centuries to allow Au-

Benaud batting in England. Benaud led the Australians in the five-match tour of India of 1959–60.

stralia to set a target of 398, and with Renneberg taking five for 39 they won by 146 runs.

The returned Pataudi, still not quite fit decided to bat at Melbourne, but good bowling by McKenzie (7–66) got India out for only 173. Simpson and Lawry opened with centuries each for Australia, Ian Chappell added another and Australia amassed 529. India's 352 lost the match by an innings and four. The Nawab of Pataudi, with 75 and 85, and Prasanna, with six for 141, did not deserve to lose.

India put Australia in at Brisbane, but they made 379, exactly 100 more than India. Prasanna's second-innings six for 104 was again in a losing cause, India being set 395 to win. They made a great effort, however, reaching 355, with Jaisimha, flown in to join the team, adding 101 to a first-innings 74.

Simpson, having been replaced by Lawry as captain in the previous Test, returned for the last Test, where India put Australia in. They made 317 and led by 49. Cowper made 165 of a total second-innings total of 292, leading to a win by Australia by 144 runs. Simpson, in his last Test before he was re-called during World Series cricket ten years later, took five for 59.

1967–68   5th Series   Aus 4, India 0

1 ADELAIDE   **Australia won by 146 runs**
Australia 335 (R M Cowper 92, A P Sheahan 81, R B Simpson 55, S Abid Ali 6–55) and 369 (R M Cowper 108, R B Simpson 103, R F Surti 5–74)
India 307 (F M Engineer 89, R F Surti 70, C G Borde 69, A N Connolly 4–54) and 251 (V Subramanyam 75, R F Surti 53, D A Renneberg 5–39)

2 MELBOURNE   **Australia won by an innings and 4 runs**
India 173 (M A K Pataudi 75, G D McKenzie 7–66) and 352 (A L Wadekar 99, M A K Pataudi 85)
Australia 529 (I M Chappell 151, R B Simpson 109, W M Lawry 100, B N Jarman 65, E A S Prasanna 6–141)

3 BRISBANE   **Australia won by 39 runs**
Australia 379 (K D Walters 93, W M Lawry 64, A P Sheahan 58, R M Cowper 51) and 294 (I R Redpath 79, K D Walters 62, E A S Prasanna 6–104)
India 279 (M A K Pataudi 74, M L Jaisimha 74, R F Surti 52) and 355 (M L Jaisimha 101, R F Surti 64, C G Borde 63, R M Cowper 4–104)

4 SYDNEY   **Australia won by 144 runs**
Australia 317 (K D Walters 94, A P Sheahan 72, W M Lawry 66) and 292 (R M Cowper 165, W M Lawry 52, E A S Prasanna 4–96)
India 268 (S Abid Ali 78, M A K Pataudi 51, E W Freeman 4–86) and 197 (S Abid Ali 81, R B Simpson 5–59, R M Cowper 4–49)

1967–68 Averages

Batting	I	No	Runs	HS	Avge
K.D. Walters (A)	4	2	254	94*	127.00
R.M. Cowper (A)	7	0	485	165	69.28
R.B. Simpson (A)	5	0	294	109	58.80
Nawab of Pataudi, jr (I)	6	0	339	85	56.50
W.M. Lawry (A)	7	0	369	100	52.71
R.F. Surti (I)	8	0	367	70	45.87
A.P. Sheahan (A)	7	0	318	81	45.42
S. Abid. Ali (I)	8	0	299	81	37.37
I.M. Chappell (A)	7	0	212	151	30.28
F.M. Engineer (I)	8	0	215	89	26.87
A.L. Wadekar (I)	8	0	212	99	26.50

Bowling	O	M	Runs	W	Avge	BB
R.B. Simpson (A)	76	20	213	13	16.38	5–59
R.M. Cowper (A)	103.2	32	239	13	18.38	4–49
G.D. McKenzie (A)	72.4	7	312	13	24.00	7–66
D.A. Renneberg (A)	66.2	8	302	12	25.16	5–39
E.A.S. Prasanna (I)	197.5	34	686	25	27.44	6–104
R.F. Surti (I)	117.4	18	528	15	35.20	5–74

Above right: The Nawab of Pataudi on-drives. He captained India and topped the averages in 1964–65, and led the tourists on the 1967–68 trip to Australia.

Right: Farokh Engineer, the Indian wicket-keeper batsman of the 1960s.

1969–70: India win a match but lose the rubber

Lawry's side played a five-Test series in India in 1969–70. The Nawab of Pataudi led India, and at Bombay in the first Test won the toss and batted. His 95 was top score as McKenzie (5–59) got the side out for 271. With Stackpole scoring 103, Australia were in front with only three men out, and eventually they needed only 64 to win by eight wickets.

G.R. Viswanath made his debut for India at Kanpur. Although he made a duck in the first innings, in the second, with Australia 28 ahead, he made 137 in a drawn match. Sheahan made an impressive 114 in Australia's first innings.

Ian Chappell's 138 was the basis of Australia's 296 against the Indian spinners at Delhi. Mallett's off-breaks (6–64) removed India for 223, but Bedi and Prasanna, who each took nine wickets in the match, then spun Australia out for 107, leaving India a reasonable 181 to win. Wadekar's 91 not out ensured they evened the series with a seven-wicket win.

McKenzie had India, who were put in, 22 for three at Calcutta. He finished with six for 67 and India with 212. Much of Australia's innings was a battle between Chappell (99) and Bedi (7–98). Connolly, at number eleven, made a quick 31, Australia led by 123, and needed only 39 in the fourth innings for an easy win.

Prasanna and Mallett each took ten wickets at Madras. Walters' first-innings century gave Australia a lead of 95. They recovered from 24 for six to set India 249, and Mallett ensured a 77-run win and a 3–1 rubber victory.

1969–70 6th Series Aus 3, India 1, Drawn 1

1 BOMBAY Australia won by 8 wkts
India 271 (M A K Pataudi 95, A V Mankad 74, G D McKenzie 5–69) and 137 (J W Gleeson 4–56)
Australia 345 (K R Stackpole 103, I R Redpath 77, E A S Prasanna 5–121) and 67–2

2 KANPUR Match Drawn
India 320 (F M Engineer 77, A V Mankad 64, A N Connolly 4–91) and 312–7 dec (G R Viswanath 137, A V Mankad 68)
Australia 348 (A P Sheahan 114, I R Redpath 70, K D Walters 53) and 95–0 (W M Lawry 56)

3 NEW DELHI India won by 7 wkts
Australia 296 (I M Chappell 138, K R Stackpole 61, B S Bedi 4–71, E A S Prasanna 4–111) and 107 (B S Bedi 5–37, E A S Prasanna 5–42)
India 223 (A V Mankad 97, A A Mallett 6–64) and 181–3 (A L Wadekar 91)

4 CALCUTTA Australia won by 10 wkts
India 212 (G R Viswanath 54, G D McKenzie 6–67) and 161 (A L Wadekar 62, A N Connolly 4–31, E W Freeman 4–54)
Australia 335 (I M Chappell 99, K D Walters 56, B S Bedi 7–98) and 42–0)

5 MADRAS Australia won by 77 runs
Australia 258 (K D Walters 102, S Venkataraghavan 4–71, E A S Prasanna 4–100) and 153 (I R Redpath 63, E A S Prasanna 6–74)
India 163 (M A K Pataudi 59, A A Mallett 5–91) and 171 (G R Viswanath 59, A L Wadekar 55, A A Mallett 5–53)

1969–70 Averages					
Batting	I	No	Runs	HS	Avge
G.R. Viswanath (I)	8	1	334	137	47.71
I.M. Chappell (A)	8	1	324	138	46.28
K.R. Stackpole (A)	10	2	368	103	46.00
K.D. Walters (A)	8	1	286	102	40.85
A.L. Wadekar (I)	10	1	336	91*	37.33
I.R. Redpath (A)	7	0	253	77	36.14
A.V. Mankad (I)	10	0	357	97	35.70

Bowling	O	M	Runs	W	Avge	BB
A.A. Mallett (A)	298.4	129	535	28	19.10	6–64
B.S. Bedi (I)	273.4	120	434	21	20.57	7–98
G.N. McKenzie (A)	222	73	441	21	21.00	6–67
A.N. Connolly (A)	215.1	67	415	17	24.41	4–31
E.A.S. Prasanna (I)	295	107	672	26	25.84	6–74
S. Venkataraghaven (I)	157.5	55	320	12	26.66	4–71

1977–78: Exciting Test series with no draws

India's visit to Australia in 1977–78 coincided with the first season of World Series Cricket, a 'private' series of matches for which many of the leading players had signed. Australia therefore fielded what was little more than a second eleven, which R.B. Simpson had been recalled to lead. There were six Test newcomers in the side dismissed for 166 in the first Test at Brisbane, Bedi, the Indian captain, taking five wickets. The total earned a 13-run lead, however, and Australia did better second time with 327, Simpson getting 89. Set 341 to win, India, with the help of Gavaskar's 113, reached 324. W.M. Clark took eight wickets in his first Test.

At Perth, India made 402, but Simpson excelled himself with 176, and Australia finished only eight short. Gavaskar made 127 and M. Amarnath followed up a first-innings 90 with 100 and India declared

Ian Chappell (above) toured India in 1969–70, and brother Greg (below) captained Australia in 1980–81.

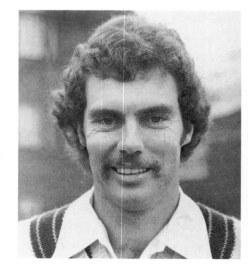

at 330 for nine. Australia found a surprising batting hero in A.L. Mann. A number eight batsman he came in as 'night-watchman' at 13 for one and made 105, steering Australia to an exciting two-wicket win. Bedi took ten wickets unavailingly.

India lost their openers for nothing at Melbourne, but reached 256 and took a lead of 43 with Chandrasekhar getting six for 52. Gavaskar's century helped India set a target of 387, and a second analysis of six for 52 for Chandrasekhar meant an Indian win by 222.

At Sydney, Simpson decided to bat on a damp wicket, and India's spinners got Australia out for 131. The Indians batted down the order for 396 for eight declared and the spinners earned India's first innings victory over Australia.

The spinners laboured hard on a good wicket at Adelaide in the deciding match, when Yallop and Simpson made centuries in a big Australian score of 505. Thomson took two wickets in 3½ overs then tore a hamstring, but even so India were out for 269. Australia batted again (it was a six-day match) and made 256, leaving India to get 493 to win. All the batsmen except number eleven reached double figures, and at 415 for six the match was even, but India fell 48 short of the target. So Australia won an exciting series 3–2.

1977–78 7th Series Aus 3, India 2

1 BRISBANE Australia won by 16 runs
Australia 166 (P M Toohey 82, B S Bedi 5–55) and 327 (R B Simpson 89, P M Toohey 57, S Madan Lal 5–72)
India 153 (W M Clark 4–46) and 324 (S M Gavaskar 113, S M H Kirmani 55, J R Thomson 4–76, W M Clark 4–101)

2 PERTH Australia won by 2 wkts
India 402 (M Amarnath 90, C P S Chauhan 88, J R Thomson 4–101) and 330–9 dec (S M Gavaskar 127, M Amarnath 100, J B Gannon 4–77)
Australia 394 (R B Simpson 176, J Dyson 53, S J Rixon 50, B S Bedi 5–89) and 342–8 (A L Mann 105, P M Toohey 83, B S Bedi 5–105)

3 MELBOURNE India won by 222 runs
India 256 (M Amarnath 72, G R Viswanath 59, W M Clark 4–73) and 343 (S M Gavaskar 118, G R Viswanath 54, W M Clark 4–96)
Australia 213 (C S Serjeant 85, G J Cosier 67, B S Chandrasekhar 6–52) and 164 (B S Chandrasekhar 6–52, B S Bedi 4–58)

4 SYDNEY India won by an innings and 2 runs
Australia 131 (B S Chandrasekhar 4–30) and 263 (P M Toohey 85, G J Cosier 68, E A S Prasanna 4–51)
India 368–8 dec (G R Viswanath 79, K D Ghavri 64, J R Thomson 4–83)

5 ADELAIDE Australia won by 47 runs
Australia 505 (G N Yallop 121, R B Simpson 100, W M Darling 65, P M Toohey 60, B S Chandrasekhar 5–136) and 256 (W M Darling 56, R B Simpson 51, K D Ghavri 4–45, B S Bedi 4–53)
India 269 (G R Viswanath 89, W M Clark 4–62) and 445 (M Amarnath 86, D B Vengsarkar 78, G R Viswanath 73, S M H Kirmani 51, B Yardley 4–134)

1977–78 Averages

Batting	I	No	Runs	HS	Avge
R.B. Simpson (A)	10	0	539	176	53.90
G.R. Viswanath (I)	9	0	473	89	52.55
S.M. Gavaskar (I)	9	0	450	127	50.00
M. Amarnath (I)	9	0	445	100	49.44
P.M. Toohey (A)	10	0	409	85	40.90
D.B. Vengsarkar (I)	9	0	320	78	35.55
S.M.H. Kirmani (I)	9	0	305	55	33.88

Bowling	O	M	Runs	W	Avge	BB
J.R. Thomson (A)	145.7	21	516	22	23.45	4–76
B.S. Bedi (I)	219.7	39	740	31	23.87	5–55
W.M. Clark (A)	198.1	27	701	28	25.03	4–46
B.S. Chandrasekhar (I)	197.3	25	704	28	25.14	6–52

Indian wicket-keeper S.M.H. Kirmani, who made a century as 'night-watchman' in the final Bombay Test in 1979–80.

1979–80: India win their first series against Australia

K.J. Hughes led Australia in India in 1979–80, and much was expected after the exciting series two years before. Gavaskar captained India.

Border (162) and Hughes (100) came together at Madras and added 222 for Australia's third wicket, 390 being reached despite Doshi's six for 103. India batted quicker and made 425 (Higgs 7–143). With Australia 175 for seven in the second innings, India had a chance to win, but dogged defence was followed by rain and the match was drawn.

Rain interrupted the second Test at Bangalore, and with batsmen on top another draw was assured. India, with centuries from Vengsarkar and Viswanath, again had the best of it.

At Kanpur, Dymock and Hogg caused India to collapse from 201 for one to 271 all out. Australia took a lead of 33, and excellent bowling by Dymock, who took 12 wickets in the match, dismissed India second time for 311; Australia needed 279 in 312 minutes but they collapsed before Kapil Dev and Yadav for 125.

One up, India consolidated at Delhi, helped by dropped catches. With Gavaskar, Viswanath and Yashpal Sharma making centuries, they made 510 for seven. Mainly through Kapil Dev (5–82), India worked through the Australian batting for 298, but sterner second-innings batting after following on saved the match for Australia.

On a slow pitch at Calcutta, Australia built up a total of 442, Yallop making 167. India batted with care to 347. The pitch turned on the fourth day and Hughes' last-day declaration at 151 for six set India 247 in 245 minutes. India were not sure whether or not to go for the runs, and ended 47 short at 200 for four.

A slow pitch at Bombay and losing the toss made Australia's task of a win very difficult. India took up most of two days over 458 for eight declared. Gavaskar and Kirmani, the 'night-watchman', made centuries. Australia, dispirited and arguing about umpiring decisions, were dismissed by Doshi and Yadav for 160 and 198 for an innings defeat. It was India's first series victory over Australia.

1979–80 8th Series India 2, Aus 0, Drawn 4

1 MADRAS Match Drawn
Australia 390 (A R Border 162, K J Hughes 100, D R Doshi 6–103) and 212–7 (A M J Hilditch 55, A R Border 50)
India 425 (Kapil Dev 83, D B Vengsarkar 65, Yashpal Sharma 52, S M H Kirmani 57, S M Gavaskar 50, J D Higgs 7–143)

2 BANGALORE Match Drawn
Australia 333 (K J Hughes 86, A M J Hilditch 62, N S Yadav 4–49) and 77–3
India 457–5 dec (G R Viswanath 161, D B Vengsarkar 112, B Yardley 4–107)

3 KANPUR India won by 153 runs
India 271 (S M Gavaskar 76, C P S Chauhan 58, D B Vengsarkar 52, G Dymock 5–99, R M Hogg 4–66) and 311 (C P S Chauhan 84, G R Viswanath 52, G Dymock 7–67)
Australia 304 (G N Yallop 89, W M Darling 59, K J Hughes 50) and 125 (Kapil Dev 4–30, N S Yadav 4–35)

4 NEW DELHI Match Drawn
India 510–7 dec (G R Viswanath 131, S M Gavaskar 115, Yashpal Sharma 100, G Dymock 4–77)
Australia 298 (D F Whatmore 77, K J Wright 55, Kapil Dev 5–82) and 413 (A M J Hilditch 85, P R Sleep 64, D F Whatmore 54)

5 CALCUTTA Match Drawn
Australia 442 (G N Yallop 167, K J Hughes 92, B Yardley 61, A R Border 54, Kapil Dev 5–74, D R Doshi 4–92) and 151–6 dec (K J Hughes 64)
India 347 (G R Viswanath 96, D B Vengsarkar 89, B Yardley 4–91) and 200–4 (Yashpal Sharma 85, C P S Chauhan 50, G Dymock 4–63)

6 BOMBAY India won by an innings and 100 runs
India 458–8 dec (S M Gavaskar 123, S M H Kirmani 101, K D Ghavri 86, C P S Chauhan 73)
Australia 160 (G N Yallop 60, D R Doshi 5–43, N S Yadav 4–40) and 198 (K J Hughes 80, A R Border 61, Kapil Dev 4–39)

1979–80 Averages

Batting	I	No	Runs	HS	Avge
G.R. Viswanath (I)	8	1	518	161*	74.00
K.J. Hughes (A)	12	2	594	100	59.40
S.M.H. Kirmani (I)	7	2	285	101*	57.00
S.M. Gavaskar (I)	8	0	425	123	53.12
Yashpal Sharma (I)	8	2	304	100*	50.66
C.P.S. Chauhan (I)	8	0	380	84	47.50
D.B. Vengsarkar (I)	8	0	372	112	46.50
A.R. Border (A)	12	0	521	162	43.41
G.N. Yallop (A)	12	1	423	167	38.45
A.M.J. Hilditch (A)	12	0	313	85	26.08

Bowling	O	M	Runs	W	Avge	BB
Kapil Dev (I)	223	52	626	28	22.35	5–74
D.R. Doshi (I)	306.2	87	630	27	23.33	6–103
N.S. Yadav (I)	234.3	63	576	24	24.00	4–35
G. Dymock (A)	212.4	46	580	24	24.16	7–67
J.D. Higgs (A)	227.3	62	702	14	50.14	7–143

1980–81: Remarkable climax to high-scoring rubber

Gavaskar's side in 1980–81 met a full-strength Australia, with Greg Chappell back as captain to face India for the first time. India made only 201 at Sydney, Lillee and Pascoe doing the damage, including sending top-scorer Patil to hospital. Chappell then exceeded this score himself, making 204. Kapil Dev and Shastri shared the wickets, but Australia made 406. India made only 201 again in the second innings and Australia won on the third day.

Australia made another big score of 528 at Adelaide after being put in. Wood (125) and Hughes (213) made most of the runs. India fought back to 419, of which Patil made 174. A cautious declaration by Chappell allowed India to scrape a draw with two wickets left.

Chappell put India in at Melbourne and had early successes, only a dogged 114 from Viswanath getting India to 237. Border made 124 and Australia's 419 appeared to make the series safe. Gavaskar and Chauhan put on 165 for India's first wicket when Gavaskar was given out lbw. He had already pointed out, sarcastically in view of Hughes' remarks in India, that Australian umpires were as good as Indian, and at this decision he took Chauhan off with him, intending to forfeit the match. The Indian manager met

Chauhan at the gate and ordered him to continue. He was soon out, and with Yadav unable to bat or bowl, India could set Australia only 143 to win. With Kapil Dev (pulled thigh muscle) not expected to bowl, and Doshi also carrying an injury, an Australian win seemed a formality. However, Ghavri struck and Australia were 24 for three overnight, which inspired Kapil Dev to go all out on the last day. He grabbed five for 28 to dismiss Australia for 83 and India won an extraordinary match to draw the series.

1980–81　9th Series　Aus 1, India 1, Drawn 1
1 SYDNEY　Australia won by an innings and 4 runs
India 201 (S M Patil 65, D K Lillee 4–86, L S Pascoe 4–61) and 201 (J D Higgs 4–45)
Australia 406 (G S Chappell 204, K D Walters 67, Kapil Dev 5–97, K D Ghavri 5–107)
2 ADELAIDE　Match Drawn
Australia 528 (K J Hughes 213, G M Wood 125, A R Border 57, N S Yadav 4–143) and 221–7 dec (K J Hughes 53, G S Chappell 52)
India 419 (S M Patil 174, C P S Chauhan 97, D K Lillee 4–80) and 135–8
3 MELBOURNE　India won by 59 runs
India 237 (G R Viswanath 114, D K Lillee 4–65) and 324 (C P S Chauhan 70, D K Lillee 4–104)
Australia 419 (A R Border 124, K D Walters 78, G S Chappell 76) and 83 (Kapil Dev 5–28)

1980–81 Averages

Batting	I	No	Runs	HS	Avge	
G.S. Chappell (A)	5	0	368	204	73.60	
K.D. Walters (A)	5	2	216	78	72.00	
K.J. Hughes (A)	5	0	330	213	66.00	
S.M. Patil (I)	6	1	311	174	62.20	
A.R. Border (A)	5	0	228	124	45.60	
C.P.S. Chauhan (I)	6	0	249	97	41.50	
G.R. Viswanath (I)	6	0	213	114	35.50	

Bowling	O	M	Runs	W	Avge	BB
L.S. Pascoe (A)	109	27	299	16	18.68	4–61
D.K. Lillee (A)	148.3	33	452	21	21.52	4–65
Kapil Dev (I)	120.5	26	333	14	23.78	5–28
K.D. Ghavri (I)	115	21	370	10	37.00	5–107
D.R. Doshi (I)	182	40	440	11	40.00	3–49

1985–86: India only draw one-sided series

Between series with New Zealand, Australia, led by Border, received the Indian tourists, led by Kapil Dev, for a three-match Test.

At Adelaide, the match was spoiled by bad weather. Boon and Ritchie made centuries for Australia in a total of 381, in which Kapil Dev, taking up where he had left off five years earlier, took eight for 106. Gavaskar scored 166 not out in a total of 520, but had retired injured for a spell, so did not carry his bat.

Australia were put in at Melbourne and made only 262, of which Matthews scored 100 not out. India reached a quick 445. A long innings of 163 by Border held up India on the last day, but they needed only 67 more at tea when rain robbed them. A disappointed Kapil Dev claimed India would have won earlier but for bad umpiring decisions in Australia's favour.

At Sydney, India's top three batsmen passed the century mark and India declared at 600 for four. Australia, beginning with 219 for the first wicket (Boon 131), lost their last five for nine, failing to avoid the follow-on by five runs. At the close, by when Yadav had taken eight in the match for 118 in 95.3 overs, Australia had hung on for a draw at 119 for six, Ritchie having batted for nearly three hours for 17.

Dennis Lillee bowled well against India in 1980–81, taking 21 wickets.

1986–87: Test cricket's second tied Test

Border's Australians toured India in 1986–87 for a three-match series of Tests. Kapil Dev led India.

Australia batted at Madras, and built up a huge score of 574 for 7 declared, D.M. Jones making 210 despite nausea and leg cramps, Boon 122 and Border 106. There were many missed catches, as there were in India's innings, which Kapil Dev rescued with 119 to 397. Border declared at 170 for five in the second innings at the end of the fourth day, leaving India to get 348 to win in one day. India were 94 for one at lunch, and 193 for two at tea. At 251 and 253 they suffered two blows with Gavaskar out for a patient 90 and Kapil Dev for only one. India pressed on and at 331 for six seemed to have swung the match their way. But Bright stepped in with wickets at 331 and 334, and then, with India four runs short, he bowled Yadav. Maninder came in as last man. In the last over Shastri scored a two and a single, leaving Maninder three balls from Matthews to score the winning run. He was lbw to the penultimate ball and the match was tied. Matthews and Bright took five wickets each in the second innings, Matthews having ten in the match. This was the second tied match in Test history.

There was only 6½ hours' play at New Delhi. At Bombay, Australia compiled a very slow 345, Marsh scoring 101. India scored quicker and went on to 517 for five declared, Gavaskar, Vengsarkar and Shastri getting centuries, the last two adding an unbeaten 298 for the sixth wicket. Australia batted out time (the players walked off with 16 overs left) and the series was drawn.

It was not a happy tour and there was much bickering between players and umpires.

Above: Alan Border, who averaged over 50 in the 1985–86 and 1986–87 series against India.

Top: Ravi Shastri, who in 1986–87 against Australia scored 231 for only once out.

Australia v Pakistan

1956–57: Pakistan win first Test in slow motion

I.W. Johnson's side which toured England in 1956 played a Test in Pakistan on the way home, the first Test between the countries. A.H. Kardar captained Pakistan, and Gul Mahomed followed his captain by making his debut for them after eight appearances for India.

The first day's play at Karachi was remarkable for only 95 runs being scored, the fewest in any full day's Test cricket. Australia were out for 80 on the matting. Fazal Mahmood (6–34) and Khan Mohammad (4–43) did the damage, bowling unchanged throughout the innings. Pakistan, 15 for two overnight, made 199 and Fazal (7–80) and Khan (3–69) followed up by dismissing Australia again, Pakistan making the 69 necessary to win by nine wickets.

1956–57 1st Series Pak 1, Aus 0
1 KARACHI **Pakistan won by 9 wkts**
Australia 80 (Fazal Mahmood 6–34, Khan Mohammad 4–43) and 187 (R Benaud 56, Fazal Mahmood 7–80)
Pakistan 199 (A H Kardar 69, Wazir Mohammad 67, I W Johnson 4–50) and 69–1

Ken Mackay, Australia's all-rounder who topped the bowling averages in Pakistan in 1959–60.

Majid Khan

Majid was born on 28 September 1946 at Ludhiana, India. He is a cousin of Javed Burki and Imran Khan and, like them, captained Pakistan (in 1972–73). He played for Lahore from 1961–62; also Punjab, PIA and, in England, Glamorgan.

He was an all-rounder: an attacking middle-order, later opening, right-hand batsman, and a medium or off-break bowler. He made his first appearance for Pakistan in 1964–65 and in 63 Tests scored 3,931 runs, average 38.92, and took 27 wickets, average 53.92.

1959–60: Australia gain revenge on second visit

Australia's next visit preceded a tour of India, and they were better prepared. Fazal and Benaud were captains, and Benaud put Pakistan in at Dacca. He and Davidson dismissed them for 200, but it needed 74 from the last two wickets to get Australia a slim lead of 25. However, Benaud and Mackay removed Pakistan for 134 next time, and Australia won by eight wickets.

At Lahore, Pakistan batted and made only 146, and without Fazal could not prevent Australia declaring at 391 for nine, O'Neill getting 134. Saeed Ahmed's 166 out of 366 set Australia a target, despite Kline's seven for 75, but they made it for a seven-wicket win.

On another matting wicket at Karachi, play was too slow for a result. Hanif made a century, Fazal and Benaud took five wickets in an innings, and Intikhab Alam took a wicket with his first ball in Test cricket. President Eisenhower watched the fourth day, in which only 105 runs were scored.

1959–60 2nd Series Aus 2, Pak 0, Drawn 1
1 DACCA **Australia won by 8 wkts**
Pakistan 200 (Hanif Mohammad 66, D Sharpe 56, A K Davidson 4–42, R Benaud 4–69) and 134 (K D Mackay 6–42, R Benaud 4–42)
Australia 225 (R N Harvey 96, A T W Grout 66, Fazal Mahmood 5–71) and 112–2
2 LAHORE **Australia won by 7 wkts**
Pakistan 146 (A K Davidson 4–48) and 366 (Saeed Ahmed 166, Imtiaz Ahmed 54, L F Kline 7–75)
Australia 391–9 dec (N C O'Neill 134) and 123–3
3 KARACHI **Match Drawn**
Pakistan 287 (Saeed Ahmed 91, Ijaz Butt 58, Hanif Mohammad 51, R Benaud 5–93) and 194–8 dec (Hanif Mohammad 101)
Australia 257 (R N Harvey 54, Fazal Mahmood 5–74) and 83–2

1959–60 Averages

Batting	I	No	Runs	HS	Avge
N.C. O'Neill (A)	6	3	218	134	72.66
Hanif Mohammad (P)	6	1	304	101*	60.80
R.N. Harvey (A)	6	1	283	96	56.60
Saeed Ahmed (P)	6	0	334	166	55.66

Bowling	O	M	Runs	W	Avge	BB
K.D. Mackay (A)	129.4	59	190	10	19.00	6–42
Fazal Mahmood (P)	96.2	32	213	11	19.26	5–71
R. Benaud (A)	224	94	379	18	21.06	5–93
A.K. Davidson (A)	146.4	34	298	12	24.83	4–42

1964–65: Even draw in Karachi

Australia, under Simpson, played again in Pakistan after a tour of England. Hanif captained Pakistan, for whom six made their debuts, most notably Asif Iqbal and Majid Khan.

Pakistan batted, and K. Ibadulla, on his debut, made 166 and shared in a Pakistani record opening partnership of 249 with Abdul Kadir (95, also on his debut). McKenzie took six for 69, but Pakistan totalled 414. Simpson made 153 out of 352, and when Pakistan declared, setting Australia 342 in 290 minutes, he followed up with 115 in a drawn match.

1964–65 3rd Series Drawn 1
1 KARACHI **Match Drawn**
Pakistan 414 (Khalid Ibadulla 166, Abdul Kadir 95, Intikhab Alam 53, G D McKenzie 6–69) and 279–8 (Javed Burki 62)
Australia 352 (R B Simpson 153, P J P Burge 54) and 227–2 (R B Simpson 115)

1964–65: Draw repeated in Melbourne

A month after the Karachi match, Pakistan played one Test in Melbourne on a tour of Australia and New Zealand. Simpson put Pakistan in, and Hanif replied with a century in 287. Australia took a big lead of 161, although Arif Butt returned six for 89 on his debut. Hanif scored 93 in the second innings, when Pakistan made 326 and set Australia 166 to win. They were 88 for two at the close. Ian Chappell made his debut for Australia.

1964–65 4th Series Drawn 1
1 MELBOURNE Match Drawn
Pakistan 287 (Hanif Mohammad 104, Saeed Ahmed 80) and 326 (Hanif Mohammad 93, Intikhab Alam 61, N J N Hawke 4–72, G D McKenzie 4–74)
Australia 448 (T R Veivers 88, R M Cowper 83, B C Booth 57, B K Shepherd 55, Arif Butt 6–89) and 88–2

1972–73: Australia win home series 3–0

The Pakistan touring party in Australia in 1972–73 was an unhappy one, torn by internal dissent.

Pakistan batted in the first Test at Adelaide, making 257 but Australia, with captain I.M. Chappell making 196 and Marsh 118, reached 585. Mallett took eight for 59 in the second innings and Australia won by an innings and 114.

Redpath and G. Chappell made centuries at Melbourne and Australia declared at 441 for five. But Sadiq (137) and Majid (158) took Pakistan to 574 for eight declared. The century-making continued in the second innings with Sheahan and J. Benaud, in his second of three Tests, hoisting Australia to 425, leaving Pakistan 293 to win. Three men were run out as Pakistan were dismissed for 200, Australia winning by 92.

Intikhab put Australia in at Sydney, and

with Mushtaq making 121, Pakistan gained a lead of 26. Salim and Sarfraz then dismissed Australia for only 184, and Pakistan wanted only 159 to win. However they made no show against Walker, who took six for 15, and fell for 106.

1972–73 5th Series Aus 3, Pak 0
1 ADELAIDE Australia won by an innings and 114 runs
Pakistan 247 (Wasim Bari 72, Intikhab Alam 64, D K Lillee 4–49, R A L Massie 4–70) and 214 (Sadiq Mohammad 81, A A Mallett 8–59)
Australia 585 (I M Chappell 196, R W Marsh 118, R Edwards 89)
2 MELBOURNE Australia won by 92 runs
Australia 441–5 dec (I R Redpath 135, G S Chappell 116, R W Marsh 74, I M Chappell 66) and 425 (J Benaud 142, A P Sheahan 127, G S Chappell 62)
Pakistan 574–8 dec (Majid Khan 158, Sadiq Mohammad 137, Intikhab Alam 68, Mushtaq Mohammad 60, Zaheer Abbas 51, Saeed Ahmed 50) and 200
3 SYDNEY Australia won by 52 runs
Australia 334 (I R Redpath 79, R Edwards 69, Sarfraz Nazaz 4–53) and 184 (Sarfraz Nazaz 4–56), Saleem Altaf 4–60)
Pakistan 360 (Mushtaq Mohammad 121, Asif Iqbal 65, Nasim-ul-Ghani 64, G S Chappell 5–61) and 106 (M H N Walker 6–15)

1972–73 Averages

Batting	I	No	Runs	HS	Avge
I.M. Chappell (A)	5	0	341	196	68.20
G.S. Chappell (A)	5	1	242	116*	60.50
I.R. Redpath (A)	5	0	240	135	48.00
Sadiq Mohammad (P)	6	0	270	137	45.00
R.W. Marsh (A)	5	0	210	118	42.00
Mushtaq Mohammad (P)	6	0	244	121	40.67
M.J. Khan (P)	6	0	239	158	39.83
Intikhab Alam (P)	6	0	227	68	37.83

Bowling	O	M	Runs	W	Avge	BB
M.H.N. Walker (A)	70	14	231	12	19.25	6–15
A.A. Mallett (A)	91.3	16	291	13	22.38	8–59
Sarfraz Nawaz (P)	84.5	16	308	12	25.67	4–53
Salim Altaf (P)	89.5	9	313	11	28.45	4–60
D.K. Lillee (A)	96.1	19	353	12	29.42	4–49

1976–77: Pakistan's first win in Australia draws series

Mushtaq led Pakistan to Australia four years later, when G.S. Chappell was Australia's captain.

At Adelaide, Pakistan made 272, not enough as I.C. Davis and Walters made centuries and Australia made 454. Pakistan fought back well with second-innings hundreds from Zaheer and Asif (152 not out), who added 87 for the last wicket with Iqbal (4), taking the score to 466. Australia needed 285, and were 228 for six with 15 overs left. But Australia then decided to bat out time for the draw.

G.S. Chappell and Cosier made centuries at Melbourne as Australia built up 517 for eight declared. Sadiq made a century in reply, but Pakistan collapsed from 270 for two to 333 all out when Lillee (6–82) put in a devastating spell of fast bowling. Australia declared a second time at 315 for eight (McCosker 105), leaving Pakistan exactly 500 to win. Lillee and O'Keeffe ensured an Australian win by 348.

With Imran taking six for 102, Australia were out for 211 at Sydney, and Asif, making 120 at number six, led Pakistan to 360. Imran took his match tally to 12 with six for 63, and Pakistan gained their first victory in Australia by an easy eight wickets.

1976–77 6th Series Pak 1, Aus 1, Drawn 1
1 ADELAIDE Match Drawn
Pakistan 272 (Zaheer Abbas 85) and 466 (Asif Iqbal 152, Zaheer Abbas 101, Javed Miandad, D K Lillee 5–163)
Australia 454 (K D Walters 107, I C Davis 105, R B McCosker 65, G S Chappell 52, Mushtaq Mohammad 4–58) and 261–6 (G S Chappell 70, K D Walters 51, Iqbal Qasim 4–84)

Lillee, Dennis Keith

Lillee was born in Subiaco, Western Australia, on 18 July 1949, and played for his state from 1969–70. An aggressive right-arm fast bowler, he made his Test debut a year later. He became the oustanding fast bowler of the 1970s. His name will be associated with Thomson, his fellow fast bowler who helped him demolish England in 1974–75, and with Marsh, who caught 95 of his Test victims. In 65 Tests he took 355 wickets, then the world record, average 23.92. He frequently attracted publicity, some of it of the worst kind.

2 MELBOURNE **Australia won by 348 runs**
Australia 517–8 dec (G J Cosier 168, G S Chappell 121, A
    Turner 82, I C Davis 56, Iqbal Qasim 4–111) and 315–8 dec
    (R B McCosker 105, I C Davis 88, G S Chappell 67, Imran
    Khan 5–122)
Pakistan 333 (Sadiq Mohammad 105, Zaheer Abbas 90, Majid
    Khan 76, D K Lillee 6–82) and 151 (Zaheer Abbas 58, K J
    O'Keeffee 4–38, D K Lillee 4–53)
3 SYDNEY **Pakistan won by 8 wkts**
Australia 211 (G J Cosier 50, Imran Khan 6–102) and 180
    (Imran Khan 6–63)
Pakistan 360 (Asif Iqbal 120, Javed Miandad 64, Haroon Rashid
    57, M H N Walker 4–112) and 32–2

1976–77 Averages

Batting	I	No	Runs	HS	Avge
Asif Iqbal (P)	5	1	313	152*	78.25
G.J. Cosier (A)	6	1	288	168	57.60
G.S. Chappell (A)	6	0	343	121	57.16
Zaheer Abbas (P)	6	0	343	101	57.16
M.J. Khan (P)	6	1	247	76	49.40
I.C. Davis (A)	6	0	294	105	49.00
K.D. Walters (A)	6	0	240	107	40.00
R.B. McCosker (A)	6	0	228	105	38.00

Bowling	O	M	Runs	W	Avge	BB
D.K. Lillee (A)	130.2	16	540	21	25.71	6–82
Imran Khan (P)	120.4	15	519	18	28.83	6–63
K.J. O'Keeffe (A)	122.1	28	341	11	31.00	4–38
Iqbal Qasim (P)	96	17	374	11	34.00	4–84

1978–79: One match each in WSC season

The 1978–79 season was influenced by World Series Cricket and Australia had many 'defectors'. They had just lost 5–1 to England when they faced Pakistan in two Tests, after Pakistan had won in New Zealand. Mushtaq and G.N. Yallop were the two captains.

Pakistan, put in, made only 196, but Australia did worse at 168. Hogg, given run out when leaving his crease before the ball was dead, wrecked the stumps in disgust. Majid made 108, and Pakistan set Australia 382 to win. They began well, with Border making a century, and at 304 for three seemed to be in control. However Sarfraz then took the last seven wickets for one run in 33 balls and Australia were out for 310. Sarfraz finished with nine for 86.

Hughes captained Australia with Yallop injured at Perth and put Pakistan in. Javed, with 129 not out, repaired early losses and they reached 277. However, Australia

passed this by 50. Asif held the tourists together in the second innings with 134 not out, but Australia needed only 236 to win, and lost only three wickets getting them.

1978–79 7th Series Pak 1, Aus 1
1 MELBOURNE **Pakistan won by 71 runs**
Pakistan 196 (R M Hogg 4–49) and 353–9 (Majid Khan 108,
    Zaheer Abbas 59)
Australia 168 (Imran Khan 4–26) and 310 (A R Border 105, K J
    Hughes 84, A M Hilditch 62, Sarfraz Nazaz 9–86)
2 PERTH **Australia won by 7 wkts**
Pakistan 277 (Javed Miandad 129, A G Hurst 4–61) and 285
    (Asif Iqbal 134, A G Hurst 5–94)
Australia 327 (A R Border 85, W M Darling 75) and 236–3 (W M
    Darling 79, A R Border 66)

1979–80: Pakistan win first rubber against Australia

The teams met again in Pakistan the following season, when the WSC players were back and G.S. Chappell was again leading Australia. Javed captained Pakistan.

Australia batted on a spinners' wicket at Karachi, and were dismissed for 225 by Qasim and Tauseef. Majid's 89 gave Pakistan a lead at 292, with Bright taking seven for 87. The same two spinners removed Australia a second time for only 140 (Qasim 7–49) and Bright had too few runs to work with, Pakistan winning by seven wickets. Qasim had 11 and Bright 10 wickets.

The match at Faisalabad began on the second day and as Greg Chappell made 235 and Yallop 172, Australia compiled a big score: 617. When Taslim Arif made 210 not out and Javed, with 106 not out, joined him in an unbeaten stand of 223, the match was drawn. All eleven Australians bowled.

On another good wicket at Lahore, Border (150 not out and 153) became the first to score 150 in each innings of a Test. Majid also made a century in another draw. Nine Pakistanis bowled in the first innings, and ten in the second, Taslim, the wicket-keeper, getting a wicket. Pakistan thus won their first rubber against Australia.

1979–80 8th Series Pak 1, Aus 0, Drawn 2
1 KARACHI **Pakistan won by 7 wkts**
Australia 225 (K J Hughes 85, Tausif Ahmed 4–64, Iqbal Qasim
    4–69) and 140 (A R Border 58, Iqbal Qasim 7–49)
Pakistan 292 (Majid Khan 89, Taslim Arif 58, R J Bright 7–87)
    and 76–3
2 FAISALABAD **Match Drawn**
Australia 617 (G S Chappell 235, G N Yallop 172, K J Hughes
    88, R W Marsh 71)
Pakistan 382–2 (Taslim Arif 210, Javed Miandad 106)
3 LAHORE **Match Drawn**
Australia 407–7 dec (A R Border 150, J W Wiener 93, G S
    Chappell 56, Iqbal Qasim 4–90) and 391–8 (A R BOrder 153,
    B M Laird 63, G S Chappell 57)
Pakistan 420–9 dec (Majid Khan 110, Mudassar Nazar 59,
    Wasim Raja 55, Imran Khan 56, R J Bright 5–172)

1979–80 Averages

Batting	I	No	Runs	HS	Avge
A.R. Border (A)	5	2	395	153	131.66
Taslim Arif (P)	4	1	307	210*	102.33
G.S. Chappell (A)	5	0	381	235	76.20
G.N. Yallop (A)	5	0	237	172	47.40

Bowling	O	M	Runs	W	Avge	BB
R.J. Bright (A)	146.5	45	354	15	23.60	7–87
Tausif Ahmed (P)	144.2	29	356	12	29.66	4–64
Iqbal Qasim (P)	201	63	475	16	29.68	7–49

Kerry O'Keefe, the Australian leg-break and googly bowler, who took 11 Pakistan wickets in 1976–77.

Left and below: Rodney Marsh, the great Australian wicket-keeper, announced his retirement after the Pakistan tour of Australia in 1983–84. He had a record number of Test victims.

Below left: Javed Miandad was the centre of controversy in Australia when involved in an altercation with Dennis Lillee.

Below: Allan Border, who averaged nearly 86 against Pakistan in 1983–84.

1981–82: Australia win 2–1 in bad-tempered series

In Australia in 1981–82, Javed put Australia in at Perth on a lively wicket, and dismissed them for 180. However, Lillee and Alderman swept through Pakistan, who were 26 for eight, before scrambling to 62. Hughes, who had lost the captaincy to G.S. Chappell after being beaten in England, then made a century as Australia declared at 424 for eight. Set 543, Pakistan were out for 256, with Yardley taking six for 84. There was an unseemly incident when Lillee appeared to obstruct Javed in a run, and then to kick him. Javed raised his bat in retaliation. Lillee was fined and suspended from two one-day matches.

At Brisbane, Chappell put Pakistan in, and they were out for 291 (Lillee 5–81). Chappell then scored 201, and declared at 512 for nine. Pakistan just saved the innings defeat, Australia having to bat for three runs.

Most of Pakistan's batsmen scored some runs at Melbourne, and they declared at 500 for eight, Yardley getting seven for 187. Despite Wood's 100, Australia made only 293 and followed on, collapsing second time for 125. It was Pakistan's first innings victory over Australia.

1981–82   9th Series   Aus 2, Pak 1

1 PERTH   Australia won by 286 runs
Australia 180 (Imran Khan 4–66) and 424–8 dec (K J Hughes 106, B M Laird 85)
Pakistan 62 (D K Lillee 5–18, T M Alderman 4–36) and 256 (Javed Miandad 79, B Yardley 6–84)

2 BRISBANE   Australia won by 10 wkts
Pakistan 291 (Zaheer Abbas 80, D K Lille 5–81) and 223 (D K Lillee 4–51, B Yardley 4–77)
Australia 512–9 dec (G S Chappell 201, G M Wood 72, Imran Khan 4–92) and 3–0

3 MELBOURNE   Pakistan won by an innings and 82 runs
Pakistan 500–8 dec (Mudassar Nazar 95, Zaheer Abbas 90, Majid Khan 74, Imran Khan 70, Wasim Raja 50, B Yardley 7–187)
Australia 293 (G M Wood 100) and 125 (B M Laird 52, Iqbal Qasim 4–44)

1981–82 Averages

Batting	I	No	Runs	HS	Avge	
G.M. Wood (A)	6	1	255	100	51.00	
G.S. Chappell (A)	5	0	251	201	50.20	
B.M. Laird (A)	6	1	246	85	49.20	
Javed Miandad (P)	5	0	205	79	41.00	

Bowling	O	M	Runs	W	Avge	BB
Imran Khan (P)	150.2	39	312	16	19.50	4–66
D.K. Lillee (A)	104.3	22	332	15	22.13	5–18
B. Yardley (A)	130.5	26	399	18	22.16	7–187
Iqbal Qasim (P)	108	33	235	10	23.50	4–44

1982–83: Pakistan win all three Tests

Two years later the sides met in Pakistan, Hughes and Imran being captains. Hughes batted at Karachi and made 284. Australian fielders were pelted with stones after Lawson had kicked up a fuss on being denied an appeal. At the end of the second day Mohsin was out 'handled the ball', the third instance in Tests. Hughes led Australia off the field twice on the third day because of political disturbances in the crowd. Pakistan led by 135 and Australia struggled second time to 179, Pakistan winning by nine wickets.

At Faisalabad, centuries from Mansoor and Zaheer allowed Imran to declare at 501 for six. Abdul Qadir then spun out Australia twice for 168 and 330, only Ritchie (106 not out) resisting for long.

Chappell, Gregory Stephen

Chappell came from a famous cricketing family. He is the grandson of V.Y. Richardson, who captained Australia, and the brother of I.M. and T.M., both of whom played for Australia. Greg and Ian both captained their country. He was born on 7 August 1948 at Unley, South Australia, and made his first appearance for his state in 1966–67, later switching to Queensland.

He was a stylish, elegant right-hand bat, a medium-pace bowler and good slip field. He made his debut for Australia in 1970–71. In 87 Tests, he was captain 48 times. He made 7,110 runs, an Australian record, at an average of 53.86. He also took 47 wickets, average 40.70. He made a century in his first and last Tests, and in his last Test he set a new career world record with 122 catches.

Australia were put in at Lahore and made 316, but then dropped some expensive catches, particularly off Javed, who made 138. Mohsin made 135 and Pakistan declared 151 ahead. Australia could make only 214 and Pakistan won by nine wickets for a clean sweep.

1982–83   10th Series   Pak 3, Aus 0

1 KARACHI   Pakistan won by 9 wkts
Australia 284 (J Dyson 87, A R Border 55, K J Hughes 54, Tahir 4–61) and 179 (Qadir 5–76)
Pakistan 419–9 dec (Zaheer Abbas 91, Haroon Rashid 82, Mohsin Khan 58, Mudassar Nazar 52) and 47–1

2 FAISALABAD   Pakistan won by an innings and 3 runs
Pakistan 501–6 dec (Zaheer Abbas 126, Mansoor Akhtar 111, Mudassar Nazar 79, Mohsin Khan 76, Haroon Rashid 51, G F Lawson 4–96)
Australia 168 (Qadir 4–76) and 330 (G M Ritchie 106, B M Laird 60, Qadir 7–142)

3 LAHORE   Pakistan won by 9 wkts
Australia 316 (G M Wood 85, G F Lawson 57, Imran Khan 4–45) and 214 (J Dyson 51, Imran Khan 4–35)
Pakistan 467–7 dec (Javed Miandad 138, Mohsin Khan 135, Zaheer Abbas 52) and 64–1

1982–83 Averages

Batting	I	No	Runs	HS	Avge	
Zaheer Abbas (P)	3	0	269	126	89.66	
Mohsin Khan (P)	5	1	297	135	74.25	
G.M. Ritchie (A)	6	1	206	106*	41.20	
J. Dyson (A)	6	0	220	87	36.66	
G.M. Wood (A)	6	0	203	85	33.83	

Bowling	O	M	Runs	W	Avge	BB
Imran Khan (P)	103.2	35	171	13	13.15	4–35
Abdul Qadir (P)	212.2	48	562	22	25.54	7–142

1983–84: End of the Chappell, Lillee, Marsh era

The teams met in Australia the following season, where at Perth Zaheer captained Pakistan in Imran's absence. W.B. Phillips (159 on his debut) and Yallop (141) added 259 for Australia's second wicket, a record between the countries as Australia reached 436 for 9 declared. Pakistan were then rushed out for 129 and 298 by Australia's fast battery, particularly Rackemann (5–32 and 6–86).

Lawson (5–49) was the main destroyer of Pakistan (156) at Brisbane, but after Border and Chappell had made centuries, rain washed out play from lunch on the fourth day, probably saving Pakistan from defeat.

On a batsman's pitch at Adelaide, Australia reached 376 for five on the first day and eventually totalled 465, with Wessels and Border making centuries. Pakistan, however, had three century-makers, Mohsin, Qasim and Javed, and reached 624. Lillee plugged away for six for 171. Hughes joined the three-figure men in the second innings, but by then the match was a draw.

Imran returned as captain of Pakistan at Melbourne, but was unable to bowl. Mohsin made 152 in a good score of 470. This was passed by Australia mainly through Yallop, whose 268 took 716 minutes, the sixth-longest innings in history. Australia led by 85 but the match was headed for a draw.

A helicopter helped dry the pitch at Sydney, and play started after tea on the first day. Pakistan were dismissed for 278 (Lawson 5–59) and Australia declared at 454 for six, with Chappell making 182. When Pakistan were dismissed for 210, Australia needed only 35 to win by ten wickets.

During or soon after the match Chappell, Lillee and Marsh announced their retirements. All had Test records. In his last match Chappell overtook Bradman and became Australia's leading run-getter, and also held the catches which enabled him to set a new Test record, outside wicket-keepers, of 122. Lillee had 355 wickets and Marsh 355 dismissals, both world records.

1983–84 11th Series Aus 2, Pak 0, Drawn 3

1 PERTH Australia won by an innings and 9 runs
Australia 436 (W B Phillips 159, G N Yallop 141, Azim Hafeez 5–100)
Pakistan 129 (C G Rackemann 5–32) and 298 (Qasim Omar 65, C G Rackemann 6–86)

2 BRISBANE Match Drawn
Pakistan 156 (Zaheer Abbas 56, G F Lawson 5–49) and 82–3
Australia 509–7 dec (G S Chappell 150, A R Border 118, K J Hughes 53)

3 ADELAIDE Match Drawn
Australia 465 (K C Wessels 179, A R Border 117, G N Yallop 68, Azim Hafeez 5–167) and 310–6 (K J Hughes 106, A R Border 66, W B Phillips 54)
Pakistan 624 (Mohsin Khan 149, Javed Miandad 131, Qasim Omar 113, D K Lillee 6–171)

4 MELBOURNE Match Drawn
Pakistan 470 (Mohsin Khan 152, Imran Khan 83) and 238–7 (Imran Khan 72, Zaheer Abbas 50)
Australia 555 (G N Yallop 268, K J Hughes 94, G R J Matthews 75, Abdul Qadir 5–166)

5 SYDNEY Australia won by 10 wkts
Pakistan 278 (Mudassar Nazar 84, Zaheer Abbas 61, Salim Malik 54, G F Lawson 5–59, D K Lillee 4–65) and 210 (Javed Miandad 60, G F Lawson 4–48, D K Lillee 4–88)
Australia 454–6 dec (G S Chappell 182, K J Hughes 76, A R Border 64) and 35–0

1983–84 Averages

Batting	I	No	Runs	HS	Avge
G.N. Yallop (A)	6	10	554	268	92.33
A.R. Border (A)	6	1	429	118	85.80
G.S. Chappell (A)	6	1	364	182	72.80
K.J. Hughes (A)	6	0	375	106	62.50
W.B. Phillips (A)	7	1	362	159	60.33
Mohsin Khan (P)	9	0	390	152	43.33
K.C. Wessels (A)	7	1	256	179	42.66
Qasim Omar (P)	9	1	327	113	40.87
Zaheer Abbas (P)	9	1	323	61	40.37
Javed Miandad (P)	9	0	302	131	33.55
Mudassar Nazar (P)	9	0	261	84	29.00

Bowling	O	M	Runs	W	Avge	BB
C.G. Rackemann (A)	52	10	177	16	11.06	6–86
G.F. Lawson (A)	188.3	40	580	24	24.16	5–49
D.K. Lillee (A)	230.2	51	633	20	31.65	6–171
Azeen Hafeez (P)	195.3	39	732	19	38.52	5–100
Abdul Qadir (P)	219.3	40	733	12	61.08	5–166

Left: Graham Yallop captained Australia against Pakistan in 1978–79. He headed the averages in the 1983–84 series.

Above: Allan Border off-driving. He is the leading Australian batsman of the post-Greg Chappell era.

West Indies v Pakistan

1957–58: Sobers breaks Test record score

Records were set in the first meeting between West Indies and Pakistan in 1957–58. F.C.M. Alexander and A.H. Kardar were the captains when Pakistan made a five-Test tour of West Indies.

At Bridgetown, Nasim-ul-Ghani made his debut at 16 years 248 days, the youngest Test cricketer at the time. C.C. Hunte made 142 in his first Test innings, and with Weekes making 197 West Indies declared at 579 for nine. Pakistan, out for 106, followed on, whereupon Hanif scored 337 in 16 hours 10 minutes, the longest innings in first-class cricket. Pakistan made 657 for eight declared, at the time their highest score, in a drawn match.

West Indies made 325 at Port-of-Spain, where L.R. Gibbs made his debut, and Pakistan recovered from 155 for eight to 282. By making 312, West Indies set Pakistan 356 – they lost by 120 runs.

Pakistan batted first at Kingston, and made 328, Imtiaz getting 122 and Atkinson five for 42. When Kanhai was out at 87, Sobers joined Hunte, and when Hunte was run out for 260, the pair had added 446, then the second highest stand in Test cricket. With two Pakistani bowlers, Nasim and Hussain, injured, Sobers went on to pass the highest individual score in Test cricket by one run before Alexander declared. Sobers was 365 not out and West Indies 790 for three declared. Wazir made 106 in the second innings but Pakistan were beaten by an innings and 174.

At Georgetown, Pakistan made 408 (Saeed 150) and West Indies 410 (Sobers 125, Walcott 145). Gibbs then took five for 80 to restrict Pakistan to 318 and West Indies won when Hunte (114) and Sobers (109 not out) knocked off most of the runs themselves. Sobers thus scored a century in each innings.

In the final Test at Port-of-Spain, West Indies were out for 268, with Fazal getting six for 83. For Pakistan, Wazir (189) put on 169 with Saeed (97) and 154 with his brother Hanif (54). Despite J. Taylor getting five for 109 on his debut, Pakistan led by 228 and won by an innings and one run when Nasim took six for 67 in the last innings.

1957–58 1st Series WI 3, Pak 1, Drawn 1

1 BRIDGETOWN Match Drawn
West Indies 579–9 dec (E de C Weekes 197, C C Hunte 142, O G Smith 78, G St A Sobers 62, Mahmood Hussain 4–153) and 28–0
Pakistan 106 (R Gilchrist 4–32) and 657–8 (Hanif Mohammad 337, Imtiaz Ahmed 91, Saeed Ahmed 65)

2 PORT OF SPAIN West Indies won by 120 runs
West Indies 325 (R B Kanhai 96, E de C Weekes 78, G St A Sobers 52) and 312 (G St A Sobers 80, F C M Alexander 57, O G Smith 51, Fazal Mahmood 4–89)
Pakistan 282 (Wallis Mathias 73, Fazal Mahmood 60, O G Smith 4–71) and 235 (Hanif Mohammad 81, Saeed Ahmed 64, R Gilchrist 4–61)

3 KINGSTON West Indies won by an innings and 174 runs
Pakistan 328 (Imtiaz Ahmed 122, Wallis Mathias 77, Saeed Ahmed 62, E St E Atkinson 5–42) and 288 (Wazir Mohammad 106, A H Kardar 57)
West Indies 790–3 dec (G St A Sobers 365, C C Hunte 260, C L Walcott 88)

4 GEORGETOWN West Indies won by 8 wkts
Pakistan 408 (Saeed Ahmed 150, Hanif Mohammad 79, R Gilchrist 4–102) and 318 (Wazir Mohammad 97, A H Kardar 56, L R Gibbs 5–80)

West Indies 410 (C L Walcott 145, G St A Sobers 125, Nasim-ul-Ghani 5–116) and 317–2 (C C Hunte 114, G St A Sobers 109, R B Kanhai 62)

5 PORT OF SPAIN Pakistan won by an innings and 1 run
West Indies 268 (O G Smith 86, E de C Weekes 51, Fazal Mahmood 6–83) and 227 (C L Walcott 62, Nasim-ul-Ghani 6–67)
Pakistan 496 (Wazir Mohammad 189, Saeed Ahmed 97, Hanif Mohammad 54, J Taylor 5–109, L R Gibbs 4–108)

1957–58 Averages

Batting	I	No	Runs	HS	Avge	
G. St. A. Sobers (WI)	8	2	824	365*	137.33	
C.L. Walcott (WI)	5	1	385	145	96.25	
C. Hunte (WI)	9	1	622	260	77.75	
Hanif Mohammad (P)	9	0	628	337	69.77	
E. de C. Weekes (WI)	8	1	455	197	65.00	
Saeed Ahmed (P)	9	0	508	150	56.40	
Wazir Mohammad (P)	9	1	440	189	55.00	
O.G. Smith (WI)	6	0	283	86	47.16	
Imtiaz Ahmed (P)	9	0	344	122	38.22	
R.B. Kanhai (WI)	9	1	299	96	37.37	
A.H. Kardar (P)	9	1	253	57	31.62	
W. Mathias (P)	9	0	251	77	27.88	

Bowling	O	M	Runs	W	Avge	BB
L.R. Gibbs (WI)	166.5	46	292	17	23.05	5–80
E. St E. Atkinson (WI)	127	21	307	12	25.58	5–42
Nasim-ul-Ghani (P)	197.1	48	508	19	26.73	6–67
R. Gilchrist (WI)	187.1	32	336	21	30.28	4–32
O.G. Smith (WI)	236	73	494	13	38.00	4–71
Fazal Mahmood (P)	319.2	96	764	20	38.20	6–83

Rohan Kanhai, one of the West Indian batsmen who ensured that the early series between West Indies and Pakistan would be high-scoring affairs.

Hanif Mohammad

Hanif was born on 21 December 1934 in Junagadh, India. He made his debut for Karachi and Bahawalpur in 1951–52, and from 1954–55 played for Karachi. He was a very steady opening right-hand batsman. He first played for Pakistan in 1952–53 and in 55 Tests scored 3,915 runs, average 43.98. He holds the record for the highest score in first-class cricket, 499 (run-out going for the 500th). Among many long innings, he played the longest in Tests, 16 hours and 10 minutes for 337 against West Indies in 1957–58. He captained Pakistan in 11 Tests. His brothers Wazir, Mushtaq and Sadiq and son Shoaib all played for Pakistan, and Hanif, Mushtaq and Sadiq appeared together against New Zealand.

WEST INDIES V PAKISTAN 1957–58
3rd Test, Kingston: West Indies won by an innings and 174

PAKISTAN

Hanif Mohammad	c Alexander b Gilchrist	3		b Gilchrist	13
Imtiaz Ahmed†	c Alexander b Gilchrist	122		lbw b Dewdney	0
Saeed Ahmed	c Weekes b Smith	52		c Gilchrist b Gibbs	44
W. Mathias	b Dewdney	77		c Alexander b Atkinson	19
Alimuddin	c Alexander b Atkinson	15		b Gibbs	30
A.H. Kardar*	c Sobers b Atkinson	15	(7)	lbw b Dewdney	57
Wazir Mohammad	c Walcott b Dewdney	2	(6)	lbw b Atkinson	106
Fazal Mahmood	c Alexander b Atkinson	6		c Alexander b Atkinson	0
Nasim-ul-Ghani	b Atkinson	5		absent hurt	–
Mahmood Hussain	b Atkinson	20		absent hurt	–
Khan Mohammad	not out	3	(9)	not out	0
Extras	(LB 5, NB 3)	8		(B 16, LB 3)	19
Total		**328**			**288**

WEST INDIES

C.C. Hunte	run out	260
R.B. Kanhai	c Imtiaz b Fazal	25
G. St A. Sobers	not out	365
E. de C. Weekes	c Hanif b Fazal	39
C.L. Walcott	not out	88
O.G. Smith	)	
F.C.M. Alexander*†	)	
L.R. Gibbs	) did not bat	
E. St E. Atkinson	)	
R. Gilchrist	)	
D.T. Dewdney	)	
Extras	(B 2, LB 7, W 4)	13
Total	(3 wickets declared)	**790**

WEST INDIES	O	M	R	W	O	M	R	W
Gilchrist	25	3	106	2	12	3	65	1
Dewdney	26	4	88	2	19.3	2	51	2
Atkinson	21	7	42	4	18	6	36	3
Gibbs	7	0	32	0	21	6	46	2
Smith	18	3	39	1	8	2	20	0
Sobers	5	1	13	0	15	4	41	0
Weekes					3	1	10	0

PAKISTAN				
Mahmood Hussain	0.5	0	2	0
Fazal	85.2	20	247	2
Khan	54	5	259	0
Nasim	15	3	39	0
Kardar	37	2	141	0
Mathias	4	0	20	0
Alimuddin	4	0	34	0
Hanif	2	0	11	0
Saeed	6	0	24	0

FALL OF WICKETS

	P	WI	P
Wkt	1st	1st	2nd
1st	4	87	8
2nd	122	533	20
3rd	223	602	57
4th	249	–	105
5th	287	–	120
6th	291	–	286
7th	299	–	286
8th	301	–	288
9th	317	–	–
10th	328	–	–

Above: Clyde Walcott, one of the great West Indian batsmen of the 1950s.

Below: Hanif Mohammad (batting) as a 19-year-old prodigy. His innings of 337 at Bridgetown in 1957–58 is the longest of all Test innings.

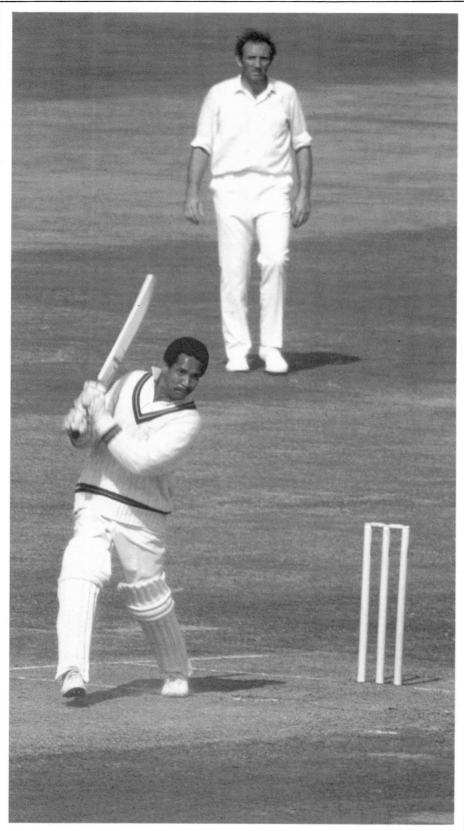

Sobers, Garfield St Aubrun

Sobers was born in Bridgetown, Barbados, on 28 July 1936, and made his debut for the island in 1952–53. He also played for South Australia and Nottinghamshire. He was a brilliant middle-order left-hand batsman, and a bowler who began as orthodox left-hand slow and developed a skill for new-ball swing bowling, and also for chinamen, and he would frequently bowl in a variety of speeds and styles in one match. He was also a brilliant field, and is acknowledged as perhaps the greatest all-rounder the game has seen. He made his Test debut in 1953–54 , and played in 93 Tests, being captain in 39, at the time a record. His greatest feat in Tests was to make the highest individual score, 365 not out, against Pakistan at Kingston in 1957–58. He was the first player to pass 8,000 runs in Tests. He made 8,032, average 57.78, and took 235 wickets, average 34.03. He was the second to score 2,000 runs and take 200 wickets in Tests. He also took 109 catches. He was knighted in 1975.

1958–59: Pakistan win series 2–1 at home

West Indies toured India and Pakistan a year later under F.C.M. Alexander. Fazal was Pakistan captain and put West Indies in in the first Test on the Karachi matting. He and Nasim, who each took four for 35, had the tourists out for 146. Pakistan made 304, with Hanif getting 103. West Indies improved second time with 245, but Pakistan won easily by ten wickets.

Without Hanif, Pakistan were 22 for five at Dacca and only recovered to 145. But Fazal took six for 34 and dismissed West Indies for their lowest score of 76. The last six batsmen failed to score. Pakistan made only 144 in the second innings but it was enough. West Indies made the game's highest score of 172 but lost by 41. Fazal took six for 66 to complete 12 for 100 in the match.

Kanhai made a brilliant 217 at Lahore, where Mushtaq Mohammad, brother of Hanif and Wazir, made his debut at 15 years and 124 days, and remains the youngest Test cricketer. West Indies' 469 was enough for an innings victory as Pakistan followed on, and with both innings interrupted by rain, could make only 209 and 104.

1958–59 2nd Series Pak 2, WI 1
1 KARACHI Pakistan won by 10 wkts
West Indies 146 (Fazal Mahmood 4–35, Nasim-ul-Ghani 4–35) and 245 (J S Solomon 66, B F Butcher 61)
Pakistan 304 (Hanif Mohammad 103, Saeed Ahmed 78) and 88–0
2 DACCA Pakistan won by 41 runs
Pakistan 145 (Wallis Mathias 64, W W Hall 4–28) and 144 (E St E Atkinson 4–42, W W Hall 4–49)
West Indies 76 (Fazal Mahmood 6–34) and 172 (Fazal Mahmood 6–66, Mahmood Hussain 4–48)
3 LAHORE West Indies won by an Innings and 156 runs
West Indies 469 (R B Kanhai 217, G St A Sobers 72, J S Solomon 56)
Pakistan 209 (W W Hall 5–87) and 104 (S Ramadhin 4–25)

1958–59 Averages

Batting	I	No	Runs	HS	Avge	
R.B. Kanhai (WI)	5	0	274	217	54.80	

Bowling	O	M	Runs	W	Avge	BB
Fazal Mahmood (P)	143.5	45	333	21	15.85	6–34
W.W. Hall (WI)	100.5	17	287	16	17.93	5–87
Nasim-ul-Ghani (P)	86	33	213	11	19.36	4–35

1974–75: Honours shared in short tour

It was 15 years since the last Test between the countries when West Indies played the first of two Tests in 1974–75 after touring India. C.H. Lloyd and Intikhab Alam were the captains.

Pakistan, put in at Lahore, made only 199 with Roberts taking five for 66. Sarfraz bowled well for Pakistan, taking six for 89, but Kallicharran's 92 not out steered West Indies to a 15-run lead. However, Pakistan made 373 for seven declared in the second innings, Mushtaq scoring 123, and West Indies were happy to draw, L. Baichan batting throughout the last day for 105 not out.

Majid and Wasim made centuries at Karachi and Pakistan declared at 406 for eight. But West Indies took a lead of 87 with Kallicharran and Julien making hundreds. At 90 for five, Pakistan were on the point of defeat, but Asif made 77 and Sadiq bravely came in at number seven to make 98 not out in 315 minutes, batting in pain from a neck injury. They saved the game, but West Indies were unlucky in that 2½ hours were lost rioting on the second day.

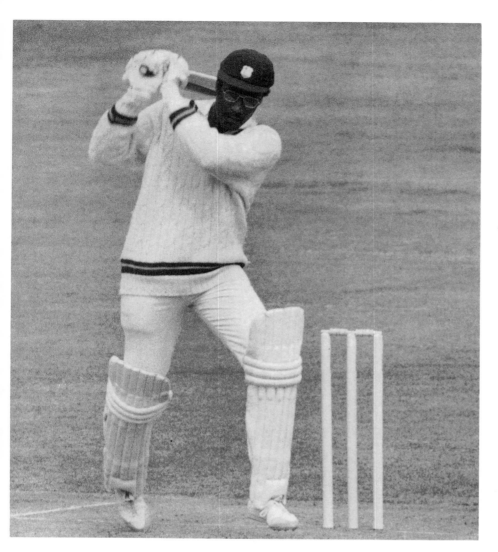

1974–75   3rd Series   Drawn 2

1 LAHORE   Match Drawn

Pakistan 199 (A M E Roberts 5–66) and 373–7 dec (Mushtaq
Mohammad 123, Aftab Baloch 60, Asif Iqbal 52, A M E
Roberts 4–121)

West Indies 214 (A I Kallicharran 92, Sarfraz Nawaz 6–89) and
258–4 (L Baichan 105, C H Lloyd 83)

2 KARACHI   Match Drawn

Pakistan 406–8 dec (Wasim Raja 107, Majid Khan 100, Wasim
Bari 58) and 256 (Sadiq Mohammad 98, Asif Iqbal 77)

West Indies 493 (A I Kallicharran 115, B D Julien 101, R C
Fredericks 77, C H Lloyd 73) and 1–0

Top left: Clive Lloyd forcing off the back foot.
Lloyd captained the first West Indian side to play
Pakistan for 15 years when he led the two-match
tour in 1974–75.

Above: Three West Indian stalwarts of the 1970s,
Andy Roberts, the leading fast bowler of his day,
Clive Lloyd, the long-serving captain, and Roy
Fredericks, the dashing opening batsman.

Top right: Javed Miandad, the dashing Pakistani
batsman who burst impressively onto the Test
match scene as a 19-year-old in 1976.

1976–77: West Indies win last Test and series 2–1

Mushtaq led a side to West Indies in 1976–77 to meet Lloyd's powerful team. C.E.H. Croft and J. Garner make their debuts at Bridgetown, but Pakistan made 435 against a battery of four fast bowlers, Wasim Raja getting 117 not out. Lloyd made 157 for West Indies but they trailed by 14. Pakistan's 291 then set West Indies 306 to win. Their total of 291 included a Test record of 68 extras. There were 173 extras in the match, including 103 no-balls. West Indies seemed certain to lose when the eighth wicket fell with about 24 overs left, but they just saved the game, with the last pair together.

At Port-of-Spain, Croft took eight for 29 and Pakistan were out for 180. Fredericks made 120 of 316, and although Pakistan fought back with a second innings 340, West Indies won by six wickets. Wasim Raja was top scorer in all four Pakistan innings to date.

It was a similar story, but with a different end, at Georgetown. Pakistan were out for 194 to the fast bowlers, then I.T. Shillingford's 120 led the way to West Indies' 448. But Majid made 167 and was well

supported all the way down, and Pakistan made 540 in the second innings, which this time was enough to save the game.

A brilliant performance by Mushtaq helped win the fourth Test. He made 121 and 56, and took five for 28 and three for 69. Pakistan were on top throughout and won by 266 to set up a decider at Kingston.

Imran grabbed quick wickets but Greenidge's 100 took West Indies to 280 (Imran 6–90). Pakistan could get only 198 and trailed by 82. West Indies made a good start in the second innings with 182 for the first wicket by Fredericks (83) and Greenidge (82) and set Pakistan 442 to win. Asif made a typically gallant 135, but Pakistan could get to only 301.

1976–77 4th Series WI 2, Pak 1, Drawn 2
1 BRIDGETOWN Match Drawn
Pakistan 435 (Wasim Raja 117, Majid Khan 88, J Garner 4–130) and 291 (Wasim Raja 71, Wasim Bari 60, C E H Croft 4–47)
West Indies 421 (C H Lloyd 157, D L Murray 52) and 251–9 (I V A Richards 92, R C Fredericks 52, Sarfraz Nawaz 4–79)
2 PORT OF SPAIN West Indies won by 6 wkts
Pakistan 180 (Wasim Raja 65, C E H Croft 9–29) and 340 (Wasim Raja 84, Sadiq Mohammad 81, Majid Khan 54, A M E Roberts 4–85)
West Indies 316 (R C Fredericks 120, Mushtaq Mohammad 4–50) and 206–4 (C G Greenidge 70, R C Fredericks 57)

Joel Garner (*above*) made his debut for West Indies in 1976–77 against Pakistan and took 4 for 48 during the series. *Left*: The West Indian opening batsman R.C. Fredericks pulls Illingworth to leg.

3 GEORGETOWN Match Drawn
Pakistan 194 (J Garner 4–48) and 540 (Majid Khan 167, Zaheer Abbas 80, Haroon Rashid 60, J Garner 4–10)
West Indies 448 (I T Shillingford 120, C G Greenidge 91, A I Kallicharran 72, I V A Richards 50, Majid Khan 4–45) and 154–1 (C G Greenidge 96, R C Fredericks 52)
4 PORT OF SPAIN Pakistan won by 266 runs
Pakistan 341 (Mushtaq Mohammad 121, Majid Khan 92) and 301–9 dec (Wasim Raja 70, Mushtaq Mohammad 56, Sarfraz Nawaz 51)
West Indies 154 (Mushtaq Mohammad 5–28, Imran Khan 4–64) and 222
5 KINGSTON West Indies won by 140 runs
West Indies 280 (C G Greenidge 100, Imran Khan 6–90) and 359 (R C Fredericks 83, C G Greenidge 82)
Pakistan 198 (Haroon Rashid 72, C E H Croft 4–49) and 301 (Asif Iqbal 135, Wasim Raja 64)

1976–77 Averages

Batting	I	No	Runs	HS	Avge
Wasim Raja (P)	10	1	517	117*	57.44
C.G. Greenidge (WI)	10	0	536	100	53.60
M.J. Khan (P)	10	0	530	167	53.00
R.C. Fredericks (WI)	10	1	457	120	50.77
C.H. Lloyd (WI)	9	1	336	157	42.00
A.I. Kallicharran (WI)	9	1	258	72	32.25
Mushtaq Mohammad (P)	10	0	314	121	31.40
Haroon Rashid (P)	10	0	300	72	30.00
I.V.A. Richards (WI)	9	0	257	90	28.55
Asif Iqbal (P)	10	0	259	135	25.90

Bowling	O	M	Runs	W	Avge	BB
C.E.H. Croft (WI)	217.5	45	676	33	20.48	8–29
Mushtaq Mohammad (P)	123.2	32	328	13	25.23	5–28
J. Garner (WI)	219.3	41	688	25	27.52	4–48
Imran Khan (P)	236.1	54	790	25	31.000	6–90
Sarfraz Nawaz (P)	197.3	54	579	16	36.18	4–79
A.M.E. Roberts (WI)	236.3	37	763	19	40.15	4–85

1980–81: West Indies' first series win in Pakistan

Javed was captain when Lloyd's team arrived in Pakistan in 1980–81.

Pakistan recovered well in the first Test at Lahore to reach 369 (Imran 123) and they got West Indies out for 297. But a whole day's play was rained off and the match drifted to a draw.

West Indies made 235 (Nazir 5–40) at Faisalabad, but Pakistan started with two for two and could reach only 176. Qasim got six for 89 when West Indies batted again, but they made 242 and set the home side 302. Pakistan could make only 145.

The match at Karachi began 1½ days late, and Pakistan were 14 for four on a drying pitch, but they made 128. West Indies in turn were 44 for five, but scrambled to 169. There were more alarms for Pakistan at 85 for five, but they batted out the limited time for a draw.

There was trouble in the last Test at Multan after Richards had made 120 not out in a total of 249 (Imran 5–62). Pakistan made only 166, during which Clarke, infuriated by the orange peel thrown at the outfielders, threw back a boundary marker brick and sent a students' leader to hospital with a direct hit. Kallicharran helped quell the crowd as play was interrupted for 20 minutes. Rain washed out most of the last two days and the chance of a result, West Indies winning their first rubber in Pakistan.

1980–81   5th Series   WI 1, Pak 0, Drawn 3
1 LAHORE   **Match Drawn**
Pakistan 369 (Imran Khan 123, Wasim Raja 76, Sarfraz Nawaz 55) and 156–7 (Majid Khan 62)
West Indies 297 (I V A Richards 75, D A Murray 50, Abdul Qadir 4–132)
2 FAISALABAD   **West Indies won by 156 runs**
West Indies 235 (I V A Richards 72, Mohammad Nazir 5–44) and 242 (I V A Richards 67, Iqbal Qasim 6–89)
Pakistan 176 (Javed Miandad 50) and 145 (M D Marshall 4–25)
3 KARACHI   **Match Drawn**
Pakistan 128 (Javed Miandad 60, S T Clarke 4–27) and 204–9 (Wasim Raja 77)
West Indies 169 (H A Gomes 61, Imran Khan 4–66, Iqbal Qasim 4–48)
4 MULTAN   **Match Drawn**
West Indies 249 (I V A Richards 120, Imran Khan 5–62) and 116–5
Pakistan 166 (Javed Miandad 57, J Garner 4–38)

1980–81 Averages

Batting	I	No	Runs	HS	Avge
I.V.A. Richards (WI)	6	1	364	120*	72.80
Wasim Raja (P)	7	0	246	77*	61.50
Javed Miandad (P)	7	0	230	60	32.85
Imran Khan (P)	7	0	204	123	29.14

Bowling	O	M	Runs	W	Avge	BB
S.T. Clarke (WI)	98	21	242	14	17.28	4–27
Mohammad Nazir (P)	122	38	283	16	17.68	5–44
C.E.H. Croft (WI)	130	32	302	17	17.76	3–27
Iqbal Qasim (P)	137.3	34	305	17	17.94	6–89
J. Garner (WI)	90.3	25	192	10	19.20	4–38
Imran Khan (P)	91	13	236	10	23.60	5–62
M.D. Marshall (WI)	98.3	12	319	13	24.53	4–25

1986–87: Shocks for both sides in drawn series

When West Indies toured Pakistan in 1986–87 Richards had succeeded Lloyd as captain. Imran led Pakistan.

Pakistan, batting at Faisalabad, were shot out for 159 by the West Indies fast battery, with Salim Malik retired with a broken bone in his hand. Although Wasim Akram bowled well for six for 91 in reply, West Indies led by 89. Wasim also made a late 66

for Pakistan when batting, hoisting the second-innings score to 328 and setting West Indies 240 to win. But the pace of Imran and wiles of Abdul Qadir totally bemused the batsmen. Some excellent catching helped Qadir (6–16), in particular, to dismiss West Indies for 53, their lowest total in Test cricket.

It was a different story on an unpredictable pitch at Lahore, with Marshall's five for 33 leading the fast men to remove Pakistan for 131. Greenidge then made a careful 75 in 4½ hours to take West Indies to 218, 87 ahead. Imran took five for 59. But West Indies did not need to bat again, Walsh with four for 21 being the most destructive bowler as Pakistan were skittled for 77.

In the decider at Karachi, West Indies made 240, Richards getting 70, on a wicket favouring spin. After a bad start to Pakistan's innings, Rameez Raja and Javed Miandad pulled them up to 239. Vice-captain Marshall upset one of the umpires with constant disagreements and he and Richards were spoken to by the manager. Imran (6–46) bowled magnificently in the second innings, but Haynes carried his bat for 88 not out in a total of 211. Pakistan

needed 213 to win the series, but were struggling at 125 for seven when bad light ended play with nine overs remaining.

1986–87   6th Series   Pak 1, WI 1, Drawn 1
1 FAISALABAD   **Pakistan won by 186 runs**
Pakistan 159 (Imran Khan 61, A H Gray 4–39) and 328 (Wasim Akram 68, Salim Yousuf 61)
West Indies 248 (R B Richardson 54, Wasim Akram 6–91) and 53 (Abdul Qadir 6–16, Imran Khan 4–30)
2 LAHORE   **West Indies won by an innings and 10 runs**
Pakistan 131 (M D Marshall 5–33) and 77 (C A Walsh 4–21)
West Indies 218 (C G Greenidge 75, Imran Khan 5–59, Abdul Qadir 4–96)
3 KARACHI   **Match Drawn**
West Indies 240 (I V A Richards 70, Abdul Qadir 4–107) and 211 (D L Haynes 88, Imran Khan 6–46)
Pakistan 239 (Javed Miandad 76, Rameez Raja 62, C G Butts 4–73) and 125–7

1986–87 Averages

Bowling	O	M	Runs	W	Avge	BB
Imran Khan (P)	106.2	23	199	18	11.05	6–46
A.H. Gray (WI)	99	27	227	14	16.21	4–39
M.D. Marshall (WI)	114	27	266	16	16.62	5–33
C.A. Walsh (WI)	97.3	27	195	11	17.72	4–21
Abdul Qadir (P)	132.2	19	361	18	20.05	6–16

Abdul Qadir, who took 6 for 16 in the 1986–87 series against West Indies, is seen in action at The Oval against England later in 1987.

New Zealand v India

1955–56: Record scoring in India

New Zealand first played Tests against India in 1955–56, when H.B. Cave captained the touring side which had earlier toured Pakistan.

In the first Test at Hyderabad, India batted and made 498 for four declared, Umrigar (223) making big stands with Manjrekar (118) and Kripal Singh (100 not out on his debut). J.W. Guy (102) failed to save the follow-on for New Zealand as Gupte took seven for 128, but B. Sutcliffe (137 not out) easily saved the match.

At Bombay, where Umrigar took over India's captaincy from Ghulam Ahmed for the rest of the series, Mankad made the same score as Umrigar (223) and India again passed 400 at 421 for eight declared. New Zealand were dismissed twice for 258 and 136, mainly by Gupte, who took eight wickets, and India won by an innings.

It was New Zealand's turn to bat at Delhi, and Sutcliffe's turn for a double-century. When New Zealand declared at 450 for two, Sutcliffe (230 not out) and Reid (119 not out) had added 222 for the third wicket. India, however, made 531 for seven declared (Manjrekar 177) and the match was drawn.

In a remarkable match at Calcutta, India were put out for 132, and despite Gupte's six for 90, New Zealand took a lead of 204 with Reid scoring 120. However India recovered so well, with Pankaj Roy and Ramchand making centuries, that they declared at 438 for seven, and New Zealand at 75 for six ended by fighting for the draw.

The last Test reverted to type. Mankad (231) reclaimed top score of the series, and

put on a world record Test opening partnership with Pankaj Roy (173) of 413. India declared at 537 for three and Gupte, with nine wickets, helped spin out New Zealand twice for an innings win.

H.B. Cave, the New Zealand medium-pace bowler, in action. He captained New Zealand in the first series against India in 1955–56.

1955–56   1st Series   India 2, NZ 0, Drawn 3

1 HYDERABAD   Match Drawn
India 498–4 (P R Umrigar 223, V L Manjrekar 118, A G Kripal Singh 100)
New Zealand 326 (J W Guy 102, A R MacGibbon 59, J R Reid 54, S P Gupte 7–128) and 212–2 (B Sutcliffe 137)

2 BOMBAY   India won by an innings and 27 runs
India 421–8 dec (M H Mankad 223, A G Kripal Singh 63)
New Zealand 258 (B Sutcliffe 73) and 136 (S P Gupte 5–45)

3 NEW DELHI   Match Drawn
New Zealand 450–2 dec (B Sutcliffe 230, J R Reid 119, J W Guy 52) and 112–1 (J G Leggat 50)
India 531–7 dec (V L Manjrekar 177, G S Ramchand 72, R G Nadkarni 68), N J Contractor 62)

4 CALCUTTA   Match Drawn
India 132 and 438–7 (G S Ramchand 106, P Roy 100, V L Manjrekar 90, N J Contractor 62)
New Zealand 336 (J R Reid 120, J W Guy 91, S P Gupte 6–90) and 75–6

5 MADRAS   India won by an innings and 109 runs
India 537–3 dec (M H Mankad 231, P Roy 173, P R Umrigar 79)
New Zealand 209 (S P Gupte 5–72) and 219 (J G Leggat 61, J R Reid 63, M H Mankad 4–65, S P Gupte 4–73)

1955–56 Averages

Batting	I	No	Runs	HS	Avge	
V. Mankad (I)	5	0	526	231	105.20	
B. Sutcliffe (NZ)	9	2	611	230*	87.28	
V.L. Manjrekar (I)	6	1	386	177	77.20	
P. Roy (I)	4	0	301	173	75.25	
J.R. Reid (NZ)	9	2	493	120	70.42	
P.R. Umrigar (I)	6	1	351	223	70.20	
J.W. Guy (NZ)	10	1	313	102	34.77	

Bowling	O	M	Runs	W	Avge	BB
S.P. Gupte (I)	356.4	153	669	34	19.67	7–128
V. Mankad (I)	167.1	66	328	12	27.33	4–65

1964–65: India win series after three draws

New Zealand's second tour of India again followed a tour of Pakistan. J.R. Reid and the Nawab of Pataudi were the captains.

At Madras, Nadkarni and Engineer added a record 143 for the eighth wicket as India made 297. Ward and Collinge added 61 for New Zealand's tenth wicket in a total of 315. There was no time for a result.

Sutcliffe made 151 and B.R. Taylor, playing in his first Test as a late replacement, 105, in New Zealand's first innings 462 for nine. Taylor followed up with five for 86, but Pataudi's captain's innings of 153 took India to 380 and again there was no time for a result.

New Zealand made 297 (Dowling 129), Desai taking six for 56, and then Taylor again bowled well to get five for 26 and

dismiss India for only 88. But in the follow-on Sardesai (200 not out) and Borde (109) batted so well that India declared at 463 for five, setting new Zealand a target of 255 in 2½ hours. New Zealand just saved the day at 80 for eight, after being 46 for seven.

Splendid bowling by Venkat and Chandra at Delhi, the former getting eight for 72, got New Zealand out for 262, and Sardesai and Pataudi centuries helped India to 465 for eight declared. More good spin bowling left India with only 70 to get to win the series.

1964–65   2nd Series   India 1, NZ 0, Drawn 3

1 MADRAS   Match Drawn
India 397 (F M Engineer 90, R G Nadkarni 75, C G Borde 68, M L Jaisimha 51) and 199–2 dec (V L Manjrekar 102)
New Zealand 315 (B Sutcliffe 56) and 62–0

2 CALCUTTA   Match Drawn
New Zealand 462–9 dec (B Sutcliffe 151, B R Taylor 105, J R Reid 82, R B Desai 4–128) and 191–9 dec
India 380 (M A K Pataudi 153, C G Borde 62, B R Taylor 5–86) and 92–3

3 BOMBAY   Match Drawn

New Zealand 297 (G T Dowling 129, R W Morgan 71, R B Desai 6–56) and 80–8

India 88 (B R Taylor 6–26) and 463–5 dec (D N Sardesai 200, C G Borde 109, Hanumant Singh 75)

4 NEW DELHI   India won by 7 wkts

New Zealand 262 (R W Morgan 82, S Venkataraghavan 8–72) and 272 (T W Jarvis 77, B Sutcliffe 54, R O Collinge 54, S Venkataraghavan 4–80)

India 465–8 dec (M A K Pataudi 113, D N Sardesai 106, C G Borde 87, Hanumant Singh 82, R O Collinge 4–89) and 73–3

1964–65 Averages

Batting	I	No	Runs	HS	Avge
D.N. Sardesai (I)	6	3	359	200*	119.66
C.G. Borde (I)	6	0	371	109	61.83
Nawab of Pataudi, jr (I)	6	0	317	153	52.83
B. Sutcliffe (NZ)	7	1	274	151*	45.66
R.W. Morgan (NZ)	7	0	260	82	37.14
G.T. Dowling (NZ)	8	1	236	129	33.71

Bowling	O	M	Runs	W	Avge	BB
B.R. Taylor (NZ)	81.5	14	276	15	18.40	5–26
S. Venkataraghavan (I)	276.3	125	399	21	19.00	8–72
R.B. Desai (I)	106	31	305	13	23.46	5–26

J.R. Reid averaged 70 for New Zealand in the 1955–56 series.

1967–68: India's first series win outside India

Pataudi led India's first touring team to New Zealand, which followed a tour of Australia. Sinclair captained New Zealand.

In the first Test at Dunedin, Dowling made 143 in a total of 350. All India's players made double figures as they took a lead of nine runs. India's spinners, led by Prasanna (6–94), got New Zealand out for 208, and India got the 200 necessary for a five-wicket win. It was India's first win outside the sub-continent.

Dowling's 239 at Christchurch was the highest innings for New Zealand and enabled them to reach 502. India were forced to follow on and New Zealand won by six wickets. Bedi, Motz and Bartlett all took six wickets in an innings.

New Zealand were dismissed for only 186 (Prasanna five for 32) at Wellington and India took a lead of 141, with Wadekar getting 143. Nadkarni and Prasanna spun out New Zealand for 199 and India won by eight wickets.

Needing to win the last Test, New Zealand put India in at Auckland and dismissed them for 252. India's spinners put New Zealand out for 140 and then set them 375 to win in 290 minutes. Spinning them out for 101, India won the series 3–1.

1967–68   3rd Series   India 3, NZ 1

1 DUNEDIN   India won by 5 wkts

New Zealand 350 (G T Dowling 143, B E Congdon 58, M G Burgess 50, S Abid Ali 4–26) and 208 (B A G Murray 54, E A S Prasanna 6–94)

India 359 (A L Wadekar 80, F M Engineer 63, R C Motz 5–86) and 200–5 (A L Wadekar 71)

2 CHRISTCHURCH   New Zealand won by 6 wkts

New Zealand 502 (G T Dowling 239, B A G Murray 74, K Thomson 69, B S Bedi 6–127) and 88–4 (B E Congdon 61)

India 288 (R F Surti 67, C G Borde 57, M A K Pataudi 52, R C Motz 6–63) and 301 (F M Engineer 63, G A Bartlett 6–38)

3 WELLINGTON   India won by 8 wkts

New Zealand 186 (M G Burgess 66, E A S Prasanna 5–32) and 199 (M G Burgess 60, B E Congdon 51, R G Nadkarni 6–43)

India 327 (A L Wadekar 143) and 59–2

4 AUCKLAND   India won by 272 runs

India 252 (M A K Pataudi 51, R C Motz 4–51) and 261–5 dec (R F Surti 99, C G Borde 65)

New Zealand 140 (E A S Prasanna 4–44) and 101 (E A S Prasanna 4–40)

1967–68 Averages

Batting	I	No	Runs	HS	Avge
G.T. Dowling (NZ)	8	0	471	239	58.87
C.G. Borde (I)	7	2	242	65*	48.40
A.L. Wadekar (I)	8	1	330	143	47.14
R.F. Surti (I)	8	1	321	99	45.85
F.M. Engineer (I)	8	0	321	63	40.12
B.E. Congdon (NZ)	8	1	240	61*	34.28
M.G. Burgess (NZ)	8	0	271	66	33.87
Nawab of Pataudi, Jr (I)	7	0	221	52	31.57

Bowling	O	M	Runs	W	Avge	BB
R.G. Nadkarni (I)	185.3	91	251	14	17.92	6–43
E.A.S. Prasanna (I)	197.5	62	451	24	18.79	6–94
G.A. Bartlett (NZ)	71.5	18	196	10	19.60	6–38
B.S. Bedi (I)	176.1	64	371	16	23.18	6–127
R.C. Motz (NZ)	148.4	41	403	15	28.86	6–63
J.C. Alabaster (NZ)	150	44	382	12	31.83	3–48

1969–70: New Zealand deprived of victory in India

Dowling led the tourists in India two years later. Rioting caused the first Test to be switched from Ahmedabad to Bombay. On an under-prepared pitch India were dismissed for 156 and New Zealand took a lead of 73. India batted much better second time for 260. Set 188, New Zealand were spun out for 127 by Bedi (6–42) and Prasanna (4–74).

At Nagpur, New Zealand made 319 and India 257 on first innings. Venkat took six for 74 to dismiss New Zealand for 214, second time, leaving India 277 to win. H.J. Howarth took five for 34, following four wickets in the first innings, to restrict India to 109.

In the decider at Hyderabad, New Zealand made 181. The second day was washed out and after a rest day India batted on a pitch which by oversight was unmown. A late 'recovery' took them to 89. After more rain and rioting, New Zealand made 175 for eight declared, allowing India the last day to make 268. Rain stopped play with India 76 for seven, and little effort was made to restart when the sun came out.

1969–70   4th Series   India 1, NZ 1, Drawn 1

1 BOMBAY   India won by 60 runs

India 156 and 260 (M A K Pataudi 67)

New Zealand 229 (B E Congdon 78, E A S Prasanna 4–97) and 127 (B S Bedi 6–42, E A S Prasanna 4–74)

2 NAGPUR   New Zealand won by 167 runs

New Zealand 319 (M G Burgess 89, G T Dowling 69, B E Congdon 64, B S Bedi 4–98) and 214 (G M Turner 57, S Venkataraghavan 6–74)

India 257 (S Abid Ali 63, H J Howarth 4–66) and 109 (H J Howarth 5–34)

3 HYDERABAD   Match Drawn

New Zealand 181 (B A G Murray 80, E A S Prasanna 5–51) and 175–8 dec (G T Dowling 60)

India 89 (D R Hadlee 4–30) and 76–7

1969–70 Averages

Batting	I	No	Runs	HS	Avge
G.T. Dowling (NZ)	6	1	257	69	51.40

Bowling	O	M	Runs	W	Avge	BB
D.R. Hadlee (NZ)	80.5	25	181	13	13.92	4–30
H.J. Howarth (NZ)	126	46	218	12	18.16	5–34
S. Venkataraghavan (I)	94	25	206	11	18.72	6–74
B.S. Bedi (I)	187.5	81	308	15	20.53	6–42
E.A.S. Prasanna (I)	204.3	69	433	20	21.65	5–51

B.S. Chandrasekhar, the Indian leg-break bowler.

1975–76: Drawn series in New Zealand

Gavaskar and Turner were captains in New Zealand in 1975–76. New Zealand batted at Auckland and made 266 (Chandra six for 95). Gavaskar and S. Amarnath made centuries for India, the latter in his first Test – he thus emulated his father, who performed the feat 42 years earlier. India led by 148, and when Prasanna took eight for 76 in the second innings, needed only 68 for an eight-wicket win. S.M.H. Kirmani and D.B. Vengsarkar also made their debuts in this match.

India made 270 at Christchurch, Collinge taking six for 63. New Zealand made a good start, with Turner getting 117, and reached 403. Kirmani, in his second Test, took six catches, equalling the record. There was no time for a result. In the last Test at Wellington, India could make only 220 and New Zealand again took a lead, of 114. R.J. Hadlee, with Gavaskar absent, then took seven for 23 (11 in the match) to dismiss India for 81. Brother D.R. Hadlee had three wickets in the match.

1975–76   5th Series   India 1, NZ 1, Drawn 1

1 AUCKLAND   India won by 8 wkts

New Zealand 266 (B E Congdon 54, B S Chandrasekhar 6–94) and 215 (J M Parker 70, B E Congdon 54, E A S Prasanna 8–76)

India 414 (S Amarnath 124, S M Gavaskar 116, M Amarnath 64, B E Congdon 5–65) and 71–2

2 CHRISTCHURCH   Match Drawn

India 270 (G R Viswanath 83, R O Collinge 6–63) and 255–6 (G R Viswanath 79, S M Gavaskar 71)

New Zealand 403 (G M Turner 117, B E Congdon 58, S Madan Lal 5–134, M Amarnath 4–63)

3 WELLINGTON   New Zealand won by an innings and 33 runs

India 220 (B P Patel 81, R J Hadlee 4–35) and 81 (R J Hadlee 7–23)

New Zealand 334 (M G Burgess 95, G M Turner 64, B E Congdon 52)

1975–76 Averages

Batting	I	No	Runs	HS	Avge	
S.M. Gavaskar (I)	5	1	266	116	66.60	
B.E. Congdon (NZ)	4	0	218	58	54.50	
G.M. Turner (NZ)	4	0	217	117	54.25	

Bowling	O	M	Runs	W	Avge	BB
R.J. Hadlee (NZ)	48.3	4	197	12	16.41	7–23
E.A.S. Prasanna (NZ)	71	13	223	11	20.27	8–76
R.O. Collinge (NZ)	68.6	5	228	10	22.80	6–63
B.S. Chandrasekhar (I)	89.7	12	294	11	26.72	6–94

1976–77: Indian spinners too good at home

The following season in India, Bedi batted at Bombay and India made 399 (Gavaskar 119). J.M. Parker made 104 out of 298 for New Zealand, and when India declared New Zealand wanted 304 in 290 minutes to win. They made only 141, Bedi, Chandra and Venkat bowling them out.

At Kanpur, India made 524 for nine declared, with 70 the highest score. Turner scored a century in reply and New Zealand reached 350. Viswanath made a quick second-innings century and India set a higher target than in the previous match: 383. The match proceeded the same way until at 134 for seven Lees and O'Sullivan came together and batted out 118 minutes for the draw.

Rain prevented play until the second morning in Madras. The match was a low-scoring version of the others, with New Zealand being set 359 and losing by 216. All but five of New Zealand's wickets in this series were taken by India's three spinners, Bedi leading the way with 22.

1976–77   6th Series   India 2, NZ 0, Drawn 1

1 BOMBAY   India won by 162 runs
India 399 (S M Gavaskar 119, S M H Kirmani 88, R J Hadlee 4–95) and 202–4 dec (B P Patel 82)
New Zealand 298 (J M Parker 104, G M Turner 65, B S Chandrasekhar 4–77) and 141 (B S Bedi 5–27)

2 KANPUR   Match Drawn
India 524–9 dec (M Amarnath 70, G R Viswanath 68, S M H Kirmani 64, S M Gavaskar 66, A V Mankad 50, B S Bedi 50) and 208–2 dec (G R Viswanath 103, A D Gaekwad 77)
New Zealand 350 (G M Turner 113, A D G Roberts 84, M G Burgess 54) and 193–7

3 MADRAS   India won by 216 runs
India 298 (G R Viswanath 87, S Venkataraghavan 64, B L Cairns 5–55) and 201–5 dec (M Amarnath 55)
New Zealand 140 (B S Bedi 5–48) and 143 (B S Bedi 4–22)

1976–77 Averages

Batting	I	No	Runs	HS	Avge	
G.R. Viswanath (I)	6	1	324	103*	64.80	
G.M. Turner (NZ)	6	0	261	113	43.50	
S.M. Gavaskar (I)	6	0	259	119	43.16	
M. Armanath (I)	6	0	229	70	38.16	
J.M. Parker (NZ)	6	0	209	104	34.83	

Bowling	O	M	Runs	W	Avge	BB
B.S. Bedi (I)	203.1	91	290	22	13.18	5–27
B.S. Chandrasekhar (I)	168.1	48	391	17	23.00	4–77
S. Venkataraghavan (I)	154	57	308	11	28.00	3–79
R.J. Hadlee (NZ)	127	18	437	13	33.61	4–95

1980–81: New Zealand at last win a series against India

Both countries played in Australia during the season, and met afterwards in New Zealand. G.P. Howarth and S.M. Gavaskar were the captains.

Gavaskar put New Zealand in at Wellington, where a new pitch was cut at right angles to the old. Howarth made 137 not out in a good total of 375. Cairns took five for 33 to obtain a lead of 152. Although New

Zealand made only 100 second time, India could not make the 253 needed and lost by 62.

Over two whole days were lost at Christchurch where Hadlee and Reid had put New Zealand on top in the little play possible.

Gavaskar batted at Auckland, where it needed a ninth-wicket stand of 105 to hoist the score to 238. Wright's century put New Zealand in command, but they found a fourth-innings target of 157 in four hours too much when drizzle interrupted play. They settled for the draw and their first series win against India.

A youthful Chandrasekhar clean bowled. A genuine No 11, in 80 Test innings he scored only 167 runs, average 4.07.

1980–81   7th Series   NZ 1, India 0, Drawn 2

1 WELLINGTON   New Zealand won by 62 runs
New Zealand 375 (G P Howarth 137) and 100 (Kapil Dev 4–34)
India 223 (S M Patil 64, B C Cairns 5–33) and 190 (R J Hadlee 4–65)

2 CHRISTCHURCH   Match Drawn
India 223 (S M Patil 64, B L Cairns 5–33) and 190 (R J Hadlee 4–65)
New Zealand 286–5 (J F Reid 123)

3 AUCKLAND   Match Drawn
India 238 (S M H Kirmani 78, J G Bracewell 4–61) and 284 (S M Patil 57, D B Vengsarkar 52, J G Bracewell 5–75)
New Zealand 366 (J G Wright 110, J F Reid 74, J V Coney 65, R J Shastri 5–125) and 95–5

1980–81 Averages

Batting	I	No	Runs	HS	Avge	
J.F. Reid (NZ)	5	1	250	123*	62.50	
J.G. Wright (NZ)	5	1	201	110	50.25	

Bowling	O	M	Runs	W	Avge	BB
B.L. Cairns (NZ)	134.2	61	203	13	15.61	5–33
R.J. Shastri (I)	147	51	277	15	18.46	5–125
R.J. Hadlee (NZ)	106.3	36	287	10	28.70	5–47

West Indies v New Zealand

1951–52: West Indies too strong on first visit

A strong West Indian side, led by J.D.C. Goddard, played two Tests in New Zealand after touring Australia in 1951–52. B. Sutcliffe captained New Zealand and batted first at Christchurch, where a ground-record 18,000 watched the second day. Nobody scored more than 71 in an innings, Ramadhin for West Indies and Burtt for New Zealand bowling well. New Zealand could set West Indies only 139 to make in the fourth innings, and the tourists won by five wickets.

West Indies, put in at Auckland, made 546 for six, with Stollmeyer, Worrell and Walcott making centuries. New Zealand made 160, but rain washed out the last day and saved them.

1951–52 1st Series WI 1, NZ 0
1 CHRISTCHURCH **West Indies won by 5 wkts**
New Zealand 236 (S Ramadhin 5–86) and 189 (S Ramadhin 4–39)
West Indies 287 (F M M Worrell 71, C L Walcott 65, S C Guillen 54, T B Burtt 5–69) and 142–5 (F M M Worrell 62)
2 AUCKLAND **Match Drawn**
West Indies 546–6 dec (C L Walcott 115, J B Stollmeyer 152, F M M Worrell 100, A F Rae 99, E de C Weekes 51)
New Zealand 160 (V J Scott 84) and 17–1

1955–56: New Zealand win first Test despite Weekes

West Indies, without Worrell and Walcott and led by D. St E. Atkinson, played four Tests while touring New Zealand in 1955–56. H.B. Cave captained New Zealand in the first Test, J.R. Reid taking over thereafter.

New Zealand were bamboozled by Ramadhin at Dunedin and out for 74, Ramadhin getting six for 74. Weekes made 123 out of 353 and West Indies won by an innings and 71.

1955–56 2nd Series WI 3, NZ 1
1 DUNEDIN **West Indies won by an innings and 71 runs**
New Zealand 74 (S Ramadhin 6–23) and 208 (J E F Beck 66)
West Indies 353 (E de C Weekes 123, O G Smith 64, R W Blair 4–90)
2 CHRISTCHURCH **West Indies won by an innings and 64 runs**
West Indies 386 (E de C Weekes 103, D St E Atkinson 85, J D C Goddard 83)
New Zealand 158 (S Ramdhin 5–46) and 164 (A L Valentine 5–32, O G Smith 4–75)
3 WELLINGTON **West Indies won by 9 wkts**
West Indies 404 (E de C Weekes 156, B H Pairaudeau 68, D St E Atkinson 60) and 13–1
New Zealand 208 (J E F Beck 55) and 208 (D D Taylor 77, D St E Atkinson 5–66)
4 AUCKLAND **New Zealand won by 190 runs**
New Zealand 255 (J R Reid 84, D T Dewdney 5–21) and 157–8 dec (D St E Atkinson 7–53)
West Indies 145 (H A Furlonge 64, H B Cave 4–22, A R MacGibbon 4–44)

1955–56 Averages

Batting	I	No	Runs	HS	Avge	
E. de C. Weekes (WI)	5	0	418	156	83.60	
J.R. Reid (NZ)	8	0	203	84	25.37	

Bowling	O	M	Runs	W	Avge	BB
D. St E. Atkinson (WI)	148.2	63	233	16	14.56	7–53
H.B. Cave (NZ)	103.4	48	186	12	15.50	4–21
S. Ramadhin (WI)	184.4	76	316	20	15.80	6–23
O.G. Smith (WI)	115.5	43	241	13	18.53	4–75
A.L. Valentine (WI)	201.4	99	283	15	18.86	5–32

West Indies batted at Christchurch and Weekes made 103, from 386. S.C. Guillen kept wicket for New Zealand, having played five matches for West Indies in Australia in 1951–52 and staying to settle in New Zealand. New Zealand were dismissed twice for 158 and 164 by spinners Ramadhin, Valentine and O.G. Smith for another innings defeat.

Weekes made 156 at Wellington from 404, but New Zealand improved, scoring 208 and 208 and losing by only nine wickets.

At Auckland, New Zealand made 255, Reid making 84, and D.T. Dewdney taking five for 21. MacGibbon (4–44) and Cave (4–22) bowled well for New Zealand to get West Indies out for 145. Atkinson fought back with seven for 53 in the second innings, but West Indies needed to get 268 to win. Cave took four more wickets as West Indies made only 77, and New Zealand won their first-ever Test match.

1968–69: Nurse plays two great innings in drawn series

After 13 years West Indies returned to New Zealand after touring Australia. Sobers was visiting captain, while Dowling led New Zealand. New Zealand began well at Auckland with B.R. Taylor getting a rapid 124 in 110 minutes to hoist his team to 323. After Carew (109) and Nurse (95) had added 172 for West Indies' second wicket, they collapsed for 276. Dowling declared at 297 for

Frank Worrell sweeping to leg. Worrell was the leading batsman in the first series between West Indies and New Zealand in 1951–52.

eight, setting West Indies 345 to win. They made them with a flourish, Nurse getting 168 and adding 174 in 142 minutes with Butcher (78).

At Wellington, Motz took six for 69 to get West Indies out for 297, but New Zealand trailed by 15 on first innings. West Indies then collapsed for 148 on a lively pitch, leaving New Zealand 164 to get. They won by six wickets, thanks to 62 not out from Hastings.

The Christchurch match was notable for a magnificent innings of 258 in his last Test by Nurse. Motz bravely took five for 113 in a total of 417. New Zealand followed on 200 behind, but Hastings made 117 not out and the match was saved with style.

1968–69 3rd Series WI 1, NZ 1, Drawn 1
1 AUCKLAND **West Indies won by 5 wkts**
New Zealand 323 (B R Taylor 124, B E Congdon 85) and 297–8 dec (G T Dowling 71, V Pollard 51)
West Indies 276 (M C Carew 109, S M Nurse 95) and 348–5 (S M Nurse 168, B F Butcher 78)
2 WELLINGTON **New Zealand won by 6 wkts**
West Indies 297 (J L Hendricks 54, B F Butcher 50, R C Motz 6–69) and 148 (B F Butcher 59)
New Zealand 282 (G M Turner 74, B E Congdon 52, R M Edwards 5–84) and 166–4 (B F Hastings 62)
3 CHRISTCHURCH **Match Drawn**
West Indies 417 (S M Nurse 258, M C Carew 91, R C Motz 5–113)
New Zealand 217 (D A J Holford 4–66) and 367–6 (B F Hastings 117, G T Dowling 76)

1968–69 Averages

Batting	I	No	Runs	HS	Avge	
S.M. Nurse (WI)	5	0	558	258	111.60	
B.R. Taylor (NZ)	5	2	209	124	69.66	
B.F. Hastings (NZ)	6	2	239	117*	59.75	
B.F. Butcher (WI)	5	1	216	78*	54.00	
M.C. Carew (WI)	5	0	256	109	51.20	
B.E. Congdon (NZ)	6	0	233	85	38.83	
G.T. Dowling (NZ)	6	0	232	76	36.66	

Bowling	O	M	Runs	W	Avge	BB
R.C. Motz (NZ)	89	11	381	17	22.41	6–69
R.M. Edwards (WI)	111.7	22	352	15	23.48	5–84

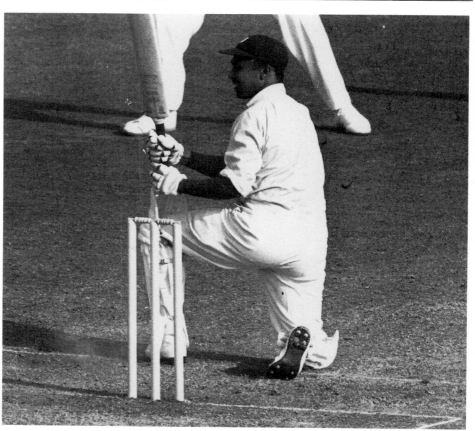

1971–72: Batsmen on top as New Zealand draw in West Indies

New Zealand were very much underdogs in their first tour of West Indies in 1971–72. Dowling and Sobers were still captains. At Kingston, Fredericks scored 163 and L.G. Rowe, in his first Test, 214. West Indies declared at 508 for four. Glenn Turner then made 223 not out and carried his bat in New Zealand's 386. It was the highest by a Test batsman carrying his bat through an innings. Rowe added to the records by getting 100 not out in the second innings: the first player to score a century in each innings on his debut and the highest scorer on his debut (314). New Zealand were set 341, and scored 236 for six to draw, Burgess making 101.

At Port-of-Spain, Congdon made 166 not out in New Zealand's 348, West Indies scoring seven fewer. Dowling declared at 288 for three but West Indies made no attempt to score 296 in 170 minutes.

B.R. Taylor was New Zealand's hero at Bridgetown, taking seven for 74 as West Indies crashed for 133. Congdon and Hastings then made centuries to hoist 422. West Indies saved the game, however, by compiling 564 for eight, Davis (183) and Sobers (142) adding 254 for the sixth wicket.

A.I. Kallicharran made his debut for West Indies at Georgetown and scored 100 not out in a total of 365 for seven declared. Turner then scored New Zealand's highest Test innings, 259, and he and Jarvis (182) put on a record 387 for the first wicket. The match was drawn. A peculiarity of New Zealand's six innings so far was that West Indies had used nine bowlers in four of them and eight in the other two – 17 different bowlers.

In the last Test at Port-of-Spain, Jumadeen made his debut and became West Indies' 17th bowler of the series. Kallicharran made 101 out of West Indies'

368, following Rowe as the second player to score centuries in his first two Test innings. Ali took five for 59 and New Zealand were 206 behind. Taylor's five for 41 removed West Indies for 194, but New Zealand needed 401 to win in 605 minutes. They drew at 253 for seven, Taylor and Wadsworth batting out the last 106 minutes. Throughout the series the batting was too strong for the bowling.

1971–72   4th Series   Drawn 5

1 KINGSTON   Match Drawn
West Indies 508–4 dec (L G Rowe 214, R C Fredericks 163) and 218–3 dec (L G Rowe 100)
New Zealand 386 (G M Turner 233, K J Wadsworth 78) and 236–6 (M G Burgess 101, D A J Holford 4–55)

2 PORT OF SPAIN   Match Drawn
New Zealand 348 (B E Congdon 166, R S Cunis 51, V A Holder 4–60) and 288–3 dec (G M Turner 95, B E Congdon 82, M G Burgess 62)
West Indies 341 (C A Davis 90, R C Fredericks 69, B R Taylor 4–41) and 121–5

3 BRIDGETOWN   Match Drawn
West Indies 133 (B R Taylor 7–74) and 564–8 (C A Davis 183, G St A Sobers 142, L G Rowe 51, D A J Holford 50)
New Zealand 422 (B E Congdon 126, B F Hastings 105, G St A Sobers 4–64)

4 GEORGETOWN   Match Drawn
West Indies 365–7 dec (A I Kallicharran 100, G A Greenidge 50) and 86–0
New Zealand 543–3 dec (G M Turner 259, T W Jarvis 182, B E Congdon 61)

5 PORT OF SPAIN   Match Drawn
West Indies 368 (A I Kallicharran 101, R C Fredericks 60) and 194 (Inshan Ali 5–41)
New Zealand 162 (Inshan Ali 5–59) and 253–7 (B E Congdon 58, G M Turner 50, V A Holder 4–41)

1971–72 Averages

Batting	I	No	Runs	HS	Avge
G.M. Turner (NZ)	8	1	672	259	96.00
B.E. Congdon (NZ)	8	2	531	166*	88.50
L.G. Rowe (WI)	7	1	419	214	69.83
C.A. Davis (WI)	9	2	466	183	58.25
R.C. Fredericks (WI)	10	1	487	163	54.11
T.W. Jarvis (NZ)	6	0	277	182	46.16
G. St. A. Sobers (WI)	8	1	253	142	36.14

Bowling	O	M	Runs	W	Avge	BB
B.R. Taylor (NZ)	172.2	39	478	27	17.70	7–74
V.A. Holder (WI)	153	52	285	12	23.75	4–41
B.E. Congdon (NZ)	200	49	446	13	34.30	3–56
H.J. Howarth (NZ)	338	100	703	14	50.21	3–70

1979–80: New Zealand victorious and West Indies bad-tempered

West Indies again toured New Zealand after winning in Australia in 1979–80. Lloyd and Howarth were captains.

At Dunedin, Hadlee (5–35) dismissed West Indies for 140, and New Zealand capitalized by getting a lead of 109. Only Haynes (105) held up Hadlee (6–68) and New Zealand in the second innings. He was top scorer and last man out in both innings – the only man to bat through two completed innings in a Test. Needing 104, New Zealand were reduced to 73 for eight and 100 for nine by West Indies' three fast bowlers, before scraping the winning run off a leg-bye. The West Indians behaved badly, Holding kicking over the stumps after one unsuccessful appeal, and only Haynes went to the post-match presentations.

There was more trouble at Christchurch. After Cairns had taken six for 85 to get West Indies out for 228, New Zealand scored 460, with Howarth and Hadlee making centuries. But after tea on the third day the West Indians refused to take the field, locking themselves in the dressing room, as a protest against an umpire. When they emerged 12 minutes late, some showed a lack of interest in fielding. On the fourth day, Croft showed dissent of a decision by barging the umpire on his next run-up. West Indies saved the match with three centuries.

When West Indies made 220 at Auckland, Edgar went a long way to ensuring the series for New Zealand by batting 432 minutes for 127, defying Garner (6–65). Troup took his match haul to ten wickets in the second innings and New Zealand easily earned the draw, which meant their first victory in a rubber at home and their first against West Indies.

Bruce Taylor at Trent Bridge in 1973.

1979–80 5th Series NZ 1, WI 0, Drawn 1

1 DUNEDIN New Zealand won by 1 wkt

West Indies 140 (D L Haynes 55, R J Hadlee 5–34) and 212 (D L
Haynes 105, R J Hadlee 6–68)

New Zealand 249 (B A Edgar 65, R J Hadlee 51, C E H Croft 4–
64) and 104–9 (J Garner 4–46)

2 CHRISTCHURCH Match Drawn

West Indies 228 (C G Greenidge 91, A I Kallicharran 75, B L
Cairns 6–85) and 447–5 (D L Haynes 122, L G Rowe 100, C L
King 100, C G Greenidge 97)

3 AUCKLAND Match Drawn

West Indies 220 (L G Rowe 50, G B Troup 4–71, R J Hadlee 4–
75) and 264–9 dec (C G Greenidge 74, G B Troup 6–95)

New Zealand 305 (B A Edgar 127, J Garner 6–56) and 73–4

1979–80 Averages

Batting	I	No	Runs	HS	Avge
B.A. Edgar (NZ)	5	1	241	127	60.25
D.L. Haynes (WI)	6	0	339	122	56.50
G.P. Howarth (NZ)	5	0	239	147	47.80
C.G. Greenidge (WI)	6	0	274	97	45.66

Bowling	O	M	Runs	W	Avge	BB
J. Garner (WI)	122.1	34	235	14	16.78	6–56
R.J. Hadlee (NZ)	161.3	50	361	19	19.00	6–68
G.P. Troup (NZ)	162.1	49	371	18	20.61	6–95
C.E.H. Croft (WI)	103	18	265	10	26.50	4–64
B.L. Cairns (NZ)	150	47	419	12	34.91	6–65

1984–85: West Indies get revenge in flurry of bouncers

Five years after their defeat, West Indies had the chance of revenge when Howarth took his side to the Caribbean, where Richards had taken over the captaincy of West Indies. Greenidge gave West Indies a good start with 100 out of 307 at Port-of-Spain. Rain meant New Zealand's reply of 262 lasted until the fourth day. West Indies' declaration at 261 for eight left New Zealand five hours to save the game, which they managed with alarms.

Richardson (187) and Martin Crowe (188) led their sides to scores of 511 for six declared and 440 respectively at Georgetown, and West Indies batted out the remaining time.

At Bridgetown, after rain delayed the start, New Zealand were put in on a green wicket, and were soon one for three. After they were out for 94, Richards scored 103 and West Indies reached 336. Amid spells of rain New Zealand just avoided an innings defeat, West Indies having to bat again for ten balls.

Howarth, needing to win the last Test at Kingston, put West Indies in. They made a solid 363. New Zealand then found themselves batting in a lively atmosphere after rain, and faced a barrage of bouncers from Marshall and Garner. Coney's arm was

broken in New Zealand's 138. In the follow-on Howarth (84) and Jeff Crowe (112) added 210 for the second wicket, but at 283 New Zealand set West Indies only 59, which were scored without loss. The West Indian manager justified the intimidatory bowling on the grounds that Hadlee began it when bowling to Garner.

Joel Garner (below) who was involved in the controversy about bouncers when playing for West Indies against New Zealand in 1984.

1984–85 6th Series WI 2, NZ 0, Drawn 2

1 PORT OF SPAIN Match Drawn

West Indies 307 (C G Greenidge 100, R B Richardson 78, I V A
Richards 57, E J Chatfield 4–51, R J Hadlee 4–82) and 261–8
dec (D L Haynes 78, I V A Richards 78, E J Chatfield 6–73)

New Zealand 262 (J J Crowe 64, M A Holding 4–79) and 187–6
(M D Marshall 4–65)

2 GEORGETOWN Match Drawn

West Indies 511–6 dec (R B Richardson 185, D L Haynes 90, P
J L Dujon 60, H A Gomes 53, A L Logie 52) and 268–6 dec
(C G Greenidge 69, R B Richardson 60)

New Zealand 440 (M D Crowe 188, J V Coney 73, I D S Smith
53, M D Marshall 4–110)

3 BRIDGETOWN West Indies won by 10 wkts

New Zealand 94 (M D Marshall 4–40) and 248 (J V Coney 83, J
G Wright 64, M D Marshall 7–80)

West Indies 336 (I V A Richards 105, M D Marshall 63, D L
Haynes 62) and 10–0

4 KINGSTON West Indies won by 10 wkts

West Indies 363 (D L Haynes 76, P J L Dujon 70, R J Hadlee 4–
53) and 59–0

New Zealand 138 (J G Wright 53, W W Davis 4–19) and 283 (J J
Crowe 112, G P Howarth 84, M D Marshall 4–66)

1984–85 Averages

Batting	I	No	Runs	HS	Avge
R.B. Richardson (WI)	6	0	378	185	63.00
I.V.A. Richards (WI)	6	1	310	105	62.00
D.L. Haynes (WI)	8	2	344	90	57.33
C.G. Greenidge (WI)	7	2	264	100	52.80
J.V. Coney (NZ)	6	1	241	83	48.20
J.J. Crowe (NZ)	7	0	252	112	36.00
M.D. Crowe (NZ)	7	0	216	188	30.85
J.G. Wright (NZ)	7	0	213	64	30.42

Bowling	O	M	Runs	W	Avge	BB
M.D. Marshall (WI)	170.1	30	486	27	18.00	7–80
W.W. Davis (WI)	63.3	11	188	10	18.80	4–19
R.J. Hadlee (NZ)	143	33	409	15	27.26	4–53
J. Garner (WI)	136.2	37	302	10	30.20	2–14
E.J. Chatfield (NZ)	152	36	441	13	33.92	6–73

1986–87: Honours shared in three-match series

West Indies returned to New Zealand in 1986–87. Richards put New Zealand (led by Coney) in at Wellington, and with Garner (5–51) the most successful of the four fast bowlers, New Zealand were out for 228. Greenidge (78) and Haynes (121) began with 150 and the tourists led by 117. A second-wicket partnership of 241 between Wright (138) and Martin Crowe (119) forced a draw.

A devastating 213 from Greenidge took West Indies to 418 for nine declared at Auckland, from which Hadlee salvaged six for 105. New Zealand collapsed against the pace bowlers to 157. In a rain-interrupted follow-on they batted with resolution, particularly Martin Crowe (104), and looked to have saved the game when bad light stopped play within the last 20 overs. But the players came back, the last two wickets fell and West Indies won by 10 wickets with 4.3 overs left.

After the first day had been lost to rain, Coney put West Indies in at Christchurch, and Hadlee (6–50) and Chatfield (4–30, bowling throughout the innings) put them out for 100, 25 of which came from the last wicket. The Crowe brothers, both dropped, then put on 156 for the third New Zealand wicket, and Coney declared at 332 for nine. On the fourth day most West Indian batsmen got a start, but wickets fell regularly, five to Snedden for 68, and at 264 New Zealand were set a target of only 33. They made a hard job of getting them, losing five men in the arc of slips and gully before winning by five wickets to level the series.

1986–87 7th Series NZ 1, WI 1, Drawn 1
1 WELLINGTON Match Drawn
New Zealand 228 (J G Wright 75, J Garner 5–51) and 386–5 dec (J G Wright 138, M D Crowe 119)
West Indies 345 (D L Haynes 121, C G Greenidge 78, E J Chatfield 4–102) and 50–2
2 AUCKLAND West Indies won by 10 wkts
West Indies 418–9 dec (C G Greenidge 213, P J L Dujon 77, R J Hadlee 6–105) and 16–0
New Zealand 157 (M D Marshall 4–43) and 273 (M D Crowe 104, C A Walsh 5–73)
3 CHRISTCHURCH New Zealand won by 5 wkts
West Indies 100 (R J Hadlee 6–50, E J Chatfield 4–30) and 264 (M C Snedden 5–68)
New Zealand 332–9 dec (M D Crowe 83, J G Bracewell 66, J J Crowe 55, J Garner 4–79) and 33–5

1986–87 Averages

Batting	I	No	Runs	HS	Avge	
C.G. Greenidge (WI)	6	1	344	213	68.80	
M.D. Crowe (NZ)	6	1	328	119	65.60	
J.G. Wright (NZ)	6	0	239	66	39.83	

Bowling	O	M	Runs	W	Avge	BB
J. Garner (WI)	77	16	205	12	17.08	5–51
R.J. Hadlee (NZ)	113.1	20	354	17	20.82	6–50
C.A. Walsh (WI)	120.2	28	306	13	23.53	5–73
E.J. Chatfield (NZ)	114.3	39	279	10	27.90	4–30

England v Sri Lanka

1981–82: England win Sri Lanka's first Test

Elected to full membership of the ICC in 1981, Sri Lanka played their first Test match against England at Colombo in 1981–82, England having just toured India. B. Warnapura was their first captain, and Fletcher led England. Underwood (5–28) was the most successful bowler as Sri Lanka were dismissed for 218. Their first 50 was scored by A. Ranatunga, who was only 18 years 78 days old. It needed 89 from Gower to give England a first-innings lead of five. Sri Lanka collapsed from 167 for three to 175 all out in their second knock, Emburey getting six for 33. England won by seven wickets.

1981–82 1st Series Eng 1, Sri Lanka 0
1 COLOMBO England won by 7 wkts
Sri Lanka 218 (R S Madugalle 65, A Ranatunge 54, D L Underwood 5–28) and 175 (R L Dias 77, J E Emburey 6–33)
England 223 (D I Gower 89, A L F de Mel 4–70) and 171–3 (C J Tavare 85)

1984: Sri Lanka get the best of a draw at Lord's

Sri Lanka played one Test in England in 1984, at Lord's. Put in by Gower, Sri Lanka made 491 for seven declared, with S. Wettimuny batting for 636 minutes, the longest Test innings at Lord's, to make 190, and the captain, L.R.D. Mendis, scoring a century in 144 minutes. Lamb made 107 for England, but at 370 they trailed by 121. S.A.R. Silva made 102 not out in the second innings, and Mendis 94, just failing to get a century in each innings. Botham took six of the seven wickets to fall before play ended in a draw.

1984 2nd Series Drawn 1
1 LORD'S Match Drawn
Sri Lanka 491–7 dec (S Wettimuny 190, L R D Mendis 111, A Ranatunga 84) and 294–7 dec (S A R Silva 102, L R Mendis 94, I T Botham 6–90)
England 370 (A J Lamb 107, B C Broad 86, D I Gower 55, V B John 4–98, A L F de Mel 4–110)

John Emburey in 1977.

Pakistan v Sri Lanka

1981–82: Sri Lanka do well until the first team return

Sri Lanka visited Pakistan for a three-Test series in 1981–82. Warnapura and Javed captained the sides.

In Sri Lanka's first Test overseas, at Karachi, Pakistan, lacking many of the side who toured Australia because of disputes over the captaincy, made 396, Haroon Rashid scoring 153. Sri Lanka batted right down the order to get 344. Salim Malik, making his debut, scored 100 not out in Pakistan's second innings 301 for four declared, and this proved too many for Sri Lanka, who were out for 149 and lost by 204.

At Faisalabad, where Mendis captained the tourists because Warnapura was injured, Wettimuny made 157 and, despite Qasim's six for 141, Sri Lanka reached 454. Pakistan, at one time 184 for eight, managed to reach 270. A Sri Lanka declaration at 154 for eight set Pakistan 339 in 330 minutes. Perhaps the declaration was too cautious, for with D.S. De Silva getting five for 59 Pakistan were hanging on at 186 for seven at the close.

Pakistan were back to full strength at Lahore, and Imran took eight for 58 after Sri Lanka were put in. R.L. Dias made a brave 109 out of 240. Pakistan declared at 500 for seven, with Mohsin and Zaheer getting centuries. Imran (6–58) did the necessary in the second innings to enable Pakistan to win by an innings and 102.

1981–82 1st Series   Pak 2, SL 0, Drawn 1
1 KARACHI   Pakistan won by 204 runs
Pakistan 396 (Haroon Rashid 153, Rashid Khan 59, Tahir Naggash 57, D S de Silva 4–102) and 301–4 dec (Salim Malik 100 not out, Javed Miandad 92, Iqbal Qasim 56)
Sri Lanka 344 (S Wettimuny 71, L R D Mendis 54, R L Dias 53) and 149 (Iqbal Qasim 4–27)
2 FAISALABAD   Match Drawn
Sri Lanka 454 (S Wettimuny 157, R L Dias 98, R S Madugalle 91, Iqbal Qasim 6–141) and 154–8 dec (H M Goonatillake 56)
Pakistan 270 (Ashraf Ali 58, D S de Silva 4–103) and 186–7 (Mohsin Khan 74, D S de Silva 5–59)
3 LAHORE   Pakistan won by an innings and 102 runs
Sri Lanka 240 (R L Dias 109, Imran Khan 8–58) and 158 (Imran Khan 6–58, Tauseef Ahmed 4–58)
Pakistan 500–7 dec (Zaheer Abbas 134, Mohsin Khan 129, Majid Khan 63)

Pakistan v Sri Lanka
1981–82 Averages

Batting	I	No	Runs	HS	Avge
Mohsin Khan (P)	3	0	215	129	71.66
S. Wettimuny (SL)	6	0	316	157	52.66
R.L. Dias (SL)	6	0	295	109	49.16

Bowling	O	M	Runs	W	Avge	BB
Imran Khan (P)	52.2	11	116	14	7.28	8–58
Iqbal Qasim (P)	151.1	46	329	15	21.93	6–141
Tauseef Ahmed (P)	96.4	22	264	11	24.00	4–58
D.S. De Silva (SL)	153	20	492	17	28.94	5–59
A.L.F. De Mel (SL)	119.2	14	488	11	44.36	3–120

1985–86: Pakistan win series 2–0 in Pakistan

After beating India in 1985–86, Hendis led the team to Pakistan, where the first Test, at Faisalabad, was played on a dead wicket. Sri Lanka made 479, P.A. de Silva top-scoring with 122, whereupon Qasim Omar and Javed Miandad, coming together at 158 for two, made the eighth-highest Test wicket partnership by adding 397, both passing

200. When Qasim Omar was out, the captains decided enough was enough.

At Sialkot, a new Test venue, Sri Lanka made only 157, and Pakistan 259, J.R. Ratnayake eight wickets for 83, a best for Sri Lanka in Tests. However, Imran Khan (5–40) took his match haul to nine as Sri Lanka were dismissed for 200, leaving Pakistan only 99 to win, which they scored easily.

The third Test was at Karachi, where Sri Lanka, batting first for the third time, were dismissed for only 162, spinner Abdul Qadir this time getting most wickets with five for 44. De Mel took the first six for Sri Lanka, but Pakistan took a lead of 133. In Sri Lanka's second knock only P.A. de Silva offered much resistance, his 105 winning him the man of the match award for the second time in the series. But Pakistan required only 98 to win and won by ten wickets. They used three captains, Javed fracturing a thumb, then Imran straining a thigh, so Mudassar was at the helm at the finish.

1985–86 2nd Series   Pak 2, Sri Lanka 0, Drawn 1
1 FAISALABAD   Match Drawn
Sri Lanka 479 (P A de Silva 122, A Ranatunga 79, R J Ratnayake 56, S Wettimuny 52)
Pakistan 555–3 (Qasim Omar 206, Javed Miandad 203, Mudassar Nazar 78)
2 SIALKOT   Pakistan won by 8 wkts
Sri Lanka 157 (Imran Khan 4–55) and 200 (R S Madugalle 65, Imran Khan 5–40)
Pakistan 259 (Mudassar Nazar 78, Mohsin Khan 50, J R Ratnayake 8–83) and 100–2
3 KARACHI   Pakistan won by 10 wkts
Sri Lanka 162 (Abdul Qadir 5–44) and 230 (P A de Silva 105, Tauseef Ahmed 5–54)
Pakistan 295 (Imran Khan 63, Javed Miandad 63, Rameez Raja 52, A L F de Mel 6–109) and 98–0

1985–86 Averages

Batting	I	No	Runs	HS	Avge
Javed Miandad (P)	3	1	306	203*	153.00
Mudassar Nazar (P)	5	2	253	78	84.33
Qasim Omar (P)	4	0	218	206	54.50
P.A. Silva (SL)	5	0	250	122	50.00

Bowling	O	M	Runs	W	Avge	BB
Imran Khan (P)	120.4	37	271	17	15.94	5–40
J.R. Ratnayeke (SL)	81.5	14	297	10	29.70	8–83

1985–86: Sri Lanka draw in return series

After the three-match series in Pakistan, the two teams returned to Sri Lanka for another. Imran led the tourists, Javed having resigned. At Kandy, Sri Lanka were rushed out in 42.4 overs for 109, and, facing a deficit of 121, were beaten by an innings when dismissed in 43 overs for 101 second time. Tauseef Ahmed took nine wickets in the match. When Ranatunga was given not out in the second innings, he was abused by the Pakistanis who considered he had been caught at short leg and left the field with Dias and the umpires. Play was held up for 30 minutes while tempers cooled.

At Colombo it was Pakistan's turn to be dismissed cheaply after they had been put in by Sri Lanka. A.K. Kuruppurachchi, making his debut, took 5 for 44 as Pakistan reached only 132. Sri Lanka made 273 and needed only 32 after removing Pakistan again for 172, this time Ratnayake taking five wickets. Sri Lanka won by eight wickets. The Pakistan team, led by some histrionics from Javed, complained about the umpires and the crowds and wanted to call off the rest of the tour.

In the third Test at Colombo, Pakistan dismissed Sri Lanka for 281 and, led by a Rameez Raja century, took a lead of 37. With Pakistan pressing for a win, rain, plus Gurusinghe and Ranatunga, who came together at 83 for 3 and were undefeated with centuries each at the close, at 323, saved the draw and the series.

1985–86 3rd Series   Sri Lanka 1, Pak 1, Drawn 1
1 KANDY   Pakistan won by an innings and 20 runs
Sri Lanka 109 and 101 (Tauseef Ahmed 6–45)
Pakistan 230 (Mudassar Nazar 81, Salim Malik 54)
2 COLOMBO   Sri Lanka won by 8 wkts
Pakistan 132 (A K Kuruppuarachchi 5–44) and 172 (Qasim Omar 52, J R Ratnayeke 5–37)
Sri Lanka 273 (A Ranatunga 77, Wasim Akram 4–57) and 32–2
3 COLOMBO   Match Drawn
Sri Lanka 281 (L R D Mendis 58, A Ranatunga 53, Imran Khan 4–69) and 323–3 (A Ranatunga 135, A P Gurusinghe 116)
Pakistan 318 (Rameez Raja 122, J R Ratnayeke 4–116)

1985–86 Averages

Batting	I	No	Runs	HS	Avge
A. Ranatunga (SL)	5	1	316	135*	79.00

Bowling	O	M	Runs	W	Avge	BB
Imran Khan (P)	116	27	270	15	18.00	4–69
J.R. Ratnayeke (SL)	74.4	14	208	11	18.90	5–37
A.L.F. De Mel (SL)	76.2	15	259	10	25.90	3–39

Australia v Sri Lanka

1982–83: Australia batsmen too strong for Sri Lanka

Australia's first Test match with Sri Lanka was at Kandy in 1982–83. G.S. Chappell and L.R.D. Mendis were the captains.

Australia batted first and most batsmen made runs, Wessels and Hookes scoring centuries, allowing a declaration at 514 for four. Lillee and Hogg reduced Sri Lanka to nine for three, whereupon Yardley (5–88) spun the rest out for 271. Ranatunga made 90 and Mendis 74. Sri Lanka followed on and although Wettimuny made 96, Hogan (5–66) worked his way through the side and Australia won by an innings and 38.

1982–83 1st Series   Aus 1, SL 0
1 KANDY   Australia won by an innings and 38 runs
Australia 514–4 dec (D W Hookes 143, K C Wessels 141, G N Yallop 98, G S Chappell 66)
Sri Lanka 271 (A Ranatunga 90, L R D Mendis 74, B Yardley 5–88) and 205 (S Wettimuny 96, T G Hogan 5–66)

New Zealand v Sri Lanka

1982–83: Defeat for Sri Lanka in first series with New Zealand

Sri Lanka visited New Zealand and Australia in 1982–83. Their side was comparatively weak, owing to 14 players having been banned for 25 years for touring South Africa, and to injuries to three of the key players remaining. D.S. De Silva captained the tourists, and G.P. Howarth captained New Zealand.

At Christchurch, De Silva put New Zealand in, and the tourists were doing well at 171 for seven, but New Zealand recovered to 344. The brothers M. de S. and S. Wettimuny opened for Sri Lanka but the side were out for 144, 200 behind, and following on made 175. Cairns took eight wickets in the match.

Put in at Wellington, Sri Lanka did better, making 240 and dismissing New Zealand for 201 (V.B. John 5–60). However, New Zealand's pace bowlers allowed Sri Lanka only 93 in the second innings and New Zealand won by six wickets.

1982–83   1st Series   NZ 2, SL 0
1 CHRISTCHURCH   **New Zealand won by an innings and 25 runs**
New Zealand 344 (W K Lees 89, J V Coney 84)
Sri Lanka 144 (S Wettimuny 63, R J Hadlee 4–33, B L Cairns 4–49) and 175 (D S de Silva 52, B L Cairns 4–47)
2 WELLINGTON   **New Zealand won by 6 wkts**
Sri Lanka 240 (R S Madugalle 79, D S de Silva 61, E J Chatfield 4–66) and 93 (R J Hadlee 4–34)
New Zealand 201 (V B John 4–60, R J Ratnayake 4–81) and 134–4

1983–84: Slow play and unhappy crowds as New Zealand win series in Sri Lanka

New Zealand, led by Howarth, toured Sri Lanka in 1983–84, playing three Tests against a side led by Mendis.

New Zealand batsmen tended to get out when set at Kandy after rain had put off the start to the second afternoon. The tourists totalled 276 (John 5–86). Sri Lanka could make only 215 however, and New Zealand's second-innings declaration set them 262 to win. Hadlee (4–8) and Boock (5–28) got them out for 97. Riot police were needed at the end to protect the team from demonstrators.

At Colombo, with police guarding the players, Howarth put Sri Lanka in, and they made only 174. J.R. Ratnayeke took five for 42 to restrict New Zealand to a lead of 24. A century from Dias allowed Sri Lanka to declare and set New Zealand a target of 266 in 350 minutes. With players injured or ill, New Zealand made no attempt, scoring 123 for four, of which a mere 117 came in the last full day's play. The crowd now directed their booing at New Zealand.

In the last Test at Colombo, Sri Lanka made 256, Hadlee and Chatfield taking five wickets each. Reid made 180 which helped New Zealand to a total of 459. Five more wickets for Hadlee for only 29 had Sri Lanka out again for 142, and New Zealand scored their first innings victory abroad.

1983–84   2nd Series   NZ 2, SL 0, Drawn 1
1 KANDY   **New Zealand won by 165 runs**
New Zealand 276 (G P Howarth 62, V B John 5–86) and 201–8 dec (G P Howarth 60)
Sri Lanka 215 (R J Hadlee 4–35) and 97 (A Ranatunga 51, S L Boock 5–28, R J Hadlee 4–8)
2 COLOMBO   **Match Drawn**
Sri Lanka 174 (B L Cairns 4–47) and 289 (R L Dias 108, S Wettimuny 65, E J Chatfield 4–78)
New Zealand 198 (J J Crowe 50, J R Ratnayake 5–42) and 123–4
3 COLOMBO   **New Zealand won by an innings and 61 runs**
Sri Lanka 256 (R S Madugalle 89, E J Chatfield 5–63, R J Hadlee 5–73) and 142 (A Ranatunga 50, R J Hadlee 5–29)
New Zealand 459 (J F Reid 180, J V Coney 92)

1983–84 Averages

Batting	I	No	Runs	HS	Avge	
R.S. Madugalle (SL)	6	2	242	89*	60.50	
J.F. Reid (NZ)	5	0	243	180	48.60	
Bowling	O	M	Runs	W	Avge	BB
R.J. Hadlee (NZ)	117.5	48	230	23	10.00	5–29
E.J. Chatfield (NZ)	80	23	203	10	20.30	5–63
V.B. John (SL)	129	28	373	16	23.31	5–86
S.L. Boock (NZ)	121.3	40	257	11	23.36	5–28

Above: Sidath Wettimuny of Sri Lanka.

1986–87: Terrorist bomb ends tour early

New Zealand, led by Jeff Crowe, were in Sri Lanka again in 1986–87.

Sri Lanka, put in at Colombo, saw a remarkable debut by their wicket-keeper and opener, D.S.B.P. Kuruppu, who scored 201 not out from a total of 397 for nine declared. It was Sri Lanka's first Test double-century and at 778 minutes the slowest in Tests. With bad light interrupting play, New Zealand were content to play for a draw, which they achieved at 406 for five, J.J. Crowe being not out 120 and Hadlee not out 151.

A terrorist bomb on the final day, which killed 100 in the city, led to the remainder of the tour being cancelled.

1986–87   3rd Series   Drawn 1
1 COLOMBO
Sri Lanka 397–9 dec (D S B P Kuruppu 201, R S Madugalle 60, R J Hadlee 4–102)
New Zealand 406–5 (R J Hadlee 151, J J Crowe 120)

Below: Ravi Ratnayeke bowling for Sri Lanka.

India v Sri Lanka

1982–83: Sri Lanka's first Test in India ends evenly poised

Sri Lanka won the toss at Madras and batted in the first series between the two countries. The two number one batsmen, Gavaskar and Warnapura, were the captains.

Mendis made 105 in the first-innings 346, Doshi getting five for 85. India, with Gavaskar and Patil making centuries, scored 566 for six declared. Mendis completed a century in each innings with another 105 when Sri Lanka batted again, becoming the first Sri Lankan to perform this feat. At 394 all out, India were set 175 to win in 53 minutes plus 20 overs, but De Mel (5–68) struck quick blows and India ended happy to draw at 135 for seven.

1982–83 1st Series Drawn 1
1 MADRAS
Sri Lanka 346 (L R D Mendis 105, R L Dias 60, D R Doshi 5–85) and 394 (L R D Mendis 105, R L Dias 97, A N Ranasinghe 77, Kapil Dev 5–110)
India 566–6 dec (S M Gavaskar 155, D B Vengsarkar 90, S M Patil 114, Arun Lal 63) and 135–7 (A L F de Mel 5–68)

1985–86: Sri Lanka deservedly win first Test series

India toured Sri Lanka in 1985–86 under Kapil Dev, who won the toss in the first Test at Colombo and batted. With Gavaskar batting at No 5 and top-scoring with 51, India were all out for 218, A.L.F. de Mel taking five for 64. Madugalle and Ranatunga each made centuries for Sri Lanka, who took a lead of 129. R.J. Ratnayake then took six for 86, and Sri Lanka were deprived of their first-ever Test victory only by Vengsarkar, who concentrated for 406 minutes for 98 not out, and rain, which robbed Sri Lanka of two hours. The final task of 123 runs in 11 overs was too much.

In the second Test Sri Lanka were again on top from the first day, which they ended at 168 for one. A.R. Silva's century headed their batting, and the team scored 385, Chetan Sharma being the leading bowler with five for 118. Gavaskar and Amarnath, batting Nos 6 and 7, were needed to save the prospect of a follow-on, after India were three for three. Even so, Sri Lanka, batting well in the second innings again, were able to declare and set India 348 to win in plenty of time. Ratnayake took five for 49 (nine in the match) and India were out in the first of the final 20 overs, a flurry of 78 from Kapil Dev at No 8 being India's last defiance. It was Sri Lanka's first Test victory in their 14th Test, less than five years after their first.

At Kandy, India tried hard to save the series, and thanks to Amarnath's second-innings century they set Sri Lanka 377 to win, with 420 minutes plus 20 overs possible for a result. But from 34 for three, R.L. Dias and the captain L.R.D. Mendis added 216, watched by a last-day crowd of 20,000. When bad light ended play seven overs early, Sri Lanka still had three wickets left and had won their first-ever Test series.

1985–86 2nd Series Sri Lanka 1, India 0, Drawn 2
1 COLOMBO Match Drawn
India 218 (S M Gavaskar 51, A L F de Mel 5–64) and 251 (D B Vengsarkar 98, L Rajput 61, R J Ratnayake 6–85)
Sri Lanka 347 (A Ranatunga 111, R S Madugalle 103, L R D Mendis 51) and 61–4
2 COLOMBO Sri Lanka won by 149 runs
Sri Lanka 358 (A R Silva 111, R L Dias 95, R S Madugalle 54, L R D Mendis 51, Chetan Sharma 5–118) and 206–3 dec (P A de Silva 75, R L Dias 60)
India 244 (K Srikkanth 64, M B Amarnath 60, S M Gavaskar 52, R J Ratnayake 4–76) and 198 (Kapil Dev 78, R J Ratnayake 5–95)
3 KANDY Match drawn
India 249 (D B Vengsarkar 62, S Ahangama 5–52) and 325–5 dec (M B Amarnath 116, R J Shastri 81)
Sri Lanka 198 (L R D Mendis 53, Maninder Singh 4–31) and 307–7 dec (L R D Mendis 124, R L Dias 106)

1985–86 Averages

Batting	I	No	Runs	HS	Avge
M. Armanath (I)	4	1	216	116*	72.00
L.R.D. Mendis (SL)	6	1	310	124	62.00
R.L. Dias (SL)	6	1	273	106	54.60

Bowling	O	M	Runs	W	Avge	BB
F.S. Ahangama (SL)	162.5	35	459	20	22.95	6–85
C. Sharma (I)	109	12	383	14	27.35	4–118
Kapil Dev (I)	129.4	30	372	11	33.81	3–74
A.L.F. De Mel (SL)	150.3	30	438	12	36.50	5–64

1986–87: India win three-match series 2–0

Sri Lanka played three Tests in India in 1986–87. Mendis led the side and Kapil Dev captained India.

At Kanpur, after an opening stand of 159, Sri Lanka batted down the order to get 420. But India easily passed this and by the close had made their highest Test total of 676 for seven declared. Gavaskar made 176, Azharuddin 199 and Kapil Dev 163. The second day was washed out, preventing hope of a result in a high-scoring game.

The second Test at Nagpur was dominated by India's spinners. Sri Lanka made 204 (Yadav 5–76), to which India replied with 451 for six declared, Amarnath and Vengsarkar making centuries. Sri Lanka were then removed for 141, Maninder Singh taking seven for 51, and completing ten wickets in the match.

At Cuttack, on a new Test venue, the match started a day late when local police were doubtful of the crowd control capabilities. Vengsarkar led the way for India with 166 from a total of 400 (J.R. Ratnayeke 5–85). Sri Lanka were then dismissed twice for 191 and 142, most of the bowlers sharing the wickets, Kapil Dev registering his 300th in Tests.

1986–87 3rd Series India 2, Sri Lanka 0, Drawn 1
1 KANPUR Match Drawn
Sri Lanka 420 (J R Ratnayeke 93, S Wettimuny 79, A Ranatunga 52, R L Dias 50)
India 676–7 (M Azharuddin 199, S M Gavaskar 176, Kapil Dev 163, D B Vengsarkar 57, J R Ratnayeke 4–132)
2 NAGPUR India won by an innings and 106 runs
Sri Lanka 204 (A Ranatunga 59, N S Yadav 5–76) and 141 (J R Ratnayeke 54, Maninder Singh 7–51)
India 451–6 dec (D B Vengsarkar 153, M B Amarnath 131, S M Gavaskar 74, R Lamba 53)
3 CUTTACK India won by an innings and 67 runs
India 400 (D B Vengsarkar 166, Kapil Dev 60, J R Ratnayeke 5–85)
Sri Lanka 191 (Maninder Singh 4–41, Kapil Dev 4–69) and 142 (R J Shastri 4–11)

Batting	I	No	Runs	HS	Avge
D.B. Vengsarkar (I)	3	0	376	166	125.33
Kapil Dev (I)	3	1	234	163	117.00
S.M. Gavaskar (I)	3	0	255	176	85.00
J.R. Ratnayeke (SL)	5	0	206	93	41.20

Bowling	O	M	Runs	W	Avge	BB
N.S. Jadav (I)	61.1	19	150	11	13.63	5–75
Maminder Singh (I)	103.5	33	279	18	15.50	7–51

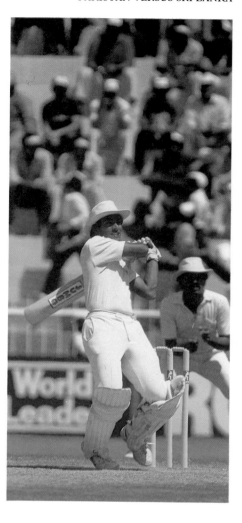

Two of Stri Lanka's most consistent strikers were Ranjan Madugalle (above) and P.A. de Silva (below).

HIGHEST AGGREGATE RUNS

	M	I	NO	Runs	HS	100s	Av
S. M. Gavaskar	125	214	16	10,122	236	34	51.12
G. Boycott	108	193	23	8,114	246	22	47.72
G. St. A. Sobers	93	160	21	8,032	365	26	57.78
M. C. Cowdrey	114	188	15	7,624	182	22	44.06
C. H. Lloyd	110	175	14	7,515	242	19	46.67
W. R. Hammond	85	140	16	7,249	336	22	58.45
G. S. Chappell	87	151	19	7,110	247	24	53.86
D. G. Bradman	52	80	10	6,996	334	29	99.94
L. Hutton	79	138	15	6,971	364	19	56.67
A. R. Border	89	157	26	6,924	196	21	52.85
K. F. Barrington	82	131	15	6,806	256	20	58.67
D. I. Gower	96	164	12	6,789	215	14	44.66
I. V. A. Richards	88	131	8	6,472	291	20	52.61
Javed Miandad	86	133	18	6,251	280	15	54.35
R. B. Kanhai	79	137	6	6,227	256	15	47.53
R. N. Harvey	79	137	10	6,149	205	21	48.41
G. R. Viswanath	91	155	10	6,080	222	14	41.93

Previous pages: A record-breaking Test wicket. Neil Hawke looks round to see Colin Cowdrey catch him in the slips in the fifth Test at the Oval in 1964. It was Fred Trueman's 300th Test wicket.

Below: Walter Hammond leading his team out at Trent Bridge against Australia in 1938. The wicket-keeper is Leslie Ames. Kenneth Farnes and Hedley Verity, following, both lost their lives in the war which followed.

Right: David Gower drives on his way to 136 in the second Australia v England Test at Perth in 1986–87. Tim Zoehrer is the wicket-keeper.

Above: Colin Cowdrey at Trent Bridge in 1964 hooking a boundary. Until passed by Gavaskar, Cowdrey's 114 Test appearances was a record.

HIGHEST TEAM TOTALS

903–7	England v Australia, the Oval, 1938
849	England v West Indies, Kingston, 1929–30
790–3 dec	West Indies v Pakistan, Kingston, 1957–58
758–8 dec	Australia v West Indies, Kingston, 1954–55
729–6 dec	Australia v England, Lord's, 1930
708	Pakistan v England, the Oval, 1987
701	Australia v England, the Oval, 1934
695	Australia v England, the Oval, 1930
687–8 dec	West Indies v England, the Oval, 1976
681–8 dec	West Indies v England, Port of Spain, 1953–54
674–6	Pakistan India, Faisalabad, 1984–85
674	Australia v India, Adelaide, 1947–48

Highest totals for other countries

644–7 dec	India v West Indies, Kanpur, 1978–79
622–9 dec	South Africa v Australia, Durban, 1969–70
553–7 dec	New Zealand v Australia, Brisbane, 1985–86
491–7 dec	Sri Lanka v England, Lord's, 1984

HIGHEST BATTING AVERAGES
Minimum 20 innings

	M	I	NO	Runs	HS	100s	Av
D. G. Bradman	52	80	10	6,996	334	29	99.94
R. G. Pollock	23	41	4	2,256	274	7	60.97
G. A. Headley	22	40	4	2,190	270	10	60.83
H. Sutcliffe	54	84	9	4,555	194	16	60.73
E. Paynter	20	31	5	1,540	243	4	59.23
K. F. Barrington	82	131	15	6,806	256	20	58.67
E. de C. Weekes	48	81	5	4,455	207	15	58.61
W. R. Hammond	85	140	16	7,249	336	22	58.45
G. St. A. Sobers	93	160	21	8,032	365	26	57.78
J. B. Hobbs	61	102	7	5,410	211	15	56.94
C. L. Walcott	44	74	7	3,798	220	15	56.68
L. Hutton	79	138	15	6,971	364	19	56.67
G. E. Tyldesley	14	20	2	990	122	3	55.00
Javed Miandad	86	133	18	6,251	280	15	54.35
C. A. Davis	15	29	5	1,301	183	4	54.20
A. R.Border	89	157	26	6,924	196	21	52.85
I. V. A. Richards	88	131	8	6,472	291	20	52.61

Above: The fifth Test at the Oval in 1938, where a large crowd saw Hutton make his record score of 364. Hutton batted over three days, his innings in all taking 13 hours and 17 minutes. England's total of 903 for seven declared remains a Test record.

Below left: Sir Jack Hobbs on his 75th birthday showing the photographer some of his trophies. Hobb's aggregate of Test runs was at the time a record.

Below: Len Hutton, another great England opener who was subsequently knighted.

HIGHEST INDIVIDUAL INNINGS

365   G. St. A. Sobers, West Indies v Pakistan, Kingston, 1957–58
364   L Hutton, England v Australia, the Oval, 1938
337   Hanif Mohammad, Pakistan v West Indies, Bridgetown, 1957–58
336   W. R. Hammond, England v New Zealand, Auckland, 1932–33
334   D. G. Bradman, Australia v England, Headingley, 1930
325   A. Sandham, England v West Indies, Kingston, 1929–30
311   R. B. Simpson, Australia v England, Old Trafford, 1964
310   J. H. Edrich, England v New Zealand, Headingley, 1965
307   R. M. Cowper, Australia v England, Melbourne, 1965–66
304   D. G. Bradman, Australia v England, Headingley, 1934
302   L. G. Rowe, West Indies v England, Bridgetown, 1973–74

Highest for other countries
274   R. G. Pollock, South Africa v Australia, Durban, 1969–70
259   G. M. Turner, New Zealand v West Indies, Georgetown, 1971–72
236   S. M. Gavaskar, India v West Indies, Madras, 1983–84
201   D. S. B. P. Kuruppi, Sri Lanka v New Zealand, Colombo 1986–87

Top: Sir Don Bradman with the Duke of Norfolk at the match between the Prime Minister's XI and the MCC at Canberra in 1962–63, when the Duke was manager of the touring party. Bradman, of course, had long since retired.

Above: Bradman's return to England after the Second World War was very much a question of carrying on where he had left off, by making a century in the first match at Worcester. Here he guides a ball through the slips.

Left: Bradman tossing up at Worcester on his last visit to England before the Second World War, in 1938. The Worcestershire captain is the Hon C.J. Lyttelton.

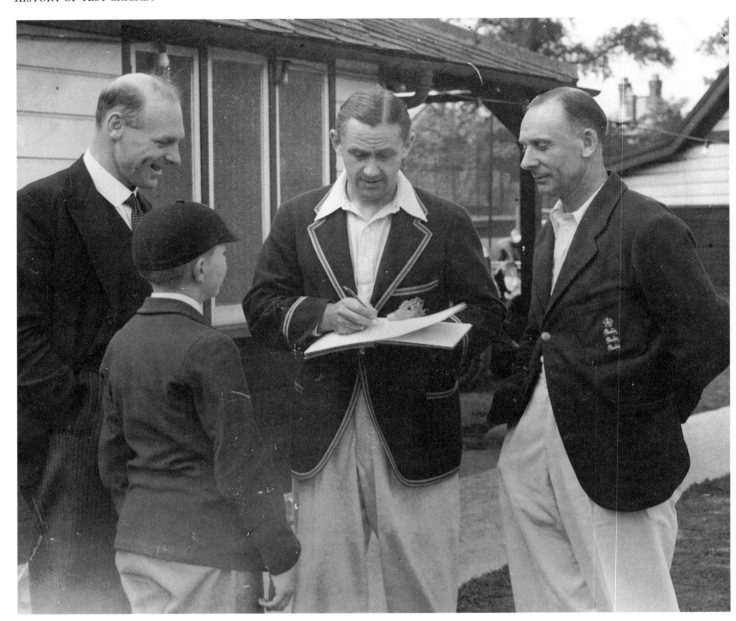

HIGHEST WICKET PARTNERSHIPS

1st 413 V. Mankad (231) and P. Roy (173), India v New Zealand, Madras, 1955–56

2nd 451 W. H. Ponsford (266) and D. G. Bradman (244), Australia v England, the Oval, 1934

3rd 451 Mudassar Nazar (231) and Javed Miandad (280), Pakistan v India, Hyderabad, 1982–83

4th 411 P. B. H. May (285) and M. C. Cowdrey (154), England v West Indies, Edgbaston, 1957

5th 405 S. G. Barnes (234) and D. G. Bradman (234), Australia v England, Sydney, 1946–47

6th 346 J. H. W. Fingleton (136) and D. G. Bradman (1270), Australia v England, Melbourne, 1936–37

7th 347 D. St. E. Atkinson (219) and C. C. Depeiza (122), West Indies v Australia, Bridgetown, 1954–55

8th 246 L. E. G. Ames (137) and G. O. Allen (122), England v New Zealand, Lord's, 1931

9th 190 Asif Iqbal (146) and Intikhab Alam (51), Pakistan v England, the Oval, 1967

10th 151 B. F. Hastings (110) and R. O. Collinge (68), New Zealand v Pakistan, Auckland, 1972–73

LOWEST TEAM TOTALS

26 New Zealand v England, Auckland, 1954–55
30 South Africa v England, Port Elizabeth, 1895–96
30 South Africa v England, Edgbaston, 1924
35 South Africa v England, Cape Town, 1898–99
36 Australia v England, Edgbaston, 1902
36 South Africa v Australia, Melbourne 1931–32
42 Australia v England, Sydney, 1887–88
42 New Zealand v Australia, Wellington, 1945–46
42 India v England, Lord's, 1974
43 South Africa v England, Cape Town, 1888–89
44 Australia v England, the Oval, 1896
45 England v Australia, Sydney, 1886–87
45 South Africa v Australia, Melbourne, 1931–32

Lowest totals for other countries

62 Pakistan v Australia, Perth, 1981–82
76 West Indies v Pakistan, Dacca, 1958–59
93 Sri Lanka v New Zealand, Wellington, 1982–83

Above: Famous Test players at a match at Woodford Wells in 1937. G.O.B. Allen, now Sir 'Gubby' Allen, a captain of England, signs autographs watched by Jack Hobbs, later Sir Jack. On the left is the famous rugby footballer, W.W. Wakefield.

Above right: Peter May on-driving at the Edgbaston Test match against West Indies in 1957. It was in this match that May and Cowdrey added on a world record 411 for the fourth wicket. May made 285 not out.

Right: Colin Cowdrey playing an almost identical shot in the same match. Cowdrey made 154. Neither picture is from the big stand, but from the first innings. May is batting with Insole, and Cowdrey with Evans.

MOST CENTURIES

Total	Player	Against							
		E	A	SA	WI	NZ	I	P	SL
34	S. M. Gavaskar (India)	4	5	—	13	2	—	5	1
29	D. G. Bradman (Australia)	19	—	4	2	0	4	—	—
26	G. St. A. Sobers (West Indies)	10	4	0	—	1	8	3	—
24	G. S. Chappell (Australia)	9	—	0	5	3	1	6	0
22	W. R. Hammond (England)	—	9	6	1	4	2	—	—
22	M. C. Cowdrey (England)	—	5	3	6	2	3	3	—
22	G. Boycott (England)	—	7	1	5	2	4	3	0
21	R. N. Harvey (Australia)	6	—	8	3	0	4	0	—
20	K. F. Barrington (England)	—	5	2	3	3	3	4	—

A dash indicates the batsman did not play against that country.

Below: Sunny Gavaskar does not worry about split flannels when he has the scent of runs in his nostrils. This square drive was in the first Test at Old Trafford in 1974 when he made 101, one of the centuries which make him the leading century-maker in Test cricket.

MOST RUNS IN A SERIES

	M	I	NO	Runs	HS	100s	Av
D. G. Bradman, Aus v Eng 1930	5	7	0	974	334	4	139.14
W. R. Hammond, Eng v Aus 1928–29	5	9	1	905	251	4	113.12
R. N. Harvey, Aus v Eng 1952–53	5	9	0	834	205	4	92.66
I. V. A. Richards, WI v Eng 1976	4	7	0	829	291	3	118.42
C. L. Walcott, WI v Aus 1954–55	5	10	0	827	155	5	82.70
G. St. A. Sobers, WI v Pak 1957–58	5	8	2	824	365	3	137.33
D. G. Bradman, Aus v Eng 1936–37	5	9	0	810	270	3	90.00
D. G. Bradman, Aus v SA 1931–32	5	5	1	806	299	4	201.50
E. de C. Weekes, WI v Ind 1948–49	5	7	0	779	194	4	111.28
S. M. Gavaskar, Ind v WI 1970–71	4	8	3	774	220	4	154.80
Mudassar Nazar, Pak v Ind 1982–83	6	8	3	761	231	4	126.83

Geoffrey Boycott receives congratulations from a supporter after making a century in the Centenary Test at Lord's in 1980. Boycott held the record aggregate of Test runs until passed by Gavaskar. He has the distinction of making his 100th century in a Test match in 1977, when he averaged 147.33 against Australia.

MOST WICKETS IN A SERIES

	T	R	W	Av	Teams
S. F. Barnes	4	536	49	10.93	England v South Africa, 1913–14
J. C. Laker	5	442	46	9.60	England v Australia, 1956
C. V. Grimmett	5	642	44	14.59	Australia v South Africa, 1935–36
T. M. Alderman	6	893	42	21.26	Australia v England, 1981
R. M. Hogg	6	527	41	12.85	Australia v England, 1978–79
Imran Khan	6	558	40	13.95	Pakistan v India, 1982–83
A. V. Bedser	5	682	39	17.48	England v Australia, 1953
D. K. Lillee	6	870	39	22.30	Australia v England, 1981
M. W. Tate	5	881	38	23.18	England v Australia, 1924–25
W. J. Whitty	5	632	37	17.08	Australia v South Africa, 1910–11
H. J. Tayfield	5	636	37	17.18	South Africa v England, 1956–57

Hugh Tayfield snicks a ball from Brian Statham to Doug Insole in the second Test at Cape Town in 1956–57. Both Tayfield and Statham figure in Test bowling records.

MOST WICKETS IN A MATCH

- 19–90 J. C. Laker, England v Australia, Old Trafford, 1956
- 17–159 S. F. Barnes, England v South Africa, Johannesburg, 1913–14
- 16–137 R. A. L. Massie, Australia v England, Lord's, 1972
- 15–28 J. Briggs, England v South Africa, Cape Town, 1888–89
- 15–45 G. A. Lohmann, England v South Africa, Port Elizabeth, 1895–96
- 15–99 C. Blythe, England v South Africa, Headingley, 1907
- 15–104 H. Verity, England v Australia, Lord's, 1934
- 15–123 R. J. Hadlee, New Zealand v Australia, Brisbane, 1985–86
- 15–124 W. Rhodes, England v Australia, Melbourne, 1903–04

MOST WICKETS IN AN INNINGS

10–53 J. C. Laker, England v Australia, Old Trafford, 1956
9–28 G. A. Lohmann, England v South Africa, Johannesburg, 189–96
9–37 J. C. Laker, England v Australia, Old Trafford, 1956
9–52 R. J. Hadlee, New Zealand v Australia, Brisbane, 1985–86
9–69 J. M. Patel, India v Australia, Kanpur, 1959–60
9–83 Kapil Dev, India v West Indies, Ahmedabad, 1983–84
9–86 Sarfraz Nawaz, Pakistan v Australia, Melbourne, 1978–79
9–95 J. M. Noreiga, West Indies v India, Port of Spain, 1970–71
9–102 S. P. Gupte, India v West Indies, Kanpur, 1958–59
9–103 S. F. Barnes, England v South Africa, Johannesburg, 1913–14
9–113 H. J. Tayfield, South Africa v England, Johannesburg, 1956–57
9–121 A. A. Mailey, Australia v England, Melbourne, 1920–21

Alec Bedser bowling in a Test trial at Canterbury in July 1946. Bedser had made his Test debut against India three weeks earlier, and taken 11 wickets. A week after this trial he played his second Test, and took another 11 wickets. By the time Bedser played his last Test in 1955, he had taken 236 Test wickets, a world record.

MOST WICKETS IN A CAREER

	M	R	W	Av
I. T. Botham	94	10,392		373
R. J. Hadlee	70	7,976		355
D. K. Lillee	70	8,493	355	23.92
R. G. D. Willis	90	8,190	325	25.20
Imran Khan	70	6,903	311	22.19
Kapil Dev	88	9.145	311	29.40
L. R. Gibbs	79	8,989	309	29.09
F. S. Trueman	67	6,625	307	21.57
D. L. Underwood	86	7,674	297	25.83
B. S. Bedi	67	7,637	266	28.71
J. Garner	58	5,433	259	20.97
J. B. Statham	70	6,261	252	24.84
M. A. Holding	60	5,898	249	23.68
R. Benaud	63	6,704	248	27.03
G. D. McKenzie	60	7,328	246	29.78
B. S. Chandrasekhar	58	7,199	242	29.74

Below: Bhagwat Chandrasekhar bowling against England at Madras in 1976–77, when he took five second-innings wickets. Of the players with 240 Test wickets, Chandra, with 58, played the fewest matches.

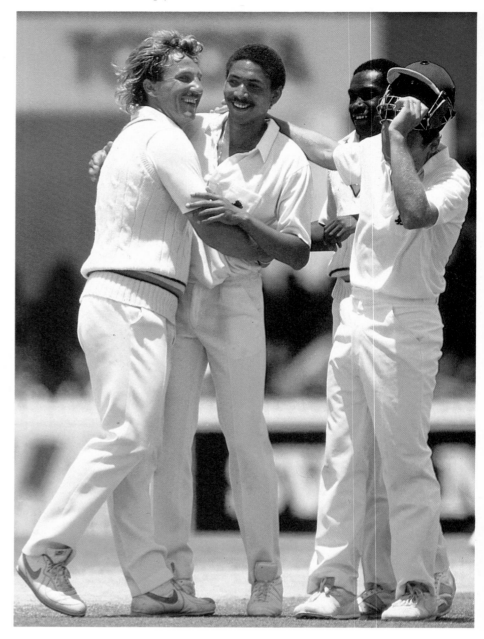

Above left: Ian Botham and Philip de Freitas celebrate a wicket in the 1986–87 Test against Australia at Perth. *Above*: A landmark for Botham the season before. Jeff Crowe of New Zealand is lbw at the Oval in 1986 and Botham takes his 356th wicket, passing Lillee's record.

Left: Derek Underwood gets in approved style at the Oval in 1974. Underwood ended his career with 297 wickets, his Packer and South African adventures preventing the total being higher.

BEST TEST AVERAGES OF BOWLERS WITH 100 WICKETS

	M	R	W	Av
S. F. Barnes	27	3,106	189	16.43
C. T. B. Turner	17	1,670	101	16.53
R. Peel	20	1,715	102	16.81
J. Briggs	33	2,094	118	17.74
C. Blythe	19	1,863	100	18.63
J. H. Wardle	28	2,080	102	20.39
A. K. Davidson	44	3,819	186	20.53
J. Garner	58	5,433	259	20.97 7
N. A. T. Adcock	26	2,195	104	21.10
J. C. Laker	46	4,101	193	21.24
F. S. Trueman	67	6,625	307	21.57
M. D. Marshall	51	5,194	240	21.64
H. Trumble	32	4,792	220	21.78

MOST WICKET-KEEPING DISMISSALS IN A SERIES

28	(all ct)	R. W. Marsh, Australia v England, 1982–83
26	(all ct)	R. W. Marsh, Australia v West Indies, 1975–76
26	(23 ct, 3 st)	J H B Waite, South Africa v New Zealand, 1961–62
24	(21 ct, 3 st)	A. P. E Knott, England v Australia, 1970–71
24	(all ct)	D. T. Lindsay, South Africa v Australia, 1966–67
24	(22 ct, 2 st)	D. L. Murray, West Indies v England, 1963
23	(22 ct, 1 st)	F. C. M. Alexander, West Indies v England, 1959–60
23	(21 ct, 2 st)	A. E. Dick, New Zealand v South Africa, 1961–62
23	(20 ct, 3 st)	A. T. W. Grout, Australia v West Indies, 1960–61
23	(22 ct, 1 st)	A. P. E. Knott, England v Australia, 1974–75
23	(22 ct, 2 st)	R. W. Marsh, Australia v England, 1972
23	(all ct)	R. W. Marsh, Australia v England, 1981
23	(16 ct, 7 st)	J. H. B. Waite, South Africa v New Zealand, 1953–54

MOST CATCHES IN A CAREER

Excluding Wicket-keepers

122	G. S. Chappell	87 matches
120	M. C. Cowdrey	114 matches
110	R. B. Simpson	62 matches
110	W. R. Hammond	85 matches
109	G. St. A. Sobers	93 matches
109	I. T. Botham	94 matches
108	S. M. Gavaskar	125 matches
105	I. M. Chappell	75 matches

TEST ALL-ROUNDER RECORDs

Century and 10 wickets

I. T. Botham	114, 6–58, 7–48, England v India, Bombay, 1979–80
Imran Khan	117, 6–98, 5–82, Pakistan v India, Faisalabad, 1982–83

2,000 Runs and 200 Wickets

	M	R	Av	Wkts	Av
R. Benaud	63	2,201	24.45	248	27.03
I. T. Botham	94	5,057	34.87	373	27.86
R. J. Hadlee	70	2,622	27.60	355	22.46
Imran Khan	70	2,770	32.97	311	22.19
Kapil Dev	88	3,668	32.17	311	29.40
G. St. A. Sobers	93	8,032	57.78	235	34.03

MOST WICKET-KEEPING DISMISSALS IN A CAREER

	M	Ct	St	Total
R. W. Marsh	96	343	12	355
A. P. E Knott	95	250	19	269
Wasim Bari	81	201	27	228
T. G. Evans	91	173	46	219
D. L. Murray	62	181	8	189
A. T. W. Grout	51	163	24	187
S. M. H. Kirmani	78	145	34	179
R. W. Taylor	57	167	7	174
J. H. B. Waite	50	124	17	141
W. A. S. Oldfield	54	78	52	130

Right: Ian Chappell skies a ball from Pocock and will be caught by wicket-keeper Alan Knott in the first Test at Old Trafford in 1968. Knott stands second in the wicket-keepers' 'most dismissals in a career' list.

Below: The man who passed Alan Knott's record, Australian Rodney Marsh, makes a brilliant leg-side catch to dismiss England opener David Lloyd off Dennis Lillee in the fifth Test at the Adelaide Oval in 1974–75.

Above: Godfrey Evans, who at one time held the record for most dismissals in a career, catches O.G. Smith off Trueman at Trent Bridge in 1957.

Right: Knott catches Ian Chappell again, this time off Chris Old in 1974–75 in Melbourne.

Below: South Africa's wicket-keeper John Waite, who with 141 dismissals heads South Africa's list, ducks below a bouncer at the Oval. Jim Parks is the wicket-keeper, Cowdrey and Barrington the slips.

A Register of
Test Cricketers
1877 to 1987

Previous pages: The West Indies touring team, 1928. Left to right: Francis, St Hill, Small, Griffith, Nunes, Brown, Scott, Bartlett, Fernandes, Hoad, Constantine and Neblett.

Left: Ron Archer of Australia bowls to the Springbok batsman-wicket keeper Henry Waite, who plays cautiously forward, during the fifth Test at Melbourne in 1952-53.

Right: Bradman leads his players onto the field at Trent Bridge for the first day's play in the first Test of 1938. Nearly 1500 runs were scored.

A Register of Test Cricketers 1877 to 1987

Aamir Malik (P) 1987-88 2 matches
Abdul Kadir (P) 1964-65 4 matches
Abdul Qadir (P) 1977-78 to 1987 48 matches
E.L. A'Beckett (A) 1928-29 to 1931-32 4 matches
S. Abid Ali (I) 1967-8 to 1974-75 29 matches
R. Abel (E) 1888 to 1902 13 matches
C.A. Absolom (E) 1878-79 1 match
E.E. Achong (WI) 1929-30 to 1934-35 6 matches
N.A.T. Adcock (SA) 1953-54 to 1961-62 26 matches
H.R. Adhikari (I) 1947-48 to 1958-59 21 matches
Afaq Hussain (P) 1961-62 to 1964-65 2 matches
Aftab Baloch (P) 1969-70 to 1974-75 2 matches
Aftab Gul (P) 1968-69 to 1971 6 matches
Agha Saadat Ali (P) 1955-56 1 match
Agha Zahid (P) 1974-75 1 match
J.P. Agnew (E) 1984 to 1985 3 matches
F.S. Ahangama (SL) 1985-86 3 matches
T.M. Alderman (A) 1981-82 to 1984-85 22 matches
F.C.M. Alexander (WI) 1957 to 1960-61 25 matches
G. Alexander (A) 1880 to 1884-85 2 matches
H.H. Alexander (A) 1932-33 1 match
Imtiaz Ali (WI) 1975-76 1 match
Inshan Ali (WI) 1970-71 to 1976-77 12 matches
J.C. Alabaster (NZ) 1955-56 to 1971-72 21 matches

Alim-ud-Din (P) 1954 to 1962 25 matches
D.W. Allan (WI) 1961-62 to 1966 5 matches
F.E. Allan (A) 1878-79 1 match
P.J. Allan (A) 1965-66 1 match
C.F.W. Allcott (NZ) 1929-30 to 1931-32 6 matches
D.A. Allen (E) 1959-60 to 1966 39 matches
G.O.B. Allen (E) 1930 to 1947-48 25 matches
R.C. Allen (A) 1886-87 1 match
M.J.C. Allom (E) 1929-30 to 1930-31 5 matches
P.J.W. Allott (E) 1981 to 1985 13 matches
K.N. Amalean (SL) 1985-86 1 match
L. Amarnath (I) 1933-34 to 1952-53 24 matches
M.B. Amarnath (I) 1969-70 to 1986-87 66 matches
S. Amarnath (I) 1975-76 to 1978-79 10 matches
Amar Singh (I) 1932 to 1936 7 matches
A.M.J.G. Amersinghe (SL) 1983-84 2 matches
L.E.G. Ames (E) 1929 to 1938-39 47 matches
Amir Elahi (I) 1947-48 1 match; (P) 1952-53 5 matches
D.L. Amiss (E) 1967 to 1977 50 matches
J.H. Anderson (SA) 1902-03 1 match
R.W. Anderson (NZ) 1976-77 to 1978 9 matches
W.M. Anderson (NZ) 1945-46 1 match
K.V. Andrew (E) 1954-55 to 1963 2 matches
B. Andrews (NZ) 1973-74 2 matches
T.J.E. Andrews (A) 1921 to 1926 16 matches
Anil Dalpat (P) 1983-84 to 1984-85 9 matches
S.D. Anurasiri (SL) 1985-86 to 1986-87 3 matches
Anwar Hussain (P) 1952-53 4 matches

Anwar Khan (P) 1978-79 1 match
R. Appleyard (E) 1954 to 1956 9 matches
A.L. Apte (I) 1959 1 match
M.L. Apte (I) 1952-53 7 matches
A.G. Archer (E) 1898-99 1 match
K.A. Archer (A) 1950-51 to 1951-52 5 matches
R.G. Archer (A) 1952-53 to 1956-57 19 matches
Arif Butt (P) 1964-65 3 matches
T. Armitage (E) 1876-77 2 matches
W.W. Armstrong (A) 1901-02 to 1921 50 matches
E.G. Arnold (E) 1903-04 to 1907 10 matches
G.G. Arnold (E) 1967 to 1975 34 matches
J. Arnold (E) 1931 1 match
B. Arun (I) 1986-87 2 matches
Arun Lal (I) 1982-83 to 1986-87 5 matches
N.S. Asgarali (WI) 1957 2 matches
W.H. Ashley (SA) 1888-89 1 match
Ashraf Ali (P) 1981-82 to 1987-88 5 matches
Asif Iqbal (P) 1964-65 to 1979-80 58 matches
Asif Masood (P) 1968-69 to 1976-77 16 matches
Asif Mujtaba (P) 1986-87 to 1987-88 3 matches
W.E. Astill (E) 1927-28 to 1929-30 9 matches
C.W.J. Athey (E) 1980 to 1987-88 29 matches
D.St E. Atkinson (WI) 1948-49 to 1957-58 22 matches
E.St E. Atkinson (WI) 1957-58 to 1958-59 8 matches
W. Attewell (E) 1884-85 to 1891-92 10 matches
R.A. Austin (WI) 1977-78 2 matches
K. Azad (I) 1980-81 to 1983-84 7 matches
Azeem Hafeez (P) 1983-84 to 1984-85 18 matches

Azhar Khan (P) 1979-80 1 match
M.A. Azharuddin (I) 1984-85 to 1986-87 21matches
Azmat Rana (P) 1979-80 1 match
S.F.A.F. Bacchus (WI) 1977-78 to 1981-82 19 matches
A. Bacher (SA) 1965 to 1969-70 12 matches
C.L. Badcock (A) 1936-37 to 1938 7 matches
F.T. Badcock (NZ) 1929-30 to 1932-33 7 matches
L. Baichan (WI) 1974-75 to 1975-76 3 matches
A.A. Baig (I) 1959 to 1966-67 10 matches
T.E. Bailey (E) 1949 to 1958-59 61 matches
D.L. Bairstow (E) 1979 to 1980-81 4 matches
A.H. Bakewell (E) 1931 to 1935 6 matches
X.C. Balaskas (SA) 1930-31 to 1938-39 9 matches
J.C. Balderstone (E) 1976 2 matches
S.A. Banerjee (I) 1948-49 1 match
S.N. Banerjee (I) 1948-49 1 match
A.C. Bannerman (A) 1878-79 to 1893 28 matches
C. Bannerman (A) 1876-77 to 1878-79 3 matches
E.A.E. Baptiste (WI) 1983 to 1984-85 9 matches
R.T. Barber (NZ) 1955-56 1 match
R.W. Barber (E) 1960 to 1968 28 matches
W. Barber (E) 1935 2 matches
W. Bardsley (A) 1909 to 1926 41 matches
E.J. Barlow (SA) 1961-62 to 1969-70 30 matches
G.D. Barlow (E) 1976-77 to 1977 3 matches
R.G. Barlow (E) 1881-82 to 1886-87 17 matches
M. Baqa Jilani (I) 1936 1 match
S.F. Barnes (E) 1901-02 to 1913-14 27 matches

S.G. Barnes (A) 1938 to 1948 13 matches
W. Barnes (E) 1880 to 1890 21 matches
B.A. Barnett (A) 1938 4 matches
C.J. Barnett (E) 1933 to 1948 20 matches
F. Barratt (E) 1929 to 1929-30 5 matches
A.G. Barrett (WI) 1970-71 to 1974-75 6 matches
J.E. Barrett (A) 1890 2 matches
K.F. Barrington (E) 1955 to 1968 82 matches
I. Barrow (WI) 1929-30 to 1939 11 matches
E.L. Bartlett (WI) 1928 to 1930-31 5 matches
G.A. Bartlett (NZ) 1961-67 10 matches
P.T. Barton (NZ) 1961-62 to 1962-63 7 matches
V.A. Barton (E) 1891-92 1 match
W. Bates (E) 1881-82 to 1886-87 15 matches
H.V. Baumgartner (SA) 1913-14 1 match
G. Bean (E) 1891-92 3 matches
D.D. Beard (NZ) 1951-52 to 1955-56 4 matches
G.R. Beard (A) 1979-80 3 matches
R. Beaumont (SA) 1912 to 1913-14 5 matches
J.E.F. Beck (NZ) 1953-54 to 1955-56 8 matches
B.S. Bedi (I) 1966-67 to 1979 67 matches
A.V. Bedser (E) 1946 to 1955 51 matches
D.W. Begbie (SA) 1948-49 to 1949-50 5 matches
A.J. Bell (SA) 1929 to 1935 16 matches
W. Bell (NZ) 1953-54 2 matches
J. Benaud (A) 1972/73 3 matches
R. Benaud (A) 1951-52 to 1963-64 63 matches
M.J. Bennett (A) 1984-85 to 1985 3 matches
M.R. Benson (E) 1986

R. Berry (E) 1950   2 matches
C.A. Best (WI) 1985-86   3
matches
N. Betancourt (WI) 1929-
30   1 match
P. Bhandari (I) 1954-55 to
1956-57   3 matches
A.R. Bhat (I) 1983-84   2
matches
G.P. Bilby (NZ) 1965-66   2
matches
J.G. Binks (E) 1963-64   2
matches
A.P. Binns (WI) 1952-53 to
1955-56   5 matches
R.M.H. Binny (I) 1979-80 to
1986-87   27 matches
M.C. Bird (E) 1909-10 to
1913-14   10 matches
J. Birkenshaw (E) 1972-73 to
1973-74   5 matches
L.S. Birkett (WI) 1930-31   4
matches
M. Bisset (SA) 1898-99 to
1909-10   3 matches
G.F. Bissett (SA) 1927-28   4
matches
J.McC. Blackham (A) 1876-77
to 1894-95   35 matches
D.D. Blackie (A) 1928-29   3
matches
T.E. Blain (NZ) 1986   1 match
R.W. Blair (NZ) 1952-53 to
1963-64   19 matches
J.M. Blanckenburg (SA)
1913-14 to 1924   18 matches
K.C. Bland (SA) 1961-62 to
1966-67   21 matches
Hon I.F.W. Bligh (E)
1882-83   4 matches
R.C. Blunt (NZ) 1929-30 to
1931-32   9 matches
C. Blythe (E) 1901-02 to
1909-10   19 matches
J.H. Board (E) 1898/99 to
1905-06   6 matches
E.G. Bock (SA) 1935-36   1
match
B.A. Bolton (NZ) 1958-59   2
matches
J.B. Bolus (E) 1963 to
1963-64   7 matches
G.E. Bond (SA) 1938-39   1
match

G.J. Bonnor (A) 1880 to
1888   17 matches
S.L. Boock (NZ) 1977-78 to
1986-87   28 matches
D.C. Boon (A) 1984-85 to
1987-88   26 matches
B.C. Booth (A) 1961 to
1965-66   29 matches
M.W. Booth (E) 1913-14   2
matches
C.G. Borde (I) 1958-59 to
1969-70   55 matches
A.R. Border (A) 1978-79 to
1987-88   92 matches
B.J.T. Bosanquet (E)
1903-04 to 1905   7
matches
I.T. Botham (E) 1977 to
1987   94 matches
J.T. Botten (SA) 1965   3
matches
M.P. Bowden (E) 1888-89   2
matches
W.E. Bowes (E) 1932 to
1946   15 matches
E.H. Bowley (E) 1929 to
1929-30   5 matches
K.D. Boyce (WI) 1970-71 to
1975-76   21 matches
G. Boycott (E) 1964 to
1981-82   108 matches
H.F. Boyle (A) 1878-79 to
1884-85   12 matches
B.P. Bracewell (NZ) 1978 to
1984-85   6 matches
J.G. Bracewell (NZ) 1980-81
to 1987-88   27 matches
W.P. Bradburn (NZ)
1963-64   2 matches
W.M. Bradley (E) 1899   2
matches
D.G. Bradman (A) 1928-29 to
1948   52 matches
W.H. Brann (SA) 1922-23   3
matches
L.C. Braund (E) 1901-02 to
1907-08   23 matches
J.M. Brearley (E) 1976 to
1981   39 matches
W. Brearley (E) 1905 to
1912   4 matches
D.V. Brennan (E) 1951   2
matches
J. Briggs (E) 1884-85 to
1899   33 matches

R.J. Bright (A) 1977 to
1986-87   25 matches
A.W. Briscoe (SA) 1935-36 to
1938-39   2 matches
B.C. Broad (E) 1984 to
1987-88   17 matches
W. Brockwell (E) 1893 to
1899   7 matches
H.D. Bromfield (SA) 1961-62
to 1965   9 matches
E.H. Bromley (A) 1932-33 to
1934   2 matches
H.R. Bromley-Davenport (E)
1895-96 to 1898-99   4
matches
D. Brookes (E) 1947-48   1
match
A. Brown (E) 1961-62   2
matches
D.J. Brown (E) 1965 to
1969   26 matches
F.R. Brown (E) 1931 to
1953   22 matches
G. Brown (E) 1921 to
1922-23   7 matches
J.T. Brown (E) 1894-95 to
1899   8 matches
L.S. Brown (SA) 1931-32   2
matches
V.R. Brown (NZ) 1985-86   2
matches
W.A. Brown (A) 1934 to
1948   22 matches
C.R. Browne (WI) 1928 to
1929-30   4 matches
W. Bruce (A) 1884-85 to
1894-95   14 matches
C.P. Buckenham (E)
1909-10   4 matches
P.J.P. Burge (A) 1954-55 to
1965-66   42 matches
C.G.de V. Burger (SA)
1957-58   2 matches
M.G. Burgess (NZ) 1967-68 to
1980-81   50 matches
C. Burke (NZ) 1945-46   1
match
J.W. Burke (A) 1950-51 to
1958-59   24 matches
J. Burki (P) 1960-61 to
1969-70   25 matches
S.F. Burke (SA) 1961-62 to
1964-65   2 matches
E.J.K. Burn (A) 1890   2
matches

F.J. Burton (A) 1886-87 to
1887-88   2 matches
T.B. Burtt (NZ) 1946-47 to
1952-53   10 matches
A.R. Butcher (E) 1979   1
match
B.F. Butcher (WI) 1958-59 to
1969   44 matches
R.O. Butcher (E) 1980-81   3
matches
H.J. Butler (E) 1947 to
1947-48   3 matches
L. Butler (WI) 1954-55   1 match
H.R. Butt (E) 1895-96   3
matches
C.G. Butts (WI) 1984-85 to
1986-87   4 matches
L.A. Butterfield (NZ)
1945-46   1 match
I.D. Buys (SA) 1922-23   1
match
M.R. Bynoe (WI) 1958-59 to
1966-67   4 matches
B.L. Cairns (NZ) 1973-74 to
1985-86   43 matches
Hon F.S.G. Calthorpe (E)
1929-30   4 matches
S.T. Callaway (A) 1891-92 to
1894-95   3 matches
I.W. Callen (A) 1977-78   1
match
G.S. Camacho (WI) 1967-68 to
1970-71   11 matches
F. J. Cameron (NZ) 1961-62 to
1965   19 matches
F.J. Cameron (WI) 1948-49   5
matches
H.B. Cameron (SA) 1927-28 to
1935   26 matches
J.H. Cameron (WI) 1939   2
matches
T. Campbell (SA) 1909-10 to
1912   5 matches
D.J. Capel (E) 1987 to
1987-88   4 match
G.M. Carew (WI) 1934-35 to
1948-49   4 matches
M.C. Carew (WI) 1963 to
1971-72   19 matches
W. Carkeek (A) 1912   6
matches
P.H. Carlson (A) 1978-79   2
matches
P.R. Carlstein (SA) 1957-58 to
1963-64   8 matches

A.W. Carr (E) 1922-23 to
1929   11 matches
D.B. Carr (E) 1951-52   2
matches
D.W. Carr (E) 1909   1 match
C.P. Carter (SA) 1912 to
1924   10 matches
H. Carter (A) 1907-08 to
1921-22   28 matches
T.W. Cartwright (E) 1964 to
1965   5 matches
R.H. Catterall (SA) 1922-23 to
1930-31   24 matches
H.B. Cave (NZ) 1949 to
1958   19 matches
G. Challenor (WI) 1928   3
matches
B.S. Chandrasekhar (I)
1963-64 to 1979   58 matches
H.S. Chang (WI) 1978-79   1
match
A.P.F. Chapman (E) 1926 to
1930-31   26 matches
H.W. Chapman (SA) 1913-14 to
1921-22   2 matches
G.S. Chappell (A) 1970-71 to
1983-84   87 matches
I.M. Chappell (A) 1964-65 to
1979-80   75 matches
T.M. Chappell (A) 1981   3
matches
M.E. Chapple (NZ) 1952-53 to
1965-66   14 matches
P.C. Charlton (A) 1890   2
matches
H.R.J. Charlwood (E)
1876-77   2 matches
E.J. Chatfield (NZ) 1974-75 to
1987-88   35 matches
W. Chatterton (E) 1891-92   1
match
C.P.S. Chauhan (I) 1969-70 to
1980-81   40 matches
J.E. Cheetham (SA) 1948-49 to
1955   24 matches
G.A. Chevalier (SA) 1969-
70   1 match
A.G. Chipperfield (A) 1934 to
1938   14 matches
N.R. Chowdhury (I) 1948-49 to
1951-52   2 matches
C.M. Christiani (WI)
1934-35   4 matches
R.J. Christiani (WI) 1947-48 to
1953-54   22 matches

Left: Ted Dexter cutting. Dexter was a dashing England captain in the 1960s.

Above: Graham Dilley, England fast bowler of the 1980s.

Right: England captain Mike Gatting lbw to Bruce Reid at Sydney during the 1986–87 Australia v England series.

S. Christopherson (E) 1884   1 match
J.A.J. Christy (SA) 1929 to 1931-32   10 matches
G.W.A. Chubb (SA) 1951   5 matches
E.W. Clark (E) 1929 to 1934   8 matches
W.M. Clark (A) 1977-78 to 1978-79   10 matches
C.B. Clarke (WI) 1939   3 matches
S.T. Clarke (WI) 1977-78 to 1981-82   11 matches
J.C. Clay (E) 1935   1 match
D.C. Cleverley (NZ) 1931-32 to 1945-46   2 matches
D.B. Close (E) 1949 to 1976   22 matches
J.A.L. Cochrane (SA) 1930-31   1 match
S.K. Coen (SA) 1927-28   2 matches
S.H.M. Colah (I) 1932 to 1933-34   2 matches
L.J. Coldwell (E) 1962 to 1964   7 matches
D.J. Colley (A) 1972   3 matches
R.O. Collinge (NZ) 1964-65 to 1978-79   35 matches
I.A. Colquhoun (NZ) 1954-55   2 matches
H.L. Collins (A) 1920-21 to 1926   19 matches
J.M.M. Commaille (SA) 1909-10 to 1927-28   12 matches
D.C.S. Compton (E) 1937 to 1956-57   78 matches
J.V. Coney (NZ) 1973-74 to 1986-87   52 matches
B.E. Congdon (NZ) 1964-65 to 1978   61 matches
A. Coningham (A) 1894-95   1 match
A.N. Connolly (A) 1963-64 to 1970-71   29 matches
L.N. Constantine (WI) 1928 to 1939   18 matches
D.P. Conyngham (SA) 1922-23   1 match
N.J. Contractor (I) 1955-56 to 1961-62   31 matches
C. Cook (E) 1947   1 match

F.J. Cook (SA) 1895-96   1 match
G. Cook (E) 1981-82 to 1982-83   7 matches
N.G.B. Cook (E) 1983 to 1987-88   12 matches
A.H.C. Cooper (SA) 1913-14   1 match
B.B. Cooper (A) 1876-77   1 match
W.H. Cooper (A) 1881-82 to 1884-85   2 matches
G.A. Cope (E) 1977-78   3 matches
W.H. Copson (E) 1939 to 1947   3 matches
G.E. Corling (A) 1964   5 matches
W.L. Cornford (E) 1929-30   4 matches
G.J. Cosier (A) 1975-76 to 1978-79   18 matches
R.M.H. Cottam (E) 1968-69 to 1972-73   4 matches
W.J. Cottam (E) 1886-87   1 match
A. Cotter (A) 1903-04 to 1911-12   21 matches
G. Coulthard (A) 1881-82   1 match
Hon C.J. Coventry (E) 1888-89   2 matches
N.G. Cowans (E) 1982-83 to 1985   19 matches
C.S. Cowdrey (E) 1984-85   5 matches
M.C. Cowdrey (E) 1954-55 to 1974-75   114 matches
J. Cowie (NZ) 1937 to 1949   9 matches
R.M. Cowper (A) 1964 to 1968   27 matches
J.L. Cox (SA) 1913-14   3 matches
A. Coxon (E) 1948   1 match
I.D. Craig (A) 1952-53 to 1957-58   11 matches
J. Cranston (E) 1890   1 match
K. Cranston (E) 1947 to 1948   8 matches
J.F. Crapp (E) 1948 to 1948-49   7 matches
J.N. Crawford (E) 1905-06 to 1907-08   12 matches

W.P.A. Crawford (A) 1956 to 1956-57   4 matches
G.F. Cresswell (NZ) 1949 to 1950-51   3 matches
G. Cripps (SA) 1891-92   1 match
R.J. Crisp (SA) 1935 to 1935-36   9 matches
C.E.H. Croft (WI) 1976-77 to 1981-82   27 matches
I.B. Cromb (NZ) 1931 to 1931-32   5 matches
J.J. Crowe (NZ) 1982-83 to 1987-88   33 matches
M.D. Crowe (NZ) 1981-82 to 1987-88   39 matches
R.S. Cunis (NZ) 1963-64 to 1971-72   20 matches
S.H. Curnow (SA) 1930-31 to 1931-32   7 matches
W.R. Cuttell (E) 1898-99   2 matches
O.C. Da Costa (WI) 1929-30 to 1934-35   5 matches
E.L. Dalton (SA) 1929 to 1938-39   15 matches
H.T. Dani (I) 1952-53   1 match
W.W. Daniel (WI) 1975-76 to 1983-84   10 matches
J.W. D'Arcy (NZ) 1958   5 matches
J. Darling (A) 1894-95 to 1905   34 matches
L.S. Darling (A) 1932-33 to 1936-37   12 matches
W.M. Darling (A) 1977-78 to 1979-80   14 matches
A.K. Davidson (A) 1953 to 1962-63   44 matches
E.Q. Davies (SA) 1935-36 to 1938-39   5 matches
B.A. Davis (WI) 1964-65   4 matches
C.A. Davis (WI) 1968-69 to 1972-73   15 matches
I.C. Davis (A) 1973-74 to 1977   15 matches
S.P. Davis (A) 1985-86   1 match
W.W. Davis (WI) 1982-83 to 1984-85   11 matches
E.W. Dawson (E) 1927-28 to 1929-30   5 matches
O.C. Dawson (SA) 1947 to 1948-49   9 matches

R.G. de Alwis (SL) 1982-83 to 1986-87   10 matches
H. Dean (E) 1912   3 matches
H.G. Deane (SA) 1924 to 1930-31   17 matches
F.I. De Caires (WI) 1929-30   3 matches
J.H. De Courcy (A) 1953   3 matches
P.A.J. De Freitas 1986-87 to 1987-88   7 matches
A.R. Dell (A) 1970-71 to 1973-74   2 matches
A.L.F. de Mel (SL) 1981-82 to 1986-87   17 matches
C.S. Dempster (NZ) 1929-30 to 1932-33   10 matches
E.W. Dempster (NZ) 1952-53 to 1953-54   5 matches
M.H. Denness (E) 1969 to 1975   28 matches
D. Denton (E) 1905 to 1909-10   11 matches
C.C. Depeiza (WI) 1954-55 to 1955-56   5 matches
D.S. de Silva (SL) 1981-82 to 1984-85   12 matches
E.A.R. de Silva (SL) 1985-86 to 1986-87   5 matches
G.R.A. de Silva (SL) 1981 to 1982-83   4 matches
P.A. de Silva (SL) 1984-85 to 1986-87   13 matches
R.B. Desai (I) 1958-59 to 1967-68   28 matches
D.T. Dewdney (WI) 1954-55 to 1957-58   9 matches
J.G. Dewes (E) 1948 to 1950-51   5 matches
E.R. Dexter (E) 1958 to 1968   62 matches
R.L. Dias (SL) 1981-82 to 1986-87   20 matches
A.E. Dick (NZ) 1961-62 to 1965   17 matches
G.R. Dickinson (NZ) 1929-30 to 1931-32   3 matches
Dilawar Hussain (I) 1933-34 to 1936   3 matches
G.R. Dilley (E) 1979-80 to 1987-88   30 matches
A.E. Dipper (E) 1921   1 match
R.V. Divecha (I) 1951-52 to 1952-53   5 matches

C.D. Dixon (SA) 1913-14   1 match
A.L.C. Doderthaide (A) 1987-88   1 match
G.H.G. Doggart (E) 1950   2 matches
B.L. D'Oliveira (E) 1966 to 1972   44 matches
H.E. Dollery (E) 1947 to 1950   4 matches
A. Dolphin (E) 1920-21   1 match
H. Donnan (A) 1891-92 to 1896   5 matches
M.P. Donnelly (NZ) 1937 to 1949   7 matches
B. Dooland (A) 1946-47 to 1947-48   3 matches
D.R. Doshi (I) 1979-80 to 1983-84   33 matches
J.W.H.T. Douglas (E) 1911-12 to 1924-25   23 matches
U.G. Dowe (WI) 1970-71 to 1972-73   4 matches
R.R. Dower (SA) 1898-99   1 match
G.T. Dowling (NZ) 1961-62 to 1971-72   39 matches
P.R. Downton (E) 1980-81 to 1986   27 matches
R.G. Draper (SA) 1949-50   2 matches
N.F. Druce (E) 1897-98   5 matches
A. D'Souza (P) 1958-59 to 1962   6 matches
A. Ducat (E) 1921   1 match
C.A.R. Duckworth (SA) 1956-57   2 matches
G. Duckworth (E) 1924 to 1936   24 matches
R.A. Duff (A) 1901-02 to 1905   22 matches
P.J.L. Dujon (WI) 1981-82 to 1986-87   43 matches
K.S. Duleepsinhji (E) 1929 to 1931   12 matches
R. Dumbrill (SA) 1965 to 1966-67   5 matches
J.P. Duminy (SA) 1927-28 to 1929   3 matches
J.R.F. Duncan (A) 1970-71   1 match
O.R. Dunell (SA) 1888-89   2 matches

J.A. Dunning (NZ) 1932-33 to 1937   4 matches

J.H. Du Preez (SA) 1966-67   2 matches

S.A. Durani (I) 1961-62 to 1972-73   29 matches

F.J. Durston (E) 1921   1 match

J.F. Du Toit (SA) 1891-92   1 match

D.V. Dyer (SA) 1947   3 matches

G.C. Dyer (A) 1987-88   4 matches

G. Dymock (A) 1973-74 to 1979-80   21 matches

J. Dyson (A) 1977-78 to 1984-85   30 matches

C.J. Eady (A) 1896 to 1901-02   2 matches

K.H. Eastwood (A) 1970-71   1 match

H.I. Ebeling (A) 1934   1 match

B.A. Edgar (NZ) 1978 to 1986   39 matches

P.H. Edmonds (E) 1975 to 1987   51 matches

J.H. Edrich (E) 1963 to 1976   77 matches

W.J. Edrich (E) 1938 to 1954-55   39 matches

G.N. Edwards (NZ) 1976-77 to 1980-81   8 matches

J.D. Edwards (A) 1888   3 matches

R. Edwards (A) 1972 to 1975   20 matches

R.M. Edwards (WI) 1968-69   5 matches

W.J. Edwards (A) 1974-75   3 matches

Ehtesham-ud-Din (P) 1979-80 to 1982   5 matches

M.K. Elgie (SA) 1961-62   3 matches

H. Elliott (E) 1927-28 to 1933-34   4 matches

R.M. Ellison (E) 1984 to 1986   11 matches

J.E. Emburey (E) 1978 to 1987-88   49 matches

R.W.G. Emery (NZ) 1951-52   2 matches

S.H. Emery (A) 1912   4 matches

G.M. Emmett (E) 1948   1 match

T. Emmett (E) 1876-77 to 1881-82   7 matches

W.R. Endean (SA) 1951 to 1956-57   28 matches

F.M. Engineer (I) 1961-62 to 1974-75   46 matches

A.J. Evans (E) 1921   1 match

E. Evans (A) 1881-82 to 1886   6 matches

T.G. Evans (E) 1946 to 1959   91 matches

A.E. Fagg (E) 1936 to 1939   5 matches

N.H. Fairbrother (E) 1987-88   2 matches

A.G. Fairfax (A) 1928-29 to 1930-31   10 matches

F.L. Fane (E) 1905-06 to 1909-10   14 matches

K. Farnes (E) 1934 to 1938-39   15 matches

Farooq Hamid (P) 1964-65   1 match

W.S. Farrer (SA) 1961-62 to 1963-64   6 matches

W. Farrimond (E) 1930-31 to 1935   4 matches

Farrukh Zaman (P) 1976-77   1 match

G.A. Faulkner (SA) 1905-06 to 1924   25 matches

L.E. Favell (A) 1954-55 to 1960-61   19 matches

Fazal Mahmood (P) 1952-53 to 1962   34 matches

J.P. Fellows-Smith (SA) 1960   4 matches

P.G.H. Fender (E) 1920-21 to 1929   13 matches

W. Ferguson (WI) 1947-48 to 1953-54   8 matches

M.P. Fernandes (WI) 1928 to 1929-30   2 matches

E.R.N.S. Fernando (SL) 1982-83 to 1983-84   5 matches

J.J. Ferris (A) 1886 to 1890   8 matches; (E) 1891-92   1 match

C.G. Fichardt (SA) 1891-92 to 1895-96   2 matches

A. Fielder (E) 1903-04 to 1907-08   6 matches

T.M. Findlay (WI) 1969 to 1972-73   10 matches

J.H.W. Fingleton (A) 1931-32 to 1938   18 matches

C.E. Finlason (SA) 1888-89   1 match

F.E. Fisher (NZ) 1952-53   1 match

L.B. Fishlock (E) 1936 to 1946-47   4 matches

J.A. Flavell (E) 1961 to 1964   4 matches

L.O'B. Fleetwood-Smith (A) 1935-36 to 1938   10 matches

K.W.R. Fletcher (E) 1968 to 1981-82   59 matches

C.E. Floquet (SA) 1909-10   1 match

W. Flowers (E) 1884-85 to 1893   8 matches

H. Foley (NZ) 1929-30   1 match

F.G.J. Ford (E) 1894-95   5 matches

F.R. Foster (E) 1911-12 to 1912   11 matches

M.L.C. Foster (WI) 1969 to 1977-78   14 matches

N.A. Foster (E) 1983 to 1987-88   21 matches

R.E. Foster (E) 1903-04 to 1907   8 matches

A.J. Fothergill (E) 1888-89   2 matches

G. Fowler (E) 1982 to 1984-85   21 matches

B.C. Francis (A) 1972   3 matches

G.N. Francis (WI) 1928 to 1933   10 matches

H.H. Francis (SA) 1898-99   2 matches

C.M. Francois (SA) 1922-23   5 matches

C.N. Frank (SA) 1921-22   3 matches

W.H.B. Frank (SA) 1895-96   1 match

T.J. Franklin (NZ) 1983 to 1985-86   2 matches

M.C. Frederick (WI) 1953-54   1 match

R.C. Fredericks (WI) 1968-69 to 1976-77   59 matches

A.P. Freeman (E) 1924-25 to 1929   12 matches

D.L. Freeman (NZ) 1932-33   2 matches

E.W. Freeman (A) 1967-68 to 1969-70   11 matches

F.W. Freer (A) 1946-47   1 match

B.N. French (E) 1986 to 1987-88   12 matches

C.B. Fry (E) 1895-96 to 1912   26 matches

E.R.H. Fuller (SA) 1952-53 to 1957-58   7 matches

R.L. Fuller (WI) 1934-35   1 match

G.M. Fullerton (SA) 1947 to 1951   7 matches

K.J. Funston (SA) 1952-53 to 1957-58   18 matches

H.A. Furlonge (WI) 1954-55 to 1955-56   3 matches

C.V. Gadkari (I) 1952-53 to 1954-55   6 matches

A.D. Gaekwad (I) 1974-75 to 1984-85   40 matches

D.K. Gaekwad (I) 1952 to 1960-61   11 matches

H.G. Gaekwad (I) 1952-53   1 match

N. Gallichan (NZ) 1937   1 match

D. Gamsy (SA) 1969-70   2 matches

A. Gandotra (I) 1969-70   2 matches

J.B. Gannon (A) 1977-78   3 matches

A.G. Ganteaume (WI) 1947-48   1 match

J. Garner (WI) 1976-77 to 1986-87   58 matches

T.W. Garrett (A) 1876-77 to 1887-88   19 matches

B.B.M. Gaskin (WI) 1947-48   2 matches

M.W. Gatting (E) 1977-78 to 1987-88   61 matches

R.A. Gaunt (A) 1957-58 to 1963-64   3 matches

S.M. Gavaskar (I) 1970-71 to 1986-87   125 matches

L.H. Gay (E) 1894-95   1 match

G. Geary (E) 1924 to 1934   14 matches

S.G. Gedye (NZ) 1963-64 to 1964-65   4 matches

D.R.A. Gehrs (A) 1903-04 to 1910-11   6 matches

K.D.Ghavri (I) 1974-75 to 1980-81   39 matches

M.E.Z. Ghazali (P) 1954   2 matches

J.M. Ghorpade (I) 1952-53 to 1959   8 matches

Ghulam Abbas (P) 1967   1 match

Ghulam Ahmed (I) 1948-49 to 1958-59   22 matches

P.A. Gibb (E) 1938-39 to 1946-47   8 matches

G.L. Gibbs (WI) 1954-55   1 match

L.R. Gibbs (WI) 1957-58 to 1975-76   79 matches

G. Giffen (A) 1881-82 to 1896   31 matches

W.F. Giffen (A) 1886-87 to 1891-92   3 matches

N. Gifford (E) 1964 to 1973   15 matches

D.R. Gilbert (A) 1985 to 1986-87   9 matches

R. Gilchrist (WI) 1957 to 1958-59   13 matches

S.R. Gillespie (NZ) 1985-86   1 match

A.E.R. Gilligan (E) 1922-23 to 1924-25   11 matches

A.H.H. Gilligan (E) 1929-30   4 matches

G.J. Gilmour (A) 1973-74 to 1976-77   15 matches

H. Gimblett (E) 1936 to 1939   3 matches

G. Gladstone (WI) 1929-30   1 match

C. Gladwin (E) 1947 to 1949   8 matches

J.W. Gleeson (A) 1967-68 to 1972   29 matches

R.A. Gleeson (SA) 1895-96   1 match

G.K. Glover (SA) 1895-96   1 match

J.D.C. Goddard (WI) 1947-48 to 1957   27 matches

Left: David Gower, the leading England batsman of the late 1970s and 1980s.

Above: Jack Hobbs, towards the end of his career in 1935. His Test career lasted from 1907–08 to 1930.

T.L. Goddard (SA) 1955 to 1969-70 41 matches

T.W.J. Goddard (E) 1930 to 1939 8 matches

H.A. Gomes (WI) 1976 to 1986-87 60 matches

G.E. Gomez (WI) 1939 to 1953-54 29 matches

G.A. Gooch (E) 1975 to 1987-88 62 matches

H.M. Goonatillake (SL) 1981-82 to 1982-83 5 matches

M.J. Gopalan (I) 1933-34 1 match

C.D. Gopinath (I) 1951-52 to 1959-60 8 matches

N. Gordon (SA) 1938-39 5 matches

A.R. Gover (E) 1936 to 1946 4 matches

D.I. Gower (E) 1978-79 to 1987 96 matches

Dr E.M. Grace (E) 1880 1 match

G.F. Grace (E) 1880 1 match

Dr W.G. Grace (E) 1880 to 1899 22 matches

H. Graham (A) 1893 to 1896 6 matches

R. Graham (SA) 1898-99 2 matches

G.C. Grant (WI) 1930-31 to 1934-35 12 matches

R.S. Grant (WI) 1934-35 to 1939 7 matches

T.W. Graveney (E) 1951 to 1969 79 matches

A.H. Gray (WI) 1987-88 9 matches

E.J. Gray (NZ) 1983 to 1986-87 8 matches

T. Greenhough (E) 1959 to 1960 4 matches

A.E. Greenidge (WI) 1977-78 to 1978-79 6 matches

C.G. Greenidge (WI) 1974-75 to 1986-87 77 matches

G.A. Greenidge (WI) 1971-72 to 1972-73 5 matches

A. Greenwood (E) 1876-77 2 matches

D.W. Gregory (A) 1876-77 to 1878-79 3 matches

E.J. Gregory (A) 1876-77 1 match

J.M. Gregory (A) 1920-21 to 1928-29 24 matches

R.G. Gregory (A) 1936-37 2 matches

S.E. Gregory (A) 1890 to 1912 58 matches

A.W. Greig (E) 1972 to 1977 58 matches

I.A. Greig (E) 1982 2 matches

M.G. Grell (WI) 1929-30 1 match

B.A. Grieve (E) 1888-89 2 matches

R.E. Grieveson (SA) 1938-39 2 matches

G.M. Griffin (SA) 1960 2 matches

C.C. Griffith (WI) 1959-60 to 1968-69 28 matches

H.C. Griffith (WI) 1928 to 1933 13 matches

S.C. Griffith (E) 1947-48 to 1948-49 3 matches

C.V. Grimmett (A) 1924-25 to 1935-36 37 matches

T.U. Groube (A) 1880 1 match

A.T.W. Grout (A) 1957-58 to 1965-66 51 matches

G.M. Guard (I) 1958-59 to 1959-60 2 matches

C.E.J. Guest (A) 1962-63 1 match

S. Guha (I) 1967 to 1969-70 4 matches

S.C. Guillen (NZ) 1955-56 3 matches; (WI) 1951-52 5 matches

Y. Gunasekera (SL) 1982-83 2 matches

Gul Mahomed (I) 1946 to 1952-53 8 matches; (P) 1956-57 1 match

R.P.W. Guneratne (SL) 1982-83 1 match

G. Gunn (E) 1907-08 to 1929-30 15 matches

J.R. Gunn (E) 1901-02 to 1905 6 matches

W. Gunn (E) 1886-87 to 1899 11 matches

B.P. Gupte (I) 1960-61 to 1964-65 3 matches

S.P. Gupte (I) 1951-52 to 1961-62 36 matches

A.P. Gurusinha (SL) 1985-86 to 1986-87 7 matches

J.W. Guy (NZ) 1955-56 to 1961-62 12 matches

D.R. Hadlee (NZ) 1969 to 1977-78 26 matches

R.J. Hadlee (NZ) 1972-73 to 1987-88 73 matches

W.A. Hadlee (NZ) 1937 to 1950-51 11 matches

N.E. Haig (E) 1921 to 1929-30 5 matches

S. Haigh (E) 1898-99 to 1912 11 matches

A.E. Hall (SA) 1922-23 to 1930-31 7 matches

G.G. Hall (SA) 1964-65 1 match

W.W. Hall (WI) 1958-59 to 1968-69 48 matches

E.A. Halliwell (SA) 1891-92 to 1902-03 8 matches

C. Hallows (E) 1921 to 1928 2 matches

C.G. Halse (SA) 1963-64 3 matches

R.A. Hamence (A) 1946-47 to 1947-48 3 matches

J.R. Hammond (A) 1972-73 5 matches

W.R. Hammond (E) 1927-28 to 1946-47 85 matches

J.H. Hampshire (E) 1969 to 1975 8 matches

P.A.M. Hands (SA) 1913-14 to 1924 7 matches

R.H.M. Hands (SA) 1913-14 1 match

Hanif Mohammad (P) 1952-53 to 1969-70 55 matches

M.A. Hanley (SA) 1948-49 1 match

Hanumant Singh (I) 1963-64 to 1969-70 14 matches

M.S. Hardikar (I) 1958-59 2 matches

H.T.W. Hardinge (E) 1921 1 match

J. Hardstaff sen (E) 1907-08 5 matches

J. Hardstaff jun (E) 1935 to 1948 23 matches

N.S. Harford (NZ) 1955-56 to 1958 8 matches

R.I. Harford (NZ) 1967-68 3 matches

Haroon Rashid (P) 1976 to 1982-83 23 matches

R.A. Harper (WI) 1983-84 to 1986-87 19 matches

Lord Harris (E) 1878-79 to 1884 4 matches

P.G.Z. Harris (NZ) 1955-56 to 1964-65 9 matches

R.M. Harris (NZ) 1958-59 2 matches

T.A. Harris (SA) 1947 to 1948-49 3 matches

J. Harry (A) 1894-95 1 match

G.P.D. Hartigan (SA) 1912 to 1913-14 5 matches

R.J. Hartigan (A) 1907-08 2 matches

A.E.V. Hartkopf (A) 1924-25 1 match

J.C. Hartley (E) 1905-06 2 matches

M.R. Harvey (A) 1946-47 1 match

R.L. Harvey (SA) 1935-36 2 matches

R.N. Harvey (A) 1947-48 to 1962-63 79 matches

Haseeb Ahsan (P) 1957-58 to 1961-62 12 matches

A.L. Hassett (A) 1938 to 1953 43 matches

B.F. Hastings (NZ) 1968-69 to 1975-76 31 matches

C.M.H. Hathorn (SA) 1902-03 to 1910-11 12 matches

Lord Hawke (E) 1895-96 to 1898-99 5 matches

N.J.N. Hawke (A) 1962-63 to 1968 27 matches

E.G. Hayes (E) 1909 to 1912 5 matches

F.C. Hayes (E) 1973 to 1976 9 matches

J.A. Hayes (NZ) 1950-51 to 1958 15 matches

D.L. Haynes (WI) 1977 to 1986-87 65 matches

T.W. Hayward (E) 1895-96 to 1909 35 matches

V.S. Hazare (I) 1946 to 1952-53 30 matches

G.R. Hazlitt (A) 1907-08 to 1912 9 matches

G.A. Headley (WI) 1929-30 to 1953-54 22 matches

R.G.A. Headley (WI) 1973 2 matches

A. Hearne (E) 1891-92 1 match

F. Hearne (E) 1888-89 2 matches; (SA) 1891-92 to 1895-96 4 matches

G.A.L. Hearne (SA) 1922-23 to 1924 3 matches

G.G. Hearne (E) 1891-92 1 match

J.T. Hearne (E) 1891-92 to 1899 12 matches

J.W. Hearne (E) 1911-12 to 1926 24 matches

P.S. Heine (SA) 1955 to 1961-62 14 matches

E.E. Hemmings (E) 1982 to 1987-88 6 matches

M. Henderson (NZ) 1929-30 1 match

E.H. Hendren (E) 1920-21 to 1934-35 51 matches

M. Hendrick (E) 1974 to 1981 30 matches

J.L. Hendriks (WI) 1961-62 to 1969 20 matches

H.S.T.L. Hendry (A) 1921 to 1928-29 11 matches

C. Heseltine (E) 1895-96 2 matches

P.A. Hibbert (A) 1977-78 1 match

J.D. Higgs (A) 1977-78 to 1980-81 22 matches

K. Higgs (E) 1965 to 1968 15 matches

A.M.J. Hilditch (A) 1978-79 to 1985-86 18 matches

A. Hill (E) 1876-77 2 matches

A.J.L. Hill (E) 1895-96 3 matches

C. Hill (A) 1896 to 1911-12 49 matches

J.C. Hill (A) 1953 to 1954-55 3 matches

M.J. Hilton (E) 1950 to 1951-52 4 matches

C.F.W. Hime (SA) 1895-96 1 match

D.D. Hindlekar (I) 1936 to 1946 4 matches

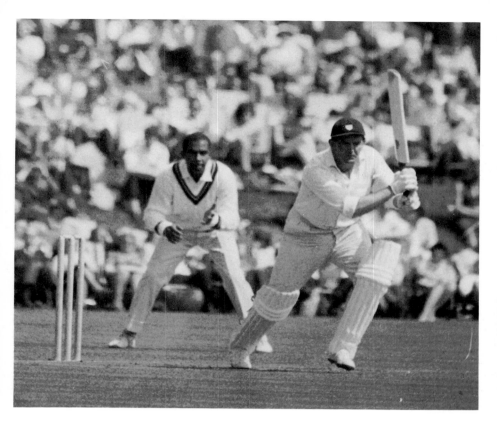

Above: An off-drive from Tom Graveney, England's elegant batsman of the 1950s and 1960s.

Right: W.G. Grace, 'the champion', who played in Tests from 1880 to 1899, usually as captain of England.

G.H. Hirst (E) 1897-98 to 1909   24 matches
J.W. Hitch (E) 1911-12 to 1921   7 matches
E.L.G. Hoad (WI) 1928 to 1933   4 matches
D.E. Hoare (A) 1960-61   1 match
Sir J.B. Hobbs (E) 1907-08 to 1930   61 matches
R.N.S. Hobbs (E) 1967 to 1971   7 matches
J.H. Hodges (A) 1876-77   2 matches
T.G. Hogan (A) 1982-83 to 1983-84   7 matches
R.M. Hogg (A) 1978-79 to 1984-85   38 matches
V.A. Holder (WI) 1969 to 1978-79   40 matches
M.A. Holding (WI) 1975-76 to 1986-87   60 matches
G.B. Hole (A) 1950-51 to 1954-55   18 matches
D.A.J. Holford (WI) 1966-67 to 1976-77   24 matches
R.G. Holland (A) 1984-85 to 1985-86   11 matches
W.E. Hollies (E) 1934-35 to 1950   13 matches
E.R.T. Holmes (E) 1934-35 to 1935   5 matches
P. Holmes (E) 1921 to 1932   7 matches
J.K. Holt jun (WI) 1953-54 to 1958-59   17 matches
L. Hone (E) 1878-79   1 match
D.W. Hookes (A) 1976-77 to 1985-86   23 matches
A.J.Y. Hopkins (A) 1901-02 to 1909   20 matches
J.L. Hopwood (E) 1934   2 matches
T.P. Horan (A) 1876-77 to 1884-85   15 matches
H.V. Hordern (A) 1910-11 to 1911-12   7 matches
A.N. Hornby (E) 1878-79 to 1884   3 matches
P.A. Horne (NZ) 1987-88   3 matches
P.M. Hornibrook (A) 1928-29 to 1930   6 matches
M.J. Horton (E) 1959   2 matches

K.W. Hough (NZ) 1958-59   2 matches
A.B. Howard (WI) 1971-72   1 match
N.D. Howard (E) 1951-52   4 matches
G.P. Howarth (NZ) 1974-75 to 1984-85   47 matches
H.J. Howarth (NZ) 1969 to 1976-77   30 matches
H. Howell (E) 1920-21 to 1924   5 matches
W.P. Howell (A) 1897-98 to 1903-04   18 matches
R. Howorth (E) 1947 to 1947-48   5 matches
K.J. Hughes (A) 1977 to 1984-85   70 matches
M.G. Hughes (A) 1985-86 to 1987-88   5 matches
J. Humphries (E) 1907-08   3 matches
W.A. Hunt (A) 1931-32   1 match
C.C. Hunte (WI) 1957-58 to 1966-67   44 matches
E.A.C. Hunte (WI) 1929-30   3 matches
J. Hunter (E) 1884-85   5 matches
A.G. Hurst (A) 1973-74 to 1979-80   12 matches
A. Hurwood (A) 1930-31   2 matches
K.L. Hutchings (E) 1907-08 to 1909   7 matches
P. Hutchinson (SA) 1888-89   2 matches
Sir L. Hutton (E) 1937 to 1954-55   79 matches
R.A. Hutton (E) 1971   5 matches
L.G. Hylton (WI) 1934-35 to 1939   6 matches
K. Ibadulla (P) 1964-65 to 1967   4 matches
K.C. Ibrahim (I) 1948-49   4 matches
J. Iddon (E) 1934-35 to 1935   5 matches
Ijaz Ahmed (P) 1986-87 to 1987-88   8 matches
Ijaz Butt (P) 1958-59 to 1962   8 matches
Ijaz Faqih (P) 1980-81 to 1986-87   3 matches

J.T. Ikin (E) 1946 to 1955   18 matches
R. Illingworth (E) 1958 to 1973   61 matches
Imran Khan (P) 1971 to 1987   70 matches
Imtiaz Ahmed (P) 1952-53 to 1962   41 matches
K.S. Indrajitsinghi (I) 1964-65 to 1969-70   4 matches
D.J. Insole (E) 1950 to 1957   9 matches
Intikhab Alam (P) 1959-60 to 1976-77   47 matches
R.J. Inverarity (A) 1968 to 1972   6 matches
Iqbal Qasim (P) 1976-77 to 1987-88   47 matches
J.K. Irani (I) 1947-48   2 matches
F.A. Iredale (A) 1894-95 to 1899   14 matches
H. Ironmonger (A) 1928-29 to 1932-33   14 matches
D.E.J. Ironside (SA) 1953-54   3 matches
B.L. Irvine (SA) 1969-70   4 matches
Israr Ali (P) 1952-53 to 1959-60   4 matches
J.B. Iverson (A) 1950-51   5 matches
R.D. Jackman (E) 1980-81 to 1982   4 matches
A.A. Jackson (A) 1928-29 to 1930-31   8 matches
Sir F.S. Jackson (E) 1893 to 1905   20 matches
H.L. Jackson (E) 1949 to 1961   2 matches
M. Jahangir Khan (I) 1932 to 1936   4 matches
L.P. Jai (I) 1933-34   1 match
M.L. Jaisimha (I) 1959 to 1970-71   39 matches
Jalal-ud-Din (P) 1982-83 to 1985-86   6 matches
K.C. James (NZ) 1929-30 to 1932-33   11 matches
J.A. Jameson (E) 1971 to 1973-74   4 matches
R.J.D. Jamshedji (I) 1933-34   1 match
D.R. Jardine (E) 1928 to 1933-34   22 matches

B.N. Jarman (A) 1959-60 to 1968-69   19 matches
A.H. Jarvis (A) 1884-85 to 1894-95   11 matches
T.W. Jarvis (NZ) 1964-65 to 1972-73   13 matches
Javed Akhtar (P) 1962   1 match
Javed Miandad (P) 1976-77 to 1987-88   89 matches
K.H. Jayantilal (I) 1970-71   1 match
R.S.A. Jayasekera (SL) 1981-82   1 match
S. Jeganathan (SL) 1982-83   2 matches
R.O. Jenkins (E) 1948-49 to 1952   9 matches
T.J. Jenner (A) 1970-71 to 1975-76   9 matches
C.B. Jennings (A) 1912   6 matches
G.L. Jessop (E) 1899 to 1912   18 matches
V.B. John (SL) 1982-83 to 1984   6 matches
C.L. Johnson (SA) 1895-96   1 match
H.H.H. Johnson (WI) 1947-48 to 1950   3 matches
I.W. Johnson (A) 1945-46 to 1956-57   45 matches
L.J. Johnson (A) 1947-48   1 match
T.F. Johnson (WI) 1939   1 match
W.A. Johnston (A) 1947-48 to 1954-55   40 matches
A.H. Jones (NZ) 1986-87 to 1987-88   4 match
A.O. Jones (E) 1899 to 1909   12 matches
C.M. Jones (WI) 1929-30 to 1934-35   4 matches
D.M. Jones (A) 1987-88 to 1986-87   13 matches
E. Jones (A) 1894-95 to 1902-03   19 matches
I.J. Jones (E) 1963-64 to 1967-68   15 matches
P.E. Jones (WI) 1947-48 to 1951-52   9 matches
S.P. Jones (A) 1881-82 to 1887-88   12 matches
P.G. Joshi (I) 1951-52 to 1960-61   12 matches

L.R. Joslin (A) 1967-68   1 match
B.D. Julien (WI) 1973 to 1976-77   24 matches
R.R. Jumadeen (WI) 1971-72 to 1978-79   12 matches
H. Jupp (E) 1876-77   2 matches
V.W.C. Jupp (E) 1921 to 1928   8 matches
B.R. Jurangpathy (SL) 1985-86 to 1986-87   2 matches
A.I. Kallicharran (WI) 1971/72 to 1980-81   66 matches
L.W. Kaluperuma (SL) 1981-82   2 matches
S.M.S. Kaluperuma (SL) 1983-84   3 matches
R.B. Kanhai (WI) 1957 to 1973-74   79 matches
H.S. Kanitkar (I) 1974-75   2 matches
Kapil Dev (I) 1978-79 to 1986-87   88 matches
A.H. Kardar (I) 1946   3 matches; (P) 1952-53 to 1957-58   23 matches
W.W. Keeton (E) 1934 to 1939   2 matches
H.J. Keith (SA) 1952-53 to 1956-57   8 matches
C. Kelleway (A) 1910-11 to 1928-29   26 matches
J.J. Kelly (A) 1896 to 1905   36 matches
T.J.D. Kelly (A) 1876-77 to 1878-79   2 matches
G.A. Kempis (SA) 1888-89   1 match
T. Kendall (A) 1876-77   2 matches
A.S. Kennedy (E) 1922-23   5 matches
R.B. Kenny (I) 1958-59 to 1959-60   5 matches
M.F. Kent (A) 1981   3 matches
E.S.M. Kentish (WI) 1947-48 to 1953-54   2 matches
D. Kenyon (E) 1951-52 to 1955   8 matches
R.B. Kerr (A) 1985-86   2 matches
J.L. Kerr (NZ) 1931 to 1937   7 matches

247

Khalid Hassan (P) 1954　1 match
Khalid Wazir (P) 1954　2 matches
Khan Mohammad (P) 1952-53 to 1957-58　13 matches
Rev E.T. Killick (E) 1929　2 matches
R. Kilner (E) 1924 to 1926　9 matches
C.L. King (WI) 1976 to 1980　9 matches
F.McD. King (WI) 1953-54 to 1955-56　14 matches
J.H. King (E) 1909　1 match
L.A. King (WI) 1961-62 to 1967-68　2 matches
S.P. Kinneir (E) 1911-12　1 match
A.F. Kippax (A) 1924-25 to 1934　22 matches
S.M.H. Kirmani (I) 1975-76 to 1985-86　88 matches
G. Kischenchand (I) 1947-48 to 1952-53　5 matches
L.F. Kline (A) 1957-58 to 1960-61　13 matches
A.E. Knight (E) 1903-04　3 matches
B.R. Knight (E) 1961-62 to 1969　29 matches
D.J. Knight (E) 1921　2 matches
A.P.E. Knott (E) 1967 to 1981　95 matches
N.A. Knox (E) 1907　2 matches
J.J. Kotze (SA) 1902-03 to 1907　3 matches
A.G. Kripal Singh (I) 1955-56 to 1964-65　14 matches
P. Krishnamurthy (I) 1970-71　5 matches
R.R. Kulkarni (I) 1986-87　3 matches
U.N. Kulkarni (I) 1967-68　4 matches
V.V. Kumar (I) 1960-61 to 1961-62　2 matches
B.K. Kunderan (I) 1959-60 to 1967　18 matches
D.S.B.P. Kuruppu (SL) 1986-87　1 match
A.L. Kuruppuarachchi (SL) 1985-86 to 1986-87　2 matches

F. Kuys (SA) 1898-99　1 match
G. Labrooy (SL) 1986-87　1 match
B.M. Laird (A) 1979-80 to 1982-83　21 matches
J.C. Laker (E) 1947-48 to 1958-59　46 matches
Lall Singh (I) 1932　1 match
A.J. Lamb (E) 1982 to 1986-87　51 matches
R.L.M. Lamba (I) 1986-87　3 matches
H.R. Lance (SA) 1961-62 to 1969-70　13 matches
G.R.A. Langley (A) 1951-52 to 1956-57　26 matches
Jas Langridge (E) 1933 to 1946　8 matches
A.B.C. Langton (SA) 1935 to 1938-39　15 matches
W. Larkins (E) 1979-80 to 1981　6 matches
J.D.F. Larter (E) 1962 to 1965　10 matches
H. Larwood (E) 1926 to 1932-33　21 matches
P.D. Lashley (WI) 1960-61 to 1966　4 matches
T.J. Laughlin (A) 1977-78 to 1978-79　3 matches
F. Laver (A) 1899 to 1909　15 matches
G.B. Lawrence (SA) 1961-62　5 matches
W.M. Lawry (A) 1961 to 1970-71　67 matches
G.F. Lawson (A) 1980-81 to 1986-87　37 matches
E. Leadbeater (E) 1951-52　2 matches
H.W. Lee (E) 1930-31　1 match
P.K. Lee (A) 1931-32 to 1932-33　2 matches
W.K. Lees (NZ) 1976-77 to 1983　21 matches
W.S. Lees (E) 1905-06　5 matches
R.A. Legall (WI) 1952-53　4 matches
I.B. Leggat (NZ) 1953-54　1 match
J.G. Leggat (NZ) 1951-52 to 1955-56　9 matches

G.B. Legge (E) 1927-28 to 1929-30　5 matches
F.L.Le Roux (SA) 1913-14　1 match
C.F.H. Leslie (E) 1882-83　4 matches
J.K. Lever (E) 1976-77 to 1986　21 matches
P. Lever (E) 1970-71 to 1975　17 matches
Sir H.D.G. Leveson Gower (E) 1909-10　3 matches
W.H.V. Levett (E) 1933-34　1 match
A.R. Lewis (E) 1972-73 to 1973　9 matches
D.M. Lewis (WI) 1970-71　3 matches
P.T. Lewis (SA) 1913-14　1 match
M. Leyland (E) 1928 to 1938　41 matches
Liaqat Ali (P) 1974-75 to 1978　5 matches
D.K. Lillee (A) 1970-71 to 1983-84　70 matches
A.F.A. Lilley (E) 1896 to 1909　35 matches
Jas Lillywhite jun (E) 1876-77　2 matches
D.T. Lindsay (SA) 1963-64 to 1969-70　19 matches
J.D. Lindsay (SA) 1947　3 matches
N.V. Lindsay (SA) 1921-22　1 match
R.R. Lindwall (A) 1946-47 to 1959-60　61 matches
W.V.S. Ling (SA) 1921-22 to 1922-23　6 matches
A.F. Lissette (NZ) 1955-56　2 matches
C.B. Llewellyn (SA) 1895-96 to 1912　15 matches
C.H. Lloyd (WI) 1966-67 to 1984-85　110 matches
D. Lloyd (E) 1974 to 1974-75　9 matches
T.A. Lloyd (E) 1984　1 match
P.J. Loader (E) 1954 to 1958-59　13 matches
G.A.R. Lock (E) 1952 to 1967-68　49 matches
W.H. Lockwood (E) 1893 to 1902　12 matches

A.L. Logie (WI) 1982-83 to 1986-87　16 matches
G.A. Lohmann (E) 1886 to 1896　18 matches
H.S.B. Love (A) 1932-33　1 match
T.C. Lowry (NZ) 1929-30 to 1931　7 matches
F.A. Lowson (E) 1951 to 1955　7 matches
S.J.E. Loxton (A) 1947-48 to 1950-51　12 matches
A.P. Lucas (E) 1878-79 to 1884　5 matches
B.W. Luckhurst (E) 1970-71 to 1974-75　21 matches
E.B. Lundie (SA) 1913-14　1 match
J.J. Lyons (A) 1886-87 to 1897-98　14 matches
Rt Hon A. Lyttelton (E) 1880 to 1884　4 matches
P.A. McAlister (A) 1903-04 to 1909　8 matches
C.G. Macartney (A) 1907-08 to 1921-22　35 matches
G.G. Macaulay (E) 1922-23 to 1933　8 matches
M.J. Macaulay (SA) 1964-65　1 match
J.C.W. MacBryan (E) 1924　1 match
S.J. McCabe (A) 1930 to 1938　39 matches
C.N. McCarthy (SA) 1948-49 to 1951　15 matches
J.E. McConnon (E) 1954　2 matches
C.L. McCool (A) 1945-46 to 1949-50　14 matches
E.L. McCormick (A) 1935-36 to 1938　12 matches
R.B. McCosker (A) 1974-75 to 1979-80　25 matches
C.J. McDermott (A) 1984-85 to 1987-88　20 matches
C.C. McDonald (A) 1951-52 to 1961　47 matches
E.A. McDonald (A) 1920-21 to 1921-22　11 matches
P.S. McDonnell (A) 1880 to 1888　19 matches
P.E. McEwan (NZ) 1979-80 to 1984-85　4 matches

C.P. McGahey (E) 1901-02　2 matches
A.R. MacGibbon (NZ) 1950-51 to 1958　26 matches
H.M. McGirr (NZ) 1929-30　2 matches
D.J. McGlew (SA) 1951 to 1961-62　34 matches
G. MacGregor (E) 1890 to 1893　8 matches
S.N. MacGregor (NZ) 1954-55 to 1964-65　25 matches
J. McIlwraith (A) 1886　1 match
A.J.W. McIntyre (E) 1950 to 1955　3 matches
K.D. Mackay (A) 1956 to 1962-63　37 matches
G.D. McKenzie (A) 1961 to 1970-71　60 matches
T.R. McKibbin (A) 1894-95 to 1897-98　5 matches
A.H. McKinnon (SA) 1960 to 1966-67　8 matches
F.A. MacKinnon (E) 1878-79　1 match
A.C. MacLaren (E) 1894-95 to 1909　35 matches
J.W. McLaren (A) 1911-12　1 match
J.A. Maclean (A) 1978-79　4 matches
R.A. MacLean (SA) 1951 to 1964-65　40 matches
C.E. McLeod (A) 1894-95 to 1905　17 matches
E.G. McLeod (NZ) 1929-30　1 match
R.W. McLeod (A) 1891-92 to 1893　6 matches
T.G. McMahon (NZ) 1955-56　5 matches
J.E.P. McMaster (E) 1888-89　1 match
Q. McMillan (SA) 1929 to 1931-32　13 matches
E.D.A.St J. McMorris (WI) 1957-58 to 1966　13 matches
D.A.N. McRae (NZ) 1945-46　1 match
P.G. McShane (A) 1884-85 to 1887-88　3 matches
C.A. McWatt (WI) 1953-54 to 1954-55　6 matches

Far left: Distinguished captains of Australia and the West Indies in the 1970s, Ian Chappell and Clive Lloyd. Lloyd made a record number of appearances as captain.

Left above: Arthur Morris, Australia's left-handed opening bat who made a century in each innings against England at Adelaide in 1946–47.

Left: Bob Massie made the most amazing debut of all modern bowlers at Lord's in 1972, when he captured 16 England wickets in the match.

Above: Dennis Lillee holds up Allan Border with his aluminium bat. This bat held up a Test match at Perth in 1979–80 when he began his innings with it.

Madan Lal (I) 1974 to 1986 39 matches
L.V. Maddocks (A) 1954-55 to 1956-57 7 matches
I.S. Madray (WI) 1957-58 2 matches
R.S. Madugalle (SL) 1981-82 to 1986-87 19 matches
J.N. Maguire (A) 1983-84 3 matches
R.S. Mahanama (SL) 1985-86 to 1986-87 3 matches
Mahmood Hussain (P) 1952-53 to 1962 27 matches
A.A. Mailey (A) 1920-21 to 1926 21 matches
Majid Khan (P) 1964-65 to 1982-83 63 matches
E.S. Maka (I) 1952-53 2 matches
J.W.H. Makepeace (E) 1920-21 4 matches
A. Malhotra (I) 1981-82 to 1984-85 7 matches
A.A. Mallett (A) 1968 to 1980 38 matches
M.F. Malone (A) 1977 1 match
Maninder Singh (I) 1982-83 to 1986-87 28 matches
V.L. Manjrekar (I) 1951-52 to 1964-65 55 matches
A.V. Mankad (I) 1969-70 to 1977-78 22 matches
M.H.(V) Mankad (I) 1946 to 1958-59 44 matches
A.L. Mann (A) 1977-78 4 matches
F.G. Mann (E) 1948-49 to 1949 7 matches
F.T. Mann (E) 1922-23 5 matches
N.B.F. Mann (SA) 1947 to 1951 19 matches
P.N.F. Mansell (SA) 1951 to 1955 13 matches
Mansoor Akhtar (P) 1980-81 to 1987 18 matches
M.K. Mantri (I) 1951-52 to 1954-55 4 matches
Manzoor Elahi (P) 1984-85 to 1986-87 4 matches
Maqsood Ahmed (P) 1952-53 to 1955-56 16 matches

L.A. Markham (SA) 1948-49 1 match
V.J. Marks (E) 1982 to 1983-84 6 matches
A.P. Marr (A) 1884-85 1 match
C.S. Marriott (E) 1933 1 match
G.R. Marsh (A) 1985-86 to 1987-88 17 matches
R.W. Marsh (A) 1970-71 to 1983-84 96 matches
M.D. Marshall (WI) 1978-79 to 1986-87 51 matches
N.E. Marshall (WI) 1954-55 1 match
R.E. Marshall (WI) 1951-52 4 matches
F. Martin (E) 1890 to 1891-92 2 matches
F.R. Martin (WI) 1928 to 1930-31 9 matches
J.W. Martin (A) 1960-61 to 1966-67 8 matches
J.W. Martin (E) 1947 1 match
E.A. Martindale (WI) 1933 to 1939 10 matches
W.F.E. Marx (SA) 1921-22 3 matches
J.R. Mason (E) 1897-98 5 matches
H.H. Massie (A) 1881-82 to 1884-85 9 matches
R.A.L. Massie (A) 1972 to 1972-73 6 matches
A.M. Matheson (NZ) 1929-30 to 1931 2 matches
Wallis Mathias (P) 1955-56 to 1962 21 matches
A.D.G. Matthews (E) 1937 1 match
C.D. Matthews (A) 1986-87 2 matches
G.R.J. Matthews (SA) 1983-84 to 1986-87 21 matches
T.J. Matthews (A) 1911-12 to 1912 8 matches
E.H. Mattis (WI) 1980-81 4 matches
P.B.H. May (E) 1951 to 1961 66 matches
T.B.A May 1987/88 1 match

E.R. Mayne (A) 1912 to 1921-22 4 matches
L.C. Mayne (A) 1964-65 to 1969-70 6 matches
C.P. Mead (E) 1911-12 to 1928-29 17 matches
W. Mead (E) 1899 1 match
T. Meale (NZ) 1958 2 matches
I. Meckiff (A) 1957-58 to 1963-64 18 matches
K.R. Meher-Homji (I) 1936 1 match
V.L. Mehra (I) 1955-56 to 1963-64 8 matches
D.J. Meintjes (SA) 1922-23 2 matches
M.G. Melle (SA) 1949-50 to 1952-53 7 matches
A. Melville (SA) 1938-39 to 1948-49 11 matches
L.R.D. Mendis (SL) 1981-82 to 1986-87 23 matches
I.L. Mendonca (WI) 1961-62 2 matches
V.M. Merchant (I) 1933-34 to 1951-52 10 matches
W.E. Merritt (NZ) 1929-30 to 1931 6 matches
C.A. Merry (WI) 1933 2 matches
K.D. Meuleman (A) 1945-46 1 match
E.M. Meuli (NZ) 1952-53 1 match
J. Middleton (SA) 1895-96 to 1902-03 6 matches
W.E. Midwinter (A) 1876-77 to 1886-87 8 matches; (E) 1881-82 4 matches
B.D. Milburn (NZ) 1968-69 3 matches
C. Milburn (E) 1966 to 1968-69 9 matches
A.G. Milkha Singh (I) 1959-60 to 1961-62 4 matches
A.M. Miller (E) 1895-96 1 match
G. Miller (E) 1976 to 1984 34 matches
K.R. Miller (A) 1945-46 to 1956-57 55 matches
L.S.M. Miller (NZ) 1952-53 to 1958 13 matches
R.C. Miller (WI) 1952-53 1 match

F.W. Milligan (E) 1898-99 2 matches
G. Millman (E) 1961-62 to 1962 6 matches
C.H. Mills (SA) 1891-92 1 match
J.E. Mills (NZ) 1929-30 to 1932-33 7 matches
C.A. Milton (E) 1958 to 1959 6 matches
W.H. Milton (SA) 1888-89 to 1891-92 3 matches
R.B. Minnett (A) 1911-12 to 1912 9 matches
Miran Bux (P) 1954-55 2 matches
F.M. Misson (A) 1960-61 to 1961 5 matches
A. Mitchell (E) 1933-34 to 1936 6 matches
B. Mitchell (SA) 1929 to 1948-49 42 matches
F. Mitchell (E) 1898-99 2 matches; (SA) 1912 3 matches
T.B. Mitchell (E) 1932-33 to 1935 5 matches
N.S. Mitchell-Innes (E) 1935 1 match
R.S. Modi (I) 1946 to 1952-53 10 matches
Mohammad Aslam (P) 1954 1 match
Mohammad Farooq (P) 1960-61 to 1964-65 7 matches
Mohammad Ilyas (P) 1964-65 to 1968-69 10 matches
Mohammad Munaf (P) 1959-60 to 1961-62 4 matches
Mohammad Nazir (P) 1969-70 to 1983-84 14 matches
Mohsin Kamal (P) 1983-84 to 1987 7 matches
Mohsin Khan (P) 1977-78 to 1986-87 48 matches
A.McK. Moir (NZ) 1950-51 to 1958-59 17 matches
A.W. Mold (E) 1893 3 matches
D.A.R. Moloney (NZ) 1937 3 matches
G.H. Moodie (WI) 1934-35 1 match

L.J. Moon (E) 1905-06 4 matches
F.L.H. Mooney (NZ) 1949 to 1953-54 14 matches
K.S. More (I) 1986 to 1986-87 13 matches
R.W. Morgan (NZ) 1964-65 to 1971-72 20 matches
D.P.B. Morkel (SA) 1927-28 to 1931-32 16 matches
F. Morley (E) 1880 to 1882-83 4 matches
J.R. Moroney (A) 1949-50 to 1951-52 7 matches
A.R. Morris (A) 1946-47 to 1954-55 46 matches
S. Morris (A) 1884-85 1 match
B.D. Morrison (NZ) 1962-63 1 match
D.K. Morrison (NZ) 1987-88 3 matches
J.F.M. Morrison (NZ) 1973-74 to 1981-82 17 matches
J.B. Mortimore (E) 1958-59 to 1964 9 matches
H. Moses (A) 1886-87 to 1894-95 6 matches
A.E. Moss (E) 1953-54 to 1960 9 matches
J.K. Moss (A) 1978-79 1 match
R.C. Motz (NZ) 1961-62 to 1969 32 matches
W.H. Moule (A) 1880 1 match
M.D. Moxon (E) 1986 to 1987 3 matches
Mudassar Nazar (P) 1976-77 to 1987-88 68 matches
V.M. Muddiah (I) 1959-60 to 1960-61 2 matches
Mufasir-ul-Haq (P) 1964-65 1 match
Munir Malik (P) 1959-60 to 1962 3 matches
W.L. Murdoch (A) 1876-77 to 1890 18 matches; (E) 1891-92 1 match
A.R.A. Murray (SA) 1952-53 to 1953-54 10 matches
B.A.G. Murray (NZ) 1967-68 to 1970-71 13 matches
D.A. Murray (WI) 1977-78 to 1981-82 19 matches

D.L. Murray (WI) 1963 to 1980   62 matches
J.T. Murray (E) 1961 to 1967   21 matches
H.A. Musgrove (A) 1884-85   1 match
S. Mushtaq Ali (I) 1933-34 to 1951-52   11 matches
Mushtaq Mohammad (P) 1958-59 to 1978-79   57 matches
R.G. Nadkarni (I) 1955-56 to 1967-68   41 matches
L.E. Nagel (A) 1932-33   1 match
S.S. Naik (I) 1974 to 1974-75   3 matches
R. Nanan (WI) 1980-81   1 match
M. Naoomal Jaoomal (I) 1932 to 1933-34   3 matches
M.V. Narasimha Rao (I) 1978-79 to 1979-80   4 match
L.J. Nash (A) 1931-32 to 1936-37   2 matches
Nasin-ul-Ghani (P) 1957-58 to 1972-73   29 matches
Naushad Ali (P) 1964-65   6 matches
J.G. Navle (I) 1932 to 1933-34   2 matches
S.V. Nayak (I) 1982   2 matches
C.K. Nayudu (I) 1932 to 1936   7 matches
C.S. Nayudu (I) 1933-34 to 1951-52   11 matches
Nazar Mohammad (P) 1952-53   5 matches
S. Nazir Ali (I) 1932 to 1933-34   2 matches
J.M. Neblett (WI) 1934-35   1 match
J.D. Nel (SA) 1949-50 to 1957-58   6 matches
C. Newberry (SA) 1913-14   4 match
W. Newham (E) 1887-88   1 match
J. Newman (NZ) 1931-32 to 1932-33   3 matches
E.S. Newson (SA) 1930-31 to 1938-39   3 matches
Niaz Ahmed (P) 1967 to 1968-69   2 matches

M.S. Nichols (E) 1929-30 to 1939   14 matches
F. Nicholson (SA) 1935-36   4 matches
J.F.W. Nicholson (SA) 1927-28   3 matches
Mahomed Nissar (I) 1932 to 1936   6 matches
H.C. Nitschke (A) 1931-32   2 matches
M.A. Noble (A) 1897-98 to 1909   42 matches
G. Noblet (A) 1949-50 to 1952-53   3 matches
J.M. Noreiga (WI) 1970-71   4 matches
N.O. Norton (SA) 1909-10   1 match
O.E. Nothling (A) 1928-29   1 match
A.D. Nourse (SA) 1935 to 1951   34 matches
A.W. Nourse (SA) 1902-03 to 1924   45 matches
R.K. Nunes (WI) 1928 to 1929-30   4 matches
E.P. Nupen (SA) 1921-22 to 1935-36   17 matches
S.M. Nurse (WI) 1959-60 to 1968-69   29 matches
S. Nyalchand (I) 1952-53   1 match
A.S.M. Oakman (E) 1956   2 matches
L.P. O'Brien (A) 1932-33 to 1936-37   5 matches
Sir T.C. O'Brien (E) 1884 to 1895-96   5 matches
A.E. Ochse (SA) 1888-89   2 matches
A.L. Ochse (SA) 1927-28 to 1929   3 matches
J. O'Connor (E) 1929 to 1929-30   4 matches
J.D.A. O'Connor (A) 1907-08 to 1909   4 matches
S.P. O'Donnell (A) 1985 to 1985-86   6 matches
A.D. Ogilvie (A) 1977-78   5 matches
K.J. O'Keeffe (A) 1970-71 to 1977   24 matches
C.M. Old (E) 1972-73 to 1981   46 matches
N. Oldfield (E) 1939   1 match

W.A.S. Oldfield (A) 1920-21 to 1936-37   54 matches
S. O'Linn (SA) 1960 to 1961-62   7 matches
N.C. O'Neill (A) 1958-59 to 1964-65   42 matches
W.J. O'Reilly (A) 1931-32 to ·1945-46   27 matches
D.R. O'Sullivan (NZ) 1972-73 to 1976-77   11 matches
G.W.F. Overton (NZ) 1953-54   3 matches
H.G.O. Owen-Smith (SA) 1929   5 matches
R.K. Oxenham (A) 1928-29 to 1931-32   7 matches
D.E.V. Padgett (E) 1960   2 matches
A.L. Padmore (WI) 1975-76 to 1976   2 matches
M.L. Page (NZ) 1929-30 to 1937   14 matches
A.M. Pai (I) 1969-70   1 match
G.A.E. Paine (E) 1934-35   4 matches
B.H. Pairaudeau (WI) 1952-53 to 1957   13 matches
L.C.H. Palairet (E) 1902   2 matches
P.E. Palia (I) 1932 to 1936   2 matches
A.W. Palm (SA) 1927-28   1 match
C.H. Palmer (E) 1953-54   1 match
G.E. Palmer (A) 1880 to 1886   17 matches
K.E. Palmer (E) 1964-65   1 match
C.S. Pandit (I) 1986 to 1986-87   3 matches
P.H. Parfitt (E) 1961-62 to 1972   37 matches
R.L. Park (A) 1920-21   1 match
G.A. Parkar (I) 1982   1 match
R.D. Parkar (I) 1972-73   2 matches
C.W.L. Parker (E) 1921   1 match
G.M. Parker (SA) 1924   2 matches
J.M. Parker (NZ) 1972-73 to 1980-81   36 matches
N.M. Parker (NZ) 1976-77   3 matches

P.W.G. Parker (E) 1981   1 match
W.G.A. Parkhouse (E) 1950 to 1959   7 matches
C.H. Parkin (E) 1920-21 to 1924   10 matches
D.C. Parkin (SA) 1891-92   1 match
J.H. Parks (E) 1937   1 match
J.M. Parks (E) 1954 to 1967-68   46 matches
D.R. Parry (WI) 1977-78 to 1979-80   12 matches
D.D. Parsana (I) 1978-79   2 matches
J.T. Partridge (SA) 1963-64 to 1964-65   11 matches
L.S. Pascoe (A) 1977 to 1981-82   14 matches
C.C. Passailaigue (WI) 1929-30   1 match
C.T. Patankar (I) 1955-56   1 match
Nawab of Pataudi sen (E) 1932-33 to 1934   3 matches; (I) 1946   3 matches
Nawab of Pataudi jun (I) 1961-62 to 1974-75   46 matches
B.P. Patel (I) 1974 to 1977-78   21 matches
D.N. Patel (NZ) 1987-88   3 matches
J.M. Patel (I) 1954-55 to 1959-60   7 matches
Maharajah of Patiala (I) 1933-34   1 match
S.M. Patil (I) 1979-80 to 1984-85   29 matches
S.R. Patil (I) 1955-56   1 match
B.P. Patterson (WI) 1985-86 to 1986-87   6 matches
T.R.O. Payne (WI) 1985-86   1 match
E. Paynter (E) 1931 to 1939   20 matches
C.O.C. Pearse (SA) 1910-11   3 matches
E. Peate (E) 1881-82 to 1886   9 matches
I.A.R. Peebles (E) 1927-28 to 1931   13 matches
R. Peel (E) 1884-85 to 1896   20 matches

S.J. Pegler (SA) 1909-10 to 1924   16 matches
C.E. Pellew (A) 1920-21 to 1921-22   10 matches
F. Penn (E) 1880   1 match
R.T.D. Perks (E) 1938-39 to 1939   2 matches
Pervez Sajjad (P) 1964-65 to 1972-73   19 matches
P.J. Petherick (NZ) 1976-77   6 matches
E.C. Petrie (NZ) 1955-56 to 1965-66   14 matches
D.G. Phadkar (I) 1947-48 to 1958-59   31 matches
H. Philipson (E) 1891-92 to 1894-95   5 matches
N. Phillip (WI) 1977-78 to 1978-79   9 matches
W.B. Phillips (A) 1983-84 to 1985-86   27 matches
P.I. Philpott (A) 1964-65 to 1965-66   8 matches
L.R. Pierre (WI) 1947-48   1 match
A.C.S. Pigott (E) 1983-84   1 match
R. Pilling (E) 1881-82 to 1888   8 matches
A.J. Pithey (SA) 1956-57 to 1964-65   17 matches
D.B. Pithey (SA) 1963-64 to 1966-67   8 matches
W. Place (E) 1947-48   3 matches
W.R. Playle (NZ) 1958 to 1962-63   8 matches
J.B. Plimsoll (SA) 1947   1 match
P.I. Pocock (E) 1967-68 to 1984   25 matches
R. Pollard (E) 1946 to 1948   4 matches
V. Pollard (NZ) 1964-65 to 1973   32 matches
P.M. Pollock (SA) 1961-62 to 1969-70   28 matches
R.G. Pollock (SA) 1963-64 to 1969-70   23 matches
W.H. Ponsford (A) 1924-25 to 1934   29 matches
C.J. Poole (E) 1951-52   3 matches
M.B. Poore (NZ) 1952-53 to 1955-56   14 matches

Above: Kerry O'Keefe in the nets. He played 24 Tests for Australia in the 1970s.

Left: England batsman John Murray surrounded by Australian close catchers as Benaud bowls to him at Sydney in 1962–63.

Right: Mushtaq Mohammad bowled middle stump at the Oval in 1974. His Test career lasted for 21 years.

R.M. Poore (SA) 1895-96 3 matches
G.H. Pope (E) 1947 1 match
R.J. Pope (A) 1884-85 1 match
J.E. Pothecary (SA) 1960 3 matches
A.D. Pougher (E) 1891-92 1 match
A.W. Powell (SA) 1898-99 1 match
M. Prabhakar (I) 1984-85 1 match
E.A.S. Prasanna (I) 1961-62 to 1978-79 49 matches
J.S.E. Price (E) 1963-64 to 1972 15 matches
W.F.F. Price (E) 1938 1 match
R.M. Prideaux (E) 1968 to 1968-69 3 matches
C.F.H. Prince (SA) 1898-99 1 match
D.R. Pringle (E) 1982 to 1986 14 matches
M.J. Procter (SA) 1966-67 to 1969-70 7 matches
H.L.E. Promnitz (SA) 1927-28 2 matches
G. Pullar (E) 1959 to 1962-63 28 matches
N. Puna (NZ) 1965-66 3 matches
P.H. Punjabi (I) 1954-55 5 matches
Qasim Omar (P) 1983-84 to 1986-87 26 matches
William Quaife (E) 1899 to 1901-02 7 matches
N.A. Quinn (SA) 1929 to 1931-32 12 matches
G.O. Rabone (NZ) 1949 to 1954-55 12 matches
C.G. Rackemann (A) 1982-83 to 1984-85 5 matches
N.V. Radford (E) 1986 2 matches
C.T. Radley (E) 1977-78 to 1978 8 matches
A.F. Rae (WI) 1948-49 to 1952-53 15 matches
K. Rai Singh (I) 1947-48 1 match
V. Rajindernath (I) 1952-53 1 match

Rajinder Pal (I) 1963-64 1 match
L.S. Rajput (I) 1985-86 2 matches
S. Ramadhin (WI) 1950 to 1960-61 43 matches
C. Ramaswami (I) 1936 2 matches
G.S. Ramchand (I) 1952 to 1959-60 33 matches
Ramiz Raja (P) 1983-84 to 1987-88 16 matches
L. Ramji (I) 1933-34 1 match
A.N. Ranasinghe (SL) 1981-82 to 1982-83 2 matches
A. Ranatunga (SL) 1981-82 to 1986-87 22 matches
D.W. Randall (E) 1976-77 to 1984 47 matches
C.R. Rangachari (I) 1947-48 to 1948-49 4 matches
K.M. Rangnekar (I) 1947-48 3 matches
V.B. Ranjane (I) 1958-59 to 1964-65 7 matches
K.S. Ranjitsinhji (E) 1896 to 1902 15 matches
V.S. Ransford (A) 1907-08 to 1911-12 20 matches
Rashid Khan (P) 1981-82 to 1984-85 4 matches
R.J. Ratnayake (SL) 1982-83 to 1986-87 14 matches
J.R. Ratnayeke (SL) 1981-82 to 1986-87 18 matches
H.D. Read (E) 1935 1 match
J.M. Read (E) 1882 to 1893 17 matches
W.W. Read (E) 1882-83 to 1893 18 matches
B. Reddy (I) 1979 4 matches
R.E. Redmond (NZ) 1972-73 1 match
I.R. Redpath (A) 1963-64 to 1975-76 66 matches
J.C. Reedman (A) 1894-95 1 match
M.R. Rege (I) 1948-49 1 match
S.F. Rehman (P) 1957-58 1 match
B.A. Reid (A) 1985-86 to 1987-88 15 matches
J.F. Reid (NZ) 1978-79 to 1985-86 19 matches

J.R. Reid (NZ) 1949 to 1965 58 matches
N. Reid (SA) 1921-22 1 match
A.E. Relf (E) 1903-04 to 1913-14 13 matches
D.A. Renneburg (A) 1966-67 to 1967-68 8 matches
H.J. Rhodes (E) 1959 2 matches
W. Rhodes (E) 1899 to 1929-30 58 matches
A.R. Richards (SA) 1895-96 1 match
B.A. Richards (SA) 1969-70 4 matches
C.J. Richards (E) 1986-87 to 1987 6 matches
I.V.A. Richards (WI) 1974-75 to 1986-87 88 matches
W.H.M. Richards (SA) 1888-89 1 match
A.J. Richardson (A) 1924-25 to 1926 9 matches
D.W. Richardson (E) 1957 1 match
P.E. Richardson (E) 1956 to 1963 34 matches
R.B. Richardson (WI) 1983-84 to 1986-87 26 matches
T. Richardson (E) 1893 to 1897-98 14 matches
V.Y. Richardson (A) 1924-25 to 1935-36 19 matches
T.L. Richmond (E) 1921 1 match
K.R. Rickards (WI) 1947-48 to 1951-52 2 matches
F. Ridgway (E) 1951-52 5 matches
K.E. Rigg (A) 1930-31 to 1936-37 8 matches
D.T. Ring (A) 1947-48 to 1953 13 matches
G.M. Ritchie (A) 1982-83 to 1986-87 30 matches
S.J. Rixon (A) 1977-78 to 1984-85 13 matches
Rizwan-uz-Zaman (P) 1981-82 to 1986-87 9 matches
C.A. Roach (WI) 1928 to 1934-35 16 matches
A.D.G. Roberts (NZ) 1975-76 to 1976-77 7 matches
A.M.E. Roberts (WI) 1973-74 to 1983-84 47 matches

A.T. Roberts (WI) 1955-56 1 match
A.W. Roberts (NZ) 1929-30 to 1937 5 matches
G.K. Robertson (NZ) 1985-86 1 match
J.B. Robertson (SA) 1935-36 3 matches
J.D.B. Robertson (E) 1947 to 1951-52 11 matches
W.R. Robertson (A) 1884-85 1 match
R.W.V. Robins (E) 1929 to 1937 19 matches
R.D. Robinson (A) 1977 3 matches
R.H. Robinson (A) 1936-37 1 match
R.T. Robinson (E) 1984-85 to 1987-88 23 matches
W.V. Rodriguez (WI) 1961-62 to 1967-68 5 matches
G.R.J. Roope (E) 1972-73 to 1978 21 matches
C.F. Root (E) 1926 3 matches
G.F. Rorke (A) 1958-59 to 1959-60 4 matches
B.C. Rose (E) 1977-78 to 1980-81 9 matches
A. Rose-Innes (SA) 1888-89 2 matches
T.W. Routledge (SA) 1891-92 to 1895-96 4 matches
A.M.B. Rowan (SA) 1947 to 1951 15 matches
E.A.B. Rowan (SA) 1935 to 1951 26 matches
C.G. Rowe (NZ) 1945-46 1 match
G.A. Rowe (SA) 1895-96 to 1902-03 5 matches
L.G. Rowe (WI) 1971-72 to 1979-80 30 matches
A. Roy (I) 1969-70 4 matches
Pankaj Roy (I) 1951-52 to 1960-61 43 matches
Pranab Roy (I) 1981-82 2 matches
V.P.F.A. Royle (E) 1878-79 1 match
F.E. Rumsey (E) 1964 to 1965 5 matches
C.A.G. Russell (E) 1920-21 to 1922-23 10 matches

W.E. Russell (E) 1961-62 to 1967 10 matches
J.W. Rutherford (A) 1956-57 1 match
K.R. Rutherford (NZ) 1984-85 to 1987-88 12 matches
J. Ryder (A) 1920-21 to 1928-29 20 matches
Sadiq Mohammad (P) 1969-70 to 1980-81 41 matches
Saeed Ahmed (P) 1957-58 to 1972-73 41 matches
R.A. Saggers (A) 1948 to 1949-50 6 matches
E.L. St Hill (WI) 1929-30 2 matches
W.H. St Hill (WI) 1928 to 1929-30 3 matches
Salah-ud-Din (P) 1964-65 to 1969-70 5 matches
Saleem Altaf (P) 1967 to 1978-79 21 matches
Saleem Yousuf (P) 1981-82 to 1987 16 matches
Salim Jaffer (P) 1987-88 1 match
Salim Malik (P) 1981-82 to 1987-88 44 matches
S.V. Samuelson (SA) 1909-10 1 match
A. Sandham (E) 1921 to 1929-30 14 matches
B.S. Sandhu (I) 1982-83 to 1983-84 8 matches
D.N. Sardesai (I) 1961-62 to 1972-73 30 matches
Sarfraz Nawaz (P) 1968-69 to 1983-84 55 matches
C.T. Sarwate (I) 1946 to 1951-52 9 matches
J.V. Saunders (A) 1901-02 to 1907-08 14 matches
R.C. Saxena (I) 1967 1 match
R.O. Scarlett (WI) 1959-60 3 matches
S.S. Schultz (E) 1878-79 1 match
R.O. Schwarz (SA) 1905-06 to 1912 20 matches
A.P.H. Scott (WI) 1952-53 1 match
H.J.H. Scott (A) 1884 to 1886 8 matches

Graham McKenzie caught by Brown at the Oval in 1968, when England beat Australia with five minutes to spare after the rain-soaked pitch had been hurriedly.dried out. All the England players are within 20 yards of the bat. Underwood is the bowler, and the fielders from the left are Illingworth, Graveney, Edrich, Dexter, Cowdrey, wicket-keeper Knott, Brown making the catch, Snow, Milburn and d'Oliveira.

Right: Chris Broad batting and Steve Waugh taking evasive action at Adelaide in the 1986–87 series, Australia v England.

O.C. Scott (WI) 1928 to 1930-31   8 matches

R.H. Scott (NZ) 1946-47   1 match

V.J. Scott (NZ) 1945-46 to 1951-52   10 matches

W.H. Scotton (E) 1881-82 to 1886-87   15 matches

B.J. Sealey (WI) 1933   1 match

J.E.D. Sealey (WI) 1929-30 to 1939   11 matches

A.W. Seccull (SA) 1895-96   1 match

T.A.P. Sekar (I) 1982-83   2 matches

J. Selby (E) 1876-77 to 1881-82   6 matches

R.H.D. Sellers (A) 1964-65   1 match

M.W.W. Selvey (E) 1976 to 1976-77   3 matches

P.K. Sen (I) 1947-48 to 1952-53   14 matches

A.K. Sen Gupta (I) 1958-59   1 match

C.S. Serjeant (A) 1977 to 1977-78   12 matches

M.A. Seymour (SA) 1963-64 to 1969-70   7 matches

D. Shackleton (E) 1950 to 1963   7 matches

Shafiq Ahmed (P) 1974 to 1980-81   6 matches

Shafqat Rana (P) 1964-65 to 1969-70   5 matches

Shahid Israr (P) 1976-77   1 match

Shahid Mahmood (P) 1962   1 match

W.A. Shalders (SA) 1898-99 to 1910   12 matches

Chetan Sharma (I) 1984-85 to 1986-87   16 matches

Gopal Sharma (I) 1984-85 to 1986-87   4 matches

P. Sharma (I) 1974-75 to 1976-77   5 matches

J. Sharp (E) 1909   3 matches

D. Sharpe (P) 1959-60   3 matches

J.W. Sharpe (E) 1890 to 1891-92   3 matches

P.J. Sharpe (E) 1963 to 1969   12 matches

R.J. Shastri (I) 1980-81 to 1986-87   54 matches

A. Shaw (E) 1876-77 to 1881-82   7 matches

A.P. Sheahan (A) 1967-68 to 1973-74   31 matches

B.K. Shepherd (A) 1962-63 to 1964-65   9 matches

J.N. Shepherd (WI) 1969 to 1970-71   5 matches

D.S. Sheppard (E) 1950 to 1963-64   22 matches

G.H. Shepstone (SA) 1895-96 to 1898-99   2 matches

P.W. Sherwell (SA) 1905-06 to 1910-11   13 matches

M. Sherwin (E) 1886-87 to 1888   3 matches

G.C. Shillingford (WI) 1969 to 1971-72   7 matches

I.T. Shillingford (WI) 1976-77 to 1977-78   4 matches

S.G. Shinde (I) 1946 to 1952   7 matches

S. Shivnarine (WI) 1977-78 to 1978-79   8 matches

Shoaib Mohammad (P) 1983-84 to 1987-88   14 matches

R.H. Shodhan (I) 1952-53   3 matches

A. Shrewsbury (E) 1881-82 to 1893   23 matches

M.J.F. Shrimpton (NZ) 1962-63 to 1973-74   10 matches

Shuja-ud-Din (P) 1954 to 1961-62   19 matches

R.C. Shukla (I) 1982-83   1 match

J. Shuter (E) 1888   1 match

K. Shuttleworth (E) 1970-71 to 1971   5 matches

A. Sidebottom (E) 1985   1 match

N.S. Sidhu (I) 1983-84   2 matches

I.J. Siedle (SA) 1927-28 to 1935-36   18 matches

M.W. Sievers (A) 1936-37   3 matches

Sikander Bakht (P) 1976-77 to 1982-83   26 matches

S.A.R. Silva (SL) 1982-83 to 1985-86   8 matches

R.B. Simpson (A) 1957-58 to 1977-78   62 matches

R.T. Simpson (E) 1948-49 to 1954-55   27 matches

G.H.T. Simpson-Hayward (E) 1909-10   5 matches

J.M. Sims (E) 1935 to 1936-37   4 matches

B.W. Sinclair (NZ) 1962-63 to 1967-68   21 matches

I.McK. Sinclair (NZ) 1955-56   2 matches

J.H. Sinclair (SA) 1895-96 to 1910-11   25 matches

D.J. Sincock (A) 1964-65 to 1965-66   3 matches

R.A. Sinfield (E) 1938   1 match

C.K. Singh (WI) 1959-60   2 matches

L. Sivaramakrishnan (I) 1982-83 to 1985-86   9 matches

W.N. Slack (E) 1985-86 to 1986   3 matches

K.N. Slater (A) 1958-59   1 match

P.R. Sleep (A) 1978-79 to 1987-88   10 matches

J. Slight (A) 1880   1 match

T.F. Smailes (E) 1946   1 match

G.C. Small (E) 1986 to 1986-87   4 matches

J.A. Small (WI) 1928 to 1929-30   3 matches

M.A. Small (WI) 1983-84 to 1984   3 matches

A.C. Smith (E) 1962-63   6 matches

C.A. Smith (E) 1888-89   1 match

C.I.J. Smith (E) 1934-35 to 1937   5 matches

C.J.E. Smith (SA) 1902-03   3 matches

C.L. Smith (E) 1983 to 1986   8 matches

C.W. Smith (WI) 1960-61 to 1961-62   5 matches

D. Smith (E) 1935   2 matches

D.B.M. Smith (A) 1912   2 matches

D.M. Smith (E) 1985-86   2 matches

D.R. Smith (E) 1961-62   5 matches

D.V. Smith (E) 1957   3 matches

E.J. Smith (E) 1911-12 to 1913-14   11 matches

F.B. Smith (NZ) 1946-47 to 1951-52   4 matches

F.W. Smith (SA) 1888-89 to 1895-96   3 matches

H. Smith (E) 1928   1 match

H.D. Smith (NZ) 1932-33   1 match

I.D.S. Smith (NZ) 1980-81 to 1987-88   40 matches

M.J.K. Smith (E) 1958 to 1972   50 matches

O.G. Smith (WI) 1954-55 to 1958-59   26 matches

S.B. Smith (A) 1983-84   3 matches

T.P.B. Smith (E) 1946 to 1946-47   4 matches

V.I. Smith (SA) 1947 to 1957-58   9 matches

G.A. Smithson (E) 1947-48   2 matches

C.A. Snedden (NZ) 1946-47   1 match

M.C. Snedden (NZ) 1980-81 to 1987-88   14 matches

S.D. Snooke (SA) 1907   1 match

S.J. Snooke (SA) 1905-06 to 1922-23   26 matches

J.A. Snow (E) 1965 to 1976   49 matches

Sir G.St A. Sobers (WI) 1953-54 to 1973-74   93 matches

S.W. Sohoni (I) 1946 to 1951-52   4 matches

E.D. Solkar (I) 1969-70 to 1976-77   27 matches

J.S. Solomon (WI) 1958-59 to 1964-65   27 matches

W.R.T. Solomon (SA) 1898-99   1 match

M.M. Sood (I) 1959-60   1 match

J. Southerton (E) 1876-77   2 matches

J.T. Sparling (NZ) 1958 to 1963-64   11 matches

F.R. Spofforth (A) 1876-77 to 1886-87   18 matches

R.H. Spooner (E) 1905 to 1912   10 matches

R.T. Spooner (E) 1951-52 to 1955   7 matches

K. Srikkanth (I) 1981-82 to 1986-87   28 matches

T.E. Srinivasan (I) 1980-81   1 match

K.R. Stackpole (A) 1965-66 to 1973-74   43 matches

R.T. Stanyforth (E) 1927-28   4 matches

S.J. Staples (E) 1927-28   3 matches

J.B. Statham (E) 1950-51 to 1965   70 matches

S.C. Stayers (WI) 1961-62   4 matches

A.G. Steel (E) 1880 to 1888   13 matches

D.S. Steele (E) 1975 to 1976   8 matches

G.B. Stevens (A) 1959-60   4 matches

G.T.S. Stevens (E) 1922-23 to 1929-30   10 matches

G.B. Stevenson (E) 1979-80 to 1980-81   2 matches

M.J. Stewart (E) 1962 to 1963-64   8 matches

R.B. Stewart (SA) 1888-89   1 match

D.A. Stirling (NZ) 1984-85 to 1986   4 matches

A.E. Stoddart (E) 1887-88 to 1897-98   16 matches

J.B. Stollmeyer (WI) 1939 to 1954-55   32 matches

V.H. Stollmeyer (WI) 1939   1 match

W. Storer (E) 1897/98 to 1899   6 matches

G.B. Street (E) 1922-23   1 match

L.A. Stricker (SA) 1909-10 to 1912   13 matches

H. Strudwick (E) 1909-10 to 1926   28 matches

C.T. Studd (E) 1882 to 1882-3   5 matches

G.B. Studd (E) 1882-83   4 matches

R. Subba Row (E) 1958 to 1961   13 matches

V. Subramanya (I) 1964-65 to 1967-68   9 matches

.H. Sugg (E) 1888 2 matches

G.R. Sunderram (I) 1955-56 2 matches

R. Surendranath (I) 1958-59 to 1960-61 11 matches

R.F. Surti (A) 1960-61 to 1969-70 26 matches

M.J. Susskind (SA) 1924 5 matches

B. Sutcliffe (NZ) 1946-47 to 1965 42 matches

H. Sutcliffe (E) 1924 to 1935 54 matches

V.N. Swamy (I) 1955-56 1 match

R. Swetman (E) 1958-59 to 1959-60 11 matches

H.B. Taber (A) 1966-67 to 1969-70 16 matches

H.M. Taberer (SA) 1902-03 1 match

Tahir Naqqash (P) 1981-82 to 1984-85 15 matches

Talat Ali (P) 1972-73 to 1978-79 10 matches

D. Tallon (A) 1945-46 to 1953 21 matches

N.S. Tamhane (I) 1954-55 to 1960-61 21 matches

A.B. Tancred (SA) 1888-89 2 matches

L.J. Tancred (SA) 1902-03 to 1913-14 14 matches

V.M. Tancred (SA) 1898-99 1 match

G.L. Tapscott (SA) 1913-14 1 match

L.E. Tapscott (SA) 1922-23 2 matches

K.K. Tarapore (I) 1948-49 1 match

Aslim Arif (P) 1970-80 to 1980-81 6 matches

F.W. Tate (E) 1902 1 match

M.W. Tate (E) 1924 to 1935 39 matches

R. Tattersall (E) 1950-51 to 1954 16 matches

auseef Ahmed (P) 1979-80 to 1987-88 22 matches

C.J. Tavare (E) 1980 to 1984 30 matches

H.J. Tayfield (SA) 1949-50 to 1960 37 matches

A.I. Taylor (SA) 1956-57 1 match

B.R. Taylor (NZ) 1964-65 to 1973 30 matches

D. Taylor (SA) 1913-14 2 matches

D.D. Taylor (NZ) 1946-47 to 1955-56 3 matches

H.W. Taylor (SA) 1912 to 1931-32 42 matches

J.M. Taylor (A) 1920-21 to 1926 20 matches

J.O. Taylor (WI) 1957-58 to 1958-59 3 matches

K. Taylor (E) 1959 to 1964 3 matches

L.B. Taylor (E) 1985 2 matches

P.L. Taylor (A) 1986-87 1 match

R.W. Taylor (E) 1970-71 to 1983-84 57 matches

Lord Tennyson (E) 1913-14 to 1921 9 matches

V.P. Terry (E) 1984 2 matches

N.H.G.de J. Theunissen (SA) 1888-89 1 match

G. Thomas (A) 1964-65 to 1965-66 8 matches

J.G. Thomas (E) 1985-86 to 1986 5 matches

G.J. Thompson (E) 1909 to 1909-10 6 matches

N. Thompson (A) 1876-77 2 matches

G.R. Thoms (A) 1951-52 1 match

A.L. Thomson (A) 1970-71 4 matches

J.R. Thomson (A) 1972-73 to 1985 51 matches

K. Thomson (NZ) 1967-68 2 matches

N.I. Thomson (E) 1964-65 5 matches

P.G. Thornton (SA) 1902-03 1 match

H.M. Thurlow (A) 1931-32 1 match

E.W.T. Tindall (SA) 1937 to 1946-47 5 matches

F.J. Titmus (E) 1955 to 1974-75 53 matches

R.W. Tolchard (E) 1976-77 4 matches

D.S. Tomlinson (SA) 1935 1 match

P.M. Toohey (A) 1977-78 to 1979-80 15 matches

E.R.H. Toshack (A) 1945-46 to 1948 12 matches

C.L. Townsend (E) 1899 2 matches

D.C.H. Townsend (E) 1934-35 3 matches

L.F. Townsend (E) 1929-30 to 1933-34 4 matches

A.J. Traicos (SA) 1969-70 3 matches

J.P.F. Travers (A) 1901-02 1 match

M.F. Tremlett (E) 1947-48 3 matches

G.E. Tribe (A) 1946-47 3 matches

J. Trim (WI) 1947-48 to 1951-52 4 matches

P.H.J. Trimborn (SA) 1966-67 to 1969-70 4 matches

A.E. Trott (A) 1894-95 3 matches; (E) 1898-99 2 matches

G.H.S. Trott (A) 1888 to 1897-98 24 matches

G.B. Troup (NZ) 1976-77 to 1985-86 15 matches

F.S. Trueman (E) 1952 to 1965 67 matches

H. Trumble (A) 1890 to 1903-04 32 matches

J.W. Trumble (A) 1884-85 to 1886 7 matches

V.T. Trumper (A) 1899 to 1911-12 48 matches

P.B. Truscott (NZ) 1964-65 1 match

L. Tuckett (SA) 1947 to 1948-49 9 matches

L.R. Tuckett (SA) 1913-14 1 match

N.C. Tufnell (E) 1909-10 1 match

M.J.L. Turnbull (E) 1929-30 to 1936 9 matches

A. Turner (A) 1975 to 1976-77 14 matches

C.T.B. Turner (A) 1886-87 to 1894-95 17 matches

G.M. Turner (NZ) 1968-69 to 1982-83 41 matches

P.S. Twentyman-Jones (SA) 1902-03 1 match

G.E. Tyldesley (E) 1921 to 1928-29 14 matches

J.T. Tyldesley (E) 1898-99 to 1909 31 matches

R.K. Tyldesley (E) 1924 to 1930 7 matches

E.F.S. Tylecote (E) 1882-83 to 1886 6 matches

E.J. Tyler (E) 1895-96 1 match

F.H. Tyson (E) 1954-55 to 1958-59 17 matches

G. Ulyett (E) 1876-77 to 1890 25 matches

P.R. Umrigar (I) 1948-49 to 1961-62 59 matches

D.L. Underwood (E) 1966 to 1981-82 86 matches

A.L. Valentine (WI) 1950 to 1961-62 36 matches

B.H. Valentine (E) 1933-34 to 1938-39 7 matches

V.A. Valentine (WI) 1933 2 matches

P.G.V. van der Bijl (SA) 1938-39 5 matches

E.A. van der Merwe (SA) 1929 to 1935-36 2 matches

P.L. van der Merwe (SA) 1963-64 to 1966-67 15 matches

C.B. van Ryneveld (SA) 1951 to 1957-58 19 matches

G.D. Varnals (SA) 1964-65 3 matches

T.R. Veivers (A) 1963-64 to 1966-67 4 matches

M.R.J. Veletta 1986-87 to 1987-88 6 matches

D.B. Vengsarkar (I) 1975-76 to 1986-87 95 matches

S. Venkataraghavan (I) 1964-65 to 1982-83 57 matches

H. Verity (E) 1931 to 1939 40 matches

G.F. Vernon (E) 1882-83 1 match

K.G. Viljoen (SA) 1930-31 to 1948-49 27 matches

C.L. Vincent (SA) 1927-28 to 1935 25 matches

J. Vine (E) 1911-12 2 matches

C.H.Vintcent (SA) 1888-89 to 1891-92 3 matches

G.R. Viswanath (I) 1969-70 to 1982-83 91 matches

S. Viswanath (I) 1985-86 3 matches

G.E. Vivian (NZ) 1964-65 to 1971-72 5 matches

H.G. Vivian (NZ) 1931 to 1937 7 matches

Maharajkumar of Vizianagram (I) 1936 3 matches

W. Voce (E) 1929-30 to 1946-47 27 matches

A.E.E. Vogler (SA) 1905-06 to 1910-11 15 matches

A. Waddington (E) 1920-21 2 matches

H.F. Wade (SA) 1935 to 1935-36 10 matches

W.W. Wade (SA) 1938-39 to 1949-50 11 matches

A.L. Wadekar (I) 1966-67 to 1974 37 matches

K.J. Wadsworth (NZ) 1969 to 1975-76 33 matches

E. Wainwright (E) 1893 to 1897-98 5 matches

J.H.B. Waite (SA) 1951 to 1964-65 50 matches

M.G. Waite (A) 1938 2 matches

C.L. Walcott (WI) 1947-48 to 1959-60 44 matches

L.A. Walcott (WI) 1929-30 1 match

M.H.N. Walker (A) 1972-73 to 1977 34 matches

P.M. Walker (E) 1960 3 matches

T.W. Wall (A) 1928-29 to 1934 18 matches

W.M. Wallace (NZ) 1937 to 1950-51 13 matches

C.A. Walsh (WI) 1984-85 to 1986-87 13 matches

K.A. Walter (SA) 1961-62 2 matches

C.F. Walters (E) 1933 to 1934 11 matches

F.H. Walters (A) 1884-85 1 match

K.D. Walters (A) 1965-66 to 1980-81 74 matches

Above: Graham Yallop of Australia, who played 39 Tests between 1975–76 and 1984–85, and captained his country.

Left: Johnny Wardle, the England left-arm spinner, driving to Lord's to appear before the MCC committee in 1958, who removed him from the tour to Australia because of a newspaper article he had written.

Waqar Hassan (P) 1952-53 to 1959-60 21 matches
Alan Ward (E) 1969 to 1976 5 matches
Albert Ward (E) 1893 to 1894-95 7 matches
F.A. Ward (A) 1936-37 to 1938 4 matches
J.T. Ward (NZ) 1963-64 to 1967-68 8 matches
T.A. Ward (SA) 1912 to 1924 23 matches
J.H. Wardle (E) 1947-48 to 1957 28 matches
B. Warnapura (SL) 1981-82 to 1982-83 4 matches
K.P.J. Warnaweera (SL) 1985-86 1 match
P.F. Warner (E) 1898-99 to 1912 15 matches
J.J. Warr (E) 1950-51 2 matches
A.R. Warren (E) 1905 1 match
C. Washbrook (E) 1937 to 1956 37 matches
Wasim Akram (P) 1984-85 to 1987-88 22 matches
Wasim Bari (P) 1967 to 1983-84 81 matches
Wasim Raja (P) 1972-73 to 1984-85 57 matches
A.J. Watkins (E) 1948 to 1952 15 matches
J.C. Watkins (SA) 1949-50 to 1956-57 15 matches
J.R. Watkins (A) 1972-73 1 match
C. Watson (WI) 1959-60 to 1961-62 7 matches
G.D. Watson (A) 1966-67 to 1972 5 matches
W. Watson (E) 1951 to 1958-59 23 matches
W. Watson (NZ) 1987-88 16 matches

W.J. Watson (A) 1954-55 4 matches
L. Watt (NZ) 1954-55 1 match
S.R. Waugh (A) 1985-86 to 1986-87 13 matches
S. Wazir Ali (I) 1932 to 1936 7 matches
Wazir Mohammad (P) 1952-53 to 1959-60 20 matches
M.G. Webb (NZ) 1970-71 to 1973-74 3 matches
P.N. Webb (NZ) 1979-80 2 matches
A.J. Webbe (E) 1878-79 1 match
E.de C. Weekes (WI) 1947-48 to 1957-58 48 matches
K.H. Weekes (WI) 1939 2 matches
C.D.U.S. Weerasinghe (SL) 1985-86 1 match
G.L.E. Weir (NZ) 1929-30 to 1937 11 matches
A.W. Wellard (E) 1937 to 1938 2 matches
D.M. Wellman (A) 1981 to 1986-87 6 matches
C. Wesley (SA) 1960 3 matches
K.C. Wessels (A) 1982-83 to 1985-86 24 matches
R.J. Wescott (SA) 1953-54 to 1957-58 5 matches
M.D. Wettimuny (SL) 1982-83 2 matches
S. Wettimuny (SL) 1981-82 to 1986-87 23 matches
A. Wharton (E) 1949 1 match
D.F. Whatmore (A) 1978-79 to 1979-80 7 matches
J.J. Whitaker (E) 1986-87 1 match

D.W. White (E) 1961-62 2 matches
G.C. White (SA) 1905-06 to 1912 17 matches
J.C. White (E) 1921 to 1930-31 15 matches
W.A. White (WI) 1964-65 2 matches
P.E. Whitelaw (NZ) 1932-33 2 matches
M.R. Whitney (A) 1981 to 1987-87 3 matches
W.J. Whitty (A) 1909 to 1912 14 matches
W.W. Whysall (E) 1924-25 to 1930 4 matches
J.M. Wiener (A) 1979-80 6 matches
C.V. Wight (WI) 1928 to 1929-30 2 matches
G.L. Wight (WI) 1952-53 1 match
R.G.C.E. Wijesuriya (SL) 1981-82 to 1985-86 4 matches
C.A. Wiles (WI) 1933 1 match
L.L. Wilkinson (E) 1938-39 3 matches
E.T. Willett (WI) 1972-73 to 1974-75 5 matches
P. Willey (E) 1976 to 1986 26 matches
A.B. Williams (WI) 1977-78 to 1978-79 7 matches
E.A.V. Williams (WI) 1939 to 1947-48 4 matches
R.G.D. Willis (E) 1970-71 to 1984 90 matches
J.T. Willoughby (SA) 1895-96 2 matches
C.E.M. Wilson (E) 1898-99 2 matches
D. Wilson (E) 1963-64 to 1970-71 6 matches
E.R. Wilson (E) 1920-21 1 match

J.W. Wilson (A) 1956-57 1 match
C.S. Wimble (SA) 1891-92 1 match
P.L. Winslow (SA) 1949-50 to 1955 5 matches
K.L. Wishart (WI) 1934-35 1 match
A. Wood (E) 1938 to 1939 4 matches
B. Wood (E) 1972 to 1978 12 matches
G.E.C. Wood (E) 1924 3 matches
G.M. Wood (A) 1977-78 to 1985 53 matches
H. Wood (E) 1888 to 1891-92 4 matches
R. Wood (E) 1886-87 1 match
A.J. Woodcock (A) 1973-74 1 match
W.M. Woodfull (A) 1926 to 1934 35 matches
S.M.J. Woods (E) 1895-96 3 matches; (A) 1888 3 matches
F.E. Woolley (E) 1909 to 1934 64 matches
R.D. Woolley (A) 1982-83 to 1983-84 2 matches
R.A. Woolmer (E) 1975 to 1981 19 matches
J. Worrall (A) 1884-85 to 1899 11 matches
Sir F.M.M. Worrell (WI) 1947-48 to 1963 51 matches
T.S. Worthington (E) 1929-30 to 1936-37 9 matches
C.W. Wright (E) 1895-96 3 matches
D.V.P. Wright (E) 1938 to 1950-51 34 matches
J.G. Wright (NZ) 1977-78 to 1987-88 52 matches

K.J. Wright (A) 1978-79 to 1979-80 10 matches
R.E.S. Wyatt (E) 1927-28 to 1936-37 40 matches
O.E. Wynne (SA) 1948-49 to 1949-50 6 matches
E.G. Wynyard (E) 1896 to 1905-06 3 matches
N.S. Yadav (I) 1979-80 to 1986-87 35 matches
J.W. Yajurvindra Singh 1976-77 to 1979-80 4 matches
G.N. Yallop (A) 1975-76 to 1984-85 39 matches
B. Yardley (A) 1977-78 to 1982-83 33 matches
N.W.D. Yardley (E) 1938-39 to 1950 20 matches
Yashpal Sharma (I) 1979 to 1983-84 37 matches
Yograj Singh (I) 1980-81 1 match
H.I. Young (E) 1899 2 matches
J.A. Young (E) 1947 to 1949 8 matches
R.A. Young (E) 1907-08 2 matches
Younis Ahmed (P) 1969-70 to 1986-87 4 matches
B.W. Yuile (NZ) 1962-63 to 1969-70 17 matches
Zaheer Abbas (P) 1969-70 to 1985-86 78 matches
Zakir Khan (P) 1985-86 1 match
T.J. Zoehrer (A) 1985-86 to 1986-87 10 matches
J.W. Zulch (SA) 1909-10 to 1921-22 15 matches
Zulfiqar Ahmed (P) 1952-53 to 1956-57 9 matches
Zulqarnain (P) 1985-86 3 matches